TALES FROM ★ THE VAULT ★

A Celebration of 100 Boxing Closet Classics

To Colonel Bob Sheridan:

Thanks so much for your faith in my book & I hope you will enjoy this trip back in time. You are a true Hall of Famer.

Lee Groves
8-6-10

FOREWORD BY STEVE FARHOOD

Lee Groves

Copyright © 2010 Lee Groves
All rghts reserved.

ISBN: 1449965601
ISBN-13: 9781449965600

★ Contents ★

Foreword – vii-ix
Acknowledgements – xi-xii
Introduction – xiii-xv

Chapter 1: Brawls
Antonio Avelar vs. Wilfredo Vazquez – 2-6
Victor Callejas vs. Loris Stecca II – 7-12
Danny Lopez vs. Ruben Olivares – 13-17
Alexis Arguello vs. Andy Ganigan – 18-23
Julio Gonzalez vs. Julian Letterlough – 24-31
Matthew Franklin vs. Richie Kates – 32-38
Kiyoshi Hatanaka vs. Pedro Decima – 39-45
Aaron Pryor vs. Dujuan Johnson – 46-53
Tony Lopez vs. Rocky Lockridge I – 54-60
William "Caveman" Lee vs. John LoCicero – 61-67

Chapter 2: Shootouts
Soo Hwan Hong vs. Hector Carrasquilla – 70-75
Juan "Kid" Meza vs. Jaime Garza – 76-80
Bobby Czyz vs. Tim Broady – 81-87
Ray Mancini vs. Arturo Frias – 88-94
Kelvin Seabrooks vs. Ernie Cataluna – 95-100
Richard Hall vs. Julian Letterlough – 101-106
Mike McCallum vs. Julian Jackson – 107-113
Ezzard Charles vs. Bob Satterfield – 114-119
Bobby Czyz vs. Willie Edwards – 120-125
Kostya Tszyu vs. Diosbelys Hurtado – 126-133

TALES FROM THE VAULT

Chapter 3: Big Man Drama
Michael Moorer vs. Bert Cooper – 136-142
Orlin Norris vs. Adolpho Washington I – 143-150
Alex Stewart vs. Ezra Sellers – 151-156
Carl Williams vs. Jesse Ferguson – 157-163
Michael Moorer vs. Alex Stewart – 164-170
Pinklon Thomas vs. Mike Weaver – 171-178
Darroll Wilson vs. Shannon Briggs – 179-185
Tommy Morrison vs. Carl Williams – 186-193
Ray Mercer vs. Bert Cooper – 194-202
Kenny Keene vs. Terry Ray I – 203-210

Chapter 4: Wars of Attrition
Oscar Larios vs. Israel Vazquez II – 212-218
Santos Cardona vs. Kevin Pompey – 219-224
Leonard Dorin vs. Raul Balbi I – 225-231
James Hughes vs. Anthony Stephens – 232-241
Ebo Elder vs. Courtney Burton – 242-249
Nestor Garza vs. Enrique Sanchez – 250-256
Jaime Garza vs. Joe Ruelaz – 257-264
Rafael Ruelas vs. Jorge Paez – 265-271
Tommy Cordova vs. Freddie Roach – 272-277
Julio Cesar Chavez vs. Roger Mayweather II – 278-286

Chapter 5: Undercard Treasures
John Tobin vs. Ferris Christian – 288-293
Leland Hardy vs. Ike Padilla – 294-299
Elvir Muriqi vs. Sam Ahmad – 300-306
Brian Hallinan vs. Kenny Blackston – 307-312
Tony Ridges vs. Roberto Cobos – 313-318
Art Jimmerson vs. Lenny LaPaglia – 319-326
Chris McInerney vs. Anterio Vines – 327-332
John Revish vs. Leo Lizarraga – 333-337
Derrick Roddy vs. Ricardo Kennedy – 338-343
Thomas Davis vs. Kendall Holt – 344-349

Chapter 6: Vengeance is Mine – Great Grudge Fights
Nigel Benn vs. Anthony Logan – 352-357
Iran Barkley vs. Michael Olajide – 358-364

Aaron Davis vs. Mark Breland – 365-372
Mark Kaylor vs. Errol Christie – 373-379
Rafael Orono vs. Chul Ho Kim II – 380-386
Bruce Curry vs. Monroe Brooks – 387-395
Wilfredo Gomez vs. Derrick Holmes – 396-403
Fernando Vargas vs. Ross Thompson – 404-410
Mike McCallum vs. Milton McCrory – 411-419
Chris Eubank vs. Nigel Benn I – 420-429

Chapter 7 – Little Big Men
Ricardo Lopez vs. Rosendo Alvarez II – 432-437
Chan Hee Park vs. Guty Espadas – 438-442
Muangchai Kittikasem vs. Jung Koo Chang – 443-449
Sung Kil Moon vs. Nana Konadu I – 450-456
Fidel Bassa vs. Dave McAuley I – 457-465
Betulio Gonzalez vs. Martin Vargas – 466-474
Amado Ursua vs. Hilario Zapata – 475-481
Masao Ohba vs. Chartchai Chionoi – 482-488
Yuri Arbachakov vs. Muangchai Kittikasem I – 489-495
Mark Johnson vs. Leon Salazar – 496-502

Chapter 8: Sudden and Violent Endings
Thomas Hearns vs. Juan Domingo Roldan – 504-509
Tommy Morrison vs. Donovan "Razor" Ruddock – 510-517
Vincent Pettway vs. Simon Brown – 518-524
Derrick Jefferson vs. Maurice Harris – 525-530
Paul Banke vs. Daniel Zaragoza II – 531-538
Prudencio Cardona vs. Antonio Avelar – 539-544
Julian Jackson vs. Herol Graham – 545-550
Alfonso Zamora vs. Alberto Sandoval – 551-557
Julian Letterlough vs. Demetrius Jenkins – 558-564
Frank Liles vs. Tim Littles II – 565-570

Chapter 9: Upsets and Unpredictability – A Walk on the Wild Side
Antwun Echols vs. Charles Brewer – 572-578
Merqui Sosa vs. Prince Charles Williams I – 579-585
Joel Casamayor vs. Diego Corrales I – 586-594
Juan Coggi vs. Eder Gonzalez I – 595-603
Vilomar Fernandez vs. Alexis Arguello I – 604-612

TALES FROM THE VAULT

Kelvin Seabrooks vs. Thierry Jacob – 613-620
Frankie Duarte vs. Alberto Davila II – 621-627
Freddie Pendleton vs. Tony Lopez – 628-633
Paul Whittaker vs. Don Lee – 634-640
Lee Roy Murphy vs. Chisanda Mutti – 641-647

Chapter 10: Back From the Brink: Great Comebacks
Danny Lopez vs. Juan Malvarez – 650-654
Rafael "Bazooka" Limon vs. Rolando Navarrete I – 655-661
Danny Williams vs. Mark Potter – 662-668
Jim Watt vs. Charlie Nash – 669-674
Kennedy McKinney vs. Junior Jones – 675-681
Kevin Kelley vs. Derrick Gainer I – 682-689
Joichiro Tatsuyoshi vs. Sirimongkol Singwancha – 690-696
John Mugabi vs. James "Hard Rock" Green – 697-704
Rolando Navarrete vs. Chung Il Choi – 705-712
Pernell Whitaker vs. Diosbelys Hurtado – 713-721

★ Foreword ★

At age 52, I'm not old, nor as young as I used to be.

(I'm not sure whether Cat Stevens first wrote that line, or maybe it was Paul Simon. Either way, I'll take credit.)

I've covered boxing for 31 years, which means that while I'm not yet cashing Social Security checks, attrition has made me a senior member of the boxing media.

In such status, there is bad and good. The bad:

- ★ Young writers sometimes refer to me as "Mr. Farhood," as if I'm old enough to be their father – which, of course, I am.
- ★ Watching hundreds of rounds of horrible heavyweight fights is a form of self-flagellation, for which I see a therapist. I've sent the bills to John Ruiz, Nikolay Valuev, and Fres Oquendo, but I've been met with – how appropriate – indifference.
- ★ I now feel guilty for ogling all those 22-year-old round-card girls. Well, maybe scratch number-three.

The good:

- ★ No one yells at me when I park myself in a better press row seat than I've been assigned.
- ★People assume I know something about this crazy sport and occasionally pay me for my worthless opinion.
- ★I've watched – and maybe, in a small way, helped – a few of the young ones grow into real writers.

And that's as satisfying as just about anything I've done.

In the '80s and '90s, I worked as editor of "KO" magazine and "The Ring," and as such, I employed a battery of overeager and underpaid freelance writers. Many were young; one was only 15 at the time of his first byline, something I learned only years later.

Some of the writers stuck with it and became significant contributors to newspapers, magazines, and websites. Others were one-and-out and as dismissible as three-dollar umbrellas.

Lee Groves most definitely belongs in the former category. It's been almost 20 years since our initial collaboration, and what's become abundantly clear is that 1) he loves boxing, 2) he loves writing, and 3) he long ago came to the realization that writing about boxing is not only worthwhile, but also wonderfully rewarding.

The British historian Arnold J. Toynbee said, "The supreme accomplishment is to blur the line between work and play." Lee and those of us who have been fortunate enough to make our livings at key fights and keyboards fully understand. Whether you fight, write, promote, manage, train, or whatever, boxing takes a hold of you and never lets go.

And when you have Lee's passion for the subject, you become a willing prisoner.

The fight's the thing, of course, and in this book, Lee details dozens of memorable bouts. What I enjoyed most is the variety of fights. Some I attended ringside, like the New York Civil War between Iran Barkley and Michael Olajide and the did-you-see-that 174-second explosion between SoCal-based Juan Meza and Jaime Garza that took place in, of all places, Kingston, New York.

Others I continue to include on the list of fights I *wish* I had attended are the first Chris Eubank-Nigel Benn grudge match in Birmingham (England, not Alabama) and Aaron Pryor-Dujuan Johnson. (If Johnson's nickname was "Mr. Excitement," how were we supposed to refer to Pryor?)

Lee adds a touch of nostalgia with his report on Ezzard Charles-Bob Satterfield, as well as Bruce Curry-Monroe Brooks, which was just one of about 500 great Los Angeles fights in the '70s, but for the most part, he writes about fights that occurred during his time on the beat.

My favorite chapter is "Undercard Treasures," which serves as a reminder of why we pay attention to the prelims when other ringsiders are arriving fashionably late, downing beers, or texting, tweeting, twittering, or twiddling their thumbs.

I had forgotten all about the heavyweight slugfest between Leland Hardy and Ike Padilla. Fortunately, Lee hasn't. I know he's a tape geek, so he can probably dig it out and watch it whenever he chooses.

And while the casual fan focuses on heavyweights, Lee pays homage to the *real* fighters by recalling strawweights and flyweights like Guty Espadas, Ricardo Lopez, Muangchai Kittikasem, and 2010 International Boxing Hall of Fame inductee Jung Koo Chang.

Real fight fans cherish the smaller guys, and Lee's stories reflect the fact that *power-punching bantamweight* and *flyweight knockout artist* are not oxymorons.

It seems like a lifetime ago that Lee wrote for me on subjects ranging from Jimmy Lennon Jr. to Pete Rademacher to Danny Lopez. But nothing's really changed: Those articles were absorbing reads, and so is this volume of recent boxing history.

No surprise to me: Lee's book is written objectively, thoroughly, accurately, and with sharp detail.

A couple of decades later, the kid's done all right.

Steve Farhood
December 15, 2009

★ Acknowledgements ★

Never in my wildest dreams – and believe me, I am capable of some real whoppers – did I ever think I'd become an author. One can never anticipate the twists and turns life will take and this book represents one of the highlights of my life thus far.

Few worthwhile pursuits are achieved without considerable help from others. First and foremost, I thank God for lending me a small slice of His infinite gifts as well as His unending patience and tolerance, for none of us are perfect and never will be.

On an earthly realm I thank my mother Linda, my father Gary and my sister Cindy for their love, support and encouragement. By the way, Cindy deserves special thanks for her technical expertise, an asset that saved my bacon many, many times during the preparatory process.

I would like to thank others who were instrumental in making this product a reality.

Christian Giudice, author of the excellent biography "Hands of Stone: The Life and Legend of Roberto Duran," provided valuable advice on my initial book proposal and the process of seeking a book agent. After absorbing a number of e-mail rejections, one agent – Matt McGowan of The Frances Golden Literary Agency, Inc. in New York City – showed faith in my vision and did everything he could to persuade the major publishing houses to take on my project. In the end, no one opted to take the leap of faith but it wasn't because of a lack of effort on Matt's part. Thanks very much for being in my corner.

When it became clear that this book was fated for the self-publishing world, Ted Sares – the author of three self-published books – provided much appreciated input on how to move forward. Through him, I was put in touch with Mabry Morrison of CreateSpace. Being the type who looks, and looks, and looks some more before he leaps, Mabry patiently answered every query and helped calm whatever nerves I had. To both I offer my heartfelt thanks.

I also would like to thank everyone else on the CreateSpace team for helping me navigate the technical nuts and bolts associated with this venture.

Stu Saks and Nigel Collins of Ring Magazine also merit my highest marks for allowing me access to their massive photo library to help spice up my book proposal.

TALES FROM THE VAULT

Thanks are also extended to every one of my fellow collectors that helped me build my archives over the years. Special thanks go to "Boxing" Bob Newman, Andy Kasprzak and Kurt Noltimier for providing specific footage that was needed to finish this book.

Since many of these stories were originally posted on MaxBoxing.com, I sought permission from Steve Kim, Thomas Gerbasi and Robert Waterman to go forward with this project. Thank you so much for offering your consent.

A big thank-you goes out to Brian Meade, a professional photographer based in Parkersburg, W.Va. who not only shot the cover photo but also came up with the concept. He was one of my very best friends during our days at Fairmont State College but it was only recently that we re-connected after more than 15 years. The timing couldn't have been better and I'm thankful that he allowed me to access his creative talents.

I also thank Steve Farhood for lending me his considerable skill and prestige by writing the foreword. He and I go back to the early 1990s when I was a young correspondent eager to prove myself to the big boys and through his guidance and faith I believe he helped me become a better writer. Of course, you, the reader, will be my judge and jury but hopefully not my executioner.

Thanks are also extended to the good people at United Bank, Inc. in Parkersburg, W.Va., for allowing Brian and me to use their vault for the cover photo. Their cooperation is very much appreciated, especially in this post-9/11 era.

Of all the people mentioned here, the single person outside my family to whom I owe the greatest debt of gratitude is CompuBox president Bob Canobbio. I met Bob through HBO's "unofficial official" Harold Lederman and through a rather jagged series of events I eventually quit my full-time job at The Parkersburg News and Sentinel in March 2007 to work for him as a writer, researcher and punch-counter. He taught me the ins and outs of the punch-counting biz and when I brought up the possibility of using his program to compile the statistics for this book he granted me his permission without hesitation. Because he invested his trust in me I've got to see places I never thought I'd get to see and meet people I otherwise never would have. In all I've visited 32 states plus Canada, the Bahamas and Germany and I couldn't have done any of it without him.

Lastly, I want to extend my thanks to you, the reader. The explosion of technology in recent years has created a multitude of ways to spend one's down time and by purchasing my book you have invested in me an irretrievable commodity – your time. My greatest wish is that when you finish reading this book you will feel as if your time was well spent and that your faith in my project was rewarded.

So without further delay, pull up a comfortable chair and transport your mind's eye to ringside where you will experience the greatest – and most underrated – fights ever staged.

★ Introduction ★

When I joined the MaxBoxing team in October 2005, I was charged with the responsibility of churning out two columns per week, every week. On the surface it didn't sound like much but once the initial energy that comes with starting a new job began to fade, fulfilling that obligation became challenging at times.

To solve that problem, I went to a tried and true formula that works with the fighters I so admire – work to your strengths. For me, finding them was easy. First, I have great reverence for boxing history. Second, I possess one of the largest private boxing video collections in the world as I have more than 20,000 fights on VHS or DVD – a number that grows daily. Third, I've been blessed with an eye for detail and the ability to vividly describe not only what I see but also why I believe it is happening. Finally, as an avid consumer of boxing publications I felt there were subjects that had been untapped.

In my 36 years as a boxing fan and nearly 25 years as a video collector, I have come across certain fights and fighters whose stories deserved the permanence of print but were bypassed for one reason or another. It was for these reasons that I began writing the Closet Classics series, and given the response I've received over the years I knew that my stories had filled a void.

So what constitutes a Closet Classic? As Supreme Court Justice Potter Stewart said when attempting to define "hard core" pornography, "I know it when I see it." First of all, it must be a fight that fulfills all the requirements of their more famous brethren – riveting two-way action and multiple momentum swings being two – but has somehow slipped through the cracks of history and memory. They are battles that don't quickly come to mind when great fights are discussed but when they do get mentioned they cause even the most devoted fan to slap his forehead and declare, "how could I have forgotten about *that* one?"

Another criterion is whether a fight or fighter boasts a compelling story line. As you will notice in the table of contents, the 100 fights are divided into 10 chapters based on several factors. Many of them are dictated by the kind of action that unfolded ("Shootouts," "Wars of Attrition," "Great Comebacks," etc.) while others are partitioned by weight class ("Little Big Men," "Big Man Drama") or by the placement on that night's fight card ("Undercard Treasures").

My favorite fights, at last in terms of writing about them, are contained in Chapter 10 – "Upsets and Unpredictability – A Walk on the Wild Side" – because while boxing under normal circumstances is exciting enough, these bouts go far beyond that. One fight, the first encounter between Juan Martin Coggi and Eder Gonzalez, represents the single worst example of hometown favoritism I have yet seen. While it was an outrage to witness, it was great fun for me to chronicle and hopefully my account will inspire a wide range of emotions.

The mission of this book is to enshrine 100 of boxing's greatest underrated and forgotten classics in an informative and entertaining format. It is the kind of book that can be wolfed down or nibbled on because each fight is an entity unto itself. In each installment, both fighters are profiled in the context of the time – what each had done up to that point in their respective careers as well as the stakes of winning and losing – and each story ends with an epilogue describing what happened to each after their fateful encounter.

Every book strives to have a unique "hook," something that either has never been tried or has seldom been attempted. That's a tough thing to pull off given the number of books produced over the years but I believe I've found something that will set this book apart. Interested? If so, read on.

Not only will each fight have detailed blow-by-blow accounts, strategic observations and storytelling aspects, it will be accompanied by official statistics detailing how many punches each man threw and landed. Due to my association with CompuBox, boxing's foremost compiler of statistics and analysis, I have received permission from company president Bob Canobbio to use his program to compile numbers on fights not already counted by CompuBox – which happens to include most of the fights in this book. Therefore, statistics for fights that either pre-date CompuBox's creation in 1985 or weren't originally covered by the company will be presented for the first time. I don't know about you, but I was extremely interested to see the punch numbers involving such luminaries as Ezzard Charles, Danny Lopez, Ruben Olivares, Matthew Saad Muhammad and Wilfredo Gomez, among others.

Of the 100 fights profiled in this book, 77 will involve bouts not originally tracked by CompuBox. Each one of the fights I counted (and I watched each video twice in order to assemble numbers for both fighters) will feature round-by-round statistics in jabs, power punches and total punches. The remainder only will have total figures because the original files containing the complete round-by-round figures no longer exist.

While most of these articles originally ran on MaxBoxing throughout the past few years, these are not verbatim reprints. First of all, the epilogues are updated to reflect what has happened as of January 2010, and several fighters' careers have either progressed or regressed since the articles' original posting. Also, I am a perfectionist

INTRODUCTION

at heart and in reviewing the copy for this book I found more than a few places where additional details and polishing needed to be done. Therefore, while the contents of this book address subjects I previously covered in my MaxBoxing articles, many of the words and impressions you read here are printed here for the first time.

Boxing is a sport rich in tradition and this book hopefully will help fill significant historical gaps by shining a light on fights that have long been overlooked – until now. Writing this book has been a most enjoyable journey and I hope that you will derive just as much pleasure reading it.

Lee Groves
February 19, 2010

★ Chapter 1 ★
BRAWLS

TALES FROM THE VAULT

Antonio Avelar vs. Wilfredo Vazquez
May 30, 1986, Miami Beach Fla.

When boxing fans gather to discuss the greatest fights in history, many matches immediately spring to mind. Battles like the Ali-Frazier, Gatti-Ward and Zale-Graziano trilogies, Dempsey-Firpo, Louis-Conn, Corrales-Castillo I and Hagler-Hearns are just a few of the dynamic scraps that make boxing such a unique spectacle.

As memorable as the above matches were, there are thousands of other fantastic fights that do not share the same historic significance or enjoy the same intense public scrutiny. Many of these bouts occurred in small arenas before hundreds of die-hard fans. Some were televised on cable channels and other weren't aired at all, yet their sheer ferocity was such that those that were lucky enough to see them chose to remember them. They are the fights that video collectors like to watch again and again to remind themselves why they became fans in the first place.

For this observer, such a bout was a bantamweight contest that took place May 30, 1986 in an intimate gymnasium in Miami Beach between Wilfredo Vazquez and Antonio Avelar, a fight that featured the greatest single round this writer has ever seen. Better than round one of Hagler-Hearns. Better than round 10 of Bowe-Holyfield I. Better than even round nine of Ward-Gatti I, though just barely. Out of the tens of thousands of rounds this author has seen in 35 years as a fan, round five of Avelar-Vazquez represents the pinnacle of this scribe's fight-watching experience.

This bout was a continuation of the never-ending fistic war between Mexico and Puerto Rico and the stakes were high for both men. The 25-year-old Vazquez (22-2-1 with 18 KO and one no-contest) turned in a brave but unsuccessful challenge against WBC champion Miguel "Happy" Lora three months before and was looking to make his case for a second chance at the Colombian champion, whom he knocked down before losing a decision. Vazquez was so eager to get back in the title picture that he took this fight just six days after scoring a third round TKO over Jose Cervantes. He entered the Avelar match as the younger, fresher, naturally bigger fighter, and, perhaps most importantly, one whose best days might still lay ahead.

On the other hand, the 27-year-old Avelar was 38-12-1 (32 KO) and was nearing the end of the line. He was more than three years removed from his brief reign as WBC flyweight champion, which ended after Prudencio Cardona produced one of the most devastating one-punch knockouts in division history, flattening the Mexican in a single round. Avelar entered this fight with a 9-3 record with seven knockouts following the Cardona loss, with his other two victories being disqualifications over Elid "Jimmy" Fernandez and future 115-pound king Gilberto Roman (which Roman avenged by seven round TKO in the rematch two months later). Avelar was coming off a four round

TKO loss to the 6-5 Arturo Mujica two months previously in Guadalajara, a result that probably prompted Vazquez's people to jump at the chance to fight the ex-champ.

The script called for the older, more shopworn Avelar to give "The Pride of Puerto Rico" a good test before eventually losing by decision or late-round TKO. For four rounds, the fight went as expected as the two warriors exchanged power shots at close range with Vazquez earning a slight advantage in each round. Vazquez appeared to stun Avelar with an overhand right in the first round and a flurry of punches along the ropes midway through the second, but the Mexican doggedly continued his pursuit and landed his share of powerful blows. Each man's punches connected with unusual force, as if their gloves housed boulders instead of human fists.

Each opened small cuts on their opponent's right eye in the third and the Puerto Rican landed hard jabs and whistling rights over the top in the fourth as Avelar caught Vazquez with lead rights and thumping body shots. Though Vazquez was winning the rounds, Avelar was forcing the fight and, as time went on, one had the feeling that Vazquez's early lead was shrinking.

Then came the unforgettable fifth.

Avelar dropped Vazquez just seven seconds into the round when his hook landed a split-second quicker than the Puerto Rican's hook. Vazquez popped up quickly and began to backpedal, popping jabs and mixing in short rights and hooks while Avelar coolly pursued. Shortly before the one-minute mark, Avelar backed Vazquez into a neutral corner and prepared to consolidate his advantage. As he did so, Vazquez lashed out with a short straight right lead that caught Avelar squarely on the jaw, causing him to fall stomach first onto the bottom rope. Like Vazquez, Avelar was up quickly but unlike the Mexican, Vazquez launched an all-out assault over the next 50 seconds. His ferocious left-rights violently snapped Avelar's head time and again, yet Avelar absorbed every rocket while somehow firing back with equal relish.

With 50 seconds remaining, Avelar turned Vazquez around and produced his own power-punching display, stunning Vazquez with his left hook-overhand right combinations as well as the considerable size of his fighting heart. The final 35 seconds saw both fighters launch simultaneous left-right combos, with Vazquez's landing with full force and Avelar's straying far off target.

Meanwhile, the crowd was screaming itself hoarse, astonished at the brutality that unfolded before them. After the bell rang, the fans gave both fighters a rousing standing ovation. Vazquez's assault raised considerable swelling over Avelar's right eye while Vazquez's face was blood-smeared and lumpy.

One would have thought that the action would slow dramatically after such a display. While the sixth and seventh rounds were nowhere near as intense as the fantastic fifth, the pace decelerated from Armageddon to mere hyper-drive. Vazquez continued to bounce rights through Avelar's porous defense, while the Mexican dug uppercuts and left hooks to Vazquez's head and body. Midway through the seventh, Avelar's hard work began to pay off as Vazquez showed signs of tiring. His punches, while still landing with authority, didn't have the same zip as before and he spent more time backing away on unsteady legs. Encouraged, Avelar pressed forward and backed the Puerto Rican into the ropes with a hard jab as the round ended.

Vazquez started the eighth round well, but it was clear his exertion had taken its toll. As he backed away from Avelar, Vazquez's arms hung limply at his sides, raising them only when he saw an incoming punch. After absorbing another Vazquez right that sent sweat spraying from his battered head, Avelar turned out Vazquez's lights with startling suddenness.

The Mexican maneuvered Vazquez to the ropes near Avelar's corner, where both men prepared to throw right hands. This time, Avelar's flyweight hand speed won out and he dumped Vazquez on his behind with the straightest right hand he threw all night.

Vazquez was up by four, but one look into his vacant eyes convinced the referee to stop the bout at the 1:10 mark. Neither the Puerto Rican nor his corner offered any argument as he was led back to this corner.

It was difficult to fathom that two bantamweights – or more accurately a bantamweight and a blown-up flyweight – could produce such heavy-handed mayhem. Fights involving the smaller-weight battlers usually emphasize speed and technique rather than raw-boned power but Avelar-Vazquez was a breathtaking exception. For one day at least, these 118-pounders showed that the little guys could deliver heavyweight-sized firepower – and heavyweight-sized drama – into the squared circle.

Epilogue: With his victory, Avelar earned a title shot against the 27-0 Lora nearly 14 months after the Vazquez victory. The most notable occurrence surrounding Avelar's four-round TKO loss was that the fight had to be interrupted midway through the first round because the boat upon which they fought began to rock back and forth due to choppy waters. Avelar never fought again, and he retired with a record of 39-13-1 with 32 KO.

Vazquez, on the other hand, fought on for 16 more years. He won his first belt after scoring a 10-round TKO of WBA bantamweight champion Chan Yong Park in October 1987, but lost it by split decision to Khaokor Galaxy six months later. Vazquez won his second world title in March 1992 by upsetting WBA 122-pound champion Raul "Jibaro" Perez by third round KO. He defended that title nine times over the next three years, beating future Hall of Famer Orlando Canizales, Thierry Jacob, Luis Mendoza and Juan Polo Perez before losing it to Antonio Cermeno in May 1995.

Three months before his 36th birthday, Vazquez captured his third divisional title by knocking out WBA featherweight champ Eloy Rojas in 11 rounds. Vazquez defended the 126-pound belt four times before being stripped for fighting WBO champ

Naseem Hamed, who KO'd Vazquez in seven in April 1998. Vazquez lost to rising lightweight star Juan Lazcano in June 2000 (TKO by 9) before ending his career at age 42 in 2002 with a pair of TKO victories over Eddie Saenz. His final record stands at 56-9-2 with 41 KO and one no-contest.

Vazquez enjoyed considerable good fortune following the Avelar fight, but despite his TKO loss, the Puerto Rican can take solace in his courageous showing. For Avelar, May 30, 1986 was a final swim in the sea of success and anyone who witnessed his come-from-behind magic against a future triple world champion will never forget it. Nor should they.

TALES FROM THE VAULT

Total Punches Landed/Thrown

Round	1	2	3	4	5	6	7	8	9	10	11	12	Total
Avelar	35/94	35/106	15/68	26/71	30/80	29/68	33/94	7/23					210/604
	37%	33%	22%	37%	38%	43%	35%	30%					35%
Vazquez	43/88	53/96	32/77	42/84	65/116	30/48	34/72	8/13					307/594
	49%	55%	42%	50%	56%	62%	47%	62%					52%

Jabs Landed/Thrown

Round	1	2	3	4	5	6	7	8	9	10	11	12	Total
Avelar	11/27	7/26	4/23	5/17	3/9	6/15	7/22	4/10					47/149
	41%	27%	17%	29%	33%	40%	32%	40%					32%
Vazquez	15/31	10/24	9/28	15/37	14/32	11/15	19/35	5/8					98/210
	48%	42%	32%	41%	44%	73%	54%	62%					47%

Power Punches Landed/Thrown

Round	1	2	3	4	5	6	7	8	9	10	11	12	Total
Avelar	24/67	28/80	11/45	21/54	27/71	23/53	26/72	3/13					163/455
	36%	35%	24%	39%	38%	43%	36%	23%					36%
Vazquez	28/57	43/72	23/49	27/47	51/84	19/33	15/37	3/5					209/384
	49%	60%	47%	57%	61%	58%	41%	60%					54%

Antonio Avelar vs. Wilfredo Vazquez, May 30, 1986, Miami Beach Fla.

Victor Callejas vs. Loris Stecca II
November 8, 1985, Rimini, Italy

Imagine yourself as a former champion seeking to regain your title against the man from whom you lost it, a fighter considered one of the sport's hardest pound-for-pound punchers. You are fighting before thousands of passionate countrymen who let you know by their roof-rattling shouts that they want you to succeed as much as you do – if not more. As you step inside the ring, you feel confident that you've done everything possible to give yourself the best chance to win. In the final moments before going into battle you think to yourself "I'm as ready as I've ever been in my life. He'll have to kill me to beat me."

Then, in the fight's opening minute, one of your opponent's blows breaks your jaw. The situation is brought into immediate focus: You have 15 long rounds to go, and you know you're in for 59 more minutes of the most excruciating pain you'll ever experience. The blood will gush out of your mouth and even your own movements will jar the jaw enough to cause you agony of the highest order. To win, you'll have to absorb dozens of flush punches from your powerful opponent while also trying to land enough of your own blows to persuade the judges to vote in your favor. Beating him while healthy would be difficult enough – after all, you lost to him by knockout the first time around – but doing so while badly injured is an exponentially tougher task.

Your options are clear – surrender and fight another day (which would be completely justified under the circumstances) or fight on and take a chance on scoring a legendary title-regaining victory, all the while risking permanent damage, or worse.

What would you do?

On November 8, 1985, former WBA junior featherweight champion Loris Stecca was confronted with this scenario and he chose to fight on, doing so in heroic fashion. His courageous stand in the face of adversity is what made his second fight with the fearsome Victor Callejas a Closet Classic.

Boxing history has seen dozens of championship rematches, but rarely does the second fight exceed the first in terms of action, emotion and drama. Alexis Arguello-Alfredo Escalera II and Roberto Duran-Esteban DeJesus II are just two examples, and Callejas-Stecca II is a worthy addition. In their first fight 17 months before, Callejas issued a methodical beating that bloodied Stecca's nose and mouth before the Puerto Rican won Stecca's WBA 122-pound belt by eighth-round stoppage. The rematch, however, would follow a far different script.

Knockouts were nothing new for Callejas – going into this, his second defense, "Luvi" had scored 19 knockouts in his last 22 fights, inspiring many to compare him to recently-departed 122-pound legend and fellow Puerto Rican Wilfredo Gomez.

The similarities were numerous: Both men had troubled pro debuts – a four-round draw to Jacinto Fuentes for Gomez and a four-round loss to Jose Parillo for Callejas. Each avenged their blemishes in subsequent fights (Gomez by second round KO in his sixth pro fight, Callejas by six-round decision in his very next outing). Gomez stood 5-5 while Callejas was 5-6, and the uppercut was an integral part of their offenses – "Bazooka" with the right, "Luvi" with the left. Finally, both fighters demonstrated the ability to box when necessary, and Callejas used those skills to carry him through some difficult moments in his 15-round win over tough Korean Seung Hoon Lee nine months before the rematch with Stecca. The 24-year-old Callejas was approaching his physical prime, and dream matches against WBA featherweight champion Barry McGuigan and WBC king Azumah Nelson were among his most lucrative options.

At 25, Stecca was still plenty young and at 39-1-1 (29 KO) he had a significant edge in experience over Callejas (21-1, 18 KO with 1 no-contest). Another huge advantage for Stecca going into the rematch was his ring activity. After taking nine months off following the Callejas loss, Stecca fought five times over the next five months, winning all of them by knockout over nondescript competition. Over the same 17 months, Callejas had the one defense against Lee before hand problems forced him to the sidelines. Needless to say, ring rust would be a concern for Callejas.

Stecca's biggest advantage, however, was the raucous, adoring fans that crowded into the Palazzetto dello Sport in Rimini, Italy who hoped to carry Stecca to the championship through a tidal wave of sound.

Both men were in excellent condition, weighing well under the 122-pound limit as Callejas was 121 ¼ while Stecca tipped the scale at 121. Each had every reason to believe they could maintain a fast pace over the scheduled 15-round distance.

Callejas came out aggressively at the opening bell, looking to back up Stecca behind a stiff jab and hooks to the head and body while Stecca bobbed and weaved while throwing his own jabs and hooks. Exactly one minute into the round, Callejas threw a four-punch combination – a right to the chin, a hook to the arm and a right hand-left hook to the chin – that clearly hurt the Italian and likely broke his jaw. After a few seconds of backpedaling along the ropes, Stecca composed himself and resumed his bob-and-weave tactics. At the 1:53 mark, Callejas' thunderbolt hook to the point of the chin sent a stricken Stecca staggering toward the ropes with Callejas in hot pursuit. The overanxious champion missed most of his follow-up blows, and Stecca got the better of a couple of furious exchanges over the final minute of the round. At the bell, the defiant Italian yelled at Callejas and gave him an "up-yours" salute as the fans roared their approval.

Callejas began the second with sharp jabs to the head and body of the stalking Stecca. Stecca then nailed Callejas with a lead right to the chin and a hook to the jaw that caused "Luvi" to back off briefly and sent the crowd into a frenzy, shouting "Loris! Loris!

Loris!" But the Puerto Rican remained cool, dodging a four-punch salvo with slick upper body movement. Another four-punch foray from Stecca was more successful and Stecca punctuated his flurry by moving his gloves in a circular fashion and opening his mouth, egging the fans to shout even louder. Stecca finished the round strongly with yet another four-punch combo, of which three got through. Encouraged by his success, a pumped-up Stecca rolled his shoulders and gloves after the round-ending bell.

Stecca continued stalking in the third, landing a right to the body and a hook to the jaw as Callejas jabbed Stecca's head and body. A few seconds later, the Italian favorite staggered Callejas with a hook to the chin that had the Puerto Rican holding on tightly and the crowd in a vocal lather. With adrenaline surging through his body – and with complete disregard for his mangled mandible – Stecca unleashed a blizzard of blows as Callejas backed away on unsteady legs. Stecca continued his assault with a brutal hook to the body and left uppercut flush on the chin.

The spectators stamped their feet and jumped up and down so mightily that the camera recording the fight shook as if an earthquake were taking place. But Callejas was able to calm himself, and near the end of the round he landed a flush hook to Stecca's splintered jaw. For the first time, Stecca's face betrayed the marks of battle as his left eye swelled and blood dripped from his mouth. A follow-up left uppercut to the jaw caused more crimson to spray out, and another left uppercut delivered from the southpaw stance proved Callejas had regained control of his faculties.

Because the crowd had shaken the television lights loose, the fourth round started in a half-lit ring. Callejas continued his steady jabbing while Stecca scored well with a right-left to the chin. Two more Stecca hooks landed cleanly, but, perhaps tellingly, they lacked the impact of previous efforts. A right-left-right by Stecca threw Callejas off balance, and the Italian unleashed yet another volley of follow-up blows, most of which were skillfully slipped by the Puerto Rican star. Between Stecca's attacks, Callejas' jab inflicted significant damage, and one of those jabs tore open a cut over Stecca's left eye. Like a matador spearing a stubborn bull, Callejas stabbed at Stecca's eyes.

The ring lights regained full illumination with 18 seconds left in the round, but darkened again as the round ended.

The ring was still semi-lit as the fifth began, and Stecca's hopes of regaining the title began to dim as well. The blood from Stecca's various injuries was smeared on his trunks and while he remained the stalker, his punch output dropped dramatically. A counter hook to the jaw forced Stecca to back away and a lead right sent what appeared to be a tooth flying from Stecca's mouth.

Despite the enormous pain he must have felt, Stecca continued to plow forward fearlessly, his only concession being that he marshaled his energy for one or two multi-punch spurts. One of those volleys began with a right to the body that caused Callejas to slip along the ropes and a follow-up hook and jab to the chin that landed flush.

Callejas appeared unhurt by the blows, but the crowd, so eager to propel their man to victory, greeted every sign of Callejas' duress with full-throated roars. For Stecca, the sequence represented an encouraging end to what had been a most brutal three minutes. Despite all of his troubles, Stecca's spirit remained buoyant, for as the bell rung Stecca pounded his gloves together as if he were applauding himself.

For those who believed in omens, they had to take comfort in the fact that the ring lights regained full illumination between rounds five and six. Did this mean that better times were ahead for the hometown hero? Stecca, injured as he was, did his best to make it so.

The sixth saw Stecca sustaining his dogged pursuit, and he made sure to keep his right hand high to protect the jaw. His punches carried plenty of heart but no longer had the heft.

Unfortunately for the Italian, Callejas' blows still packed enormous power, and that power manifested itself with startling suddenness when he dropped Stecca with a lead right-left hook to the head. Stecca arose at the count of three, but the damage was now obvious to everyone. Blood poured from the Italian's mouth and his face was a mass of lumps and bumps. Another right-left combo added to Stecca's agony and a crushing hook to the jaw sent the Italian flying to the floor, both of his legs folded underneath him as he landed on the canvas. It was a knockdown so melodramatic that Sylvester Stallone would have been proud, but for this "Italian Stallion" the agony was all too real.

The fight appeared over, but the incredibly courageous Stecca arose at five and convinced referee Stanley Christoudoulou to let the fight continue. After absorbing a steady stream of hooks from Callejas, the bell signaled the end of another chillingly violent round.

Callejas' sixth-round assault opened another cut around Stecca's right eye, adding to the Italian's avalanche of troubles. As he sat on the stool between the sixth and seventh rounds, Stecca's left eye was swollen and raw and his mouth was a crimson mess. One look at Stecca's badly beaten visage was all that trainer Elio Ghelfi needed to see to make his decision. Enough was enough.

At the time of the knockout, Callejas was ahead by 57-56 (Carol Polis), 58-55 (Lou Moret) and 58-57 (Charles Williams). While Callejas performed well in the face of a hostile audience, it was Stecca's raw courage and indomitable spirit in the midst of crisis that made this fight so memorable. Stecca's showing was just another example that real fighters will endure just about anything to achieve the ultimate objective. While his plaque will never hang on the walls of Canastota, Stecca proved, at least on this day, that he was a fighter in the truest sense of the term – mind, body and soul.

Epilogue: Despite his tender years Callejas fought just six more times and never engaged in another 122-pound title fight. The WBA stripped Callejas after failing to reach an agreement to fight mandatory challenger Louie Espinoza, who stopped

Tommy Valoy for the vacant belt on January 16, 1987. After tune-ups against Cleo Garcia (W 10) and Pedro Nolasco (KO 1), Callejas rose in weight to fight Jeff Fenech in Sydney, Australia, for the WBC featherweight title vacated by Azumah Nelson. Though he nailed Fenech with a trademark left uppercut in the first round, Callejas was slowly worn out by Fenech's all-out attack before being stopped in the 10th round. After scoring two wins in 1989 over Juan B. Torres (KO 7) and Brian Roche (W 10), Callejas ended his career on September 6, 1990 with a 10-round loss to Francisco Alvarez. His final record was 26-3 (22 KO).

Stecca laid off nearly eight months to allow the jaw to heal then proceeded to make up for lost time. Stecca fought 17 fights in just 29 months before retiring in December 1988 with a six-round TKO victory over Jorge Alvarez in Sassari, Italy. Stecca enjoyed considerable success during the final stretch of his career, going 16-0-1 with eight knockouts. The level of competition was mediocre, with the most recognizable names being Ron Cisneros (W 8) and Sonny Long (W 8). The draw came against Francisco Arreola and Stecca garnered his third and final disqualification win against Cesar Almonte November 27, 1987. Stecca's retired with an excellent 55-2-2 mark with 37 knockouts.

TALES FROM THE VAULT

Total Punches Landed/Thrown

Round	1	2	3	4	5	6	7	8	9	10	11	12	Total
Callejas	29/72	18/52	9/44	12/40	16/47	21/50							105/305
	40%	35%	20%	30%	34%	42%							34%
Stecca	20/59	14/57	21/66	16/38	20/54	13/36							104/310
	34%	25%	32%	42%	37%	36%							34%

Jabs Landed/Thrown

Round	1	2	3	4	5	6	7	8	9	10	11	12	Total
Callejas	6/17	14/38	2/27	9/25	11/29	7/19							49/155
	35%	37%	7%	36%	38%	37%							32%
Stecca	5/17	5/25	2/16	5/11	6/18	5/15							28/102
	29%	20%	12%	45%	33%	33%							27%

Power Punches Landed/Thrown

Round	1	2	3	4	5	6	7	8	9	10	11	12	Total
Callejas	23/55	4/14	7/17	3/15	5/18	14/31							56/150
	42%	29%	41%	20%	28%	45%							37%
Stecca	15/42	9/32	19/50	11/27	14/36	8/21							76/208
	36%	28%	38%	41%	39%	38%							37%

Victor Callejas vs. Loris Stecca II, November 8, 1985, Rimini, Italy

Danny Lopez vs. Ruben Olivares
December 4, 1975, Inglewood, California

During the 1960s and 1970s, Southern California was the place to be if you wanted to see the world's best smaller men trade leather in all-out turf wars. Inglewood had the Fabulous Forum while Los Angeles boasted the Olympic Auditorium, Coliseum and Memorial Sports Arena. The roster of champions who graced those rings reads like a Who's Who of Latin greats: Jose Napoles, Roberto Duran, Rodolfo Gonzalez, Mando Ramos, Romeo Anaya, Alfonso Zamora, Carlos Zarate, Chucho Castillo, Bobby Chacon, Alexis Arguello, Lupe Pintor and many more.

The fans demanded action for their hard-earned money. Those who complied were showered with coins as well as love and respect that continued long after retirement. Those who didn't were showered by cups of warm beer, or even worse, warm liquids made of far more personal ingredients.

This high-octane match between two of the biggest fan favorites from that era, Ruben Olivares and Danny "Little Red" Lopez, took place at the Forum and for both it was a crossroads fight. The 28-year-old Olivares (79-6-1, 71 KO) had lost his WBC featherweight title to Ghanaian David "Poison" Kotey nine weeks earlier at this same venue. Meanwhile, the 23-year-old Lopez (27-3, 26 KO) was seeking to rebuild his reputation after suffering losses to Chacon (KO by 9), Shig Fukuyama (KO by 9) and Octavio Gomez (L 10) between May 1974 and January 1975. "Little Red" came into the Olivares fight on a three-fight winning streak, knocking out a faded Chucho Castillo (KO 2), Raul Cruz (KO 6) and Antonio Nava (KO 6). Beating Olivares would certify Lopez as a legitimate title threat while for Olivares, knocking off "Little Red" would justify return matches with either Kotey or WBA champion Alexis Arguello, who stopped Olivares in 13 rounds the previous November to win his belt.

The fans that filled the Forum to see Lopez-Olivares carried high expectations because the combatants' predatory styles were made for each other. Both were aggressors whose one-punch power could end the fight at any moment – and both men also had leaky defenses and shaky chins. The fight may have been scheduled for 10 rounds, but everyone *knew* the fight wasn't going to last that long. The only question on everyone's mind was "who's going down?"

The answer: Both of them.

Lopez and Olivares went right to work after the opening bell sounded, with Lopez having the faster hands and Olivares the more proven. "Little Red" fired quick one-twos while "Mr. KO" winged his famous left hooks, though they were thrown slowly and inaccurately at first. Two sharper hooks by Olivares turned Lopez into the ropes, and the Mexican took advantage by landing another hook to the jaw, a right to the face and a hook to the body before Lopez managed to spin away.

While exchanging hard blows at ring center, Olivares slammed Lopez with an overhand right to the ear that dropped the younger man on his right side. Early knockdowns weren't new for the notoriously slow-starting Lopez and at times it looked as if he needed these crises to get himself into the fight.

"(Getting knocked down) actually stirred me up and infuriated me," Lopez said years later. "I'd think, *'who is this guy to knock me down?'* All those times I got knocked down and jumped back up, I was never really hurt or dazed. The thing that went through my mind was to just get up and get that knockdown back."

Lopez leapt to his feet before referee Dick Young even had a chance to count and as Young tolled the mandatory eight, Lopez stalked around the ring, anxious to exact revenge. Knowing Lopez wasn't seriously hurt, "Mr. KO" didn't go for the KO. Maybe he should have, for just 16 seconds after the action resumed Lopez got his revenge – and more.

"Little Red" threw three soft jabs and countered Olivares' wide hook with a pinpoint right to the chin that dumped Olivares near his own corner. Furious, the Mexican pounded the canvas with his fist before rising at six. Unlike Olivares seconds earlier, Lopez went for the kill. He tore into Olivares, missing an overhand right and a left hook before exploding a lead right off the head. A hook to the jaw caused Olivares to stumble backward before crashing to the canvas posterior-first. Down for the second time, "Rockabye Ruben" shook his head to clear the cobwebs and pounded his fist on the canvas in self-chastisement. As he took the count on one knee, he stared at Lopez with a mixture of exasperation, frustration and bewilderment. A split-second after Olivares arose at eight, the bell signaled the end of an incredible first round.

His pride stung, Olivares wanted nothing more than to make amends. He nailed Lopez with a wide hook to begin round two, but Lopez, his chin now warmed up, took the punch well. Though Olivares was able to bull Lopez to the ropes, "Little Red" got the better of the exchanges with his quick-fisted combinations. A solid right backed Olivares off and a follow-up right to the temple consolidated his advantage.

When at his best, Lopez is a punching machine whose volume attack is designed to keep his opponents occupied with defense while also allowing him to set the table for even harder punches. That formula worked perfectly here as a counter right over Olivares' hook positioned him to throw a hook and a right uppercut that decked Olivares for the third time in the fight. The Mexican looked badly hurt this time and he took every available second to clear his head before arising at nine.

Olivares barreled his way inside to smother Lopez's follow-up shots and even got in a good hook late in the round. Meanwhile, Lopez could not draw a bead on Olivares' chin and because of that the veteran two-division champ escaped without suffering further damage.

The Mexicans in the crowd tried to spark Olivares by chanting "Mexico, Mexico" as the third round began but their favorite was too busy fending off a steady stream of jabs, hooks, uppercuts and crosses to launch his own offensive. Olivares knew Lopez couldn't possibly maintain his fast pace, so he bided his time until he saw the opening he wanted. For all his power, Olivares was a smart ring man who could box when necessary, and his on-the-fly blueprint for survival soon began to pay dividends. The tide slowly started to turn in the round's final minute as Olivares, his back on the ropes, landed two rights to the chin that backed Lopez off. Another overhand right capped his mini-rally and Lopez returned to the corner sporting a cut over his right eye.

Encouraged by his late-round success, Olivares opened the fourth sharply, landing jabs to the face and body while mixing in lead rights and left hooks that targeted Lopez's cut. Fighting with much improved rhythm, Olivares began to find the zone where he could land punches while also eluding Lopez's. A snappy overhand right jolted Lopez's head and when the fourth round bell sounded, Olivares knew he had turned a corner.

The Mexican continued his rally early in the fifth as he landed an arcing right to the jaw and a hook that drove Lopez to the ropes. Though Olivares was starting to dominate, an element of danger was always present for Olivares because Lopez had already proved he could turn the tables with a single punch. But for now, Olivares' experience was the dominant factor.

Both men picked up the pace in round six as Lopez tried to offset Olivares' boxing with more pressure. A lead right and a jab to the chin backed up Olivares and another right to the jaw landed with force. Olivares responded with a solid right and a hook to the body. The pulsating give-and-take action continued throughout the session and the fans were getting more than their money's worth as the two world-class fighters dug in their toes and exchanged powerful blows in ring center. Olivares punctuated the round with two flush rights to the jaw that Lopez absorbed without ill effect.

Even though Olivares was more than holding his own, the tenor of the fight was shifting against Olivares in two ways. First, for someone reputed to have a "glass jaw," Lopez fielded Olivares' power shots with aplomb while the naturally bigger Lopez's punches had a clear effect on the former bantamweight champion. Second, the fight was evolving into a battle of attrition, a bad equation because Olivares carried the wear-and-tear of 86 fights into the ring while Lopez was six years younger and 56 fights fresher. If Olivares were to win, he'd have to do it soon.

With that in mind, Olivares opened the seventh with a strong right that brought oohs and aahs from the Forum faithful. The Mexican feinted a left to the body to bring Lopez's hands down, then nailed him with a solid right. Another right crashed on Lopez's jaw but the Utah native absorbed the blows without flinching because Olivares was not the puncher at featherweight that he was at 118.

Just when everyone thought Olivares was on the road to victory, the Mexican ran headlong into a brick wall – one encased in a boxing glove, that is. Lopez's light, range-finding jab set up a scorching right cross that caught Olivares coming in. With his quarry stunned, Lopez then applied the *coup de grace* – a gorgeous six-inch right to the jaw that drove Olivares to the canvas.

The discouraged Mexican shook his head twice as he listened to Young's count and pondered his fate. At seven, a kneeling Olivares made his decision. He covered his eyes with his gloves, then crawled on his hands and knees as the final seconds were tolled. Only after Young counted "ten" and waved off the fight at the 1:59 mark did Olivares pull himself upright, after which he walked over to Lopez and congratulated him. It was clear that Olivares wanted no more of Lopez, and while Olivares will always be known as "Mr. KO," he seemingly passed the torch to a younger, stronger and – on this day – better man.

Epilogue: The Olivares victory was just the beginning of a great run for Lopez, who won his next 14 fights in the ensuing four years. In his next outing, "Little Red" knocked out 17-year-old future lightweight champion Sean O'Grady in four rounds. Three fights later, Lopez traveled to Accra, Ghana and, before a crowd of more than 100,000, dethroned Kotey over 15 rounds. Lopez said years later that his performance was so dominant that the Ghanaian government burned the fight film. "Little Red" defended the WBC title eight times, often rallying from the brink of doom to knock out his opponents. His 15-round TKO over Mike Ayala was named Ring's Fight of the Year in 1979 and Lopez's fights were "must-see TV" on Saturday and Sunday afternoons.

Lopez ran out of miracles on Groundhog Day 1980 against classy counter puncher Salvador Sanchez, who stopped him in 13 dominant rounds. Lopez fared better in the rematch four months later, even holding a slight lead after 10 rounds. But Sanchez's late-round strength snuffed out Lopez's dreams of regaining the title and the fight was stopped in the 14th.

"Little Red" retired on the advice of trainer Bennie Georgino, a decision he later regretted. After spending several years working in construction, a 39-year-old Lopez returned to the ring against Jorge Rodriguez. Lopez left the ring for good after suffering a two-round TKO. Lopez, a member of the International Boxing Hall of Fame's Class of 2010, retired with a record of 42-6 (39 KO).

Olivares took six months off before resuming his career with a one-round KO over Pajet Lupikanet. The Mexican made one more run at a title, going 7-2-1 (5 KO) before meeting WBA featherweight champion Eusebio Pedroza July 21, 1979 in Houston. Olivares didn't have nearly enough in the tank to deal with Pedroza, who was at the peak of his powers. The 12-round TKO loss was Olivares' final title fight. The Mexican legend fought six more times in the next nine years, going 2-3-1 (2 KO). The 41-year-old Olivares ended his career with a four-round TKO loss to Ignacio Madrid in Mexico City March 12, 1988. The Hall of Famer's career record is 88-13-3 (78 KO).

BRAWLS

Total Punches Landed/Thrown

Round	1	2	3	4	5	6	7	8	9	10	11	12	Total
Lopez	32/78 41%	39/111 35%	28/97 29%	22/95 23%	26/106 25%	39/104 38%	16/45 36%						202/636 32%
Olivares	35/62 56%	27/73 37%	29/68 43%	40/90 44%	31/62 50%	29/63 46%	16/40 40%						207/458 45%

Jabs Landed/Thrown

Round	1	2	3	4	5	6	7	8	9	10	11	12	Total
Lopez	9/30 30%	1/22 5%	5/38 13%	3/43 7%	4/38 11%	11/40 28%	5/23 22%						38/234 16%
Olivares	3/8 38%	1/6 17%	2/9 22%	6/16 38%	4/8 50%	5/10 50%	3/12 25%						24/69 35%

Power Punches Landed/Thrown

Round	1	2	3	4	5	6	7	8	9	10	11	12	Total
Lopez	23/48 48%	38/89 43%	23/59 39%	19/52 37%	22/68 32%	28/64 44%	11/22 50%						164/402 41%
Olivares	32/54 59%	26/67 39%	27/59 46%	34/74 46%	27/54 50%	24/53 45%	13/28 46%						183/389 47%

Danny Lopez vs. Ruben Olivares, December 4, 1975, Inglewood, California

TALES FROM THE VAULT

Alexis Arguello vs. Andy Ganigan
May 22, 1982, Las Vegas, Nevada

The line that separates the great from the very good is an extremely thin one. Over the years, many fighters have assembled outstanding records, especially during the early stages when their superior skills overwhelm handpicked opposition. Upon seeing this, those well versed in the sport would nod their heads and say "yes, he's done well, but let's see what happens when his opponents start fighting back."

It may sound harsh, but only the proverbial baptism in fire can bring out those special qualities that either certify greatness or expose fatal flaws.

Alexis Arguello had his first taste of world-class adversity when he challenged Ernesto Marcel for the WBA featherweight title February 16, 1974 in Panama City. The 21-year-old Arguello weighed an improbably light 122 ½ pounds against the seasoned Marcel and his lack of strength hurt him as the Panamanian rocked him time and again before winning a clear-cut 15-round decision. Marcel, though just 25, announced his retirement shortly thereafter.

Great fighters don't necessarily succeed the first time around, but they do learn from past mistakes. Nine months after the Marcel loss, Arguello got a second crack at the WBA belt against the legendary Ruben Olivares, who won Marcel's vacated belt by knocking out Zensuke Utagawa in seven rounds. Out-boxed and trailing on the scorecards, Arguello patiently walked Olivares down and seized on an opening early in the 13th. Two knockdowns later, Arguello was the new champion.

Over the next eight years, Arguello faced several more tests of his mettle, and he was up to the task each time. Alfredo Escalera pushed back hard against Arguello's classical skills in both of their fights, but the Nicaraguan prevailed with a pair of 13th round knockouts. Bobby Chacon enjoyed many good moments against Arguello, but the Nicaraguan came through with a seven round KO. The young, fiery Ray Mancini offered a stern challenge for Arguello's WBC lightweight title in 1981, yet the savvy Arguello waited patiently until he lowered the boom on "Boom Boom" in the 14th.

By the time Arguello (74-4, 60 KO) met Andy Ganigan May 22, 1982 at the Aladdin Hotel in Las Vegas, he was an expert on how to handle difficult situations in the ring, and he would need every one of those skills against the wild-swinging Hawaii-based Filipino. The 29-year-old Arguello was now a triple champion, winning belts at featherweight and junior lightweight before winning the WBC lightweight title from Jim Watt 11 months before meeting Ganigan. To this point, Arguello had won 18 consecutive title fights, having vacated his other two belts due to weight-making difficulties.

Ganigan (34-3, 30 KO) was the mandatory challenger to Arguello's strap, earning his opportunity by knocking out former WBA lightweight champion Sean O'Grady in two rounds for the spurious World Athletic Association belt October 31, 1981. The WAA was the brainchild of Pat O'Grady, who sought to give his son a title after Sean was stripped for not fighting mandatory challenger Claude Noel, but Ganigan upset the apple cart by scoring three knockdowns in the second round before the fight was stopped. Predictably, Ganigan never defended the WAA bauble.

Arguello was coming off a sixth round TKO of James "Bubba" Busceme, who just happened to defeat Ganigan at the National Golden Gloves in 1972. The fight was originally scheduled for April 3, but a viral infection forced Arguello to push the fight back six weeks – the first postponement of Arguello's long career. Ironically, it was Ganigan, not Arguello, who experienced problems making weight. Arguello checked in at 134 ¾ while Ganigan was one pound over at the 7 p.m. weigh-in the day before the fight. Ganigan hit the 135-pound limit on his second try and seemed none the worse for wear.

Few nicknames have ever been better suited for a pair of fighters. Arguello was known as "El Flaco Explosivo" – The Explosive Thin Man – while Ganigan carried the sobriquet "The Hawaiian Punch." The Nicaraguan was a man of diverse skills. While he wasn't slicing through opponents' defenses with precise jabs, he was laying them out with an assortment of heavy hooks, thunderous crosses and draining body blows. Ganigan was a pure predator that charged in behind winging hooks and powerful left crosses. The jab was merely a rumor as he used it to blind opponents to the charges that invariably followed.

Arguello began the fight by advancing to ring center with his hands high, chin tucked downward and making himself as tall as his 5-10 frame allowed. The southpaw Ganigan, faced with 2 ½-inch disadvantages in height and reach, probed with half-speed jabs while ducking low to find a way inside. Ganigan landed the fight's first punch, a right hook to the body, but Arguello spun away to ring center where Ganigan missed with a wild right and left. Ganigan was the aggressor out of necessity, and Arguello spent much of the round trying to catch Ganigan barreling in.

For all his virtues, Arguello was a habitually slow starter and Ganigan was about to exploit that flaw to the fullest.

With 35 seconds left in the round, Ganigan bulled Arguello into the ropes, where he landed a right hook to the body and a pinpoint left to the button that floored Arguello for only the second time in his career. Jose Luis Ramirez had turned the trick six fights earlier while losing a razor-thin 10-round decision. Up at two, Arguello wore a tiny smile of embarrassment but also had fire in his eyes as he glared at Ganigan. The message was loud and clear: *"Okay, good shot. But now the fight really begins. Let's see if you can handle it."*

Ganigan had only 22 seconds to finish the job, and he stormed in behind wild punches. The challenger landed a good left cross to the ear but Arguello countered with a stiff right to the forehead. Neither man could line up the other for the remainder of what was an action-packed and shocking opening round.

His pride stung by the knockdown, Arguello was determined to get to work as the second round opened. A lead right smacked against Ganigan's forehead but the charging Hawaiian bounced back behind a left to the chin. Another charge resulted in a landed left to the body and a right hook to the jaw.

By being so aggressive, Ganigan was playing a risky game because of Arguello's masterful countering ability, but for now he was finding great success. His confidence was surging, and even after Arguello caught him with a left hook that spun his head Ganigan nodded forcefully and smiled as if to say *"Good punch! But I can take anything you can throw, and then I'll take you out."*

Arguello started the third quickly, firing a jab and landing a right that caught Ganigan at the end of the punch. The challenger roared back, throwing a three-punch combo of which one, another short solid left, connected. Ganigan pressed ahead and muscled Arguello to the ropes with a left to the body and another to the jaw. Arguello bit down and drove Ganigan away with a four-punch salvo that ended with a right to the forehead. The champion missed a right to the chin, but another one to the cheek forced Ganigan to retreat.

Arguello then unleashed a hair-trigger lead right to the jaw that caught Ganigan reaching in with his jab and dropped the Hawaiian on his right side. Like Arguello before him, Ganigan arose very quickly while the Nicaraguan stalked slowly from the neutral corner.

Unhurt, Ganigan stormed in again, landing a right to the body but missing with a wild right-left that allowed Arguello to land an overhand left. As Ganigan advanced, Arguello shot a thudding right to the body that made Ganigan wince and a cross that smacked against his jaw. An Arguello right to the head drove Ganigan to Arguello's corner and the champion turned on the jets, firing a torrent of blows designed to finish the job. Ganigan weaved his body from side to side to avoid the brunt of Arguello's attack while firing back heavy shots of his own. A tremendous right hook gave Ganigan enough room to return to ring center. While there, Ganigan uncorked a right hook-left cross combo but Arguello countered with a short hook. Ganigan then exploded a short left cross that made Arguello's knees buckle.

The action was furious and while Arguello was getting the better of it, Ganigan remained dangerous. The experience of 78 fights proved valuable as the Nicaraguan maintained a cool head while fighting off Ganigan in the eye of the storm. His head buzzing, Arguello went back to basics as he snapped a jab to the face and ripped a hook to the ribs. Another hook caught Ganigan moving to his right and a straight right wobbled Ganigan into the turnbuckle as a most tumultuous third round ended. A charged-up Arguello bounced on his toes while his eyes bore a hole through Ganigan as the challenger made his way back to the corner.

The fans were roaring in both appreciation and surprise at the strength of Ganigan's challenge as well as Arguello's furious response to it. The styles dictated a good action fight, but the gulf in class was thought to be so wide that a one-sided fight could result. Despite the mountains he faced, Ganigan was able to lift his game to a new level and the back-and-forth action offered the crowd and the CBS audience an unexpected thrill.

Ganigan again came out throwing in the fourth, but Arguello deftly deflected the blows with his gloves and forearms. Arguello zipped in an uppercut to the chin and bounced a right off Ganigan's jaw. The challenger pulled Arguello into a clinch and popped him with a left, drawing a warning from Carlos Padilla for holding and hitting. Perhaps still feeling the effects of the third-round knockdown, Ganigan began backing away and tossing light, but inaccurate jabs. The challenger missed with two lefts but landed a light right hook to the body.

Arguello now was walking down the challenger, firing a jab and catching him with a solid hook coming in. The champion was slowly imposing his will and talent on Ganigan, keeping him at his preferred punching range and pummeling him with his full arsenal of blows in a calm, measured, yet devastating manner. He mixed his punches between head and body with the care of a master craftsman and soon Ganigan didn't know from where the next punch would be launched. Arguello went about his work with no burst of emotion or a dramatic fusillade of punches. They came one at a time but over time the accumulation began to take a toll on Ganigan's physical strength and mental resolve. And yet, the Hawaiian/Filipino was stubborn and determined as he pumped away with passion but without precision. After the bell ending the fourth, Ganigan walked back to the corner with a significant nosebleed, plus a first-hand education of why Arguello rated among the world's top pound-for-pound fighters.

The fifth round provided a graphic illustration of why height and reach are so valuable to boxers. To be effective, the shorter Ganigan had to lunge in while the angular Arguello had the luxury of landing his blows while also maintaining proper balance and leverage. Arguello nailed Ganigan coming in with a jab that had the force of some fighters' right hands, and another lead right bounced off the forehead. Ganigan continued to march forward, landing a right to the body that had less juice than a few minutes earlier.

Arguello worked steadily, his clinical but violent blows breaking down Ganigan bit by bit.

Three solid jabs cracked off Ganigan's jaw and he retreated to the ropes with 13 seconds remaining. At that point, Arguello assembled a final bouquet of brilliance – a jab, a short right, a hook to the chin, a left uppercut to the jaw, a hook to the ear, a monstrous right to the body, another hook to the ear, a crunching right to the pit of the stomach, a third hook to the ear and a final right to the jaw as Ganigan collapsed to the canvas. Nearly every one of those 10 punches landed and the result was the valiant Ganigan grimacing in pain and spitting out his mouthpiece as Padilla tolled "ten."

"In the earlier two rounds, he was giving me a lot of trouble because he has a really weird, difficult style," Arguello told CBS' Tim Ryan. "I always say that each fighter has our own style and Ganigan is one of those guys that has his own style. I knew in the first round how he was going to counter punch me. In the third I really knew what was going on. Eddie Futch told me what to do and I paid really good attention."

"I thought I had a chance to finish him off, but I was wrong," Ganigan said. "He's a great champion and he knows how to handle himself really good. I congratulate him."

Ending the interview with a wry smile, Ganigan declared "I shall return."

Epilogue: Ganigan would return, but only for one more fight. Thirteen months after the loss to Arguello, Ganigan fought future IBF lightweight champion Jimmy Paul for the vacant USBA belt and was knocked out in the sixth round. His final record was 34-5 (30 KO).

Arguello gave up his WBC lightweight title after beating Ganigan and moved up to 140 in an attempt to become the first boxer to win championships in four weight classes. Two months after the Ganigan victory, Arguello splattered Kevin Rooney in two rounds with a scorching right cross to the jaw. But Arguello's pursuit of history was brutally stopped by WBA junior welterweight champion Aaron Pryor, who unflinchingly absorbed dozens of Arguello's best bombs before knocking the triple-crown king unconscious in the 14th round.

Arguello was never the same fighter after losing to Pryor, though he decisioned Vilomar Fernandez to avenge an earlier loss and knocked out former WBA lightweight king Claude Noel in three rounds to earn a second chance at Pryor. In an underrated slugfest, Arguello again lost to "The Hawk," this time in the 10th round, and announced his retirement.

But the Nicaraguan great couldn't stay away. Twenty-five months after the second loss to Pryor, Arguello stopped Pat Jefferson in five rounds. Arguello was nearing a shot at WBA champion Patrizio Oliva after knocking out former WBC champion Billy Costello in four rounds, but he had to abort the comeback after doctors found an abnormality with his heart. In 1992, Arguello was inducted into the International Boxing Hall of Fame.

Still, Arguello's desire to fight wasn't fully sated. At age 42, Arguello became only the second IBHOF member (after Sugar Ray Leonard) to emerge from retirement to fight again. Arguello's return got off to a decent start when he overcame a broken right hand to score a majority decision over Jorge Palomares. On January 21, 1995 in Las Vegas, Arguello's ring career came to a final end after losing a comprehensive 10-round decision to Scott "Pink Cat" Walker. His final record is 82-8 (65 KO).

Total Punches Landed/Thrown

Round	1	2	3	4	5	6	7	8	9	10	11	12	Total
Arguello	9/25	12/32	34/69	22/44	31/54								108/224
	36%	38%	49%	50%	57%								48%
Ganigan	15/63	24/77	26/87	14/72	12/71								91/370
	24%	31%	30%	19%	17%								25%

Jabs Landed/Thrown

Round	1	2	3	4	5	6	7	8	9	10	11	12	Total
Arguello	3/7	4/12	5/14	6/13	13/25								31/71
	43%	33%	36%	46%	52%								44%
Ganigan	3/36	6/45	5/38	5/41	5/45								24/205
	8%	13%	13%	12%	11%								12%

Power Punches Landed/Thrown

Round	1	2	3	4	5	6	7	8	9	10	11	12	Total
Arguello	6/18	8/20	29/55	16/31	18/29								77/153
	33%	40%	53%	52%	62%								50%
Ganigan	12/27	18/32	21/49	9/31	7/26								67/165
	44%	56%	43%	29%	27%								41%

Alexis Arguello vs. Andy Ganigan, May 22, 1982, Las Vegas, Nevada

Julio Gonzalez vs. Julian Letterlough
February 2, 2001 – Columbus, Ohio

In boxing, there are few sure things – at least on the positive side. Fans and media alike often are frustrated by decisions that defy logic while the omnipresent promotional infighting has prevented many great matches from materializing. Moreover, prospects that carry the "can't-miss" label end up missing the mark.

So when a positive "sure thing" like Julian Letterlough came along, many fans eagerly latched on because they knew what they were going to get. Whenever his name appeared on the marquee, it was a virtual lock that whatever the result the route getting there was going to be wildly entertaining. His thrill-a-minute fights against, among others, Sam Ahmad, Max Heyman, Richard Hall and Demetrius Jenkins earned Letterlough lasting respect and admiration. But the one fight for which he will be best remembered came against Julio Gonzalez February 2, 2001 at the Celeste Center in Columbus, Ohio.

The man known as "Mr. KO" was raw and unpolished, but there were two good reasons for that. First, Letterlough had no amateur background and second, he entered the pro ranks at the advanced age of 28 after serving a seven-year prison term for assault. Following his release, Letterlough made a concerted effort to get his life on track and boxing provided the means by which he could improve his family's lot. Despite his personal and professional obstacles, the 31-year-old Letterlough carried a 15-0-1 (15 KO) mark into the ring against the 24-year-old Gonzalez (25-0, 16 KO), who was ranked ninth by the WBA.

Unlike Letterlough, Gonzalez was an accomplished amateur who represented Mexico in the 1996 Olympics – though he lost in a first-round fight to eventual gold medalist (and future cruiserweight champion) Vassiliy Jirov. Gonzalez also enjoyed huge physical advantages over Letterlough – four inches in height and 11 inches in reach. To win, Gonzalez needed to suppress his natural tendency to brawl and operate behind the jab while trying to catch Letterlough coming in with uppercuts. Meanwhile, Letterlough had to find a way inside for two reasons – to establish proper range for his bombs and to smother Gonzalez's long-armed punches. Gonzalez's people might have wanted a boxing match, but everyone present knew that a slugfest was all but inevitable. After all, "Mr. KO" was in the house.

Letterlough marched forward as the opening bell rang, moving his torso side to side to slip past Gonzalez's jab while Gonzalez took small steps back to establish proper punching range. As Letterlough briefly stepped back toward the corner with his hands down, Gonzalez swiftly capitalized. A right uppercut snapped Letterlough's head and a follow-up one-two dropped him to a knee.

Only 21 seconds had elapsed when Letterlough hit the floor, and with Gonzalez quickly proving he had the power to drop "Mr. KO," any chance of a technical match went out the window. Letterlough arose at two, and Gonzalez wobbled Letterlough again by beating him in an exchange of hooks. As Letterlough backed to the ropes Gonzalez stunned the Pennsylvanian a third time by slamming in two overhand rights and a crunching hook to the ribs. Mindful of Letterlough's well-honed recuperative powers, Gonzalez fought with some caution and Letterlough validated Gonzalez's prudence by winging powerful, but inaccurate blows.

As the seconds passed, Letterlough steadily regained his equilibrium. A terrific overhand right cracked Gonzalez's chin with a minute to go, but he soon was clutching Gonzalez's head with both hands. With Letterlough voluntarily immobilized, Gonzalez blasted away at Letterlough's exposed ribs with both hands and a body right-head hook combo broke Letterlough's grasp. As the round closed, Gonzalez peppered Letterlough with a lead right to the body, hooks to the ribs and jaw, a one-two to the head and a final hook to the body to punctuate a dominant round.

In the first round, Gonzalez unleashed 92 blows, landing 31 of them for 38 percent accuracy. Letterlough, who was in survival mode most of the round, landed only six of his 46 punches. But if anyone was equipped to overcome a slow start, it was Letterlough.

Letterlough started the second well with a lunging right-left that backed Gonzalez away, but Gonzalez turned the tables with a right-left to the body and a left uppercut to the head that turned Letterlough toward the ropes.

As Gonzalez and Letterlough bombed away, the Mexican was winning the exchanges with his harder, sharper blows, but Letterlough had gained a significant strategic advantage by having the fight take place at close range. The intensity of the exchanges increased steadily and it wasn't long before both men were swapping full-strength power shots. Ironically, by getting hurt early, Letterlough was able to draw Gonzalez into the type of inside war in which he excelled.

As the second round neared an end, Letterlough turned Gonzalez toward the ropes and whaled away, but his shots still lacked Gonzalez's accuracy as most were either blocked or slipped. By out-landing Letterlough 58-17 while connecting on 52 power shots, Gonzalez had established firm control of the bout.

The third started at long range with Gonzalez snapping jabs and Letterlough bobbing and weaving in search of openings. Letterlough's jabs fell short but then again he wasn't about jabs, he was about power. Forty seconds into the round, Letterlough dramatically drove that message home.

After breaking from a clinch, Gonzalez returned inside with a right-left to the body and a missed right uppercut. As Gonzalez prepared to throw another right, Letterlough unleashed a well-timed hair-trigger right that caught Gonzalez in his windup and dropped him to a knee. Up at two, Gonzalez walked to a corner looking slightly dazed and he opened his mouth wide to alleviate the numbness as he took the eight count.

At last, "Mr. KO" had a chance to do his thing.

His first overhand right missed, but the second landed sharply and a left hook glanced off the forehead. Gonzalez managed to spin Letterlough back onto the ropes and nicely ducked under a pair of hooks. They resumed trading bombs until they entangled themselves enough to force a break. By the round's midway point, Gonzalez had regained his balance, and therefore the balance of power. A thumping hook to the body and a follow-up right uppercut-left hook prompted Letterlough to drop his gloves and fire a hard stare.

Though Gonzalez possessed the height and reach to keep Letterlough at bay, he couldn't resist the temptation to yield to his brawling instincts. But going toe to toe with Letterlough was working for Gonzalez as he continually blasted in combinations, plus he absorbed most of Letterlough's blows with enviable aplomb. A strong right to the ear jerked Letterlough's head to the side but Letterlough retaliated with a right to the ear, a hook to the jaw and another right to the ear that forced a rare clinch. As the round wound down, the two men continued to trade and any doubts that this fight would live up to the hype were dismissed.

The bout, while undeniably thrilling, was also a statistical wipeout. Through three rounds, Gonzalez had out-landed Letterlough 118-38 while throwing only 69 more punches. Gonzalez was busier and far more accurate, but the Pennsylvanian puncher was secure in the knowledge that he could instantly turn the fight at any moment. Moreover, he was willing to put in the work to make that happen.

Both men went straight to close quarters in the fourth with Gonzalez on the attack and Letterlough on the ropes. Gonzalez fired faster and landed harder and though Letterlough offered stiff resistance, he still wasn't able to land cleanly or consistently. Gonzalez's pedigree enabled him to more easily find the range and successfully target vital areas. Meanwhile, Letterlough continued to pound away in the hopes that something good would happen along the way.

Midway through the round, Letterlough landed a thudding right uppercut-left cross combo and a snappy overhand right jerked Gonzalez's head. Letterlough's rally was short-lived and Gonzalez hurt Letterlough with a sizzling hook, two overhand rights and a left uppercut. The follow-through on a home-run overhand right sent Gonzalez off-balance, and Letterlough smartly parked himself at extremely close range to smother Gonzalez's follow-ups. Letterlough ripped a good left uppercut, but Gonzalez recovered quickly enough to line up a solid left-right.

The pace was hot, the action never waned and it made for excellent viewing. But seconds into the fifth Letterlough made even better TV by landing his money punch – a crunching counter hook – that sent Gonzalez face first onto the lower rope. This time

Gonzalez took the full eight, but his pride commanded him to fight back and his rally convinced Letterlough – an expert in knockout situations – that Gonzalez needed more tenderizing before serving up the finisher.

Gonzalez rallied strongly, backing Letterlough to the ropes with a hook to the body and stunning him with a six-punch volley. But like Gonzalez, Letterlough's instinct was to fight when hurt and while his blows lacked accuracy he still gave Gonzalez plenty to think about.

In the sixth, Gonzalez continued to fire away but Letterlough remained persistent and competitive, whaling away with gusto and resolve. He was staying true to his talent and was willing to take everything to give himself the chance to land that one precious equalizer. With 56 seconds remaining, Gonzalez landed a right to the ear, but Letterlough answered with an overhand right and a crunching hook that spun Gonzalez's head around. It was a testament to Gonzalez's strength that he not only took it but that he fought back. In the final seconds, Letterlough began to show the first telltale signs of fatigue and the blood flow from his mouth was increasing. Seeing this, Gonzalez stepped on the gas and finished the round strongly.

Gonzalez began the seventh on his toes, driving Letterlough to the ropes with jabs. Letterlough grimaced as he soaked up hook after hook to the ribs, but he drove himself forward, turned Gonzalez to the ropes and blasted away at his flanks. At the midway point, both retreated to long range to give themselves a break from the draining chest-to-chest combat. The shorter Letterlough wasn't doing badly, matching the more ring-wise Gonzalez jab for jab. But almost inevitably, the fight moved back inside with one minute remaining and, like most of the fight so far, Gonzalez threw and landed more often.

With 13 seconds remaining, Gonzalez sunk a short hook to the liver that left Letterlough doubled over and wincing in pain. Gonzalez climbed all over Letterlough, who opted to keep his hands high and wait out the storm instead of clinching. After absorbing a second liver hook, Letterlough rode out the round by slowing backing away with arms down and a smile on his face to conceal the waves of searing pain that racked his body.

The one-minute rest did Letterlough much good – a testament to his conditioning – and he began the eighth by cracking a hook to the body and peppering Gonzalez with short inside punches. A right-left to the torso struck forcefully and he backed Gonzalez to the ropes with a follow-up volleys punctuated with a heavy hook.

Letterlough was enjoying his longest sequence of success and Gonzalez sought to recover from his strenuous seventh by inducing more clinches and retreating to ring center. Gonzalez picked up the pace in the final round's final minute and kept it up throughout the ninth.

Both men tested the other's resolve in different ways and both had scored passing grades. Gonzalez proved his fighting heart by continually forcing the fight despite being knocked down twice. Letterlough was used to being floored, but he was also accustomed to putting those opponents away. Gonzalez proved to be far more resilient and yet Letterlough didn't get frustrated or discouraged. An interview conducted by ESPN2 before the fight offered an explanation for his unwavering self-belief.

"You hit a guy with your best shot, you knock him down and he gets right back up, gets right back in your face, he's not running and he's not looking for an easy way out," Letterlough said. "You go *'I just hit this man with my best shot, so what's next?'* It's pressure. It's that constant pressure that breaks your opponent down. It's like *'wow, man'* Then he gets careless, he drops his hands, you hit him with a good shot and he's down. Even if he can get back up, sometimes he's like *'hey, I don't even want to get back up.'*" After absorbing another pounding in the 10th, Letterlough's persistence paid off.

In the final minute, Gonzalez backed up Letterlough with a heavy jab and he followed his retreating opponent with a lunging jab to the body. Letterlough missed with a hook over the head but launched a screaming overhand right that caught Gonzalez on the jaw as he started his own right.

Boom!

Suddenly, Gonzalez was spread-eagled on the canvas, his vacant eyes staring up into the ring lights. He briefly lifted his head off the canvas but put it down again. At that point, the fight seemed over, as most fighters who act this way often resign themselves to defeat. Most people in Gonzalez's position calculate the risks and rewards of getting up to pursue an unlikely knockout and find that they don't have the energy or the desire to turn the momentum. Letterlough and Gonzalez had proven their superior courage by fighting on despite suffering earlier knockdowns, so there was ample reason to suspect the fight would go on. But this trip to the canvas was different – Gonzalez was caught coming in during a late round when energy supplies are depleted. Gonzalez was ahead on the scorecards, but the knockdown didn't help matters on that front either.

The decision was easy for Gonzalez. He closed his eyes, took a couple of deep breaths and hauled himself up by nine. As he watched the fallen Gonzalez from the neutral corner, Letterlough was determined to make his rival pay the price for not taking the easy way out.

The instant the fight resumed, Letterlough ran in and smacked a lead right off Gonzalez's jaw, missed with a big hook and drove Gonzalez to the ropes with another huge right cross-left uppercut combination. Gonzalez's hands were dangerously low as another sharp right to the ear spun his head. Letterlough was rampaging now, hungry for the kill, and Gonzalez was unable to contain the storm for several long seconds. But contain it he did, as Gonzalez soon clamped down on Letterlough, his body bent over and racked with pain. He was clearly looking to survive as Letterlough winged punch after punch, most of which missed the target but carried fight-ending intent.

As the round wound down, Letterlough fell off balance after landing yet another right to the jaw and the referee correctly called the tumble a slip. But for the first time in the fight, Letterlough had seized the momentum and he had two more rounds to pull out a most memorable – and perhaps miraculous – victory.

Though weaker than before, Gonzalez was on his toes as the 11th began, throwing jabs followed by volleys to the head and body. Letterlough spent a lot of time rolling underneath Gonzalez's blows while winging hooks that mostly caught air. Gonzalez chose to respond to the previous round's knockdown by going to his strength – his physical strength. It was about to pay off in a big way, and once again the fight's momentum would take another titanic turn.

With 1:21 left, a sharp short hook sent Letterlough stumbling off-balance toward a neutral corner and a long right that just missed the target completed Letterlough's second knockdown and the fight's fifth. As Letterlough arose at four, he insisted the fall was a slip but the referee ruled the initial hook produced a legitimate knockdown. The pendulum had swung back Gonzalez's way and for the rest of the round he pounded long lefts and rights at Letterlough, who continued to pump away with little precision.

Gonzalez, feeling confident he had a big lead on the scorecards, started the final round at long range. But like two magnets they shortly returned to the inside where they pushed, pulled, grappled, wrestled and threw short but not especially sharp blows. Given the frenetic pace, their weariness was perfectly justified.

In the final minute, Gonzalez raked Letterlough with a variety of long, sharp blows from the outside. Letterlough, his energy spent but his courage at full strength, lost his mouthpiece and soaked up the punishment until the final bell. The fight over, a smiling Letterlough embraced Gonzalez in recognition of a good fight and Gonzalez, in turn, nodded his approval.

The scorecards hardly reflected the bout's numerous twists and turns. Gonzalez captured a unanimous decision by 114-109 (twice) and 113-109 margins, but in the ring it was a fight to remember and cherish as both victor and vanquished were covered in glory. After all, it was a "sure thing" that once again came true.

Epilogue: Since the war with Letterlough Gonzalez fought 21 more times, going 15-6 (9 KO). After polishing off Konstantin Semerdjiev in five rounds, Gonzalez earned a shot at dominant light heavyweight champion Roy Jones Jr. Though he lost a lopsided decision, Gonzalez put forth a worthy effort. Gonzalez bounced back with seven consecutive wins (including a majority decision over future IBF champion Glen Johnson) to earn a chance at WBO (and linear) light heavyweight king Dariusz Michalczewski. On October 18, 2003, Gonzalez made history by winning a split decision in Michalczewski's home turf of Hamburg while inflicting the first blemish on the German's perfect 48-0 record.

Gonzalez's reign as WBO champ lasted only three months as Zsolt Erdei lifted the belt by unanimous decision. Wins over Orlando Rivera (W 10) and David Telesco (KO 8) led to an IBF title eliminator against former champion Montell Griffin. The bout ended on technical decision after six rounds with Gonzalez holding a sizeable lead on two of the three cards.

Four months later Gonzalez lost a unanimous decision to IBF champion Clinton Woods, but he positioned himself for another title shot with a 12-round win over Jason DeLisle for the IBF's number-two slot. Two more KO wins against Rodney Moore (KO 3) and Vitali Kopitko (KO 3) earned Gonzalez a rematch with Woods, which he lost by 12 round decision. Gonzalez ended his career following two more defeats Reggie Johnson (L 12) and undefeated prospect Tavoris Cloud (KO by 10) in 2008. His record stands at 41-6 (25 KO).

Letterlough fought 12 more times after the Gonzalez fight, going 7-4-1 (5 KO). Amazingly, Letterlough returned to the ring just nine weeks later and won a six-rounder against Dennis McKinney. A two-round KO of Ka-Dy King followed, and Letterlough received an unexpected crack at undefeated IBF cruiserweight champion Vassiliy Jirov on HBO. Letterlough fought Jirov with his typical courage, but the 1996 Olympic champion was simply too big and strong as he registered an eighth round TKO.

Over the next three years, Letterlough continued to thrill audiences – win, lose or draw. His two-round TKO loss to Richard Hall was particularly memorable as both hit the canvas in the first round, but his final ring appearance was successful as he polished off Eric Starr in two rounds October 1, 2004 in Reading, Pa. His record is 21-5-3 (20 KO).

Letterlough's final chapter in life was also written in Reading. On July 8, 2005 was shot in the back and killed after leaving a bar with his wife and was pronounced dead at the scene. Letterlough was just 35 years old.

A few days before the Gonzalez fight, Letterlough explained his outlook on life to MaxBoxing's Thomas Gerbasi.

"I look at life like this," he said. "If I should happen to lose, I'm still winning because I'm setting examples for my kids. I'm doing positive things at home as well as on TV. I'm showing people that you can have positive things after going through negative experiences. I don't think I'm ever going to be a loser. If the judges happen to say someone else is the winner in a bout, I'm still a winner."

Indeed he was. Rest in peace, Julian.

BRAWLS

Total Punches Landed/Thrown

Round	1	2	3	4	5	6	7	8	9	10	11	12	Total
Gonzalez													401/1029
													39%
Letterlough													193/908
													21%

Jabs Landed/Thrown

Round	1	2	3	4	5	6	7	8	9	10	11	12	Total
Gonzalez													71/290
													24%
Letterlough													32/158
													20%

Power Punches Landed/Thrown

Round	1	2	3	4	5	6	7	8	9	10	11	12	Total
Gonzalez													330/739
													45%
Letterlough													161/750
													21%

* Fight originally done by CompuBox, but the original HTML files with complete round-by-round statistics no longer exist.

Julio Gonzalez vs. Julian Letterlough February 2, 2001 – Columbus, Ohio

TALES FROM THE VAULT

Matthew Franklin vs. Richie Kates
February 10, 1978, Philadelphia, Pa.

Matthew Saad Muhammad has always been a fighter, both in life as well as inside the ropes. As WBC light heavyweight champion from 1979 to 1981, he thrilled fans with a series of breathtaking comebacks against Marvin Johnson, John Conteh, Alvaro "Yaqui" Lopez, Murray Sutherland, Vonzell Johnson and Jerry Martin, with the Lopez bout declared 1980's Fight of the Year by Ring magazine.

But before he was Matthew Saad Muhammad, he was born Maxwell Antonio Loach, though Saad didn't learn of this until adulthood. After his mother died, Loach and an older brother moved in with an aunt. Because she could not afford to raise both boys, the aunt instructed the older brother to abandon his sibling. Led to the Benjamin Franklin Parkway, his brother broke into a sprint and five-year-old Maxwell couldn't keep up. When the police found him, he was taken to Catholic Social Services where they bestowed him the name Matthew Franklin, the first name because the nuns misunderstood the pronunciation of his first name and the surname for the parkway where he was found.

Franklin turned pro at age 19 with a two round knockout of Billy Early on January 19, 1974 and while mostly successful, his early career was dotted with several imperfections. Against Wayne McGee, Franklin lost a decision and fought to a 10 round draw and suffered blemishes to future champions Mate Parlov (D 10) and Marvin Camel (L 10). But a 10-round split decision defeat to Eddie Gregory (later known as Eddie Mustafa Muhammad) prompted Franklin to overhaul his style.

Tired of losing decisions he felt he won, he transformed himself from boxer to bomber. The switch resulted in consistent – and exciting – wins. Two fights after losing to Gregory, Franklin captured the vacant North American Boxing Federation light heavyweight title by stopping Marvin Johnson in the 12th and final round of a spectacle so brutal it almost defied description.

Franklin successfully defended his crown by knocking out Billy Douglas (father of heavyweight champion James "Buster" Douglas) in six rounds and won a non-title 10-rounder over Lee Royster six weeks later. On February 10, 1978 at Philadelphia's Spectrum, the 23-year-old Franklin (18-3-2, 11 KO) risked his belt against Richie Kates. The 26-year-old Kates (35-3, 19 KO) was perceived to be a serious threat to Franklin's crown because of his two stirring but unsuccessful challenges for Victor Galindez's WBA title. The first Galindez encounter was one of the 175-pound division's most memorable fights. A vicious but accidental butt in the third round produced a monstrous gash on Galindez that flowed freely throughout the rest of the fight. Holding a slight lead on the cards, Galindez knocked Kates out with one second remaining in the 15th round.

After losing the rematch to Galindez a year later, Kates sought to re-establish his championship credentials and the NABF title would provide justification for a third world title opportunity. Two months after losing the rematch to "Vicious Victor," Kates tuned up for Franklin by knocking out journeyman Harold Carter in three rounds.

The Spectrum was filled with 6,586 charged-up fans ready to see if their favorite son would knock off the dangerous New Jersey interloper.

Franklin began the fight on the move while Kates rolled his upper body and probed for openings. Franklin darted to his right and landed a long right to the jaw, then landed a left uppercut-right cross combination. After Franklin tagged Kates with another long lead right, Kates landed two jabs and countered a Franklin jab with a four-punch salvo to the midsection. With Kates assuming the role of aggressor, Franklin connected with another lead right and consolidated his advantage with a solid one-two to the jaw.

Coming out of a clinch, Kates nailed Franklin with a hook and got the better of the ensuing infighting. At ring center, Franklin speared Kates with a jab, and a full-extension right prompted a clinch where Kates hammered four rights to the body. Franklin absorbed the blows well and countered with a wide hook and an overhand right to the face.

Franklin wanted to use his boxing skills to feel Kates out, but his early success encouraged him to shift into a slugging mode and he ended a good first round with a lead hook and a right that whizzed past Kates' chin.

The NABF champ opened the second on his toes, falling short with jabs and double jabs. Kates eluded a lead right by ducking inside to land a hook to the ribs, a punch that sparked an exchange of clubbing body blows. Franklin appeared to be the more versatile fighter, smoothly alternating between boxing and bombing while Kates constantly moved forward.

Franklin flashed his considerable hand speed by coupling two hooks to the body with two more to the head in a quick burst. That volley set up a crunching one-two to the jaw that sent Kates falling heavily to the canvas. Somehow, referee Charlie Cirillo ruled Franklin had pushed Kates to the canvas, but Franklin wasn't fooled as he fired a wild home run hook and a chopping right once the action resumed. Another overhand right to the temple caused Kates' legs to sag and Franklin unleashed his full arsenal. Kates coolly rolled underneath most of Franklin's bombs, but two overhand rights deepened his distress along the ropes. A heavy right to the ear triggered another all-out assault with the highlight being a left hook that spun Kates' head. But as the round wound down, Kates' legs gained strength while Franklin's blows lost steam.

A split-second after the bell, Kates landed two blows, the last of which caught Franklin walking away, but Franklin not only kept his cool he didn't even acknowledge the blow as he trudged toward his corner.

It was a huge round for Franklin, both physically and psychologically. He had proven he could hurt any fighter regardless of class or past accomplishment, and the first Johnson fight had already certified his ability to bounce back from adversity.

That attribute would come in handy later.

Kates appeared fresher as the third began as he nailed Franklin coming in with a counter right to the jaw. Franklin drove a hard right to the ribs and just missed with a countering hook. But that miss helped set up a chopping right to the jaw and he went back to the winning formula of using his superior speed and jab to set up his power punches. Kates slipped in a couple of body blows after Franklin missed a right over the head.

Kates landed two hard jabs to the face and in a clinch he fired two right uppercuts to the pit of the stomach. Franklin answered with a rifle shot right to the jaw whose sound reverberated around ringside. After a long exchange of jabs, Franklin nailed Kates with a right to the forehead coupled with a left uppercut-right cross combo that knocked the challenger back a half step. Kates ended a decent comeback round with a solid left uppercut-right cross to the head.

Franklin started well in the fourth by circling and pot-shotting Kates with two hooks delivered while leaning back. Kates ducked inside behind two slapping hooks to the body and followed with a hard right moments later. The two exchanged rights with Kates' landing first and harder, and the challenger tagged Franklin with a crisp counter hook. Kates appeared completely recovered from his second-round battering and he proved it by catching Franklin with two jabs, a cross and a hook in quick succession. Two more Kates jabs preceded a heavy left uppercut to the body and two more hooks to Franklin's jaw. After a third hook drove Franklin to the ropes, it was evident that Kates was surging and was ready to administer a severe test to the youngster.

With 12 seconds remaining in the round, Kates delivered the ultimate pop quiz.

A split second after Franklin landed a 45-degree hook to the jaw, Kates came over the top with a massive overhand right that twisted Franklin's head and caused his body to pitch forward like a fallen oak. The champion smacked the canvas face first and the fight appeared over.

Hall of Fame trainer Gil Clancy often said that a fighter who fell face first hardly ever gets up and most times that statement is true. But Matthew Franklin never was one to be grouped with "most fighters" and he proved it by hauling himself up by Cirillo's count of five. Cirillo looked deeply into Franklin's eyes for several seconds to gauge his condition and by the time he ruled the fight could continue the bell rang.

The crowd's roaring drowned out the bell and when Cirillo led Franklin to the corner Kates thought the fight had been stopped. But Cirillo told Kates in the strongest terms that the fight was still on.

Convinced he had Franklin at his mercy, Kates showed none as he roared out of the corner to start the fifth. Kates drove Franklin to the ropes with a heavy right to the body, then uncorked a hook to the ribs, a short hook to the head and a left uppercut to the jaw before Franklin managed to grab him. A right-left-right slammed off Franklin's face and the veteran campaigner unleashed an array of power punches.

The volume and intensity threatened to overwhelm Franklin, who could do no more than pin his elbows to his ribs and take whatever Kates dished out. Most of the blows ripped through Franklin's guard, yet his vast reservoir of resilience enabled him to gradually free himself from the ropes while also turning Kates toward the strands.

The roles reversed, Franklin also sought to reverse the fortunes – a trait that would become the stuff of legend during his subsequent title reign. It began with a short hook to the body and a second one to the jaw that connected solidly. An overhand right to the ear, a hook to the body and a second overhand right to the ear found the mark and Kates, perhaps weary from his earlier outburst, showed the slightest sign of weakening. Demonstrating incredible presence of mind, Franklin not only perceived the sign but also acted on it in most violent fashion.

After Franklin hurt Kates with a right-left-right to the jaw, the crowd leaped to its feet and screamed in full-throated ecstasy. They had seen Franklin do something very similar during the Marvin Johnson fight, and now the Comeback Kid was at it again. Kates connected with two strong rights and a solid left jab, prompting Franklin to beckon Kates in with his left glove and lifted his arms in the air as if to say *"come on and fight me, will you?"* When Kates did, Franklin nailed him with a sharp left-right that stunned the challenger and a follow-up jab-cross-hook combo forced Kates to seek a clinch. The fight had transformed into a contest of wills and resilience, and Franklin was about to show everyone that he was the master of this domain.

With 13 seconds to go, after lining up Kates with a light jab to the face, Franklin reared back and crushed Kates with a pulverizing right cross to the jaw. As Kates fell face first to the canvas, Franklin marched to his own corner with arms upraised, convinced his night's work was done. But just like Franklin three minutes before, Kates defied logic and struggled to his feet at Cirillo's count of seven. And just like Franklin three minutes before, Kates was saved by a bell drowned out by the crowd's deafening din.

Kates' corner man ran toward his stricken fighter and dragged his virtually unconscious charge to the corner. Fifty seconds later, Kates somehow pulled himself together and, to the amazement of many, awaited the sixth round bell bouncing lightly on his toes.

Franklin tested Kates' resiliency by firing a hard right to the jaw, but Kates unleashed a spring-loaded counter right that caught Franklin on the ear. Franklin worked the jab well and soon coupled the jabs with full-strength crosses.

The knockout can come in many ways. Most times it arrives with the suddenness of a lightning bolt but other times they are the product of trial and error. Throughout the fight a boxer is in constant assessment mode as he discerns the effectiveness of each punch while also gauging the strength of his opponent's blows. From time to time he attempts various combinations in the hopes of latching on to the one that will unlock the keys to victory.

Although Franklin and Kates had swapped many punishing blows, this cerebral back-and-forth was still in full swing. And at this juncture, almost out of nowhere, Franklin found the final pieces of the puzzle. Ironically enough, it was the most basic of combinations – the old one-two – that paved the way to success.

The champion fired a trio of left-rights – the first set landed but without full effect. He then shuffled a half-step forward and tried again; this time both blows landed with more force. Now at proper range the third set connected with concussive impact and Kates was in a terrible state. As two more left-rights whizzed by, Kates' upper body leaned back awkwardly, but physics (and a small push by Franklin) sent Kates to the canvas.

Kates pushed his body up at five, and retreated to a neutral corner to wait out Franklin's follow-up assault.

Franklin measured Kates with three light jabs to establish proper range, then splattered him with a monstrous right cross to the face. Kates, who was winding up a right at the time, couldn't have been hit more solidly. His body was giving him mixed signals – his brain told Kates to shut down but his legs commanded him to stay upright. Kates managed a compromise by staggering five steps toward his corner, his upper body leaning forward and his right shoulder dipping toward the floor. Kates may have been fit to fight a battle with his own body but he was in no shape to fight another man. Knowing this, referee Cirillo correctly stopped the fight at 1:35 of round six.

With the victory, Franklin had stamped himself as a world title threat and in the post-fight interview he called out the division's best. But first he paid tribute to his brave victim.

"Kates is a good fighter, man," Franklin said. "He's the most experienced fighter I ever fought. I can't take anything away from Kates – he's good."

When asked if Kates hurt him, Franklin replied "He did. Then I got determination and I got guts. I want Galindez. I want Galindez. I gotta have Galindez next or Mate Parlov, to win the world championship."

Epilogue: Franklin never fought Galindez or Parlov for the title, and it would be 14 months before he got his championship opportunity. After disposing of Dale Grant (KO 5) and Fred Bright (KO 8), Franklin won a classic war with Alvaro "Yaqui" Lopez for the NABF belt, knocking him out with one second remaining in the 11th round. Six months after beating Lopez, Franklin overcame several serious eye cuts to knock out Marvin Johnson to win the WBC title. Over the next 32 months, Franklin, who announced his name change to Matthew Saad Muhammad immediately after winning the championship, would put together one of boxing history's most exciting and tumultuous reigns before losing the belt in his ninth defense to fellow Muslim Dwight Muhammad Qawi. He never challenged for a title again and his decade-long slide was a sad spectacle for his legion of fans. He won just eight of his final 20 fights and retired at age 37 with a 39-16-3 (21 KO) record after losing by two round TKO to Jason Waller in Fredericksburg, Va., on March 21, 1992.

Nine months after losing to Franklin Kates knocked out Carlos Marks in nine rounds and though he never again fought for a belt of any kind he enjoyed a run of success before his retirement. He won 12 of his final 14 fights, including wins over Sutherland (W 10), Jerry Celestine (KO 5), Pat Cuillo (KO 5) and future cruiserweight champion Jeff Lampkin (W 10). His only losses were to Celestine (KO by 8) and James Scott (KO by 10). Kates won his final five fights, including his swan song, a 10-round split decision over Jerry Martin in Atlantic City October 26, 1983. The 32-year-old Kates retired with a 45-6 (23 KO) record.

TALES FROM THE VAULT

Total Punches Landed/Thrown

Round	1	2	3	4	5	6	7	8	9	10	11	12	Total
Franklin	23/61	36/108	19/65	20/56	24/61	13/46							135/397
	38%	33%	29%	36%	39%	28%							34%
Kates	18/46	17/45	10/36	29/65	37/91	1/11							112/294
	39%	38%	28%	45%	41%	9%							38%

Jabs Landed/Thrown

Round	1	2	3	4	5	6	7	8	9	10	11	12	Total
Franklin	7/31	8/45	8/42	10/37	1/16	5/25							39/196
	23%	18%	19%	27%	6%	20%							20%
Kates	6/17	4/12	1/16	9/21	1/15	0/3							21/84
	35%	33%	6%	43%	7%	0%							25%

Power Punches Landed/Thrown

Round	1	2	3	4	5	6	7	8	9	10	11	12	Total
Franklin	16/30	28/63	11/23	10/19	23/45	8/21							96/201
	53%	44%	48%	53%	51%	38%							48%
Kates	12/29	13/33	9/20	20/44	36/76	1/8							91/210
	41%	39%	45%	45%	47%	12%							43%

Matthew Franklin vs. Richie Kates February 10, 1978, Philadelphia, Pa.

Kiyoshi Hatanaka vs. Pedro Decima
February 3, 1991, Nagoya, Japan

When observers decry the multitude of weight classes these days, the junior featherweight division is often mentioned as one that should be removed from boxing's firmament. After all, they say, there's only four pounds separating it from bantamweight and featherweight, so those who occupy it should be able to adjust by either shedding or adding a few pounds.

But in the three decades since the division's creation, the 122-pounders have provided an effective argument for their collective existence by producing some of the greatest fights ever staged. The 1982 war between Wilfredo Gomez and Lupe Pintor stole the thunder from main-eventers Thomas Hearns and Wilfred Benitez while the first fight between Erik Morales and Marco Antonio Barrera ranks among the most savage fights of the decade — any decade.

There are, however, a cornucopia of classics that have flown under the radar. One such fight took place when Pedro Decima and Kiyoshi Hatanaka engaged in one of the division's most explosive slugfests.

The 27-year-old Decima (26-2, 18 KO) was making the first defense of the WBC super bantamweight title, a belt he won by knocking out Paul Banke in four rounds at the Great Western Forum in Inglewood, California less than three months earlier. Though he looked overwhelming against Banke, Decima did himself no favors by picking the 23-year-old Hatanaka (21-1-1, 14 KO) as his first challenger. First, the fight was taking place in Hatanaka's hometown and second, Hatanaka was aggressive, quick-handed and a good puncher.

Decima's brain trust, however, knew Hatanaka had failed the only other time he attempted a big jump in class — the then 15-0 Hatanaka had feasted on obscure Asian opponents before losing a lopsided decision to WBC super flyweight champion Gilberto Roman 29 months earlier. Another bad omen for Hatanaka was that the Decima fight was taking place at Rainbow Hall, where his only previous visit was the loss to Roman. Still, Hatanaka would enjoy the benefits of nearly unanimous crowd support but Decima wasn't concerned. After all, he won his title on the road, did he not?

The bout promised an interesting clash of styles. Hatanaka was a long-limbed boxer who flashed plenty of speed and employed solid and economical movement while Decima was a powerfully built battler who, while armed with a numbing punch, also boasted excellent technique.

A pumped-up Hatanaka raced out of the corner and launched a hook to the jaw that Decima blocked. Hatanaka assumed the role of stalker while Decima jabbed to establish distance and moved side to side in both directions to offset the challenger's aggression.

With 1:10 gone in the round, Decima landed two sharp hooks and a left-right to the jaw but an unimpressed Hatanaka continued to march forward behind jabs. A solid hook by Decima got a rise from the pro-Hatanaka crowd and the challenger answered with his own hook that Decima smothered.

The fighters spent the next minute studying one another with the jab, but study hall came to an abrupt end near the end of the round when Decima dropped Hatanaka to a knee with a perfectly delivered one-two to the jaw. Up immediately, Hatanaka raised his right glove to signal he was OK and walked back and forth and tried to kick some life into his legs. The bell prevented any more punches from being thrown, but Decima sent a powerful message to Hatanaka: *"Roman was too much for you and so am I."*

Because the knockdown was of the flash variety, Hatanaka didn't look the worse for wear as the second round started. Decima found a good boxing rhythm as he popped Hatanaka with a jolting hook-right to the jaw and a sharp right to the cheek a few moments later. Hatanaka appeared disorganized, not sure whether to use his height and reach or to return to the natural aggression that resulted in his being knocked down. While Hatanaka pondered his options, Decima got in a good chopping right to the jaw and a hard jab knocked Hatanaka back a half step. Decima carried the rest of the round with his smooth boxing and it appeared as if he had already conjured the formula for victory.

Hatanaka continued to have trouble solving Decima's in-and-out, bob-and-weave style in the third, and the Argentine took full advantage as he landed a solid jab, a left-right to the face and a ripping hook to the ribs. A swift overhand right and hook found Hatanaka's jaw and a few seconds later a pinpoint right to the chin buckled the challenger's knees. Slowly, Decima assumed the role of aggressor and Hatanaka appeared to be at a loss as to what to do beyond throwing occasional jabs to the head and body. Decima didn't give him much of a target and he couldn't react quickly enough to seize upon any openings. As a result, Hatanaka's punch rate dipped to a dangerously low level.

As the third round progressed, Decima increased the pressure and backed up the challenger behind quick two- and three-punch bursts. Everything was working for Decima as a precision right jacked Hatanaka's jaw and a hook to the body caused the challenger to cringe. Decima was in the zone and after landing a triple jab and a full-extension right it was difficult to conceive how he missed punches. He wasn't hurting Hatanaka but he was piling up points and inflicting damage as blood trickled from the Japanese's nose.

Hatanaka knew he had to change the momentum so instead of wrestling between two styles, he picked one and went with it. When the fourth bell sounded, Hatanaka came out moving side to side and allowed Decima to take the lead. The move paid immediate dividends as he beat the champion to the punch with a lead right to the jaw and a shotgun jab to the face that was answered by a long right and a one-two.

Up to this point, the fight was clearly Decima's, but that would change a little more than a minute into the round. Decima fired a jab, but because he left it out too long Hatanaka countered over it with a snappy right cross. Decima ducked underneath a hook but when he began to straighten up he left his arms at his side. That split-second opening allowed Hatanaka to land a scorching right that stiffened Decima's legs and sent him skittering in retreat. Hatanaka chased Decima to the ropes but the champ somehow fended him off for a few seconds by firing back furiously.

Hatanaka, fueled by encouragement, ignored Decima's charge and when the champion again threw a lazy jab Hatanaka blasted him with a right cross that dumped Decima on his behind. Decima slowly regained his feet at three and looked somewhat dazed as he took the mandatory eight count. As the count reached seven, Decima nodded his head and appeared steadier. Exactly half the round remained when the battle resumed, giving Hatanaka plenty of time to take advantage while offering Decima a daunting challenge. Hatanaka chased after Decima but the anxious challenger's blows lacked sufficient accuracy. Decima could have frittered away the round to preserve himself, but astonishingly he opted to launch an all-out assault.

As Jose Torres often said in his book "Sting Like A Bee," fighters lie to one another and Decima tried to lie about his true state through accelerated activity.

Hatanaka didn't buy the deception. After Decima ducked under a hook, he again left his arms down when he straightened himself. And once again Hatanaka cracked a pulverizing right to the jaw and a follow-up hook that dropped Decima heavily on his back. Decima regained his feet at six and this time he appeared more stricken, but Decima received a slightly longer respite because Hatanaka had strayed from the neutral corner.

Hatanaka swarmed the champion, landing three rights that forced Decima to his knees along the ropes. Hatanaka pumped his fist as he ran toward the corner because he thought he had won the title on the automatic three-knockdown rule. However, the rule was not in effect for this fight and as Decima arose at four he got several more seconds of rest as the referee thrice pointed Hatanaka back to the neutral corner.

Hatanaka raced in for the finish, but Decima grabbed him and Hatanaka wrestled him to the ground. Decima smartly took his time regaining his feet. The badly dazed champion somehow smacked the charging Hatanaka with a right, but the Japanese walked right through it and a hook-cross combination caused Decima to stumble back toward the ropes. A follow-up flurry punctuated with a right to the ear floored Decima for the fourth time in the round with five seconds remaining.

For Decima, the round-ending bell was the sound of salvation – however temporary – while for Hatanaka it only delayed what he felt was the inevitable. Still, Hatanaka returned to the corner with a left eye that was starting to swell and was badly discolored.

Few fighters have ever come back from four knockdowns to win a title fight – much less four in a single round – but one of them was another 122-pound classic when Soo Hwan Hong defeated Hector Carrasquilla in November 1977. That was the formidable challenge that faced Decima, and he got off to a surprisingly good start in the fifth as he backed up Hatanaka with combinations punctuated with a sharp counter hook to the jaw. Frustrated by Decima's unexpected surge, Hatanaka deliberately butted Decima in a clinch, which drew a warning from the referee.

A tremendous left-right-left not only staggered Hatanaka, it opened a cut at the corner of the left eye. Remarkably, Decima had regained the in-and-out movement and precise punching of the first three rounds and he ended the fifth by spearing Hatanaka with a pair of jabs.

Decima stayed on the attack in the sixth as he bounced a long right off the face and pumped a multitude of jabs. Hatanaka circled and worked his own jab, but Decima's upper body movement caused many of them to miss the target. Decima's jabs were harder and more accurate and they set up several power shots to the head and body. With 1:48 gone, Hatanaka connected with a lead hook to the jaw, but Decima proved he was fully recovered from his fourth-round nightmare by absorbing it without trouble and continuing to work effectively. A pair of one-twos knocked Hatanaka off balance and Decima closed the round with a flurry along the ropes. It was a big round for Decima and though he may well have been down on the scorecards it appeared he had regained a solid foothold.

Hatanaka, however, was not going to fold easily, especially before his hometown fans with the title on the line. He certified his comeback capacity earlier in the fight by scoring four knockdowns after losing the first three rounds and as the seventh began he found himself having to rally again.

And rally he did.

A lead right sent a spray of water and sweat off Decima's head and he dug a hook to the body after slipping Decima's jab. A few moments later, the challenger landed a light overhand right to the ear and a hook to the jaw. Decima didn't seem overly concerned with Hatanaka's offensive surge as he continued to work his offense.

But 57 seconds into the round, Hatanaka gave him good reason to be concerned.

Hatanaka feinted a one-two, then landed a shotgun jab to the jaw that dropped Decima for the fifth time in the fight. Up at two, Decima walked to a neutral corner and took the mandatory eight with aplomb. Decima worked the jab and landed a crisp overhand right to the jaw, but Hatanaka answered with a hook and a flush jab. Just as he did in the fourth round, Decima was eager to prove to Hatanaka that he wasn't hurt by the knockdown by cranking up his offense. His short combinations to the face bounced off a charging Hatanaka, and the challenger fired back with gusto as they produced the longest sustained exchange of the fight.

Hatanaka knocked Decima back to the neutral corner with a right-left and the action was halted with five seconds remaining when Decima lost his mouthpiece while following through with a right. When the referee led Decima to the corner to get the mouthguard replaced, confusion entered the arena.

Hatanaka walked toward his corner and both sets of corner men came into the ring to tend to their fighters. The round card girl, following the corner men's lead, stepped into the ring and began her circuit. The bell had never sounded to end the seventh round, but because the sequence of events offered no advantage to either fighter, the rhythms of routine were allowed to continue.

Both men operated behind their jabs as the eighth began, but it didn't take them long to again bring out the heavy artillery as Decima landed a left uppercut and Hatanaka countered with an overhand right. Despite the punishment both men absorbed, they still retained their boxing skills while also maintaining a high-energy pace. The action was crisp and compelling, with Decima throwing more punches and Hatanaka landing the harder blows.

Decima's jab worsened Hatanaka's cut and blood was smeared all over the left side of the challenger's face. Two left-rights connected cleanly for Decima and Hatanaka appeared somewhat stunned. But when Decima moved in to throw a hook, Hatanaka slipped it and landed a hard hook that stopped Decima in his tracks.

Hatanaka moved in to attack, but Decima caught Hatanaka with a flush left-right to the jaw that snapped his head back and a left-right-hook thrown while on the retreat found the target. As he threw the punches, Hatanaka sensed Decima had weakened by the smallest fraction, so he decided to escalate his attack.

A hook to the body backed up Decima, who exhaled visibly. An overhand right connected a few moments later and an inside hook landed forcefully. As Decima threw an overhand right, Hatanaka fired a beautifully timed jab that caught Decima off-balance. It was a punch the champion did not see and he slowly fell backward toward the canvas, landing hard on his behind. It was the sixth knockdown Decima suffered in the fight and like all the others, he managed to get to his feet. But when the referee commanded him to raise his gloves, the Argentine did nothing but stare straight ahead. At that point the referee waved his arms and declared the fight over.

A joyous Hatanaka did a somersault on the canvas and leaped into the arms of his trainers. His eye was a mess and his mouth was full of blood, but he was also the new WBC super bantamweight champion. Unlike his last visit to Rainbow Hall, Hatanaka emerged victorious over a talented champion in a tough fight, which is the perfect way to exorcise the ghost of past championship failure. No matter what might occur in the future, Hatanaka would know that his title-winning fight would be rated among the best ever waged at 122 pounds, one that tested his skill and resolve like few others will. All in all, that's not a bad slice of history to claim.

Epilogue: Hatanaka returned to Rainbow Hall four months later to defend against Mexican veteran Daniel Zaragoza, and unfortunately for him it was Zaragoza who was the Rainbow Warrior as he lifted the title by split decision. The Zaragoza fight would prove to be Hatanaka's last, and at 23 he is among the youngest fighters ever to retire and never return. His final record is 22-2-1 (15 KO).

Decima fought seven more times in the next two years, going 5-1 with one no-contest. After losing to Hatanaka, Decima waited 10 months before returning with a three-round KO win over Hugo Escudero in Buenos Aires. After two more wins in Buenos Aires, Decima took on the streaking Rudy Zavala at Caesars Palace in Las Vegas. Zavala snuffed out Decima's final drive toward a title by stopping the Argentine in six rounds. Decima's final fight took place October 23, 1993 when he stopped Almir Fernandes de Oliveria in five rounds in Buenos Aires. The 28-year-old Decima's final record is 31-4 (21 KO) with one no-contest.

Total Punches Landed/Thrown

Round	1	2	3	4	5	6	7	8	9	10	11	12	Total
Hatanaka	12/49	8/35	12/45	31/71	29/65	18/46	33/83	32/76					175/470
	24%	23%	27%	44%	45%	39%	40%	42%					37%
Decima	16/52	23/82	34/95	16/61	28/87	28/89	33/81	44/100					222/647
	31%	28%	36%	26%	32%	31%	41%	44%					34%

Jabs Landed/Thrown

Round	1	2	3	4	5	6	7	8	9	10	11	12	Total
Hatanaka	6/32	3/19	6/27	5/16	7/18	12/29	10/33	11/37					60/211
	19%	16%	22%	31%	39%	41%	30%	30%					28%
Decima	5/26	10/40	17/58	9/36	14/41	12/55	16/49	23/68					106/373
	19%	25%	29%	25%	34%	22%	33%	34%					28%

Power Punches Landed/Thrown

Round	1	2	3	4	5	6	7	8	9	10	11	12	Total
Hatanaka	6/17	5/16	6/18	26/55	22/47	6/17	23/50	21/39					115/259
	35%	31%	33%	47%	47%	35%	46%	54%					44%
Decima	11/26	13/42	17/37	7/25	14/46	16/34	17/32	21/32					116/274
	42%	31%	46%	28%	30%	47%	53%	66%					42%

Kiyoshi Hatanaka vs. Pedro Decima February 3, 1991, Nagoya, Japan

TALES FROM THE VAULT

Aaron Pryor vs. Dujuan Johnson
November 14, 1981, Cleveland, Ohio

Some fights have a way of jumping out and grabbing a fan by the throat before a punch is ever thrown. The mere announcement that a certain fight has been made inspires mental images so powerful and inviting that one can't help but get excited. When two dynamic, explosive punchers armed with uncompromisingly violent mindsets get together, it is the closest thing to a sure bet that boxing can offer. Because most fighters aren't wired in this way this type of encounter is extremely rare, so when it does occur it is an occasion worthy of being savored.

When Aaron Pryor crossed paths with Dujuan Johnson at Cleveland's Public Auditorium on November 14, 1981, everyone in the arena (and all who were watching on CBS) knew they were in for something special. Pryor, who was defending his WBA junior welterweight title for the third time, boasted a record of 28-0 with 26 ending inside the distance – including the last 20 in succession. Pryor initially made his mark on the world stage at 135, but because he was unable to secure a lightweight title shot he jumped at the chance to lift Antonio Cervantes' WBA title at 140 before his hometown fans in Cincinnati on August 2, 1980.

Though Cervantes scored a flash knockdown in the opening seconds, Pryor proceeded to overwhelm the aging "Kid Pambele" before putting him away with an overhand right to the jaw in round four. Pryor's ferocious approach proved to be a ratings winner and his first two defenses against Gaetan Hart (KO 6) and Lennox Blackmoore (KO 2) were featured on CBS and ABC respectively. Slowly but surely, Pryor was becoming the star he knew he had always been.

So imagine the excitement when Pryor signed to fight Johnson, whose nickname was, by the way, "Mister Excitement." Johnson was just one month shy of his 21st birthday, though his receding hairline made him appear much older. Nevertheless, the Detroit native's power-packed style was a perfect fit for the offense-minded approach favored by his trainer/manager Emanuel Steward, the mastermind behind the Kronk Gym juggernaut that produced newly crowned champions Thomas Hearns and Hilmer Kenty.

Both Pryor and Johnson were accomplished amateurs. Pryor amassed a 204-16 record but his goal of making the 1976 Olympic team fell short with a pair of losses to eventual gold medalist Howard Davis Jr.

Johnson began boxing at age 12 and won two Michigan AAU championships, a Golden Gloves title and the 1978 National Sports Festival title while putting together a 107-17 mark. Johnson's biggest victory as a pro was a 10-round decision over perennial contender Miguel Montilla 11 months earlier and he entered the Pryor fight fresh off a pair of one-round knockouts over Sonny Perez and Joey Robles. Johnson was rated second by the WBA and eighth by the WBC, but he was nearly Pryor's equal when it came to sheer explosiveness.

Each man was aware of the other's power and both were respectful enough to say they wanted to take a more cautious approach.

"This fight we're going to work a different strategy out, maybe doing a bit of bobbing and weaving in the first round and counter-punching," Pryor said. "Then in the middle rounds, do a little punching. Then, in the later rounds, moving on my toes and seeing how I feel, if it goes that far. He's looking for a lucky shot because he knows the odds of beating me are like 10 to 1. But a lucky shot happens every day. In the Larry Holmes-Renaldo Snipes fight, that was nothing but a lucky shot. It woke me up; it put me on my Ps and Qs. That's why you're going to see a different Aaron, a cautious Aaron, a for-sure Aaron. All of my punches will be direct and on target and I'll show the public what I really can do."

"I expect Aaron to run out across the ring swinging all the best shots he has the first two rounds," Johnson replied. "But I'm going to stick to my basic boxing, keep my hands up and go straight down the middle. I can box or I can slug. Ain't no thing that says I have to stand there and slug punch for punch. But we both won't still be standing after four rounds."

Stick and move? Basic boxing? As Mike Tyson would say years later, everyone has a plan until they get hit. And given the styles of Pryor and Johnson, there was going to be some serious hitting.

The fight almost began before the bell. Pryor made Johnson wait in the ring nearly 10 minutes before he made his entrance, but once "The Hawk" hit the ring he was a human storm. He cut a series of quick circles around the ring – and around Johnson – with a menacing look on his face, but Johnson would have none of it as he danced with Pryor and pivoted his body so that he was always facing the champion. Pryor took a swipe at Johnson with a jab that fell short and when Johnson advanced, one of Pryor's corner men stepped between them. But Pryor broke away and continued to circle and fire jabs.

By this time, Johnson's seconds, including Steward, were smiling because they knew that Pryor was simply firing himself up and playing to the crowd. So Johnson decided to go with the flow. As Pryor shimmied his shoulders, Johnson pantomimed a left-right and raised his arms over his head as if he just scored the knockout. Despite Pryor's attempt to unnerve the young challenger, Johnson remained calm, relaxed and even playful, a good sign for a 20-year-old about to take part in the biggest fight of his young life.

A split second after the opening bell Johnson, 140, ran out of the corner to meet Pryor, 139¼, but put on the brakes a few feet short. Pryor, as promised, ran around the ring at hyper speed with arms dangling at his side. Pryor's jab fell short but Johnson's hit the mark and snapped "The Hawk's" head back. A few seconds later, Johnson caught the circling Pryor with a wide hook to the jaw and a right-left to the body. Though Pryor was in full reverse gear, the tactic did nothing to help his defense.

That was amplified several seconds later. As Pryor reached in to throw an overhand right, Johnson fired a quick one-two that dropped the champ to one knee, then on his stomach. The instant Pryor's torso hit the canvas, he scrambled to his feet, did an Ali shuffle and circled the ring, nodding his head and smiling ruefully all the while. He danced to within a couple of feet of Johnson to taunt him and referee Jack Keough, knowing it was futile to administer a standing eight count, stepped away and let the fight continue.

So much for the boxing; the slugfest was officially on.

Pryor immediately reverted to his typical windmilling style and nailed Johnson with a hook that forced the fight's first clinch. In that clinch, Johnson looked over Pryor's shoulder at the crowd, smiled broadly and pointed at Pryor with his right glove as if to say *"see, I knocked this man down and I have him right where I want him."*

Pryor tore after Johnson, who caught the challenger with a smashing hook that prompted Pryor to veil his pain with a modified version of the Jersey Joe Walcott step-away shuffle.

Imagine that: The Ali Shuffle and the Walcott Shuffle in the same round.

As Pryor backed toward the ropes, Johnson unleashed a long right that promised severe damage had it landed, but the champ rolled away at the last second to avoid the brunt. With 1:19 remaining in a frenetic first, Pryor tagged Johnson with two hooks but Johnson answered with an even stronger hook that wobbled Pryor. Try as he might to cover his distress with mugging and posturing, "The Hawk" was far more hurt than he had been on the knockdown – and Johnson knew it. The challenger missed wildly with an overhand right and left hook intended to finish matters, but Pryor's incredible recuperative powers began to kick in just seconds after Johnson's hook put him in danger. Pryor pressed forward behind three jabs and a solid right, a missed hook, and a tremendous right-left that shook Johnson to his foundation. Johnson tried to grab, but Pryor shook him off and connected with another combination. Johnson attempted to slide away but Pryor cut off his escape route and zipped in a right-left to the body just before Johnson clinched and pushed Pryor toward ring center.

Both men had expended tons of energy in the fight's initial stages and they took a few seconds to catch their breath. Pryor broke the brief respite by landing an overhand right and left hook to the jaw. As the round neared an end, Johnson cranked hooks to the body and head and missed with a home run right that could have ended matters. After the bell sounded, Pryor looked down at ringsiders and shook his head as if to say *"I'm not hurt at all and I'll prove it to you in the next round."*

"The Hawk" was in full flight to start the second as he tore after Johnson with a dizzying array of power shots that spun his head in several directions. Johnson weathered the furious start and landed a power hook to the body that forced Pryor to back away, a grimace creasing his features. A right to the body strayed low as Pryor pivoted away, and the champ immediately leaped in behind a strong hook to the jaw.

The frantic pace slowed a bit as Pryor settled down to work behind a pawing jab and an occasional overhand right. Johnson moved steadily forward, intent on landing the one bomb that would make him a champion. Pryor fired four hooks, the last of which landed and set up a head-snapping right uppercut and left hook. Johnson's work rate slowed precipitously, allowing Pryor to begin and end virtually every exchange.

The champ constantly used his superior foot speed to create punching angles and his swifter hands to take advantage of the openings his angles created. "The Hawk" fired crisp blows from all angles – and in combination. Like a boa constrictor, Pryor's high-energy pace was starting to squeeze the air out of Johnson. Though Johnson landed a solid right-left to end the round, the stanza clearly belonged to the champion as he punctuated his dominance with a parting right to the jaw.

Awash with renewed confidence, Pryor sauntered around the ring with his arms in the air. The area around Johnson's left cheek was swelling and he sucked in several deep breaths to try and regain some of the energy he would need to overcome Pryor's dynamic attack.

Both men started the third operating behind their jabs, but Pryor was doing him one better by weaving in combinations behind his. Johnson drilled a hard, but low, left but Pryor didn't complain; he made him pay with a solid hook to the jaw that forced Johnson to back away.

As Pryor inched forward, Johnson reared back and nailed Pryor with a huge right to the jaw that would have hurt, if not put away, most other men. Though Pryor was dropped often in a fight's earliest stages, that changed once he properly warmed up. Then Pryor possessed an almost inhuman capacity to absorb singular bombs without noticeable effect. Instead of falling as most men would have, Pryor moved to his right and tagged Johnson with a sharp hook to the face before darting away.

Johnson's inexperience was beginning to manifest itself as he continued to plod straight ahead while Pryor used his superior maneuverability to work the angles. A Pryor jab set up a strong lead right-left hook combo, but as the champ chased Johnson to the ropes, the challenger blasted in a right that caused Pryor to stumble into the ropes. As soon as Pryor regained his balance, he pantomimed brushing his hair with his right glove, then pelted Johnson with a sneaky right. A miffed Johnson sunk a nasty hook into Pryor's side and followed with a right to the head and left to the body that had the champ in some distress. Even when hurt, Pryor moved his hands to keep

Johnson occupied while he tried to recover. With 10 seconds remaining, Pryor landed a strong right before clinching away the rest of the round.

Even corner man Panama Lewis was concerned about Pryor's state, but the champ assured him that he was in fine working order. To prove it, he answered the fourth-round bell wearing a confident smirk.

Johnson fired long-range jabs while Pryor continued his shifty footwork. When Johnson countered a Pryor jab with a booming right Pryor couldn't have been hit much harder but the champ remained upright, his only concession to the pain being a brief clinch. Pryor retreated to the ropes, darted to his right and pelted Johnson with a right-left before dashing to the left toward ring center; showing everyone he still was in full control of his motor skills.

After Pryor landed another hook, Johnson connected with a fierce right that made Pryor stumble forward. Amazingly, Pryor shook off the effects within seconds and danced around the ring on shockingly springy legs. But Johnson suspected Pryor was just covering up his hurt, and his suspicions were confirmed after he landed three terrific rights. Believing he had a renewed chance to spring the upset, Johnson began to throw even harder. But because he threw them too hard, his accuracy suffered and Pryor was able to dodge the blows while waiting for his own batteries to recharge.

Pryor looked better at the start of the fifth as he connected on two hooks and a left-right. As the seconds ticked by Pryor pieced together the formula he needed to achieve ultimate success: Short, quick, unpredictable combinations that exploited his edge in hand speed and Johnson's defensive liabilities. An eight-punch salvo backed Johnson to the ropes, and after ducking under a Johnson right Pryor snapped off a hurtful hook to the jaw. A right-left jerked Johnson's head and another right-left caught the challenger cleanly. Johnson was doing his best to force another toe-to-toe slugfest, but Pryor was now channeling his entire range of skills in the proper direction. Along with his quick-fisted combinations, Pryor used his feet to dart in and out and his experience to blend everything into a successful package.

A six-punch flurry backed Johnson to the ropes and he then let his hands fly, but Johnson showed flashes of defensive prowess by weaving his upper body away from most of Pryor's blows before grabbing the champion. Back at ring center, Johnson blasted Pryor with a right but whiffed on a second one. With Johnson throwing two punches at a time and Pryor unleashing six-to-eight-punch attacks, the numbers game was quickly sapping the challenger's strength.

After a bad start, Pryor had seized the momentum. He had already taken the best punches Johnson could throw and not only did he survive, he flourished. The champion now came at Johnson in waves, alternating between jabbing and moving and wading in behind dazzling combinations. In the sixth, Pryor was particularly effective with lead rights that bounced off Johnson's reddening face. Johnson still landed some of his blows, but they lacked the firepower of previous rounds.

When the bell sounded for round seven, it marked the farthest Pryor had to fight since his 10th round KO of Leonidis Asprilla two years earlier. But Pryor was still spry as he bounced around the ring with remarkable freshness. A little more than a minute into the round, Pryor connected with by far his best punch of the fight, a looping overhand right that jerked Johnson's head violently. Seeing his prey desperately hurt, "The Hawk" swooped in for the kill. Thirty-four blows followed and Johnson had no chance to retaliate. Referee Keough had little alternative but to stop the potential massacre at the 1:49 mark of round seven.

"(When I got knocked down) I was thinking that my title was on the line and that this guy wasn't a playmate," Pryor told CBS' Tim Ryan. "I got serious after I got knocked down in the first round. But it was good for me and it disciplined me and it made me a better champion just like it did Larry Holmes."

When asked about whom he would like to fight next, Pryor was emphatic.

"I hope that the next fight will be the biggie," he said. "I want to fight (Sugar Ray) Leonard because I feel like I'm the king of the junior welterweights for what I've already done. Don King promised me that if he can't get Leonard to sign that he would go for (WBC lightweight champion) Alex Arguello, so I'm going to wait in line and see if he puts it together."

Epilogue: King couldn't get Leonard to sign on the dotted line, and it would be a while before Pryor would fight "the biggie." Four months after beating Johnson, Pryor experienced some difficulty before stopping Montilla in 12 rounds. In his next fight, Pryor again had to overcome a first-round knockdown to take out Akio "KO" Kameda in six rounds.

Finally, Pryor got the superfight against Arguello, who was trying to win a then-unprecedented fourth divisional crown. In a fight that was deemed 1982's Fight of the Year, Pryor traded bombs with the "Explosive Thin Man" before putting him away with a ferocious flurry in round 14. Pryor's moment of triumph was overshadowed by the appearance of a mysterious "black bottle," the contents of which Pryor swallowed. The controversy led to a rematch with Arguello five months after his three round knockout of former champ Sang Hyun Kim. Though Arguello overcame knockdowns in the first and fourth rounds to battle his way back into the fight, Pryor put Arguello down for good in round 10.

Pryor's life outside the ring descended into chaos, and drug use had become part of his life. He was unimpressive in subsequent fights against Nick Furlano (W 15) and Gary Hinton (W 15) before leaving the ring for two years. Pryor returned to the ring in 1987 but was stopped in seven rounds by Bobby Joe Young. Despite severe damage to his retinas, Pryor returned to the ring two-and-a-half years later to knock out former sparring partner Daryl Jones in three rounds. The 35-year-old Pryor's final fight was a seven round knockout win over Roger Choate on December 4, 1990 in Oklahoma City.

After a debilitating battle with cocaine addiction, Pryor again demonstrated his tremendous recuperative powers by overcoming drugs and regaining his life. Pryor rededicated himself to Christianity, serving as a deacon at the New Friendship Baptist Church in Cincinnati before being installed as an associate minister in June 2005. Pryor was inducted into the International Boxing Hall of Fame in 1996 and seven years later he married his longtime companion Frankie Wagner to christen the IBHOF's new outdoor pavilion. His final ring record is 39-1 (35 KO).

Life did not proceed as happily for Johnson. He fought only six more times, winning four and losing two. His final fight took place June 1, 1984 in Brisbane, Australia against Brian Janssen. After eight savage rounds that saw both men bloodied, Johnson roared from behind and flattened Janssen with a tremendous hook to the jaw that led to the fight being stopped in the ninth.

Less than four months later, on September 19, 1984, the 23-year-old Johnson was shot to death during a robbery. His final record is 21-3 (17 KO).

BRAWLS

Total Punches Landed/Thrown

Round	1	2	3	4	5	6	7	8	9	10	11	12	Total
Pryor	18/50	48/89	27/58	40/72	52/88	52/105	29/60						266/522
	36%	54%	47%	56%	59%	50%	48%						51%
Johnson	16/45	14/36	18/48	18/54	12/44	16/49	9/27						103/303
	36%	39%	38%	33%	27%	33%	33%						34%

Jabs Landed/Thrown

Round	1	2	3	4	5	6	7	8	9	10	11	12	Total
Pryor	4/13	7/20	11/25	6/13	9/22	14/33	3/16						54/142
	31%	35%	44%	46%	41%	42%	19%						38%
Johnson	4/17	5/13	8/26	4/19	3/23	5/20	4/15						33/133
	24%	38%	31%	21%	13%	25%	27%						25%

Power Punches Landed/Thrown

Round	1	2	3	4	5	6	7	8	9	10	11	12	Total
Pryor	14/37	41/69	16/33	34/59	43/66	38/72	26/44						212/380
	38%	59%	48%	58%	65%	53%	59%						56%
Johnson	12/28	9/23	10/22	14/35	9/21	11/29	5/12						70/170
	43%	39%	45%	40%	43%	38%	42%						41%

Aaron Pryor vs. Dujuan Johnson November 14, 1981, Cleveland, Ohio

Tony Lopez vs. Rocky Lockridge I
July 23, 1988, Sacramento, California

A fighter's career consists of a series of crossroads that lead to places to where no one can be sure. Of course, everyone wants to take the path that leads toward victory, success, riches and perhaps the Hall of Fame, but the forces in charge of destiny often steer a fighter toward defeat, disappointment and financial ruin, for there are far more ways to fail than to succeed.

Only the special ones blessed with supreme talent, wild card intangibles or sheer luck find the roads they seek. Many of them can point to the single day and the single fight that confirmed their worth as fighters and forever separated them from the millions who did their best but fell short of the mark. For Tony "The Tiger" Lopez, that day came July 23, 1988 before thousands of his best friends and millions of new friends watching on CBS.

Up until then, Lopez was popular in Sacramento but was a virtual stranger to TV viewers beyond its borders. The 25-year-old Lopez had won 29 of his 30 fights with 22 knockouts and the IBF viewed Lopez as the 10th best junior lightweight in the world. The only blemish came via seventh-round disqualification to Ramon Rico, a defeat that was avenged just 24 days later by second round knockout. Meanwhile, his most notable victories came against Tommy Cordova (W 10), Arnel Arrozal (KO 2), Gerardo Velazquez (KO 3) and, in his most recent outing four months earlier, Tony Pep (KO 3).

The 29-year-old Lockridge was a much better known quantity, for his busy style and perpetual aggression had made him a TV favorite. Lockridge, in just his eighth pro fight, decisioned dangerous spoiler Gerald Hayes (W 10) and that victory helped paved the way toward a title shot with an eight-fight KO streak that included victories over Fel Clemente (KO 7) and Richard Rozelle (KO 2). Many observers felt Lockridge had done enough to dethrone longtime WBA champ Eusebio Pedroza when they first met on October 4, 1980 in McAfee, N.J., but the Panamanian's trademark late charge secured a split decision win.

Following a shocking two-round KO loss to Juan LaPorte five fights later, it was thought that Lockridge was a spent force, but Rocky proved them wrong as he racked up nine straight wins to earn a second crack at Pedroza. Weighing a shockingly light 122 ½, Lockridge lost another razor-thin decision. The determined Lockridge soldiered on, and his 10-round decision upset over Cornelius Boza-Edwards on the undercard of Pryor-Arguello II paved the way for a third title chance against WBA junior lightweight champion Roger Mayweather. Lockridge, again an underdog, pulled off another surprise as an overhand right to the jaw took out the "Black Mamba" in just 91 seconds.

Lockridge defended his belt three times against Tae Jin Moon (KO 11), Julio Llerena (KO 6) and Kamel Bou Ali (KO 6) before venturing to San Juan, Puerto Rico to take on the legendary Wilfredo Gomez. Lockridge was strong in the first two-thirds of the fight, but the resourceful Gomez kept plugging away and the judges saw enough good moments in the late rounds to award Gomez a highly debatable split decision. Lockridge secured a shot at Julio Cesar Chavez's WBC title three fights later, and though he fought well he lost a majority decision. But the phoenix-like Lockridge rose yet again as three fights later he beat IBF junior lightweight titlist Barry Michael into an eighth-round submission, and Lopez represented the third title defense of Lockridge's second 130-pound reign.

Though Lockridge was fighting in decidedly hostile territory, he was expected to turn away his charismatic challenger. The stamina demands that dogged Lockridge against Pedroza were reduced for this fight due to a jurisdictional conflict. Though the IBF would continue to hold 15-round title fights until September 1, this bout was to be contested over 12 rounds because the rules in California took precedence. That good omen was countered by another, more sinister one: Lockridge tipped the scale at 128 even though he had not worked in the gym for the last few days of training. This brought back memories of Lockridge's second fight with Pedroza in which he was noticeably weaker in the final five rounds. Lockridge would need every ounce of strength he could muster to turn back this Tiger.

Lockridge opened the fight by landing a jab to Lopez's body and after Lopez answered with two jabs and an overhand right, they dug their toes into the canvas and began trading on the inside. Lopez ripped a right uppercut as Lockridge cranked hooks to the body. Lockridge just missed with his trademark punch – a looping right to the jaw – but Lopez countered with one on the ear that prompted Lockridge to clinch.

It didn't take long for both men to pump up the pace, and it was Lopez who won the early test of strength and territory. It was apparent Lockridge was not going to bulldoze Lopez like he had so many other opponents, and as he speared Lockridge with jabs he was showing himself to be a versatile, physically strong and dangerous performer.

The air of mystery that surrounded Lopez was beginning to fade as he kept pace with the free-swinging Lockridge and smoothly alternated between long and short range fighting.

Lopez cracked a charging Lockridge with a hard right to the cheek in the opening seconds of round two and a second big right capped off a tough exchange. Moments later, a short lead right buckled the champion's legs, but the resourceful Lockridge fell inside and dug a right to the body. A hammering right to the ear caught Lockridge rolling away. A big round for Lopez became towering when a short left to the face forced Lockridge to take a stutter-step backward. The champion remained persistent, however, as he worked the body and caught Lopez with occasional rights over the top.

But it was Lopez who took the play away from the champion as he ended the round by blasting a right-left to Lockridge's body.

Amidst the biggest moment of his life, both inside and outside the ring, Lopez couldn't have dreamed of a better scenario. Before 11,000 boisterous fans chanting his name, Lopez had seized the early advantage against perhaps the most physically strong 130-pounder in the world. Fighting at a pace that matched the 100-degree temperatures outside Arco Arena, Lopez remained cool and relaxed yet was very active with his hands and feet. His blows were sharper, straighter and carried more authority, and the crowd's full-throated bellows made his already overwhelming home-field advantage even more pronounced. His physical and psychic energy were perfectly linked and he carried the bulletproof confidence that only a man with pristine, uncut brows and a chin that had yet to absorb a knockdown punch could possess.

But Lockridge was not about to meekly surrender to the inevitable because that was not the way of champions. He knew himself well enough to realize that he needed several rounds to properly warm up his engine, and once he did he would be all right. As Lopez piled up the early rounds on the scorecards, Lockridge continued to plug away with roundhouse punches under and over in the hopes that their cumulative effect would eventually tell on his stubborn challenger.

The champion's fortunes began to turn for the better at the start of the fifth as he accelerated his charge and began finding the range with more consistency. Lockridge began and ended most of the bristling exchanges and his blows possessed previously unseen sharpness. With under a minute remaining, Lopez rallied behind a right to the ear and a right-left-right that forced Lockridge to the ropes. A brief clinch was all Lockridge needed to recover and despite Lopez's rally Lockridge still enjoyed his best round so far.

The firefight in the trenches continued in the sixth as both men demonstrated terrific conditioning and focus. It was a surprise to see Lopez backing up the physically stronger Lockridge, but because the champion's motor was properly warmed up it was he that was getting off his punches first more often. It was Lopez, however, who possessed the greater single-shot power on this day and a right to the jaw forced Lockridge, who now had blood at the corner of his right eye, to spin toward the ropes on unsteady legs.

Lockridge successfully returned to the sanctuary of close range, all the while banging away at Lopez's body. Lockridge was also landing blows to the head, for Lopez now sported a bruise on the bridge of the nose.

The crowd was on its feet as Lopez rocked Lockridge with a right to the head, and more layers of drama were piled on as Lockridge responded with his own surge. A heavy right with 30 seconds remaining forced Lockridge to slump into a clinch, but the champion kept digging away at the body for the rest of an extraordinarily exciting round.

The break between rounds six and seven was extended by 46 seconds so that the doctor could properly inspect Lockridge's cut while giving his seconds the full minute to work on the gash; a recently adopted rule in California. The Golden State crowd voiced its disapproval, for they felt Lopez was being denied a golden opportunity, but the boos turned into cheers early in the seventh as Lopez bounced several crisp rights off Lockridge's jaw.

The challenger was fighting with a serenity born of confidence and it didn't take Lopez long to reopen Lockridge's cut. Lockridge drove both hands hard to the body, but his offerings had little effect on Lopez, who was gulping in air because he was putting everything he had behind every punch.

Lopez's double jabs in the eighth worsened Lockridge's cut, and while Rocky was shortening up his punches and putting more speed on them, Lopez was still dictating the pace behind a triple jab followed by a unusual right-jab-jab combination. Lopez's beautiful clusters of punches produced blood in Lockridge's mouth.

Everything seemed to be going Lopez's way, but with 1:10 remaining in the round, Lockridge showed why he was a champion. A right hand that scraped off the side of Lopez's ear caused the challenger's body to fall straight down to the canvas in most awkward fashion. It was a precision punch that struck Lopez in the tiny area that controlled his equilibrium, and as a result his knees folded double while the rest of his body remained erect. The rest of his body then surrendered to gravity and crashed hard on the right side. Up at four, Lopez's eyes and mouth were wide open and his face wore an uncertain expression as he took the rest of referee Robert Byrd's count.

With a single punch, Lockridge had swung the pendulum his way and he raced after Lopez to finish the job. The crowd's enthusiasm was instantly transformed into shrieks of alarm as an overhand right slammed against Lopez's head. For Lopez, this was his first real test of his survival skills and he was moving his upper body just enough to prevent Lockridge from drawing a bead on him. A huge overhand right nearly toppled the Tiger again near the end of the round, but his follow-up punches didn't land cleanly.

The ringside physician took an extra 30 seconds to examine Lockridge's eye cut, enhancing Lopez's chances of recovery. Lopez made the most of his extended rest period as he gave as good as he got in the ninth, though Lockridge still dictated the pace. Still, Lopez appeared tired, shaken and unsteady as he leaned against the ropes with hands held high as Lockridge pounded the body. Lockridge, long criticized for his lack of stamina in his losses to Pedroza and Gomez, was now the one putting together a late charge.

Lockridge had the fight he wanted entering the 10th, a toe-to-toe slugfest along the ropes against a steadily weakening opponent. Blood stained both men's trunks but their resolve was as strong as ever as they maintained an incredibly fast pace. As each minute passed, Lopez was gaining the second wind he needed if he wanted to go the distance.

But not only did Lopez go the distance, this Tiger roared in the "championship rounds."

Though Lopez had never seen the 11th round in his boxing life, it was he who proved stronger down the stretch. A right-left-right buckled Lockridge's knees and an overhand right had Lockridge holding on. Though Lockridge's face was a mess – it now sported a new cut under the left eye – his spirit remained sturdy as he ended the round with two vicious rights.

Lockridge answered the bell for the final round with a glob of cut medicine hanging from his face, and he pushed the pace even harder because he knew he needed a big finish to save his title. He pushed Lopez toward the ropes and whaled away at his body, but the challenger pushed right back and knocked out Lockridge's mouthpiece with a sharp blow. The two men hammered each other relentlessly and every second was crammed with action as the crowd's roars lifted the combatants toward the finish line. The instant the final fell sounded Lopez spread his arms wide to embrace Lockridge to congratulate him for a battle well waged.

The decision was unanimous as Barry Yeats and Mike Glianna saw the bout 115-112 while Frank Rustich viewed it 116-112 for the new champion Tony Lopez.

As Survivor's "Eye of the Tiger" blared over the loudspeakers, boxing fans both at the arena and all over the United States knew that the sport had just witnessed the emergence of not only a new champion but of a potential star. Lopez had stared into the face of adversity and came through it a better competitor. No matter what would happen to Lopez in the future, he could point to this day as the one he showed everyone that he was not a club fighter but a champion in every way.

Epilogue: Although Lopez-Lockridge was named Ring Magazine's 1988 Fight of the Year, it remains one of the more obscure fights in terms of fame, so that's why it was included in this collection. Following a successful – and controversial – defense against John-John Molina, Lopez met Lockridge again in March 1989. Lopez won a more convincing decision and would notch another successful defense against mandatory challenger Tyrone Jackson (KO 8) before dropping the belt to Molina via 10th round TKO. Lopez won the rubber match by decision seven months later, capping off the win with an 11th round knockdown.

Lopez continued to provide action in his second reign against Jorge Paez (W 12), WBA champion Brian Mitchell (D 12) and Lupe Gutierrez (KO 6) before losing the IBF belt for good in his rematch against Mitchell (L 12). To ease his weight-making difficulties, Lopez moved up to 135 and notched three KO wins to earn a shot at Joey Gamache's WBA belt. Lopez, fighting in pro-Gamache Portland, Maine, was behind on two cards and even on the third before dropping Gamache and scoring an 11th round TKO. Lopez retained the belt by controversial decision over Dingaan Thobela in Sacramento but dropped a close nod to Thobela in the rematch in South Africa four months later.

Lopez challenged for a belt once more, losing by 10th round TKO to WBC super lightweight champion Julio Cesar Chavez in December 1994. Lopez lost two more fights to Freddie Pendleton (KO by 8) and Charles Murray (L 12), but put together a five-fight winning streak to set up a fight with the 25-3-1 Hector Quiroz in Coachella, Calif. Four days short of his 36th birthday, Lopez lost by first round TKO and retired with a record of 50-8-1 with 34 knockouts.

Lockridge fought just three more times following the rematch loss to Lopez. Three months after that fight, Lockridge knocked out Mike Zena in eight rounds but he then took more than two years off before returning against hot prospect Rafael Ruelas in January 1992. Though Lockridge fought credibly, Ruelas pounded out a 10 round decision, and following a 10-round loss to Sharmba Mitchell three months later, the 33-year-old Lockridge left the sport with a record of 44-9 with 36 knockouts.

TALES FROM THE VAULT

Total Punches Landed/Thrown

Round	1	2	3	4	5	6	7	8	9	10	11	12	Total
Lopez	28/60	22/68	20/68	27/72	24/73	20/78	25/77	20/58	33/83	36/86	35/80	35/88	325/891
	47%	32%	29%	38%	33%	26%	32%	34%	40%	42%	44%	40%	36%
Lockridge	26/89	23/73	27/87	25/98	41/103	27/99	25/88	31/91	32/115	18/92	30/93	27/98	332/1126
	29%	32%	31%	26%	40%	27%	28%	34%	28%	20%	32%	28%	29%

Jabs Landed/Thrown

Round	1	2	3	4	5	6	7	8	9	10	11	12	Total
Lopez	9/26	8/33	8/34	5/25	9/25	7/29	13/44	11/42	3/16	10/39	6/26	6/30	95/369
	35%	24%	24%	20%	36%	24%	30%	26%	19%	26%	23%	20%	26%
Lockridge	9/35	9/30	8/34	3/32	9/25	3/18	4/36	6/25	1/9	5/36	7/26	8/29	72/335
	26%	30%	24%	9%	36%	17%	11%	24%	11%	14%	27%	28%	21%

Power Punches Landed/Thrown

Round	1	2	3	4	5	6	7	8	9	10	11	12	Total
Lopez	19/34	14/35	12/34	22/47	15/48	13/49	12/33	9/16	30/67	26/47	29/54	29/58	230/522
	56%	40%	35%	47%	31%	27%	36%	56%	45%	55%	54%	50%	44%
Lockridge	17/54	14/43	19/53	22/66	32/78	24/81	21/52	25/66	31/106	13/56	23/67	19/69	260/791
	31%	33%	36%	33%	41%	30%	40%	38%	29%	23%	34%	28%	33%

Tony Lopez vs. Rocky Lockridge I July 23, 1988, Sacramento, California

William "Caveman" Lee vs. John LoCicero
July 9, 1981, Detroit, Michigan

The defining moment. If an athlete can't achieve the ultimate goal of lasting greatness, this slice of excellence is the next best thing. It allows him or her to rise above the teeming masses of mediocrity and obscurity and be remembered for all time.

Joe Namath's successful guarantee of victory before Super Bowl III propelled him all the way to the Hall of Fame and a level of celebrity that continues to this day. Bobby Thompson – and Ralph Branca for that matter – will always be remembered for "The Shot Hit Around the World" that won Thompson's New York Giants the 1951 pennant and a spot in the World Series. Even legendary players like hockey's Mark Messier are fondly recalled for singular moments, like his pre-game declaration before Game 6 of the 1994 Eastern Conference championships against the New Jersey Devils that his Rangers would win, after which he produced a hat trick. It didn't hurt that Messier then led the Rangers to the Stanley Cup to break the team's 54-year drought.

In boxing, the name Buster Douglas will always be linked to arguably the greatest upset in the history of sports when the 42-1 underdog overcame personal tragedy to knock out undisputed heavyweight champion Mike Tyson. This one act erased everything that had happened before and relegated to the background virtually all that has transpired since. As far as casual sports fans are concerned, Douglas will always be known as the man who destroyed "Iron Mike's" pristine aura of invincibility.

While Douglas' feat earned him worldwide acclaim, other defining moments have allowed lesser lights to enjoy a measure of notoriety decades after the fact. When boxing fans bring up the names of William "Caveman" Lee and John LoCicero, their collective minds are immediately transported back to the Twenty Grand Showroom in Detroit. It was there that their scheduled 10-round middleweight bout was transformed from an ordinary "ESPN Top Rank Boxing" main event into an instant classic, mostly on the power of one unforgettable round.

The Lee-LoCicero bout was a crossroads encounter that had important ramifications for both in terms of their viability as contenders. Lee (20-0, 19 KO) was a 24-year-old bomber from Emanuel Steward's Kronk Gym riding a six-bout knockout string following a four-round KO loss to top contender Frank "The Animal" Fletcher. Lee was a man used to going home quickly as 15 of his 19 knockouts came within the first two rounds, and most of them came courtesy of his tremendous left hook. Ironically, Lee's most noteworthy win was the one that came by decision – an eight-round verdict over O'Dell Leonard, who was said to be related to one Sugar Ray Leonard, but really wasn't.

While Lee was close to regaining contender status, the 24-year-old LoCicero (17-5, 13 KO) was in desperate need of a victory – any victory – to keep his career going. Like Lee, LoCicero had been a knockout machine with his most notable scalps being those of Willie Classen (KO 8), Carlos Betancourt (KO 1) and a certain Brooklyn middleweight who went on to make a much bigger mark in show business, Tony Danza. But LoCicero entered the Lee bout with no momentum; his last outing was a nationally televised 10-round defeat to the 16-0 Norberto Sabater nine months earlier and his last somewhat significant win (against Betancourt) had taken place nearly a year-and-a-half ago. LoCicero did have one thing going for him: An exciting, bombs away style that television executives love, and given Lee's penchant for toe-to-toe combat, LoCicero had the playing field he needed to cash in on his last, best chance at revitalizing his career.

The two fighters began by circling one another and poking out lefts, but LoCicero quickly broke the strategic tension by sneaking in a short hook to the jaw. Lee paid him back with one of his own moments later, then bulled LoCicero across the ring with an inaccurate flurry. LoCicero spun Lee toward the ropes and threw hard to the body before Lee escaped to ring center. LoCicero shot a jab and straight right to the body while Lee's solid jab popped back LoCicero's head. The shorter LoCicero lowered his head and bodied Lee to the ropes and fired a jab to the body, a right cross to the jaw, and a hook-cross-hook to the head.

Lee, though, was unhurt and he proved it by landing a hard hook during LoCicero's salvo and returning to the center of the ring. Lee slipped inside LoCicero's jab with a sharp counter hook, after which he returned to long range and pumped several jabs. Those jabs set up a crisp right to the ear that wobbled LoCicero, but the New Yorker regained enough of his equilibrium to convince Lee to back off and to end the round jabbing to the head.

At least on this night, the normally aggressive Lee was a more highly evolved "Caveman" as he smartly used his height and reach advantages to forge an early lead, and LoCicero was at a loss on how to get inside Lee's jabs. LoCicero didn't help matters much by lifting his chin every time he jabbed, the result of having to lunge after Lee at every turn.

Early in the second, Lee drove LoCicero back with a right to the body, a right uppercut to the jaw and a heavy jab. LoCicero managed to spin Lee toward the corner pad, where he landed a chopping right to the jaw and a hook to the ribs.

With that, the terms of battle changed from a long-distance battle to one that favored LoCicero's talents in the trenches. But Lee adjusted well to his new circumstances by catching LoCicero with four solid uppercuts. LoCicero got in his own right uppercut and followed with a strong left-right to the body. Lee shifted his upper body back and forth to set up more uppercuts and escape the ropes, but LoCicero bullied him back with a hook-right-hook. As the second round neared its end, the two fighters began to produce the fireworks expected of them by trading heavy artillery until the bell.

The third saw more of the same as LoCicero banged in a solid lead right to the side of the head. The New Yorker then tried to push Lee toward the ropes but the "Caveman" spun away and fired a double jab, a third jab that forced LoCicero to the ropes and a fourth that snapped his opponent's head to the side. LoCicero tried to burrow his way inside, but Lee nailed him with a right uppercut and two more forced LoCicero to back away and reset himself. Instead of letting LoCicero catch his breath, Lee charged in and sunk a hook to the ribs.

Though there were brief segments when both men sought to fence at long range, one didn't have to dig deeply to know each had just one goal on his mind – knockout.

LoCicero again pushed Lee toward the ropes, and once again Lee made him pay with several uppercuts. A crunching hook off one of those uppercuts hurt LoCicero seriously and as LoCicero tried to smother him, Lee banged the body and connected with a pair of follow-up jabs. Instead of retreating and collecting his thoughts, LoCicero continued to press forward and Lee took advantage with a trio of uppercuts. Lee couldn't seem to miss with the uppercut, but LoCicero's sheer toughness and unwillingness to show weakness gave Lee reason to throttle down his attack for the rest of the round.

The fourth began with a jabbing contest, with Lee's longer spears trumping LoCicero's. A right to the ear forced Lee toward the ropes but Lee kept his hands working as LoCicero closed in, landing a right uppercut and left hook before pivoting out. Though LoCicero was taking most of the punishment, he bested Lee continuously in terms of ring positioning as he used his lower center of gravity to move Lee toward the corners and ropes, and Lee had no choice but to engage LoCicero on his terms. As long as LoCicero could dictate the course of action, it gave him reason to hope that the fight would eventually turn in his favor.

Midway through the fourth, LoCicero saw his chance. After muscling Lee to the ropes, LoCicero kept his hands working and his effort started to pay off. LoCicero ripped a six-punch flurry to Lee's head and followed with an overhand right. After Lee pushed him off, LoCicero pumped in a hook to the head, a hook to the ribs and a right to the body. LoCicero fired a right to the ear and a hook to the body as Lee tried to play "rope a dope." Though LoCicero was mounting the first sustained attack of the fight, Lee didn't seem seriously hurt.

All that changed in the final minute of the fourth.

After LoCicero lashed out with a lead overhand right to the temple, he pushed Lee off to create more punching room. He opened just enough space to unload a booming hook-right uppercut combination that stiffened Lee's legs and had him in deep trouble. An adrenaline-charged LoCicero chased Lee to the ropes behind an overhand right and seven more punches crashed through Lee's guard before Lee could spin away and back up toward another set of ropes. LoCicero blasted in a right to the chin that caused Lee to seek refuge, but LoCicero gave him none as a counter right-left hook combo to the face, a right to the ear, a hard left and a huge right deepened Lee's crisis. LoCicero pounded away furiously as Lee secured a saving clinch that enabled him to ride out the final seconds. Lee walked back to the corner with blood coming out of his nose while LoCicero now sported a growing mouse under his right eye.

Up until now, Lee had dominated the fight in every way but LoCicero's grit had delivered him to the doorstep of a phenomenal comeback victory. The closing seconds of the fourth saw Lee on the verge of athletic extinction but one would have never known it if the opening seconds of round five were the first images he saw of the fight. The one-minute respite did Lee a world of good as he opened with an extra spring in his step and renewed strength on his punches. He was determined to turn the fight back in his direction – and put LoCicero away once and for all.

Lee opened with a hook to the chin and a right to the temple while also targeting his stiff jabs at LoCicero's swollen right eye. LoCicero struggled mightily with his vision and he seemed unable to recapture his fourth-round magic. Emboldened by his success, Lee pressed forward behind a right uppercut to the jaw, a hook to the body and a right uppercut. A right-left-right followed by a right uppercut sent LoCicero reeling toward the ropes. Lee worked LoCicero over with right uppercuts, and the New Yorker could do nothing more than lean in with his upper body and hope for a break.

LoCicero tried a five-punch flurry, but that burst of energy went for naught as every blow missed. Lee spun him around and dug two rights to the ribs and a fierce hook to the jaw. LoCicero attempted a hook, but Lee stepped in and snapped LoCicero's head with a harder one. Lee's finely honed instincts as a knockout artist kicked in with full force as a right uppercut-jab-overhand right-left uppercut-right uppercut-overhand right salvo left LoCicero sprawled at Lee's feet.

LoCicero groped for consciousness before regaining his feet at nine and the end seemed near. LoCicero tried to hold on, but Lee shook him off and kept firing away. An overhand right had LoCicero all but out.

Of all the traits that separate good fights from great, multiple shifts of momentum are the strongest of all. Usually these ebbs and flows unfold over a number of minutes or even several rounds, as was the case of the first Sugar Ray Leonard-Thomas Hearns bout. It is rare, indeed, when a fight changes course more than once over the course of a single round, but, as you are about to read, it actually happened *twice*.

As Lee tried to apply the finishing touches to an almost semi-conscious LoCicero, the fifth round took its first dramatic – and potentially legend-making – turn.

As a badly stricken LoCicero managed to duck under a Lee left hook, the New Yorker lashed out with a hook to the body and a Hail Mary right to the jaw that stiffened Lee's legs and forced him to seek cover on the ropes. A suddenly re-energized LoCicero pursued and unloaded a massive overhand right that spun Lee's head violently. Had it not been for the ropes, Lee surely would have fallen to the floor. But the strands offered no salvation for the hometown hero; instead LoCicero connected with a scorching right uppercut-left hook combination. Lee tried to retaliate on instinct alone, but LoCicero fought like a man possessed as his fists produced dizzyingly powerful combinations. A hook-cross-hook was followed by 14 more savage punches that had Lee on the verge of unconsciousness.

LoCicero was poised to complete a most improbable comeback, but no one could have known that one act of seeming impossibility would be immediately followed by another.

LoCicero's barrage had depleted him of his entire energy supply, and because he stopped punching for a precious moment Lee was able to slap on the briefest of clinches. Once the referee separated them, LoCicero dropped his arms to chest level and attempted to catch his breath.

Big mistake.

Lee, still in a semi-conscious haze, uncorked a short right to the jaw that set up a hook that made LoCicero's body visibly shudder. That one image instantly snapped Lee out of his fog, and he seized the situation by landing a short right uppercut that made LoCicero stumble forward into a clinch. As the referee separated the two, both fighters' upper bodies resembled flaccid water hoses as they tried to force themselves to keep going. LoCicero attempted to save himself with an all-or-nothing overhand right and Lee responded with one of his own. The crowd was electrified by the extraordinary shifts in momentum, and thoughts of that rarest of birds – a double knockout – seemed within the realm of possibility. Both fighters appeared ready to collapse at any moment.

One would.

Lee dug in his toes and ripped a left hook to the body and a second to the jaw, and LoCicero dropped straight down to the canvas. LoCicero was a spent force as he sat on the floor and shook his head, and he was facing his corner on one knee as the referee tolled the fateful "ten."

The crowd roared at the finish, many applauding as others wore awestruck expressions. A rush of Kronk acolytes, led by their mentor Emanuel Steward, rushed across the ring and congratulated Lee on his hard-earned triumph.

Lee-LoCicero was the kind of action-packed, drama-filled, see saw affair worthy of being remembered long after the television cameras were shut down. The fifth round was mandatory material on all ESPN retrospective shows, and the two fighters would forever be linked with a hyphen just like all the other legends. For the rest of time, Lee-LoCicero would conjure images of desire, determination and drama for boxing fans everywhere, especially for those who were privileged to see it unfold as it happened.

Epilogue: Neither man would ever again reach the heights of their unforgettable evening together, but as the winner Lee would eventually get the opportunity to fulfill the ultimate professional dream. Four months after stopping Reyes Escalera in four rounds on November 19, 1981, Lee received a shot at Marvin Hagler's world middleweight championship at Bally's Park Place in Atlantic City. But Lee's aspiration of becoming a champion was snuffed out in extremely short order as Hagler blew Lee out in just 67 seconds.

Lee took a four-year break from the sport following the Hagler defeat, resurfacing at Detroit's Cobo Arena with a one-round knockout of Orlando Pauling. But Lee failed to follow up that victory quickly, instead taking another two years off before making his final ring appearance. On January 3, 1988 at the Pellazza dello Sport in Genoa, Italy, Yawe Davis stopped the 30-year-old Lee in four rounds. Lee's final record is 23-4 with 22 KO.

Four months after his loss to Lee, LoCicero scored a 10th round KO over the solid 24-3 Bruce McIntyre. Unfortunately for LoCicero, this would prove to be his final victory as over the next four months he dropped a pair of 10 round decisions to Mike Baker and Sugar Ray Seales. The 25-year-old LoCicero ended his career on November 18, 1982 in Atlantic City against Tony Suero, who stopped LoCicero in three rounds. LoCicero's final record is 18-9 (14 KO).

BRAWLS

Total Punches Landed/Thrown

Round	1	2	3	4	5	6	7	8	9	10	11	12	Total
Lee	25/63	30/64	27/56	8/27	48/86								138/296
	40%	47%	48%	30%	56%								47%
LoCicero	20/43	19/56	10/43	32/72	29/50								110/264
	47%	34	23%	44%	58%								42%

Jabs Landed/Thrown

Round	1	2	3	4	5	6	7	8	9	10	11	12	Total
Lee	13/33	12/33	6/20	3/9	7/20								41/115
	39%	36%	30%	33%	35%								36%
LoCicero	9/23	5/26	4/21	4/21	4/8								26/99
	39%	19%	19%	19%	50%								26%

Power Punches Landed/Thrown

Round	1	2	3	4	5	6	7	8	9	10	11	12	Total
Lee	12/30	18/31	21/36	5/18	41/66								97/181
	40%	58%	58%	28%	62%								54%
LoCicero	11/20	14/30	6/22	28/51	25/42								84/165
	55%	47%	27%	55%	60%								51%

William "Caveman" Lee vs. John LoCicero July 9, 1981, Detroit, Michigan

★ Chapter 2 ★
SHOOTOUTS

TALES FROM THE VAULT

Soo Hwan Hong vs. Hector Carrasquilla
November 26, 1977, Panama City, Panama

The junior featherweight class has seen more than its share of thrilling fights since the World Boxing Council revived it in 1976 following a five-decade hiatus. Wilfredo Gomez and Lupe Pintor put on a fight for the ages on the undercard of Thomas Hearns-Wilfred Benitez in 1982 while Marco Antonio Barrera and Erik Morales staged an epic battle in the first installment of their trilogy in 2000. Leo Cruz-Sergio Palma II and Lupe Pintor-Juan "Kid" Meza were brutal wars of attrition while Meza's one-round, one-punch KO over Jaime Garza in 1984 was highly-concentrated TNT.

The fight between Soo Hwan Hong and Hector Carrasquilla November 26, 1977 in Panama City, had the explosiveness of Meza-Garza as well as a plot twist that would rival any Hollywood screenplay. The fight boasted several historic angles – it was the first 122-pound title fight conducted by the World Boxing Association and the Panamanian challenger, at 17 years 186 days, was attempting to become history's second-youngest world champion. Wilfred Benitez was 17 years 180 days old when he won the WBA junior welterweight championship from the legendary Antonio Cervantes March 6, 1976. Benitez's record still stands more than three decades later.

With the fight taking place in his hometown of Panama City against a battle-worn veteran, one would think the road to success was being paved for the hotshot kid with the 10-0 (10 KO) record. Carrasquilla turned pro 27 days before his 16th birthday with a first round KO of Pedro Reyes. His list of opponents were dotted with names like Guillermo Shakespeare ("Guillermo" is the Spanish equivalent of "William") and Esparragoza (the first name being Jesus, not onetime WBA featherweight champ Antonio). None of his fights lasted more than three rounds and his three-round KO over Esparragoza was not only his first scheduled 12 rounder, it earned him the right to fight for the vacant belt.

At 27, Hong (38-4-3, 12 KO) had already experienced success at every level of the sport. He won the Korean bantamweight title by knocking out Young Suh Park in four rounds and won the vacant Oriental and Pacific Boxing Federation 118-pound belt by beating Al Diaz over 12 rounds. After defending the OPBF strap against Shigeyoshi Ohki (W 12), Hong began stepping up the level of competition. He avenged an earlier loss to Ushiwakamaru Harada (W 10) then knocked out future world title challenger Thanomchit Sukothai in eight to keep the OPBF title. A three-round KO of Susumu Inuoe was followed by his biggest win to date, a 10-round decision to fading former WBA flyweight champion Berkrerk Chartvanchai.

Four fights after the Chartvanchai win, Hong beat Arnold Taylor by 15-round decision to capture the WBA bantamweight title in Durban, South Africa in one of the division's more exciting championship encounters. Following a non-title victory over Genzo Kurosawa and a defense against Fernando Cabanela, Hong lost the WBA belt to Alfonso Zamora, who, like Carrasquilla, was a young power-punching phenom. The fourth round KO upped the 21-year-old Zamora's record to 21-0 (21 KO) and Hong was left to pick up the pieces of his career.

Hong earned a rematch with Zamora by going 9-0-1 in his next 10 fights, regaining the OPBF bantamweight title by decisioning former WBC flyweight champion Venice Borkhorsor along the way. Zamora-Hong II took place October 16, 1976 in Inchon, Korea and Hong fought competitively before the fight was stopped controversially in the 12th, prompting the overwhelmingly pro-Hong crowd to riot. Disappointed, Hong had to find a way to get back into the title picture – any title picture.

Hong found hope in the newly created junior featherweight division. After two 10-round decisions over Conrado Vasquez in Honolulu and former WBC super bantamweight champion Dong Kyun Yum in Seoul, Hong earned a spot in the WBA elimination tournament to determine who would take part in the sanctioning body's first title fight at 122. Carrasquilla had already reserved his place in the final by knocking out Jesus Esparragoza six weeks before, and Hong grabbed the other slot by decisioning Futaro Tanaka over 12 rounds in Seoul.

As Carrasquilla and Hong received their final instructions at ring center, the source of the Panamanian's power could be seen in his thicker chest and shoulders while Hong's long, lean muscles were perfectly suited for his volume punching attack. The crowd at the Gimnasio Nuevo Panama in Panama City knew it was going to witness history of some sort but nobody could have anticipated the fireworks that were about to be detonated.

The fight began calmly enough with Carrasquilla sizing up Hong, throwing half-speed jabs and rolling his upper body. Hong landed well with his jab and he smartly mixed in hooks to the body followed by right uppercuts to the chin. A three-punch combination by Hong – a right to the body, a hook to the ribs and a hook/uppercut to the chin – was particularly effective and two more hooks to the body a few seconds later helped Hong seize the momentum.

Late in the round, Carrasquilla concentrated on landing lead rights to Hong's ear, connecting with three of them. The Panamanian showed unusual composure for a 17-year-old, and those rights to the ear laid the foundation for the success that followed a few minutes later.

Carrasquilla started the second by energetically working the jab to the head and body while Hong dug the body from long range. The two engaged in a test of strength at ring center by exchanging powerful blows in the trenches. The veteran Hong tempted fate by trading with the precocious Panamanian and Fate was about to strike Hong hard.

Following another lead right to the ear, Carrasquilla unleashed three short, powerful hooks. The last two exploded off Hong's chin and the bridge of the nose and the South Korean crashed to the canvas with startling suddenness. Sensing the kill – and the crowning of a new Panamanian world champion – the crowd leaped to its feet and roared its encouragement.

Up at two, Hong tried to kick some life into his legs as he took referee Jay Edson's mandatory eight-count. Hong immediately went inside to smother Carrasquilla's follow-up blows, but the youngster would have none of it because he found the key to solving Hong – rights to the ear followed by hooks to the jaw. Carrasquilla landed the combination squarely as Hong rushed inside and seconds later he tried it again. The right missed, but the hook produced a second knockdown. Up at seven, Hong didn't seem badly hurt. His eyes may have been focused but his legs told another story.

Clearly in survival mode, Hong again sought refuge on the inside, bulling Carrasquilla to the ropes and trying to re-establish respect. Respect was nowhere to be found as Carrasquilla connected with a right to the body and a right to the jaw. When Hong fell the third time, the crowd jumped in jubilation and the ringside commentator shouted, "the fight is over!" because bouts were normally stopped after three knockdowns in a round. But Edson did not stop the fight, instead issuing another count over Hong. While the three-knockdown rule has become the standard by which most fights are stopped, in this instance the decision to end matters rested solely on Edson's discretion.

Hong, up at four, was badly hurt this time and while he continued to throw punches, his legs could no longer hold him upright. When Hong collapsed to the floor from yet another right-left to the chin, the crowd didn't know how to react because they thought the fight should have been over by now. It was four knockdowns and counting, and the courageous Hong arose again at six.

Carrasquilla backed Hong to the ropes and landed volleys of power shots. Hong valiantly tried to fight back, but his punches did nothing to deter the raging teen-ager that was seconds away from achieving every fighter's dream. Two hooks and a right crashed off Hong's jaw and after two more rights and a hook, Hong's hellish second round finally ended.

Hong's corner desperately tried to revive their stricken warrior by applying an ice bag to the back of his neck, but it appeared their efforts were only delaying the inevitable.

Then came round three, destined to be the final round of the fight...but for whom?

Incredibly, Hong charged out of his corner and met Carrasquilla two-thirds of the way across the ring. He landed the round's first two punches as he ripped a right to the body and a left to the liver. Hong's legs looked surprisingly fresh as he circled

Carrasquilla, and he showed no signs of the beating he had just absorbed. How was this possible?

A hook to the body and a right to the temple stunned the hometown favorite. Smelling blood, the shark-like Hong pressed forward and poured in blows with remarkable energy and snap. After Hong landed two uppercuts, a right to the jaw backed Carrasquilla to the ropes and it was evident the pendulum had swung in a big way toward the seasoned pro.

Hong landed a 45-degree angle right uppercut to the chin and a searing hook to the ribs buckled Carrasquilla's legs. The Korean then aired it out, landing an overhand right to the chin, a cuffing hook to the head and another right uppercut to the head. After missing a hook, Hong pushed off Carrasquilla to give himself more punching room.

Once he had the room, Hong lowered the boom.

A crackling hook on the point of the chin snapped Carrasquilla's head straight back and after missing a follow-up right, a final hook to the jaw caught the Panamanian as he was crumbling to the canvas. Carrasquilla was flat on his back along the ropes just a few feet from his corner and didn't begin to move until Edson's count of seven. Hong, meanwhile, paraded around the ring with his right fist in the air and never retreated to the farthest neutral corner. When the count reached seven, Hong was just five feet from his fallen opponent, but, smart cookie that he was, he quickly retreated to the center of the ring an instant before Edson waved the fight over and declared him the WBA's first junior featherweight champion.

It was a comeback of mind-blowing proportions. Just two minutes before, Carrasquilla was poised to become boxing history's second 17-year-old champion and Hong looked all but out. But Hong drew upon his vast reservoir of experience and courage to snatch victory and a second world title just 64 seconds after the ensuing round began. Hong-Carrasquilla was just another episode in boxing's perpetual story line of young up-and-coming lion versus older but still viable lion. This time, guile and fortitude won out.

Epilogue: Carrasquilla was never the same fighter after losing to Hong. He did, however, get another chance to make history April 7, 1979 in Panama City when he challenged fellow Panamanian Eusebio Pedroza for the WBA featherweight title. Had he beaten Pedroza, he would have become the youngest featherweight champion at 18 years 347 days, 15 days younger than Tony Canzoneri when he won the belt from Johnny Dundee October 24, 1927. But Pedroza was too strong, too durable and too good for Carrasquilla, who was stopped in 11.

Carrasquilla lost a three-round shootout to 43-0 Ruben Castillo July 21, 1979 in his last high-profile fight, but he did end his career on a high note as he decisioned Victor Brown May 16, 1981. He was only 21 when he retired.

TALES FROM THE VAULT

Hong fought just three more times after the war with Carrasquilla. He defended his new belt against Yu Kasahara in Tokyo February 1, 1978, scoring five knockdowns en route to an impressive 15-round decision. He wasn't so lucky three months later as Ricardo Cardona stopped him in Seoul. His final fight was a rematch with Dong Kyun Yum Dec. 19, 1980 in Seoul, which ended in a 10-round draw. His final record was 40-5-4 (13 KO).

SHOOTOUTS

Total Punches Landed/Thrown

Round	1	2	3	4	5	6	7	8	9	10	11	12	Total
Hong	31/63 49%	19/67 28%	21/42 50%										71/172 41%
Carrasquilla	14/52 27%	47/98 48%	6/16 38%										67/166 40%

Jabs Landed/Thrown

Round	1	2	3	4	5	6	7	8	9	10	11	12	Total
Hong	9/20 45%	1/11 9%	2/5 40%										12/36 33%
Carrasquilla	7/38 18%	6/21 29%	2/6 33%										15/65 23%

Power Punches Landed/Thrown

Round	1	2	3	4	5	6	7	8	9	10	11	12	Total
Hong	22/43 51%	18/56 32%	19/37 51%										59/136 43%
Carrasquilla	7/14 50%	41/77 53%	4/10 40%										52/101 51%

Soo Hwan Hong vs. Hector Carrasquilla November 26, 1977, Panama City, Panama

TALES FROM THE VAULT

Juan Meza vs. Jaime Garza
November 3, 1984, Kingston, New York

Boxing, like most other pursuits, can serve as the canvas upon which life's dramas are played out. Most fights are decided because one fighter possesses an overwhelming edge in physical skills, but there are times when other factors determine the outcome.

Some fights are won because one fighter is more willing to endure – and overcome – more punishment. Others earn the "W" by superior application of experience; for example one fighter may spot and exploit a flaw while the other man is unable to conjure an antidote. On rare occasions, fights are won even before the combatants step into the ring. Muhammad Ali used schoolyard taunts to rattle his opponents while Sonny Liston, the young George Foreman and the prime Mike Tyson were so physically intimidating that they didn't have to say a word to plant the seeds of fear.

Sometimes, the Teddy Roosevelt philosophy of "speak softly but carry a big stick" will get the job done. That was the case when Juan "Kid" Meza challenged Jaime Garza for the WBC super bantamweight title inside the Mid-Town Neighborhood Center in Kingston, N.Y.

On paper, Meza-Garza was merely the appetizer for hometown hero Billy Costello's WBC super lightweight title defense against Saoul Mamby but to many hard-core boxing fans this bout, which aired on CBS, was the first nationally-televised opportunity to scout a superstar-in-the-making.

The 25-year-old Garza sported an eye-popping 40-0 record that included 38 knockouts – an awesome .950 KO percentage. Under the tutelage of John Montes Sr. and Bennie Georgino, Garza's all-offense, no-defense ring persona reminded many West Coast observers of another Georgino product – Danny "Little Red" Lopez. Garza won his title in dramatic fashion 17 months before by coming off the floor in the first round to blast out Bobby Berna in the second for the belt vacated by the legendary Wilfredo Gomez. Few opponents could withstand Garza's swift, power-packed combinations for long – 30 of his 38 knockout victims were taken out in three rounds or less, including 13 in the first round.

The 27-year-old Meza (40-6, 31 KO) was cast a supporting role in Garza's debut on the national stage. Many fans had seen his brave challenge of Gomez more than two years earlier in which he acquitted himself honorably before being stopped in the sixth. The Mexicali native worked his way back to title contention with wins over Roberto Castillo (KO 8), the 20-1 Pongpan Sorphayathai (KO 3) and two 10-round decisions over Javier Barajas. Like Garza, Meza was a quick starter as 21 of his 31 knockouts ended in three or fewer rounds – nine of which were one-rounders. One other point of conflict: Meza had never been knocked down as a pro, but Garza's prodigious punch figured to change that.

Several hours before they entered the ring, Meza got in the first blow. Only it landed in Garza's most vulnerable spot – his psyche.

Shortly after both men weighed in at 121 ½ pounds the morning of the fight, they retreated to the hotel dining room to get some much-needed nourishment. Garza and manager Georgino were already eating when the usually reserved Meza approached their table.

"Jaime had a full plate, steak and eggs," CBS boxing consultant Mort Sharnik said in the May 1985 issue of KO. "Meza nodded his approval and then said, 'It's good that you're eating well, you'll need it.' In effect, he was saying, *'You'll be eating humble pie later.'* And Meza's voice never rose above (a normal tone)." Most fighters, especially those at the championship level, would have dismissed Meza's remark with a shrug of the shoulders. But Garza, perhaps feeling the pressure of performing before a national audience, shouted back at Meza, rose from his seat and lunged toward him. The mind game worked better than Meza could have imagined, and Garza continued his slow burn when he stepped between the ropes six hours later.

After the first bell sounded, Meza reached out to touch gloves in the age-old gesture of sportsmanship. Garza, however, would have none of it and kept his hands in a defensive position. Meza brushed off the snub and fired a home run hook that missed wildly. Garza answered with a snappy counter hook to the jaw and another that glanced off the forehead. Garza then landed a jab to the body, a hook to the ear and an overhand right to the face that landed solidly.

Garza was encouraged by his early success, and he edged in closer by feinting a hook to the body. A right uppercut barely missed the target, but a wide hook crashed off Meza's temple and dumped the Mexican on his behind for the first time in his 47-fight career. Only 40 seconds had elapsed and Garza had already proven beyond doubt that his blows could knock *anyone* off his feet.

As Meza sat on the canvas for what seemed like an eternity, he seemed in perfect control of his senses. His facial expression was almost placid as he glanced at Garza standing in the neutral corner, then deliberately scanned his surroundings before picking up referee Johnny LoBianco's count. For a man who had never been floored, Meza handled the situation with uncommon poise as he took advantage of every precious second before rising at eight.

Garza, who definitely wasn't placid, charged in behind a jab and a right uppercut to the jaw. Two hooks drove Meza back toward the ropes, but as Garza barreled in to consolidate his advantage, Meza dipped and ripped a torrid hook to the jaw that served notice that he remained a dangerous man.

As Garza cracked a jolting one-two to the jaw, CBS analyst Gil Clancy marveled at the instant plot twist. "Garza is the guy who is usually susceptible early," he said. "He's been on the deck four times, always in an early round, and has gotten up to win. This time the other guy's on the deck."

Garza continued to fire away with little regard for defense, nor for what Meza threw back at him.

Meanwhile, Meza kept his cool as he fired jabs that sliced through Garza's porous defense. As Garza dipped low after tossing a one-two, Meza uncorked a right uppercut-left hook combo that landed forcefully. Garza connected with a piercing jab to the face, but Meza answered with a hook to the nose seconds after whiffing on a four-punch flurry.

A jab to the stomach pushed Meza toward the ropes, but Meza countered with a looping hook that caught Garza rushing in and just missed with a wide arcing overhand right. Garza popped Meza on the ear with a right, but Meza knocked the overanxious Garza off-balance with a right to the ribs and an overhand right to the side of the head. As Garza missed with a winging right, Meza found the mark with a jab to the face and another over the right eye.

"Garza's making the mistake of falling in with his hands down," CBS analyst Sugar Ray Leonard noted as Garza stumbled into the corner after missing a wild hook. As Meza pursued, Garza spun away and landed a cuffing hook that sent Meza to the canvas. LoBianco ruled the incident a slip after Meza quickly arose and pointed his gloves toward the canvas to indicate he had been pushed instead of punched.

Garza landed another jab, but his right uppercut-left hook combo whizzed over Meza's head. As if to deliver an object lesson to his younger opponent, Meza proceeded to land that very combination to Garza's face before the champion danced away.

"The big difference that I see so far is that Garza is much the shorter puncher of the two," Clancy noted. "He'll beat Meza to the punch because Meza is a wide puncher."

The instant after Clancy uttered those words, Meza made the veteran trainer eat them.

After Meza missed with a short hook-right combo over Garza's head, Garza began to launch a counter hook. In the process of doing so, the champion kept his right arm too low, which created a crucial opening. Meanwhile, Meza's missed right hand put the Mexican in perfect position to launch his own hook – and his blow was triggered just before Garza's.

Meza planted his feet, rotated his hips and beat Garza to the mark with devastating effect. The massive blow struck Garza on the point of the jaw and snapped the champion's head violently to the side. His body spun to the right as he crashed hard to the canvas, his head bouncing sickeningly off the floor. As LoBianco led Meza to the neutral corner, Garza waged a battle with his own body, and he was losing it. As he struck the canvas, Garza's eyes rolled up into his head and his body desperately attempted to reassemble its working parts quickly enough to beat the 10-count. Garza rolled to his left onto his hands and knees in an effort to get his body near the ropes, but he wasn't close enough yet to grab the strands. He rolled onto his back underneath the ropes, and he managed to pull himself upright. His effort was for naught as LoBianco completed his count and waved off the fight a split-second before Garza fully regained his feet.

The superstar-in-the-making was undone, and a new champion had taken his place.

Meza, who had maintained a veneer of calm and composure throughout the fight, exploded with joy, jumping thrice into the air with his arms upraised. As he ran around the ring, he pounded his gloves together in triumph and raced into the arms of his rapturous handlers. After seven years as a pro, Meza had finally achieved his dream, and did so in spectacular fashion before an audience of millions. And like Teddy Roosevelt before him, Meza's big stick was everything it was cracked up to be.

Epilogue: Meza fought only seven more times after the Garza fight, which was named 1984's Knockout of the Year by KO magazine. Meza overpowered perennial contender Mike Ayala in six rounds five months later, but shockingly dropped the belt to prohibitive underdog – and former WBC bantamweight champion– Lupe Pintor in a thrilling 12-round slugfest.

Sixteen months after losing to Pintor, Meza challenged for a world title for the final time against Pintor's successor Samart Payakaroon in Bangkok. The slick-boxing Thai built a huge lead on the scorecards before stopping Meza a mere five seconds before the final bell.

Eight months later, Meza dusted Lenny Valdez in one round but was stopped in eight rounds by Javier Marquez two months after that. The Mexican launched a two-fight comeback nine years later at age 40, stopping Esteban Lozoya in four, but being stopped in a single round by Wilfredo Negron five weeks later. Meza retired for good after that, and his final record stands at 45-9 (37 KO).

Garza never again fought for a world title, and his rise to featherweight had mixed results. Garza notched four straight knockouts following the Meza defeat, but against Darryl Thigpen his chin let him down four times before being stopped in six rounds. Garza then entered the Stroh's featherweight tournament in the Forum in Los Angeles, and he advanced with decision wins over Dwight Pratchett and Joe Ruelaz. George Navarro ended Garza's road toward the grand prize by decisioning Garza over 10 rounds.

Garza went 2-3 in his final five fights, beating James Manning (KO 6) and Rosendo Alonso (KO 1) while losing to Marcos Villasana (KO by 5) and Mark Smith (KO by 2). The 35-year-old Garza called it a career after being knocked out in six rounds by lightweight Jose Luis Madrid February 16, 1995. Garza's final record is 48-6 (44 KO).

TALES FROM THE VAULT

Total Punches Landed/Thrown

Round	1	2	3	4	5	6	7	8	9	10	11	12	Total
Meza	30/60												30/60
	50%												50%
Garza	27/68												27/68
	40%												40%

Jabs Landed/Thrown

Round	1	2	3	4	5	6	7	8	9	10	11	12	Total
Meza	10/18												10/18
	56%												56%
Garza	14/38												14/38
	37%												37%

Power Punches Landed/Thrown

Round	1	2	3	4	5	6	7	8	9	10	11	12	Total
Meza	20/42												20/42
	48%												48%
Garza	13/30												13/30
	43%												43%

Juan Meza vs. Jaime Garza November 3, 1984, Kingston, New York

Bobby Czyz vs. Tim Broady
January 18, 1985, Houston, Texas

When Bobby Czyz turned pro in 1980 at age 18, he seemed to have it all. He was part of NBC's "Tomorrow's Champions" along with Tony Ayala Jr., Johnny Bumphus and Alex Ramos. His telegenic visage and well-spoken intelligence inspired others to describe him as "The Matinee Idol" and "white, bright and polite." But most importantly Czyz backed up the hype by winning his first 20 fights, 15 by knockout. The quality of opposition was pretty good as his victims included former champions (Elisha Obed and Oscar Albarado) as well as solid pros and fellow prospects (Teddy Mann, Robbie Sims, Bobby Coolidge and Bruce "The Mouse" Strauss).

But by age 20, the troubles began for Czyz. On November 20, 1982 before a prime-time NBC audience, a weight-drained Czyz lost a lopsided decision to perennial contender Mustafa Hamsho and suffered greatly for it. He fought listlessly throughout the bout, and a broken right hand just added to his woes. Losing the perfect record in that fashion also inflicted great harm to his marketability.

But for Czyz the problems were only beginning.

The injury kept Czyz on the shelf for 10 months, and shortly after the Hamsho loss he was dealt a crushing blow: His father committed suicide. Czyz had little choice but to fight on to support his family and he was successful, beating Bert Lee (KO 3) and Bill Medei (KO 4) in 1983 and Jimmy Baker (KO 1), Mark Frazie (W 10) and Marvin Mack (W 10) in 1984. But the agony continued as Czyz contracted mononucleosis when he was scheduled to fight for a title. Czyz and Main Events parted ways and NBC no longer wanted to showcase him, so his post-Hamsho fights were shown on small cable TV outlets. If that wasn't enough, Czyz also had several legal issues to address in his personal life that were eventually resolved in the courts.

It was a lot for a 23-year-old to take, but as Czyz entered 1985 he was ready to make another run at the top, this time as a light heavyweight.

The victories over Frazie and Mack helped Czyz (25-1, 18 KO) vault to the number two slot in the IBF and he looked to solidify his championship credentials by taking on the sixth ranked Tim "TNT" Broady, whose 17 wins in 19 fights were all by knockout. The fight took place January 18, 1985 at The Summit in Houston, and the winner was scheduled to fight Willie "Sandman" Edwards for the NABF title. But the real prize for Czyz and Broady (who turned 26 eight days earlier) was a potential world title shot against the dominant Michael Spinks, who was scheduled to defend against David Sears the following month.

Broady's most significant win to date took place June 27, 1984 when he scored a ninth round TKO over Charles Singleton, who was ranked third in the world at the time, and the Tacoma, Wash., native was known for his powerful left hook. However, Broady's last fight was a 10-round draw to Tyrone Booze just seven weeks earlier. Also, Broady was a notoriously slow starter while Czyz had no problems with firing early and often. Against Hamsho, Czyz showed a great chin but his ability to absorb an above average 175-pounder's punch was still unknown. The styles suggested a dramatic fight was in store, and in the end no one was disappointed.

Czyz came out jabbing at the opening bell while a wide-eyed Broady quickly swayed his upper body in search of openings. Czyz's jabs were sharp, accurate and diversified as he occasionally doubled it up. Broady landed his own jab but missed with a right to the jaw. Czyz countered a Broady right with a one-two that backed the Washingtonian to the ropes and a hair-trigger right over a Broady jab landed solidly.

The fight's pattern was established quickly: Czyz was clearly in counter-punching mode as he used his superior hand speed and technique to pounce on every opening Broady's slower, wider blows presented. Broady, for his part, adopted a wait-and-see attitude as he gauged Czyz's speed and sought to overcome yet another slow start.

With 1:18 remaining in the opening stanza, Czyz bulled Broady to the ropes with his most impressive string of punches yet: A jab, a right to the body, a hook, an overhand right to the head and a digging right to the ribs. Another overhand right caromed off Broady's head and a left hook-right hand combo tore through his defense. Broady wasn't hurt by any means, but he was in danger of digging too deep of a hole for himself. Late in the round, "TNT's" fuse finally sparked as he snapped jabs to Czyz's face and connected with a right to the body. While Broady enjoyed pockets of success, Czyz was still winning every mini-battle. Czyz ended a dominant first round by snapping a right-left-right to the body and a hook-left uppercut-right salvo.

Not only was Czyz out-quicking Broady, he was doing so with style. His pedigree shone through as he unleashed precise, calculated combinations in unpredictable patterns. Though Czyz was still in his early 20s, he fought like a seasoned pro whose mind and body was in perfect symmetry. Despite losing the first round badly, Broady didn't panic because he knew it was just a matter of time before he would get the chance to test Czyz's chin – and courage.

Broady opened the second with a crisp jab that brought a nod of acknowledgement from Czyz, but "Chappie" retaliated with two strong jabs that snapped back Broady's head. Broady cranked up a hook to the ribs and Czyz answered with a strong hook to the jaw. The fight quickly shifted out of feeling-out mode as both men planted their feet and mixed powerful hooks and crosses to the head and body in an early test of strength. The fight resembled a particularly violent form of chess in which they spent the first round moving out their pawns to establish position before introducing the rooks, knights and bishops.

Let the real games begin.

A terrific Czyz right caught Broady coming out and a right-left to the body caused Broady to cover up. Broady connected with a crunching hook to the ribs, but Czyz landed an excellent counter hook to the chin. Two stinging jabs snapped Broady's head and another double jab caused him to wince. A 45-degree hook rotated Broady's head violently and Czyz, convinced Broady was hurt, leaped in with both hands blazing.

Broady convinced Czyz otherwise as a heavy hook and an overhand right drove the former Matinee Idol to the ropes. Off the break, Broady strung together a six-punch flurry that was answered with a swift Czyz combination.

The naturally bigger Broady was losing the fight on points, but he had Czyz exactly where he wanted him – exchanging power shots at close range – and he sought to take advantage by investing full strength into every blow. Sooner or later, he thought, one of those bombs would turn the momentum in his favor.

With 25 seconds to go in the round, Broady was proven right.

A tremendous overhand right-left hook combo caught Czyz flush in the face and his tree-trunk legs went numb as he stumbled toward the neutral corner to buy time. Fueled by a fresh wave of killer instinct, Broady chased after Czyz and unloaded bomb after bomb. Though hurt badly, Czyz demonstrated his resourcefulness as he ducked under most of Broady's blows and even stunned him with a wide hook to the face. The man known as "TNT" was determined to detonate and as the round ended, he buried Czyz under artillery that was long on power but short on accuracy.

Broady flew out of the corner at the start of round three and blasted Czyz with a left-right to the body and an overhand right to the ear. Broady was single-minded in his pursuit to take Czyz out; his eyes were wide open and his hands fired like destructive pistons. Still, Broady couldn't line up the equalizer, and Czyz seized on every opening with sharp jabs and body volleys. While Czyz was lauded for his offensive firepower, his overlooked defensive skills were what saved him here. In one sequence, he deftly avoided a six-punch combo by keeping his hands high while bending slightly at the knees at the appropriate moment. As good as Czyz's defense was, his offense was even better as he cracked a double jab-right hand combo as well as a rifle shot right that spun Broady's head. Czyz was recovering nicely from his second-round difficulties due to his devotion to fundamentals. It was beautiful, textbook boxing but the pulsating toe-to-toe action was enough to satisfy any fan's "sweat" tooth.

But the danger for Czyz had not yet passed as Broady snapped a jab and connected well with an overhand right that twisted Czyz's neck. Another right-left glanced off Czyz's head, but Czyz ducked under a winging right and sprang up behind a hook and overhand right before darting away.

Midway through the round, Czyz stunned Broady with a huge right, and as Broady retreated to the ropes, Czyz worked the body with a pair of rights. However, Broady stayed persistent and whaled away when Czyz found himself near the corner pad.

Broady exploded a brutal left uppercut-right cross combo off Czyz's jaw, and Czyz fired back an equally huge hook to the face.

The fight was no longer a showcase for Czyz's skills against a perfect foil; it turned into what it really was – a crossroads fight between two highly-rated contenders that carried real danger for both men.

Broady slammed a right-left-right to the body and a hook to the jaw drove Czyz to the turnbuckle. An overhand right caused Czyz's knees to dip toward the floor but the Jersey Man's pride kept him upright. With 30 seconds remaining, the boxers were locked in the most extended toe-to-toe exchange of the bout, and it was about to get wilder.

After being stunned by Broady's right, Czyz roared out of the corner and drove Broady back to ring center behind a sizzling right-left-right. An overhand right to the head and a hook to the solar plexus had Broady holding on, but Broady ended a tremendous third round by cranking a hook to the hip, a right to the body and a right hook to the ear.

The Summit crowd was on its feet and roaring with appreciation. The winner might have been scheduled to fight Willie Edwards next, but at this pace there might not have been enough of the winner left for "The Sandman" to fight.

The breathtaking end to the third led to a quieter beginning in the fourth as both men exchanged jabs. As was the case in everything else in this fight, even the jabbing contest was intense as both connected flush. Another constant was Czyz's decided edges in hand and foot speed, which was illustrated by a triple jab that knocked Broady a step back. Still, Broady remained devoted to a body attack that created occasional openings for power blows to the head.

Czyz wanted to use this fight to prove he was a serious threat to capture light heavyweight world honors – and he was about to make his case in a most emphatic way.

As Broady set himself to throw his next volley, Czyz dipped slightly to his left and uncorked a short, explosive hook to the jaw that sent Broady crashing to the floor. Broady rolled onto all fours with his right arm bent awkwardly behind him, but as he arose at five he bounced on his toes well enough to allow the fight to continue. Czyz, tasting victory, leaped in with a huge right, a left uppercut to the jaw, a crunching hook and a monstrous right that left Broady's head and neck draped over the top rope. Czyz landed two more punches to Broady's unprotected jaw before referee Chris Jordan was able to leap in and stop the carnage.

At the 1:41 mark of round four, Bobby Czyz had taken a huge step toward fulfilling the promise expected of him, and he knew it. After Jordan stopped the fight, Czyz stood over the unconscious Broady and raised his arms in a gesture of primal triumph. After absorbing several frightening shots from Broady – and in his life outside the ring – Czyz was as close to his championship dreams as he had ever been.

"As far as I'm concerned, it's the best fight I've ever had," Czyz said in the August 1985 issue of KO. "I matched Broady punch for punch, strength for strength, and took him right out. It's the best I've ever looked."

But Czyz knew he was in a battle, saying of Broady "I had never been hit that hard before. When he hit me, my left leg was kind of uncontrollable. I still had my mental faculties, I could think, but when your legs aren't cooperating with your mind, you've got problems. So I backed into the ropes because I knew another shot was coming, so the first thing I did was duck. The stuff started coming, I put my hands up, and tried to minimize the amount of space he could hit. I started moving to minimize the ease with which he could hit me. I threw a few punches back, tried to work the ropes the best I could, and eventually got out of trouble. I've got great recuperative powers. Then I saw he was missing a lot that round too, except for the last 30 seconds. He didn't land anything but that one clean shot. You know, I had been training with cruiserweights. I was hit by cruiserweights in the gym, but my body never quite responded like that."

Maybe so, but Czyz found the strength within himself to overcome his crisis and come out on top like the star he hoped to become.

"The Matinee Idol" was now ready for his championship close-up.

Epilogue: After Spinks polished off Sears (KO 3) and "Diamond" Jim MacDonald (KO 8), he vacated the world light heavyweight title to pursue a shot against IBF heavyweight champion Larry Holmes, which led to the three major belts being splintered. Slobodan Kacar captured the IBF strap by decisioning Eddie Mustafa Muhammad. Meanwhile, Czyz earned a shot at Kacar by decisioning Mike Fisher and Murray Sutherland over 10 rounds.

Czyz was out of the ring another 14 months before finally fighting Kacar, and on September 6, 1986 "Tomorrow's Champion" became today's champion by blitzing the Yugoslavian in five rounds. Czyz defended the title three times against good opposition and looked impressive each time – David Sears (KO 1), Willie Edwards (KO 2) and MacDonald (KO 6). Czyz's stock was rising, and his next defense against Prince Charles Williams in October 1987 was the main supporting bout of the Thomas Hearns-Juan Roldan pay-per-view telecast. Czyz started well, knocking Williams down multiple times in the early rounds. But Williams rallied strongly behind a seemingly endless stream of uppercuts that raised a massive swelling over Czyz's eye, a swelling that led to the fight being stopped in the ninth.

For the next two years, Czyz's career raced wildly between victory and defeat. He lost a majority decision to Dennis Andries but notched solid wins over Leslie Stewart (W 10) and Mike DeVito (KO 7). Then he lost back-to-back title shots to Williams (KO by 10) and Virgil Hill (L 12). Czyz then won three fights against Uriah Grant (W 10), Andrew Maynard (KO 7) and Horacio Brandan (KO 6) to earn an unexpected title shot against WBA cruiserweight champion Robert Daniels. "Chappie" captured his second divisional belt via split decision and defended it twice against Bash Ali (W 12) and Donny Lalonde (W 12).

After winning a 10-rounder over George O'Mara, Czyz shockingly lost to undefeated Nigerian David Izeqwire due to complications from a back injury. He then moved up to heavyweight, where he beat Tim Tomashek (KO 4), Jeff Williams (W 10) and Richard Jackson (KO 6) before losing to Evander Holyfield (KO by 5). On June 12, 1998, the 36-year-old Czyz ended his career with a two-round stoppage loss to Corrie Sanders. His final record stands at 44-8 (28 KO).

Broady maintained an incredibly busy schedule following the Czyz bout as he fought seven times in the next 12 months. Less than two months after the Czyz loss, Broady rebounded with a two-round KO over David Todt, but was stopped in five rounds by Andries. Two solid wins over Darryl Spain (KO 5) and Jerome Clouden (KO 2) was followed by a loss to Marvin Mack (L 8) and a victory over Tim Williams (KO 10) to finish 1985. But TKO losses to Jeff Lampkin and Grover Robinson prompted Broady to take six years off. The comeback started well as he dusted Bernard Boyce (KO 1) and Bernard Littman (KO 2), but the 34-year-old Broady couldn't sustain the momentum as on June 11, 1993 he suffered a fourth round TKO to Ray Alberts. His final record is 21-7-1 (20 KO).

Total Punches Landed/Thrown

Round	1	2	3	4	5	6	7	8	9	10	11	12	Total
Czyz	34/56	44/65	56/81	22/37									156/239
	61%	68%	69%	59%									65%
Broady	19/62	27/95	35/88	13/38									94/283
	31%	28%	40%	34%									33%

Jabs Landed/Thrown

Round	1	2	3	4	5	6	7	8	9	10	11	12	Total
Czyz	14/25	20/28	22/39	12/18									68/110
	56%	71%	56%	67%									62%
Broady	11/49	10/45	11/35	7/26									39/155
	22%	22%	31%	27%									25%

Power Punches Landed/Thrown

Round	1	2	3	4	5	6	7	8	9	10	11	12	Total
Czyz	20/31	24/37	34/42	10/19									88/129
	65%	65%	81%	53%									68%
Broady	8/13	17/50	24/53	6/12									55/128
	62%	34%	45%	50%									43%

Bobby Czyz vs. Tim Broady January 18, 1985, Houston, Texas

TALES FROM THE VAULT

Ray Mancini vs. Arturo Frias
May 8, 1982, Las Vegas, Nevada

The realization of a dream is one of life's most powerful moments, especially when that moment is preceded by years of hard work and sacrifice. It is even more so after one fails the first time on the big stage, only to have fate (and the powers that be) smile on you and provide a second chance.

Now imagine the dream coming true in most spectacular fashion before a roaring crowd, a national TV audience and – most importantly – his parents, and one will have a sense of what Ray Mancini must have felt as he was declared the new WBA lightweight champion. The explosion of joy, the flowing of tears and the pure satisfaction had the feel of an old-time Hollywood movie, so it is fitting that the man known as "Boom Boom" in the ring is now spending his time making movies.

But the Mancini story began before Ray was even born. During the late 1930s and early 1940s, a dynamic young lightweight named Lenny "Boom Boom" Mancini was blowing through one opponent after another, and eventually he earned a non-title fight with lightweight champion Sammy Angott in 1941. Angott won a decision that most observers thought Lenny deserved. A rematch – this time for the title – was being negotiated when Lenny received his draft notice from selective service on January 15, 1942. The Army, unmoved by Lenny's story, said no furloughs or delays would be offered and it rejected his offer to donate his title fight purse to the war effort.

While fighting in Metz, Lenny was hit by mortar fire. Thirteen pieces of shrapnel were lodged in his body and doctors predicted he would be paralyzed. By the time he recovered from his injuries, the 5-2 Lenny carried heavyweight poundage, but through his typical perseverance he returned to the ring as a welterweight. Over the next three years Lenny won 14 of his next 16 fights, six by knockout, and a match with Rocky Graziano was discussed but never signed. Lenny lost his last four fights, the last two coming to Rocky Castellani. His final record was 42-12-3 (16 KO).

Upon retirement, Lenny eloped with his girlfriend Ellen and began a career with General Fireproofing in Youngstown. Ray was born when Lenny was 42, and while Ray was a child he heard the stories of his father's life as a boxer. A scrapbook detailing Lenny's career was kept in the attic and though Ray wasn't allowed to see it unattended he managed to sneak up from time to time and look through it. It was in that attic that the seeds of a dream were sown.

At age 15, Ray surprised everyone by announcing he wanted to train for the Junior Olympics. It represented the first step to fulfilling a plan aimed at winning a professional world championship for his father, who warned Ray about the hardships a boxing career might produce. Undeterred, Ray enjoyed a stellar amateur career and turned pro on October 18, 1979 with a one-round KO of Phil Bowen in Struthers, Ohio. Mancini knocked out 10 of his first 11 opponents and survived his first "step-up" fights by beating Johnny Summerhays (W 10) and later Norman Goins (KO 2) and Al Ford (W 10).

Mancini won the NABF lightweight title by knocking out Jorge Morales in nine rounds to earn a bout with the 71-3 Jose Luis Ramirez, with the winner promised a title shot with WBC champion Alexis Arguello. Given the styles, Mancini-Ramirez promised to be an all-out war but "Boom Boom" surprised everyone by turning boxer, jabbing and moving his way to a lopsided 12-round decision.

At age 20, Mancini was in position to fulfill what he felt was his destiny. On October 3, 1981 in Atlantic City, Mancini began the Arguello fight strongly and was ahead at the halfway point. But Arguello gathered himself and proceeded to pick Mancini apart with an exquisite array of jabs and power punches that eventually scored a knockdown in the 12th. Mancini suffered bad beatings in the 13th and 14th before referee Tony Perez called a halt at the 1:44 mark of round 14 after being floored by a final right cross to the jaw.

Heartbroken, Mancini thought he had lost his one and only opportunity to win a championship. But his strong challenge of Arguello – combined with his exciting style, good looks, charisma and dramatic story – enabled Mancini to secure a second chance against WBA champion Arturo Frias following wins over Manuel Abedoy (KO 2) and Julio "Diablito" Valdez (KO 10).

While Mancini's story made him a natural fan favorite, Frias was also a feel-good story. Born in East Los Angeles, Frias fell in love with boxing when he received his first set of gloves at age six. His early idol was Mando Ramos and when he heard Ramos was going to appear at the Resurrection Athletic Club near his home, he had to be there.

"I rushed down there to see him," Frias said in the April 1982 edition of International Boxing. "Just being near the champ and seeing other kids my age box settled it. I was going to be a boxer! I asked the program director if I could be in the next tournament and he told me okay – if I helped take care of the gym. He handed me a broom, and that's how I got started."

Frias began his amateur career at age 10 and won 102 of his 111 amateur fights before turning pro in 1975. He won 16 straight to begin his career, then laid off for 25 months because of hand injuries. While he waited for his hands to heal, he drove a truck for a linen company. When he returned to the ring in June 1980, he won four more fights to earn a crack at former WBA lightweight champion Ernesto Espana. Frias gave all Espana could handle, but because the fight was held in Caracas, Venezuela, the home country fighter emerged with a controversial majority decision win. Undeterred, Frias fought three months later and scored a 10-round win over Rosendo Ramirez, then rebounded from a first-round knockdown to bludgeon highly touted Mexican Juan Graciano in five rounds.

Then fate smiled on Frias.

Gonzalo Montellano was to fight champion Claude Noel for the WBA title, but "Sonny" suffered an injury in training. The number-five Frias had been preparing for a fight to take place the week after the December 5, 1981 Noel-Montellano bout, so Frias eagerly accepted the once-in-a-lifetime opportunity. Seizing the day, Frias applied ceaseless pressure and dominated throughout. In the eighth round, Frias slammed home a counter right that caught Noel winding up on a right uppercut. The Trinidad native was unable to beat Mills Lane's 10-count and at the 1:52 mark Frias had scored one of the year's big surprises.

"It felt beautiful," Frias said of the knockout punch. "It's the proudest day of my life. I'm proud to be an American and I'm proud to be lightweight champion of the world."

Two months later, Frias avenged his loss to perennial lightweight title challenger Espana by winning a technical decision in nine rounds, then signed to defend against Mancini May 8, 1982 in Las Vegas. Mancini-Frias matched two physically strong brawlers whose styles guaranteed fistic fireworks. For Frias to win, he had to exploit Mancini's easily penetrated defense and the scar tissue above his eyes. Mancini, by far the physically stronger man, wanted to use his superior work rate and punching power to overwhelm the champion. Also, Mancini had to like his chances to win because this time he didn't have a legend standing in the other corner.

As the opening bell rang, Frias quickly kneeled in his corner and crossed himself while Mancini advanced to ring center behind a bob-and-weave defense. Both men exchanged jabs, with Mancini's heavier and more accurate. The feeling-out phase lasted less than 20 seconds as Mancini ripped a right to the body and a double hook to the body and head and Frias connected with a one-two. Encouraged, Frias jumped in with another one-two and followed it with a scorching hook that exploded off Mancini's cheek. "Boom Boom" staggered toward the ropes with Frias pursuing him, but Mancini managed to grab Frias and turn him toward the ropes.

Frias landed a right to the body and a right to the jaw while Mancini countered with a hook to the face. Mancini ducked under a Frias right and connected with another hook. Frias whaled away with rights under and over while Mancini worked the left overtime. Frias nailed Mancini with two jabs and an inside right to the jaw and a second right deflected off Mancini's upraised arms.

The fight might as well have been scheduled for three rounds instead of 15 because both men fought with no regard for anything beyond that. Mancini and Frias were engaged in a high-speed firefight that could only end in an early knockout. The only questions now were "who" and "when."

Surprisingly, Frias was getting the better of the exchanges and he even managed to back up the bull-strong "Boom Boom" a few steps. Frias tagged Mancini with a sharp one-two and ducked under a wide Mancini hook, then dug a right to the solar plexus, a second one to the ribs and countered a Mancini body hook with a short right to the jaw. The champion, briefly in a southpaw stance, landed a left cross to the jaw, then switched back and missed with a one-two.

Despite getting the worst of the early chest-to-chest warfare, Mancini continued to engage the champion in the trenches. He missed with a short hook over Frias' head but drove a right to the ribs. Mancini whiffed on a wide hook, then shifted slightly to his right and nailed Frias with a compact hook to the jaw that caught the champion in mid-punch. Frias, momentarily stunned, latched on and referee Richard Greene broke them for the first time in the match.

Mancini slipped a Frias jab and fired a right to the body and landed a cuffing hook to the chin. Frias connected with a jab at long range, but the action swiftly returned to the inside. Mancini missed a hook but a right to the ribs and a hook to the jaw enabled "Boom Boom" to back up the champion for the first time.

Frias emerged with a slice under the left eye but that didn't stop him from cranking five consecutive rights to the body followed by a right uppercut to the jaw and a cross to the head. Through it all, Mancini unleashed left after left, missing with most but forcing Frias to expend more energy than he surely wanted.

After Mancini cracked a hook off Frias' jaw, Frias sprung a right uppercut that landed cleanly. Mancini landed a counter hook to the head and banged two more at short range while bulling Frias to the ropes. With his back to the ropes, Frias fired two rights to the body and blasted a right-left to the head, sparking a furious exchange that brought the crowd to its feet and roaring. The two men resembled pinwheels blown by gale-force winds and there was no sign of letup.

Frias didn't sport the sculpted upper body of Mancini, but he proved he was his equal in terms of desire and physical strength. He was winning the exchanges and was showing the experts that he was more than a club fighter who became a champion as a result of being at the right place and the right time. Given his style, however, he couldn't have fought Mancini any other way and he was about to pay the price for his courageous stand.

At ring center, Mancini unleashed a scorching four-punch combination that shifted the momentum powerfully and irreversibly. A looping hook and overhand right crashed in and a wicked hook wobbled Frias. Seeing this, Mancini swooped in and connected with a tremendous inside hook to the jaw that dumped Frias on his behind.

Up at three, Frias suddenly looked the worse for wear. A glob of mucous hung from his upper lip and more blood flowed from underneath his left eye. When Greene asked Frias if he was OK he nodded his assent, and the fight continued.

Mancini stormed in behind a wild right and a hook to the body steered Frias to the ropes. Smelling victory and the realization of his dream – "Boom Boom" emptied his guns and unleashed a hailstorm of blows under which no one could be expected to weather. Over the next 16 seconds, Mancini fired 34 blows – landing 23 of them – and Frias was unable to respond with a single blow. At the 2:54 mark, Greene stepped in and stopped the fight, sparking a wild celebration. A jubilant Mancini leaped into the arms of his handlers and blew a kiss to the crowd. As he was lifted into the air, one look at Mancini's left eye proved Frias wasn't the only one who suffered. A mouse below and a cut above framed Mancini's eye, but at this juncture he felt no pain whatsoever.

He fought through the crowd to congratulate Frias on his stirring effort, and a few seconds later Mancini's parents Lenny and Ellen joined the new champion in the ring. When Mancini spotted them, he no longer was the rough, tough champion but a proud son who wanted nothing more than to share his triumph with the man who served as his inspiration and the woman who gave him unconditional support and encouragement. Overcome with emotion, Ray wept as he hugged his parents simultaneously. Only they – and Mancini's siblings – could fully grasp the significance.

"I thank God for the strength and power he gave me to win (Frias') title," Mancini said after the fight. "I've been on both ends of the coin and I know how it feels to win and to lose. Art is still a champion. Nobody can take that away from him."

Addressing Frias' effort, Mancini said, "Art stung me early; he was all over me. I was hoping to just get through the first round. But then when I got him on the ropes I just kept throwing punches until the referee stopped the fight. Who knows what would have happened if the fight had gone onto the second and third round? This is the greatest thing in my life, and I will be a true champion. I will give everyone who deserves it a shot at my title. And I certainly will give Art a rematch. He gave me a chance at his title. Now I will give him a chance at mine."

Epilogue: There would be no rematch with Frias, but Mancini fulfilled his promise of being a fighting champion. Ten weeks after winning the title, he knocked out Ernesto Espana in six rounds before an adoring crowd in Warren, Ohio. But that triumph was followed by tragedy as Mancini knocked out Deuk Koo Kim after 14 action-packed rounds. Kim died four days after the bout and a grotesque twist of fate Kim's mother and referee Richard Greene committed suicide within four months after the bout. The Mancini-Kim result prompted the WBC to reduce its championship fights from 15 rounds to 12.

Mancini, a deeply sensitive man, would never be the same. Less than two months later he decisioned George Feeney in a non-title fight, then struggled at times against Orlando Romero before blasting him out with a single hook to the jaw. "Boom Boom" was more impressive against Johnny Torres (KO 1) and Bobby Chacon (KO 3) but Livingstone Bramble surprised many by ripping the title away by 14th round stoppage on June 1, 1984 in Buffalo. In the rematch in Reno eight months later, Mancini put forth a determined stand, fighting through a multitude of cuts before losing a highly controversial split decision to Bramble.

Only three weeks short of his 25th birthday, Mancini announced his retirement. But Mancini couldn't resist the urge to make a comeback – or two. On March 6, 1989, "Boom Boom" looked surprisingly good in a 12-round split decision loss to Hector Camacho. Unfortunately for Mancini, it wasn't his swan song – that event came on April 3, 1992 against Greg Haugen, who knocked him out in seven rounds. Mancini's final record was 29-5 (23 KO). Mancini was just one month past age 31 at the time of the Haugen fight.

Like Mancini, Frias re-entered the ring two months later but wasn't nearly as successful as Ruben Munoz stopped him in five rounds. But Frias bounced back nicely with wins over Joe Perez (W 10), Javier Rios (KO 3), Jerry Lewis (TD 4) and Jose Torres (W 10). Frias' momentum was stopped cold as the 15-17-2 Kelvin Lampkin scored a nine-round TKO. Frias ended his career on August 15, 1985 in Sacramento by losing to Bobby Chacon in five rounds. At age 28, Frias retired with a 28-5 (8 KO) mark.

TALES FROM THE VAULT

Total Punches Landed/Thrown

Round	1	2	3	4	5	6	7	8	9	10	11	12	Total
Mancini	63/114												63/114
	55%												55%
Frias	45/93												45/93
	48%												48%

Jabs Landed/Thrown

Round	1	2	3	4	5	6	7	8	9	10	11	12	Total
Mancini	9/16												9/16
	56%												56%
Frias	14/27												14/27
	52%												52%

Power Punches Landed/Thrown

Round	1	2	3	4	5	6	7	8	9	10	11	12	Total
Mancini	54/98												54/98
	55%												55%
Frias	31/66												31/66
	47%												47%

Ray Mancini vs. Arturo Frias May 8, 1982, Las Vegas, Nevada

Kelvin Seabrooks vs. Ernie Cataluna
November 18, 1987, San Cataldo, Italy

Fate is capable of dealing strange and unexpected hands. Just when the course of one's life seems set, an array of circumstances intersect to create a different reality as well as the ability to reach a plateau once thought unreachable.

For most of his career, Kelvin Seabrooks was a fighter whose purpose was to make others more favored than himself look good. Instead of being allowed to build his own reputation, he was thrown in with the undefeated Jerome Coffee and the more experienced Kenny Mitchell in his fifth and sixth pro fights respectively. Predictably, Seabrooks ended up losing a pair of decisions. The Charlotte, N.C. native bounced back with seven wins over lower-level foes and he was rewarded with a crossroads fight with highly regarded puncher Carmelo Negron. But after suffering a seventh round TKO, his place in the boxing firmament appeared to be locked in. Seabrooks was talented enough to provide seasoning for those higher up in the pecking order but not good enough to seize their spots for himself.

Over the next several years, his boxing life assumed that of a gatekeeper. Seabrooks shined against club fighters and he was good enough to expose prospects whose substance didn't match their glossy records. But when he stepped up in class he always fell short. To fighters like Calvin Grove (L 10), Pat Cowdell (KO by 5), Harold Petty (L 12) and Gaby Canizales (L 12), Seabrooks was just another stop on the road to a title shot, a necessary roadblock to negotiate before getting to their desired destination. Once disposed with, Seabooks would go on to the next assignment in the hopes that Fate would shoot him a favorable glance.

On March 10, 1986 – in Sydney, Australia no less – the 18-13 (14 KO) Seabrooks stood across the ring from Freddie "The Pebble" Jackson, who was looking to regain his stature after being disqualified for a blatant head butt against Daniel Zaragoza for the vacant WBC bantamweight title 10 months before.

Jackson was expected to polish off Seabrooks quickly, but the underdog turned the tables in a most violent way in scoring a two-round TKO.

Buoyed by his success, Seabrooks iced Tony Reyes in one round five months later and captured the USBA bantamweight title in his next outing, decisioning undefeated 1976 Olympian Louis Curtis over 12 rounds. The Curtis victory vaulted Seabrooks into a match for the IBF bantamweight belt vacated by Jeff Fenech. Again, he was thrust into the role of underdog road warrior as he took on 16-2-2 Colombian Miguel Maturana in Cartagena, but five rounds later he took out the hometown favorite and became one of boxing's most unlikely champions.

Given his past, he was seen as a titular caretaker ripe for the picking against his first challenger – any challenger. Just six weeks after capturing the crown, Seabrooks was in Calais, France, to take on the 21-0 Thierry Jacob. The night had the air of a coronation and Jacob looked the part as he knocked Seabrooks down three times. But in the 10th, Fate again smiled on Seabrooks as he shocked the crowd – and Jacob –with a Saad Muhammad-like resurrection en route to a TKO victory.

It was under this backdrop that the 24-year-old Seabrooks would engage in his second defense against 28-year-old Filipino southpaw Ernie Cataluna (24-4-7, 9 KO). Just five weeks before this fight, Cataluna struggled to a 10-round draw with Sam Yong Kim but ostensibly earned the shot by avenging an earlier loss to Ki-Yul Kang eight months before the draw. Unlike most of Seabrooks' foes, Cataluna wasn't viewed as an overwhelming favorite but his aggressive style promised to provide an exciting counterpoint to Seabrooks' well-rounded abilities.

Cataluna had to draw encouragement from Seabrooks' career – after all, if he was able to become a champion, why not him? So when the bell rang for round one he decided to forego any thoughts of going 15 rounds. He wanted the championship and he wanted it now.

After a few seconds of looking one another over, Cataluna dove in with a right hook to the body and a wild overhand left that sent him stumbling off balance. Cataluna bulled Seabrooks to the ropes with another left to the body, then trapped Seabrooks in the corner with a second left and whacked away at the champion's high guard. A couple of left crosses pierced Seabrooks' defense and the champion backed away on slightly unsteady legs. A glancing left uppercut off the forehead propelled the champion toward the ropes and Cataluna pursued behind a strong body attack punctuated by three left uppercuts to the jaw.

Knowing Seabrooks' history of slow starts, Cataluna sensed his opportunity to become the new champion was already at hand. Over the next 34 seconds, the Filipino unleashed a tidal wave of power punches to the head and body. In all, Cataluna fired 50 unanswered blows and Seabrooks was in danger of crumbling. But referee Al Rothenberg temporarily halted Cataluna's assault to issue a warning for elbowing. The brief respite did nothing to slow Cataluna down as he cranked a right hook to the body before shoving Seabrooks to the canvas, earning another warning from Rothenberg.

Cataluna was in a fighting froth, and as Rothenberg wiped Seabrooks' gloves he wandered from the neutral corner and was less than five feet away when the referee called them back into action. Finally given a little room to operate, Seabrooks fired his first real punch, a lead right to the face, but a follow-up right-left missed and soon he was back on the ropes with Cataluna firing away with a stream of left uppercuts to the face. The Filipino threw six, then seven consecutive uppercuts as he tried to take out the champion, who now sported a cut over the right eye.

With a little more than a minute remaining, Cataluna's avalanche approach finally paid dividends as an overhand left to the ear sent Seabrooks flying nearly seven feet toward the neutral corner before falling near the corner pad. Up at two, Seabrooks was given a few more seconds of recovery time because Cataluna refused to stay in the neutral corner. Still, the champion was in a world of trouble – blood was dripping directly into his eye while more crimson stained his moustache and lips.

The mandatory eight-count completed, Cataluna raced back to the attack, landing a right hook to the body, an overhand left to the ear and a left cross to the jaw. Seabrooks managed to get off two right-lefts that missed, but was countered by two long left crosses. After two more left uppercuts landed for Cataluna, Seabrooks answered with his two best punches so far, a snappy right cross-jab combination that earned the challenger's attention. After Cataluna connected with yet another left uppercut, Seabrooks fired a three-punch combo that found only air but served notice that he still had plenty of energy despite absorbing a frightful beating.

Between rounds Cataluna breathed deeply and often as he tried to replenish his energy but it was Seabrooks who remained in his corner an extra 15 seconds because his seconds were slow to leave the ring.

Cataluna wisely decelerated his assault and Seabrooks, finally seeing his chance to get his motor running, began to fire. The champion landed a sharp one-two during a six-punch flurry and connected with a solid hook following a missed right.

Though Seabrooks sported a swelling under his right eye, everything else was remarkably intact. His legs had regained their bounce and his combinations were swift, if not particularly accurate. Seabrooks worked the lead right constantly, and though many of them fell short they helped keep Cataluna at a safe distance. The fight settled into a quieter place as Seabrooks sought to regain his legs while Cataluna waited for his body to provide him a second wind. Late in the round, Seabrooks' lead rights began to find the mark and he punctuated a good comeback round by landing a follow-up left as the round closed.

As the champion sat in his corner, his visage bore the scars of battle but his eyes were bright and alert. His mere presence gave him a tremendous physical and psychological boost – after all, the first round beating he absorbed would have been enough to finish most fighters. Not only did he survive it, he arguably won the second round.

But Cataluna was far from finished as he roared out of his corner and tagged Seabrooks with three lefts. The Filipino muscled Seabrooks into the ropes and whacked away but this time the champion smartly spun out to his right and retreated to ring center. Given room to operate, Seabrooks tagged Cataluna with a right-left and ducked under a counter right hook. What started as an all-out brawl became a boxing match and Seabrooks' superior array of skills asserted themselves. Seabrooks countered a left cross with a quick one-two to the jaw. Another one-two fell short but a jab-cross-hook combo didn't. As Seabrooks bounced a lead right off Cataluna's face, the difference in hand speed was evident and the competitive gulf Cataluna had created in the first round was closing quickly.

The foundation for Seabrooks' comeback was being built with an accumulation of point-scoring flurries instead of one tide-turning blow, and a byproduct of that was his improved fighting rhythm. He weaved his upper body to better position himself to fire his fast-handed blows and Cataluna had no answers for Seabrooks' strategic adjustment. The Filipino challenger often stayed on the outside, his offense inhibited by Seabrooks' offense as well as his own confusion.

As the round closed, Seabrooks continued to chip away at Cataluna's shell, driving him to the ropes and landing a hook to the head and three right crosses to the jaw during a dizzying nine-punch flurry. As Seabrooks walked back to his corner, his visage wore a more confident look and the area around his injured eye seemed under better control.

But Cataluna was nowhere near ready to give up his challenge. He had traveled thousands of miles to chase his dream and he was determined to make it come true. As the fourth opened, Cataluna dug a right to the body and bulled Seabrooks near the ropes. But his attempt to duplicate his first-round success didn't have the same strength or zip. Meanwhile, Seabrooks was on his toes – all the better to position himself to land lead rights to the jaw. A left hook to the ear caused Cataluna to pause momentarily and another hook following a missed left-right weakened the challenger's legs ever so slightly.

That was all Seabrooks needed to see.

Seabrooks charged in, firing a volley of punches while driving him into one of the corner pads. Cataluna escaped and muscled Seabrooks to the opposite corner, all the while throwing weary lefts that the champion easily blocked with his elbows. The champion continued to fight well at short range as he landed compact lefts and uppercuts to the jaw while inching backward. A left hook to the temple bounced off Cataluna's head and a follow-up right caused the challenger to grimace. Fueled by Cataluna's distress, Seabrooks summoned a barrage that drove Cataluna to the ropes. The challenger managed to fire two left crosses but his efforts seemed futile. Some in the French crowd, moved by the American's courage, began chanting "U.S.A! U.S.A.!"

After Cataluna was warned for butting he wearily stumbled backward toward the corner, the picture of exhaustion. He had shot his mighty bolt in the first and under most circumstances it would have earned him a championship, but Seabrooks' durability enabled him to persevere. A left cross, the final ingredient of a seven-punch volley, forced Cataluna to the ropes and a follow-up five-punch flurry caved in the challenger.

Usually fighters fall to the canvas in sections, but Cataluna was so spent he arose in sections. He rolled off his behind to both knees, then lurched his left knee forward to give him a base upon which he could push himself up. He tottered back a few steps as he regained his feet at the count of seven. Looking deeply into Cataluna's eyes, referee Rothenberg asked, "Are you all right? Can you see OK?" After several seconds, he commanded in a voice dripping with resignation, "all right…let's go."

Seabrooks buried a right to the body and a light right forced Cataluna to the ropes. A final hook to the short ribs extinguished the final embers of Cataluna's competitive fire. The challenger was on his knees and wore a dazed expression when Rothenberg tolled "ten" and declared the fight over at 2:52 of round four.

Seabrooks, his championship safe and sound, was too weary to stage the wild celebration his incredible comeback warranted. Instead, he calmly stood in his corner as his second wiped the grease and cut medicine from his face and he almost collapsed as a well-wisher gave him a hug. The champion possessed an air of quiet satisfaction, knowing he had already progressed further than his humble professional beginnings ever suggested. Another championship fight – and another championship-sized payday – awaited him.

Epilogue: Seabrooks returned to France less than three months after the Cataluna fight, disposing of Fernando Beltran in two rounds. His next defense proved to be his last as Orlando Canizales scored a 15th round TKO. True to form, however, Seabrooks did not make things easy for the future great. Though knocked down in the first and 15th rounds, the North Carolinian gave everything he had and made Canizales earn every point. Ever the sportsman, Seabrooks helped fasten the new belt around Canizales' waist and wished him well. Seabrooks earned a rematch with Canizales 11 months (and two fights) later, but this time Canizales was dominant in registering an 11th round TKO.

From then on, Seabrooks returned to being a stepping stone, winning just one of his final eight fights, the last five by TKO. His final bout was a two-round TKO defeat to Jimmi Bredahl in Copenhagen, Denmark on March 17, 1995, and Seabrooks, just one week past his 32nd birthday, retired with a 27-22 (22 KO) mark.

A complete record on Cataluna is not available, but incredibly he returned to the ring just one month and one day after his fight with Seabrooks. He traveled to Chinju, Korea to take on the 20-1 Chun Huh and lost a 12-round decision. Then, just six weeks later, he lost a 10-rounder to former WBC flyweight champion Frank Cedeno. According to Boxrec.com, Cataluna fought 13 more times, going 9-4 (6 KO). His final recorded bout took place November 23, 1994 when he lost a 12-rounder to future WBC super flyweight champion Satoshi Iida in Nagoya, Japan. The 35-year-old Cataluna retired sporting a record of 34-11-7 (16 KO).

TALES FROM THE VAULT

Total Punches Landed/Thrown

Round	1	2	3	4	5	6	7	8	9	10	11	12	Total
Seabrooks	8/34	16/60	22/61	37/105									83/260
	24%	27%	36%	35%									32%
Cataluna	65/112	16/36	15/33	17/39									113/220
	58%	44%	45%	44%									51%

Jabs Landed/Thrown

Round	1	2	3	4	5	6	7	8	9	10	11	12	Total
Seabrooks	2/6	2/18	8/20	6/29									18/73
	33%	11%	40%	21%									25%
Cataluna	1/3	1/3	2/3	0/1									4/10
	33%	33%	67%	0%									40%

Power Punches Landed/Thrown

Round	1	2	3	4	5	6	7	8	9	10	11	12	Total
Seabrooks	6/28	14/42	14/41	31/76									65/187
	21%	33%	34%	41%									35%
Cataluna	64/109	15/33	13/30	17/38									109/210
	59%	45%	43%	45%									52%

Kelvin Seabrooks vs. Ernie Cataluna November 18, 1987, San Cataldo, Italy

Richard Hall vs. Julian Letterlough
July 18, 2003, Hyannis, Massachusetts

If one watches boxing long enough, he'll find that the sport is not just about the action in the ring. Many fights, whether it be a four-round preliminary or a pay-per-view championship attraction, are laced with a multitude of underlying "stories" that are played out time and again. The natural sense of conflict enables many of these tales to assume the air of an athletic soap opera, and if the episode is a particularly good one it will encourage fans to stick around and find out what will happen next time.

For example, the "story" behind many fights scheduled for less than 10 rounds is the tale of Prospect against Journeyman – with the preferred ending being Prospect moving ahead and Journeyman moving on after taking his lumps. But sometimes Journeyman springs a Surprise, so another "story" comes about – the Rematch and the chance for Redemption. If Prospect reverses the result, his story will continue uninterrupted but if Journeyman duplicates his feat, the roles reverse themselves. With stunning swiftness, Journeyman is transformed into a belated Prospect while the former Prospect finds himself flirting with Oblivion – and the unpleasant task of having to find a Job.

Another one of boxing's favorite "stories" is the Crossroad Fight, which can take many forms. Often, the Crossroad Fight signifies the Day of Reckoning as Prospect takes on Proven Contender or even Champion. Other Crossroad Fights, however, offer a more harrowing scenario. After two Contenders fail against Champion, they are pitted against one another for one purpose: To see which man gets to stay a Contender and which one is turned into a Journeyman, or worse yet, a Stepping Stone.

This was one of the stories that were told on July 18, 2003 at the Cape Cod Melody Tent in Hyannis, Massachusetts when light heavyweights Richard Hall and Julian Letterlough met in a scheduled 10 rounder. Both men had already experienced a peek at the summit as they took on a pair of Champions, but for a variety of reasons they weren't able to plant the flag.

For the 33-year-old Letterlough (19-3-2, 18 KO), it was because of his desire to fight anyone, anytime and at any weight. "Mr. KO" was one of boxing's most exciting television fighters and his pulsating encounters with Demetrius Jenkins (KO 7), Sam Ahmad (D 10), Max Heyman (KO 5) and especially Julio Gonzalez (L 12) made him a favorite on ESPN. But all of those fights came at light heavyweight and neither Roy Jones nor Dariusz Michalczewski had any plans to fight Letterlough anytime soon. So on September 8, 2001, the Reading, Pa., native accepted a fight with IBF cruiserweight champion Vassiliy Jirov on HBO. Letterlough gave it his best shot, but Jirov proved himself too big, too strong and too good in registering an eighth round TKO.

Letterlough's slide toward Journeyman continued four months later when he lost a 10-rounder to Contender David Telesco. After knocking out Lloyd Bryan in two rounds, Letterlough was held to a surprising draw to the 2-8-2 John Douglas. Letterlough entered the fight with Hall coming off a one-round knockout of Stacy Goodson four months before.

The 31-year-old Hall (25-4, 24 KO) had three opportunities to transform himself from Contender to Champion. In May 2000 Hall fought Jones for three of the four light heavyweight belts, and though he fought bravely he lost every round before referee Wayne Kelly stopped the beating in round 11. In his two previous fights before meeting Letterlough, Hall fought Michalczewski in consecutive bouts for the one belt Jones didn't hold. The first fight in Berlin in December 2001 was stopped in the 10th round due to a huge swelling over Hall's left eye. Ten months later, Hall received another shot at "The Tiger" in Braunschweig, Germany and over the first eight rounds the Jamaican native opened nasty cuts over both of Michalczewski's eyes and his left eye was badly discolored and nearly shut. But the Polish-German hero rallied in the 10th, hurting Hall, driving him to the ropes and pelting him with flurries until referee Rudy Battle stopped the fight. Hall felt he was robbed in both fights and was anxious to get back on the winning track against Letterlough.

Though Hall, 177, and Letterlough, 176, were vicious punchers, their dimensions provided a stark contrast. The thickly built Letterlough, who bore a strong resemblance to former Pittsburgh Steelers running back Jerome Bettis, was 5-10 with a 68-inch reach and fought out of the orthodox stance. Hall, a southpaw, was long and lean at 6-4 and his reach was nine-and-a-half inches longer. Their body types dictated the expected strategies. For Hall to win, he needed to keep Letterlough at distance with a ramrod jab and long lefts while tying Letterlough up whenever he managed to get inside his reach. Letterlough, for his part, had to find a way inside and whack away at Hall's torso. Of course, he would have to walk through plenty of enemy fire to get there but Letterlough was not the type to let that concern him.

Both men followed their fight plans in the opening seconds as Hall operated at long range, bouncing on his toes while feinting right jabs to keep Letterlough at a safe distance. Letterlough weaved his upper body to create an angle of entry. Letterlough nipped out of range after missing a wild right to the body, clearly respectful of Hall's power. Hall speared Letterlough with a left cross, the last of a right-right-left combo, and followed up with a sharp jab. Letterlough dove in with a hook under the elbow and Hall immediately moved out of range, for he, too, was mindful of Letterlough's punch.

Though Letterlough wasn't landing much, he remained persistent. He caught Hall reaching in after throwing a left cross with a hook to the side of the head. A few moments later, Letterlough dug a right to the ribs that drove Hall a step backward.

Given the explosive power both men possessed, it was only a matter of time before the bombs would start flying – and before one would score the crucial First Strike. No one knew, however, that it would happen within the first 74 seconds.

Letterlough fired a long lead right that sailed wide of the target, but his follow-through left the Pennsylvanian in a southpaw stance. Hall tried to take advantage of the off-balance Letterlough by catching him with a jab coming in, but all it did was leave a crucial split-second opening. Letterlough took a big step to his right, and, while still in the lefty stance, clocked Hall with a long left to the ear. Hall fell heavily to the canvas, his left foot folding dangerously underneath him. Hall was able to extricate his foot before any serious damage was done. His foot may have been fine but the rest of him was in a fog as he struggled to his feet at referee Richard Flaherty's count of four. His equilibrium was compromised but by the time Flaherty reached eight Hall appeared ready to resume the battle.

Letterlough chased Hall into a corner and blasted away, but while his blows carried plenty of kick they lacked precision. Still, Hall was clearly in survival mode as he ducked his head, grabbed Letterlough around the waist and wrestled him to the canvas.

Letterlough scrambled to his feet and raced to a corner, smartly recognizing Hall's move was a ploy to gain more recovery time. Once the action resumed, Letterlough bulled Hall to the ropes behind a right-left to the body, but Hall managed to spin out and force Letterlough to the ropes, where Hall grabbed on and rested for several seconds before Flaherty broke them.

Back at ring center, Hall caught Letterlough coming in with a light right hook to the ear, but "Mr. KO" was still primed for the kill as he walked through the blow and bulled Hall to the ropes.

A puncher of Hall's caliber is dangerous at any moment, and especially so when he's hurt. Hall would prove that axiom true with 54 seconds remaining in the round.

Letterlough had just followed through with a right to the body and was winding up a hook to get back on balance. But Hall beat him to the punch with a short hair-trigger left to the button that drove Letterlough to a knee. Letterlough wore a dazed look as he immediately regained his feet, but as the seconds ticked by his face hardened back to normal and was ready to go again.

Unlike Letterlough, Hall didn't go for the kill. He saw the knockdown as a chance to recover further from his own knockdown without Letterlough bearing down on him. Still, Hall nailed Letterlough with a left to the jaw that drove the American to the ropes and this time it was Letterlough who was holding on. The respite didn't last long as they began to trade bombs, with Letterlough's aimed for the jaw and Hall's targeting the body. Both ended a most exhilarating first round at ring center, knowing full well what they knew going in; that the other man was cut from the same power-punching cloth as he.

The statistics prove that statement as well – every blow that landed was a power punch. And there was more to come.

Letterlough came out strong in round two as he charged forward and landed a hook to the body as Hall tried to land right-lefts to the head. The first two attempts failed to hit the target, but like Letterlough, Hall was a stubborn sort who had complete faith in his ability and especially in his power. So Hall tried the right-left a third time and this time the left was a bull's eye. The shock waves rippled through Letterlough's body and instantly stiffened his legs.

To knockout punchers, the stiffening of an opponent's legs is as powerful a sight as blood is to a shark. And like the shark, the pugilistic predator in Hall immediately leaped to action. Hall drove Letterlough to the ropes and whaled away with heavy blows to the head and body. Letterlough tried to fend off the assault by bobbing and weaving but Hall's attack was overwhelming. With Letterlough propped against a corner pad, Hall landed a huge left cross to the jaw. Letterlough's upper body pitched forward, and while his legs were still strong it was clear he was nearing a helpless state. Two more right hooks crashed against Letterlough's head and Flaherty jumped in to spare him further punishment.

The fight was stopped just 3 minutes 47 seconds after the opening bell, and in that short time one man's career was revived while the other's took a significant step back. Letterlough wore an expression of disbelief as he sought an explanation from Flaherty. Blood was coming out of his nose but his spirit appeared to be more damaged. Given his history for rebounding strongly from adversity, he felt he should have been given more of an opportunity to fight his way out of trouble. After all, he did just that a couple of minutes before.

Meanwhile, Hall was exultant and the raw emotion of his comeback victory was pouring out of him. He twice unleashed a throat-slashing gesture and he leaped to the second strand of ropes and pounded his chest. As his handlers lifted him skyward, he shouted, "I am back! I am back! I am back!" – as in back in the championship picture.

"I feel good," Hall said after the fight. "I've been wanting to come back for the longest time. I've been hoping and praying that I'd get a fight in the United States after going what I've been going through in Germany. I'm glad that Julian Letterlough accepted my challenge."

As for his trip to the canvas, Hall said, "it was a flash knockdown. I didn't get hurt or nothing, but I got up and I said *'I'm going to kill him.'*"

Hall credited studying videos of Letterlough's fights for the victory, something he hadn't done with any previous opponent.

"I studied a couple of his films and it really paid off," Hall said. "I know he always tried to jump in (during) the first round with the left hook and he tricked me with the right hand and then jumped in with the left hook. Tonight I fell for it and he stunned me a little bit and put me on the canvas. But I got up and put him back down and that's the way it's supposed to be."

Those were the words of a true Destroyer…and, once again, of a Contender.

Epilogue: Four months later, Hall continued his climb toward a fourth championship chance by decisioning Rodney Moore over 10 rounds. That victory earned Hall an IBF light heavyweight title elimination fight against the 16-0 Rico Hoye May 15, 2004 at Mandalay Bay in Las Vegas on the undercard of Antonio Tarver-Roy Jones II. Hall was blasted out in four rounds, prompting a 21-month hiatus. Once he returned he lost decisions to Glen Johnson (L 12) and Shaun George (L 8) but he ended his career on a high note as the 36-year-old stopped Byron Mitchell in four rounds on November 21, 2007 in Miami. Hall retired with a record of 28-7 (26 KO).

Letterlough returned to the ring just 42 days later, losing a six-round majority decision to Faustino Gonzalez – in "Mr. KO's" hometown of Reading, Pa. Letterlough scored a good win by knocking out the 77-17-1 Tony Menefee in five rounds the next time out. He then held the 19-0-2 Daniel Judah (brother of former two-division champion Zab Judah) to a 12-round draw, knocking down Judah in the fifth round. His final fight took place October 1, 2004 with a two-round knockout of Eric Starr in Reading. On July 8, 2005 was shot in the back and killed after leaving a bar with his wife and was pronounced dead at the scene. Letterlough was just 35 years old.

TALES FROM THE VAULT

Total Punches Landed/Thrown

Round	1	2	3	4	5	6	7	8	9	10	11	12	Total
Letterlough													8/39
													21%
Hall													18/62
													29%

Jabs Landed/Thrown

Round	1	2	3	4	5	6	7	8	9	10	11	12	Total
Letterlough													0/1
													0%
Hall													1/18
													6%

Power Punches Landed/Thrown

Round	1	2	3	4	5	6	7	8	9	10	11	12	Total
Letterlough													8/38
													21%
Hall													17/44
													39%

* Fight originally done by CompuBox, but the original HTML files with complete round-by-round statistics no longer exist.

Richard Hall vs. Julian Letterlough July 18, 2003, Hyannis, Massachusetts

Mike McCallum vs. Julian Jackson
August 23, 1986, Miami Beach, Florida

The road to recognition and respect is an individual journey. For those who find favor with the right people, the correct doors can be made to swing wide open. If a fighter's life provides a good story and if his personality and charisma can translate to the small screen, the road can be paved with gold – provided he keeps winning.

For others, like Mike McCallum, the journey to stardom and riches is more difficult. What makes the situation baffling is that talent has little to do with whether that special light will shine on a fighter, though it certainly would help him garner that important first look. The decision on whether a fighter has that elusive quality called "it" is often a snap judgment and if that one decision maker perceives that someone doesn't have that unique magnetic quality at that one moment in time, he is tossed aside, never to be given another chance. It is a cruel and many times unfair process, but it is also a reality of life in big-time sports.

McCallum certainly had the ability; as an amateur he fought in the 1976 Olympics for his native Jamaica and advanced to the welterweight quarterfinals before dropping a 3-2 decision to eventual bronze medalist Reinhard Skricek of Germany. McCallum was in line to try again in 1980, but because Jamaica was one of the many countries to join the U.S. boycott McCallum was unable to compete in the Moscow games and turned pro in January 1981 with a four-round knockout of Rigoberto Lopez in Las Vegas.

McCallum continued to enjoy success inside the ropes, knocking out the 10-1-1 Rocky Fabrizio in one round in his second pro outing. Over the next three years, McCallum added the notable scalps of Bruce "The Mouse" Strauss (KO 2), Jimmy Haeir (KO 2) and former junior middleweight champion Ayub Kalule (KO 7) in building a 21-0 (19 KO) record. McCallum's skills and Emanuel Steward's managerial skills helped the Jamaican rise to the top spot in the WBA rankings. He was the mandatory challenger for Roberto Duran, and a victory over the legendary Panamanian would provide a mighty boost to his standing in the boxing world – as well as his moneymaking potential.

But McCallum's stablemate, WBC super welterweight champion Thomas Hearns, needed a superfight to aid his pursuit of middleweight champion Marvelous Marvin Hagler and Duran certainly fit the bill. Hearns had plenty of regard for McCallum's ability, after all it was he who first called McCallum "The Bodysnatcher" for his vaunted body attack. But Steward had a decision to make – either allow McCallum to receive his crack at Duran or pave the way for the "Hit Man" to fight "Manos de Piedra" in a big money unification showdown. Because Steward judged that Hearns had "it" and McCallum didn't, he opted for the sure bet and made Hearns-Duran. The WBA stripped Duran for not defending against McCallum, so the Jamaican fought number-two contender Sean Mannion for the vacant belt October 19, 1984 at Madison Square Garden. Fifteen lopsided rounds later, McCallum had reached his professional pinnacle but he couldn't help but wonder what could have been.

Enraged by being rendered the odd man out, McCallum ended his association with Steward and signed with Main Events. McCallum successfully defended the belt against fellow 1976 welterweight Olympian Luigi Minchillo (KO 13) and former Kronk stablemate David Braxton (KO 8) to earn a small measure of revenge against Steward.

If McCallum wasn't fated to earn stardom the easy way, he was determined to use all of the weapons at his disposal to get it any way he could. One reliable way is to travel the road Marvelous Marvin Hagler took – by mowing down a succession of tough challengers and letting the numbers speak for him. McCallum took a step in that direction by meeting the dangerous Julian Jackson in his third title defense on the undercard of WBC bantamweight champion Miguel "Happy" Lora's defense against top contender Enrique Sanchez.

If one goes by records alone, McCallum-Jackson promised to be one of the great "high octane" matches of all time. The 29-year-old McCallum entered the bout with a sterling record of 26-0 (23 KO) while the 25-year-old Jackson was 29-0 (27 KO). Under the promotional guidance of Don King Productions, Jackson built his record on championship undercards against a succession of obscure opponents. The best-known names included faded former WBA junior middleweight champion Eddie Gazo (KO 2) and fringe contenders Jake Torrance (KO 5) and Curtis Ramsey (KO 12). His most recent outing was typical of this phase in his career as he blasted out Derrick Drane in two rounds at Madison Square Garden three months earlier. Still, he not only beat his opponents, he smashed them with style as his heavy hands produced spectacular pyrotechnic displays of raw power.

There were two points of intrigue surrounding McCallum-Jackson. First, it was a Caribbean turf war that pitted Jamaica (McCallum) and the U.S. Virgin Islands (Jackson). Second, with two huge punchers, it was likely that the man who landed the first big shot would be the winner.

Jackson, 153, was determined to be that man as he raced from his corner and connected with an overhand right to McCallum's jaw, but McCallum, 152 ½, managed to smack a hook off Jackson's chin as he recoiled from Jackson's blow. Jackson bulled McCallum into the ropes, but the Jamaican returned to ring center and banged a right-left to the body after Jackson's wild right curled around the back of McCallum's head.

Jackson's every punch was launched with the intent of tearing McCallum's head from his shoulders, but the champion handled Jackson's opening rush with a veteran's cool as he ripped a hook to the head and body after ducking an overhand right.

A second overhand right by Jackson clanged off McCallum's temple, but the champion quickly recovered with a right uppercut to the jaw.

Jackson forced a frenetic pace to neutralize McCallum's advantage in ring craft, but McCallum was more than eager to swap powerful blows at ring center. It was power against power, and given the two men's records it was just a matter of time before one would connect with a fight-turning punch. Jackson landed two hard rights in a four-punch flurry and at the 52-second mark a wicked hook wobbled McCallum and forced him to clamp on tightly. Jackson broke free and landed two more heavy rights that caused McCallum to take a step back.

McCallum tried to turn down the heat by working his jab but Jackson would have none of it as he tore in behind an overhand right to the jaw. A left hook glanced off McCallum's shoulder but a right landed like an ice pick over the champ's left eye. It was fire versus ice and chaos versus calm – and disorder was slowly becoming the order of the day. Every blow seemed to trigger an even stronger response from the other. A missed overhand right by Jackson brought back a hook to the body by McCallum, which in turn drew a hook to the jaw by Jackson. Jackson's hook to the body was answered with a McCallum right that strayed low, but that punch created an opening big enough for Jackson to land a heavy overhand right over the top. They cranked up simultaneous rights that missed but left hooks that connected – Jackson's to the head and McCallum's to the body. But the body hook strayed low, drawing a caution from referee Eddie Eckert.

McCallum worked more steadily behind the jab, but Jackson had no use for such niceties and continued to fire away. McCallum thumped a right-left to the body and banged a short right uppercut to the jaw while holding Jackson's head with his left glove. The move drew a second caution from Eckert, and a third warning came seconds later when McCallum's right strayed low after Jackson pulled his head down. A pulsating first round ended with McCallum spearing Jackson with three jabs and connecting with a hook to the ribs.

Jackson walked to his corner and quickly raised both arms, and he had plenty of reason to feel good about his situation. He forced McCallum out of his comfort zone by forcing a fast pace and making him trade power shots for all three minutes. He wobbled McCallum with his best punch, the left hook, and he was confident that it was just a matter of time before he would land the one shot that would bring him a championship.

Things were not as cheerful in McCallum's corner. Trainer Lou Duva was enraged over Eckert's low blow warnings, correctly pointing out that Jackson's trunks were several inches above the bellybutton.

McCallum and Jackson went right back to business in round two as they launched simultaneous hooks, Jackson's to the head and McCallum's to the ribs. Jackson nailed the champ with an overhand right to the jaw but McCallum retaliated with a right to the hip – a blow that drew no warning from Eckert this time. Jackson bulled McCallum to the ropes behind a hook that was blocked and a left-right to the body that hit the mark. McCallum connected with a sharp counter hook and spun out to ring center to fire off several jabs.

From Jackson's standpoint the fight had to be won with brute force – the less science the better. Every punch he threw was launched with incredible speed and ferocious power. He did everything he could to turn the boxing match into a firefight and was succeeding beyond all expectation. But it takes two to make a fight, and McCallum was a willing accomplice as he eagerly matched Jackson shot for shot.

Jackson banged a right to the body and McCallum returned the favor with a hook to the belly. The challenger whiffed with a left-right over the top but found the target with his own hook to the stomach. The rugged give-and-take action was beyond exciting but the human body could only take so much punishment in such a short period of time before one or the other had to give.

Jackson thought he reached McCallum's limit in the first minute of the fight, but now it was McCallum's turn to test Jackson's.

McCallum countered a Jackson jab with an overhand right to the jaw and a left to the bicep that sent an off-balance Jackson hard to the canvas. Eckert called the fall a knockdown and Jackson, who was up immediately, offered no argument as he took the mandatory eight. McCallum backed Jackson to the ropes with an overhand right and began to go to work. McCallum blasted a low right and a legal hook to the belt line and snapped Jackson's head with a right to the jaw. McCallum won an exchange of hooks and a solid left to the solar plexus kept Jackson pinned to the ropes. A whipping left-right snapped Jackson's head and the Virgin Islander somehow managed to get off the ropes. But McCallum was in full fighting heat as he forced Jackson to a different set of ropes and continued his whirlwind attack.

McCallum unleashed a torrent of well-mixed blows to Jackson's head and body, and several rights to the ribs shook Jackson to his very foundation. The champion fired every punch in his considerable arsenal and the inexperienced Jackson was unable to conjure the correct counterstrategy. Two tremendous rights to the body caused Jackson's body to double over and seek the refuge of a clinch.

With 1:21 remaining, Eckert took a long look at Jackson, who nodded his willingness to continue fighting. A McCallum hook clanged off Jackson's temple and a follow-up right-left hook exploded off the challenger's jaw. A heavy right-left rattled Jackson's ribs and a flurry of hooks caused Jackson to stumble backward across the ring and into the ropes, even bumping into Eckert along the way. Jackson was in bad shape and was ripe for the taking – and McCallum was primed to take him.

A right-left-right powered through Jackson's arms and two more lefts split the guard. McCallum dug a right to the hip while Jackson missed wildly with a hook over the top. A heavy right twisted Jackson's head and a pretty left-left-right-uppercut combo snapped Jackson's head violently. That salvo prompted Eckert to move in but before he could do so McCallum fired off four final blows. When Eckert stepped between them at the 2:03 mark of round two, Jackson spread his arms wide and protested but it was all in vain. McCallum's handlers hoisted him in the air and the champion proudly held a tiny Jamaican flag in his right glove.

It was the picture that McCallum had played in his mind's eye ever since he began boxing and now it had come true. He had emerged victorious in a vicious give-and-take war against a dangerous opponent and he believed that he had taken a big step toward the star status – and the millions of dollars – that would come with it. For Jackson, it was his first taste of defeat as a professional and he could treat it in one of two ways: He could pick himself up and learn from his mistakes or let his failure consume him like a cancer. But no matter what turns McCallum and Jackson would make in the future, the day their points converged in Miami Beach was to serve as a career touchstone for years to come.

Epilogue: Jackson chose to learn from the McCallum loss and as a result he enjoyed a highly successful career. Four months after the McCallum fight, Jackson got back on the winning track with a one-round KO of Khalif Shabazz and two fights later he won the vacant WBA junior middleweight title by stopping In-Chul Baek in three rounds. Jackson defended the belt three times, scoring spectacular knockouts of Buster Drayon (KO 3), Francisco DeJesus (KO 8) and Terry Norris (KO 2)

Jackson vacated the belt to move up to middleweight, and he won the vacant WBC belt in most emphatic fashion. After losing the first three rounds and suffering a badly swollen eye, Jackson flattened Herol Graham in the fourth with one of the most frightening right hand bombs ever seen in championship competition. Graham went down like a shot and stayed there for several minutes, and just like that Jackson had captured his second divisional belt. Jackson defended that belt four times, blasting out Dennis Milton (KO 1), Ismael Negron (a 50-second KO) and Ron Collins (KO 5) before struggling to win a decision against Thomas Tate.

Jackson lost the belt to fellow power-puncher Gerald McClellan in five rounds and lost the rematch a year later by first round KO. By this time, Jackson was nearing the end of the line yet he managed to win a belt one final time by blasting out Agostino Cardamone in two rounds to win the WBC title vacated by McClellan. Jackson lost the title in his first defense by sixth round TKO to Quincy Taylor and never fought for a major championship again. The 37-year-old Jackson's final fight took place May 24, 1998 at The Palace in Auburn Hills, Michigan, where he lost to Anthony Jones by ninth round TKO. His final record stands at 55-6 with 49 KO and he was inducted into the World Boxing Hall of Fame's Class of 2006.

McCallum's next fight took place just 23 days later against Irving Hines, who he stopped in four rounds. After beating Said Skouma in nine rounds, McCallum's career was ready to take a quantum leap upward. On April 19, 1987 in Phoenix, Arizona before a nationwide audience on ABC, McCallum impressively stopped former WBC welterweight champion Milton McCrory in 10 rounds, earning him a chance to defend his belt against Donald Curry on HBO three months later.

Trailing on all cards after four rounds, McCallum cold-cocked Curry with a smashing hook that put "The Cobra" down for the count in the fifth. After the fight McCallum said, "this is the day that I will finally get my recognition." And for a while, he did.

McCallum vacated the WBA belt, a title Jackson would claim by knocking out Baek, and moved up to middleweight to take on Sumbu Kalambay in Kalambay's adopted home country of Italy on March 5, 1988. McCallum, a heavy favorite, lost a close unanimous decision to Kalambay but four fights later McCallum won the WBA belt stripped from Kalambay for taking on IBF champion Michael Nunn by beating Herol Graham by split decision. After two non-title wins, McCallum fought IBF champion James Toney to a draw and lost the rematch by disputed majority decision two fights later.

The 37-year-old McCallum moved up to light heavyweight in search of a third world title and found it after he impressively dismantled the tough Jeff Harding for the WBC title. McCallum shined in stopping Carl Jones in his first defense but surprisingly lost the belt in defense number two to Frenchman Fabrice Tiozzo. McCallum would get one last crack at a world title, but a prime Roy Jones was simply too much for McCallum, who was just 15 days short of his 40th birthday. His final fight took place February 22, 1997 at the Mohegan Sun Casino in Uncasville, Connecticut, where he lost a 12-round decision to Toney for a minor cruiserweight belt. McCallum's final record is 49-5-1 with 36 knockouts and in 2003 he finally got the recognition he had long sought when he was inducted into the International Boxing Hall of Fame.

SHOOTOUTS

Total Punches Landed/Thrown

Round	1	2	3	4	5	6	7	8	9	10	11	12	Total
McCallum	49/103	60/109											109/212
	48%	55%											51%
Jackson	29/86	14/44											43/130
	34%	32%											33%

Jabs Landed/Thrown

Round	1	2	3	4	5	6	7	8	9	10	11	12	Total
McCallum	29/65	10/34											39/99
	45%	29%											39%
Jackson	5/15	3/8											8/23
	33%	38%											35%

Power Punches Landed/Thrown

Round	1	2	3	4	5	6	7	8	9	10	11	12	Total
McCallum	20/38	50/75											70/113
	53%	67%											62%
Jackson	24/71	11/36											35/107
	34%	31%											33%

Mike McCallum vs. Julian Jackson August 23, 1986, Miami Beach, Florida

TALES FROM THE VAULT

Ezzard Charles vs. Bob Satterfield
January 13, 1954, Chicago, Illinois

Boxing is a sport steeped in lineages. Up until a few years ago, one can trace the parade of champions all the way back to the sport's beginnings and the phrase "the man who beat the man" had real meaning. The proliferation of alphabet groups has made that task much more difficult, if not impossible, but there is one group of fighters whose lineage has remained untainted: The television fighter.

Before there was an Arturo Gatti, before there was Matthew Saad Muhammad, and before Saad there was Danny "Little Red" Lopez. Before Lopez, there was Emile Griffith and before Griffith, there was Chicago light heavyweight Bob Satterfield. While Satterfield's career can't compare to those of Gatti, Saad Muhammad, Lopez and Griffith, he was their equal – if not their superior – in terms of providing pure adrenaline-pumping excitement. He was that rarest of commodities, a one-punch KO artist who was not afraid to risk being knocked out in pursuit of his goal. There was no room for compromise with Satterfield; either he got you or you got him but either way someone was going to go through hell.

The quintessential Satterfield fight took place on January 30, 1952 in Chicago Stadium when he fought the 30-2-1 Clarence Henry. Satterfield knocked Henry down with his first thrown punch but Henry put Satterfield on the deck soon after. Henry would score two more knockdowns and Satterfield sported a nasty gash over the left eye when the fight was stopped just 101 seconds after it began.

This do-or-die approach made Satterfield immensely popular but it took its toll on his record. Save for a stretch in his early career in which he scored nine consecutive knockouts – seven of which took place in the first two rounds – Satterfield was the prototypical hot-and-cold fighter. He was willing to fight anyone at any weight, but when he stepped up in class he failed more often than he succeeded. His conquerors include Holman Williams (L 10), Jake LaMotta (KO by 7), Sam Baroudi (KO by 2), Joey Maxim (L 10), Archie Moore (KO by 3), Rex Layne (KO by 8) and Harold Johnson (KO by 2). But Satterfield also came out on the winning end on a few occasions as he won a split decision from Johnson, a 10-round nod over the 75-8-2 Tommy Gomez and a sixth round KO over heavyweight Lee Oma.

When Satterfield signed to fight former heavyweight champion Ezzard Charles on January 13, 1954, he again was cast in the role of prohibitive underdog. But the 30-year-old Satterfield had several things going for him. For one thing, he entered the fight on a roll of four consecutive knockout wins, the most recent of which was an eighth-round KO over the 62-12-4 Ray Augustus that came courtesy of one titanic left hook.

Also, the fight took place at Chicago Stadium, where the 32-14-2 (25 KO) Satterfield possessed a 12-4-1 (7 KO) record.

Though the 32-year-old Charles (85-10-1, 53 KO) was viewed as a fighter who had already seen his best days, he presented a formidable challenge for Satterfield because he still possessed many of the skills that led him to glory in two weight classes. Several historians regard Charles as the greatest 175-pounder who has yet lived, and there is plenty of evidence to support that assertion. He held victories over Anton Christoforidis (KO 3), Charley Burley (W 10, W 10), Joey Maxim (five times), Jimmy Bivins (three out of four), Lloyd Marshall (two of three) and three wins over the legendary Archie Moore (including an eighth-round KO in their last encounter.)

Despite his great success at 175, Charles was unable to secure a title shot so he moved up to heavyweight to pursue greater challenges. After heavyweight champion Joe Louis announced his retirement, Charles won the vacant belt by beating Jersey Joe Walcott over 15 rounds. Charles retained the title by beating Gus Lesnevich (KO 7), Pat Valentino (KO 8) and Freddie Beshore (KO 14) before beating a comebacking Louis over 15 rounds to gain universal recognition. Charles continued to roll with defenses against Oma (KO 10), Walcott (W 15) and Maxim (W 15) before shockingly losing the belt to Walcott via one-punch KO in the seventh. Charles secured a fourth fight with Walcott 11 months later, but the 38-year-old wonder scored a 15-round decision.

Charles posted a 10-3 (6 KO) record since the second Walcott loss, but a 10th round KO over Coley Wallace in his last fight rekindled his hopes for another shot at the heavyweight title, this time against Walcott's conqueror Rocky Marciano. In fact, Charles was reportedly in line for a crack at Marciano in June – provided he beat Satterfield in this nationally televised fight.

The opening bell saw both men immediately trying to execute their game plans. Charles, 189, worked behind the jab while Satterfield, 180, fought out of a surprisingly exaggerated crouch. Satterfield missed a winging right and a wild hook before landing a jab to the body. Charles missed with two jabs and a swooping right to the body but hit the target with a solid jab. Charles sneaked in a right to the pit of Satterfield's stomach before falling into a clinch.

At his best, Charles was a pinpoint boxer who possessed plenty of spring in his legs, but here he spent more time milling at close range. From time to time, Charles returned to the outside and speared the bobbing Satterfield with jabs and those jabs enabled him to weave in behind a hook that landed slightly below the belt line. Charles paid for his unintentional foul by giving Satterfield the opening he needed to launch his first good hook of the fight, a punch that made Charles beat a hasty retreat.

Back at long range, Charles fired a long right cross to the chin. But because he lunged with the punch, Satterfield connected with a short, snappy hook that appeared to stun the former champion. Instead of backing away, Charles lunged in behind a sweeping hook that missed badly and Satterfield charged in behind a right to the body, a hook to the jaw, a pile-driving right and a solid hook that clearly hurt Charles.

Satterfield's hometown crowd cheered as Charles backed toward the ropes and awkwardly held out both arms in search of a clinch. Satterfield didn't allow that to happen as he shook off Charles and blasted another right that dislodged the ex-champ's mouthpiece. Charles quickly stuffed the mouth guard back in while managing to grab Satterfield and smartly spinning himself toward the relative safety of ring center.

Charles sought to clear his head by sticking out long range-finding jabs as Satterfield missed with a home-run right over the top. The ever-dangerous Satterfield struck again with a right uppercut-left hook to the chin, and two more rights to the temple again forced Charles to clinch.

Charles was hurt and appeared totally out of sorts while the surging Satterfield was fueled by the prospect of scoring an earth-shaking upset. Charles may not have been in his prime, but every sportswriter at ringside still predicted an easy Charles victory. After all, this fight was supposed to make the case for a Marciano-Charles showdown, but Satterfield had an entirely different agenda – and he was carrying it out with stunning success.

A buzzed Charles sought to catch his breath in the clinches, often looking over the shorter Satterfield's head and shoulder. He released his grip just long enough to launch one punch before grabbing again, and the tactic allowed him to set a trap. After yet another break, Charles sought to surprise Satterfield with a big right-left hook combo and while the right missed, the hook jerked Satterfield's head. But Satterfield had a trap of his own as plunged forward behind a looping right-left-right that buckled Charles' knees.

Charles recovered quickly and both men briefly returned to long range. Just before the end of an explosive and surprising first round, Charles cranked a long hook to the solar plexus and followed with an equally wide hook to the jaw. It had been a perilous opening session for Charles and only his experience and savvy allowed him to survive Satterfield's unexpected storm.

Charles went right back to the double hook to the body and head as the second round opened. Both punches found the target and Satterfield was forced to take his first involuntary backward steps of the fight. Satterfield quickly reset his feet and launched a right to the face, a hook to he jaw and a heavy right to the temple that made Charles grab, then stumble toward the ropes. Satterfield shook off Charles and fired two more rights that prompted yet another clinch.

Though Satterfield was well known for his savage hook, he found great success with the right, and this extra dimension forced Charles to keep his eyes peeled on both gloves. One of the great appeals of Satterfield's fights – and of boxing in general – is the ever-present potential for a stunningly quick and dynamic conclusion. One never knew whether Satterfield would be the one standing in the neutral corner or if he would be left prostrate on the canvas, but against Charles one had to assume that the Chicagoan was having one of the best nights of his career. He proved in the first round that he owned the power to hurt the highly ranked former champion while Charles had yet to dent Satterfield's notoriously vulnerable chin.

But Charles would soon demonstrate why he was nicknamed "The Cincinnati Cobra."

Moments after missing with a lunging right, Charles shifted his feet and threw a range-finding jab. Seeing his chance, Charles dug his toes into the canvas and launched a crushing right cross-left hook combo to Satterfield's jaw. Satterfield, who was cranking up his own right-left combo, never saw them coming and upon impact his body was instantly anesthetized. Satterfield stiffened, then fell in sections. The back of his head hit the canvas with a thud, and aside from his slightly elevated right glove and his left forearm and glove pointed skyward, his body was totally flat on the canvas. Satterfield didn't move a muscle until referee Mike Gilmer reached the count of eight when Satterfield lowered his left arm and managed to raise his head slightly. But the waves of dizziness shooting through his cranium prevented Satterfield from proceeding any further and the fight was declared over exactly one minute into the second round.

In victory, Charles proved beyond doubt that he remained a major player in the heavyweight title picture while in defeat, Satterfield showed why he remained the king of the small screen.

Epilogue: Five months after fighting Satterfield, Charles received his shot at Marciano at Yankee Stadium. Though Charles lost a 15-round decision, he fought well enough to warrant a second crack exactly three months later, again at Yankee Stadium. Though Marciano was well ahead on the scorecards, a Charles elbow opened a vertical cut on Marciano's nose that produced perhaps the greatest threat to the "Brockton Blockbuster's" perfect record. Told to either produce a knockout or lose his championship, Marciano came up big and scored the title-saving KO in round eight.

Charles never received another heavyweight title shot, and because financial problems forced him to fight longer than he should have, his form took a nosedive. In the five years after the second Marciano fight, Charles won just 10 of his final 23 fights. Weighing a bloated 201 pounds, the 38-year-old Charles ended his career at Municipal Auditorium in Oklahoma City with a 10 round unanimous decision loss to Alvin Green. Charles' decline may well have been caused by the onset of amyotrophic lateral sclerosis (ALS), also known as Lou Gehrig's Disease, the illness that would eventually kill the 53-year-old Charles in 1975.

Charles was among the original enshrinees at the International Boxing Hall of Fame in 1990 and his final record was 96-25-1 with 58 knockouts.

Satterfield continued to live up to his nickname of "The Bombardier" as he continued to beat – and be beaten – in unforgettable shootouts. Over the next three years, Satterfield would knock out the fearsome Cleveland Williams in three rounds and defeat Nino Valdez (W 10) and Johnny Summerlin (W 10). He spun his wheels in multi-fight series that saw a two-fight split with the slick Marty Marshall (KO by 2, W 10), a 2-1 edge over with John Holman (KO 10, KO 1, KO by 8) and a 0-1-2 split with Harold Carter.

Though Satterfield continued to thrill, his inconsistency prevented him from making any serious run at a championship.

Satterfield's final fight took place November 21, 1957 at the Auditorium in Oakland, where the 34-year-old captured a 10-round split decision over Howard King. Satterfield retired with a record of 50-25-4 with 35 knockouts, and, like Charles, he was taken far too soon as he died in 1977, also aged 53.

SHOOTOUTS

Total Punches Landed/Thrown

Round	1	2	3	4	5	6	7	8	9	10	11	12	Total
Charles	19/53	8/14											27/67
	36%	57%											40%
Satterfield	30/66	9/23											39/89
	45%	39%											44%

Jabs Landed/Thrown

Round	1	2	3	4	5	6	7	8	9	10	11	12	Total
Charles	7/27	3/7											10/34
	26%	43%											29%
Satterfield	5/10	2/6											7/16
	50%	33%											44%

Power Punches Landed/Thrown

Round	1	2	3	4	5	6	7	8	9	10	11	12	Total
Charles	12/26	5/7											17/33
	46%	71%											52%
Satterfield	25/56	7/17											32/73
	45%	41%											44%

Ezzard Charles vs. Bob Satterfield January 13, 1954, Chicago, Illinois

TALES FROM THE VAULT

Bobby Czyz vs. Willie Edwards
February 21, 1987, Atlantic City, New Jersey

Many times, a fighter who moves up in weight is either making a concession to Father Time or showing signs of a lagging commitment to conditioning, but there are also occasions when putting on pounds is an absolute necessity.

For Bobby Czyz, adding 15 pounds to his frame was the best thing he could have done.

Czyz began his pro career at middleweight in April 1980 with a one-round KO over Hank Whitmore at Totowa, N.J.'s Ice World. Blessed with rugged good looks and a crowd-pleasing style, NBC packaged Czyz – along with Tony Ayala, Johnny Bumphus and Alex Ramos – under the banner of "Tomorrow's Champions." Czyz justified that buildup by amassing a 20-0 (15 KO) that included victories over Bruce "The Mouse" Strauss (KO 3), Teddy Mann (W 8), former junior middleweight champions Oscar Albarado (KO 3) and Elisha Obed (DQ 6) as well as Robbie Sims (W 10).

Because the 20-year-old Czyz's body was still maturing, he found it far more difficult to stay near 160 pounds and as time went on his system began to rebel. By the time Czyz met veteran Mustafa Hamsho in a prime-time bout on NBC, the effects of squeezing down to 159 ¾ – and Hamsho's roughhousing pressure – were graphically evident. Hamsho systematically dismantled Czyz en route to a 10-round decision and slammed the brakes on "Chappie's" championship express.

Following two KO wins over Bert Lee (KO 3) and Bill Medei (KO 4) at 162 and 163, Czyz moved up to super middleweight to score victories over Jimmy Baker (KO 1) and Mark Frazie (W 10) before becoming a full-time light heavyweight. The move worked wonders for Czyz's physical and psychological well being and the results inside the ropes provided ample evidence. Wins over Marvin Mack (W 10), Tim Broady (KO 4) and Murray Sutherland (W 10) earned Czyz a shot at undefeated IBF king Slobodan Kacar on the undercard of Michael Spinks-Steffen Tangstad at the Hilton Hotel in Las Vegas in September 1986. Czyz steamrolled the awkward Kacar in five rounds with an aesthetic blend of power and precision.

Czyz's brilliant form continued three months later – on Boxing Day 1986 no less – as he plowed through David Sears in just 61 seconds. In the midst of the greatest roll of his career, Czyz (30-1, 21 KO) signed to defend against the powerful Willie Edwards (22-2-1, 16 KO) at the Convention Hall in Atlantic City's Trump Plaza on February 21, 1987.

The "Sandman" was aptly named because he either knocked his opponents out or was put to sleep himself. His most notable knockout victims included Willie Monroe (KO 3), Len Hutchins (KO 3), Dale Grant (KO 10), Pete McIntyre (KO 7), former light heavyweight champions Matthew Saad Muhammad (KO 11) and Donny Lalonde (KO 9) to win the NABF belt. His knockout of McIntyre avenged a KO defeat seven months earlier and his only other loss was to the hard-punching "Diamond" Jim McDonald (KO by 4). The draw occurred against Sears, and that blemish was also avenged by 12 round decision in his most recent outing 11 months before.

Edwards was a banger who carried most of his weight in his muscular upper body while the more technically proficient Czyz produced power from his thickly muscled legs. Their mutually aggressive ring styles promised a pleasing mesh for both the live crowd and for those watching on CBS.

Edwards began the fight working behind jabs that Czyz easily blocked with his high-held guard. His gloves also deflected a lunging hook-cross combo and an instant later he popped back Edwards' head with a powerful jab. The pair spent the first minute gathering reconnaissance for the attacks that were inevitable given their temperaments.

As the bout entered its second minute, the heavy artillery began to emerge as Czyz landed a right uppercut-left hook combo that got a rise from the heavily pro-Czyz crowd. A follow-up one-two backed Edwards to the ropes, where Czyz connected with a right to the ear. Another right uppercut-hook sent Edwards wobbling away and a subsequent right to the side of the head stiffened his legs and widened his eyes.

In just a few seconds' time, Czyz apparently had found the keys to solving Edwards' style while also establishing his superior hand speed and punching technique. He also proved himself powerful enough to hurt the naturally bigger Edwards, which gave the champion a vital psychological edge.

But at that moment, Czyz wasn't thinking about long-term strategy – he wanted a quick and efficient kill. Czyz roared after the challenger behind a wild hook that sailed over the ducking Edwards' head. Edwards, though clearly stunned, was able to steady himself quickly enough to convince Czyz to throttle down his assault.

The action soon moved to close quarters, where Edwards landed a light right-left followed by a much heavier one-two to the face. Now it was Czyz who sought refuge as he retreated behind his guard. Edwards sliced a piston-like jab through the gloves that set up two hooks and a thudding cross. The challenger used his rock-like upper body to create punching angles on the inside, and his work paid off in the form of a right uppercut, left uppercut and a right to the ribs.

Edwards had regained his footing following a rocky start. But no one could have guessed that the challenger was about to rock Czyz's world in a big way.

With just three seconds remaining in an action-packed first, Edwards snapped off a right-left-right followed by a pile-driving right to Czyz's lightly stubbled chin. The blow whip-lashed Czyz's head and collapsed his legs, but because he was near his own corner the ropes prevented the champion from hitting the canvas. Instead, Czyz's behind hit the bottom strand and he somehow boomeranged upright – right into the path of a booming hook to the jaw. Czyz's shock-absorber neck fielded the punch and then he had enough presence of mind to execute the following moves: Slip under an Edwards right, grab the challenger from behind, spin him toward the ropes and blast a right to the face. The final blow arrived just before referee Rudy Battle separated them to end the round.

Czyz only had to walk a couple of steps to reach his stool, but even they seemed labored. Still, he assured longtime trainer Tommy Parks he was OK as Parks worked on a bruise under the champ's left eye.

As Edwards pondered his situation between rounds, he was locked in a physiological and psychological battle. The "Sandman" earned his nickname by blowing out troubled opponents, and his experience told him that Czyz was ready to be taken out. His lifelong dream was potentially seconds away from being realized, and he couldn't help but feel the surge of adrenaline and ambition within him.

But this was not just any opponent – this was a once-beaten champion who proved himself a resilient sort both in victory and defeat. Tim Broady blasted his best Sunday punches off Czyz's jaw but the New Jersey native made him pay a steep price when he tried to follow up his advantage. The result: A fourth round KO for Czyz.

The 15-round distance was also a factor in his decision making – did Edwards have enough stamina to last the full route if necessary? Edwards didn't know for sure because he had only been past 10 rounds four times, an 11th round TKO over Saad Muhammad, a 12-round draw and a route-going win with Sears and a 12-round victory over Witherspoon. The difference between 12 and 15 rounds consists of more than just nine more minutes of action – it's having to fight nine more minutes when tired. Exhaustion has a way of slowing and expanding an athlete's sense of time and the grind is as much mental as physical.

Fighters often try to simulate championship conditions by going 15 rounds – or more – with a continuously fresh supply of sparring partners. Clearing this hurdle might make the fighter feel better about his stamina but on fight night there is still the specter of the unknown. It's one thing to run the championship course with 16-ounce gloves, headgear and an opponent hired to help, not harm. It's a completely different proposition when the man you're fighting is hell-bent on keeping his championship and the financial riches it generates while also destroying you in the process.

All of those factors were in play as Edwards assessed his situation. He had a big decision to make: Go for it all now, or marshal his energies for another attack down the line. Each option had consequences, both good and bad, and he had less than 60 seconds to make the call. His seconds were there to provide input, but in the end it is the fighter who is the ultimate master of his fate.

Though the fight was taking place inside a casino, Edwards wasn't yet willing to gamble.

Edwards began the second cautiously, but soon found that Czyz was still in a weakened state as his right cross down the middle made the champion's legs dip. Instead of following up, Edwards chose to pump jabs. Just as Edwards quickly recovered from Czyz's assault, such was also the case for Czyz as he countered one of Edwards' jabs with a whipping hook to the jaw.

Edwards' grimace injected renewed strength in Czyz, who followed up with a chopping right that buckled the challenger's legs. Edwards tried to crank a right uppercut but Czyz's overhand right to the ear got there first. Czyz lunged in behind a right but Edwards caught him coming in with a pair of torrid rights, the first of which was an uppercut and the second a cross. Czyz fell inside to work Edwards' body while also neutralizing the challenger's six-inch reach advantage.

Both men's faces sported damage — Edwards was cut underneath his left eye while Czyz had blood on the corner of his left eye. Any concerns about the 15-round distance were mutually tossed aside as the all-out back-and-forth action demanded a quick — and violent — conclusion.

The follow through on a missed Edwards right sent Czyz stumbling toward his own corner and Edwards moved in behind a solid left uppercut-right-cross-left hook combo. After milling in close to catch a few seconds of rest, the two boxers returned to ring center to set up shop. While there, Edwards strung together a beautiful left uppercut to the body followed by a clean hook-cross combo.

One of Czyz's most underrated weapons was his shotgun jab — a straight-from-the-shoulder thrust whose power was augmented by the forward momentum generated by his tree-trunk legs. Most fighters use the jab as a range finder, but for Czyz it was a battering ram that broke down defenses as well as his opponents' wills.

Edwards sought to consolidate his advantage by jabbing his way in, but Czyz's ramrod jab forced the challenger to retreat toward his own corner. As Edwards fell short with a jab, Czyz lined him up with two light jabs and unloaded a chopping right to the temple that shook the "Sandman" to his core. Edwards tried to regain his balance by shifting his upper body from side to side, but his trembling legs told Czyz everything he needed to know — get him and get him now.

After Czyz snapped a right to the jaw, Edwards moved toward his own corner with the intent of propping himself up against the corner pad. But Czyz wouldn't let him get there, for he whipped over a right to the jaw that connected with full force.

Edwards fell first on all fours, then crumbled to the floor. At Battle's count of seven, ringside physician Dr. Frank B. Doggett climbed through the ropes to save Edwards, who was now flat on his face. Still, Battle completed the 10-count and the fight was declared over at 2:16 of round two.

Though victorious, Czyz knew he had just passed a most demanding test. He didn't have the time or energy to engage in post-fight histrionics aside from a fist-pump; instead he walked over to the scrum around Edwards to make sure his rival was OK. Satisfied that he was being well taken care of, Czyz calmly walked to his corner to accept congratulations.

Czyz needed every ounce of strength to turn back Edwards' challenge. When he was an up-and-coming middleweight, Czyz was billed as "The Matinee Idol" because of his combination of looks and intelligence. But now, armed with a new body and a fortified fighting spirit that comes with being a battle-tested champion, the matinee idol was on his way to becoming a real star.

Epilogue: Czyz defended his title once more, a sixth round TKO of McDonald, before surprisingly losing the belt to Prince Charles Williams in one of 1987's most exciting fights.

Czyz made two attempts to regain a light heavyweight titlet but lost both by decision to Williams and WBA king Virgil Hill. Following three more wins against Uriah Grant (W 10), Andrew Maynard (KO 7) and Haracio Brandan (KO 6), Czyz rose to cruiserweight and won his second divisional championship by upset split decision over WBA titlist Robert Daniels. After defenses against Bash Ali (W 12) and Lalonde (W 12), Czyz vacated the belt with an eye on a big-money heavyweight title shot.

Czyz aggravated a back injury during his final cruiserweight fight, a four-round loss to undefeated David Izeqwire. Victories over heavyweights Tim Tomashek (KO 5), Jeff Williams (W 10) and Robert Jackson (KO 6) set up a fight with Evander Holyfield in May 1996 at Madison Square Garden. With a possible fight with Mike Tyson looming, Czyz lost by fifth round knockout, though he alleged a substance that got into his eye had more to do with the loss than Holyfield did. Those allegations never got the traction Czyz sought and the matter was eventually dropped.

The 36-year-old Czyz ended his career with a second-round TKO loss to South African southpaw Corrie Sanders on June 12, 1998 at the Mohegan Sun in Uncasville, Conn. His final record is 44-8 with 28 knockouts.

Williams returned to the ring two months later with a fifth-round knockout of Tony Morrison, but lost two months after that to undefeated NABF light heavyweight titlist Tony Willis via fourth-round TKO. Williams launched a comeback following a five-year absence and after scoring three quick knockout wins, it ended after undefeated NABF champ Egerton Marcus polished off Williams in one round. His final record stands at 26-5-1 with 20 knockouts.

SHOOTOUTS

Total Punches Landed/Thrown

Round	1	2	3	4	5	6	7	8	9	10	11	12	Total
Czyz	23/45 51%	20/48 42%											43/93 46%
Edwards	30/86 35%	18/53 34%											48/139 35%

Jabs Landed/Thrown

Round	1	2	3	4	5	6	7	8	9	10	11	12	Total
Czyz	8/16 50%	5/13 38%											13/29 45%
Edwards	9/46 20%	5/27 19%											14/73 19%

Power Punches Landed/Thrown

Round	1	2	3	4	5	6	7	8	9	10	11	12	Total
Czyz	15/29 52%	15/35 43%											30/64 47%
Edwards	21/40 52%	13/26 50%											34/66 52%

Bobby Czyz vs. Willie Edwards February 21, 1987, Atlantic City, New Jersey

TALES FROM THE VAULT

Kostya Tszyu vs. Diosbelys Hurtado
November 28, 1998, Indio, California

In boxing, few things are set in stone – especially one's opposition. Last-minute changes are common even at the highest levels of the sport as short notice training injuries, contract and promotional disputes and other unforeseen circumstances force matchmakers to burn up the phone lines in search of a suitable replacement. Many times the name they find is nowhere near the quality of the original fighter, but every once in a while the late sub turns out to be better than anyone could have imagined.

On November 28, 1998 at the Fantasy Springs Casino in Indio, California, Kostya Tszyu was to have fought Miguel Angel Gonzalez for the vacant WBC super lightweight title to fill the void left by Oscar de la Hoya. Gonzalez, who lost a 12-rounder to the "Golden Boy" on January 18 1997, tried to fill the vacancy in March 1998 against the venerable Julio Cesar Chavez, but because the pair fought to a draw the title was still unoccupied. Because he didn't lose to Chavez, Gonzalez remained the WBC's number one challenger and thus had the right to again fight for the belt against the second-rated Tszyu.

Just 13 days before Gonzalez-Tszyu, the deck was unexpectedly shuffled when the Mexican suffered a rib cage injury in training. Instead of calling off the HBO-televised card, an attractive and high quality substitute was found in the fifth-rated Diosbelys Hurtado.

Hurtado's face was familiar to HBO viewers. On January 24, 1997 Hurtado fought WBC welterweight champion Pernell Whitaker, who already was scheduled to defend against De La Hoya on April 12. But the Cuban expatriate nearly pulled off a superfight-destroying upset by scoring two knockdowns and leading on all scorecards entering the 11th. Whitaker saved the big-money showdown by hammering Hurtado into helplessness with nine consecutive overhand lefts that left him draped on the ropes and just four minutes short of achieving immortality.

Now, nearly two years and eight wins later, Hurtado again stood at the doorstep of dreams. Despite decisioning Manuel Gomez over 10 rounds at Miami's Mahi Shrine just 15 days earlier, Hurtado's management jumped at the chance to fight Tszyu, who was in the midst of his own comeback story.

The Australian-based Russian was headed toward his own showdown with De La Hoya when Vince Phillips scored a shocking 10th round TKO at Atlantic City's Taj Mahal on May 31, 1997. In the 18 months that followed he scored three impressive wins against Ismael Armando Chaves (KO 3) and former champions Calvin Grove (KO 1) and Rafael Ruelas (KO 9).

The Tszyu-Hurtado fight was for an "interim" title, a concept originally designed to keep a title active while a champion recuperates from an extensive injury but eventually evolved into an additional revenue stream for the sanctioning bodies. The winner of Tszyu-Hurtado was obligated to fight Gonzalez in his next fight for the still-vacant "full" title.

The bout was a rare encounter between two fighters who could box and punch with equal effectiveness. At 5-11 with a 74-inch reach, the 26-year-old Hurtado had the physical dimensions of a speedy long-range boxer, and he accessed those attributes freely. But, as he proved against Whitaker, he possessed a potent punch, and that was borne out by his 28-1 (19 KO) record.

Because the 29-year-old Tszyu (21-1-1, 17 KO) was five inches shorter and owned a seven-inch shorter wingspan, he was forced into the role of heavy-handed aggressor. Tszyu, however, was not a face-first fighter by any means. His lightning-quick reflexes and highly developed sense of distance enabled him to skillfully evade his opponents' blows while also allowing him to position himself perfectly to fire his cannon-like right cross. Both fighters had amateur backgrounds as Tszyu, a 1988 Olympian and the gold medalist at the 1991 World Championships, won 259 of his 270 bouts while Hurtado, who had hoped to compete in the 1992 games, was 220-20.

The fight began as expected, with Hurtado on the move behind his jab and Tszyu coming forward and trying to force the action. The cat-and-mouse game didn't last long as Hurtado planted his feet long enough to uncork two lead rights to the head. Tszyu was unruffled and proved it moments later by firing a lead right to the cheek that sent a stunned Hurtado to the ropes and a sizzling left uppercut to the face that would have floored the Cuban had he not hooked his arm around the second rope. Just 40 seconds into the fight, Dr. James Jen Kin correctly ruled a knockdown and a chagrined Hurtado hoisted himself upright at three.

Tszyu charged in for the finish, but he quickly paid a price for his wildness. Hurtado, with his back to the ropes, unleashed a hair-trigger right lead that sent Tszyu, who was launching his own right, crumbling to the floor on one knee. Like Hurtado, Tszyu quickly regained his feet and flashed a sheepish grin. He knew he had been careless and though he was unaffected by the flash knockdown he chose to pursue Hurtado with more care.

Following an exchange on the ropes midway through the round, Hurtado had just enough room to unload a booming right cross that sent Tszyu falling forward toward the floor. Because both gloves touched the canvas, the referee ruled a second knockdown. Tszyu again rose quickly, but this time he appeared unsteady. Still, Tszyu doggedly moved forward but Hurtado planted his feet more often and ran off combinations while still keeping his distance with the jab. Tszyu managed to block a four-punch volley but Hurtado's missiles raised a dangerous looking swelling underneath Tszyu's right eye.

The pair exchanged right hands, but because Tszyu's was shorter and a bit quicker, it inflicted more damage. As Hurtado fell back into the ropes, an open-mouthed Tszyu was on him instantly. A big right knocked Hurtado into the corner pad and the Russian pressed for the finish like a wild man, but Hurtado temporarily stemmed the tide by whipping in his own flurry. As the round closed, Tszyu got the better of an exchange of rights and connected with a final looping left-right as the bell sounded. As both fighters walked toward their corners, they did so with a slowness that suggested they had fought much longer than just three minutes of a scheduled 36-minute contest.

Given each man's wealth of experience and knowledge, a wild all-out opening round peppered with three knockdowns was the last thing most observers expected. When one strips away the layers of pugilistic nuances and technical skills from a highly developed fighter, most times he will find a raging monster whose thirst for combat is insatiable and can only be silenced by another, more fortified member of the same species. Still, it is rare to see two highly rated ring men shed their fistic inhibitions in such breathtaking fashion. There was little science involved; just pursuit and instincts.

In Hurtado's corner, Lou Duva knew trading punch-for-punch with Tszyu was a losing proposition. Height, reach and speed were the keys to victory and it was his job to make sure he reined in his primal instincts enough to use them.

"Explain to him he's winning the fight and he can do anything he wants with this guy," Duva told the Spanish translator. "But he's got to find his range. He's got to jab, he's got to move. Box, box, box!"

Tszyu started the second by whiffing on an overhand right, allowing Hurtado to slap on a clinch. Hurtado retreated to the ropes, squared his shoulders and tried to jab. Tszyu sneaked in a right to the body and pulled away from a counter right. Tszyu connected with a solid jab, after which Hurtado got on his bicycle and fired a four-punch flurry, two of which landed.

As the round proceeded, Hurtado started to put together the awkwardly unpredictable combinations that had befuddled Whitaker, but Tszyu walked through them and landed rights over the top. The action was ungainly at times as Hurtado motored in both directions and Tszyu attempted to cut off the ring with arms held out in front.

Though Hurtado was on the move, his gait appeared shaky as if he was still affected by the early knockdown. Despite this, he still managed to connect with a solid hook during an exchange, after which he smothered Tszyu in a clinch. Tszyu had trouble lining up Hurtado as the Cuban either kept him at arm's length or muzzled his offense with well-timed clinches. In the corner between rounds, Johnny Lewis urged Tszyu to remain patient.

"No chances at all, mate. Just be intelligent," Lewis calmly said. "Keep off the ropes and out of the corners."

Hurtado began the third much as he did the second, by retreating to the ropes and setting up shop. Hurtado missed with a lunging overhand right while Tszyu missed with his own winging right. Tszyu marched forward with little head movement but with plenty of hand movement as he sought the combination that would turn the fight. Hurtado didn't make matters easy as he slid left and right in herky-jerky fashion, leaned away from counters and fired in bursts that seldom adhered to the bounds of predictability. The "book" says to attack a swollen eye with hard jabs, but Hurtado curiously stayed away from Tszyu's injury.

With 33 seconds to go, Tszyu's heavy right sliced through Hurtado's gloves, but Hurtado weathered it well and kept on the move and snapped in his own hard right. Tszyu fired in a right lead and Hurtado responded with a hook that backed Tszyu away. Tszyu regrouped and barreled in behind a burst highlighted by a solid jab and hook, but Hurtado spun away and connected with a right to the side of the head before clinching. A hard Hurtado jab ended a round marked with plenty of wild-swinging action.

Neither man seemed to be fighting with a long-term strategy in mind nor did they seem to be following a template; they just did what felt right at the moment. After three rounds Tszyu and Hurtado threw almost nearly the same number of punches (168-164 for Tszyu) but the Russian-Australian was far more accurate as he landed 75 for 47 percent to Hurtado's 46 for 28 percent.

Lewis also spotted another trend late in the third; that Hurtado's legs had lost some of their spring. And Lewis knew exactly what his man needed to do to exploit that.

"When you get him on the ropes, smash it into his body," he said. "He's starting to tire a little bit."

Tszyu obediently began the fourth by following a solid jab with a hook to the body and pressing Hurtado toward the ropes. An overhand right to the jaw and a right to the ribs connected, and that was followed by a burst capped off by a solid hook that forced Hurtado to retreat. Tszyu was ratcheting up the pressure and the effects were slowly showing on Hurtado. The Cuban initiated more clinches in an effort to buy time, and he succeeded as the fight devolved into wrestling mode.

Hurtado jacked Tszyu's jaw with a jolting jab but Tszyu nailed the Cuban with a right to the forehead as he tried to launch a right-left-right. Tszyu caught the final right rolling away but he swiftly regained his balance and moved in behind a solid right to the ribs. The action was sloppy but full of energy as each tried to impose his strength, will and power on the other. Tszyu was inexorably getting the better of the action as he connected sharply with a crunching hook to the body and a right over the top. Though Hurtado's desire was as strong as ever, his punches were no longer thrown with the same speed and snap, thanks to Tszyu's concerted body assault. And what's worse, the sharply observant Tszyu knew it.

Riding the wave of momentum to its fullest, Tszyu roared out of the corner in round five and pushed Hurtado to the ropes with a missed left-left-right. He then chased the Cuban to the corner pad and connected with an overhand right before falling into a clinch. Tszyu pawed out a range-finding left to line up two solid rights. A shotgun jab drove Hurtado to the ropes and a second one moments later did the same thing. Hurtado missed with a right uppercut to the body but a follow-up overhand right tagged Tszyu solidly. Undeterred, Tszyu kept coming.

Tszyu whipped in a jab, pushed Hurtado away with his left forearm and smacked a right to the face. A thunderous jab snapped the grimacing Hurtado's head and forced him to make an involuntary whooshing sound and that was followed by a left hook and left uppercut to the head. A right-left thudded into Hurtado's body and a pair of right uppercuts put Hurtado in full retreat mode.

The relentless Tszyu knew the end was near, and he systematically dissected Hurtado with withering, devastating accuracy. Six consecutive jabs brought blood from Hurtado's mouth and a left uppercut split the Cuban's gloves. A loud, heavy hook to the body and a right to the ribs buckled Hurtado, and a right-left-right snapped back Hurtado's head and had the Cuban wiping away more blood from his face.

As Hurtado tried to cover up on the ropes, Tszyu prepared the finishing touches: A left-left-right followed by a searing hook to the body. The agony was too much for Hurtado as he voluntarily took a knee along the ropes to provide a temporary respite. After Hurtado rose at six, Tszyu resumed his assault. A range-finding jab and a glancing right to the head gave Tszyu enough room to drill a knifing hook to the ribs that sent Hurtado to the canvas again. Referee Jen-Kin halted the count at three and Tszyu was declared the winner at 2:35 of the fifth round. Though the area beneath Tszyu's right eye was discolored and swollen, it ultimately proved to be a non-factor as he landed 39 of the last 47 connected punches of the fight. At the time of the knockout, Tszyu led on two of the three scorecards, and he held a 136-67 connect edge overall despite throwing only 50 more punches (292-242). In power shots alone, Tszyu racked up a massive 90-37 advantage.

When HBO's Larry Merchant asked Tszyu his thoughts about the two early knockdowns, he replied with his usual candor – and a bit of word play.

"That was a stupid thing for me," he said. "I remember I told you in the press conference that I'm rushing always too much. I'm from Russia and I was rushing too much. I had to calm myself down because he's a great puncher and I had forgotten about that."

Tszyu believed his chance to come back was inevitable because he knew Hurtado had to eventually settle down and engage with him.

"It doesn't matter if you have to run, you have to stop to punch, and we'd wait for the opportunity all night," he told Merchant. "You can't run and punch at the same time. When he stops he has to punch and fight me."

He was also unconcerned about the swelling.

"It's a scratch," he scoffed. "I'm the man, I'm the boxer. I don't care about this kind of thing. It don't look good right now, but to lose the title on a scratch wouldn't be fair." Seeing it as a badge of honor, he added, "it's an enjoyable part of being world champion."

Epilogue: Despite Tszyu's post-fight statement, the Hurtado victory only gave him the interim belt, but he would make his belt "full" nine months later when he stopped Gonzalez in 10 rounds. His second reign as a 140-pound titleholder was a fruitful one as he followed defenses against Ahmed Santos (KO 8) and Chavez (KO 6) by adding Sharmba Mitchell's WBA belt via seventh-round TKO and Zab Judah's IBF title via spectacular second round TKO five months after decisioning Oktay Urkal.

Tszyu's reign as a three-belt champion lasted just two fights against Ben Tackie (W 12) and Jesse James Leija (KO 6) before injuries forced him to take a nearly two-year hiatus. With IBF belt still in hand, Tszyu was an underdog against Mitchell in their rematch in November 2004 because of age and the prospect of ring rust. Tszyu exploded those myths by dropping Mitchell four times en route to a third round TKO.

The 35-year-old Tszyu then went to the lion's den of the M.E.N. Arena in Manchester, England to take on undefeated hometown demigod Ricky Hatton on June 4, 2005. Following a bruising battle, Tszyu retired on the stool – and ultimately from boxing – before the final round. Despite rumors to the contrary, Tszyu never returned to the ring and is considered by many a future Hall of Famer. His record stands at 31-2 with 25 knockouts.

Seven months after losing to Tszyu, Hurtado returned to the victory column by decisioning former 140-pound champion Lonnie Smith over 10 rounds and followed with a three round TKO of Dillon Carew. Just one week after beating Carew in Miami, Hurtado traveled to Carolina, Puerto Rico to fight future welterweight champion Ricardo Mayorga. That bout was declared a technical draw after an accidental head butt stopped the fight in the second round.

Four victories over Cosme Rivera (W 12), Fray Luis Sierra (KO 1), Henry Cokes (KO 1) and Ricky Quiles (W 12) led to a confrontation with WBA junior welterweight king Randall Bailey on May 11, 2002 in San Juan. Hurtado's third title shot would be the charm as he registered a come-from-behind seventh round TKO.

Unfortunately for Hurtado, his reign was short-lived. In another wild affair, he dropped the belt to Vivian Harris in a two-round shootout. He returned to the ring following a one-year layoff and knocked out Rudy Lovato in three rounds and he followed with a eight round decision over Joshua Smith seven months later and a two round TKO over Leo Edwards. Hurtado then launched a comeback three years later and as of March 2010 he is 4-0 as he defeated Rafael Chiruta (W 6), Eugen Stan (W 6), Arturo Morua (W 12) and Manuel Garnica (W 12). His record stands at 42-3-1 with 25 knockouts.

SHOOTOUTS

Total Punches Landed/Thrown

Round	1	2	3	4	5	6	7	8	9	10	11	12	Total
Tszyu													136/292 47%
Hurtado													67/242 28%

Jabs Landed/Thrown

Round	1	2	3	4	5	6	7	8	9	10	11	12	Total
Tszyu													46/101 46%
Hurtado													30/118 25%

Power Punches Landed/Thrown

Round	1	2	3	4	5	6	7	8	9	10	11	12	Total
Tszyu													90/191 47%
Hurtado													37/124 30%

* Fight originally done by CompuBox, but the original HTML files with complete round-by-round statistics no longer exist.

Kostya Tszyu vs. Diosbelys Hurtado November 28, 1998, Indio, California

★ Chapter 3 ★
BIG MAN DRAMA

Michael Moorer vs. Bert Cooper
May 15, 1992, Atlantic City, N.J.

During the height of his reign as WBO light heavyweight champion, Michael Moorer told an interviewer "I crave violence." He loved watching slasher movies and wondered what it would be like to cave in an opponent's cheekbone. Moorer spoke in an unsettlingly quiet voice but the intensity behind his words was unmistakable – and downright chilling.

Moorer's taste for combat was sorely tested in his heavyweight brawl with "Smokin'" Bert Cooper May 15, 1992 at the Taj Mahal Casino in Atlantic City. The bout was for the vacant WBO heavyweight title and the match between top-rated Moorer and second-ranked Cooper was one that featured two men whose careers were going in different directions.

Moorer was the one being groomed for future heavyweight stardom. He had already built a fearsome reputation by knocking out all 22 of his light-heavyweight opponents, winning the WBO crown by stopping Ramzi Hassan in five. He made nine defenses of his belt, and several well-known names were among his victims – Frankie Swindell (KO 6), former WBA champ Leslie Stewart (KO 8), veteran trialhorse Mike Sedillo (KO 6) and "Diamond" Jim McDonald (KO 3). His success came with a steep price, for every time Moorer prepared for a title defense, he tortured his body to squeeze his muscular 6-2 frame down to 175 pounds. By the time he knocked out Danny Stonewalker in eight rounds December 15, 1990 in Pittsburgh, Moorer's body was barely able to function. He won all right, but he was no longer able to fight with the same verve.

Fed up with starving himself, Moorer zoomed past the cruiserweight division and began anew as a 213-pounder against Terry Davis four months later. The two-round knockout confirmed he could take out heavyweights and his thrilling four-round KO over Alex Stewart July 27, 1991 confirmed his mean streak was also intact. After blitzing Bobby Crabtree in one round, Moorer's knockout streak ended at 26 after winning a 10-round decision over seven-footer Mike "The Giant" White February 1, 1992.

Questions about Moorer's ability to take a heavyweight wallop surfaced during his 10-round win over Everett "Bigfoot" Martin, who floored Moorer only 62 days before he stepped in the ring with Cooper, a more than respectable puncher himself.

Of all the fighters who trained under Joe Frazier, Cooper was the one who came closest to duplicating "Smokin' Joe's" hard-driving, power-packed style. In his 27 wins entering the Moorer fight, 26 came by knockout. By this time, however, Cooper had already experienced a number of ups and downs in his career – both professionally and literally. Cooper stopped his first eight opponents and was 10-0 when Reggie Gross scored a stunning eight-round TKO. Six more wins followed, most notably over a pair of Olympians in Henry Tillman (W 12) and Willie de Wit (KO 2) in de Wit's backyard of Regina, Saskatchewan.

The nationally televised victory over de Wit earned Cooper a fight with Carl "The Truth" Williams for the vacant USBA title. But Cooper couldn't handle "The Truth," losing by eight-round TKO. Cooper returned to cruiserweight and won the vacant NABF belt by knocking out Andre McCall in six, but a 10-round loss to the 16-5-1 Everett "Bigfoot" Martin began the next phase in Cooper's career – a "name" fighter used to pad others' records.

Sometimes he played his role perfectly as losses to Nate Miller (KO by 7), George Foreman (KO by 3), Mike Cohen (NC 8) and Riddick Bowe (KO by 2) attested. But once in a while, Cooper's smoke would choke his favored opponents. Orlin Norris was knocked out in eight rounds and Cooper gave Ray Mercer fits – and fists – before dropping a 12-round decision in a classic heavyweight slugfest.

When an injured Francesco Damiani was unable to fight undisputed champion Evander Holyfield, Cooper stepped in on short notice and nearly stepped out with the heavyweight title around his waist. Before "The Real Deal's" hometown fans in Atlanta, an inspired Cooper got off the floor in the first and decked Holyfield for the first time in his career in round three. Seconds away from scoring one of the biggest upsets in sports history, Cooper swarmed over the champ, landing blow after blow. But Holyfield regained his bearings and stopped a tiring Cooper in the seventh. It was this performance that earned Cooper (27-8, 26 KO) the number-two ranking he needed to fight Moorer (28-0, 26 KO) for the WBO crown.

The left-handed Moorer came out boxing while Cooper immediately sought to get inside to neutralize Moorer's two-and-a-half inch height advantage. "Smokin' Bert's" strategy was immediately apparent – wing as many lead rights as possible and hope one of them connects with Moorer's suspect chin. Cooper whipped five consecutive rights to the head and body and two of them pushed a slightly wobbly Moorer to the ropes. Two more rights, one to the temple and one to the jaw, left Moorer off-balance. Cooper pounced landing a flurry of power shots that forced Moorer to turn away and crumple to the canvas just 41 seconds into the fight.

Moorer arose at Joe O'Neill's count of five but he received several extra seconds to recuperate because Cooper had wandered from the neutral corner. By the time action resumed, Moorer's eyes were clear and his legs sturdy. Hungry for the knockout, Cooper bulled Moorer to the ropes and unleashed a torrent of wild right hands. The composed Moorer kept his hands high and bided his time in search of an opening.

The opening he sought revealed itself quickly.

A compact lead left cross found Cooper's chin and the Philadelphian's legs shook as if experiencing a mini-earthquake. With that blow, Moorer got the time he needed to further clear his head while making Cooper content to rest and recover.

After a few seconds of R&R, they went at it again. A right-left-right rattled Moorer's ribs while the "Kronk Krusher" cracked a left off Cooper's jaw. Both men pushed off to establish more punching room with the same thought in mind – throw the right hand. Cooper's sailed by harmlessly, but Moorer's hit the bull's eye. A follow-up left missed, but another Moorer right hook sent Cooper flying backwards to the canvas and his mouthpiece tumbling to the floor.

Cooper got up at six and after O'Neill completed the mandatory eight-count, Cooper said "mouthpiece" and pointed to his open mouth with his glove. O'Neill retrieved the gumshield and gave it to Eddie "The Clot" Aliano to wash out. But Cooper didn't wait for Aliano to finish the job, instead walking toward Moorer to resume fighting. Moorer took advantage by raking Cooper's body with wicked power shots followed by lefts to the jaw. A right hook to the stomach and another to the face sent Cooper stumbling across the ring with Moorer in hot pursuit. A five-punch combination had Cooper leaning forward at the waist, his glove nearly touching the canvas. But Cooper pulled himself upright and soaked up more punishment.

The pace was already far quicker than most heavyweight fights and the strain started to show. O'Neill stopped the action when the pair didn't punch for 10 seconds and replaced Cooper's mouthpiece. After Moorer slammed Cooper with a right to the body, Cooper countered with a hurtful right hook that made Moorer dizzy.

Finally, a most memorable first round came to an end. Moorer patted Cooper on the behind as if to say *"great round."* After all, he knew good carnage when he saw it.

Fueled by his late-round success, Cooper roared out of the corner and planted two lead rights and a hook to Moorer's face. The 224 ½-pound Cooper pushed the 217-pound Moorer against the ropes and whacked the body. Moorer spent most of the round with his back on the ropes, and while Cooper landed the heavier blows Moorer peppered Cooper's face and body with an assortment of short, precise punches designed to slowly wear down his opponent.

The first two rounds featured the type of brutal action expected of most heavyweight fights but rarely achieved. The pattern established in round two continued in the third, with Cooper pushing Moorer to the ropes and "Double M" popping Cooper with counters. Suddenly, a hook and a wide-swinging right crashed on Moorer's chin, hurting him visibly. Cooper attacked viciously, unleashing a nine-punch flurry (of which eight landed) that drove Moorer to his knees.

Moorer, up at four, didn't appear seriously hurt. Cooper, perhaps winded by his energy-sapping flurry, was content to back Moorer toward the ropes, inch by inch, instead of trying to apply the finisher. While on the ropes, Moorer landed a heavy double hook to the body and a short uppercut to the chin. The short bursts of punches kept Cooper at bay while allowing Moorer time to regain his equilibrium. Moorer concentrated on being sharp, accurate and busy in the hope that Cooper's fatigue would overcome him. Moorer received instant evidence that his short volleys were effective as one of them opened a cut over Cooper's right eye.

Cooper continued to push Moorer against the ropes in the fourth and Moorer continued to be effective fighting off the ropes. Moorer ripped a right hook to the body and fired two sharp jabs while Cooper dug a hook to the ribs and drove a right uppercut to the jaw. A sharp hook snapped Moorer's head, but the number-one contender was taking Cooper's shots better. A left to the liver backed Cooper a few inches, allowing Moorer the range to land another right uppercut-left cross combo. Cooper roared back with a right to the chin and hook to the jaw that drove a buzzed Moorer into the corner pad. A small swelling sprouted under Moorer's left eye as Cooper's rights kept bouncing off his face. Moorer finished the fourth strongly, landing a quick double hook to the chin and two light uppercuts.

Cooper's weight advantage enabled him to push Moorer to the ropes, but as the fight entered the fifth the added poundage became a burden on his stamina. Though his blows were still strong enough to force Moorer against the strands, they no longer had the same speed or snap. Emanuel Steward told Moorer to work behind the jab, but Moorer was content to do his best Wilfred Benitez impression and counter Cooper's wider punches with his uncommonly straight and technically superior punches.

With fatigue bearing down, Cooper began grunting with each blow much like his old boss Joe Frazier did. He also emulated Frazier's legendary resolve as he continued to press forward. A right drove Moorer to a corner pad and two more rights to the body kept him there. Moorer pushed Cooper away and landed jabs and short lefts to the chin.

With 1:07 left in the round, Moorer pushed Cooper off and snapped a right hook and left cross that clearly hurt. For the first time, Moorer backed Cooper to the ropes and threw punches with abandon. A thunderous right uppercut to the jaw and a follow-up left cross left Cooper sprawled in the corner, his upper body draped over the lowest strand of rope. At seven, Cooper reached out his right arm as if to ask referee O'Neill to help him up, but O'Neill did his job and kept counting.

After Cooper pulled himself upright at nine, O'Neill asked him "are you all right?"

"Yeah," Cooper said softly.

"Are you sure?" O'Neill asked. Cooper nodded, but without conviction. O'Neill waved the fight over at 2:21 of round five.

The CompuBox numbers bore out what everyone already knew: Moorer-Cooper was a memorable, bombs-away affair. Overall Moorer landed 137 of 240 punches and 108 of 188 power shots for 57 percent accuracy in both categories. Cooper landed 114 of his 281 attempts for 41 percent accuracy and all but two of his connects were power shots. Of the 251 punches landed between the pair, an incredible 88 percent were power shots and their 22 connects per round is double the heavyweight average.

When TVKO's Joe Goosen asked about Moorer's strategy of fighting off the ropes, he replied "it was my strategy because I can see the shots better than I can on the outside. I picked my shots and I came through. Bert's a tough guy and I take my hat off to Mr. Cooper. I guess I was hurt a little, but this is boxing, you're going to get hurt. I went down, but it's a sign of a good fighter to get up and come back. I always have confidence in myself because I'm a strong-minded person. I just went in there and I did it."

Epilogue: Both men had plenty more fights in them. The Cooper fight was one of the last examples of Michael Moorer the savage executioner. As he matured emotionally, his fighting style also became far less reckless – and sometimes downright boring to fans expecting to see more of the old Moorer.

Moorer continued to enjoy success following the Cooper win, beating Bonecrusher Smith (W 10), Frankie Swindell (KO 3) and Mike Evans (W 10) before challenging Holyfield for the WBA and IBF titles April 22, 1994. Though Moorer was a natural right-hander who fought as a lefty, he technically became boxing history's first southpaw heavyweight champion after capturing a majority decision over Holyfield.

In his next fight, Moorer made history again – except he was on the losing end of it. At 45 years 10 months, George Foreman became the oldest heavyweight champion after knocking Moorer out with a single right hand on November 5, 1994. After a 10-round win over Melvin Foster, Moorer won the vacant IBF belt by decisioning Axel Schulz in Dortmund, Germany. He defended the IBF belt twice, knocking out Alexander Zolkin in 12 and scoring a pedestrian decision over Vaughn Bean.

Moorer regained his old fire against WBA/IBF champ Holyfield November 8, 1997, showing considerable courage and resolve. Though knocked down five times, Moorer gained his feet each time and came out firing. The eighth-round TKO loss actually enhanced Moorer's standing as a fighter. He never again fought for a heavyweight title, but he enjoyed success against lesser lights Lorenzo Boyd (KO 4), Terrence Lewis (KO 2), Terry Porter (KO 4), Otis Tisdale (W 10), Rogerio Lobo (KO 1) and Jose Arimatea Da Silva (KO7). David Tua knocked Moorer out in a single round August 17, 2002 in Atlantic City and a 251-pound Moorer was decisioned by Eliseo Castillo July 3, 2004.

Unlike most champions, Moorer went out a winner as he won seven of his final eight fights and at age 40 he retired with a record of 52-4-1 (40 KO).

Cooper fought 22 more times, winning nine and losing 13. Over the next 10 years, Cooper served as fodder for up-and-comers Joe Mesi (KO by 7), Fres Oquendo (L 10), Derrick Jefferson (KO by 2), Samson Po'uha (KO by 4), Chris Byrd (L 10), Alexander

Zolkin (KO by 8), Jeremy Williams (KO by 7), Larry Donald (KO by 7) and Corrie Sanders (KO by 3).

Occasionally, Cooper upset the best-laid plans of pugilists and promoters, most notably against 16-4-1 Rocky Pepeli (KO 8), 18-0 Richie Melito (KO 1) and 19-5 Derek Williams (W 10). Cooper ended his roller-coaster career at age 36 with a four-round KO loss to Darroll Wilson Sept. 20, 2002. His final record was 36-22 (30 KO).

TALES FROM THE VAULT

Total Punches Landed/Thrown

Round	1	2	3	4	5	6	7	8	9	10	11	12	Total
Moorer													137/240
													57%
Cooper													114/281
													41%

Jabs Landed/Thrown

Round	1	2	3	4	5	6	7	8	9	10	11	12	Total
Moorer													29/52
													56%
Cooper													2/22
													9%

Power Punches Landed/Thrown

Round	1	2	3	4	5	6	7	8	9	10	11	12	Total
Moorer													108/188
													57%
Cooper													112/259
													43%

* Fight originally done by CompuBox, but the original HTML files with complete round-by-round statistics no longer exist.

Michael Moorer vs. Bert Cooper May 15, 1992, Atlantic City, N.J.

Orlin Norris vs. Adolpho Washington I
March 17, 1995, Worchester, Massachusetts

During the mid- to late-1970s, the World Boxing Council and World Boxing Association unleashed an unprecedented expansion. Within the space of five years, the WBA and WBC established four new divisions, most of which filled perceived gaps between long-established weight classes and all of which provided new sources of sanctioning fees.

Of the new arrivals, the one that made the most sense was cruiserweight. By this time, the gulf between light heavyweights and viable heavyweights had ballooned to more than 40 pounds and smallish heavyweights seeking the big money regularly had to concede 20 pounds or more. Moreover, their smaller frames had to absorb the punches of bigger, stronger men to get ahead, and that's never a good equation – neither for the boxer nor a sport in which safety is paramount to its survival in modern society.

Ever since Marvin Camel beat Mate Parlov in their rematch to become the sport's first cruiserweight champion March 31, 1980, the division has been somewhat star-crossed. Camel-Parlov I was supposed to crown the division's first champion, but the fight ended in a draw. For a time, there was confusion about the division's name as the WBC called it cruiserweight while the WBA used "junior heavyweight" before dropping it. Also, the division evolved into a haven for onetime light heavyweights who could no longer make the 175-pound weight limit and lighter heavyweights who wanted to win a belt to improve their marketability for an eventual return to the land of the giants.

From time to time, however, this stepping-stone provided some excellent fights. The first bout between Evander Holyfield and Dwight Muhammad Qawi remains the gold standard, but there have been others that have stirred fans' passions – among them Carl Thompson-Chris Eubank I, James Toney-Vassiliy Jirov and Lee Roy Murphy-Chisanda Mutti, the latter of which produced a rare double knockdown.

Another excellent scrap was the first meeting between WBA champion Orlin Norris and mandatory challenger Adolpho Washington. Norris-Washington I pitted a former light heavyweight (Washington) against a smaller heavyweight who experienced some success before moving down (Norris.)

For the 27-year-old Washington (24-2-2, 15 KO), the Norris fight was his third chance at a world title and his previous two championship encounters produced bizarre results. His first shot against WBA light heavyweight king Virgil Hill ended in 11 rounds when Washington was cut after bumping his head against a ringside TV camera and was unable to continue. In his second opportunity against WBC cruiserweight champion Anaclet Wamba in Monte Carlo, Washington fought well enough to earn at least a draw. However, it was discovered that a penalty point for an accidental butt was not deducted from Wamba's scorecard – yet the draw stood and Washington was again denied a championship.

Nearly four months after the Wamba disappointment, Washington grabbed the fringe IBO title by stopping David Izeqwire in eight rounds. That, and his past performances at 175, enabled Washington to become the mandatory contender for Norris.

The move down from heavyweight proved to be an excellent career move for the 29-year-old Norris (42-3, 1 no-decision, 24 KO). After losing a 12-round decision to Tony Tucker, Norris dropped 23 pounds in 10 weeks and knocked out Jesse Shelby in 10 rounds. Norris won his next seven fights to secure a chance at the vacant WBA title against Marcelo Figueroa. Six rounds later, Figueroa was knocked out and Orlin joined his brother Terry among the ranks of world champions.

The Washington fight was Norris' fourth defense, and though Wamba and IBF king Al Cole would argue, the Lubbock, Texas, native was generally regarded as the world's best 190-pounder. "Juice" notched two wins over Arthur Williams (W 12, KO 3) and James Heath (KO 2) to run his cruiserweight record to 13-0 (9 KO).

To be successful against Washington, Norris had to impose his superior strength and exert constant pressure to wear down the naturally smaller man. For Washington, his prospects for victory depended on how well he utilized his edges in hand speed and mobility. Though he was coming up from 175, Washington enjoyed a one-inch height advantage and a four-inch edge in reach.

The challenger's longer arms paid dividends seconds into the fight as Washington introduced himself with a snappy jab to Norris' face. Norris tossed his own jabs to find his best range, and he ended a brief feeling-out period with a solid hook to the jaw. The champion tried to maneuver Washington to the ropes, but Washington smartly spun away and continued to bounce jabs off Norris' head and body while weaving in an occasional hook to the body.

Washington was off to a good start, and in the final minute he diversified his attack even further. He landed a nice left uppercut to the belly and his lead rights regularly penetrated Norris' usually tight defense. Norris, however, had the last laugh as he ended the round with a solid counter hook to the body.

Washington started the second on the move, but Norris was through surveying the situation as he bulled the challenger toward the ropes more frequently. Washington maintained a high work rate as he snapped jabs and lead rights that didn't hurt the thickly built Norris but scored plenty of points. Midway through the round, Norris worked his way inside and landed a four-punch combination to Washington's head and body. None of the blows were struck with Norris' full weight, but he was laying the groundwork toward establishing a foothold inside Washington's reach.

Norris pushed Washington to the ropes and ripped a hook to the body, but Washington spun out after Norris' wide hook missed and connected with a solid one-two. Norris' high guard caught most of the challenger's follow-up blows, but the already quick pace was starting to heat up even more. Wary of Norris' inside strength, Washington went back on the bicycle, snapping jabs and ducking underneath Norris' counters. The champion usually exhibited good punching technique, but Washington's movement caused Norris to lunge off-balance and leave himself open for counters.

"You're trying to kill him with that right hand," trainer Abel Sanchez told Norris between rounds. "Don't try to hit him so hard. Just set him up for the right hand and the hook." It wasn't a strategy designed to reap quick rewards, but a long-range plan that sought to wait out Washington's early-rounds spurt and take advantage when fatigue's poisonous effects set in.

As the third round began, Norris exerted steadier and more composed pressure. A quick jab set up a hook-right-hook combo that forced Washington back and another double jab kept the ball rolling. Washington answered with a solid counter right to the point of the chin. Two missed jabs set up a stronger right by Norris, and a follow-up hook landed slightly low, drawing a caution from Canadian referee Hubert Earle. Washington continued to exhibit strong ring generalship, throwing hard and straight with a variety of blows while moving left and right in tight circles.

While not explosive, the fight radiated championship intensity as both men seamlessly blended offensive and defensive skills while never taking a second off to rest.

Washington's trainer Goody Petronelli kept his instructions simple between the third and fourth rounds – follow the jab with a one-two to counteract Norris' steady pressure. Washington opened the round moving well to his right, but Norris cut the ring off and maneuvered the challenger to the ropes where he landed a lead hook to the head and a right that was deflected. Moments later a strong left uppercut sliced through Washington's guard but the durable challenger spun away to ring center and continued his stick-and-move tactics.

One minute into the fourth, the action shifted back to the ropes where Washington landed a sticky right-left to the body, but Norris countered with a head-jerking left uppercut to the chin and a right hook to the head. Another hook-right combo connected solidly but Washington's sturdy chin absorbed the blows extraordinarily well. Make no mistake, the punches Norris landed had felled other cruiserweights but against Washington they had no discernable effect. Moreover, the determined challenger was firing back and piling up points.

A pattern was soon established: Whenever the fight was at long range, Washington dictated the terms of combat with his long, stabbing shots but at close range, the stockier Norris' strength and well-grounded punching fundamentals proved superior.

The fight was even after four rounds, but in the fifth and sixth rounds, Washington enjoyed one of the best stretches of his career. Washington was in constant motion, shifting directions by the second. In the fifth, he smoked a one-two through the guard and a follow-up hook-right combination connected sharply on a seemingly mesmerized Norris. A swelling erupted around Norris' right eye and while he continued to apply pressure he wasn't getting off his blows as quickly. Meanwhile, Washington was bouncing combinations off Norris' head, and while they weren't thrown with full power they helped him establish a working margin on the judges' scorecards. Washington was blending all aspects of his game, setting up his combinations with unpredictable lateral movement in both directions. It wasn't that Norris was fighting badly, Washington was just fighting better.

With 45 seconds remaining in the sixth, Washington, perhaps feeling his oats, began to engage Norris at shorter range as he whacked a right-left to the body. Norris countered with a sharp jab and a hook that caused saliva to shoot from the challenger's mouth. Norris followed with a solid jab to the face but Washington ended the round strongly with a chopping right to the ear.

"He's putting the pressure on you a little bit," Petronelli told Washington in an effort to maintain his fighter's momentum. "You have to throw more flurries, more combinations. He's edging you in that damn round because he's aggressive." Petronelli knew the bout was evolving into one of attrition and given Washington's history with close decisions, the trainer wanted his charge to grab as many points as possible. Washington obeyed his trainer's instructions and opened the seventh aggressively. But after the initial wave of energy gained by the one minute's rest, Washington's performance receded ever so slightly and Norris was right there to take advantage by landing a strong one-two that made the Worchester crowd react. Washington threw punches freely, but Norris' gloves caught most of them. Norris moved inside behind a clean hook to the body and a right to the head but Washington blunted Norris' rally temporarily by countering a jab with a heavy hook to the stomach.

The flow of the fight was slowly shifting toward the champion. The strategic seeds that were planted in the difficult early rounds began to sprout through the ground and see the light of day – or in this case, the television lights above the ring. Though Washington remained the busier fighter, Norris looked the stronger man.

As the eighth round began, the battle shifted to close range, where Norris landed a quick left uppercut-right hand to the head. Another short hook found the mark and a four-punch bouquet to the head and body was capped with a solid right uppercut that jerked Washington's head. Norris backed to the ropes and let the challenger pepper away as the champion blocked most of the blows. A few seconds later, Norris sprung the trap, leaping off the ropes with a lead overhand right to the jaw. Two more thudding rights to the temple had Washington holding on and Norris fought off a Washington clinch by firing two uppercuts to the chin.

After several difficult early rounds, Norris had the fight he wanted. At short range, Norris was within reach of his taller opponent, whose longer arms prevented him from gaining proper leverage. Plus, Norris' earmuffs defense blocked many of Washington's punches. Norris looked strong and invulnerable and it appeared the tortoise was finally catching up to the hare.

Washington sought to turn the momentum in the ninth as he got up on his toes and tried to replicate the formula that worked so well in rounds five and six. But soon, the fight returned to close quarters where the two engaged in an extended toe-to-toe exchange. Washington showed signs of "hitting the wall" as he blew air from his cheeks. Washington threw a lead right-left uppercut combo, both of which missed, and Norris took advantage by landing a hook, a chopping right to the ear and a short right uppercut to the jaw that stunned Washington. After a wide hook and a right to the body connected, Washington spread out his arms as if to say *"is that all you got?"*

Norris' answer: *Nope, I've got more.* Two more rights to the ear crashed home before Washington found the safety of a clinch.

During that clinch, Washington drew on his determination to become a champion. Once he broke free with 20 seconds remaining in the round, he expressed that resolve with stunning swiftness.

A pair of hard double hooks froze Norris temporarily and a short hook to the jaw and right to the temple forced the champion back to the ropes. Though not hurt badly, Norris appeared stunned and the crowd rose in surprise at the sudden shift of fortune. A final hook – and the ninth-round bell – ended Washington's mini-flurry.

There's nothing like a little success to turn a fight around, and Washington, who minutes before seemed to have reached his physical limit, now had "Big Mo" in his corner. As the 10th round opened, the life returned to Washington's legs and his jabs regained their snap. Two of them landed flush and an overhand right to the ear connected well.

Older fighters have been known to turn back the clock several years, but for Washington all he needed to do was turn it back by 20 minutes.

After a brief lull on the inside, the pair again saved the best action for the last 20 seconds. A four-punch combo pushed Norris toward the ropes and the champion answered with his own flurry. A solid hook landed on Washington's jaw, but the challenger did Norris two better by landing a pair of jolting hooks as the round ended.

Norris knew he needed a big finish to preserve his championship and he opened the 11th on his toes to give himself time to marshal the energy he wanted to expend in the 12th. Washington took advantage by landing jabs and putting more mustard behind his rights.

As the fight entered the final round, both knew that whomever won it would likely win the fight.

Washington began strongly, beating Norris twice to the punch with a lead right and a left that caught the champion coming in. Norris advanced behind the jab but Washington again caught the advancing Norris with two sneaky, jolting hooks. The champion ripped an overhand right to the head and Washington countered with a hair-trigger right. Norris drove a right to the ear and a fierce left uppercut-right cross combination to the head.

With the fight still in the balance after two minutes, the fight shifted inside and the two men were ready to empty their chambers. Emerging from a clinch, Norris tagged Washington with a left-right to the head as Washington roared back with a strong right uppercut, a hook to the temple, another hook to the jaw and a right to the back of the head before forcing a clinch.

After Earle separated them, Washington took a deep breath as he braced himself for his final assault. Norris was ready for him and the boxers tore into each other in the final 10 seconds, desperate to affix a final, positive image for judges Julio Roldan, Fernando Viso and Waldemar Schmidt.

After the final bell sounded, Norris smiled and stood still for a few seconds as he waited for Washington to come over. When he did, he gave the champion a "well-done" embrace.

Despite all the back-and-forth action, the judges came up with identical scores: 115-114 for the winner and still champion, Orlin "Juice" Norris.

The fans let their feelings be known, and they weren't saying "Juuuuuuuuice" either.

An exasperated and depressed Washington agreed, telling Showtime's Ferdie Pacheco "It's not like I've never been hit before. Why even train? Why not let the judges pick who they want to win and stop the f***ing fight? It's awful."

"This was a little tough," Norris acknowledged. "But I expected a tough fight out of him, otherwise I don't think I would've made it through it. I knew he was going to change up his tactics because he just couldn't keep running like that to continue to stay in the fight. He's a smart fighter. He stunned me with a few shots, but I was never in jeopardy. I knew it was close and I started to pour it on. I knew I had to keep throwing punches."

When asked if he would give Washington a rematch, Norris said, "I'll fight him again. He's a tough fighter and he deserves it."

Epilogue: The two would fight again three years later, but not for one of the three major belts. On May 22, 1998 in Monroe, Michigan, Norris won a 12-round decision to capture the vacant IBA super cruiserweight title.

Washington took nearly a year off after the first fight with Norris before capturing a 10-round decision over Art Pendergrass and earning a chance at the vacant IBF cruserweight title. On his fourth try at a title, Washington finally came through with a 12-round decision over the 15-0 Torsten May in Palma de Mallorca, Spain August 31, 1996.

Washington's reign didn't last long, however, as he lost a majority decision to the 25-12 Uriah Grant 10 months later. From then on, he suffered a drop in form, and though he knocked out the 20-5 Paul Phillips in three rounds Washington's career was dotted with more losses than wins. Some of the more notable losses were against May (TD 9), James Toney (KO by 10) and Vassiliy Jirov (L 10). Washington's final fight took place September 28, 2001 when the 34-year-old decisioned Mike Peak at Applebee Park in Lexington, Kentucky. His final ring record is 31-9-2 (17 KO).

Four months after beating Washington the first time, Norris lost the WBA belt by eighth round TKO to Nate Miller. With the title gone, Norris returned to heavyweight and enjoyed some success, beating among others Tony Tucker (W 10) and Marion Wilson (W 10) before losing a 12-rounder to Henry Akinwande in a WBA elimination fight.

After beating Washington in the rematch, Norris avenged his loss to Miller (W 12) and knocked out Pele Reid (KO 1) to earn a fight with Mike Tyson Oct. 23, 1999. The fight was declared a no-contest after Norris was hit after the first round bell and in the process of falling injured his knee. From then on, Norris' career was hot-and-cold as he defeated clubfighters Bradley Rone (W 10), Brian Yates (W 8), Henry Funmaker (KO 5), Troy Weida (KO 3), Robert Coelho (W 8), Mike Peak (W 8) and Ken Murphy (KO 6). Whenever he stepped up the level of competition, Norris was found wanting as he was defeated by Andrew Golota (L 10), future champion Vitali Klitschko (KO by 1), Brian Nielsen (L 12), the 36-1 Albert Sosnowski (L 6) and Vassiliy Jirov (D 8). Norris' final fight took place November 3, 2005 in his adopted hometown of San Diego, where he was TKO'd in seven rounds by Ola Afolabi. His record stands at 57-10-1 (31 KO).

TALES FROM THE VAULT

Total Punches Landed/Thrown

Round	1	2	3	4	5	6	7	8	9	10	11	12	Total
Norris	17/44	14/46	22/60	20/58	19/55	22/59	13/45	27/57	34/67	32/70	28/69	21/59	269/689
	39%	30%	37%	34%	35%	37%	29%	47%	51%	46%	41%	36%	39%
Washington	13/63	9/58	16/69	12/60	18/69	23/58	19/73	18/69	25/72	26/80	27/80	33/76	239/827
	21%	16%	23%	20%	26%	40%	26%	26%	35%	32%	34%	43%	29%

Jabs Landed/Thrown

Round	1	2	3	4	5	6	7	8	9	10	11	12	Total
Norris	9/30	8/28	9/37	6/29	7/27	7/24	5/24	8/19	10/24	13/32	8/25	8/25	98/324
	30%	29%	24%	21%	26%	29%	21%	42%	42%	41%	32%	32%	30%
Washington	9/52	7/40	11/53	8/43	7/44	13/38	7/45	11/48	7/33	10/38	9/36	8/30	107/500
	17%	18%	21%	19%	16%	34%	16%	23%	21%	26%	25%	27%	21%

Power Punches Landed/Thrown

Round	1	2	3	4	5	6	7	8	9	10	11	12	Total
Norris	8/14	6/18	13/23	14/29	12/28	15/35	8/21	19/38	24/43	19/38	20/44	13/34	171/365
	57%	33%	57%	48%	43%	43%	38%	50%	56%	50%	45%	38%	47%
Washington	4/11	2/18	5/16	4/17	11/25	10/20	12/28	7/21	18/39	16/42	18/44	25/46	132/327
	36%	11%	31%	24%	44%	50%	43%	33%	46%	38%	41%	54%	40%

Orlin Norris vs. Adolpho Washington I March 17, 1995, Worchester, Massachusetts

Alex Stewart vs. Ezra Sellers
October 8, 1998, Kansas City, Missouri

Most boxing matches quickly settle into a pattern that rarely changes for as long as it lasts. That's because fighters usually follow strategies that are laid out weeks in advance and aside from a few small modifications, the boxer stays within tight parameters. In short, if a fight starts dull it'll likely stay dull.

One of the reasons the first Sugar Ray Leonard-Thomas Hearns fight was so memorable was the startling 180-degree turn both boxers took strategically. After Leonard hurt Hearns in the sixth, the speedy Sugar Ray turned into a relentless slugger while the predatory "Hit Man" turned into the "Hit-and-Run" man – and both assumed their roles with stunning fluency.

It is rare indeed when a bout begins at a normal pace only to morph into a memorable and explosive spectacle. Such was the case when Alex Stewart and Ezra Sellers met at the Harrah's Hotel Casino in Kansas City, Mo. What started out as typical heavyweight fare changed with head-snapping suddenness into a power-punching extravaganza with thrills and plenty of spills.

When Stewart-Sellers was signed, the story line was an all-too-familiar one: A step up in class for a prospect against an established veteran whose biggest weapon was thought to be the drawing power of his name. At age 34, Stewart (42-8, 39 KO) had faced some of the best heavyweights of his era – Evander Holyfield, Michael Moorer, Mike Tyson and George Foreman. But with the exception of Tyson, who knocked Stewart out in 147 seconds, "The Destroyer" provided the others with many anxious moments before losing. Stewart was quite athletic in his youth – at age 16 he was a member of the Jamaican national rugby team – and he hoped his 211 rounds and 12 years of experience would be enough to get past the upstart Sellers.

The 30-year-old Sellers (15-2, 14 KO) had been a pro nine years, but he endured long stretches of inactivity due to what he called bad management. Sellers grew up in Washington, D.C., but only after he moved to North Carolina did he blossom as a fighter. While there, he received high-quality sparring from Tim Witherspoon, Oliver McCall and Bert Cooper – and Witherspoon returned the favor by helping him prepare for the Stewart bout. With only 51 rounds of experience, he was far fresher than Stewart. But was he also too green?

Stewart-Sellers took place outdoors amid temperatures in the 40s, which made it difficult for the fighters to work up a sweat and establish a good rhythm. The southpaw Sellers began the fight on his toes, moving in tight circles around the stalking Stewart. Shortly after Stewart missed with a left-right, Sellers staggered Stewart with a sharp left cross to the jaw. Stewart, long prone to early-round knockdowns, took Sellers' blow well and responded with two good straight rights to the body.

With each man sampling the other man's power, they settled into a wait-and-see mode. Sellers connected with occasional straight lefts but didn't follow up while Stewart stalked with hands high and missed with occasional jabs. Sellers ended a quiet first round by popping Stewart with a quick left to the face, and as he walked back to his corner he was secure in the knowledge that he could land his bread-and-butter power punch against his more experienced opponent.

The somewhat cautious fighting continued in round two, with Stewart driving Sellers to the ropes 50 seconds in with a right-left-right that missed, and nailing Sellers with a cross to the nose and two hooks to the jaw. Sellers rolled away from the brunt of those blows and responded with a strong left cross-right uppercut combination. Sellers clearly had the faster hands, which allowed him to slice through Stewart's defense time and again. However, Stewart remained in the fight because Sellers' punch output was low.

Up to this point, the action was pedestrian but for heavyweights it was fairly typical. Most fights would have proceeded along the same path until its conclusion, but every once in a while a fight takes a turn for the better. Yet Stewart-Sellers would go beyond even that. What happened in the next three minutes and 48 seconds of action was nothing short of astounding.

As Sellers spun away to his right from a Stewart jab, Stewart caught a slightly off-balance Sellers with a solid right cross. Sellers stumbled toward Stewart's corner and fell heavily in the neutral corner. Up at seven, Sellers shook his head in discouragement but as the referee wiped his gloves the fighter was eager to continue the battle.

Sellers retreated to his right with Stewart in hot pursuit. With arms held high, Sellers blocked two blows and responded with his own sharp right to the jaw. Stewart was hell-bent on destruction, wading through a Sellers right to land a thudding right of his own. As Stewart charged in to unload another right, Sellers uncorked a sneaky right hook that caught Stewart on the button and caused him to fall forward into the neutral corner with 38 seconds remaining in the round.

It was an astonishing turn of events. Just seconds before, Sellers was moments away from becoming another Stewart knockout victim but his sudden rebound placed him on the cusp of his biggest win as a pro.

But it was not to be – at least for now – as Stewart arose at three. He wore a look of composure because he had suffered early-round knockdowns before and went on to perform well. Sellers, however, had much to say about that as he landed with a left cross and a right uppercut to the jaw. Stewart pressed ahead behind his jab and following a solid one-two, Sellers countered with a big right hook that twisted Stewart's head violently. After Stewart landed another one-two, Sellers caught Stewart falling in with a scorching four-punch combination that decked Stewart with vicious force. Sellers' flurry was particularly devastating: A right hook caromed off Stewart's head and a second right uppercut glanced off the temple. But a torrid left uppercut straightened up Stewart and a final right hook sent "The Destroyer" to the floor in sections.

Unlike the earlier knockdown, Stewart was badly hurt. His fighting instincts commanded him to rise but his body wasn't yet ready to comply. At four he tried to get up but instead he rolled onto his back underneath the ropes. At seven, Stewart used the strands to help him get to his feet by nine. Meanwhile, Sellers was in the neutral corner, crouched over at the waist as if he was about to start a 100-meter dash.

The referee gave Stewart a good long look and when the boxer offered an emphatic "yes" to the referee's query, the bout was allowed to go on. But before Sellers could follow up, the bell sounded to end a most tumultuous round. In the final minute alone the fighters combined for three knockdowns and given Stewart's condition, the fight's conclusion seemed close at hand.

In the corner, however, Stewart's recuperative powers kicked in. Though he was unsteady while walking to the corner, he talked freely with trainer Kevin Rooney by the 10-second mark. When the referee saw this after walking to the corner to check on Stewart, he was convinced that the Jamaican/New Yorker was fit to fight.

Sparked by his late-round success, Sellers tore out of the corner as the third began. He flashed a jab and a right uppercut-left uppercut combo barely missed the target. As Sellers landed another left cross, Stewart connected with a tremendous right to the button. Sellers stumbled to the corner pad and Stewart quickly followed him, throwing two short jabs, a right to the head and a heavy right to the ribs at close range. As Stewart rushed in, Sellers countered with a right uppercut and a right to the temple that backed Stewart off on unsteady legs back to ring center. As Stewart sought the refuge of a clinch, Sellers nailed him with a crushing left cross to the jaw and two right uppercuts.

The fight's momentum was shifting wildly, and with both men's legs in a compromised state it was difficult to predict what would happen next.

Sellers put everything he had behind his blows, but he was unable to draw a bead on the off-balance Stewart. Stewart used his bulk to drive Sellers to the ropes, where he dug a hook to the body and a right uppercut to the chin. The uppercut jolted Sellers into landing an even better right hook that caused Stewart's legs to tremble and a right uppercut to the jaw that sent Stewart falling into the ropes.

Though Stewart never touched the canvas, he was judged to be in a helpless enough state to prompt the referee to administer a mandatory eight count. As Stewart took his third eight-count of the fight, his left eye was nearly swollen shut and he was brought over to the doctor for a brief examination.

For Stewart, things were going downhill – and fast. But that would change.

The fight was allowed to continue but Sellers was bent on putting an end to it. He landed a home-run left cross to Stewart's jaw but as both men ducked low, Stewart landed a powerful jab that caught Sellers coming in. Because the impact of Stewart's jab was doubled by Sellers' momentum, Sellers fell awkwardly to the canvas. As he regained his feet by nine, Sellers looked out of it and his surviving the final 1:15 seemed a formidable task.

Stewart chased Sellers into his corner and landed a hook, a cross and a huge hook to the ribs, but Sellers ripped a right uppercut that whizzed by dangerously. Stewart ignored the warning shot and whaled away at his stricken foe with a speed that reminded many of a younger "Destroyer." Stewart fought like a man desperate to get everything done before the next turn of momentum and given the fight's pattern, his concern was justified. A right uppercut, a snappy one-two, a big hook to the jaw and a right to the pit of the stomach dumped Sellers for the second time in the round and the third time in the fight.

Up at six, Sellers trudged to a neutral corner but was able to compose himself enough to convince the referee of his fitness. Sellers tried to buy time with his legs, but Stewart's momentum was too strong to overcome. Stewart landed a teeth-rattling one-two and a ripping hook to the body. A lead right powered through Sellers' gloves and another hook had Sellers ducking low and seeking a clinch. Stewart emptied his guns, and three rights to the ribs sent Sellers stumbling across the ring and falling face first into another set of ropes, which prompted the referee to wave the fight over at the 2:43 mark due to the three-knockdown rule.

The fight's final 3:48 had the look of a speeding car careening wildly on a dangerous mountaintop road. In all, the fighters combined for seven knockdowns and provided the Kansas City audience with an unbelievable spectacle.

The bout's conclusion came in the nick of time – for the winner. Along with a virtually closed left eye, Stewart sported a hematoma on the side of his head. Neither fighter showed an ounce of quit, and Stewart was the first to lead the applause for Sellers.

"This guy was a tough guy," Stewart said after the fight. "He came out prepared. He had six weeks to train. I'm not making any excuses, he was ready tonight."

As for the punch that turned the fight in his favor, Stewart said, "A jab hurt him. I know that I have a good jab and he left himself open. Boom! It landed right on the chin and put him down. It was the only way because he had a lot of savvy. He was boxing me and beating the hell out of me. I take nothing away from him. He was hitting me some tremendous shots and I felt like I had to do what I had to do. This guy was dangerous. He was a southpaw, which aren't my favorites because they pump me on my seat. I don't want any more southpaws, please."

Epilogue: The good news for Stewart was that he got his wish of never again facing a left-hander. Unfortunately for him, the Sellers fight would prove to be his final victory. Stewart would fight twice more and was a knockout loser in both. Three months after fighting Sellers, Lance "Mount" Whitaker stopped Stewart in seven rounds, and on June 6, 1999 in Las Vegas, Stewart's career ended with a two-round stoppage loss to Jorge Luis Gonzalez. Stewart's final record is 43-10 (40 KO).

The younger Sellers had more fights left in the tank – 16 in all. Three months after losing to Stewart, Sellers got back on the winning track with a fourth round KO over Danny Woffard. Sellers then dropped to cruiserweight and found success by winning his next six fights, five by knockout. His step-up fight against former Cuban amateur star Ramon Garbey ended just 105 seconds after it began, with Garbey the victor. Two fights later, Sellers engaged in another classic brawl with Carl Thompson. Sellers and Thompson combined for six knockdowns before the Washington, D.C. native emerged with the victory.

Sellers' next fight was against WBO titleholder Johnny Nelson, who stopped Sellers in eight rounds. Sellers scored three wins over Kevin Tallon (KO 2), Jason Robinson (KO 1) and Joseph Awinongya (W 8) to earn a shot at Kelvin Davis for the vacant IBF cruiserweight belt. But Sellers' championship dreams weren't to be as Davis stopped him in eight rounds. His last fight was a two-round KO loss against future world cruiserweight champion O'Neil Bell on September 4, 2004 at Mandalay Bay in Las Vegas. The loss precipitated a three year hiatus and the comeback was initially successful as he stopped Troy Beets (KO 6) and Kenny Craven (KO 3) in 2007. On January 19, 2008 on the undercard of Roy Jones-Felix Trinidad in New York, however, Emmanuel Nwodo stopped the 39-year-old Sellers in two rounds. Sellers' record stands at 29-8 (26 KO).

TALES FROM THE VAULT

Total Punches Landed/Thrown

Round	1	2	3	4	5	6	7	8	9	10	11	12	Total
Stewart	4/32	15/42	29/59										48/133
	12%	36%	49%										36%
Sellers	10/35	12/39	12/34										34/108
	29%	31%	35%										31%

Jabs Landed/Thrown

Round	1	2	3	4	5	6	7	8	9	10	11	12	Total
Stewart	1/18	6/18	5/14										12/50
	6%	33%	36%										24%
Sellers	3/22	4/17	1/2										8/41
	14%	24%	50%										20%

Power Punches Landed/Thrown

Round	1	2	3	4	5	6	7	8	9	10	11	12	Total
Stewart	3/14	9/24	24/45										36/83
	21%	38%	53%										43%
Sellers	7/13	8/22	11/32										26/67
	54%	36%	34%										39%

Alex Stewart vs. Ezra Sellers October 8, 1998, Kansas City, Missouri

Carl Williams vs. Jesse Ferguson
August 31, 1985, Atlantic City, New Jersey

When looking back on fighters' records, one can see a handful of bouts that determined the course of the rest of their careers – good or bad.

Sugar Ray Leonard weathered an unexpected storm against middleweight Marcos Geraldo and blitzed respected contender Andy Price in one round before capturing his first title against Wilfred Benitez. His 1976 Olympic teammate Howard Davis survived two knockdowns to beat Norman Goins and toughed out a difficult decision against Vilomar Fernandez to earn his chance against WBC lightweight champion Jim Watt, a fighter he was heavily favored to beat. But the gritty Scot, fighting before his adoring fans in Glasgow, dominated Davis in winning a 15-round decision. Though he had good performances after that, Davis never fulfilled the promise others saw in him.

August 31, 1985 was a day of reckoning for heavyweights Carl "The Truth" Williams and Jesse "Thunder" Ferguson, who were scheduled to fight a 10-rounder in Atlantic City. For Williams (16-1, 12 KO), it was a chance to re-establish his credentials following a stirring – but losing – challenge against IBF heavyweight champion Larry Holmes. In that fight, the 25-year-old Williams built an early lead behind a long, snapping jab that reminded many of a young Holmes. But the 35-year-old "Easton Assassin" dug deep in the middle and late rounds to pull out a unanimous decision.

For the 28-year-old Ferguson (13-0, 10 KO), the Williams fight was the one he had to win to earn his own chance at the brass ring. Two fights before, he won his first step-up fight by 10-round majority decision over future heavyweight champion James "Buster" Douglas and in his last outing he knocked out Tony Anthony in 10 to win the ESPN Eastern Heavyweight Tournament. Ferguson was a man on the rise and the Williams fight would serve as his barometer on how far his talent could take him.

The fight plans for each was easy to decipher. The 6-4 Williams needed to use his two-inch height advantage and eight-inch reach edge to keep Ferguson at bay while Ferguson had to fight through Williams' long arms to get in range to unleash his thunderous left hook. In other words, whoever dictated the distance would win the fight.

Williams began the fight pumping the jab to Ferguson's head and body, and a solid jab knocked Ferguson back a half step. Ferguson missed with a wild hook but landed a hard jab and hook to the body. After an extended clinch, Williams snapped in a jab and Ferguson winged in three punches, all of which missed the retreating Williams. "The Truth" was off to a fast start as he controlled the pace with superior output.

That start got even faster a minute into the round as Williams' right to the temple caused Fergsuon's knees to dip toward the canvas. Ferguson scrambled to a corner on wobbly legs, but fought his way out behind two rights to the body. Williams maintained the pressure by landing two jabs, a left-right-right to the body, a left-right to the ribs and an overhand right to the jaw, but Ferguson again stormed his way out behind a winging hook and a glancing right to the ear.

At ring center, Williams continued to score with jabs, but Ferguson connected with a good overhand right over one of them and another big right prompted a brief clinch. Williams landed a solid hook to the body, a one-two, a hook-right combo and a pair of one-twos. "The Truth" was clearly the faster man and was far quicker on the trigger than Ferguson, whose offense was limited to occasional looping hooks.

With 12 seconds to go in the round, however, Ferguson broke through with an overhand right that brought oohs and aahs from the crowd and a powerful hook drove Williams back several feet.

Though Williams clearly dominated the round, Ferguson exploited the one element of Williams' game that wasn't world-class – his ability to absorb a heavy punch. Thus, Ferguson figured, he had a chance to win as long as he was able to stand.

Williams began the second strongly with jabs followed by rights to the body but in doing so he carried his hands at chest level, leaving him vulnerable to Ferguson's dangerous hook. "Thunder" cracked Williams with one as he moved straight back and a harder one forced Williams into full retreat. Fortunately for Williams, his legs were still viable enough to carry him away from Ferguson's follow-up punches. Williams regained the momentum behind a solid one-two and a right to the body while also smothering Ferguson's digs to the body by grabbing his head and holding on tight.

A pattern was emerging, and for Williams each round was a microcosm of the Holmes fight: Quick, impressive starts that showcased his superior weaponry followed by late fades that cast doubt on his dominance. Meanwhile, Ferguson applied steady pressure behind forceful but inaccurate punches, fighting with a belief that Williams would stop hitting him long enough to give him the one opening he needed to obliterate Williams' numerical and stylistic advantages.

He got such an opening a minute into round three.

Williams forced Ferguson into the corner with a flurry of blows, but as he contemplated his next punch sequence he left his hands perilously low. Ferguson leaped out of the corner behind a sizzling hook to the jaw that had Williams retreating awkwardly toward ring center. As Williams scampered away, Ferguson unleashed another monstrous hook and a right cross that dumped Williams on his rump. Up at three, Williams turned his back and walked toward his own corner, shaking his head in disappointment. Referee Larry Hazzard administered the mandatory eight count and determined Williams was fit to continue.

Williams validated Hazzard's judgment by snapping jabs – both to keep Ferguson at a safe distance and to clear his foggy head. Ferguson chased Williams to a corner behind two winging rights that missed, but after Williams spun out and retreated to ring center, Ferguson nailed him with two crunching hooks to the jaw and an overhand right that put Williams back in trouble. Williams galloped into his corner and managed to grab Ferguson to buy recovery time. A long clinch ensued and Williams took advantage of every second.

Ferguson's inaccurate power punching rendered "Thunder" silent and unable to follow up his advantage. Williams, for his part, let his hands go and as the round closed he drove Ferguson back with a right uppercut, a solid cross and two left-rights to the head.

Despite his strong finish, Williams was still dazed as he had problems finding his corner. Once he did, he stared long and hard at Ferguson with a look that said *"how did he do that to me?"*

Williams continued his rally in the fourth, stunning Ferguson with a left-right followed by a hook to the body and a right to the temple. Ferguson escaped from the corner behind a winging hook and charged in behind a left-right to the body. But Ferguson continued to fight in spurts and Williams seized on Ferguson's lethargy by firing four jabs, a right to the body, an overhand right to the jaw and another one-two. In the closing moments, Williams hit Ferguson with a pulverizing right uppercut to the jaw and a follow-up left-right that polished off a good comeback round for "The Truth."

Williams continued to ratchet up the aggression in the fifth, driving the phlegmatic Ferguson to the ropes with a right uppercut and a one-two. Another left-right connected and a left uppercut-overhand right combo appeared to stun Ferguson.

But what Williams – or anyone watching the fight – didn't know was that "Thunder's" lightning was about to strike for a second time.

As Williams lathered him with follow-up punches, Ferguson dipped low, lined up his shot with a light right to the body, then sprang up with a tremendous hook that sent sweat flying from Williams' head. "The Truth's" body spun 90 degrees to the right before crashing to the floor.

In that instant, Ferguson's tactics crystallized: Unable to match Williams' weaponry, Ferguson played a waiting game. He quickly realized that Williams was a "one-mode" fighter in that he was either all-offense or all-defense. When Williams' attacked Ferguson, his low-held hands rendered him vulnerable to Ferguson's mighty hook. So it was entirely possible that Ferguson had engaged in a dangerous game of possum to lure Williams into a trap – and in the fifth, that trap snapped shut.

Up at two, Williams was frustrated and muttering to himself. To that point Williams was winning the round handily and one Ferguson blow had obliterated all his good work in the judges' eyes. Also, he had to survive another 90 seconds to earn a respite.

But a funny thing happened on the way to a Ferguson knockout victory – Ferguson stopped fighting. After a brief chase, "Thunder" became scattered showers as he hung back and waited for another opportunity to strike. This allowed Williams to recover quickly and soon he was banging Ferguson with rights to the ribs and jaw while sidestepping the occasional Ferguson hook. Soon, his legs regained their strength and he ran out the clock behind long jabs.

Williams started the sixth quickly, whipping in quick blows to the head and body, but Ferguson stemmed the tide with a hook to the jaw. Ferguson was landing the hook at will, but doing so came with a hefty price tag – working through a thicket of Williams' combinations. Because of that, Ferguson continued to pursue behind a defensive shell. Meanwhile, Williams operated behind solid jabs – one of which hit Ferguson's eye and made him wince. Four Williams jabs preceded a heavy right to the body that prompted Ferguson to again set his trap along the ropes. This time the big hook missed, and Williams retreated to ring center. Ferguson countered a three-punch salvo with a hook to the ribs, and as the bell sounded he connected with another hook to let Williams know he was still in the danger zone.

"The Truth" bolted out of his corner in the seventh and backed Ferguson to the ropes with a strong, head-jerking jab. A double right to the head and belly triggered another all-out assault by Williams and Ferguson again laid the trap by giving him just enough of his head and body to induce Williams to continue the attack.

Williams took the bait and Ferguson snapped the trap – again.

Ferguson unloaded two freight train hooks to the jaw and a follow-up right sent Williams galloping toward ring center in a desperate attempt to escape. Ferguson ran after Williams and landed another sizzling hook and it appeared Williams was about to make a third trip to the canvas. But this time, Williams managed to grab Ferguson and buy precious recovery time. That clinch, however, also stopped Ferguson's momentum cold.

With the crisis suddenly over, Williams regained his equilibrium and began to rally. A snappy double right to the body and head caused Ferguson to sag into the ropes and a vicious right to the belly briefly doubled Ferguson over. Ferguson missed with a huge hook, and a right uppercut pierced Ferguson's guard. Williams spent the rest of the round strafing Ferguson with a continuous stream of offensive firepower that kept Ferguson's thunder at bay.

By this point, Ferguson had become a one-trick pony. In his mind, his only hope was to reel in the big fish with his hook while waiting Williams out behind his defensive cocoon. Williams took advantage of this in the eighth and ninth rounds by firing away at will, gaining momentum with every passing second. He wasn't hurting Ferguson but he was in the process of building a mathematical mountain so high that Ferguson couldn't reach its summit without the knockout.

Midway through the ninth, the mountain of punishment started to cave in on Ferguson. A right to the nose sent Ferguson into full retreat and Williams increased the pressure. His volley drove Ferguson to the ropes, the scene of so many sprung traps. But there would be no more trickery from Ferguson as he fell forward onto his knees after fielding a swinging right to the temple with five seconds remaining in the round. As referee Larry Hazzard kneeled on the canvas and shouted the count into Ferguson's ear, Ferguson touched his eyes and nose with his left glove while contemplating whether to get up. After he arose at nine, the round-ending bell sounded.

There would be no more miraculous comebacks for Ferguson in the 10th and final round. Williams maneuvered Ferguson into the corner with two stiff jabs after which Ferguson answered with a decent right-left to the body. A final arcing right to the jaw by Williams left Ferguson face down. His will broken, Ferguson arose a split-second after Hazzard completed the 10 count. At the 37-second mark of round 10, Jesse "Thunder" Ferguson permanently exited the ranks of the undefeated while Carl "The Truth" Williams took another step toward a second title opportunity.

"That Ferguson was very game," Williams told ABC's Keith Jackson before providing an apt description on why he struggled. "He was throwing left hooks and wide punches and I was keeping my right hand very low and I should have been picking it up. He came over the top and caught me several times."

He blamed his troubles on inadequate warm-up time due to the demands of live television.

"I didn't get a chance to loosen up in the back," he said. "I came down here and they brought me right out. So I really came into the ring cold. Everybody knows that when a fighter is cold, he can come out here and get decked. The same thing happened with 'Quick' Tillis. I came out cold and he decked me. But when I loosen up I'm a completely different fighter. Not to make any excuses, because I did my job and I did what I had to do – I took him out."

Epilogue: Indeed he did. This fight was a foreshadowing of things to come for both men. Ferguson beat Oscar Holman over 10 rounds less than four months after losing to Williams, but from then on his career took a serious nosedive. Over the next 13 years Ferguson fought 30 times and went just 12-18 (6 KO). Between fights Ferguson made a good living serving as a sparring partner for many of the world's top heavyweights, and his lethargic approach in many of his subsequent fights led many critics to say he had a "sparring partner mentality." But Ferguson was good enough to spring upsets from time to time, most notably a 10-round decision over Ray Mercer in February 1993. That victory led to title shot against WBA champion Riddick Bowe three months later, but "Big Daddy" blew "Thunder" away in two rounds.

As a heavyweight gatekeeper, Ferguson fought the best the division had to offer and often lost to them. His high-quality losses came to Mike Tyson (KO by 6), James "Bonecrusher" Smith (L 10), Orlin Norris (L 12), Oliver McCall (L 10), Bruce Seldon (KO by 5), Michael Dokes (L 10), Tony Tubbs (L 10), Mercer in a rematch (L 10), Frank

Bruno (KO by 1), Larry Holmes (L 10), Jeremy Williams (KO by 7), Alex Stewart (L 10), Dannell Nicholson (KO by 8) and Hasim Rahman (L 12).

Still, Ferguson got work because he was durable and was talented enough to upset several promoters' best-laid plans. For instance, in a four-fight stretch between September 1996 and May 1997, Ferguson beat the 18-0 Bobby Harris (W 10) in addition to Everton Davis (W 10), Thomas Williams (KO 8) and Samson Po'uha (KO 8) to earn the fight with USBA champion Rahman. Ferguson's final fight was a 10-round decision loss to Andrew Golota January 30, 1999 in Atlantic City. Ferguson, two months short of his 42nd birthday, retired with a 26-18 (16 KO) record. Still, one has to wonder what course Ferguson's career would have taken had he beaten Williams to maintain his undefeated record.

Nearly six months after surviving Ferguson, Williams faced former WBA heavyweight champion Mike Weaver. Weaver was supposed to be a "name" opponent for the rising star but instead "Hercules" finished the job Ferguson started. In the second round, Weaver floored the charging Williams with a tremendous hook to the jaw, just as Ferguson had done. Two knockdowns later, the fight was over and his reputation as a dangerous offensive force with a suspect chin was firmly set in stone.

Williams picked himself off the canvas and earned his second title opportunity by winning his next five fights, including a victory over former WBC champion Trevor Berbick (W 12). Some observers (including this one) believed Williams possessed the size, speed and skill to give undisputed champion Mike Tyson a run for his money, but they (and I) were proven wrong as Tyson wiped out Williams in 93 seconds July 21, 1989. He never again fought for a championship, but he continued to entertain fans for the next eight years. He won some (Melton Bowen, Marshall Tillman, Ossie Ocasio and Marion Wilson among others) and he lost some (Tommy Morrison, Tim Witherspoon, Frank Bruno, Alexander Zolkin and Melvin Foster), but he always gave it his best shot.

Just 12 days shy of his 38th birthday Williams fought his final bout, a seven-round TKO loss to 271-pound Anthony Green in Port Chester, N.Y. October 30, 1997. His record stands at 30-10 (21 KO).

Total Punches Landed/Thrown

Round	1	2	3	4	5	6	7	8	9	10	11	12	Total
Williams	36/83	14/42	23/65	26/56	16/45	16/42	26/52	22/41	32/65	3/8			214/499
	43%	33%	35%	46%	36%	38%	50%	54%	49%	38%			43%
Ferguson	18/49	21/52	10/29	13/30	13/27	11/26	15/30	8/24	6/13	1/3			116/283
	37%	40%	34%	43%	48%	42%	50%	33%	46%	33%			41%

Jabs Landed/Thrown

Round	1	2	3	4	5	6	7	8	9	10	11	12	Total
Williams	15/35	7/29	10/31	11/27	4/15	5/21	7/14	14/26	12/26	0/4			85/228
	43%	24%	32%	41%	27%	24%	50%	54%	46%	0%			37%
Ferguson	2/10	4/16	2/9	1/9	1/5	1/6	0/3	2/9	0/4	0/1			13/72
	20%	25%	22%	11%	20%	17%	0%	22%	0%	0%			18%

Power Punches Landed/Thrown

Round	1	2	3	4	5	6	7	8	9	10	11	12	Total
Williams	21/48	7/13	13/34	15/29	12/30	11/21	19/38	8/15	20/39	3/4			129/271
	44%	54%	38%	52%	40%	52%	50%	53%	51%	75%			48%
Ferguson	16/39	17/36	8/20	12/21	12/22	10/20	15/27	6/15	6/9	1/2			103/211
	41%	47%	40%	57%	55%	50%	56%	40%	67%	50%			49%

Carl Williams vs. Jesse Ferguson August 31, 1985, Atlantic City, New Jersey

TALES FROM THE VAULT

Michael Moorer vs. Alex Stewart
July 27, 1991, Norfolk, Virginia

After Mike Tyson won the WBC heavyweight title in late 1986 and added the WBA and IBF titles in 1987, it was thought that the future of boxing's most glamorous division – and the sport itself – was secure for years to come. Tyson's combination of prodigious punching power, extraordinary hand speed, scintillating defensive skills and a charismatic personality ensured that his fights wouldn't just be boxing matches, but also must-see events.

But as the 1980s turned into the 1990s, Tyson's world fell apart. His personal life was reduced to rubble and his professional life soon followed as James "Buster" Douglas shockingly lifted the title. By June 1991, Evander Holyfield had succeeded Douglas as champion and Tyson was facing rape charges that would eventually land him in jail for three years. While Holyfield possessed the warrior's spirit fans loved, his low-key personality hindered his effort to become the crossover star Tyson had been. Thus, the heavyweight division was in a state of flux.

Meanwhile, the rumblings made by a quintet of heavyweights proved the division's future would remain in capable hands should Holyfield be beaten. 1988 Olympic silver medalist Riddick Bowe had a charming personality, an undefeated record and knockout power in both hands. "Big Daddy's" Olympic conqueror Lennox Lewis was winning crowns in Europe while fellow gold medalist Ray Mercer was doing the same in the States, winning the minor WBO title in the process. Tommy Morrison possessed a left hook from hell and achieved mainstream success with his portrayal of Tommy Gunn in "Rocky V."

The most recent addition to the heavyweight sweepstakes was Michael Moorer, a former WBO light heavyweight champion who grew weary of boiling his 6-2 frame down to 175 pounds. Following an eighth round TKO over Danny Stonewalker, Moorer and his trainer Emanuel Steward decided to bypass the money-starved cruiserweight class and make the big jump to heavyweight. Moorer made his divisional debut April 19, 1991 with a second round KO of Terry Davis and followed it with a third round knockout of tough Levi Billups.

By the time the 23-year-old Moorer (24-0, 24 KO) signed to fight fellow knockout artist Alex Stewart there already was a groundswell of opinion among experts that Moorer could be the best of the emerging heavyweights. The knockouts of Davis and Billups proved Moorer possessed big-man power while retaining much of his light heavyweight hand speed. His near-perfect punching technique would prove to be a big edge against most heavyweights, who often threw in wide, sloppy arcs. The only question remaining for the heavyweight version of Moorer was this – could he take a legitimate big man's best punch?

Enter 27-year-old Alex "The Destroyer" Stewart (27-2, 27 KO), who a few years earlier had made big noise by racking up 24 consecutive knockouts to start his career. But against Holyfield on November 4, 1989, Stewart hit the wall, fighting bravely before ultimately losing by eighth round TKO. Victories over Mark Young (KO 5) and Jamie Howe (KO 7) earned Stewart a chance at redemption against Tyson, who was making his second ring appearance since the Douglas debacle. Two minutes twenty-seven seconds later, it was over and Stewart was relegated to the role of stepping stone against Moorer.

A tough stepping stone? Absolutely. Twenty-seven knockouts in 27 wins proved that. But to most observers, the two losses to Holyfield and Tyson spoke louder than his victories.

Still, Moorer-Stewart was an intriguing crossroads fight that promised explosive action. The match pitted two genuine knockout punchers, one with a questionable chin and the other with a prodigious mean streak. Most of the fans inside The Scope were there to see hometown hero Pernell Whitaker defend his lightweight title against undefeated Poli Diaz, but while they waited for "Sweet Pete" do to his thing, the appetizer ended up a four-course banquet.

The fighters set up shop at ring center, shuffling in tight circles around one another. Moorer opened hostilities by spearing Stewart with a sharp jab while Stewart's jabs fell short of the target. Moorer connected with a straight left to the jaw and Stewart answered with a lead right – the textbook punch against a southpaw.

Moorer may have fought as a southpaw, but he wasn't a lefty in the truest sense. He did everything else right-handed and thus his right hook was his most potent punch. As Stewart moved inside, Moorer caught Stewart with that right hook, but "The Destroyer" was undeterred as he dug a right to Moorer's ribs. "Double M" retreated a step to set up two crisp jabs but Stewart caught Moorer well with a one-two.

Neither man was in the mood for a feeling-out period. It already was a high-contact fight as both men blasted away and inflicted damage. One minute into the fight, Moorer already had a bloody nose, but Stewart also made sure to punish the body. Twice Stewart countered Moorer's jab by dipping underneath and whipping rights to the rib cage.

With 51 seconds left in the round, Moorer countered a missed Stewart hook with two right hooks that sent the London native stumbling toward the ropes. Moorer swooped in and uncorked a fusillade of short, precise and powerful blows. A right uppercut ripped through the guard and sent Stewart tumbling to the canvas on all fours. Up at referee Chris Wolleson's count of four, Stewart sported a cut over his left eye.

As a light heavyweight, Moorer was regarded as an excellent finisher, and with 39 seconds remaining Stewart had some big work ahead if he wanted to get back to his corner. Stewart countered two missed jabs with a nifty lead right. Moorer connected with a left cross to the body and a right hook to the head, but Stewart's short lead right backed Moorer away momentarily. As an exciting first round neared its end, Moorer's perfect one-two forced Stewart to the ropes and a heavy left snapped Stewart's head back and splayed his upper body over the top rope before crumbling in the corner. As Wolleson counted, Stewart slowly regained his feet at seven and the round-ending bell temporarily spared Stewart further punishment.

Moorer resumed his attack in the second, staggering Stewart with a hard jab and backing him away further with a one-two. Stewart forced a clinch, and it was a testament to his conditioning that he quickly collected himself after absorbing Moorer's opening blows. Stewart jabbed to keep Moorer at range before clubbing him with an overhand right. Stewart zinged Moorer with a sharper right, but Moorer remained devastatingly accurate with his crisp jabs, virtually all of which landed. Stewart continued to concentrate on Moorer's body while "The Kronk Krusher" threw bouquets of laser-like combinations that showcased his edge in hand speed.

With one minute to go in a round he was losing big, Stewart followed two jabs with a scorching right to the bridge of the nose that drove a wobbly Moorer to the ropes. Moorer answered with a short left cross and the two big men traded wild, power-laden punches in a heated exchange that sent the Scope crowd into an uproar. Instead of clinching, Moorer fired back but after Stewart's bulk prevented him from escaping the ropes, Moorer reluctantly clamped down and forced a break.

As the second round ended, it was clear that both had earned the other's respect. It was also evident that Stewart was buzzed, for he walked toward the wrong corner. It was a strange scene as Stewart and Moorer walked together toward the same stool with Stewart a half step ahead of Moorer. The Brit was a couple of feet away from sitting on Moorer's stool before Emanuel Steward waved him away with his left hand and used his right to point toward the correct corner.

Moorer's breathtaking marksmanship continued in the third as his jabs sliced through Stewart's defense and a right uppercut pierced his guard. Stewart plowed ahead, digging both hands to the body and driving Moorer back time and again. Moorer was the busier fighter by far but Stewart's pressuring tactics began to test Moorer's strength, both physically and emotionally.

Following several seconds of milling along the ropes, Moorer sprung off behind a snapping right to the body and right uppercut to the jaw, after which Stewart hammered Moorer with a heavy right to the temple. By now, Stewart had adjusted to Moorer's power and was taking his blows much better. As Stewart leaned in and ripped rights to the head and body, the look of dejection he wore in the second turned into one of self-belief. He still fielded plenty of punches, but as the round progressed Moorer showed signs that his frenetic pace was taking a toll. Instead of creating punching angles with his legs, Moorer chose to languish on the ropes as Stewart whacked away for the remainder of the round.

As Moorer sat on the stool, Steward lightly tapped his fighter's face with his left hand to get his attention. "Stay off the ropes," he intoned. "Let's get back to the right jab this round. Very important: You've got to go back to the right hand." At this point, cut man Ralph Citro amplified Steward's remarks: "When he gets you to the ropes, tie him up and when the ref breaks you, stay off the ropes. You've got to use your jab. It's perfect, but you're not using it."

The CompuBox numbers for Moorer's jab proved Steward and Citro correct – his jab *was* nearly perfect. In the first round, Moorer landed 27 of 34 (79 percent) while 30 of his 36 second-round jabs hit the target (83 percent). But in the third, Moorer threw only nine jabs and landed three of them.

Meanwhile, Stewart's corner urged him to go to the body to hasten Moorer's demise. Stewart enjoyed his best statistical round in the third, landing 35 of his 76 attempts (46 percent), including 29 of 57 power shots (51 percent). Both men sought to apply their respective strategies in the fourth.

Moorer walked to ring center and promptly snapped two gorgeous jabs and countered a missed Stewart jab with a right hook. Stewart bulled Moorer to the ropes and worked him over before Moorer applied Citro's advice and induced a clinch. Back at ring center, Moorer connected with a sharp left cross and blood flowed from the bridge of Stewart's nose. Two jabs and a right backed Moorer to the ropes and a heavy, winging right to the jaw line snapped Moorer's head and stunned the Kronk disciple. As Stewart whaled away, he leaned too far forward and Moorer zipped in a short right uppercut that jerked Stewart's head and prompted a clinch.

At ring center, Moorer impaled Stewart with a jab and followed with a solid left to the belly while Stewart countered with jabs and a thudding right to the jaw. Moorer and Stewart gave the crowd – and HBO's audience – everything they could want in a heavyweight fight. But as with all good things, it was about to end.

With 1:22 left, Moorer dug in his toes and ripped a right uppercut that caused Stewart to pitch forward. A second right uppercut straightened Stewart and a follow-up left cross sent him tumbling forward to the canvas for the third time in the fight. Stewart slowly regained his feet, a dazed look on his face and a severe vertical cut over his right eye. Referee Wolleson took several seconds to look into Stewart's eyes and determined he was no longer fit to continue. With a look of disappointment and discouragement, Stewart offered no argument as he trudged toward his corner.

It was a statistical tour de force for Moorer as he landed 149 of his 267 punches for 56 percent accuracy. In round four, Moorer applied his corner's advice in landing eight of his 12 jabs. He launched 67 punches per round and connected on 37 of them, far outstripping the heavyweight averages of 46 and 18 respectively. Stewart threw nearly the same number of punches as Moorer with 264 but connected on 56 fewer for 35 percent accuracy.

When asked by Larry Merchant if he was surprised at the way Stewart came back after being hurt in the first round, Moorer said, "Yes I was. That shows the sign of a veteran and a good fighter. A lot of people doubted me because they think I'm a blown-up light heavyweight but I think we proved the point that I am a legitimate heavyweight. I took some good shots, he hurt me once and I exchanged some good blows with him."

Moorer said he wasn't hurt badly in the third and added "Emanuel was telling me to throw a right uppercut on the inside – a short punch – and that's what I did. I had to wait for the special moment to throw it." As he watched the replay of the knockout punch, he shouted, "Damn, I'm pleased!"

"This was a good fight for me," Moorer continued. "For instead of going short distance, it went four good, hard rounds and I appreciate it."

So did everyone else.

Epilogue: Stewart took seven months off before returning to the ring, stopping Joey Christjohn in three rounds in Katowice, Poland. Six weeks later, Stewart again assumed the stepping stone role against George Foreman. Stewart climbed off the canvas and proceeded to turn Foreman's face into a grotesquely swollen, bloody mask before dropping a 10-round majority decision.

Four more KO wins followed, earning Stewart a rematch with Holyfield. Though he dropped a comprehensive 12-round decision, Stewart acquitted himself honorably and continued to earn steady work. Stewart won his next seven before suffering a surprising eight-round TKO loss to Craig Peterson on the Foreman-Crawford Grimsley undercard. From then on, Stewart ran hot and cold, going 4-4 (2 KO), including three losses in his final four bouts. His last in-ring engagement was a two-round TKO defeat to Jorge Luis Gonzalez June 6, 1999 in Las Vegas. Stewart retired three weeks short of his 35th birthday with a 43-10 (40 KO) mark.

Four months after the Stewart victory, Moorer continued to climb the heavyweight ladder with a one-round KO over 67-fight veteran Bobby Crabtree. Moorer's knockout streak ended at 26 when 275-pound Mike "The Giant" White took him the full 10 rounds, but just barely. As the bell sounded to end the fight, Moorer scored a knockdown but no count was issued because the bell saved White.

Seven wins followed, including a classic brawl with "Smokin'" Bert Cooper, and on April 22, 1994 he stood across the ring from WBA/IBF champion Holyfield. Moorer arose from a second round knockdown to jab his way to a majority win and become the first southpaw fighter (if not the first natural lefty) to win the heavyweight title.

Moorer lost the title in his first defense to 45-year-old Foreman, who lost almost every second of every round before landing a thudding right to the point of the jaw that dumped Moorer for the full count. Two fights later Moorer became a two-time titleholder after capturing a split-decision over Axel Schulz in Dortmund, Germany June 22, 1996 for the vacant IBF belt. After notching two successful defenses against Frans Botha (KO 12) and Vaughn Bean (W 12), Moorer and Holyfield met for the second time for the WBA and IBF belts. Knocked down five times, Moorer proved his courage beyond doubt by rising five times before the fight was stopped in eight rounds. The Holyfield rematch was Moorer's last title fight.

Moorer retired for nearly three years after losing to Holyfield, but returned to stop trialhorse Lorenzo Boyd in four rounds. Following a second round TKO over Terrence Lewis, Moorer won a five-round technical decision over Dale Crowe after an accidental butt opened a fight-ending cut.

Moorer beat Terry Porter (KO 4) and Robert Davis (W 10) to earn an HBO date with David Tua August 17, 2002. In the shortest fight ever televised by HBO, Tua dusted Moorer in 30 seconds. But Moorer's career ended on a happier note as he won seven of his final eight fights, the most significant of which came against former cruiserweight champion Vassiliy Jirov December 9, 2004. Trailing badly on all three cards, Moorer summoned a final burst of his old power and stiffened Jirov in the ninth round. Moorer subsequently added victories over Cliff Couser (KO 1), Sedreck Fields (W 10), Rick Boruff (KO 1), Roderick Willis (KO 10) and Shelby Gross (KO 1). At 40, Moorer retired with a record of 52-4-1 (40 KO).

TALES FROM THE VAULT

Total Punches Landed/Thrown

Round	1	2	3	4	5	6	7	8	9	10	11	12	Total
Moorer	55/83	47/80	25/67	22/37									149/267
	66%	59%	37%	60%									56%
Stewart	13/76	22/73	35/76	23/39									93/264
	17%	30%	46%	59%									35%

Jabs Landed/Thrown

Round	1	2	3	4	5	6	7	8	9	10	11	12	Total
Moorer	27/34	30/36	3/9	8/12									68/91
	79%	83%	33%	67%									75%
Stewart	3/37	9/38	6/19	10/17									28/111
	8%	24%	32%	59%									25%

Power Punches Landed/Thrown

Round	1	2	3	4	5	6	7	8	9	10	11	12	Total
Moorer	28/49	17/44	22/58	14/25									81/176
	57%	39%	38%	56%									46%
Stewart	10/39	13/35	29/57	13/22									65/153
	26%	37%	51%	59%									42%

Michael Moorer vs. Alex Stewart July 27, 1991, Norfolk, Virginia

Pinklon Thomas vs. Mike Weaver
June 15, 1985, Las Vegas, Nevada

Throughout boxing history, the heavyweight division's hold on the masses has been based on perpetual possibility. The image of two huge athletes exchanging hammering blows is a sure-fire sell because of the world's fascination with raw power. Even in its down cycles, big-man boxing thrives due to a simple logical progression: The bigger the man, the bigger the punch and the bigger the punch, the more spectacular the results will be. For boxers and the men who promote them, the equation reads as follows: Power equals money, and money equals power.

But boxing is about much more than trading leather; it is a skill that requires years of discipline and hard work both in and out of the gym. Naturally gifted fighters who are humble enough to heed the advice of knowledgeable teachers have a much better chance to ascend to heights even they couldn't have imagined. Plus, they will be able to produce fights that give fans the best of both worlds – precision and punch.

The WBC heavyweight title bout between champion Pinklon Thomas and challenger Mike Weaver on June 15, 1985 at the Riviera Hotel and Casino in Las Vegas was one that provided fans an excellent exhibition of boxing fundamentals, shifting tides of fortune and – that rarest of birds – an explosive one-punch ending. Yet when great heavyweight title fights are discussed, Thomas-Weaver remains far in the background for a variety of reasons. But by the time the fight ended, those inside the casino and those who saw it live on HBO knew they had just witnessed an excellent scrap.

Ten months earlier Thomas, a converted southpaw, lifted the belt from Tim Witherspoon with a thudding, powerful jab that inspired comparisons to those owned by Sonny Liston and IBF champ Larry Holmes. In fact, the 27-year-old Thomas' performance against Witherspoon was so impressive that talk of a unification bout with Holmes was the subject of intense speculation and this bout with Weaver was to serve as a showcase to help pump up that contest. Though there were questions about the heft he carried in his fists, Thomas entered the bout with seven knockouts in his last 11 victories.

Weaver, a former WBA champ, was engaging in his fifth fight since losing the belt to Michael Dokes under politically-tainted circumstances in December 1982. Referee Joey Curtis' controversial 63-second stoppage prompted a rematch six months later, but Dokes kept the belt with a 15-round draw in a fight most observers thought Weaver deserved to win. Weaver returned to the winning track with knockouts over Stan Ward (KO 9) and Billy Joe Thomas (KO 7), but his most recent outing was a bizarre one-round disqualification victory over Tony Anthony.

Shortly after the bell sounded, Anthony ran across the ring and struck Weaver with a left hook to the back of the head. When Weaver couldn't continue, the fight was called off. Yes, it was a victory, but it wasn't the ideal way for him to arrive at a heavyweight championship fight. The 33-year-old was installed as a 2-to-1 underdog, based on his age and the fact that at 221¼ he was 10 ¾ pounds heavier than he was against Anthony. There was sentiment among seasoned observers, however, that Weaver was capable of inflicting serious damage with his superior single-shot clout.

Thomas began the fight circling and pumping out his vaunted jab while Weaver stalked and attempted to jab with the champion. Weaver was a notoriously slow starter and before the fight he said he would do his best to rev up his engine earlier. Though two inches shorter at 6-1, his 78½-inch reach was two inches longer and he took full advantage as he snapped in double jabs and forced Thomas to focus more on defense. By the end of the first minute Weaver's jabs had bloodied Thomas' mouth, but Weaver in turn had a slight abrasion around his left eye.

The fighters circled one another in tight arcs and fired stiff, heavy and purposeful jabs that often landed flush. Thomas tried a right after his jab and missed, but moments later Weaver followed his landed jab with a hard right that made Thomas back off. In another sequence, Thomas missed a left-right and a stronger right as Weaver pulled away, and Weaver answered with yet another double jab to the face.

The bomber had turned boxer, and he was more than holding his own. In fact, he was outdoing him as those punches that followed the jab landed with more authority. Weaver was carrying out a well conceived plan: Thomas' best weapon was his jab, and the best way to neutralize a great jabber is to jab at the same time because it throws off a fighter's rhythm and keeps him from stepping in with it. It was a strategy Ken Norton employed perfectly in his first fight with Muhammad Ali, and Norton's fellow Californian was looking to duplicate that success.

The younger champion soon got fed up with the situation and did something about it in most dramatic fashion. Thomas followed a solid left-right with a 13-punch explosion that left Weaver sprawled at Thomas' feet. Weaver arose at three and trudged toward the ropes with a disgusted, downcast expression. Once the action resumed, however, Weaver continued to execute as if nothing had happened as he connected with a hard double jab. At this, Thomas took his time, landing his own jab and following it with a chopping right that forced Weaver to the ropes. A left-left-right missed for Thomas but he was able to punctuate a successful round with a thudding jab to the face.

As Weaver walked slowly to his corner, he shook his hanging head. Yes, he enjoyed strategic success but the knockdown brought back bitter memories of other slow starts in heavyweight championship fights, one of which cost him the title against Dokes.

While disgusted with himself, he wisely limited his moping to the time spent in the corner.

Thomas started the second on his toes, whipping in jabs that had plenty of pop. Weaver ducked inside and connected with two thudding hooks to the body that brought a nod of acknowledgement. Moments later Weaver landed another hook to the ribs and drove in a right during the ensuing clinch.

All the ingredients were coming together for the challenger. Weaver worked the left well to both head and body; the jabs nullified Thomas' best weapon and the body punches slowed Thomas' legs to the point where he had to engage Weaver at close range. Unfortunately for Weaver, his progress would be impeded.

Midway through the round, an open-handed flicking jab accidentally caught Weaver's left eye and he backed toward the ropes wincing and complaining to referee Carlos Padilla. Since they were wearing thumb-attached gloves, thumbing shouldn't have been possible but since the webbing was halfway up the thumb and not all the way up on the glove, Weaver paid the price. Thomas took full advantage as he ripped an uppercut as Weaver wiped at his eye, and later threw a four-punch burst capped off by a slapping hook to the jaw. Weaver landed a hook to the ribs and two more to the jaw but Thomas came back with his own three-punch salvo. Near the end of the round, another flicking jab by Thomas landed cleanly and prompted Padilla to tell Thomas to close his glove.

Weaver appeared recovered from the thumbing and proved it by jolting Thomas' head back with a jab. Thomas moved side to side behind harder jabs, but Weaver slowed him down enough to induce a clinch and land a hook to the ribs. After separating, Weaver tagged Thomas with a one-two and a glancing right.

By the second minute, Thomas was off his bicycle and trading hard quick blows with Weaver at close range. Back and forth they went: A Weaver hook brought back a solid Thomas right. A double jab by Weaver was followed by a left-left-right by Thomas. The champion was getting off quicker with more variety but he was still tagged regularly by Weaver, especially with jabs. An already fast-paced heavyweight fight was about to get even faster.

Two cuffing hooks by Thomas followed by a harder third one sparked a fierce toe-to-toe exchange at point-blank range. As Thomas fired away, Weaver connected with three strong rights that rocked the champion. At this, Thomas shoved Weaver a full five feet away, drawing a warning from Padilla, boos from the crowd and several precious seconds of recovery time for the challenger. Not that it did much good for Thomas; Weaver landed a long glancing right, then moved inside and ripped a hook and a chopping right that stunned Thomas with 10 seconds remaining in the round. A looping hook slammed Thomas' jaw, but Thomas fired back just enough to fall into a clinch and ride out the final seconds. Still, Thomas emerged from that clinch with a cut at the corner of his left eye.

It was a terrific bounce-back round for Weaver, and trainer Don Manuel sought to keep the momentum going.

"Don't back up; lay your head on his chest and drive them shots to the body," he growled. "After that, come up with short left hooks and right hands through the middle." Meanwhile, another drama was taking place outside the ring: Weaver's mother was involved in a scuffle with someone in the crowd.

The result of that skirmish was unknown, but her son began the fourth strongly by knocking Thomas back with a double jab and a right cross-left hook combo moments later. The crowd's focus instantly shifted to the action in the ring, and they quickly got behind the underdog by chanting "Weaver! Weaver!"

Thomas made for an inviting target as he stood at long range with his left arm dangling by his hip, but for whatever reason Weaver didn't press his attack. By mid-round Thomas was back to jabbing effectively and the cut around his eye was no longer an issue. As both men sought to regroup, the fight became an intense jabbing contest, a situation that normally favored Thomas. As it turned out, Weaver's double jabs were just as quick and powerful as Thomas', and he more than held his own.

While Weaver enjoyed a good round four, his trainer wasn't satisfied. He knew that a challenger had to engage the champion to score points with the judges and force the titleholder to fight outside his comfort zone.

"You've got to keep taking it to him," Manuel said. "You jab, jab, you hurt him and then you back off. That gives him the initiative, you understand? Stay with this guy. Keep jabbing, but two jabs all the time. And you've got a body, keep hitting that body."

In the other corner, Angelo Dundee was hardly happy with what his man was doing either.

"If nothing else, tie up the left hook in close, OK?" he said. "C'mon now, you're fighting a bad, bad fight, son. Now pick it up; step up to him. Go to work. Let's go to work!"

At this, HBO's analyst Larry Merchant chuckled, "looks like they're working pretty hard to me." And he was right; Thomas-Weaver was fought at a demanding pace, especially for heavyweights who tended to fight within comfortable envelopes. Each forced the other to engage every second of the round, and any questions concerning Weaver's weight gain were long discarded. This was not the usual plodding, elephantine heavyweight fight; it was an athletic contest that demanded speed, skill, intelligence and conditioning, and both men were up to the task.

The fifth saw Thomas dancing and jabbing, but Weaver still knocked him back with a double jab and a hook, after which Thomas connected with a jolting jab. Thomas sneaked in a hook during a follow-up flurry and smartly worked his jab to the head and body, but Weaver soon piled in behind a right to the body that set up a solid hook-uppercut combination. Thomas quickly shook off the punches and drilled a right to the jaw. At ring center they continued their jabbing contest, with Weaver landed a double jab while Thomas followed with four of his own. For a period, Weaver looked to be tiring, but in the final 10 seconds he rocked Thomas with a hook to the body and a pair of jab-hook-cross combinations.

In a division best known for spectacular displays of power, Thomas and Weaver were proving that ring science can also be a spectacle. Both men were dishing out and taking punishment in equal portions, but they were doing so in a thoughtful way. Every offensive burst was set up by the jab and each punch that followed had a specific target and underlying purpose. The sixth round saw the pace slow, but by only a little, as they unleashed a steady stream of textbook jabs that snapped the other man's head back. Weaver again finished strongly as he followed a jab with a hook to the jaw to perhaps steal a close round.

The champion knew the flow of the fight was going against him, and worse yet his opponent was using his own tactics against him. A change needed to be made if he wanted to keep his championship, and early in the seventh round he produced a potential solution.

Weaver began the round by landing a hard jab, but Thomas answered by feinting a jab with his left shoulder and driving home a lead right to the jaw. Two more right leads nailed Weaver and a third caused Weaver's legs to buckle slightly. Weaver slipped in his own right, but Thomas avoided two jabs, pulled away from a hook and connected with a one-two. An exchange of jabs ended when Thomas cracked in another right.

Thomas was now moving Weaver back consistently and doing more with his hands. With Weaver on the retreat, Thomas' jab connected with more strength and his aggression projected confidence to the judges. Thomas punctuated his comeback in the final 20 seconds by landing a left-right-hook combo, a second hook to the head, a pair of jabs to the stomach, a left-right uppercut salvo and a final jab to the face.

Encouraged by his rally, Thomas started round eight moving better than he had at any point in the fight and firing jabs at the stalking Weaver, who now took deeper breaths. The challenger's double jab connected, but they didn't disturb Thomas, who sneaked in a right uppercut before Weaver landed a hook and clinched. When they separated, they again fell into the intense jabbing contest of previous rounds with both men working lefts to the head and body.

Midway through the round, however, the crisp boxing match would instantly revert back to more typical heavyweight fare.

The attribute that separates heavyweight boxing from all other divisions reappeared with dramatic effect. Thomas stuck out a probing jab, after which he stepped in and delivered a crushing right to the forehead. Weaver's body went limp and fell heavily back first to the floor. At three Weaver rolled onto his left elbow and listened to Padilla's count. At eight he tried to rise but at nine he fell backward, forcing Padilla to count him out at 1:42 of round eight.

Just like that, it was over. In a match filled with ring intelligence and finely honed skills, the heavyweight division's indelible trademark ended up determining its winner. It was a fitting end to a fight that had everything, and both winner and loser were elevated in the process. Thomas proved himself a champion – and a star – on the rise and it was the kind of performance that could do nothing but help with his pursuit of a unification fight with Holmes. Conversely, Weaver did nothing to diminish his standing as a world-class competitor. Yes, he was defeated by a one-punch knockout, but the judges' scorecards revealed that he was in the fight right up to the final moment. Herb Santos and Dick Cole saw the fight 66-66 while Dave Moretti had Thomas leading by just 67-66.

In the end, however, it was the power of a single punch that had the final say.

Epilogue: As impressive as Thomas' knockout of Weaver was, that's how unimpressive he looked against Trevor Berbick just nine months later. The charged-up Berbick out-hustled a listless Thomas and captured a narrow but proper unanimous decision. Thomas rebuilt his standing with three knockout wins, earning a crack at WBA/WBC champ Mike Tyson. Tyson stopped Thomas with a ferocious combination highlighted by three flush, scorching hooks to the jaw that not only left the former heavyweight champion flat on the canvas, but out of the heavyweight title picture as he never again fought for a belt.

Now a name steppingstone, Thomas lost four of his next five fights to Evander Holyfield (KO by 7), Mike Hunter (L 10), Riddick Bowe (KO by 9) and Tommy Morrison (KO by 1). Thomas looked all but finished after the Morrison defeat, but starting in May 1992 the resilient Thomas picked himself up and began a whirlwind tour that saw him win 13 consecutive times in the next six months, including five times in a 36-day span. That streak ended with a split decision victory over Craig Payne to capture a fringe belt.

Just one month short of his 35th birthday, Thomas fought Lawrence Carter for another minor title on January 29, 1993 in Columbia, South Carolina, but Carter's seventh round TKO convinced the former champion to hang up his gloves for good. His final record stands at 43-7-1 with 34 KO.

As for Weaver, he took an eight-month hiatus before returning against Carl "The Truth" Williams, who was fresh off his stirring challenge for Larry Holmes' IBF title. A heavy underdog, Weaver scored a shocking second round TKO that resurrected his status as a viable heavyweight contender. But just as he blitzed Williams, James "Bonecrusher" Smith blitzed him in one round less than two months later.

Over the next several years, Weaver's fights would be impossible to predict. Donovan "Razor" Ruddock defeated Weaver on split decision four months after losing to Smith, but after disposing of Dave Jaco (KO 2), he upset unbeaten prospects James Pritchard (KO 6) and Johnny DuPlooy (KO 7). Weaver lost the return to DuPlooy (KO by 2), but three more victories earned him a rematch with the Bonecrusher on a pay-per-view show at Madison Square Garden. The 38-year-old Weaver was again shackled by lethargy as Smith won a wide decision.

Even into his 40s, Weaver was a risky proposition for all but the best. Weaver lost only once in his next eight fights from July 1990 to March 1996, and that was a sixth round TKO to future champion Lennox Lewis in July 1991. Father Time eventually wore down Weaver and he lost his final two fights. His last ring effort saw the 49-year-old Weaver lose a 10 round decision to 51-year-old Larry Holmes on November 17, 2000 in Biloxi, Miss. He retired with a record of 41-18-1 with 28 KO.

TALES FROM THE VAULT

Total Punches Landed/Thrown

Round	1	2	3	4	5	6	7	8	9	10	11	12	Total
Thomas													202/419
													48%
Weaver													159/342
													46%

Jabs Landed/Thrown

Round	1	2	3	4	5	6	7	8	9	10	11	12	Total
Thomas													146/308
													47%
Weaver													103/227
													45%

Power Punches Landed/Thrown

Round	1	2	3	4	5	6	7	8	9	10	11	12	Total
Thomas													56/111
													50%
Weaver													56/115
													49%

* Fight originally done by CompuBox, but the original HTML files with complete round-by-round statistics no longer exist.

Pinklon Thomas vs. Mike Weaver June 15, 1985, Las Vegas, Nevada

Darroll Wilson vs. Shannon Briggs
March 15, 1996, Atlantic City, New Jersey

Self-belief is one of mankind's most formidable weapons. It can prove to be the crucial ingredient one needs to push himself past challenges that others see as too daunting and not worth pursuing.

This is especially true when that person has yet to be beaten in his chosen endeavor. A lawyer who has never lost a murder case possesses an unwavering and justified confidence that he will do whatever is necessary to maintain his aura of invincibility. That feeling often extends to his opponents, who are burdened by the responsibility of blazing a new trail, of conquering the unconquered, of defeating one who has never been defeated. In a way, that is an even more difficult feat than establishing and maintaining perfection.

In sports – and particularly in boxing – the ultimate status symbol is having the number "zero" occupy one's loss column. It proves beyond doubt that no one has ever gotten the best of you in hand-to-hand combat, and the resulting air of superiority has impact on other aspects of life. It affects how others perceive you, and if the victory string is long enough it will determine how many zeroes will be written on your paychecks. For a number that represents the concept of nothingness, it can be immensely powerful.

A well-worn boxing truism states that an undefeated fighter is tough to beat because he doesn't know what it is like to lose. But what happens when two fighters with perfect records collide? That was the question that confronted Darroll Wilson and Shannon Briggs when they met on March 15, 1996 at the Atlantic City Convention Center in Atlantic City, N.J. as part of HBO's "Night of the Young Heavyweights" telecast.

Wilson and Briggs were part of a show that pitted rising stars David Tua and John Ruiz as well as Andrew Golota and Dannell Nicholson. The undercard also featured Courage Tshabalala and Michael Grant in separate fights, and the intent of this card was to separate the wheat from the chaff in terms of who would eventually challenge Mike Tyson, Evander Holyfield and Lennox Lewis for supremacy a few years down the road.

Of all the fighters on the televised portion of the show, Wilson, a former supermarket security guard, was by far the least celebrated. Born and raised in Danville, Va., Wilson was a onetime high school baseball and football star who turned to boxing at a relatively late age. A well muscled 6-footer, the 215-pound Wilson was a converted southpaw with a powerful jab and hook, and he rode those weapons to a 15-0-2 (10 KO) record after turning pro in May 1993. The two draws came against Levon

Warner in his fifth pro fight and against fellow unbeaten Terry McGroom in August 1995, but going into this high-profile bout against Briggs he projected the unshakable confidence of a man who had never been officially bested as a pro. He declared before the bout that Briggs couldn't beat him on his worst day – Wilson's worst day, that is.

For the most part Wilson's boasts fell on deaf ears because Briggs' fame was the equal of Wilson's anonymity. Briggs possessed all the ingredients for success, not only in the athletic arena but also in venues far beyond it.

At 6-4 and 227 sculpted pounds, Briggs owned excellent hand speed that produced devastatingly effective combinations and one-punch knockout power in both fists. Like Wilson, Briggs was a late bloomer, as he didn't take up the sport until age 18. In a two-year amateur career, Briggs was a finalist at the 1991 Pan American games and in 1992 was the United States amateur champion. Though he was regarded as a top prospect for the Barcelona Olympics, Briggs decided to turn pro in July 1992 with a first round knockout of John Basil Jackson. In the four years since, Briggs sailed to a sparkling 25-0 (20 KO) record, registering 15 first round knockouts along the way.

Besides the obvious athletic talent, Briggs had the look and air of a future great. The first element was geographical – he was born in the Brownsville section of Brooklyn, an area that produced three previous heavyweight champions in Floyd Patterson, Mike Tyson and Riddick Bowe – and being a native of the media capital of the world did wonders in terms of raising his profile. Two other favorable elements were his unique hairstyle – orange dreadlocks – and his media-friendly personality. Additionally, Briggs was under the tutelage of Teddy Atlas, who had already guided Michael Moorer to a heavyweight championship.

With his fame also came critics. Many observers questioned his level of competition, and their feelings were backed up by the fact that of the six fighters featured on the card, Briggs' opposition in his last five fights was the weakest in terms of winning percentage (68-43-2, 60 percent). Seventeen of his 25 foes had losing records, and while Briggs shined against them they still wondered what would happen when he made the inevitable step up. Though Wilson was a decided underdog, he still represented the biggest test of Briggs' career.

Also, rumors about Briggs' shaky chin were running rampant around the New York gyms. According to the whispers Briggs had been dropped twice in sparring sessions, including once by Lou Savarese, another unbeaten heavyweight prospect. That aside, a confident-looking but focused Briggs entered the ring at Bally's Park Place a prohibitive favorite. One reason for that was because the man called "Doin' Damage" hadn't been doing damage lately as his last five fights had gone the distance while Briggs was fresh off three consecutive one-round blowouts.

As the fight began, Briggs immediately went to work as he missed with a left-right over the top but clanged a hard hook off the side of Wilson's head. Wilson sneaked in a hard jab in the midst of Briggs' follow-up flurry, which had the look of a blender set on "obliterate." Three big hooks and an overhand right caught the crouching Wilson, who remained composed throughout Briggs' opening storm as he occasionally whipped in body shots and cuffing blows to the head.

A seven-punch salvo highlighted by a hook staggered Wilson and a lightning-quick one-two deepened Wilson's distress. Wilson propped himself against the ropes and did his best to bob and weave away from the artillery instead of clinching. Briggs' opening assault petered out after 45 seconds and Wilson finally had a chance to regain his bearings. Briggs missed with a roundhouse hook over Wilson's head that threw off him balance, allowing Wilson to escape to ring center.

The fight instantaneously slowed to a tactical pace with both men studying the other at long range. Briggs missed a jab-cross combo but blasted a hook to the ribs. Wilson bided his time as he inched back and threw an occasional jab, but the most important development for him was that he was clear-eyed and competing. As the round neared its final minute the two exchanged punches at short range, with Wilson connecting with jab and a hard right-left that snapped Briggs' head and moved him backward for the first time in the fight. Briggs grinned at Wilson and snapped in a pair of jabs and a left hook to the ear. Two more shotgun jabs found Wilson's face, and moments later Briggs won an exchange of jabs. But as the round closed, Wilson caught Briggs' attention by snapping in a left hook-right cross combo, three jabs, an overhand right, a left hook and a final overhand right to the jaw. Briggs' answered with a short jolting hook to the chin as the bell rang, but a wobbled Wilson showed his defiance by yelling at Briggs before he turned to go to his corner.

The ever-observant Atlas noticed something was wrong with Briggs during the round, but the problem wasn't just physical but also emotional. He sensed that his charge had lost his confidence because his opening assault didn't produce its usual early stoppage.

"Relax," Atlas said. "Do not allow yourself to panic. Do not allow yourself to doubt yourself. This is no different than when a guy tries to make a run at the gym. There's no difference. You understand?"

"Gotcha," Briggs replied.

Despite losing the round, Wilson had to feel good about the way he handled himself. He withstood the charge and fired back, showing Briggs he wasn't going to be just another record-padding patsy.

The second round began slowly with Wilson moving nimbly in both directions and Briggs cautiously stalking. By the second minute the battle moved inside and they began to let their hands go as Wilson connected with a short right to the ribs and three soft hooks to the jaw while Briggs replied with a thumping hook to the body. Wilson won an exchange of jabs and popped Briggs' head back with another shotgun jab. As

Wilson fired a one-two, one could sense his confidence growing by the second – and the perceived talent gap between the two shrinking. Briggs was no longer the hurricane that was bent on destruction; now he stood straight up in front of Wilson, moving neither his feet nor his hands in any significant way. When he did, Wilson was there with his answer.

Wilson ducked under a right hand and made Briggs pay with a hefty hook to the ribs. Briggs jabbed twice, and the second jab knocked Wilson back several feet. Briggs rushed in behind a right to the body, but Wilson immediately nailed Briggs with a left hook to the chest and a right to the jaw before moving inside. While there, Wilson pumped in a hook-uppercut-hook-cross combo and Briggs retaliated with a hook that spun Wilson's head. Wilson's left uppercut landed cleanly, and Briggs' answering hook glanced off Wilson's shoulder. The round ended with the pair trading jabs.

Though Briggs managed to land several good punches, there was a growing sense that Wilson had seized a semblance of control. He had not only survived Briggs' patented first-round bull rush – something few fighters had done to this point – but he showed he was capable of offering stiff resistance. This round heralded the start of an important moment in Briggs' development as a fighter because Wilson was in the process of asking Briggs a crucial question – what will happen when an opponent takes your best and doesn't go away? To this point, Wilson's status as an unbeaten fighter gave him the mental strength he needed to weather the initial storm and Atlas knew that it was Briggs' turn to come up with the proper reply.

"Pull yourself together and be a pro," Atlas said. "I know what talent you have. I know what size you have. I know what strength you have. Act like a g*****n pro. Do you understand what I mean by that? This is what I want: His greatest defense is to get you to think that you've got to throw one and to get you to think that he's doing more than he's doing. He's just steady, that's all he is. Use your jab, don't look for one punch and when you miss a right hand, come back with a hook to the body. And no posing…no posing."

Briggs began the third round standing erect and poking out a jab, but Wilson replied with a double jab. Another Briggs jab brought back a triple jab from Wilson. He was determined to outdo Briggs in every department, for that was his way of imposing his will.

Wilson slipped a jab and connected with a glancing left uppercut to the chin. Wilson jabbed the body but Briggs answered with a jab and a hard right to the ear – then he stood back and admired his work. That was what Atlas meant by "posing." Wilson took advantage by moving inside and initiating exchanges at close range. A right, two hooks and a right-left crashed off Briggs' jaw, prompting the taller man to return to the outside and twice shaking his head as if to clear cobwebs from his head. That told

Wilson that all was not right, so Wilson dove back inside and rattled off a series of short crisp blows to the head and body that opened a cut above Briggs' right eye.

The area where the cut had opened up had tiny bruising as early as round one, but Wilson's peppering punches had now inflicted visible damage. The sight of crimson trickling down Briggs' cheek further energized Wilson as the round entered its final minute. As Briggs languished on the ropes, he poked out a weak lead right that provided a split-second opening that Wilson instantly seized upon. Behind a range-finding jab, Wilson unleashed a huge right and a monstrous left hook that landed flush on Briggs' jaw and the big man fell heavily on his right side.

The crowd roared its surprise as Briggs rolled onto his back and stared blankly at the ceiling. At six, referee Tony Orlando looked down at Briggs and waved his arms, completing an upset as massive as the punches that felled the favorite.

The flush of success flowed freely through Wilson's body as he wildly celebrated his triumph. He twice fell to the floor in wonder and he climbed the ropes, proudly pounding his chest. As the scene unfolded, everyone inside the arena and those watching on HBO was forced to quickly reshuffle the pecking order of perceptions. Briggs had entered the ring as a celebrated prospect while Wilson was cast as his foil. But because, as Larry Merchant said, "undefeated fighters are hard to defeat," the foil had foiled everything.

Wilson-Briggs was just another example of another sports truism: Legends die hard, but those who think they are die harder.

Epilogue: Wilson followed up his gigantic victory over Briggs four months later with a 10-round decision over trial horse Rick Sullivan, after which he was matched with Tua on another HBO "young heavyweights" card September 20, 1996. Wilson's shield of invincibility fell victim to Tua's lethal hook in the first round but Wilson revived his career two months later when he overcame two first-round knockdowns to polish off Tshabalala in four rounds. A two-round KO of journeyman James Pritchard followed, but Wilson suffered an upset in his next bout when Terrence Lewis stopped him in the fifth. From that point forward, Wilson was stamped as a gatekeeper who still owned dangerous power.

After stopping Anthony Willis in five, Wilson dropped the durable David Izon in the first before being stopped himself in the fourth. Wilson went on to lose to Zuri Lawrence (L 10), Tim Witherspoon (KO by 2), Jean Francois Bergeron (L 10), Ray Mercer (L 10) and Oliver McCall (KO by 4) with his only notable victory being a fourth round TKO over a faded Bert Cooper in September 2002. Wilson's last recorded fight took place on December 2, 2006 in St. Charles, Mo., when the 40-year-old was stopped in seven by Sedrick Fields. Wilson's final record stands at 27-10-2 (21 KO).

Briggs got back on the winning track six months later with a first-round blowout of Tim Ray. Three knockouts later, Briggs won recognition as the linear heavyweight champion by capturing a highly controversial majority decision over George Foreman on November 22, 1997. In his next outing against WBC titlist Lennox Lewis four months later, Briggs showed plenty of courage in suffering three resounding knockdowns and a fifth-round TKO loss.

From there, Briggs mixed in plenty of early knockout victories with uneven performances and upset losses. A one-round TKO of Marcus Rhode was followed by a 10-round draw with Francois Botha and a shocking eight-round decision loss to Sedreck Fields two fights later. Four KO wins was followed by a 10-round loss to Jameel McCline in April 2002.

Over the next four years, Briggs slowly rebuilt his career by winning 11 consecutive fights, all by knockout and eight within three rounds or less. That streak got him a shot at newly crowned WBO king Sergei Lyakhovich on November 4, 2006 in Phoenix, Ariz. The solidly built 268-pound Briggs was trailing on all three scorecards entering the final round when he benefited from one of the strangest endings in heavyweight championship history. With less than a minute remaining Briggs stunned Liakhovich with a series of rights that culminated with a knockdown. Up at five, the champion looked out on his feet when the fight resumed, and Briggs hammered him through the ropes and onto the scorer's table with five more clubbing rights. Liakhovich tried to get back into the ring, but referee Bobby Ferrara waved off the contest with one second remaining in the fight.

Briggs first defense came seven months later against the undefeated Sultan Ibragimov, but because the 273-pound champion only fought in infrequent spurts, he lost a unanimous decision.

Briggs returned to the ring following a two-and-a-half year hiatus with a one-round knockout over Marcus McGee and as of December 2009 the 38-year-old Briggs' record stands at 49-5-1 (43 KO).

Total Punches Landed/Thrown

Round	1	2	3	4	5	6	7	8	9	10	11	12	Total
Wilson													53/109
													49%
Briggs													33/96
													34%

Jabs Landed/Thrown

Round	1	2	3	4	5	6	7	8	9	10	11	12	Total
Wilson													22/41
													54%
Briggs													12/40
													30%

Power Punches Landed/Thrown

Round	1	2	3	4	5	6	7	8	9	10	11	12	Total
Wilson													31/68
													46%
Briggs													21/56
													38%

* Fight originally done by CompuBox, but the original HTML files with complete round-by-round statistics no longer exist.

Darroll Wilson vs. Shannon Briggs March 15, 1996, Atlantic City, New Jersey

TALES FROM THE VAULT

Tommy Morrison vs. Carl Williams
January 16, 1993, Reno, Nevada

Adversity is, by design, a difficult taskmaster. It never gives its target any warning of its arrival and it demands an instinctive and immediate response. Because of this phenomenon, adversity exposes the contents of a person's spirit at that particular juncture – will he confront it head on or will he shrink before its challenge?

Once the test is taken, there is much time for contemplation; to reflect on what happened and, if one fails, how to better address it in the future. The beauty of adversity – if one can call it beauty – is that it will return to administer another exam and provide a future opportunity to conquer it.

Tommy Morrison and Carl Williams had encountered their share of adversity and both had experienced success and failure. For Morrison, the first big test of his mettle came against WBO heavyweight champion Ray Mercer October 18, 1991. "The Duke" swept the first three rounds but a combination of energy expended and situational stresss sapped his strength prematurely. In the fifth, Mercer pummeled Morrison into semi-consciousness with a frightening barrage of power punches. His championship dreams were halted temporarily but his undefeated record was gone permanently, and Morrison was forced to reassess his professional standing.

Five fights and eight months later against Joe Hipp, Morrison endured one of the most severe physical and emotional tests imaginable when he overcame a broken jaw and a fractured right hand to score two knockdowns and register a ninth round KO victory. Morrison took six months off to heal his wounds and prove himself fully recovered as he iced Marshall Tillman in one round. At 24, Morrison (34-1, 30 KO) was ready to make another run at a championship fight and his next assignment was against Carl "The Truth" Williams at the Reno Sparks Convention Center in Reno, Nevada. Morrison-Williams was the main support to George Foreman-Pierre Coetzer, with the winners scheduled to meet for the vacant WBO title.

Like Coetzer, the 33-year-old Williams was supposed to serve as cannon fodder for his more marketable opponent. But at his best, Williams was quite formidable. At 6-4 with a seemingly endless 85-inch reach, his boxing skills were such that his friends deemed him "The Truth." Williams vaulted into the spotlight eight years before when he fought IBF heavyweight champion Larry Holmes before the last nationwide audience to witness a heavyweight title fight on free, over-the-air network TV in 1985. Williams built an early lead behind his long, snapping jab and the 25-year-old's skills reminded many of Holmes in his youth. But the 35-year-old remnants of Holmes' greatness rose up in the middle and late rounds to produce a narrow, hard-fought 15 round decision. The results of his first trip through championship fire were mixed he lost the fight on the scorecards, but won respect and credibility as a potential champion capable of producing greatness.

But that was not to be. He was flattened in two rounds by Mike Weaver and six fights later he was controversially stopped by Mike Tyson in just 93 seconds. A dispirited Williams, who at his best weighed between 215 and 225, began fighting in the mid-230s and as a result his performances suffered. He was 236 when he lost a 12-round split decision to Tim Witherspoon and 236½ when he reached his nadir, a 10-round decision loss to Jerry Jones.

Williams could have given up his quest for a title at this point. He was now in his 30s and his physical zenith had come and gone. This adversity was of a more permanent nature, but he felt there was time to make one more big push. Williams entered the Morrison fight off two wins, a 10-round decision over Ossie Ocasio and a three-round KO over Jerry Lee Smith, and he was a fit 226 for both of them. For Morrison, Williams (26-5, 20 KO) trained for 10 weeks and whipped himself into terrific shape at 225 while Morrison, who set up camp at Fort Huachuca, Arizona, was a rock-hard 228.

Williams and Morrison were gifted offensive machines. Williams' hand and foot speed combined with a stinging and accurate left jab made him a most formidable foe while Morrison, despite his thick muscle-man's physique, possessed extraordinary speed and snap as well as one of the most lethal left hooks the sport had ever seen. But they also harbored significant flaws – for Morrison it was stamina and maintaining composure while Williams' were a fragile chin and tendency to leave his right hand too low while punching. Because Williams' weaknesses played right into the younger and fresher Morrison's strengths, "The Duke" was thought to be a prohibitive favorite.

The stakes were high and both fighters' demeanors indicated they knew it. Williams said before the fight that this was his last chance to achieve credibility and the same could be said for Morrison, who was so eager to get the fight started that he touched gloves with Williams and walked to his corner midway through referee Mills Lane's final instructions.

Williams opened with fight by snapping the jab while moving in small circles around Morrison, who bulled Williams to the ropes behind a hard right. Williams immediately grabbed Morrison and "The Duke" hit Williams on the break with a right hand, prompting a warning from Lane.

At ring center, Williams threw a soft four-punch flurry that culminated with a sidearm right to the head. That right produced just enough of an opening for Morrison to come over the top with a hook to the temple that sent Williams crashing to the canvas just 46 seconds after the opening bell. It wasn't his best hook, but it was more than enough to get the job done.

Up at two, Williams shook his head in embarrassment and self-chastisement. He had been here many times before and he knew what to do to whether the storm.

Conversely, Morrison had been here many times as well and his 15 previous first-round knockouts proved he knew how to close the show. Morrison drove a hard right to the body but Williams answered with a snappy jab and a strong right uppercut before clinching. Williams fired hooks to the head and body but Morrison made Williams shudder with a counter hook. A high-contact first round ended with Williams nailing Morrison with a right cross and "The Duke" ringing Williams' bell with a right uppercut to the jaw and an overhand right to the ear. Williams wavered but he remained upright, a small victory in itself.

Williams began the second with a hard jab and a harder right uppercut to the body as Morrison stalked. Williams needed to establish respect after his rocky start and he chose to do so by coupling his jabs with a variety of hooks, crosses and uppercuts. When he wasn't punching, Williams was clinching, and he was doing so for two reasons. First, Williams needed to kill the clock and get a tired Morrison into the later rounds; and second, to prevent Morrison from getting the room he needed to crank full-leverage hooks. His head clearing, Williams turned up the pressure by landing two hooks and a one-two before ducking under a winging hook. With 37 seconds remaining, they landed simultaneous hooks that forced both to wobble back a step. Because Williams stayed upright, he felt he had achieved a moral victory, so he smiled at Morrison as if to say *"See? I can take your best shot. And mine's not bad either, isn't it?"*

The third began the same way the second did, with Williams moving and Morrison walking him down – and doing little else. Morrison was caught in a strategic trap: If he fought naturally, he could burn out and leave himself vulnerable to another mid-rounds collapse. But if he laid back too much, he could find himself in a deep points hole against a man smart enough to clinch away the final couple of rounds on his way to a points win. Morrison's answer was simple: Keep the punch rate down to preserve strength but also make sure whatever blows land get big results.

Twenty-five seconds into the round, he got big results.

As Williams stepped in with a jab, Morrison triggered a short shotgun jab to the button that floored Williams heavily for the second time in the fight. Arising slowly at six, Williams was ripe for the taking and Morrison rushed in to finish the job. A right uppercut forced Williams to the ropes but "The Truth" snapped off a one-two before grabbing Morrison's arms. A big overhand right caromed off Williams' head, but Williams shook his head dismissively.

The weeks of hard work were paying dividends for Williams as he quickly regained strength and resumed his diversified attack. As if there were any doubts, this was the "good" version of Carl "The Truth" Williams, the one that inspired so many experts to declare him Holmes' logical successor. Meanwhile, though Morrison still appeared dangerous and strong, the first signs of weariness were surfacing as he fought with his mouth open. This wasn't lost on Williams' trainer John Davenport between rounds.

"He's wearing down, baby, he's wearing down," Davenport said. "You can hit him, you see that right? He's just a big wide-body. You can hit him, he's one-dimensional and he's got only the left hook. Stay out in the center of the ring. It's still early and you're getting there."

Williams was on target with the jab in the fourth while Morrison continued to wait. "The Truth" had found a good boxing rhythm as he moved in and out while firing occasional three- and four-punch bursts. He nailed Morrison with a right uppercut as "The Duke" ducked and he even kept his right hand high to block Morrison's infrequent hooks. One hook, however, nearly knocked out Williams' mouthpiece but Williams showed his bravado by talking to Morrison. He was enjoying his best round of the fight so far, but it would get even better in the fifth.

With 1:50 to go, Williams leaped in with a hook to the ear, took a half step back to reset his feet and fired a sharp right to the jaw that drove Morrison to his knees. "The Duke" calmly rested on one knee before rising at nine but the opportunistic Williams unleashed a wicked right uppercut to the jaw that rocked Morrison to his core. Desperate to stay upright, Morrison tried to grab Williams' waist but instead he crumbled at his feet. This time, Morrison was in deep trouble and thoughts of another Mercer-type debacle swirled through many heads. After all, Mercer also stopped Morrison in the fifth and "The Duke" was just one knockdown away from having his professional nightmare play out a second time. The crowd's higher-pitched roars indicated they sensed a mighty upset was brewing and it almost came true as a right to the ear made Morrison totter a step forward.

Williams landed a heavy hook-right combo but Morrison answered with his own hook to stop Williams' rally. With 12 seconds left, a thunderous Morrison hook stopped Williams in his tracks. Thinking that Lane was about to break the ensuing clinch, Williams relaxed and Morrison took advantage by nailing Williams with another powerful hook.

When Morrison threw, he landed well but he was woefully inactive as he threw only 35 punches in the previous two rounds combined. Morrison, painfully aware of his stamina problems, was overcompensating and as a result Williams had seized control of the fight. The pace slowed noticeably in the sixth as Williams continued to bounce punches off Morrison's head and body while Morrison's power-laden punches whizzed dangerously past Williams' chin.

With 30 seconds to go, Morrison stunned Williams with a lead right to the jaw and a second right landed after Williams again relaxed his guard in anticipation of a break in the action that never came. Williams smartly grabbed on and smothered away the rest of a round that saw Morrison throw only 25 punches.

Urged by his corner to pick up the pace, Morrison began the seventh throwing hard jabs that set up a right to the body and a hook to the jaw. Williams intelligently employed a jab-and-grab offense that kept Morrison from finding his rhythm. Coming out of a clinch with 45 seconds remaining, Williams hurt Morrison with a right uppercut-left hook-right cross combo that caused "The Duke's" upper body to pitch forward. A big right crashed off Morrison's chin and a follow up hook and jab spun his head. Morrison regained his composure quickly and snapped two heavy jabs off Williams' face but "The Truth" ran out the round with his longer, more fluid jabs.

After a very rocky start, Williams found himself in a perfect situation. He had survived Morrison's early barrage and made it a close fight on the scorecards. Morrison had only been past six rounds once while Williams had 13 such fights. He had proven he could hurt Morrison and put him on the canvas, plus the younger man was intentionally inhibiting his offense, causing the fight to slow to a pace beneficial to the 33-year-old Williams.

By this point, Morrison was reduced to a home run hitter who stands in the box and patiently waits for his pitch before hitting it out of the park. For all his power, Morrison was by nature a counter puncher who was one of the most devastating "trap fighters" of his era. Despite his blocky physique, Morrison possessed incredibly quick hands and superior timing, and he used those attributes to wait until his opponent threw a pre-determined punch, after which he unleashed his explosive counter. Time and again Morrison keyed on Williams' right hand, whether it was a cross or an uppercut, because that scenario presented the best chance for his monstrous left hook to come into play.

But Morrison was running out of time as the fight entered the eighth. The momentum had clearly swung to Williams and to make matters worse, an unintentional head butt opened a cut on top of Morrison's head early in the round. A moment of power, however, can make all wrongs right again and with 1:17 remaining in the eighth that moment arrived for Tommy Morrison.

After Williams landed a slinging right to Morrison's head, "The Duke" let fly with a whipping hook to the jaw and a right to the head, causing Williams to clinch. Again anticipating a break, Williams turned his head to look for Lane and Morrison capitalized on Williams' defensive lapse by driving a huge right uppercut to the jaw that put Williams in deep trouble.

The shark-like Morrison tore after Williams and landed a right to the body, a right uppercut to the jaw and a howitzer hook that caused Williams to wobble into the ropes. A right-left crashed home and Williams' body sagged. But most importantly for Morrison, Williams' fighting spirit sagged as well as he shook his head in the general direction of Lane after absorbing two more booming overhand rights. After a momentary pause, Morrison raced in and drilled five more punches before backing away a second time. Convinced the fight was not yet over, Morrison drove in a final left hook and overhand right to persuade Lane to stop the fight at 2:10 of round eight.

Williams, who had come so close to pulling off a big upset, wore a dazed look as he sat on a stool in Morrison's corner. Though he didn't win, he gave notice that when in shape he was still a capable and attractive opponent worthy of several more sizeable paydays.

For Morrison, a potential fight with George Foreman awaited, which was ironic because it was Foreman who gave Morrison valuable advice on how to relax in the ring following his devastating loss to Mercer. He took that advice to heart against Williams – almost dangerously so – and ended up with a most important win. When he was asked by HBO's Larry Merchant whether he wanted to fight "Big George," Morrison replied "not just 'yes,' but 'hell yes!'"

Against Mercer, Morrison faced adversity and came up short but against Joe Hipp and now against Carl "The Truth" Williams a new truth emerged – by overcoming adversity not once but twice, Tommy Morrison was a "finished" fighter who was far from finished.

Epilogue: Foreman knocked Coetzer out in the eighth round to set up the Morrison-Foreman fight June 7, 1993 in Las Vegas. Morrison surprised virtually everyone by adopting a stick-and-move style to out-point Foreman and win the vacant WBO title. After knocking out Tim Tomashek in four rounds to defend the belt, Morrison was nearing a multi-million dollar payday against Lennox Lewis, but Michael Bentt destroyed those plans by blasting out Morrison in 93 seconds.

Morrison went 7-0-1 (6 KO) over the next two years to earn his long-awaited crack at Lewis, but when he met in Atlantic City on October 7, 1995 it was Morrison who was cracked before losing by sixth-round TKO.

In February 1996 Morrison announced he had tested HIV positive, and a three-fight $38.5 million deal with Don King that was to have culminated with a fight against Mike Tyson fight was voided. However, Morrison did land one final bout November 3, 1996 against the 15-1 (15 KO) Marcus Rhode on the undercard of Foreman-Crawford Grimsley in Japan, which had no prohibition against HIV-positive fighters. Morrison said at the time his comeback was not a career move but a two-fight comeback designed to raise AIDS awareness. Morrison wanted the second fight to be against Foreman to not only gain financially but to provide publicity for the Knock Out AIDS Foundation he had recently established.

The bout with Rhode was conducted under special rules that addressed Morrison's HIV-positive status. If Morrison had suffered a cut, the fight would be stopped and his corner would be given one minute to receive treatment. If that failed, the fight would be stopped immediately. But there was no need for the rules to be applied as Morrison stopped Rhode via the three-knockdown rule 98 seconds after the opening bell. The Foreman rematch never materialized.

TALES FROM THE VAULT

But Morrison did fight again, not just once but twice. On February 22, 2007 at the Mountaineer Race Track in Chester, W.Va., Morrison fought John Castle with the blessing of the state athletic commission. Morrison lost the first round handily only to instantly turn the fight around in the second with a trademark hook. Then on February 9, 2008 in Leon, Mexico he stopped Matt Weishaar in three rounds to raise his record to 48-3-1 (42 KO) as of January 2010.

Williams fought eight more times over the next four-and-a-half years, going 4-4 (1 KO). Three months after he lost to Morrison, Williams took one last stab at regaining a foothold in the heavyweight title chase by fighting Frank Bruno. A 10th round TKO loss took him out of contention for good and his final fight was a seven-round TKO loss to Anthony Green in Port Chester, N.Y., October 30, 1997. Williams, 12 days short of his 38th birthday, retired with a record of 30-10 (21 KO).

BIG MAN DRAMA

Total Punches Landed/Thrown

Round	1	2	3	4	5	6	7	8	9	10	11	12	Total
Morrison													114/196
													58%
Williams													131/280
													47%

Jabs Landed/Thrown

Round	1	2	3	4	5	6	7	8	9	10	11	12	Total
Morrison													35/69
													51%
Williams													51/141
													36%

Power Punches Landed/Thrown

Round	1	2	3	4	5	6	7	8	9	10	11	12	Total
Morrison													79/127
													62%
Williams													80/139
													58%

* Fight originally done by CompuBox, but the original HTML files with complete round-by-round statistics no longer exist.

Tommy Morrison vs. Carl Williams January 16, 1993, Reno, Nevada

Ray Mercer vs. Bert Cooper
August 5, 1990, Atlantic City, New Jersey

Every prospect that aspires to become a champion ideally must face a day of reckoning where his character is challenged like never before. It is a day that reveals all in two important ways; first, whether the lessons learned in the gym have paid off and second, if the fighter possesses the inborn courage and wherewithal to overcome the severest situations.

For Ray Mercer, his biography alone offered a partial answer. A sergeant in the U.S. Army, Mercer didn't take up the sport until age 23 yet he cut a powerful swath through his competition. He won the 1988 U.S. National Championships to earn a spot in the Olympic Trials, then – as an underdog – he defeated Michael Bent in both the trials and the box-offs to earn a ticket to the Seoul games as the 201-pound representative. Mercer proceeded to destroy the field, scoring four stoppages over Rudolf Gavenciak of Czechoslovakia (RSC 3), Italy's Luigi Gaudiano (RSC 1), Arnold Vanderlyde of the Netherlands (RSC 2) and finally South Korea's Baik Hyun Man for the gold (RSC 1). The mental and physical toughness honed by his military service no doubt contributed to his success in overcoming obstacles.

Mercer turned pro on February 24, 1989, joining Olympic teammates Michael Carbajal, Kennedy McKinney and Andrew Maynard – along with Kenyan representative Robert Wangila – on the undercard of Roberto Duran-Iran Barkley. Mercer continued his destructive ways by stopping Jesse McGhee in three rounds and knocking out the next eight out of nine opponents. From that point forward Mercer's competition was raised and though he had some difficult moments against Ossie Ocasio (W 8) and Kimmuel Odom (W 12) he managed to keep his perfect record intact. A fourth round TKO over Lionel Washington upped Mercer's record to 15-0 (11 KO) and on August 5, 1990 at the Convention Hall in Atlantic City he was scheduled to fight NABF champion Bert Cooper. The Cooper fight was intended to establish a world ranking for the 29-year-old Mercer, who was put on the fast track toward a title shot due to his advanced age.

Though five years younger than Mercer, "Smokin' Bert" was perceived to be an older fighter because of his vast edge in experience against world-class opposition and his occasional troubles against them. The thickly built Cooper first made his mark as a power-punching cruiserweight who stopped eight of his first nine opponents before suffering a shocking eighth round TKO to Reggie Gross, who at 212 outweighed Cooper by 12 pounds.

Two fights after losing to Gross, Cooper won the NABF cruiserweight belt with a 12 round decision over previously unbeaten 1988 Olympian Henry Tillman. It was the second of a six-fight winning streak that culminated in another big upset, this time a two-round KO of Canadian Olympian Willie deWit before a hostile crowd in Regina, Saskatchewan in February 1987. That victory earned Cooper a crossroads fight with Carl "The Truth" Williams for the vacant USBA heavyweight title four months later, but Williams hammered Cooper into an eighth round TKO defeat.

From that point forward, Cooper was an astoundingly unpredictable fighter. For every good victory over previous unbeaten Andre McCall (KO 3) and the 37-1-1 Tony Fulillangi (KO 4) there were defeats to Everett Martin (L 10) and Nate Miller (KO by 7).

Cooper's lowest point happened nearly four months after losing to Miller when he fought George Foreman in June 1988. A sleep-deprived Cooper offered virtually no resistance before being stopped in the third round, and there was talk immediately after the bout of holding up his purse and imposing a suspension.

After stopping Rick Hoard in one round and scoring an eight-round no decision against Mike Cohen, the "good" Cooper re-emerged on February 17, 1990 when he stopped the heavily-favored 22-1 Orlin Norris in eight rounds to win the NABF heavyweight title, after which he signed to defend against Mercer. At 5-11 and 217 pounds, he was two-and-a-half inches shorter and just three pounds lighter, but the real wild card was not Cooper's body but his mind. If Cooper (22-5, 19 KO with one no-decision) was "all there," he was more than capable of springing another mighty upset, but if he wasn't it would have meant a short afternoon for all concerned.

The reality of the situation from Cooper's perspective was revealed during the pre-fight introductions when he, the champion, was introduced before his challenger, a telling departure from tradition. Another detour from standard procedure took place before the fight even made air as most of the audience watching on CBS never saw the bout's first 98 seconds. A tape of the raw feed revealed that blow-by-blow commentator Tim Ryan believed the opening bell was being delayed to allow another long-running live event to finish. Unfortunately for Ryan – and ultimately the fight fans tuning in – the timekeeper rang the bell prematurely.

Mercer and Cooper tore into each other from the opening second, with Mercer digging to the body and Cooper tagging the former Olympian with a pair of lead rights to the jaw. Mercer retaliated with a sizzling right cross-left hook combination after which the duo moved into point-blank range. Cooper ended the exchange with a whistling right uppercut that ripped open a deep vertical gash on Mercer's lower lip and darting back to long range. Mercer plowed back inside behind a one-two, and after Cooper connected with another lead right, Mercer bulled him to the ropes and fired a pair of three-punch flurries. Only after all this did the first clinch take place. When they separated, Mercer nailed Cooper coming in with a right cross. His follow-up seven-punch salvo was mostly blocked, and Cooper roared back with his own counter attack.

The heated pace and furious action was worthy of far lighter men but Mercer provided a jolting reality check when a perfectly delivered one-two to the chin dropped Cooper on the seat of his pants. After Cooper arose at three, Mercer rushed in for the finish but he kept his cool well enough to mix in a driving right to the body among his many accurate head shots. Cooper tried to fight his way out by targeting several rights to the ribs as Mercer leaned on him. The two milled evenly at close range, with Cooper landing a head-spinning overhand right to spark another fierce exchange.

At this point, the clock read 42 seconds remaining in a spectacular first round and it was here that CBS beamed the first images of the fight to most of the country. But all of the round's excitement had already taken place, and the two men spent the rest of the stanza pushing, pulling and punching.

Both men worked the jab to start round two, but Cooper broke the pattern with a leaping hook to re-establish the bombs-away approach of the first. Mercer ripped a five-punch combination to the head and body but Cooper burrowed inside with a right to the body, a knifing left uppercut to the face and a pair of overhand rights. Mercer cranked a right to the body that Cooper blocked and a follow-up hook that wasn't.

The two continued to trade punches – and momentum – throughout and each fought with an energy and drive uncommon in heavyweight contests. They strung together effective combinations, both at long range and in close, instead of the usual slow-pace mauling typical of the division. In short, these big men were fighting big – and in some ways "small."

The violent template continued in the third as Mercer used his bigger frame to force Cooper back. Mercer shifted his focus to Cooper's body with hooks and straight rights while Cooper largely aimed for the head. Each threw sharp hard blows at close range and with terrific variety. Mercer's consistency carried the round while Cooper fought in spectacular spurts. Mercer ensured himself a successful round with an 11-punch outburst highlighted by a right-left-right and two more crosses that sent Cooper wobbling toward his own corner.

Cooper bounced back from his late-round adversity early in the fourth when he connected with a pair of sledgehammer rights to the side of the head. Not only did Mercer stand up to them, he drove Cooper back to the ropes with his own five-punch flurry, taking a huge right to the face while doing so. With that very sequence, Mercer forever established his reputation as the owner of a jaw that rivaled diamonds for hardness, for he couldn't have been hit harder by a confirmed big puncher, yet he showed the fortitude to punch back.

The duo moved inside and ripped heavy punches to the flanks, and the effects of the hard pace started to show on Mercer. A left hook-straight right spun Mercer's head, which sported swellings around both eyes. Some of the snap had left Mercer's punches while Cooper's were peppy and powerful. Mercer's breathing was more labored and he had the look of a man who was facing a physical and emotional crossroads.

Just when one thought Mercer was showing the tell-take signs of lasting fatigue, he produced a shockingly hard burst with 20 seconds remaining. A right-left-right cracked home and a rippling right to the ribs combined with a right uppercut to the jaw had Cooper in duress. Seven more clean and punishing blows ravaged Cooper, who took them all with the resiliency of a two-ton boulder.

Mercer continued his rally 37 seconds into the fifth when he came over a missed Cooper hook with a hurtful right cross to the jaw. Cooper tottered back a couple of steps, but no more as he planted his feet and covered up in a cross-armed shell. A hefty hook-right-right combination stunned Cooper further and a hook sent a telling shudder through the champion's body. Cooper still had the presence of mind to bob and weave under Mercer's follow-up bombs and to grab Mercer at the first opportunity.

There had been questions about Cooper's willingness to fight hard at all times and to train properly for his fights – and for good reason. On this day, however, he was the best he could be and he brought all of his best stuff. His plan was to take the inexperienced Mercer into the later rounds, and while his blueprint was starting to pay dividends he had to pay a high physical price.

As Cooper popped in short punches on the inside, Mercer spent more time leaning in and resting his head on Cooper's shoulder. While there he stole several deep breaths, but at the crack of the 10-second hammer he again tried to rally. But after a five-punch flurry capped by a right to the body, it petered out after a couple of seconds. Cooper, who now had a nick over the left eyebrow, had survived an early nightmare and was starting to close the gap on the scorecards.

With the underdog rallying, the crowd commenced the sixth by chanting "Bert! Bert! Bert!" After milling on the inside for the first 20 seconds, it was Mercer who broke free and wobbled Cooper with four full-strength rights to the jaw and a wicked hook to the ribs. Mercer then fell into a clinch and Cooper responded with a right cross that sent his challenger to the ropes. When Mercer sought another clinch, Cooper flashed a smile and proceeded to fire short punches at close range.

Mercer's face, already cut and swollen, had a new problem: The area around the left side of his jaw was puffing up. The first signs erupted in the previous round but now it was more pronounced. Cooper wasn't without his own issues as the eye cut dripped more blood that smeared his cheek and caused him to blink.

A ferocious Cooper hook broke up the inside mauling but Mercer kept coming on, showing little sign of the pain he must have been in. Mercer only threw occasionally as he dropped his head forward and used it to push back Cooper, who was hitting him with peppery punches. Cooper closed the round strongly with a hook-cross-hook to the body that forced Mercer to retreat. A final right cross-left hook salvo at the bell enabled Cooper to claim yet another round.

As his corner worked on his various swellings with an Enswell, Mercer's face resembled a chipmunk with a month's worth of nuts stuffed in its cheek. Yet it was Mercer who started the seventh well by landing a hook from long range that knocked Cooper back. Weariness forced Mercer to return to the inside, though now he moved his hands whenever he pushed Cooper back. Cooper retaliated with a couple of sharp right-lefts with his back to the ropes before spinning out.

Mercer threw several slapping rights to dislodge the Avitene that coated Cooper's left eye, but Cooper created enough space to connect with a right to the swollen jaw. Though stunned, Mercer answered with a fierce right-left-right to beat Cooper off him. Two big rights came back from Cooper and suddenly the back-and-forth war was on again.

Mercer snapped Cooper's head straight back with a right and the crowd urged Cooper to fight back by chanting "Cooper! Cooper! Cooper!" Mercer stayed on the throttle with a right uppercut-left hook-right cross combo that shook Cooper, and several more right crosses over the top deepened Cooper's troubles. As was the case throughout the fight, Cooper summoned up his courage and fought back, but Mercer's heavier blows enabled him to win the round.

Mercer began the eighth by driving Cooper back with a knifing left to the jaw, causing Cooper to flash a defiant smile. His jaw was ballooning to grotesque proportions, yet he was the one dictating the action as he pressed Cooper against the ropes and pounded the body and head. Cooper seized back the momentum behind two heavy rights and a hook to the jaw, but Mercer snatched it back seconds later with a right to the chin and a second thudding one moments later.

"The punishment these guys are taking is amazing," marveled CBS analyst Gil Clancy, who surely was speaking for the millions of viewers who tuned in. "We know they're both good punchers."

A portion of the crowd began a chant for Mercer, but the Cooper partisans soon drowned them out. Second later, Cooper landed a big right directly on Mercer's swollen jaw, but Mercer walked through it and continued to bull Cooper. Following a brief lull, Mercer snapped out of his lethargy with a quick hook to the body, another to the head and a right cross to the jaw before returning to the mauling tactics for the remainder of the round.

Mercer returned to long range early in the ninth round and found success with a pair of double jabs that snapped back Cooper's head. Cooper answered with a hook-right, but Mercer re-established control with a three-punch burst before falling back inside. A tiring Mercer only had the energy for a few spurts but he made them count – and made them hurt. Cooper, while not looking as tired and beaten as Mercer, wasn't able to summon a sustained response, though the punches he unleashed still had plenty of steam.

Cooper started the 10th with a change in approach; he now worked behind the jab while circling Mercer. That, however, lasted less than a half minute when Mercer bulled him to the ropes with a flurry and slapped on a clinch. When they separated, they mutually decided to let punches go, and Mercer got by far the best of it as he landed an effective right cross-left uppercut combo as Cooper unloaded a hook. Two more rights to the temple wobbled Cooper and Mercer gunned for the finish behind several more full-shouldered punches. Cooper kept his composure and waited for a weakened Mercer to run down. When he did, he gladly accepted the clinch Mercer initiated. As Perez broke them up, Cooper smiled ruefully before driving in a right to Mercer's disfigured mandible. Mercer did more leaning than punching and Cooper took advantage with several intermittent offerings for the rest of the round.

Both men sought a breather at the start of the 11th by staying at arm's length and pumping out jabs, but Mercer soon added a pair of rights to move Cooper back. Cooper cranked two hooks that persuaded Mercer to hold. A strong straight left following a right snapped Cooper's head and another combination pushed the NABF champ toward his own corner. A few moments later, the usually stoic Mercer showed his surging confidence by dropping his arms and mugging at Cooper before returning to business and landing a long right. At that moment, Mercer realized he was close to the end of this most harrowing test of endurance and that he would not only survive it but also emerge as a better fighter. That epiphany made him almost joyous, and he celebrated it by landing a concrete-like hook.

At this, the Mercer fans chanted and this time the dispirited Cooper fans couldn't override them. Cooper tried to rally in the final seconds but Mercer's reply was instantaneous – and better. At the bell, an effusive Mercer smiled and pumped his arms overhead in triumph as an important mental barrier was now in his rear view mirror.

At the one-minute mark of the final round, Mercer laced a right to the jaw and fell inside. It was obvious to all that exhaustion gripped both men, yet they sought to push through it the best they could. Mercer's jaw stuck out gruesomely and the slice on his lower lip was now a gash through which a river of blood flowed, but he continued to punish himself by continuing and punish Cooper with his punches. A searing right uppercut-left hook pairing stunned Cooper, but the champion withstood it and pumped three light rights to the ribs.

With the clock running out, Mercer got on his toes and landed a double jab and a leaping right-left to the face. As he connected on another one-two to the face, Mercer showed the energy that comes from knowing his mission was at an end, though one final wild hook at the bell nearly hit Perez.

It was the kind of fight that elevated both winner and loser because of the courage and tenacity each demonstrated. The decision was unanimous – and unfairly wide given the punishment dished out and the contest's ebb-and-flow. Vincent Rainone saw it 119-108 while Phil Newman saw it 117-110 and Sid Rubinstein viewed it 117-106 for the winner and new NABF champion, Ray Mercer.

One of boxing's greatest appeals is its ability to expose all secrets about an athlete's character. Through this brutal war of attrition, each transported the other to the bowels of their athletic souls, and both realized that they had what it took to withstand – then overcome – the punishment that had been meted out. For Mercer, it validated his status as a world-class fighter and a title threat while for Cooper it quieted those who labeled him a quitter and a choke artist. For all of his problems with consistency, he showed that he had the goods to put forth his best when it really counted.

Epilogue: Cooper's sterling showing earned him a bout with Mercer's Olympic teammate, the 19-0 Riddick Bowe, just 11 weeks later. The future heavyweight champion blasted out Cooper in two rounds and from that point forward he remained the heavyweight division's symbolic hand grenade in that one couldn't tell by sight only whether it was a dud or a recipe for instant death.

Cooper won four consecutive fights, including a fifth round knockout of the 21-1 Joe Hipp, to earn a surprise shot at WBA/IBF champ Evander Holyfield. Cooper was a last-minute sub for the injured Francesco Damiani and he nearly pulled off one of history's greatest upsets by scoring a knockdown and nearly taking out "The Real Deal." But Holyfield, showing his trademark courage, rallied to stop Cooper in the seventh.

Three months after stopping Cecil Coffee, Cooper again fought for a belt, this time against WBO champ Michael Moorer. A pumped-up Cooper decked Moorer in the first and third rounds, but Moorer, who also scored a knockdown in the first, got the last laugh as he flattened Cooper in the fifth.

Cooper never again fought for a major belt and over the next 10 years he went 9-13 (6 KO). On September 20, 2002 at the Blue Horizon in Philadelphia, Darroll Wilson stopped the 36-year-old Cooper in four rounds to snuff "Smokin' Bert's" fire for good. He retired with a record of 36-22 with 30 knockouts.

Five months after beating Cooper, Mercer stopped Damiani in nine rounds to win the WBO title. He defended the belt just once, spectacularly knocking out Tommy Morrison in five rounds before relinquishing it to fight 42-year-old grandfather Larry Holmes, who derailed Mercer's hopes for a showdown with new champion Bowe by capturing a shocking 12 round decision.

Knockouts of Mike Dixon and Jerry "Wimpy" Halstead positioned Mercer for another crack at Bowe, but the chance fell away forever when he lost a decision to Jesse Ferguson in a bout that brought accusations of bribery. The charges were dropped, and

Mercer gained a measure of revenge by beating Ferguson in a rematch three fights and nine months later.

After settling his issues with Ferguson, Mercer slumped as he drew with Marion Wilson and lost a pair of exciting and competitive decisions to Holyfield and Lennox Lewis. Mercer won his next seven fights, including a decision victory over Tim Witherspoon, to earn a shot at Wladimir Klitschko's WBO belt on June 29, 2002. The 41-year-old Mercer was stopped in six rounds and he never again fought for a major title.

Ironically, the man who was put on a fast track to a title shot due to his advanced age fought on until age 48. In January 2008 he lost a 12 round decision to Derric Rossy in Macao, China and eight months later he won a six-round majority nod over Richel Hersisia in Karlstad, Sweden. His record stands at 36-7-1 with 26 knockouts.

TALES FROM THE VAULT

Total Punches Landed/Thrown

Round	1	2	3	4	5	6	7	8	9	10	11	12	Total
Mercer	34/87	28/75	32/77	29/61	30/54	20/48	29/61	29/57	15/49	25/59	33/70	16/42	320/740
	39%	37%	42%	48%	56%	42%	48%	51%	31%	42%	47%	38%	43%
Cooper	29/55	38/75	27/53	20/43	22/51	34/59	18/41	21/43	17/34	26/43	22/47	9/26	283/570
	53%	51%	51%	47%	43%	58%	44%	49%	50%	60%	47%	35%	50%

Jabs Landed/Thrown

Round	1	2	3	4	5	6	7	8	9	10	11	12	Total
Mercer	7/27	2/20	4/20	3/16	3/11	1/7	3/15	5/15	5/24	1/9	8/23	7/21	49/208
	26%	10%	20%	19%	27%	14%	20%	33%	21%	11%	35%	33%	24%
Cooper	3/10	0/9	2/10	1/8	5/10	2/5	1/4	1/7	1/5	2/8	5/12	1/8	24/96
	30%	0%	20%	12%	50%	40%	25%	14%	20%	25%	42%	12%	25%

Power Punches Landed/Thrown

Round	1	2	3	4	5	6	7	8	9	10	11	12	Total
Mercer	27/60	26/55	28/57	26/45	27/43	19/41	26/46	24/42	10/25	24/50	25/47	9/21	271/532
	45%	47%	49%	58%	63%	46%	57%	57%	40%	48%	53%	43%	51%
Cooper	26/45	38/66	25/43	19/35	17/41	32/54	17/37	20/36	16/29	24/35	17/35	8/18	259/474
	58%	58%	58%	54%	41%	59%	46%	56%	55%	69%	49%	44%	55%

Ray Mercer vs. Bert Cooper August 5, 1990, Atlantic City, New Jersey

Kenny Keene vs. Terry Ray I
October 8, 1994, Terre Haute, Indiana

Throughout boxing history, the most celebrated figures are those who either possess special abilities or have achieved extraordinary feats. Jack Dempsey is remembered for his uncompromising savagery while Willie Pep is lauded for his peerless defensive skill. Joe Louis is honored for his prodigious power, his technical brilliance and his quiet dignity; Rocky Marciano for his "Suzy Q" and his 49-0 record and Muhammad Ali for his dazzling speed of hands, feet and mouth. And if one wanted to show a young fan what the perfect fighter looked like, all he had to do was pop in a tape or a DVD of Sugar Ray Robinson.

There is, however, one category of fighter that is often overlooked – the honest workman. He is the gladiator who is not blessed with the superlative talent that attracts multi-million dollar TV contracts and the attention of Hall of Fame trainers and promoters. Though he emerges victorious time after time, the media refrains from writing stories on him because he is considered too bland. Instead, he makes do with what he has and makes the best of it.

He is the fighter who clocks in at the gym every day and quietly goes about his business. He absorbs whatever instructions are given to him and he does the best he can within his skill set to carry them out. His greatest assets are those that can't be seen but only perceived: Steadiness, reliability and tenacity.

Kenny Keene and Terry Ray are two members of this proud but understated fraternity. Going in, they had two firm footholds in this pantheon: First, they campaigned in the necessary but perennially maligned cruiserweight division and second, Keene hailed from Emmett, Idaho and Ray from Terre Haute, Indiana, not exactly hotbeds for world class boxers. But it was the way Keene and Ray fought and conducted themselves that made them full-fledged members of this tribe and that was never more in evidence than on October 8, 1994, the day they produced one of the most bruising and action-packed fights this division has ever known.

On the line was Keene's lightly regarded World Boxing Federation cruiserweight title, a belt he won seven months earlier by stopping Bobby Crabtree in four rounds. Since then, Keene decisioned John McClain in a non-title 10 rounder and stopped Vincent Boulware in 10 rounds two months before taking on Ray. Keene was not without credentials: As an amateur he compiled an 86-20 record, winning the 1984 Junior Olympic championship along with six Golden Gloves titles and a spot in the finals of the 1988 national Golden Gloves. He continued his success after turning pro in August 1990, running off 28 consecutive victories that included 19 knockouts. His best victories before taking out Crabtree were against former champions Ricky Parkey

(W 10) and J.B. Williamson (KO 4) as well as fringe heavyweight contender James Pritchard (W 10).

Much of Keene's approach had to do with his choice of role model – former middleweight champion Gene Fullmer. Soft-spoken and humble outside the ring, both Fullmer and Keene used their relentless ruggedness to methodically break down opponents in it. His balding head and flat speech pattern resembled Fullmer's, and like him Keene was honest about his abilities.

"Usually I'm shorter than the other guy but I can out-jab them," he said. "I've got decent power and I take a pretty good shot. I'm not the greatest boxer but I do OK when I have to. My weaknesses? I'm sure I got a few. I'm not the fastest guy, I'm not the hardest puncher, I'm not the best boxer but I do what I have to do to win."

Ray, who at 31 was five years older than Keene, also had a long association with boxing. He took up the sport at age 12 and learned his craft at Terre Haute's Glenn Youth Center and Ryves Hall Youth Center and had a successful amateur career before turning pro in June 1986. Over the next eight years Ray crafted a 25-1 (14 KO) record against an assortment of journeymen, with the only loss coming against Mike Peak at a very early stage in both men's careers. The Keene fight represented a quantum leap upward in competition, but three factors helped bolster his chances. First, the fight was being held in Ray's hometown of Terre Haute on the campus of Indiana State University, from where he graduated in 1989. Second, his corner man was the legendary Angelo Dundee. Finally, at 6-2 ½ and armed with a 74-inch reach, Ray held advantages of 5 ½ inches in height and seven inches in reach.

As the fight began, Ray, 190, sought to use those edges as he stood straight up and worked behind the jab while popping in occasional rights to the head and body. Keene, 189 ½, his hands high and upper body hunched forward, was surprisingly effective with his jabs and a follow-up overhand right snapped Ray's head. The feeling-out fencing didn't last long, and both men soon set the terms of battle: Whether at close range or at arm's length, both men were punching – and punching often. Ray's stiff jabs penetrated Keene's peek-a-boo style guard while the champion smartly fired in blows from his bob-and-weave. In the final minute both picked up the pace and scored heavily with bombs at close range, Keene working more to the body while Ray targeted the head, especially with right uppercuts.

Ray started the second continuously pumping the jab but Keene rolled under most of them and scored with his own jabs. Ray was trying his best to establish a big man's game of fighting at a distance, but his temperament – and his vocal hometown crowd – commanded him to trade punch for punch. A right to the jaw nailed Keene in the final minute but Keene bounced back with a pair of rights. Ray answered that salvo with a right-left and the champion responded with a head rattling overhand right. It was a vicious, sustained exchange seldom seen in big men as CBS boxing analyst Gil Clancy duly noted.

"Keene's style is to out-tough the other guy, but he's in with another very tough guy," he said.

Given the extraordinarily tough pace and the damage both men inflicted, it was difficult to imagine that this would last for long. As the pair hammered away, Clancy told blow-by-blow man Tim Ryan he'd buy him a hat if the fight went the distance. Ryan pointed out that he didn't wear hats, but Clancy said he'd be getting one anyway. He was that sure he was right.

The bruising action continued in the third with Keene's body attack gaining steam and Ray catching the champ with lead rights and right uppercuts. This was a fight – and a pace – to which Keene was accustomed; of his 28 fights he had gone 10 rounds seven times while Ray had never got beyond eight, a mark he reached just five times in his 26 bouts. At this early juncture Ray was already breathing hard and Keene's thumping body shots didn't make things any easier. A right to the ribs made Ray wince and a left to the pit of the stomach moments later only added to his duress. The crowd, sensing Ray was weakening, tried to lift his spirits and while Ray continued to work the third was clearly Keene's best thus far.

Keene worked both hands with surprising speed as he rattled off a double jab to the head followed by a double jab-right to the body combo to begin the fourth. His body punches were delivered with accuracy and hurtful leverage, the kind that saps an opponent's energy and resolve. But every time Keene mounted a surge, Ray soaked up the punishment and produced his own answer, especially during those sequences when the fight was waged at arm's length. Though he wasn't scoring quite as often as Keene, Ray managed to open a cut under the champion's right eye while also producing blood from Keene's nostrils.

The fifth was waged at a withering pace more suited to lightweights than cruiserweights as there were neither clinches nor rest for either man. Keene's sharpness and underrated quickness still carried the day as he sliced through Ray's defense. Ray, unmoved, still stood tall while inching forward behind jabs and clubbing rights.

Ray, perhaps pacing himself, had fought a patient fight up to now and that patience began to pay off midway through the session when Keene initiated a pair of clinches and Ray started to land with more effect. Keene coped by going back to the body, but now Ray's shots to the ribs made Keene pause and take a deep breath. Nevertheless, neither was willing to cede control for more than a few seconds, but one could sense a small shift in fortune as Ray landed a left-right-left uppercut combo in the round's final moments.

Keene knew his jab was the best weapon to use when awaiting a second wind, and his success with it fueled several follow-ups that enabled him to regain a semblance of control in the sixth.

His combinations – especially to the body – were pure Fullmer. He knew he wasn't the fastest or the most powerful, but he had faith in his ability to endure anything his opponent could dish out. The body blows adroitly set up opportunities to the head, which he partook with relish. Still, Ray stayed with Keene every second of every round, trading with a challenger's resolve. Together, they were two workmen who were in the mood to put forth an honest day's work that far exceeded their honest day's pay.

A short hook on the inside backed Keene off, who shook his head at the challenger to signal he was unaffected. Neither Ray nor the crowd was fooled by Keene's uncharacteristic show of bravado; he jumped in and went after the champion. But Keene answered Ray's burst with a solid lead right that quelled the mini-rally.

Keene switched tactics early in the seventh as he backed away in small circles and pelted Ray with long range punches, much like Fullmer did in his first fight with Carmen Basilio in 1959. He slipped under Ray's blows and brought up rights to the gut and overhand rights to the head. In the final minute, Keene surged forward and stepped up his offense. A huge overhand right-left hook-straight right combo caused Ray's legs to quiver and Keene tore after him. A solid right opened a nasty cut along Ray's left eye and for the first time Ray looked ready to be taken. But Ray, ever game, rode out the storm and mounted a rally in the final moments with a counter right-hook combo that stunned Keene. Here, the champion's calm came in handy as he regrouped and fought his way out of trouble.

The hard pace told on both men as they wearily walked back to their respective corners. But Dundee wanted more from his man.

"Don't look at this guy," Dundee commanded. "Back him up!"

Ray did his best to heed Dundee in the eighth, and his rights began to take more of a toll. The blood flowed more freely from Ray's eye because Dundee's cut medicine had not yet taken hold and Keene's nosebleed also increased in severity. Even though their faces were breaking apart, their wills remained resolute. Ray surged at the midway point as he connected with a right uppercut-left hook that knocked Keene slightly off balance, but was hard enough to ignite a roar from the crowd. The champion quieted them with three consecutive overhand rights, a one-two and a full-shouldered jab.

With a minute left, referee Sean Curtain stopped the action and asked the ringside physician to examine Ray's cut – a move that prompted loud boos. The bout was allowed to continue, but the possibility of the fight being stopped caused both men to go for the kill. Keene landed a right-left-right-right to the face while Ray answered with a pair of heavy lefts and a one-two that drove the champion back.

The two fighters hammered away remorselessly, each believing he had the other on the edge of defeat. Clancy marveled at the action, saying "I don't think I've ever seen more action in a fight with big men than in this fight, and that's some statement, but that happens to be true." This fight may have been for a belt whose worth was not highly regarded, but the two men fighting for it put forth an effort worthy of an undisputed championship.

Up to this point, Keene had built an edge on the scorecards due to his sharper combination punching and slightly superior work rate but his effort was about to come with a high price. Starting late in the eighth, Keene's technique became more ragged and his mouth started to hang open. By the ninth, the ever-observant Dundee pounded the ring mat and shouted, "Jump on him! Jump on him!" At the end of the round, Ray did as he was told and slammed a heavy right that made the champion clinch.

Fueled with renewed energy and confidence, Ray began the 10th snapping jabs while moving strategically in both directions. Ray initiated most of the exchanges and landed the harder punches, and he punctuated the trend with a left hook that sent Keene reeling toward the ropes. Though the champion continued to throw, his punches no longer had snap and were unleashed more on reflex than with any conscious purpose. A wicked hook following a missed right stopped Keene in his tracks and a subsequent flurry sent him wobbling to the ropes and holding on. Keene's only saving grace was that Ray couldn't draw the perfect bead for a knockout punch, but in any case the 10th represented by far the challenger's best round.

Knowing their man was putting together a potential title-winning drive, the crowd sought to push Ray toward the finish line. Ray worked the left and connected with a good counter right as a weary Keene remained at long range, his offensive output eroding noticeably. A snappy hook nailed Keene during an exchange, and the champion's resistance decayed dangerously. Realizing the crisis before him, Keene summoned his bread and butter – his strong body attack – to keep Ray from applying the finishing touches as the round closed.

Ray was performing well for a man who was about to engage in his fourth round beyond his longest previous distance. The conventional wisdom indicated that Ray's best chance was an early knockout, but here he was, in the most physically demanding fight of his professional career, and he was the one who was coming on stronger against a man renowned for his stamina. On the other hand Keene realized that the lead he had built was rapidly shrinking and that he needed to summon one more massive effort to prevent a changing of the guard.

Ray started the final round well as he landed a right uppercut-left uppercut-overhand right combo while Keene answered with a jab-jab-right before falling into a clinch. Keene somehow unleashed a five-punch salvo, but Ray connected with a terrific hook in the midst of an exchange. With the carrot of the final three minutes upon them, both men put forth their best selves. As tired as Keene appeared in the 11th, he had regained a measure of accuracy and effectiveness. Yet Ray maintained the form that fueled his late round rally as he slammed in a pair of right uppercuts and a hook as

Keene rushed in. Another right uppercut strafed Keene's head and a follow-up one-two buckled the champion's knees ever so slightly.

Each man laid everything on the line in pursuit of a common goal – victory – and the fight ended much like it began, with the pair throwing and landing hard blows until the last moment.

Judge Mark Snow saw the bout a draw at 115-115, but Gary Merritt and Deacon Bower overruled him by scoring it 116-112 and 118-113 for the winner – and still – champion Kenny Keene.

When Ryan asked Keene if he was relieved he had won a decision in his challenger's hometown, he replied, "yes I am. And I couldn't really tell how the fight was going because every time he hit me the crowd was going crazy. But who cares? He has nothing to be ashamed of and I don't either."

Keene was surprised at his opponent's stamina considering his inexperience with long distances.

"My plan kind of backfired on me," he said. "I've been the rounds and he hasn't so I thought once I got him in the later rounds I'd be in control, but it backfired on me."

The disappointed Ray believed he had done enough to deserve the decision.

"I thought I won the fight to be honest with you," he told Ryan. "I thought I won it pretty clearly. It was close and Kenny is a very tough individual. I may be a better fighter than Kenny Keene thought and maybe he's got a little more respect for me."

It was the kind of fight that not only caused the combatants to elevate their respect for one another, but also the public appreciation for fighters who, in essence, are much like themselves – hard-working, earnest and always striving to be their best.

Epilogue: The two met again nine months later, this time for the vacant IBC belt, but the result was as anticlimactic as the first fight was scintillating as Keene won a five-round technical decision due to an unintentional head butt. Before the rematch, Keene knocked out Martin Lopez in three, lost the WBF belt back to Crabtree by split decision and stopping Herman Delgado in three. Meanwhile, Ray was similarly active as he stopped Tim Johnson (KO 12), Robert Straw (KO 5) and Keith Williams (KO 7) before losing his second fight to Keene.

Ray ran off five straight victories before losing a 10-round decision to Robert Daniels, yet the defeat didn't keep him from earning a crack at Crabtree's WBF belt on March 2, 1997. This time Ray made good as he stopped the southpaw bomber in three. Ray's reign lasted only three months as the 18-0 Don Diego Poeder halted Ray in 10 rounds.

Ray's only chance at a major title came against WBA champion Fabrice Tiozzo, who stopped Ray in just 60 seconds. Four months later he fell victim to the 40-0 Brian Nielsen in five rounds. He returned to his sphere of familiarity and found success in it, regaining the WBF title by stopping Samson Cohen in two rounds on January 23,

1999 and defending it three months later against Ron Bensonhaver (TD 9). Vincenzo Cantatore stopped Ray in three for the WBU belt but Ray won the WBF bauble for the third time by decisioning Bensonhaver for the vacant title. After losing the belt to Bash Ali (TD 7), the 37-year-old Ray won his final fight on February 27, 2001 when he stopped Brian Yates in four rounds. His final record is 41-9 with 25 knockouts.

Keene fought on for 11 more years after the Ray rematch, and while he never fought for a "major" title he was largely successful as he went 19-3 (7 KO). His best victories were against Crabtree (KO 9), Mike Sedillo (W 10), Rich LaMontagne (W 12), Rocky Gannon (KO 11), Dominick Carter (W 12, KO 5), Rob Calloway (W 12) and Tony Menefee (KO 1). Only Saul Montana (L 12), Robert Daniels (L 12) and Arthur Williams (KO by 10), all of whom made their marks on the world stage, managed to best him.

The Williams defeat took place July 29, 2006 at the Qwest Arena in Boise, Idaho eight days after Keene's 38th birthday. It was to be his final outing as he retired with a record of 51-4 (28 KO).

TALES FROM THE VAULT

Total Punches Landed/Thrown

Round	1	2	3	4	5	6	7	8	9	10	11	12	Total
Keene	43/84	42/84	43/80	26/69	26/52	38/70	39/79	40/74	26/51	21/60	14/39	19/61	377/803
	51%	50%	54%	38%	50%	54%	49%	54%	51%	35%	36%	31%	47%
Ray	42/106	27/90	19/80	19/60	21/69	19/71	13/54	29/80	22/57	29/70	20/49	23/58	283/844
	40%	30%	24%	32%	30%	27%	24%	36%	39%	41%	41%	40%	34%

Jabs Landed/Thrown

Round	1	2	3	4	5	6	7	8	9	10	11	12	Total
Keene	11/31	17/37	11/36	10/39	9/25	15/38	13/33	24/41	17/34	14/33	7/26	7/31	155/404
	35%	46%	31%	26%	36%	39%	39%	59%	50%	42%	27%	23%	38%
Ray	19/47	10/44	7/31	10/25	10/24	7/28	7/22	15/36	11/30	10/24	13/29	9/26	128/366
	40%	23%	23%	40%	42%	25%	32%	42%	37%	42%	45%	35%	35%

Power Punches Landed/Thrown

Round	1	2	3	4	5	6	7	8	9	10	11	12	Total
Keene	32/53	25/47	32/44	16/30	17/27	23/32	26/46	16/33	9/17	7/27	7/13	12/30	222/399
	60%	53%	73%	53%	63%	72%	57%	48%	53%	26%	54%	40%	56%
Ray	23/59	17/46	12/49	9/35	11/45	12/43	6/32	14/44	11/27	19/46	7/20	14/32	155/478
	39%	37%	24%	26%	24%	28%	19%	32%	41%	41%	35%	44%	32%

Kenny Keene vs. Terry Ray I October 8, 1994, Terre Haute, Indiana

★ Chapter 4 ★
WARS OF ATTRITION

TALES FROM THE VAULT

Oscar Larios vs. Israel Vazquez II
May 17, 2002, Sacramento, California

EDITOR'S NOTE: *This article was written in December 2005, the week of the third – and ultimately final – encounter between Larios and Vazquez and at the time the boxing world was abuzz with anticipation. The fight was the main support for the rematch between Bernard Hopkins and Jermain Taylor but for the hard-cores, Larios-Vazquez III was the real reason to purchase the pay-per-view because the second fight was so terrific. Therefore, the impressions of the original were maintained, although the third fight much resembled the first – a quick but spectacular blowout that took three rounds instead of one.*

* * *

In a way, boxing fans are just like small children – once they see something they like, they want to see it again and again. For today's kids, it's Elmo, Blues Clues and Clifford the Big Red Dog while for boxing fans of all ages they are action-packed brawls that give us that special buzz of excitement and remind us why we love our sport so much.

Some fights are so good that they not only have to fight again but again still. Barrera-Morales and Gatti-Ward left us breathless and wishing they could have fought every month.

On December 3 at the Mandalay Bay in Las Vegas, Oscar Larios and Israel Vazquez hope they will join the pantheon of great "thrillogies" when they step into the ring on the undercard of Jermain Taylor-Bernard Hopkins II. Another great selling point is that their second fight was one of 2002's best. The bristling back-and-forth action and the sudden dramatic ending is the reason Saturday night's third fight is happening. It's also why it's a perfect Closet Classic.

The Larios-Vasquez series proves one can't judge a book by its cover or a potential trilogy by the first fight. Their first meeting took place April 12, 1997 in Mexico City and while it was explosive, it was also brief. Larios was 20-0 with 15 knockouts while Vazquez (who won all 58 of his amateur fights by KO) was 11-1 with 10 KO, so both were already gaining notice on the Mexican boxing scene. But Vazquez's superior power ruled the day as he scored two knockdowns en route to a first round KO. Vazquez knew what it was like to be caught early, as six months earlier he was polished off in one round by the 9-6 Ulises Flores.

Larios and Vazquez continued their upward path following their brief encounter. Larios maintained a busy schedule, winning the Sinaloa junior featherweight title in his next outing by knocking out Israel Melendez in two rounds. He notched seven more victories before Agapito Sanchez stopped him in five rounds on cuts, something that would become a persistent problem for him. Only 29 days after the Sanchez loss, Larios captured the Mexican super bantamweight title with a two-round KO over Javier Calderon and proceeded to defend the belt eight times. His most noteworthy win to date, however, was a 12-rounder over Cesar Soto in a WBC super bantamweight title eliminator. After icing Sammy Ventura in one round, Larios got his chance at WBC champion Willie Jorrin January 19, 2001 in Jorrin's home base of Sacramento, California.

Jorrin-Larios was a fast-paced war and many who saw it thought Larios had done enough to lift the belt. Keith McDonald agreed, judging the fight 113-112 for the challenger. But Doug Tucker and Glen Trowbridge overruled him as they saw Jorrin a dominant 115-110 winner.

Again, Larios was left to pick himself up and move forward. And he did, beating John Lowey (W 10), Angel Chacon (W 12), Ivan Alvarez (W 12) and Darryl Pinckney (W 8) to maintain his number two ranking in the WBC and earn the rematch with Vazquez.

After being Larios, Vazquez won nine fights before dropping a 12-round split decision to Marcos Lincona for the vacant WBO/NABO junior featherweight title. Instead of moping, Vazquez kept pressing forward, running off 12 more victories, including solid wins over Hector Velazquez (W 10), Javier Varguez (KO 3) and Ever Beleno (KO 2). He rose through the rankings, finally reaching No. 1 in the WBC and earning a fight with Jorrin. But because Jorrin kept sustaining injuries, the fight was pushed back three times. In fact, Vazquez was to have fought Jorrin on the night of the Larios rematch, but an ankle injury forced the champion to the sidelines yet again.

The WBC, hungry for a sanctioning fee, made Larios-Vazquez II a bout for the "interim" WBC belt with the winner earning a mandatory shot at Jorrin for the "full" WBC title. Larios and Vazquez, though young at 25 and 24 respectively, had plenty of seasoning. Larios entered the ring with a 43-3-1 (30 KO) mark while Vazquez was 32-2 (24 KO).

The taller Larios came out on his toes, throwing a busy jab and tossing lead right uppercuts to the body and hooks to the head before inducing brief clinches. Vazquez stalked and tossed harder jabs, constantly looking to cut the ring in half while moving his upper body from side to side. Vazquez dug in a good lead right to the ribs followed by a jab to the face while Larios landed lighter but more frequent punches before spinning away. Both men established a quick pace as Larios threw 90 punches to Vazquez's 67, but though Vazquez's blows were heavier, Larios earned an edge because his superior movement dictated how the action unfolded.

The second round followed the same pattern: Vazquez the aggressor and Larios mixing his attack between head and body while on the retreat. Midway through the round, Vazquez opened a cut over Larios' right eye and referee Pat Russell immediately ruled the cut was caused by a punch, meaning if the fight was stopped because of the cut, Vazquez would win by TKO. Concerned, Larios accelerated his pace, digging harder to the body and landing a good counter hook to the jaw. Vazquez remained patient, working his way inside from time to time behind his solid jab. Both men were in constant motion, each answering the other's blows with counters. Larios' solid one-two induced a Vazquez lead right to the chin, but Larios' activity and his mastery at long range continued to carry the fight throughout the second and third rounds.

Larios was playing a numbers game, throwing more punches and appearing more effective. But if one saw the CompuBox figures, his effectiveness was merely a mirage for in round three, Vazquez outlanded Larios 35-30 despite throwing nine fewer blows (93-84). Because Larios' punches were longer and more easily seen, his work was more appreciated by the fans and judges.

In the fourth, Larios began to land harder, and a one-two to the chin forced Vazquez to clinch. Midway through the round, two more rights crashed on Vazquez's jaw and it appeared the number-one contender was in trouble. A good illustration of Larios' lack of one-punch power occurred with less than 10 seconds left as Larios caught Vazquez coming in with a full-impact right to the jaw, the kind of blow that would usually put an opponent in big trouble – if not on the canvas. But after a brief clinch, Vazquez shook off its effects and continued applying pressure. The message was clear: If Larios wanted victory, he'd have to work long and hard to get it.

Larios began round five on the inside, whipping hard shots to the body. The Guadalajara product was standing much closer to Vazquez than in the first four frames, and Vazquez took advantage by landing a rising hook to the jaw, by far his best punch of the fight. Smartly, Larios retreated to the outside and resumed his stick-and-move tactics. Vazquez continued to concentrate his attack to the body in an effort to drain the strength from Larios' lively legs. Both men were in constant motion, always thinking about what move to try next while also figuring what to do to counter his opponent's tactics.

The CompuBox statistics confirmed the high-energy nature of the contest as after five rounds, Larios landed 135 of his 446 punches (nearly 90 per round) while Vazquez connected on 127 of 383 blows (almost 77 per round). The junior featherweight average is 59 punches a round.

Larios opened the sixth with strong jabs followed by a looping right to the forehead and a hook to the chin, but Vazquez walked through them and continued to whack Larios' body. Late in the round, Larios dug in his toes and ripped to the body, then switched to southpaw – an unusual maneuver for him. Vazquez was unconcerned as his consistent bodywork sought to build the foundation for a second-half rally.

That rally began in the seventh, as Vazquez countered a Larios uppercut with a short, direct right to the jaw. Larios' chin, however, withstood the punch well. Vazquez countered Larios' jabs with his own jabs, only his were stiffer and more effective. Vazquez was gaining strength while Larios began to sling his punches, losing the excellent form he showed in the bout's first half.

The fight was engaged at close range in round eight and Vazquez began to impose his superior strength by bouncing rights off the jaw and unleashing withering shots to the ribcage. Larios remained active, but his balance was beginning to erode and he found himself squaring his body more often, exposing more punching area for Vazquez to attack.

The Mexico City native was feeling good about things now, and as they separated from a rare clinch he tapped his gloves together, nodded and smiled at Larios before winging another hook to the body. Vazquez wasn't dominating the action, but the pendulum of fortune was swinging his way.

As the fight entered the final four rounds, the two fighters lifted themselves to an even higher level of intensity. They ignored the punishment of earlier rounds as they engaged in a long series of bristling, power-packed exchanges at long range as well as in close. Larios regained his earlier brilliance, masterfully mixing his blows to the head and body while moving his torso like a Slinky to evade Vazquez's counters. Vazquez continued to march forward, firing hard to the body and maintaining an unshakable determination. He was finding success, landing 38 of 105 blows (36 percent), but Larios was better as he connected on 46 of his 107 punches (43 percent).

The breathtaking action continued in the 10th and 11th and Larios' sheer volume and intensity backed Vazquez to the ropes. But it wasn't a one-way street as Vazquez was in his face, answering every attack with one of his own. Both were scientifically savage, remorselessly tearing away at one another but doing so with a mental energy that rivaled what they were doing physically. As the round closed, Larios gritted his teeth, stepped on the gas and drove Vazquez to the ropes with a blizzard of blows. And like the stubborn rival he was, Vazquez resisted the temptation to quit, determined to see the fight out until the very end.

Larios started the final round throwing punches like a blender set on "pulverize" and a left hook hurt Vazquez badly as he staggered into the ropes. Larios pounced, but Vazquez smartly clinched and cleared his head. A lead right to the ear turned Vazquez's legs to jelly and he clinched again. As they separated, Vazquez complained to Russell, claiming the painted logo on the canvas caused him to slip. After taking an appropriate pause, Larios jumped in and nailed Vazquez with a scorching lead right that dumped the top contender hard on his rump.

Up at seven, Vazquez grabbed Larios in desperation, but Larios shook him off and drove him to the ropes. With 1:09 remaining in the fight, Larios crashed a pair of overhand rights to the jaw that drove Vazquez to the canvas like a woodworker hammering a nail into a 2-by-4. Vazquez was left on all fours, and after counting to four, Russell took one look into Vazquez's eyes and stopped the fight. Only 63 seconds remained.

In all, the two fighters exchanged 2,049 punches, fourth all-time among 122-pound bouts tracked by CompuBox. The numbers also confirmed the bruising, exhausting nature of the fight in two ways: First, Larios landed an average of 26 power punches a round while Vazquez connected on 21 and secondly, in rounds 9-11, Larios averaged 109 thrown punches to Vazquez's 100.

Larios carried a WBC "interim" title belt from the ring, but he knew he had one more mountain to climb before he could feel like a real champion. That mountain's name was Willie Jorrin.

Epilogue: After polishing off Manabu Fukushima in eight to defend his interim belt, Larios finally got his second crack at Jorrin, again at the ARCO Arena in Sacramento. Leaving nothing to chance, Larios overwhelmed Jorrin, stopping him just 88 seconds after the opening bell sounded.

Over the next three years, Larios assembled a distinguished title reign, amassing seven defenses. After notching a non-title win over Marcos Lincona (W 10), Larios overcame a broken jaw to beat Shigeru Nakazato (W 12). Less than five months later, he returned to Japan to knock out Kozo Ishii (KO 2). From there, he defended the belt regularly, defeating Napapol Kiattisakchokchai (KO 10), Nazakato (W 12), Nedel Hussein (W 12) and two wars with former WBC bantamweight champion Wayne McCullough (W 12, KO 10). Between the wins over Nakazato and Hussein, Larios won two non-title affairs over Jesus Perez (W 10) and Ivan Alvarez (W 10) to set up the third meeting with Vazquez.

With a solid chance to elevate his pound-for-pound ranking, Larios fell to Vazquez's power in three rounds, then lost a decision to Manny Pacquiao in July 2006. Despite that result, the Mexican continued to be in the championship mix. Following three wins, Larios lost a decision to Jorge Linares for the vacant WBC featherweight title in July 2007 but earned another crack by winning three fights, including a fifth-round knockout of Marlon Aguilar for the interim WBC featherweight belt. That set up a fight with "full" champion Takahiro Aoh in October 2008, which he won by split decision. The uproar over the verdict set up a rematch the following March, which saw Larios drop a comprehensive decision. As of January 2010, the 33-year-old "Chololo's" record is 63-7-1 with 39 knockouts.

Vazquez has been less active than Larios but more successful. Four months after losing to Larios the second time, Vazquez easily decisioned Justo Almazan and knocked out former WBA bantamweight champion Jorge Eliecer Julio in 10 rounds as well as Trinidad Mendoza (KO 7). Vazquez captured the IBF title vacated by Manny Pacquiao by stopping Jose Luis Valbuena in 12 rounds. He defended the belt twice, dominating Art Simonyan (KO 5) and overcoming a slow start to decision Armando Guerrero May 31.

After taking a 2-1 lead over Larios, Vazquez polished off Ivan Hernandez (KO 4) and Jhonny Gonzalez (KO 10) to set up another trilogy, this time against longtime IBF bantamweight champion Rafael Marquez. Their three fight series turned out to be among the most thrilling the sport has ever seen as Marquez won the first slugfest by seventh round corner retirement while Vazquez won the final two (KO 6, W 12) in brutal spectacles that almost defy description. The third installment was so good that a fourth bout was discussed but then scrapped as each took long breaks to heal.

Vazquez returned to the ring in October 2009 with a ninth round TKO of Angel Priolo, setting up a fourth fight with Marquez. As of January 2010, the bout was scheduled for May 22 and the 32-year-old Vazquez enters the bout with a record of 44-4 with 32 knockouts.

TALES FROM THE VAULT

Total Punches Landed/Thrown

Round	1	2	3	4	5	6	7	8	9	10	11	12	Total
Larios													387/1080 36%
Vazquez													332/969 34%

Jabs Landed/Thrown

Round	1	2	3	4	5	6	7	8	9	10	11	12	Total
Larios													77/348 22%
Vazquez													77/424 18%

Power Punches Landed/Thrown

Round	1	2	3	4	5	6	7	8	9	10	11	12	Total
Larios													310/732 42%
Vazquez													255/545 47%

* Fight originally done by CompuBox, but the original HTML files with complete round-by-round statistics no longer exist.

Oscar Larios vs. Israel Vazquez II May 17, 2002, Sacramento, California

Santos Cardona vs. Kevin Pompey
April 11, 1991, Albany, New York

One of the many attributes that separates boxing from other sports is its capacity to lay bare what is inside an athlete's heart. There's nothing like one-on-one combat to expose how someone will react when he meets an opponent that matches his determination, drive and fighting spirit. When two fighters of nearly equal ability meet, the result often rests on which one can go beyond his physical self and unleash his inner beast. More often than not will, not skill, determines the ultimate result.

It is a rare occurrence when both winner and loser gain in stature following a fight, and that was the case when Santos Cardona and Kevin Pompey met for Pompey's IBC welterweight title in Albany, N.Y. The fans who packed the Knickerbocker Arena and those who watched the fight on ESPN were treated to an extraordinary battle of indomitable courage.

The fight pitted two boxers who can best be described as solid pros – men who enjoyed success at the middle range of the sport but found themselves wanting when they sampled the elite level. The 26-year-old Pompey (22-3-1, 10 KO) won 17 of his first 20 fights before meeting Tyrone Trice for the WBA Americas welterweight title January 14, 1990 in Atlantic City. After 12 rounds of tremendous action, Trice came away with a close unanimous decision and a second shot at IBF champion Simon Brown while Pompey exited with a loss – and valuable experience. Pompey entered the Cardona fight on a five-fight winning streak that began following the Trice loss, including a split decision over Darryl Lattimore to capture the IBC belt. Pompey's last outing was a 10-round non-title win over Tim Rabon 10 weeks before.

The 25-year-old Cardona (20-3, 14 KO) followed a similar route to Pompey's – early success followed by credible failure at higher levels. Cardona captured the Puerto Rican lightweight title by decisioning Angel Luis Garcia and the WBC Fecarbox junior welterweight title by knocking out Albert Mieses in three rounds. Armed with a 16-0 (9 KO) record, Cardona entered the Stroh's junior welterweight tournament at the Great Western Forum in Los Angeles. It was there that he ran into Sammy Fuentes and his considerable power, which turned out the lights in two rounds.

From that point on, Cardona ran hot-and-cold against the better fighters. He lost a 10-round decision to Terrence Alli but defeated former WBA lightweight champion Livingstone (a.k.a. Ras-I Aluja) Bramble by majority decision five weeks later to capture the NABF junior welterweight title. Cardona lost the belt in his next outing to John Wesley Meekins but came into the Pompey fight on a positive note by knocking down Miguel Santana four times before scoring a five-round TKO.

Both Cardona and Pompey had already shown the ability to bounce back from adversity, but they couldn't have known how much they needed to draw upon that reservoir when they stepped between the ropes.

The fight began at a high tempo with Pompey immediately working the body with hooks and rights while mixing in short punches to the head while Cardona circled to his left, probing with jabs and occasional lead rights to the head. Cardona wanted to use his two-inch height advantage to catch Pompey coming in, but midway through the round Cardona began targeting the body while maintaining his preferred distance. Pompey repeatedly whacked away at Cardona's ribs, but the Puerto Rican captured the round with his slightly more effective punching.

Neither man bothered with the jab in round one, with Pompey landing only three of his 20 jabs while Cardona connected on only one of his 30 attempts. Overall, Cardona landed 17 of 67 blows while Pompey was 12 of 50.

Perhaps bothered by his lack of success with the jab, Cardona started the second snapping out the left and landing more against the advancing Pompey, who remained committed to bodywork with hooks and tightly-thrown rights. Pompey countered Cardona's body hooks with his signature hooks to the jaw. In the final minute, both men shifted the battle to close range and initiated a long, uninterrupted stream of powerful blows. Neither man was badly hurt by the other and they were eager to see who would win this test of strength. An excellent right by Pompey briefly put Cardona back on his heels, but the Puerto Rican maintained a slight edge because of his superior activity. In round two, Cardona out-landed Pompey 33-22 while nearly doubling the New Yorker's punch output 103-56.

The two men resumed their inside war in the third, putting their heads on the other man's shoulder and pounding away. Cardona was getting off his blows slightly quicker but Pompey was far more accurate. Pompey's jab landed flush on the face and snapped Cardona's head back and he continually sunk hooks into the body. Cardona, for his part, dished out a steady stream of blows that bounced off Pompey's head and body.

In the final minute, the two men accelerated their attacks, going punch for punch in a breathtaking display of stamina and stubbornness. A double right by Pompey was answered with hooks and straight rights to the jaw. Cardona gradually forced Pompey backward throughout the round and his blows carried a little more force as a result.

The fight took on the appearance of a pot of water placed just above a stove's flame and by the end of the third the fight was beginning to heat up. The two men landed a combined 96 punches in the third round with Cardona landing 48 of his 124 punches and Pompey 48 of 78 for 62 percent accuracy.

The boiling point got a whole lot closer in the fourth.

Pompey found the range with his one-twos and more of his body blows penetrated Cardona's guard. But the New Yorker always got stiff resistance from Cardona, who was always there with an answer for Pompey's attacks. The question was who was going to crack – and get cracked – first.

With 1:21 left in the round, Cardona nailed Pompey with an overhand right to the temple that had Pompey stumbling along the ropes. Another right snapped Pompey's head and still another caught the IBC champion as he spun off the ropes and retreated to ring center on unreliable legs. Another hook forced Pompey to the ropes and Cardona fired away with abandon. But as the seconds passed, Pompey gathered himself, his head clearing gradually as he fielded Cardona's follow-up blows on his arms and gloves. Meanwhile, he kept his arms in constant motion in the hopes that he could turn the tide. A precise right uppercut split Cardona's guard with 28 seconds remaining and his bobbing and weaving kept Cardona's attack at bay. A series of quick double rights to the head certified that Pompey was back in the fight and the two men traded quick-fisted volleys until the bell rang.

Pompey's comeback signaled that the real war was on, and the numbers bore that out. Cardona threw 125 punches in the round, landing an incredible 60 of them while Pompey's 48 of 75 output translated to an astounding 64 percent accuracy.

But if the fans thought the fourth was great, the fifth threatened the scrape the stratosphere.

Pompey roared out of the corner and immediately raked Cardona's body and ripped right uppercuts to the jaw. Cardona was unmoved as he continued to throw volleys of punches without pause. An inside right to the jaw snapped Pompey's head, and in an effort to physically clear the cobwebs he shook his head from side to side. While fighting off the ropes, Pompey dug a hook to the head, another to the body and a right to the jaw and Cardona answered with body punches and a short right uppercut to the chin. Another scintillating right crashed off Pompey's jaw and he mixed in two searing hooks to the ribs.

While Cardona enjoyed an edge on the scorecards, the fight was hurtling toward Pompey's specialty – give-and-take wars determined by drive, desire and willpower. The incredible fifth ended with both men tearing into each other with no regard for the punishment inflicted or absorbed.

The fifth round's brutality was evident in the CompuBox numbers. The two men landed a combined 140 punches with Cardona landing 67 of 121 (55 percent) and Pompey connecting on an incredible 73 of 101 for an eye-popping 72 percent. All but 13 of the combined 222 blows were power punches.

The ceaseless action ratcheted up another notch in the sixth as they continued their war on the inside as Cardona pitted his slightly superior power and higher work rate against Pompey's withering body attack and extraordinary accuracy. The pace soared to incredible heights and the level of warfare escalated with every passing second. With 45 seconds remaining, an inside hook prompted Pompey to physically shake away the cobwebs and a second one backed him to the ropes. Pompey's fighting heart remained strong as he valiantly fired back against the avalanche of blows coming at him. Finally, Pompey spun off the strands and landed a cuffing right to the neck and a hook to the jaw, but Cardona was always there to counter whatever Pompey tried.

After the sixth round bell rang, the crowd gave the fighters a standing ovation – with good reason. Through six rounds, the fight was almost even with Cardona out-throwing Pompey 652 to 459 but only out-landing him 276-273. Somehow, neither man bore any marks of battle.

In the seventh, Pompey went back to the attack but was starting to feel the effects of Cardona's sixth-round assault. His legs looked less steady and the zip on his punches wasn't as evident. He shook his right hand following an exchange, perhaps suffering the same injury he incurred two fights before against Lattimore. Yet Pompey continued to throw and land a steady stream of powerful and precise blows. Cardona sustained his attack as well, but his punches lacked the sharpness of previous rounds. The tide of the fight wasn't shifting from round to round, but second by second.

The seventh was a statistical tour de force by Pompey as he landed 78 of his 97 punches – an almost unheard of 78 percent accuracy. Cardona was no bystander as he unleashed 125 blows, landing 66 of them for 53 percent.

Pompey's inside work gave him the momentum as round eight began, and he hustled on the retreat as Cardona advanced and stayed busy. Suddenly, Cardona shifted his attack to long range and the move paid immediate dividends as he rattled a right-left-right off Pompey's face. Another one-two landed well for the circling Cardona and a jab connected stiffly. Two more jabs snapped Pompey's head and a lead overhand right to the jaw found the target. Cardona had finally found the key to Pompey's persistence – do what you do best and let the chips fall however they may.

Happily for Cardona, it wasn't chips that were about to fall.

With 54 seconds to go, a lead overhand right caromed off Pompey's temple and the New Yorker collapsed to the canvas with stunning suddenness. It was as if the accumulation of Cardona's attack had fallen onto his shoulders like a giant sack of concrete and he no longer had the strength to resist it. Up unsteadily at eight, Pompey looked out into the crowd and turned his head toward referee Joe Santarpia. The clouded look in his eyes told Santarpia what he needed to know and he waved off the fight at the 2:16 mark with no complaint from Pompey.

Cardona may have won the IBC belt, but the more important victory was the one over himself. Pompey pushed him to his physical and emotional limit and he emerged with the precious "W" by his name.

Cardona hit Pompey 379 times while Pompey answered with 391 connected blows. While Cardona's 45 percent accuracy would be outstanding in most cases, his figure paled to Pompey's 63 percent rate. But no matter how the numbers stacked up, the fans already knew they had witnessed a fight to remember.

Epilogue: Five months after beating Pompey, Cardona continued the best stretch of his career by knocking out Tim Rabon in five and decisioning David Taylor and Martin Quiroz. Five knockouts later, he earned a chance at Pernell Whitaker's WBC welterweight title on April 9, 1994. Whitaker, like he did against everyone else, pitched a 12-round shutout. After losing to Whitaker, Cardona lost two consecutive 12-round decisions for the WBO welterweight title against Verno Phillips and was defeated in a third chance for the belt against Bronco McKart (KO by 9).

After losing to McKart, Cardona won seven straight, knocking out Oscar Gabriel Gonzalez (KO 5) for the WBO/NABO welterweight belt and Willie Wise (KO 9) to defend it. He lost a WBO welterweight title shot at 24-1 Ahmed Kotiev (L 12) and wound up his career going 2-2, beating Anthony Ivory (W 8) and Santiago Samaniego (W 12) and losing to 25-1 Lavell Finger (L 8) and Tony Ayala Jr. (L 10) in his final fight July 31, 2001. Cardona retired with a 39-10 (26 KO) record.

Pompey rebounded nicely from the Cardona loss as he won his next six fights, the biggest of which was a 12-round decision over the 123-2-2 Buck Smith for the USBA welterweight belt. From then on, Pompey suffered a dramatic drop in form as he went 4-14-2 in his final 20 fights. His last best fight was a 12-round split decision over Harold Brazier to defend his USBA belt, but lost the belt to Brazier 10 weeks later via 10 round TKO. He became a stepping stone as he put up credible losing efforts to Buddy McGirt (L 10), Anthony Stephens (KO by 9), Troy Waters (KO by 4), Markus Beyer (L 8), Eric Lucas (L 10), Laurent Boudouani (L 8), comebacking Don LaLonde (L 8) and Omar Sheika (KO by 8). His final fight was a three-round KO loss to future WBA super middleweight champion Anthony Mundine July 10, 2001 and his record dropped to 32-18-3 (12 KO).

TALES FROM THE VAULT

Total Punches Landed/Thrown

Round	1	2	3	4	5	6	7	8	9	10	11	12	Total
Cardona													379/837
													45%
Pompey													391/621
													63%

Jabs Landed/Thrown

Round	1	2	3	4	5	6	7	8	9	10	11	12	Total
Cardona													59/224
													26%
Pompey													65/138
													47%

Power Punches Landed/Thrown

Round	1	2	3	4	5	6	7	8	9	10	11	12	Total
Cardona													320/613
													52%
Pompey													326/483
													67%

* Fight originally done by CompuBox, but the original HTML files with complete round-by-round statistics no longer exist.

Santos Cardona vs. Kevin Pompey April 11, 1991, Albany, New York

Leonard Dorin vs. Raul Balbi I
January 5, 2002, San Antonio, Texas

The quest to determine the limits of human performance has always been a source of fascination. Mickey Mantle's reported 565-foot bomb in April 1953 inspired the term "tape measure home run" and though track and field is no longer a marquee sport in the United States, we still want to know how fast the "world's fastest human" ran the 100 meter dash. When someone shatters a record, the feat is often described as "Beamonesque," referring to Bob Beamon's 29-2 ½" long jump that had broken the existing world record by nearly two feet. The Olympic motto of "swifter, higher, stronger" succinctly captures our never-ending drive to push toward places once thought impossible.

The flow of action in most boxing matches has peaks and valleys as the fighters summon bursts of energy while looking to recover from those bursts during the down times. But is it possible for a fighter to put forth all-out effort every second of every round? And what would happen if two such fighters were pitted against one another?

Theory and reality seldom meet in their purest forms, but when they do the results can be memorable – if not legendary. When WBA lightweight champion Raul Balbi met Romanian-turned-Canadian Leonard Dorin at Freeman Coliseum in San Antonio, few in attendance knew who they were at the start but by the time they finished their names were burned into their collective memories. Balbi-Dorin was the main support for Jesse James Leija-Micky Ward on a card entitled "Real Men, Real Fights." No one could have ever anticipated that an undercard fight could be so good that it would make a battle involving Leija or Ward pale in comparison.

The 28-year-old Balbi (48-4-1, 33 KO) was making his first defense of the WBA title he won by majority decision from Frenchman Julien Lorcy – in Paris, no less. The Argentine was making his first appearance in America and was riding a 19-fight unbeaten streak. Though Dorin had only 19 pro fights in an unbeaten pro career, the 31-year-old had 254 amateur fights on his odometer. As Leonard Doroftei, he won bronze medals in the 1988 and 1992 Olympics and his body punching was so good that NBC "Triplecast" boxing analyst Wally Matthews took to calling him "Smokin' Joe." His high-pressure style was sure to test Balbi's conditioning, but more importantly his determination to stay champion.

Dorin began the fight moving forward and jabbing behind a high guard while Balbi probed with light blows. It didn't take long for their engines to warm up and they began unleashing their blows freely. At 5-4, Dorin was three inches shorter and his 63-inch reach forced him to burrow inside Balbi's four-inch reach advantage. Balbi countered Dorin's aggression by inching back just enough to maintain his preferred range. All the while, they fired crisp, pinpoint blows with speed and proper technique. Balbi was especially effective throwing jab-right-hook volleys followed by hooks to the ribs while Dorin tagged the champion with overhand rights.

The two men traded bristling combinations on the inside, but the infighting also produced a pair of head butts that caused Balbi to complain and turn away. Between the head clashes, they were doing plenty of punching – in the first round Balbi threw 82 while Dorin fired 96.

Balbi began the second throwing long lead rights that Dorin easily blocked while the Romanian tossed light double hooks to the face. Balbi won an exchange of jabs and followed with a heavy hook to the ribs and a right-left to the stomach a few moments later. Dorin continued to chug ahead, catching Balbi with rights. Balbi was effective with hooks to the body of Dorin, who kept his torso square when fighting at extreme close range. This tactic allowed him to unload his punches more quickly because they required less distance to travel but it also sacrificed what little power he already possessed. Still, Dorin applied relentless pressure like a termite determined to eat through a three-story building by himself. A right-left-right jerked Balbi's head and Dorin's superior upper body strength allowed him to bull Balbi wherever he pleased.

The suffocating pressure was doing nothing to weaken Balbi's resolve, and he proved it by throwing a five-punch flurry. The fight was turning into a game of "can you top this" as one man would throw a combination only to have the other produce an even better one in return. The punches were laser quick and the two men were conducting a clinic on infighting technique as they fired blow after blow. As the round ticked under 30 seconds, Balbi turned up the heat even more by pelting Dorin's head and body with combinations, after which three left uppercuts sliced through Dorin's gloves.

The action was incredible and the crowd, who didn't know anything about either man a few minutes before, stood and roared their appreciation after the bell ended the second round. This type of ovation is usually reserved for the final round of a great fight, and the good news for them was that the fight was scheduled for 10 more rounds.

"This may end up being the fight of the year," HBO analyst Emanuel Steward exclaimed. "The first fight may be the best fight!"

Balbi appeared to control the action with his heavier blows but the second round was a statistical blowout for Dorin as he uncorked an incredible 122 blows to Balbi's 96 and out-landed the champion 58-23. But Dorin paid a price as a corner man pressed a towel against a cut over the challenger's left eye. Cuts had been a persistent problem for Dorin, but just like he knew how to counteract the problems associated with his 5-3 height, he also was well equipped to deal with the effects of brittle skin. His answer for these problems was the same as for every other boxing-associated problem he encountered – action, action and more action.

Balbi and Dorin went immediately to close quarters and blasted away at one another as the third began, and the champion appeared to seize the upper hand as his crisp blows were delivered with more power. Balbi hooked to the body incessantly as the two men worked shoulder to shoulder and fired seldom-seen combinations. Balbi pumped in a pair of five-punch flurries and a three-punch salvo within seconds of one another and Dorin retaliated with a three-punch reply. A heavy overhand right caused Balbi to fall inside and a double hook that split Balbi's gloves triggered a torrent of blows by Dorin. But whenever one man tried to surge ahead, the other would fire back with even more gusto. Dorin landed a big right to Balbi's jaw that precipitated an all-out assault by both men. Balbi appeared to cringe after absorbing a Dorin body hook, but his punch rate never slowed as they traded until the bell.

In just three rounds, Balbi and Dorin threw a combined 603 blows and connected on 224 of them. In the third, both exceeded the 100-punch mark as Dorin landed 44 of 109 and Balbi 39 of 101. Dorin was the more consistent worker, but Balbi's eye-catching and slightly heavier blows conveyed the image that he was dictating the ever-changing flow of action.

Balbi turned up the pressure in the fourth as he whaled away with left uppercut-right cross combos, but Dorin snapped the champion's head with a searing hook-uppercut that prompted Balbi to beckon him forward with his gloves. Dorin complied by banging two hooks to the jaw and hitting on the break, which produced only a command to continue when Balbi complained. Moments later, Balbi tried to hit Dorin on the break, which prompted a warning and a subsequent apology. After touching gloves, Balbi drove a right to the body and after another exchange Dorin emerged from close quarters with a cut underneath the right eyebrow. With Dorin's face a mask of blood, an energized Balbi nailed the challenger with a right-left uppercut-right, a strong one-two and a big right to the jaw. Dorin came out of the ensuing infighting with cuts over the left eye and the bridge of the nose, prompting referee Rafael Ramos to bring Dorin over to ringside physician Andres Hernandez.

For the first time in the bout, the crowd booed.

After Hernandez allowed the fight to continue, Dorin charged in behind a right to the body but Balbi closed the round by raking the aggressive champion with short, straight punches to the face while on the retreat.

Dorin opened the fifth with a jolting hook to the jaw, but Balbi walked through the blow and continued to engage Dorin in a brutal game of give-and-take. The action pulsated back and forth with the momentum changing every few seconds. The two lightweights were producing a magnificent display of man-sized, full-blooded, bell-to-bell fighting. Balbi was winning the rounds but Dorin's steady work was building the foundation for a potential late-round rally. The burning question was whether Dorin's cuts would allow him to complete his mission.

Being a short, cut-prone pressure fighter with little punching power made every fight a struggle for Dorin, but his years of experience taught him that persistence, toughness, focus and desire was more than enough to overcome all his physical disadvantages. His ring record alone was proof of that. Balbi, however, proved a tough nut to crack – not only was he nailing Dorin with sharp combinations, his stamina appeared to be at least the equal of Dorin's. Plus, the Argentine champion's brows had been untouched by cuts, not only in this fight but also throughout his entire boxing life. It all seemed to be too much for Dorin to overcome.

Hernandez examined Dorin's cuts between the fifth and sixth, and the champion was told to pick up the pace in the seventh to make it more difficult for the doctor to stop the fight. But every time he put on a surge, Balbi went with him and to make matters worse blood poured out of Dorin's nose. Yet Dorin pressed on, and midway through the seventh Dorin smacked a left-right, then nipped out and landed two more one-twos and a sharp left uppercut. Balbi, however, out-threw and out-landed Dorin for the first time in round seven and his perceived edge on the scorecards grew ever wider.

Most fights have peaks and valleys, but this one only contained peaks. Balbi and Dorin appeared to revel in the robust action as they snapped off combination after combination with a crispness that belied the level of physical exertion. If either man had great power, the fight would have been unspeakably brutal – and probably long over by this point.

The tremendous pace continued into the eighth as Balbi dug three consecutive hooks to the body, then connected with a swinging left-right. Dorin loaded up a right to the jaw that landed perfectly as Balbi was coming in. But in a graphic display of Dorin's lack of pop, Balbi walked through a blow that didn't even jerk his head measurably.

Through the first eight rounds, Balbi was thought to have the edge because each of his blows was perceived to be harder and his flashier combinations overshadowed Dorin's consistency. As he stood in his corner for the first 20 seconds between the eighth and ninth rounds, Balbi wanted to project an aura of strength. The Romanian challenger, however, wasn't the type who was swayed by mind games. To him, psychological warfare was just a show for the paying customers that had no relevance to the job at hand.

"If you want to beat me, then beat me," Dorin's style said. *"But to do it, you're going to have to go through hell and I don't think you have the stomach for it. So let's fight!"*

Dorin needed to put together a title-winning rally in the final four rounds and with 35 seconds remaining in the ninth the challenger built the foundation. A strong right bounced off Balbi's jaw and two hooks had Balbi holding on. An overhand right and left to the head caused Balbi's upper body to lean forward in pain and Dorin pounced as he unleashed a blizzard of blows. A solid hook forced Balbi to retreat to the ropes, and he smartly grabbed Dorin when the challenger raced in to follow up his advantage. Even though Balbi launched a good mini-burst to close the round, it was clear Dorin had taken the round. The stats bore that out as Dorin out-landed Balbi 43-28 while connecting on 48 percent of his blows.

Balbi began the 10th strongly with jabs, hooks and uppercuts with the left but midway through the round, Dorin revved up another scorching attack. An overhand right to the jaw jolted Balbi but his follow-up hook landed slightly below the belt. Because Balbi winced in pain, Ramos was persuaded to deduct one point from Dorin. A few seconds later, another Dorin blow landed low and Balbi again reacted strongly but this time no penalty was assessed.

As Ramos issued the warning, Dorin's face was in an appalling state. Blood seeped from both eyes, the bridge of his nose and his nostrils, the claret forming a gory moustache. While his visage bore the scars of combat, his fighting spirit remained resolute and unrelenting. In the final seconds of the 10th, Dorin unleashed two terrific overhand rights to the jaw that might have been enough to neutralize the mathematical damage of the point penalty.

In all, 177 punches were thrown in the 10th, with 171 of them power shots. This was a fight for the masses, where courage, tenacity, heart, conditioning and willpower would separate victor from vanquished. With every passing second, the fight soared toward rarely approached heights.

Meanwhile, Dorin continued to rally in the 11th as a short right stunned Balbi momentarily. But another blow strayed low and Dorin was fortunate to avoid another point penalty. Dorin took advantage by catching Balbi with more rights and the Argentine finally showed small signs of weariness as he leaned in from time to time. Still, Balbi nailed Dorin with several rights that appeared to buzz the challenger, but Dorin bounced back with hurtful rights to the ribs as the round closed.

By stringing together three good rounds, Dorin had closed the gap on the scorecards and a strong 12th might be enough to lift Balbi's belt. But the proud Argentine was not going to wilt for anyone, and he was determined to do all he could to bring the belt back to Buenos Aires. The constant action made judging the fight a formidable task, and neither man was in a position to feel comfortable about his standing. Because of this, Balbi and Dorin wanted to make a persuasive final argument.

Dorin began the 12th by catching Balbi with a lead overhand right and a left to the jaw that caused the champion to lean forward. Dorin bounced rights off Balbi's head and body and a right-left-right backed the Argentine to the ropes. Sensing his title was slipping away, Balbi reached deep and tried to summon a final rally. Though Balbi fired relentlessly, Dorin was the stronger man and he showed it by nailing Balbi with a lead right that made the champion bull Dorin into the ropes. Another lead right smacked off the jaw and the crowd arose as one to applaud the fighters as the final seconds ticked away.

The final CompuBox numbers were staggering. Balbi landed 345 of his 927 punches for 37 percent accuracy while Dorin unleashed 1,083 blows and connected on 476 of them for 44 percent accuracy. It was a brutal give-and-take slugfest and the action suggested a close and controversial decision was likely.

Gale Van Hoy saw the bout 115-112 for Dorin while Ray Hawkins scored it 115-112 for Balbi. Duane Ford cast the deciding ballot of 114-113 for the winner and new WBA lightweight champion Leonard Dorin.

The decision may have been split, but the opinion that it was a great fight was undoubtedly unanimous.

Epilogue: Dorin-Balbi I was so spectacularly action-packed that a rematch was immediately arranged for May 31, 2002 in Dorin's backyard of Bucharest, Romania. The rematch didn't come close to living up to the first fight as Dorin won a lopsided unanimous decision.

Dorin didn't fight again for nearly a year, and the WBA champion appeared to do more than enough to add Paul Spadafora's IBF belt. However, the bout was fought in Pittsburgh before thousands of highly charged Spadafora supporters, so the bout was ruled a draw. Over the next several months, Dorin vacillated on his decision to retire so the WBA made the decision for him as they declared the belt vacant and had Miguel Callist and Lakva Sim fight for it. After Dorin knocked out Charles "Chucky T" Tschorniawsky, he fought Arturo Gatti for the WBC super lightweight belt on July 24, 2004 at Boardwalk Hall in Atlantic City. Memories of the first Balbi fight stirred up visions of another Gatti-Ward Armageddon, but "Thunder" snuffed out those thoughts with one devastating hook to the liver in the second round. The punch not only took the wind out of Dorin's body but his career as well as the 34-year-old Dorin retired with a 22-1-1 (8 KO) record.

After losing the Dorin rematch, Balbi appeared washed up as he was TKO'd in eight rounds by Jose Joaquin Rosa Gomez 10 months later. Balbi took the next two years off, and he returned with a convincing two-round KO over Norberto Acosta on March 12, 2005. Over the next nine months, Balbi notched five wins over Carlos Jerez (W 10), Carlos Donquiz (KO 5), Guillermo de Jesus Paz (W 10), Walter Diaz (KO 6) and Jorge Luis Medrano (KO 2) to earn a shot against Souleymane M'baye for the vacant WBA junior welterweight title. M'Baye blasted Balbi out in four rounds, a result that prompted a 13-month hiatus. In October 2007 he stopped Diego Jesus Ponce in two rounds but as of January 2010 the 36-year-old was on a three-fight losing streak. He lost bouts to the unbeaten Ionut Dan Ion (KO by 3) and Denis Shafkiov (TD 6) in 2008 as well as to the 14-18-3 Guillermo de Jesus Paz in September 2009 (L 6). His record stands at 55-11-1 (38 KO).

WARS OF ATTRITION

Total Punches Landed/Thrown

Round	1	2	3	4	5	6	7	8	9	10	11	12	Total
Dorin													476/1083 44%
Balbi													345/927 37%

Jabs Landed/Thrown

Round	1	2	3	4	5	6	7	8	9	10	11	12	Total
Dorin													23/128 18%
Balbi													20/114 18%

Power Punches Landed/Thrown

Round	1	2	3	4	5	6	7	8	9	10	11	12	Total
Dorin													453/955 47%
Balbi													325/813 40%

* Fight originally done by CompuBox, but the original HTML files with complete round-by-round statistics no longer exist.

Leonard Dorin vs. Raul Balbi I January 5, 2002, San Antonio, Texas

TALES FROM THE VAULT

James Hughes vs. Anthony Stephens
October 26, 1994, Bossier City, Louisiana

Over the past few decades, boxing has developed an obsession for perfection, especially when it comes to the records of superstars and those who aspire to join their ranks. During the heyday of free over-the-air TV boxing in the 1970s and 1980s, fighters' records were carefully built and the glossy records were prominently displayed in pre-fight commercials and during the broadcast. After all, logic says, if a fighter is undefeated in 20-plus fights, he has to be good and if he is that good he must be worth watching. If enough people come to that conclusion, the ratings go up, the dollars from advertising flow freely and everyone ends up happy.

The flip side to that coin is that a single loss, no matter how that came about, would destroy everything. It is said that nobody likes a loser and even if a fighter has a record of 33-1, the "1" stands out more prominently than the "33." This "all-or-nothing" approach had a profound effect on the sport, both physically and psychologically. Many fighters who might have eventually become stars had their dreams snuffed out prematurely, and the people around them were denied the riches that would have come from a more tolerant and patient environment. Also, managers were less willing to put their charges in risky fights, which in turn hindered their fighters' development and altered their career paths. While discretion is often the better part of valor as far as management is concerned, the fans end up being the losers because they are denied consistent matches pitting the best against the best.

To be fair, this hard-line stance has softened in recent years. As Arturo Gatti can attest, the powers-that-be will not penalize fighters as long as they perform honorably and bravely in defeat – and a little charisma doesn't hurt either. Gatti, as well as others, have proven that a fighter with an imperfect record can still give the paying audience all the thrills they can ask for – and in Gatti's case much more.

When Anthony Stephens (23-6-2, 16 KO) and James Hughes (23-8, 15 KO) met for Stephens' USBA welterweight title at the Bossier Civic Center in Bossier City, Louisiana on October 26, 1994, the records might not have been pretty but the attitude was gritty – and full of promise. When Stephens was asked what his fight plan was, he said simply – and with plenty of menace – "My plan tonight is to bust this guy's a**. He's in trouble." Hughes, who called himself "The Modern Day Outlaw," responded in kind, saying "every time he moves or breathes, I'm going to be throwing punches. I'm not going to give him no break, at least for the first eight rounds. He's gonna be smothered in punches."

The fight was a homecoming for Stephens, who hailed from nearby Shreveport, Louisiana, and he earned that reward by beating Harold Brazier over 12 rounds to win the title three months before. The Brazier win avenged a comprehensive 10-round loss in August 1990 and he felt his career was back on the ascent. Entering the Hughes fight Stephens was on a three-fight winning streak and his most recent loss was an honorable one as he scored an early knockdown of IBF welterweight champion Felix Trinidad before being stopped in the 10th.

Hughes was a colorful character who entered the ring in full Western regalia, topped off with a black cowboy hat and a blood-and-guts attitude. The native of Mobile, Alabama did just fine against lower-level fighters but when he stepped up to world-class competition, his considerable fighting spirit wasn't enough to overcome his opponents' superior skills. He lost to future champions Maurice Blocker (L 10) and Vincent Pettway (KO 3) and was one of Buddy McGirt's final victims when he lost a 10-rounder in January 1994. The Stephens fight was Hughes' sixth fight of 1994, which followed an interesting pattern. After losing to McGirt, Hughes knocked out Paul Blount (KO 1), lost to Stephane Ouellet (L 10), defeated Tocker Pudwill (retirement after seven rounds) and in his last fight two months earlier he lost a decision to Eric Holland. If form held, Hughes was due to have a good night but if he were to gain the victory, he would have to overcome a difficult opponent and a hostile atmosphere.

Hughes, 146, had worked himself into a fighting froth, and he made sure Stephens, also 146, knew it when they received their final instructions at ring center. After referee Johnny Femia commanded them to touch gloves, Hughes hammered Stephens' gloves and yelled menacingly. The unrattled Stephens was enough of a veteran to know that pre-fight pyrotechnics was just show business and that an opponent's true state would emerge when the real fighting started.

True to his word, Hughes came out hard and sought to muscle his way inside by crouching, pushing and burrowing with his shoulders and forearms. Stephens tied up Hughes at first, then punched his way out with four consecutive hooks. Hughes wrestled Stephens to the ground and after he popped back to his feet he popped Hughes with a hook on the break. Femia issued no warning for the obvious infraction and in Hughes' mind it confirmed his suspicion that this out-of-towner wasn't going to receive a fair shake. So Hughes pressed ahead and continued to wrestle in the clinches and spin him into the ropes with relative ease. Hughes' strategy was clear: Since he couldn't compete with him in a classic boxing match, Hughes wanted to take Stephens out of his comfort zone and make him fight instead of box.

Despite Hughes' bullying, Stephens was getting in more than his share of good shots. Two hard jabs knocked Hughes back and a short left uppercut snapped his head back. Stephens connected on a nifty jab-cross-hook combo while Hughes continually whiffed on his wild hooks. As the round closed, Stephens clipped Hughes' jaw with a crisp hook, which brought nothing but a smile and a shake of the head from Hughes – and a likely 10-9 round from the judges.

Hughes continued to pressure in round two, using his jab to get inside. Hughes slung Stephens to the ropes with his left arm when Stephens tried to pivot away from the ropes, and Femia was quick to issue a warning for his roughhouse tactics. Stylistically, Hughes had little choice because whenever they engaged at long range Stephens was the master as he stabbed Hughes' faces with pinpoint jabs. Those jabs opened a small cut underneath Hughes' right eye and swelling soon erupted under the orbit. Hughes continued to march forward behind inaccurate left-rights and Stephens made him pay with a heavy right to the jaw, a left-right-hook combo and a punishing right-left to the jaw to close a strategically dominant round.

The gulf in success could be seen in the CompuBox numbers in round two as Stephens out-landed Hughes 34-17 and connected on 55 percent of his 62 blows. Hughes unleashed 55 punches, but landed only at a 31 percent clip.

The ringside physician briefly inspected Hughes' cut between rounds, saying the slice wasn't severe enough for the fight to be halted. Hughes didn't seem concerned with his slow start as he smiled and winked at Stephens as he awaited the third-round bell. Hughes roared inside behind a crab-like crouch and applied heavy pressure, but Stephens continued to nail Hughes with jabs and counter hooks. His blows weren't hurting the rough-hewn Arkansan, but he was administering a boxing lesson. Stephens would nip in, land a couple of sharp blows then escape before Hughes could even react. In terms of sheer talent it was a mismatch but in terms of toughness it was much closer as Hughes unflinchingly absorbed the punishment and kept coming.

And what punishment it was. In the third round, Stephens was 39 of 62 for an outstanding 63 percent connect rate while Hughes managed to land 17 of his 52 attempts for 33 percent. The math – and the fight – was definitely not going Hughes' way.

But Hughes had little use for math. He had complete faith in his durability and his plan was designed to achieve long-term results. He knew if he could absorb Stephens' initial attack, his pressure eventually would break down Stephens physically and emotionally. With 1:46 remaining in the fourth round, Hughes' faith would be rewarded.

Hughes countered Stephens' jab with two swift overhand rights that caught the champion off-balance and sent him flying to the floor along the ropes. Stephens muttered to himself as he arose at three, and because the knockdown punch had knocked out Stephens' mouthpiece the hometown lad received a 25-second rest while the mouthpiece was rinsed and replaced.

Hughes turned up the heat considerably as an overhand right to the temple made Stephens woozy. A right uppercut and an overhand right put Stephens in deeper trouble. Hughes' strength was finally making an impact on the fight, but Stephens was nowhere near ready to concede. The USBA champ weathered the storm and by the end of the round he was spearing Hughes with jabs and a concluding right-left jolted the challenger's head.

The statistical landslide of the first three rounds was history. In round four, Hughes landed 25 of 57 blows for 44 percent while Stephens landed 18 of 42 for 43 percent. The war was finally on, and Stephens' camp knew it.

"You gotta suck it up!" yelled Stephens' trainer Les Bonano. "Nobody ever said it was easy. Every time you land a couple of quick punches, you come up straight in front of him and you want to swap with him. Land what you want to and then step across." Then, pointing a finger at him, Bonano said, "You're not going to take the easy way out. You can beat this guy but you're gonna be smart. Jab, and step to the side. You're the man. You can do it."

It didn't look that way early in the fifth as two huge right uppercuts wobbled Stephens and a right to the jaw prompted the champ to take a knee. Up at seven, blood was trickling out of Stephens' mouth and he looked ripe for the taking as his wide-eyed expression betrayed his vulnerable state.

Hughes pursued his quarry with uncharacteristic calm, as if he wanted to set up the perfect finish. While Hughes waited, Stephens was slowly recovering. A jolting right uppercut-left hook combination seemed to snap Stephens out of his fog and he responded with an overhand right to the ear, a left-right-hook to the jaw and a clipping right to the point of the chin to close out the round. The fifth was a huge scoring round for Hughes but Stephens' late rally proved that the "Modern Day Outlaw" had missed a golden opportunity to gun down his man.

As the sixth round opened, Stephens was moving better but his blows lacked their usual accuracy. Hughes still steamed forward but this time his jabs set the table for power punches that found the target from time to time. Hughes was already enjoying his best form of the fight so far and as the seconds ticked by Stephens was regaining his good technique. A shotgun left snapped Hughes' head and the cut underneath Hughes' right eye again trickled blood. By round's end Stephens was boxing at full capacity and it was clear that "The Untouchable" had successfully staved off Hughes' earlier threat.

As exciting and eventful as the first half of the fight had been, it was about to get even more so.

Hughes ran across the ring to open the seventh and exerted smothering pressure, but his punches found mostly air. Stephens worked the jab well, catching Hughes with full impact as he roared in. The rock-hard Hughes seemed impervious to anything Stephens threw, and because he had scored two knockdowns he showed he could hurt the champion but the champion had not yet hurt him. Hughes rocked Stephens back with a right uppercut and walloped him with a hook to the point of the chin and sunk a right to the body. Hughes invested every ounce of his 146 pounds behind every blow, even the jab, and it appeared Stephens was just a few punches away from becoming an ex-champion.

Driven to the corner pad, Stephens told Hughes "not so fast." With 30 seconds left in the round, two solid hooks and a stiff one-two cracked off Hughes' jaw and for the first time in the fight Hughes appeared a bit shaken. Hughes retreated on legs that weren't quite right and a re-energized Stephens leaped to action. In his haste to finish off the challenger, Stephens was caught cleanly with a short left. While Stephens fell to the floor, Femia correctly ruled that his fall was not caused by the punch.

With seven seconds remaining, the champion reared back and nailed Hughes with a powerful cross to the jaw. Incredibly, Hughes was unmoved. But Stephens was undeterred as he capped off a big rally with a one-two followed by a right to the body and a left to the jaw. When the bell rang, Hughes stared and jutted out his chin at Stephens as if to say, *"I took your best and I'm still here."*

Hughes' trainer Wally Denkins was beside himself. "Not enough pressure! Not enough pressure!" he yelled. Hughes nodded his agreement as Denkins began to work on the cut under the right eye. "You got him ready to go, boy. You ain't throwing enough g****** punches. When he ties you up and you have that right hand free, work it!"

Hughes ran out of the corner to start the eighth and body blocked Stephens to the corner. Hughes landed a right to the body, and as he looked for another opening Hughes clocked him with an electric right to the jaw and pivoted away. Hughes was caught flush and couldn't have been hit any harder but to the uninitiated eye he appeared unaffected. But Stephens' years of experience told him otherwise and when he followed up with a flurry of punches, he forced Hughes to reveal his true status as he unsteadily retreated across the ring. Hughes was in big trouble and he sought to hold on, but Stephens broke loose and nailed him with a monstrous hook that sent the challenger skittering across the ring. Stephens hammered away with rights to the body as Hughes desperately sought to hold on.

Finally securing a firm grip, Hughes walked Stephens around the ring for a few seconds and during the clinch Stephens' face took on the appearance of a man with a depleted gas tank. After all, he had absorbed two knockdowns earlier in the fight and he had spent the entire bout dealing with Hughes' immense pressure. After missing with an overhand right, it was now Stephens who initiated the clinch and he took full advantage as he clamped on, walked Hughes to a corner and rested his head on the challenger's right shoulder for several long seconds. Stephens' mouthpiece also fell out of his mouth during the long walk, so he bought even more rest time while Femia had the mouthpiece rinsed and reinserted.

After being so energetic just moments earlier, Stephens' body was in free-fall as the effects of exhaustion gripped him. During the mouthpiece-inspired break, Stephens took two deep breaths and Bonano told him to go after Hughes' body.

Seeing Stephens' obvious weakness, Hughes turned up the pressure and drove a hook to the body. But the rest also did Stephens some good as he fired a right to the head and a second one to the ear. His rally proved temporary as an excellent overhand right by Hughes caught Stephens coming in and a second lead right shook the champion. A third right drove Stephens to the canvas like a hammer driving a nail into a piece of wood. As he rested on his back along the ropes, Stephens turned his head and told his corner "I'm all right, I'm all right."

After rising at seven, Femia found that the mouthpiece had once again fallen out of Stephens' mouth and that the hometown man would receive yet another extended rest. No point penalty, however, was assessed, and a second look at the action revealed that Stephens had not spat out the mouthpiece intentionally. Still, circumstances conspired to give the champion a fortunately timed rest.

At first, Hughes thought the delay meant the fight was being stopped and he raised his arms, but after an additional 15-second break the two fighters were once again brought together. In the few seconds remaining in the round, Hughes managed to land a couple of more rights, but his chance to end the fight at this juncture had been cut short.

Stephens left his corner energetically for round nine, eager to show Hughes he had recovered from his late-round beating. But Hughes wasn't deceived as he pressured the champion and worked the right overtime to the head and body. A right caught Stephens' jaw and a straight left buckled his legs slightly. A heavy chopping right hit the mark and it appeared his brute strength was starting to crack Stephens' resolve.

This was Hughes' plan all along. He knew he had to take a lot of punishment early but he also knew he was tough enough to handle it. He was bonded to his fight plan and he stuck with it in good times and in bad – and his faithfulness was starting to pay off. He was cutting off the ring at will and he hurt Stephens with a jolting hook that twisted his head awkwardly. Stephens' energy was ebbing away and at one point he hooked both gloves around the top ropes and trapped Hughes for several seconds to get a much-needed breather.

Hughes finally had the champion right where he wanted him.

Round nine was a statistical wipeout for Hughes as he landed 39 of his 77 punches for 51 percent accuracy while Stephens was just 11 of 36 (31 percent). In terms of power punches, Hughes landed 30 of them with Stephens connecting on just one.

Hughes continued his surge in round 10 as he powered an overhand right to the jaw that buckled Stephens' right leg awkwardly and twisted his body 180 degrees toward the ropes. Somehow, Stephens stayed on his feet but Hughes sought to take advantage with two torrid right uppercuts. The champion fought his way out of the corner and clamped down on Hughes. Then, for the fourth time in the fight, Stephens' mouthpiece hit the floor and this time it was intentionally spat out. However, Femia, though it appeared he saw it, let the fight continue without interruption, preventing Stephens from getting the long rest he sought.

So what did Stephens do? He fought back – hard.

A chopping right to the ear initiated a clinch by Hughes and he began to look a bit winded. Another chopping right put Hughes on the retreat and a third one made Hughes' body sag into the corner. Hughes gathered himself by circling away from the corner and nailing Stephens with a shotgun jab and a heavy right several seconds later that made him back away a few steps. The champion roared back strongly behind a left-right, an upward arcing hook to the face and a chopping right to the temple. The two exchanged brutal rights, with Hughes' driving Stephens back to the ropes and Stephens' hitting Hughes flush in the face. A right to the body drove Hughes toward the ropes and Stephens followed up with two left uppercuts to the jaw that pushed him to the corner. As he pursued his advantage, Stephens' right glove got tangled in the rope that separated the top and second ropes. But he didn't let that stop him as he crashed in two more lefts as he extricated his other arm. As the bell ended a tumultuous 10th, both men trudged to their corners, utterly spent.

It was a brutal round statistically. Both men landed 57 percent of their punches, with Stephens landing 50 of 88 and Hughes 34 of 60.

Stephens jabbed out of a crouch as the 11th began, and while his spirit was more than willing and his body wanted to comply, what was produced didn't seem all there. His feet were wide apart and his punches lacked their earlier crispness. Hughes was the fresher man and he took advantage of Stephens' fatigue in the first 30 seconds by throwing a right-left-right that dropped the champion for the fourth time. Up at five, Femia stopped the count and waved the two fighters back together, but then stepped between them to wipe off Stephens' gloves. Hughes hurt Stephens with a looping right to the jaw and as he backed to ring center his legs were in a sorry state. But Stephens wanted to keep his title badly and he was willing to put everything on the line to keep it.

A torrid right uppercut snapped Stephens' head back and another right forced Stephens to take a step back. But Hughes was also weary and he hooked his left arm on the rope to buy a little rest time. Midway through the round, they exchanged heavy blows and while Hughes landed a solid hook, Stephens' right-left was even better and a hard jab sent Hughes retreating to ring center. Astonishingly, Stephens began forcing the fight and Hughes was taking in huge breaths whenever he got the chance.

It was an extraordinary display of will by both men. Stephens was doing everything humanly possible to save his championship while Hughes had invested every ounce of himself into winning the belt. With fatigue racking both of their bodies, they were fighting on nerve alone and while the action wasn't pretty, the spirit and resolve were riveting to watch. In the final 10 seconds, Stephens' mouthpiece again dropped to the canvas but that didn't stop him from muscling Hughes across the ring with a series of fatigue-laden blows. As the bell rang, Stephens had again defied logic by mounting a strong comeback in a round in which he was knocked down.

Hughes' trainer Bonano knew his fighter was in need of a lift as the fight entered the final three minutes, and he sought to whip his fighter into a final frenzy by breaking out the verbal whip and reminding him of the perceived political mountain he still had to surmount.

"This is it baby, this is it!" he urged as Hughes took in deep gulps of air. "You've got to have this round. You know how they'll do you. You got four knockdowns but you know how they'll do you. You've got to have it. Don't stop throwing g****** punches! Never! Get up off your a** and show them what you're about! Show them now! Take this round!"

As Femia commanded them to touch gloves, Hughes extended his gloves at waist level but the instant after Stephens hurriedly tapped the gloves, the hometown hero ambushed Hughes with a left hook to the jaw and drove him to the ropes with a flurry of jabs. Hughes spun out and worked his jab, and when Stephens slipped to the canvas, Hughes showed the sportsmanship Stephens didn't by stepping away and giving him a chance to regain his feet unmolested.

Still, Stephens continued to push himself forward and he was the one throwing more blows while Hughes initiated more of the clinches. But Hughes was just biding his time before lowering the boom.

Hughes countered Stephens' jab with his own jab, and both men set themselves to throw right hands. Stephens' whizzed by harmlessly while Hughes' hit the bull's eye. A smashing hook immediately followed and Stephens fell for the fifth time. Both of his legs folded underneath his body and his torso slumped to the canvas. Femia gave Stephens every opportunity to rise, but he could only get to one knee by Femia's count of 10. With just 70 seconds left in the fight, Hughes sprung the upset and became the new USBA welterweight champion.

With renewed energy that could come only from his deep sense of exhilaration and accomplishment, Hughes raised his arms, ran from the neutral corner and was lifted by his handlers, a broad smile spreading across his face. He marched around the ring, climbed the ropes and yelled out in triumph and perhaps a bit of defiance as scored the biggest victory of his career on the road.

"I knew I had to be the judge, I'm in his back yard," Hughes told ESPN's Dave Bontempo. "I've been fighting in other people's back yards and I've been robbed on a bunch of occasions. I kept a lot of pressure on him and I knew he would fade in the later rounds. I kept the pressure on and I caught him."

Despite having eight losses on his record, James Hughes was no longer a journeyman but a real player in the welterweight division. He was one step closer to his dream and he couldn't have been happier. As for Stephens, he fought with a champion's bravery but he ended up falling just short. The real winners, however, were those who watched the fight and even though the hometown fighter didn't win they were treated to one of 1994's most exciting contests. Pretty records are nice to look at, but to fight fans actions speak louder than numbers.

Epilogue: The loss to Hughes wasn't the end of Stephens' career – not by a long shot. Four months after losing to Hughes, Stephens stopped Kevin Pompey in nine rounds. Five more victories – including one over Aaron Davis – earned him a crack at the vacant IBF title against Raul Marquez April 12, 1997. Marquez stopped Stephens in nine rounds, but that wouldn't be Stephens' last opportunity at a title. That would come two fights later against IBF junior middleweight king Luis Ramon "Yory Boy" Campas on March 23, 1998, and the fight ended in heartbreaking fashion for Stephens as a dislocated left shoulder forced him to retire on his stool after the third round.

Over the next eight years, Stephens fought 14 times, winning only four. But Stephens left the sport a winner, for on October 24, 2006 at the Petroleum Club in Shreveport, Louisiana the 41-year-old 197-pounder stopped the 0-16 Glen Brown in three rounds to raise his final record to 33-19-2 with 18 knockouts.

Five months after the victory over Stephens, Hughes continued to roll as he stopped the previously unbeaten (13-0-1) Adrian Stone in 10 rounds to defend the belt. Two months later he iced Kenny Lewis in one round and on July 7, 1995 in Bossier City, he notched another successful title defense by stopping Nick Rupa.

Eighteen days after the Rupa fight, the 29-year-old Hughes' body was found in a swamp but the circumstances surrounding his death remain a mystery. The autopsy revealed that Hughes had received blunt trauma to the head but not one that would have resulted in his death. Trace amounts of cocaine were found in his liver but the amount wouldn't have killed him or caused him serious harm in their judgment. No stab wounds or bullet holes were found on his body. No cause of death was ever determined and speculation has run rampant. No definitive answers have ever emerged and the entire truth may never be known.

Hughes final record reads 27-8 with 19 KO.

WARS OF ATTRITION

Total Punches Landed/Thrown

Round	1	2	3	4	5	6	7	8	9	10	11	12	Total
Hughes													347/741 47%
Stephens													281/640 44%

* Fight originally done by CompuBox, but the original HTML files with complete round-by-round statistics no longer exist.

James Hughes vs. Anthony Stephens October 26, 1994, Bossier City, Louisiana

TALES FROM THE VAULT

Ebo Elder vs. Courtney Burton
December 17, 2004, Santa Ynez, California

Many ingredients need to be present if a boxer wants to squeeze out every bit of potential he possesses. Talent, of course, is the biggest and most obvious of these but the intangibles of desire, faith, stubbornness, knowledge and will are just as important – and in some cases, even more so.

When a fighter encounters an opponent who has nearly the same talent, he must call upon the foundations of his personality and experience to overcome the challenges set before him. Even if he emerges triumphant in the end, it doesn't necessarily mean he is the superior man for all time; he just performed better on that day. History is replete with examples of boxers reversing the results of their first encounters, so the glory of winning and the stigma of losing should only be limited to that slice of time.

When Ebo Elder and Courtney Burton met at the Chumash Casino in Santa Ynez, California, they not only exhibited their physical skills but also the contents of their characters both during the fight and afterward. It was a fight that was made for television because of the drama in both the sporting and human sense.

Before Elder was a "Contender," he was a prospect. The native of Newnan, Georgia and resident of Atlanta had a solid amateur foundation as he won 125 fights and captured the silver medal at the Goodwill Games. As a young pro, the man known as the "X-treme Machine" maintained an extreme schedule as he fought 17 times in his first 17 months, with his best win being a 10-round decision over future title challenger Emmanuel Clottey on July 3, 2001. But fight number 17 proved to be a shock to Elder's system as Ubaldo Hernandez blasted him out in a single round and toppled him from the ranks of the unbeaten.

Elder's hectic schedule burned him out on boxing and his relationship with father/trainer Greg suffered. The 22-year-old desperately needed a break from the sport and for the next 26 months he did everything but box, even joining a rock-and-roll band. But Elder's roots in boxing ran deep and the time away allowed him to regain his love for the sport as well as reaffirm his relationships with both his biological and spiritual fathers. Elder returned to the ring by stopping Tyrone Wiggins in the third round and a lopsided 10-round decision over fellow unbeaten Oscar Diaz two months later propelled his career skyward. Three more victories, including a sixth round KO over Ricardo Fuentes two months earlier to win the vacant NABO/WBO lightweight belt, set up the match with Burton.

Burton got his start in boxing – and a big jump-start in life – through a chance encounter when he was eight years old. He was involved in a street fight in which he was outnumbered and was being beaten with a baseball bat when trainer Napolean

Lark happened to drive toward the scene. Lark jumped out of the car and scared away Burton's attackers, then asked Burton if he would like to learn how to defend himself. Burton accepted Lark's invitation and stopped by the local community center the next day. Lark and his wife eventually would become the legal guardians of Burton and his younger brother Bill.

Like Elder, Burton had an excellent amateur career as he won 87 of his 91 fights and turned pro as a welterweight in July 1996 with a four round majority decision win over Sam Mahmoud. Following the victory, Burton didn't fight again for the next 38 months.

He returned in September 1999 as a 140-pounder and proceeded to reel off wins against nondescript Midwest competition. Burton was 16-0 with one no-contest when Eleazar Contreras Jr. dropped Burton five times en route to a fifth-round stoppage.

Burton rebounded strongly from the defeat as he registered back-to-back eighth round knockouts of Gabriel Ruelas and Angel Manfredy. The Manfredy win vaulted Burton into world prominence, but from that fight forward his form began to suffer. He struggled to a 12-round split decision win over Francisco Lorenzo and four months later Julio Diaz stopped him in 11 rounds in an IBF elimination fight. His most recent outing five months earlier resulted in a highly controversial split decision win over Emanuel Augustus, a verdict that many have called among the worst of the decade.

So Elder-Burton is a tale of two fighters going in different directions but whose desire to win were at a similar point. For Elder (21-1, 13 KO), a win meant advancement while for Burton (21-2, 11 KO with one no-contest) it meant career survival.

Both men began the fight working the jab and Burton, known for his constant switch-hitting, started in the right-handed stance. Burton, 135, began reaching Elder with lefts while Elder, 134 ½, found success with several left crosses. Burton momentarily switched to lefty to land a lead right, then immediately switched back. Elder was picking his spots, throwing right-lefts then moving to the side after landing bustling combinations to the body. As Elder dug a left to the body, Burton nailed him with a left over the top. The briefly stunned Elder reacted instantly by shoe-shining Burton's body. As the round closed, they exchanged on the inside with some of the blows landing below the belt. Neither man gained a discernable advantage but the action planted a strategic seed about future tactics.

Elder landed the first significant punch of round two with a straight left and he immediately followed up with several body shots. The unhurt Burton tagged the charging Elder with a strong right and pushed him back toward the ropes with a series of jabs and dug a good right-left to the body. On the inside, Burton switched to southpaw and caught Elder with a short left to the cheek and a long right that made Elder back out to long range. Back at ring center Burton was committed to the left-handed stance and Elder used his quicker hands to pepper Burton with combinations.

Midway through the round, Burton's heavier hands came into play as a right-left – mixed with an accidental head butt to the face – made Elder briefly stumble back. Eager to prove he wasn't hurt, Elder threw a six-punch flurry that included two solid left uppercuts to the body before backing away.

Though Burton was more effective as a southpaw, he was determined to use the switch-hitting approach, and he showed why as he nailed Elder with a lead right, then a split-second later hitting him with another right as he turned lefty.

As each man tried to gain a foothold on the inside, the action sometimes got messy and at one point both men tumbled to the canvas. Elder sought to regain the momentum with several flashy flurries but Burton, again as a southpaw, landed a solid right hook as the round ended.

Elder attempted to regain his rhythm in the third as he connected with a sharp right-left followed by a four-punch flurry capped by a right to the ribs. More body shots from Elder set up a quick right hook, and a second hook connected a few seconds later. The orthodox Burton caught Elder ducking in with a straight right to the jaw, then switched to connect with a double right hook to the head and body. Burton switched stances freely and effectively and took advantage of any openings Elder provided while not trying to do too much.

The intensity of the exchanges escalated with every passing second with Elder using his faster hands and more educated combinations and Burton utilizing his superior single-shot power. Midway through the round, Burton opened a cut around Elder's right eye and Burton worsened it by landing a chopping left. Elder remained composed as he nailed Burton with a right hook and a solid right-left. Burton's right hook hit the target forcefully but Elder fired right back with a right, a right-left and two jabs.

As Elder sat in the corner between rounds, not only did he have the cut over the right eye, a common problem for him, the area around his left eye was discolored and slightly swollen.

Burton started the fourth strongly by landing a lead right to the jaw and backing Elder off with a looping right to the body as a righty and a ripping jab as a southpaw moments later. Burton was building momentum and Elder sought to stem it with bursts of body blows followed by a sharp left uppercut to the face. Burton was determined to draw Elder into a firefight and he slowly was finding success as the action morphed from a boxing match to a toe-to-toe slugfest.

It was not the kind of fight that Greg Elder wanted to see from his son.

"I want to see presence of mind in there," he told him between rounds four and five. "Head feints, head movement, short shots, use the ring a little bit. Catch him coming to you and don't make a big fight out of it, OK? When he goes right-handed, throw left hooks to the body and when he goes left-handed, throw right hooks to the body."

The two met at ring center and launched simultaneous punches – with Burton's landing with far more impact. Elder landed a short hook to the body and began to follow his father's advice by using his speed at long range. A long left to the stomach by Elder hit the borderline and Burton jumped in behind a right hook to the jaw. Elder retaliated with a stinging right-left to the jaw that made Burton back away for the first time in the fight. Burton recovered quickly by shooting a right through Elder's guard and landed a chopping left directly on Elder's cut right eye. Elder connected on an on-the-move triple jab and another three-punch flurry seconds later.

The blood was now running into Elder's eye but he remained composed as he worked behind the jab. Burton's solid right jab knocked out Elder's mouthpiece and a sweeping right hook to the forehead wobbled Elder in the closing seconds. As the bell sounded, Burton fired a long hard stare as if he intended to land a blow to Elder's psyche. The nonplussed Elder returned the stare by briefly glancing over his shoulder.

Elder began the sixth by firing a triple jab and looping a left uppercut to the stomach while Burton worked the angles with his constant switch-hitting. "The X-treme Machine" turned up the speed in this round, unleashing a four-punch combo capped by a sharp left cross that caught Burton pulling out. A few seconds later, Elder strung together another four-punch flurry and ended it with a solid right hook to the jaw.

Elder was landing the cleaner punches but they lacked the steam to deter Burton for long. For Elder, his plan for victory was a long-term strategy that involved chipping away at Burton little by little while Burton had the luxury of short-circuiting everything with a single blow. That was demonstrated in part when Burton hurt Elder with a right hook, but Elder was in no mood to back away and collect himself, instead opting to fire back immediately.

With 1:05 remaining, Elder blasted a right hook that caused Burton to double over and back away to the ropes. Elder rushed in to throw a left but referee Jerry Cantu held him back, led him to a neutral corner and deducted a point for a low blow. The replay showed the blow in question landed on the belt line, but Burton's reaction enabled him to induce Cantu's action. During the 40-second time-out, corner man Malcolm Garrett told Burton to take his time and it paid dividends when he cracked Elder with a chopping left, a right hook and a left cross that forced Elder against the ropes. Elder flurried busily to the body, but Burton neutralized it with a thumping right to the head and left to the body. They finished with round with a rousing exchange, yet it appeared Burton had regained the momentum after a difficult start to the round.

Elder landed a strong combination to force Burton against the ropes early in the seventh, but a good counter left by Burton put an immediate stop to it. Whenever one man launched an attack, the other would instantly retaliate to neutralize its effects. Elder landed the quicker, flashier punches while Burton used his superior upper body strength to maneuver Elder into position and his heavier punches to counteract Elder's point-scoring.

After they frenetically traded blows in the final moments of round seven, the pace slowed in the eighth. Blood still seeped from Elder's right eye, but his peppery combinations raised small swellings under and over Burton's right eye. A quiet ninth turned noisy when Burton first stunned Elder with a lead right to the chin and again with a right hook to the jaw as well as a left cross. The pace dramatically slowed as Burton followed his corner's advice to "rest this round and pick him apart." Still, Elder's face was turning into a grotesque mask. Not only was blood coming out of the right eye, the area around the right side of his mouth was swollen and misshapen.

Burton accelerated his attack in the final minute and Elder went with him with his bustling combinations. A split-second before the bell, Burton nailed Elder with a whistling left cross to the jaw and followed with a right uppercut a tad after the gong. The punch spun Elder's body 180 degrees and forced him to stumble back to his corner.

Burton continued to roll at the start of the 10th when he rocked Elder with a counter right hook. But Burton, mindful of his own stamina, didn't press for the knockout, instead choosing to tag Elder with occasional single punches. Elder used the respite to recharge his batteries, following Burton around the ring and firing jabs. He was being given the most valuable commodity he could have had at this point – time.

Early in the 11th, a Burton rooter in the crowd yelled, "come on Burton, he ain't got no heart left." One of the greatest insults a fighter can hear is that he lacks courage, and the instant after Elder heard it he sprung into action behind a strong left cross. A second one moments later drove Burton to a corner, and though he had regained the upper hand his face hardly had the look of a resurgent fighter. Both eyes and the area around his mouth were swollen and he had to have felt searing pain, but both he and Burton drove themselves forward because they knew the winner would be the man who was willing to dig deeper into his reservoir of courage and desire. Elder's successful sequences were longer lasting and more consistent, but Burton may have stolen the round with a tremendous round-ending flurry that forced Elder to give ground.

The start of the final round saw both men pick up the pace and put more energy into every punch. A Burton combination made Elder bend over at the waist with his gloves at his side. He was clearly in pain and was desperately tired but his will would not permit him to slump to the canvas. With a minute gone, Elder made a last stand as he fired off combinations and backed Burton up. Several in the crowd now chanted Elder's name but soon his rally slowed down, albeit briefly.

Knowing his son needed energy down the stretch, the deeply religious Greg Elder had prayed with his equally devout son several times between rounds, asking for strength to allow the fighter to do what he had to do. With Elder seemingly on his way to a stoppage defeat, those prayers were answered in a most dramatic way.

With 1:15 left in the fight, Elder, who had just missed a three-punch combination, sprang out of a crouch and nailed Burton with a left cross that sent him flying to the corner pad. Burton was in huge trouble and he desperately clung to Elder's waist as they stumbled to ring center. After breaking, Elder snapped Burton's head with a massive left to the chin that sent Burton stumbling forward to the canvas near the ropes. Up at five, he was able to walk forward well enough to satisfy Cantu.

Elder rushed forward and missed with his first flurry. The second one, capped with a final straight left, caused Burton to fall into the ropes in a sitting position. Because Burton hadn't fallen all the way to the canvas, Elder hammered him to the floor with a final left. At that point – with just 50 seconds left on the clock – Cantu declared the fight over.

Elder, his face a gargoyle-like mass of swellings, discolorations and blood, raced to his corner and immediately dropped to his knees, closed his eyes and offered his thanks. His earthly father told him "you knocked him out. You had to have it and you did it."

As Elder rejoiced and the crowd chanted "Ebo! Ebo!," Burton was flat on his back and he wasn't in a good state. Exhaustion racked his body and he remained on the canvas for several minutes as he attempted to collect himself. As soon as Burton was deemed well enough to sit on a stool, Elder made his way over to his freshly vanquished foe.

Elder got on one knee so he could look directly into Burton's eyes and he asked "do you want to pray with me?"

"Yeah," Burton said.

"Lord, I thank you for this gladiator, this man with such heart and such skill, such determination," Elder began. "I pray that you make this loss for him a benefit like you did for me three-and-a-half years ago. Make it the best thing that ever happened to him so that he'll turn his life completely to you, God. I pray that you touch his heart. Make him have no pain, no hurt and no misunderstanding, and let him know that I love him as a brother in Christ. In Jesus' name, amen."

"Amen," Burton said.

Though some may object to this public display of religious faith, one can't argue that this was a genuinely touching and human scene borne of pain, emotion and mercy. Just minutes before, each man was inflicting terrible punishment on the other in the pursuit of a singular goal. But as violent as the action was at times, there was no malevolence in either man's heart, and their actions after the fight proved it beyond doubt.

Though the result propelled one man's career upward while inflicting a setback upon the other, the human element remained refreshingly the same. It is one of boxing's unique ironies that a hard, competitive and punishing fight can bring two fighters closer together as human beings. Only they could ever know the suffering they went through and their shared knowledge, more often than not, translates to everlasting admiration.

Epilogue: The 28-year-old Burton fought three times since the loss to Elder, and he has lost all three fights by knockout. Eight months after the Elder fight, Burton returned to the Chumash Casino, but the result was unfortunately the same as Rolando Reyes stopped him in eight rounds. Four months after that, Juan Lazcano scored a ninth round TKO and his final outing took place in September 2006 in Tulsa, Oklahoma against Emanuel Augustus, who knocked out Burton in eight rounds. His final record reads 21-6 (11 KO).

Elder fared no better in the two fights he had since beating Burton. Nine months later Lakva Sim stopped Elder in the final round of their WBA lightweight eliminator, after which Elder joined the cast of "The Contender" during its second season. On January 27, 2006 at the Contender Gymnasium in Pasadena, Calif., Elder won the first three rounds against Michael "No Joke" Stewart, only to suffer a one-punch knockout in the fourth. The 28-year-old Elder's record reads 22-3 (14 KO).

WARS OF ATTRITION

Total Punches Landed/Thrown

Round	1	2	3	4	5	6	7	8	9	10	11	12	Total
Elder	25/74	22/74	31/88	33/98	30/88	33/91	31/93	29/87	18/77	19/67	26/77	24/80	321/994
	34%	30%	35%	34%	34%	36%	33%	33%	23%	28%	34%	30%	32%
Burton	16/51	22/59	22/65	16/64	21/59	25/71	19/71	20/66	17/46	14/47	26/56	15/39	233/694
	31%	37%	34%	25%	36%	35%	27%	30%	37%	30%	46%	38%	34%

Jabs Landed/Thrown

Round	1	2	3	4	5	6	7	8	9	10	11	12	Total
Elder	7/27	7/26	10/39	11/42	12/39	9/32	9/31	14/46	2/34	4/31	9/32	5/29	99/408
	26%	27%	26%	26%	31%	28%	29%	30%	6%	13%	28%	17%	24%
Burton	7/27	4/27	4/32	5/35	6/24	4/30	5/28	11/36	3/21	5/26	6/23	2/7	62/316
	26%	15%	12%	14%	25%	13%	18%	31%	14%	19%	26%	29%	20%

Power Punches Landed/Thrown

Round	1	2	3	4	5	6	7	8	9	10	11	12	Total
Elder	18/47	15/48	21/49	22/56	18/49	24/59	22/62	15/41	16/43	15/36	17/45	19/51	222/586
	38%	31%	43%	39%	37%	41%	35%	37%	37%	42%	38%	37%	38%
Burton	9/24	18/32	18/33	11/29	15/35	21/41	14/43	9/30	14/25	9/21	20/33	13/32	171/378
	38%	56%	55%	38%	43%	51%	33%	30%	56%	43%	61%	41%	45%

Ebo Elder vs. Courtney Burton December 17, 2004, Santa Ynez, California

TALES FROM THE VAULT

Nestor Garza vs. Enrique Sanchez
December 12, 1998, Indio, California

All fights, especially those for a championship, represent a melding of individual wills. Each combatant has an objective – victory – and to achieve it they must invest the entirety of their knowledge, talent, skill and courage. Ideally, the fighter will possess 100 percent of every capability but in practice one or more areas will be lacking. During those times it is up to the fighter to find ways to make up for his shortcomings. Those who are successful will be remembered in boxing lore and if both participants in a given fight achieve it, their encounter should earn its rightful place in history.

The 122-pound division, though only three decades old in its most recent incarnation, has had more than its share of memorable fights. The 14-round war between Wilfredo Gomez and Lupe Pintor is regarded by many as the greatest junior featherweight title fight ever and the first fight between Marco Antonio Barrera and Erik Morales ranks among history's most savage regardless of division. The unforgettable bout between Barrera and Kennedy McKinney launched HBO's "Boxing After Dark" series, helping greatly to cement the lower weights' presence on "The Network of Champions."

For whatever reason, other fights have slipped through the chronological cracks. Soo Hwan Hong's incredible four-times-off-the-floor KO of Hector Carrasquilla is largely forgotten, as is Leo Cruz's title-winning victory over WBA champ Sergio Palma. Another underrated 122-pound brawl was the December 12, 1998 battle between defending WBA champ Enrique Sanchez and Nestor Garza at the Fantasy Springs Casino in Indio, California.

Sanchez (24-0-1, 17 KO) won the vacant title by decisioning Rafael Del Valle nearly 10 months earlier, and the Garza fight was his first defense. At 5-8, Sanchez was very tall for his weight class and he utilized his natural advantages by keeping his foes at a distance with snappy, precise jabs and producing quick, crowd-pleasing knockouts with straight, needle-sharp lefts. He raced to a 13-0 (11 KO) record before making his U.S. debut, a two-round knockout of Horacio Ramirez in Las Vegas. Sanchez continued to impress as he piled up victories in the U.S. against mid-level competition. Those wins led to a crack at the vacant WBA super bantamweight title against the 23-1-1 Del Valle. Though Sanchez won the belt, he didn't enter the Garza defense on the best of notes as he fought a surprising 10-round draw with the 21-17-3 Ricardo Medina in a non-title go five months earlier.

At just 22, Garza had already engaged in 35 pro fights, winning 34 and scoring 27 knockouts. The man known as "El Tigre" tore through his early competition as he scored 17 knockouts in his first 18 fights, including 15 in the first two rounds and six consecutive one-rounders. He, too, prospered after making his U.S. debut with a three-round KO of Julio Cesar Cardona at the Great Western Forum. His best wins came against Roland Gomez (KO 5), Cruz Carvajal (W 12) and Freddie Cruz (W 10), which led to his successful challenge of WBO/NABO super bantamweight champion Jesus Sarabia (W 12) 10 weeks before challenging Garza for world honors.

Both men began the fight throwing fast range-finding jabs with Sanchez finding the mark with a pair of light left crosses. But it didn't take long for Garza to close the gap and initiate a toe-to-toe exchange. He tagged Sanchez with hooks to the body and a right to the chin and Sanchez immediately retaliated to neutralize Garza's advantage. A few moments later, Garza again charged with fists flying and pushed Sanchez to the ropes with a flurry, but Sanchez smartly spun off and set up shop at ring center.

Sanchez used his boxing skills as a precursor to sudden, explosive bursts of power and Garza was about to get a taste of that. After Garza missed with a wild right, both men prepared to crank lefts. Sanchez beat Garza to the punch as he planted a perfect cross to the jaw, driving Garza back-first to the canvas with 45 seconds remaining. As the crowd roared, Garza appeared ready to rise at two but as he began to pull himself up with the ropes he thought better of it and waited until referee Lou Filippo's count of seven before getting to his feet. Garza sported a tiny cut on the forehead above the right eye, and as Filippo signaled him to continue he banged his gloves together determinedly.

Because Garza appeared clear-eyed, Sanchez didn't press his advantage and was content to snap jabs at long range. A quick left jerked Garza's head back in the closing seconds, but he did nothing more to consolidate his edge. As he sat in the corner between rounds, Sanchez's nose and the corner of his mouth leaked blood.

Though he suffered an early knockdown, Garza would not let that prevent him from probervially putting his head into the lion's mouth. He had no choice because he was three inches shorter and sported a two-inch reach disadvantage, so he leaped in behind a quick hook-right combo and pushed him toward the ropes. Garza dug in a nasty hook to the ribs and fired a flurry but Sanchez put a stop to it by blasting him with a pinpoint counter left cross that made Garza's legs dip dramatically. Thinking Garza was on his way down for the second time, Sanchez walked toward the neutral corner. But Garza kept his feet and charged toward the nonchalant Sanchez. Sanchez looked over his shoulder and seemed surprised as he saw Garza running in behind an overhand right to the jaw. Sanchez braced himself just in time; he took the blow well and pivoted to ring center.

The bout soon assumed a pattern; the sudden explosions of power were preceded by long stretches of careful, cerebral boxing with jabs, feints, moves and counter moves. This was the case when Sanchez scored the knockdown in round one and the champ would soon learn that turnabout was fair play.

Sanchez began round three with a counter right-left that tagged Garza, but seconds later the challenger would really get Sanchez's attention. Moments bouncing a left off Garza's nose, Sanchez fired a jab that missed. Garza then unleashed a trip-hammer counter right on the button that sent Sanchez sprawling to the canvas.

The champ was up immediately but Garza's blow inflicted horrible damage. Blood poured out of Sanchez's nose and mouth and combined with a cut around the left eye his face was a crimson mask. He might have looked awful but his legs were strong and steady and his mind clear.

Sanchez smartly used his reach to make it difficult for Garza to press his advantage. Garza's lead rights were now wild and short of the target and Sanchez countered nicely with a snappy right hook that followed a missed lead left. Garza ducked inside and cracked a swooping hook to the face that made Sanchez retreat on slightly wobbly legs and a follow-up right propelled him into the ropes. Sanchez staved off the attack behind a solid right hook and he managed to spin off and jab the round away at ring center.

Sanchez continued to jab well to start the fourth, illustrating how powerful a weapon height and reach can be. They gave him strategic options that Garza simply didn't have. He could choose to box and jab his way to victory or use his power to bomb out Garza, all within the parameters of his preferred distance. Though Garza possessed good speed and skill, he was forced to fight only one way if he wanted to take Sanchez's title. Also, because he was the challenger, he carried the burden of proof; he had to show the judges through his aggression and power that he deserved to become the new champion.

Garza added an exhibit for his case in the fourth round as he buckled Sanchez's knees with a sweeping hook. With 30 seconds remaining he nailed Sanchez with two consecutive rights to the jaw, a hook to the temple, a driving left to the side, a right hook and a piercing jab to the eye that had Sanchez holding on. Garza bulled Sanchez to the ropes and unleashed another flurry but Sanchez ended the round with a snappy right-left to the chin, delivering a not-so-friendly reminder that he still needed to be wary of the champ's power.

Sanchez started the fifth by delivering a stinging right-left, but Garza soon bulled Sanchez to the ropes with another combination. Garza was trying to force a firefight while Sanchez wanted a controlled boxing match. Sanchez demonstrated his talent by not just throwing, but landing, an unusual right uppercut-left cross combo. Though Garza had to be aggressive, he was willing to wait for the right opportunity to present itself.

Midway through the round Garza smacked a hook-cross combination and a follow-up three-punch flurry sent Sanchez skittering along the ropes. Garza pummeled the champion with a torrent of blows and caught Sanchez with a solid hook and a rattling right as the champ tried to escape to ring center.

It was Garza's best and most sustained attack of the fight and the grimacing Sanchez, who had always fired back immediately when attacked previously, now sought to clinch. He managed to nail the charging Garza with an overhand left that had the challenger clinching briefly, but Garza regained control seconds later with more bustling combinations on the inside and he carried that momentum for the rest of the round.

Sanchez worked the jab feverishly to start the sixth but Garza walked through them and knocked Sanchez into the ropes with a strong right hook to the jaw, and two more propelled him into further retreat.

As Garza pelted Sanchez with short punches on the inside, it was clear the fight's momentum had swung his way. He had finally found the avenue by which he could get past the champion's long arms, and it didn't take much for Garza to draw blood from Sanchez's nose and mouth. Garza pushed a fast, grueling pace that forced both men to unleash hard, thumping shots. While Sanchez had the luxury of height and reach, Garza neutralized it by forcing the control-conscious champion to fight harder and faster than he wanted, especially considering the facial injuries.

Though the flow of the fight suited Garza more, Sanchez adjusted to his new environment as he strung together a right hook-left cross-straight right combo that made the challenger take a step back. As the round closed, Garza fired a trio of left-rights that fell short but still kept Sanchez moving backward.

The intense boxing at close range continued in the seventh with Garza landing straight rights and Sanchez connecting with left crosses. The gap between them shrunk and the pace accelerated as they exchanged leads and counters that landed with almost frightening flushness. A short right hook to the face early in the eighth sent Garza stumbling forward but the challenger rebounded instantly behind a solid counter hook. Garza found pay dirt with several straight rights but the stoic Sanchez calmly retaliated with stiff jabs followed by a left cross. In the final 35 seconds, Garza ratcheted up the pace behind a slew of overhand rights that mostly missed the target but forced Sanchez to remain in a defensive mode.

Garza continued his charge in the ninth as he drove Sanchez back with punches thrown with a strength and speed that belied the intense action that preceded them. A right hook late in the second minute of the 10th spun Sanchez's head and caused him to slump into the ropes. Sanchez tried to whirl off toward ring center as he had in earlier rounds, but this time Garza wouldn't let him do so without paying a price as he blasted a hook to the jaw.

Retreating on wobbly legs, Sanchez tried to clinch but Garza shook him off and continued to press. Sanchez was now in survival mode as he tried valiantly to hold off his surging opponent. Though Sanchez continued to hold his form by keeping his hands high and throwing needle-straight punches, his face was becoming a hideous sight. The areas above and below both eyes were badly discolored and blood was smeared all over his face as he absorbed Garza's whirlwind attack. Garza opened a deep slice above Sanchez's left eye late in the round, and the blood only added fuel to Garza's already raging fire.

Garza was taking advantage of the innate psychological edge all challengers possess when the skill level is relatively even: He was striving toward a higher plateau that represented his profession's ultimate summit while Sanchez struggled to keep something he already owned. Human nature suggests that we invest more of ourselves when we try to attain a higher goal as opposed to defending what is already ours, and that equation was definitely at work here. Garza was attempting to make history by adding his name to the roll of champions while Sanchez's reward was to push himself a notch higher among his peers, much like a third-degree black belt in karate works to earn fourth-degree status. While Sanchez did the best he could, he didn't have the extra boost of ambition Garza enjoyed.

Still, Sanchez literally was willing to give his last drop of blood to emerge victorious, and though his face as a grotesque sight he continued to fire away. A strong left in the 11th made Garza nod his head in recognition and a second one snapped his head back and drove him to the ropes. But Garza was too close to his dream to let anything stop him and he continued to press forward for the rest of the round.

Knowing the end was at hand, Garza stepped up the pace even more as the final round began, pelting him with lead rights to Sanchez's misshapen face. Sanchez's shoulders, chest and back were blood-spattered yet he produced a strong left cross that made Garza blink – but only for a moment. He fought like a man consumed with the idea of victory and the rewards that would come with it. Both men tore through the finish line with vicious exchanges and when the final bell sounded they lifted their arms in victory.

The decision was unanimous. Duane Ford saw the fight 116-111 while James Jen Kin and Jesus Covan judged it 115-112 and 114-112 for the winner – and new – champion Nestor Garza.

Garza beamed as the belt was fastened around his waist while Sanchez lowered his battered visage in disappointment. Blood caked his mouth and nose and his eyes sported ugly purple bruises. But his was the face of a champion, a warrior who invested everything he had only to come up short on the scorecards. He may have lost the fight but in no way was he a loser. He had stayed true to the fighter's code and because of that he, along with Garza, produced one of the greatest fights his weight class had ever seen. If he does nothing else in his career, at least he would have that.

Epilogue: Sanchez's next fight took place six months later and he scored a three-round KO over Eugenio Ventura. Two more victories over Eddie Saenz (KO 3) and former champion Juan Polo Perez (KO 4) followed but then his tender skin began getting in the way of progress. An accidental clash of heads resulted in a seven-round technical draw with Carlos Contreras and he would suffer three others later on his career.

Following a six-round TKO to Marco Antonio Barrera, Sanchez fought twice against Nelson Ramon Medina and butt-induced cuts played a big role in both bouts. The first was a technical decision victory for Sanchez while the rematch two-and-a-half months later resulted in a two-round technical draw. Four months later, Sanchez was again involved in a butt/cut-induced technical draw with Jorge Martinez and it became clear that while Sanchez's spirit was willing, his face could no longer handle the stress of combat. His final fight came on June 3, 2004 against future IBF featherweight champion Robert "The Ghost" Guerrero in Lincoln City, Ore., where he lost by eighth round TKO. The 31-year-old Sanchez retired with a record of 30-3-4 with 21 knockouts.

Garza returned to the ring five months later and would notch successful defenses against Carlos Barreto (KO 8) in Las Vegas and Kozo Ishii (KO 12) in Tokyo. Following a non-title tune-up against Hugo Torres (KO 6), Garza lost the title to Clarence "Bones" Adams by unanimous decision on March 4, 2000. An eighth-round TKO of Armando Arriaga followed three months later but then he would suffer two consecutive TKO losses to Hector Mancina. A three-and-a-half year hiatus followed but Garza, just a few months past 29, launched a one-fight comeback February 17, 2006 in McAllen, Texas as a junior welterweight. He polished off clubfighter Mikkel Williams in one round, and his record stands at 41-4 with 33 knockouts.

TALES FROM THE VAULT

Total Punches Landed/Thrown

Round	1	2	3	4	5	6	7	8	9	10	11	12	Total
Garza	13/51	9/51	6/33	24/74	24/83	14/67	17/81	18/73	16/65	28/100	12/82	18/85	199/845
	25%	18%	18%	32%	29%	21%	21%	25%	25%	28%	15%	21%	24%
Sanchez	11/62	9/57	11/65	9/63	19/70	15/82	22/78	13/66	14/70	15/82	15/73	11/57	164/825
	18%	16%	17%	14%	27%	18%	28%	20%	20%	18%	21%	19%	20%

Jabs Landed/Thrown

Round	1	2	3	4	5	6	7	8	9	10	11	12	Total
Garza	0/9	1/12	2/12	0/8	0/7	1/12	2/15	0/10	1/9	2/10	2/30	2/17	13/151
	0%	8%	17%	0%	0%	8%	13%	0%	11%	20%	7%	12%	9%
Sanchez	1/40	3/42	6/49	4/44	6/34	7/46	11/50	4/42	7/45	4/43	10/48	6/36	69/519
	2%	7%	12%	9%	18%	15%	22%	10%	16%	9%	21%	17%	13%

Power Punches Landed/Thrown

Round	1	2	3	4	5	6	7	8	9	10	11	12	Total
Garza	13/42	8/39	4/21	24/66	24/76	13/55	15/66	18/63	15/56	26/90	10/52	16/68	186/694
	31%	21%	19%	36%	32%	24%	23%	29%	27%	29%	19%	24%	27%
Sanchez	10/22	6/15	5/16	5/19	13/36	8/36	11/28	9/24	7/25	11/39	5/25	5/21	95/306
	45%	40%	31%	26%	36%	22%	39%	38%	28%	28%	20%	24%	31%

Nestor Garza vs. Enrique Sanchez December 12, 1998, Indio, California

Jaime Garza vs. Joe Ruelaz
May 18, 1987, Inglewood, California

Sports are fueled by our innate competitiveness, which was honed and perfected during the era when hunting and gathering was not a hobby but the means by which we survived. Athletes pit their skills against one another in individual and team settings while their fans invest their territorial zeal — and their hard-earned money — in the hope that their group of athletes will emerge with the ultimate prize, a championship.

Many times, the lengthy regular season only serves as an appetizer to the main event, the playoffs. There, the intensity is ratcheted up because every defeat represents one step closer to seasonal oblivion. The NCAA men's basketball tournament personifies all the best elements of tournament play — Davids competing against, and often beating, the sport's Goliaths in the opening rounds of play but in the end, more often than not, the best teams rise to the top.

In one sense, boxing is the greatest sport of all because every fight is a "one and done" situation, especially at the elite level. The winner moves on to bigger fights and larger paychecks while the loser is left to pick up the pieces and begin again — or perhaps not. Still, boxing has operated within the tournament concept on several occasions. When the WBA stripped Muhammad Ali of his heavyweight title for the second time for refusing military induction, the sanctioning body put together an eight-man tournament to crown Ali's "successor." Jimmy Ellis defeated Jerry Quarry over 15 rounds to win WBA recognition but was stopped by New York State champion Joe Frazier when he tried to win the undisputed title. In the 1980s, both ESPN and the Great Western Forum regularly staged tournaments. The Forum's tournament, then sponsored by Stroh's beer, consisted of eight (and sometimes 16) fighters and the prize was twofold — a $100,000 check and a top-10 world ranking. Both prizes served as powerful motivation and more often than not it resulted in memorable and riveting spectacles.

Such was the case when Jaime Garza and Joe Ruelaz met in the quarterfinals of the Stroh's featherweight tournament at the Great Western Forum. This was the second fight for both in the tournament; just five weeks earlier Garza (45-2, 42 KO) scored a somewhat lackluster decision over Dwight Pratchett while Ruelaz (20-3, 16 KO) impressively KO'd former WBA bantamweight champion Julian Solis in three rounds. It was fitting that their fight took place in a tournament setting because both stood at a career crossroads.

For the 24-year-old Ruelaz the Garza fight was another chance to push himself past a higher level of opponent, a level that often proved to be beyond his grasp. Though he had won the NABF featherweight title in 12-round war with Tommy Cordova, two of his three losses came to his most prominent opponents: Freddie Roach (KO by 4) and

Bernard Taylor (L 12) eight months earlier. A victory over Garza would raise Ruelaz's stock considerably, and should he win he might get the chance to fight red-hot prospect and tournament favorite Hector Lopez – who just happened to be at ringside taking notes.

At one time, the 27-year-old Garza was one of boxing's budding superstars. The Texas native moved to California to train under Bennie Georgino, and soon he launched a meteoric rise toward world prominence. His early fights featured both offensive fireworks and defensive disasters as he often rebounded from early knockdowns to score spectacular stoppages. Many observers compared Garza to another one of Georgino's proteges, Danny "Little Red" Lopez. Garza rolled to a 37-0 (35 KO) record, including 20 consecutive knockouts, to earn a crack at the WBC super bantamweight title vacated by Wilfredo Gomez. His opponent that day was Filipino Bobby Berna, and the fight assumed a familiar pattern. Berna stunned the Olympic Auditorium crowd – and perhaps Garza himself – by flooring him in the first, but Garza quickly rebounded to score his own knockdown later in the round and stopped Berna in the next round.

Garza stopped Austreberto Perez in five in a non-title fight and had problems with the freakishly tall southpaw Felipe Orozsco before scoring a one-punch knockout in the third. The 40-0 (38 KO) Garza earned a national showcase when CBS aired his defense against Juan "Kid" Meza on the same card as Billy Costello's WBC super lightweight defense against Saoul Mamby. Meza-Garza featured the usual pyrotechnics, but not the usual result. After Garza floored Meza with a wide hook just 40 seconds into the fight, Meza flattened Garza with a torrid hook to the jaw. The superstar-in-the-making had come undone, and he spent the next 15 months contemplating his future.

Garza returned as a full-fledged featherweight and he regained his footing while upsetting Miguel Arrozal's to score a three-round KO. Following three more knockouts Garza ran into a buzzsaw in the form of Darryl Thigpen, who scored four knockdowns en route to a sixth round TKO. But Garza was determined to soldier on, and three months later he entered the Stroh's tournament and defeated Pratchett to set up the fight with Ruelaz. Garza was rated 12th by the WBC while Ruelaz was 13th and number two by the NABF.

Much was at stake for both men, and once the opening bell rang they fought like it.

After a brief feeling-out period, Ruelaz opened the festivities with a sharp left-left-right to the jaw and landed a good counter jab after Garza feinted with the right. Both worked at long range to gauge the other's weaponry and early on it was Ruelaz who appeared to have the quicker hands and the faster trigger.

Garza was by far the harder hitter and it proved to be an early wild card. As Ruelaz leaned in to deliver a less-than-snappy left-right, Garza countered over the top with a quick double hook that shook Ruelaz slightly. Encouraged, Garza followed with a right uppercut and an overhand right followed by a chopping right to the jaw and a thumping right to the belly. The crowd's volume rose as they sensed what Garza already knew – Ruelaz was stunned and vulnerable.

A sharp jab popped Ruelaz's head back, but the Santa Ana, California product served notice that he wasn't ready to depart as he cracked Garza with a chopping lead right cross as Garza prepared to launch a hook. Garza regrouped quickly behind a double jab, and another powerful one-two forced Ruelaz to back away. Garza ripped a right cross to the jaw and a hook to the liver and followed moments later with a lead hook and an overhand right to the temple. Garza closed a resounding first round by winning an exchange of jabs.

Though many hard punches landed, they were launched within the context of a boxing match instead of a brawl. Both men were light on their feet and they operated as if they were following definitive plans. That wasn't a surprise when one considered that Georgino trained Garza and Jackie McCoy guided Ruelaz. Incidentally, this fight marked the first time in their 30-year association that Georgino and McCoy worked opposite corners. Much like boxers in the same situation, Georgino and McCoy said their friendship would continue after the fight but would work with all their might to secure victory on fight night.

Buoyed by his first-round success, Garza came out more aggressively in round two. But his looping blows allowed Ruelaz to land a good jab and a solid left-right to the jaw. Ruelaz smacked a looping right to the jaw and connected with another long right moments later.

For Garza, an all-or-nothing fighter with little defensive prowess, this was an occupational hazard but more often than not his power was enough to see him through almost any situation. Whether that power would serve him as well at featherweight was one of the more intriguing questions surrounding the bout.

A little more than a minute in, Garza received a partial answer. Moments after Ruelaz landed a chopping fight and a double hook, Garza snapped a counter right to the jaw that buckled Ruelaz's legs ever so slightly. While Ruelaz was able to fire back immediately, Garza was secure in the knowledge that his punch was capable of at least stunning a naturally stronger fighter.

The hard clean punches landed by both men stirred their mutual thirst for combat and they soon were locked in a heated exchange at ring center. Garza's double right forced Ruelaz to break off the assault briefly, but Ruelaz returned to the fray several seconds later behind his own overhand right. Garza's experience was coming to the fore as his attack was far more diversified.

While Ruelaz concentrated on Garza's vulnerable jaw, the Texas native raked Ruelaz's body and head with an unpredictable array of jabs, hooks, uppercuts and crosses. That experience also showed itself as Garza popped Ruelaz several times while holding his opponent's neck. Still, Ruelaz proved to be a durable sort as he absorbed Garza's best punches and fired back with plenty of his own. As the round closed, Ruelaz cranked a tremendous hook to Garza's jaw but Garza weathered it well and exchanged freely until the bell.

The furious back-and-forth action had many in the crowd applauding with hands over their heads to register the intensity of their appreciation. The fighters obliged at the start of round three as Garza backed up Ruelaz with a five-punch combination and a hurtful hook had Ruelaz covering up along the ropes. Ruelaz spun from the ropes and got on his bicycle, but Garza followed up by countering a wide hook with a crisp left-right-body hook combination and pulling away from Ruelaz's answering hook. Ruelaz sneaked in a short right but Garza continued to string together effective flurries. The boxing was very intense and both men set a very hard pace, though Garza was generally getting the better of the action.

Ruelaz mounted a brief rally midway through the round by landing a pair of double hooks. The first set connected to the head and body while the second pair to the jaw appeared to stun Garza. With about 45 seconds remaining, the two men exchanged hard blows at ring center when Garza whipped in a short, thudding hook to the chin that acted like a time-release capsule. Ruelaz managed to duck under two Garza hooks but then the effects of Garza's hook set in dramatically. His legs shuddered, his upper body slumped and he desperately tried to grab Garza's shoulders. Garza shook Ruelaz off and Ruelaz limply fell to the canvas in sections. Ruelaz received valuable recovery time when referee Vince Delgado ruled the fall a slip and wiped off Ruelaz's gloves. Garza rushed in and nailed Ruelaz with a right but Ruelaz managed to keep Garza at arm's length for the rest of the round.

"You hurt him, and that's good," Georgino told Garza between rounds. "But you've got to keep the jab going. That's the thing that's throwing him off. Use the jab and come back with strong, short combinations on the inside. Lay in close, keep it going but stay together – don't try to knock him out. It's gonna happen." As Georgino stepped out of the ring, he admonished Garza to keep using the left.

Garza began the fourth following Georgino's instructions to the letter as he burrowed inside and popped Ruelaz with short, snappy punches. Ruelaz sought to keep Garza at a distance with his own jabs, but Garza found the mark with a hook-right to the jaw and a digging right to the ribs that made Ruelaz briefly stumble. Ruelaz found some success with the jab but his follow-up blows failed to hit the target. Ruelaz, however, was a persistent sort and he knew as long as he kept throwing that he would eventually break through.

A little more than halfway through the round, Ruelaz found Garza's chin with a lead right and a sharp left-right to the face, but Garza immediately retaliated with an even heavier right and a searing hook to the body. A strong right made Ruelaz fall into the ropes but Ruelaz rebounded by nailing Garza with a hook to the cheek.

Garza closed the round with a left-left-right and a right uppercut to the jaw that made Ruelaz's legs totter.

Garza was off to a strong start, and he was showing his best form since his championship days. He dictated the pace and he fought with a confidence he didn't show in his most recent outing against Pratchett. Whenever Ruelaz nailed him with a punch, Garza immediately snatched back the momentum. While he felt he led on the cards, he also knew that his night's work was far from over.

Garza speared Ruelaz's body with a pair of wide rights to open the fifth while Ruelaz worked a jab that often fell short. Garza banged a short hook and a sweeping right glanced off Ruelaz's face. Ruelaz nailed Garza with a right but Garza answered with his own right.

Though Garza's attack was far more seasoned, Ruelaz's sheer doggedness presented a formidable challenge. The mouse erupting under Garza's right eye was evidence that Ruelaz was landing his fair share of punches.

A good left hand drove Ruelaz to the ropes early in the sixth, but Ruelaz fought his way out, only to be punished with a hard straight left to the face. Garza fought with patience, versatility and quickness while also demonstrating an intelligence that had not been needed during his bomb throwing days early in his career. Against Ruelaz, Garza was making it look easy – almost too easy.

With about a minute left in the sixth, the tenor of the fight took a dramatic turn. Ruelaz smacked a hook directly on Garza's growing mouse and a follow-up right-left-left hit the target. They cranked up hooks and this time, Ruelaz's connected with far more impact. Suddenly Garza was in trouble as his legs wavered under Ruelaz's bombardment. In past fights, Garza might have fallen but here he stood tall and fielded more blows before grabbing Ruelaz around the shoulders.

The surging Ruelaz would have none of it as he shook Garza off and drove him from corner to corner with a steady stream of punishment. A chopping right nearly dropped Garza with 21 seconds remaining but four seconds later Garza nailed Ruelaz with a swinging short hook to the jaw that spun Ruelaz's head. A second Garza hook landed with authority but the pumped-up Ruelaz walked through it and traded power punches until the bell. The crowd again rewarded the fighters with ear-splitting cheers and a standing ovation, for this was the kind of two-way war that real fans relish.

"That, ladies and gentlemen, might be as good a round as we've ever had at the Fabulous Forum," Prime Ticket blow-by-blow man Chick Hearn declared. "That was a sensational round. The action was non-stop, both men were scoring, both men were being hurt and *neither* went down!"

Both men remained transfixed on offense as the seventh round began. Ruelaz continued to find the mark with several chopping rights while Garza put every bit of strength behind his punches. Neither man was in a mood to clinch as the punches freely flew. Ruelaz's jabs pierced Garza's guard while Garza reared back and blasted a right cross and a left uppercut to the jaw. Amazingly, Ruelaz didn't budge and he nailed Garza with a hook mixed with the top of his head that sent Garza back on his heels. A right-left to the chin and a one-two to the jaw kept Garza at bay. But Garza wouldn't be held off for long and they spent the rest of the round in a thrilling game of give and take.

With the Forum crowd chanting "Go! Go! Go!" Garza and Ruelaz went, went went in the eighth. Ruelaz knocked Garza back with a strong right-left and after Delgado separated them Garza's legs wobbled. Garza had invested a lot of energy in building his numerical lead and the toll began to show. Ruelaz shoved him into a corner and emptied his guns, blasting him with right after right. Garza was forced to fight back fiercely just to keep Ruelaz from burying him but it was Ruelaz that was the sharper, harder and more effective puncher. Ruelaz was now surging and one had to wonder if Garza had enough energy left to last the distance.

"Keep that chin down and make those shots hard," McCoy told Ruelaz. "Let's see that hook. Really rip that hook. You know how every once in a while you throw those little fast flurries with three, four, five shots? Do that with him."

Ruelas began the ninth by landing a sharp right, but moments later Garza turned the pendulum dramatically when a sneaky left hook sent Ruelaz reeling halfway across the ring and into the ropes. Garza was all over him but when Ruelaz grabbed him about the shoulders Garza shoved him down with his left glove. Nevertheless, Delgado ruled Ruelaz's heavy fall to the canvas a knockdown and began to count. Up at four, Ruelaz convinced Delgado he was fit to continue.

Garza showed further evidence of his maturity by not going all out for the KO. The former champ took his time and picked his shots. He strung together combinations and Ruelaz, who was now holding on for dear life, was an open book. Another heavy left sent Ruelaz back to the ropes on failing legs but Ruelaz again clinched and walked Garza to ring center.

Delgado was looking at Ruelaz very closely, and for good reason. Not only was he being pummeled, both cheekbones were black and blue and he was drawing in deep gulps of air whenever he had the chance. As Garza continued to apply pressure, all Ruelaz could think about was seeking well-timed clinches. The thought of quitting, however, never entered his mind.

McCoy, ever the straight shooter, told Ruelaz the obvious between rounds nine and 10.

"The only way you're going to win is to get the guy," he said. "You've got to hurt him."

Ruelaz did his best to do just that at the start of the 10th, landing a left-right and another chopping right moments later. A right-left hit the tip of Garza's jaw, but Garza answered by digging several punches into Ruelaz's ribs. Ruelaz jarred Garza with a right but Garza retaliated with his own right to stem the tide. Garza popped Ruelaz's head back with sharp jabs and it appeared he was going to successfully run out the clock. He appeared fresher and stronger, and the flush of victory was soon at hand.

But Ruelaz had one more trick up his sleeve. With 26 seconds left, Ruelaz landed a heavy chopping right and suddenly Garza's body resembled a balloon whose contents were being emptied. After Delgado broke the clinch, Ruelaz nailed Garza with another right as the former champ sought another clinch. Garza now awkwardly stumbled forward as he desperately tried to get inside and prevent Ruelaz from getting valuable leverage on his follow-up blows. The crowd roared at the prospect of witnessing a potential miracle.

But Garza dug down and found what he needed to survive. With just six seconds remaining, Garza cranked up a big hook that blasted off Ruelaz's jaw and a follow-up right allowed Garza to run out the clock. Both men embraced wearily after the final bell sounded, and who knows what would have happened had this fight had been a 12-rounder. Thankfully for Garza, he didn't have to find out.

As was the custom following a great fight, the crowd tossed coins and bills into the ring, some as large as $20. This show of appreciation has a dangerous side, and both corners put towels on their fighter's head to prevent damage from a flying coin.

The decision was split. Chuck Hassett saw it 95-94 for Garza while Raul Caiz viewed it 96-95 for Ruelaz. The deciding vote came from Larry Rozadilla who saw the fight 96-95 for the former WBC super bantamweight champion Jaime Garza. Had it not been for the ninth round knockdown, the bout would have been ruled a draw.

It was a close, hard-fought contest befitting a tournament atmosphere and while Garza would advance to fight another hot prospect in George Navarro, Ruelaz would move on to the next assignment. Such is the finality of tournament action.

Epilogue: Ruelaz would fight just twice more. Three months after losing to Garza, Ruelaz defeated Kelvin Lampkin by unanimous eight round decision. His final fight took place September 30, 1988 when he stopped the 11-1 Andre Smith in six rounds at the Aviation Gym in Redondo Beach, Calif. Ruelaz was just eight days past his 26th birthday when he retired with a record of 22-4 (17 KO).

Garza lost his semi-final bout against Navarro by comprehensive unanimous 10-round decision. Garza rebounded with a six-round KO of James Manning but he lost three of his final four fights, all by KO. The 35-year-old Garza retired following a six-round TKO loss to Jose Luis Madrid at the Olympic Auditorium February 16, 1995. His final record stands at 48-6 (44 KO).

TALES FROM THE VAULT

Total Punches Landed/Thrown

Round	1	2	3	4	5	6	7	8	9	10	11	12	Total
Garza	32/96	43/116	35/102	48/128	29/96	33/100	33/108	26/110	36/111	34/105			349/1072
	33%	37%	34%	38%	30%	33%	31%	24%	32%	32%			33%
Ruelaz	20/52	33/89	19/67	17/73	13/55	36/87	29/84	31/80	8/22	26/80			232/689
	38%	37%	28%	23%	24%	41%	35%	39%	36%	32%			34%

Jabs Landed/Thrown

Round	1	2	3	4	5	6	7	8	9	10	11	12	Total
Garza	20/71	13/42	17/57	19/64	6/45	11/39	13/52	7/51	10/48	14/35			130/504
	28%	31%	30%	30%	13%	28%	25%	14%	21%	40%			26%
Ruelaz	17/45	12/40	9/39	8/51	6/35	6/31	14/48	9/33	5/19	8/35			94/376
	38%	30%	23%	16%	17%	19%	29%	27%	26%	23%			25%

Power Punches Landed/Thrown

Round	1	2	3	4	5	6	7	8	9	10	11	12	Total
Garza	12/25	30/74	18/45	29/64	23/51	22/61	20/56	19/59	26/63	20/70			219/568
	48%	41%	40%	45%	45%	36%	36%	32%	41%	29%			39%
Ruelaz	3/7	21/49	10/28	9/22	7/20	30/56	15/36	22/47	3/3	18/45			138/313
	43%	43%	36%	41%	35%	54%	42%	47%	100%	40%			44%

Jaime Garza vs. Joe Ruelaz May 18, 1987, Inglewood, California

Rafael Ruelas vs. Jorge Paez
November 6, 1992, Inglewood, California

A prospect's route to a championship is usually well defined. After disposing of a series of "easy" opponents to showcase the skills that initiated the careful buildup, his management gradually moves up the scheduled distances of his fights as well as the quality of opposition. If all goes well, and it usually does, an important character in his development will inevitably appear – the former champion.

Such was the path taken by 21-year-old Rafael Ruelas, a native of Yerba Buena, Mexico who made his residence in Sylmar, California. Ruelas and brother Gabriel emigrated to the United States as pre-teens and, as the story goes, sold candy door-to-door to bring extra money to the household. One of their prospective customers was Joe Goossen, head trainer of the Ten Goose Gym in Van Nuys. Once the brothers got a taste of the gym environment they instantly knew what their future occupation would be.

Rafael turned pro after an amateur career that included two victories over eventual 1992 gold medalist Oscar de la Hoya. He and Gabriel tore through their early opposition in spectacular fashion, inspiring one magazine writer to compare the 5-7 Gabriel to Roberto Duran and the 5-11 Ruelas to Alexis Arguello.

But the brothers would not go through the first phase of their careers unscathed. On April 14, 1990 in Las Vegas, the 21-0 (12 KO) Gabriel, noted for his ferocious left hook, was on his way to a victory over Jeff Franklin when he suffered an injury to his right elbow in the sixth round. It was obvious that Gabriel was suffering as his arm hung limply at his side but he somehow managed to lift it – with a subtle assist from Goossen – when the doctor commanded him to do so between rounds.

Seeing a chance to score a huge upset, Franklin locked the arm in a clinch and pulled his own arm toward his body. The effects of his next move were sickening and devastating – Franklin twisted Gabriel's injured elbow at a grotesque angle and the waves of pain forced a screaming Gabriel to pull away. He could no longer conceal his agony and referee Richard Steele was forced to stop the fight. Because Franklin executed his blatant foul outside of Steele's vision, he was awarded an seventh round TKO instead of a disqualification.

The first blemish on Rafael's record came under equally bizarre circumstances. On July 31, 1991 at the Country Club in Reseda, the 27-0 (22 KO) Rafael fought a 10-rounder with the 45-15-5 Mauro Gutierrez in a bout televised on USA. Ruelas won the first round and was on his way to doing the same in the second when Gutierrez shockingly scored a knockdown. Rafael initially wanted to arise immediately, but then he spied Goossen in his corner urging him to stay on a knee until the referee reached eight. But Goossen misread the referee's count, thinking he had reached eight when he actually had tolled 10. Rafael immediately jumped to his feet the instant the referee ended the fight and tried, to no avail, to convince him to continue the fight.

Both brothers bounced back from their adversities. Gabriel won his next 12 fights en route to a 1993 title shot against Azumah Nelson while Rafael prevailed in his next six fights, including a 10-round decision over Gutierrez, to set up the next step in his fistic progression – an encounter with his first former champion.

The colorful Jorge Paez was known as "Maromero" in honor of his past in the family circus. He was later dubbed "The Clown Prince of Boxing" for his in-ring antics that included break-dancing routines, kissing round-card girls between rounds, occasionally profane hip-thrusting maneuvers during clinches as well as wild hairstyles, oversized hats and glittering robes and trunks.

Paez's showmanship overshadowed the fact that he was an excellent fighter who had credentials to back up his good-natured bluster. He captured the IBF featherweight title from Calvin Grove in one of boxing history's most stunning turnarounds. The 34-0 Grove had built an almost unassailable lead entering the 15th and final round but the heat generated both by Paez and the 120-plus degree ringside temperatures wore Grove out. Three knockdowns enabled Paez to put together the 10-6 round he needed to score an unlikely majority decision.

Paez proved to be an active and entertaining champion as he racked up eight defenses while also mixing a pair of non-title wins. Severe weight-making difficulties prompted Paez to vacate his 126-pound title in favor of an immediate title shot against IBF junior lightweight king Tony Lopez, also a staple of NBC's airwaves. After losing a comprehensive decision to Lopez, Paez continued on his merry way by moving up to 135 pounds and staying active. Paez fought five times in 1991, capping that year with an entertaining majority decision win over Tracy Spann but losing a 12-rounder to world lightweight champion Pernell Whitaker. Paez fought five more times in 1992, winning all of them to set up the crossroads fight with Ruelas.

At age 27, Paez was on the tail end of his physical prime and since he was still a winning fighter it was thought he would provide an accurate barometer of both Ruelas' progress and his own prospects for future title glory.

The contrast in personalities was on stark display during the ring entrances. The stoic Ruelas was the first to enter and he calmly walked to the ring in a fashion that perfectly suited his no-flash, all-substance persona. Ruelas was coolly shadowboxing in his corner when the strains of "Rocky" began pumping through the loudspeakers and the equally loud Paez emerged from the tunnel. A giant sombrero with the words "Viva Mexico" adorned his head and as he twirled several times a few feet from his corner, the bottom of his sequined robe resembling a huge hula hoop. When he removed the sombrero, the back of his otherwise normal-looking locks sported a shaved message:

"Clinton TLC." The "Clinton" was the surname of the U.S. President-elect while "TLC" was a message encouraging "fair trade" with Mexico.

While Paez's showmanship was in full display during the pre-fight festivities, that all changed once the opening bell rang because he realized fighting Ruelas would demand his full concentration. Paez immediately set up shop at close range where he and Ruelas wrestled for position while throwing lefts to the body. After a brief break, Paez tried to fall in and grab Ruelas but the youngster man instead banged left and right uppercuts to the jaw. Paez retaliated by driving hooks to the head and body and soon the fight assumed a frenetic pace.

Less than a minute into the round Ruelas uncorked his "money punch," a searing left uppercut to Paez's nose. The blow sent Paez tumbling onto his back and he immediately brought his right glove to his injured proboscis. Up at seven, referee Marty Denkin sent Paez back into battle with a light slap to the face.

Ruelas blasted Paez's body while the stricken "Maromero" sought to fight at a longer distance. Paez fired a lead right over Ruelas' jab that drove the prospect to the ropes but Ruelas instantly unloaded an almost ceaseless succession of hooks and uppercuts. Ruelas was like a threshing machine as he sought to shred Paez's crossed-arm defense. A hook to the jaw twisted Paez's head and a follow-up five-punch flurry capped by a left uppercut sent Paez crashing heavily on his rump.

Paez sat on the canvas with a bewildered expression until he arose at Denkin's count of six. Ruelas, realizing his biggest and most spectacular win of his career was at hand, went after Paez with a youthful exuberance but the wily Paez rolled away from most of Ruelas' shots. Paez sprung from his crouch behind a strong hook that moved Ruelas back, but Ruelas' retreat lasted only for an instant. Ruelas then rained blow after blow on Paez until the end of a most savage first round. The Forum crowd was electrified as they stood, applauded and yelled with full-throated rapture following a round that exceeded the already soaring expectations.

Paez began the second by burrowing inside with the intent of smothering the long-armed Ruelas' punches, but Ruelas proved once again that he was most comfortable in close quarters as he ripped short punches in all directions. He also found that Ruelas possessed underrated hand speed as those short punches came with unsettling rapidity. A right-left uppercut combination spun Paez's head but because the veteran was bent on applying pressure it made for tremendous two-way action. The crowd roared its approval as Paez unloaded a whipping right to the jaw but Ruelas fired back a flurry that made Paez give ground grudgingly. The two men stood head-to-head and swapped dozens of punches. They didn't care that 10 more rounds were scheduled; they lived for the here and now and all that mattered was coming out on top instant by instant.

Ruelas was uncommonly calm in the midst of the storm that he created. In the weeks before the fight, Paez tried to rattle the youngster with his usual verbal blasts but through it all the kid remained his serene and studious self. Ruelas saved his responses for the ring and Paez was finding out just how dangerous and formidable a proposition he could be.

Ruelas continued to throw his cluster bombs in the third as Paez covered up and tried to pick his spots. Paez had seen whirlwind attacks before and his experience told him that the storm would eventually run its course. But Ruelas showed there were plenty more storms to come as he took a half-step back and unloaded stinging uppercuts to the forward-leaning Paez's jaw. Paez soaked up the punishment as if it had no impact and he continued to move forward behind looping shots under and over. As the round progressed, Paez began to gain strength while Ruelas showed the first signs of arm weariness. A right and two lefts broke through for Paez while the still aggressive Ruelas' punches lacked their previous snap. Nevertheless, a heavy right-left to the chin by Paez brought back nine unanswered punches from Ruelas that produced a thin ribbon of blood from Paez's nose.

Ruelas began the fourth by keeping Paez at arm's length with long probing jabs but Paez found his way inside with a winging right and a left uppercut that turned Ruelas' head. Paez bulled Ruelas across the ring with a flurry but the indestructible Ruelas kept firing even when he was being forced back.

Midway through the round, Paez changed the course of battle when he buckled Ruelas' knees with a hook-cross combo and another salvo drove Ruelas to the ropes on weakened legs. Seeing his chance to seize control, Paez pounced and unleashed a torrent of punches from every conceivable direction while Ruelas planted his back on the ropes and used his high guard to deflect as many blows as he could. It was, by far, Paez's best sequence of the fight and it upped the ante on an already pulsating war.

After absorbing another Paez barrage, Ruelas wobbled toward the ring post in Paez's corner, bringing up a roar from Paez's partisans. Paez pounded away with both hands with a fury seldom seen in the fun loving "Clown Prince." But Paez proved that the clown within still lurked near the surface by mixing in a right-handed bolo punch among the serious blows.

Paez was so eager to finish off his young challenger that the mouthpiece dropped out, prompting Denkin to call a time-out to Paez's disgust. The temporary respite did Ruelas some good as he landed several light shots on the charging Paez, but the veteran's punches carried far more pop as a left to the chin sent Ruelas staggering to the ropes. Though his balance was badly compromised, Ruelas continued to fire back determinedly until the bell.

Goossen told Ruelas between rounds not to let Paez back him up and to make sure he began every exchange, and Goossen's charge obeyed as he planted his feet and popped Paez's head with short, quick shots to begin the fifth. Paez responded with thudding hook to the body and a second one forced Ruelas toward the ropes. The two men played a brutal game of tug-of-war with momentum being the prize as they traded withering punches at point-blank range.

Because the 5-6 Paez was five inches shorter than Ruelas, he had to fight this way in order to be effective, but frenetic toe-to-toe exchanges was a game tailor-made for the ambition of youth, not the sage of age. Ruelas' rat-a-tat attack soon produced a cut under Paez's right eye and the weariness of round four was beginning to transform into a second wind that made Ruelas' volume-punching attack take on the look of a termite fueled by Red Bull. Punch after punch strafed Paez's skull and it was clear that if Paez were to win he would have to utilize another strategy.

Paez began the sixth at long range to give himself time to wipe away the blood but the relentless Ruelas showed him no pity as his attacks constantly forced him backward. Blood covered nearly the entire right side of Paez's face, and the veteran's attack began to slow perceptively. Paez tried to distract the youngster by backing toward a neutral corner and pantomiming a matador holding out a cape for the bull to charge through, but this was a fight – and Ruelas was a fighter – that had no room for any bull.

Paez was at a loss as to what to do with Ruelas. He even turned southpaw for a few moments in the seventh, anything to grab a few seconds of rest against a man who simply didn't want to take a break. The eighth was a resting round for both as Paez used his legs and Ruelas decelerated his attack – at least for the first half of the round. At the midway point the scene returned to close quarters and the taller man again began to shine with ripping uppercuts that dramatically popped back Paez's head. One of those uppercuts opened a gash over Paez's left eye to match the one underneath the orb.

With blood staining his face and his pace ebbing, Paez had the look of a shopworn veteran as he brushed the crimson away. Though he fought valiantly, Paez began to feel the effects of holding off a bigger, stronger, fresher, harder-hitting volume puncher bent on fulfilling still unrealized dreams.

Paez used the ninth to collect himself as the fickle crowd booed his cautious tactics. Ruelas continued to attack in the hopes of sapping Paez's final energy reserves. And his tactics were working: As if the blood encircling his left eye didn't present enough problems, his right eye was starting to swell shut.

Paez continued to slip and slide in the 10th as the blood poured from his nose and into his mouth. The remorseless Ruelas pushed Paez against the ropes and blasted away while the crowd, sensing the kill, rose in anticipation. As the bell sounded, Ruelas landed a final right-left to the jaw that drove the proud veteran back.

That right-left proved to be the final punches of the bout as Paez's corner called a merciful end on behalf of their brave but battered warrior. Paez honored the fighter's code by giving it his best effort, but it wasn't enough to deny the younger man his place among the world's best lightweights.

Ruelas had successfully bulldozed his way through a crucial doorway in his development and for him bigger, better and more financially rewarding dates lay ahead. For Paez, despite his defeat, he still demonstrated why he had his day in the sun. But only he could determine whether this fight would represent the sunset of his career.

Epilogue: The Ruelas loss was hardly the last boxing fans would see of "Maromero" as he would fight 46 more times in the next 11 years. He received two more cracks at a title; the first was a 12-round loss to IBF champ Freddie Pendleton eight months later and the other was a second round TKO to Oscar de la Hoya for the WBO belt a year later. Paez won more than he lost, and more often than not his defeats came against quality opposition like Genaro Hernandez (KO by 8), Angel Manfredy (KO by 8), the 21-1 Augie Sanchez (KO by 7) and Jose Luis Castillo (KO by 5).

Following the Castillo loss, however, Paez experienced a renaissance of sorts that lasted for the remainder of his career. Against mostly modest opposition Paez was 15-0-1 in his final 16 bouts, the last of which took place at the Dodge Theater in Phoenix, Arizona when the 38-year-old Paez scored a 10-round split decision over Scott McCracken. Paez's final record is 79-14-5 with 51 KO.

Ruelas continued his rise by scoring five victories to earn a crack at Pendleton on February 19, 1994 at The Forum. "Fearless Freddie" shocked Ruelas by dropping him twice in the first, but Ruelas' volume-punching attack enabled him to make up ground and eventually win a 12 round decision.

Ruelas notched title defenses against Mike Evgen (KO 3) and Billy Schwer (KO 8) to set up a title unification showdown with WBO champ De La Hoya on May 6, 1995 at Caesars Palace in Las Vegas. "The Golden Boy" was golden as he blew Ruelas away in two rounds.

Many pundits thought Ruelas was a spent force following his next outing, a 12-round loss to the 26-1 George Scott. But Ruelas would bounce back with nine consecutive wins over mostly nondescript competition save for Jaime "Rocky" Balboa (KO 5) and a faded Livingstone Bramble (W 10). The streak earned Ruelas a crossroads match against rising Australian/Russian star Kostya Tszyu in a stark role reversal of Ruelas-Paez. The prospect inflicted a frightful beating on Ruelas before scoring a ninth round TKO.

The 28-year-old Ruelas would fight once more, a 10-round split decision win over Hicklet Lau at the New Frontier Hotel in Las Vegas on August 8, 1999. His final record is 53-4 (42 KO).

WARS OF ATTRITION

Total Punches Landed/Thrown

Round	1	2	3	4	5	6	7	8	9	10	11	12	Total
Ruelas	60/138	61/159	58/157	36/120	92/189	19/106	24/83	49/130	15/87	42/111			456/1280
	43%	38%	37%	30%	49%	18%	29%	38%	17%	38%			36%
Paez	9/36	27/50	20/43	24/60	17/43	9/29	2/18	5/22	4/26	6/22			123/349
	25%	54%	47%	40%	40%	31%	11%	23%	15%	27%			35%

Jabs Landed/Thrown

Round	1	2	3	4	5	6	7	8	9	10	11	12	Total
Ruelas	0/17	3/18	5/39	4/37	1/6	7/51	3/30	2/33	5/34	4/17			34/282
	0%	17%	13%	11%	17%	14%	10%	6%	15%	24%			12%
Paez	0/1	0/2	4/12	3/10	1/1	2/13	0/7	1/3	1/9	0/3			12/61
	0%	0%	33%	30%	100%	15%	0%	33%	11%	0%			20%

Power Punches Landed/Thrown

Round	1	2	3	4	5	6	7	8	9	10	11	12	Total
Ruelas	60/121	58/141	53/118	32/83	91/183	12/55	21/53	47/97	10/53	38/94			422/998
	50%	41%	45%	39%	50%	22%	40%	48%	19%	40%			42%
Paez	9/35	27/48	16/31	21/50	16/42	7/16	2/11	4/19	3/17	6/19			111/288
	26%	56%	52%	42%	38%	44%	18%	21%	18%	32%			39%

Rafael Ruelas vs. Jorge Paez November 6, 1992, Inglewood, California

TALES FROM THE VAULT

Tommy Cordova vs. Freddie Roach
June 12, 1984, Las Vegas, Nevada

During the early years of ESPN's "Top Rank Boxing" series, the network showcased fighters who would later become stars. One of the most notable was Dwight Braxton, who skyrocketed to world title contention en route to winning the ESPN light heavyweight tournament. After capturing the WBC light heavyweight title from Matthew Saad Muhammad, Braxton changed his name to Dwight Muhammad Qawi and later won the WBA cruiserweight belt en route to his eventual enshrinement in the International Boxing Hall of Fame.

Through consistent network exposure, other fighters gained a measure of stardom, not because of whether they won or lost but how they fought the fight. Tommy Cordova was one such fighter, and it was his all-out war with Freddie Roach at the Showboat Hotel and Casino in Las Vegas that vaulted him toward prominence on the world scene and set the stage for a memorable run on the network.

The prize on this night was the vacant ESPN junior lightweight title, whose purpose was similar to the NABF, USBA, EBU and OBPF belts – getting its owner into the world rankings. Cordova-Roach was a classic crossroads fight between prospect and veteran that also featured a pleasing mix of styles. The 22-year-old Cordova (10-1, 6 KO) was a 5-3 whirlwind who owned massive reserves of stamina while the 24-year-old Roach (33-5 with 11 KO) was a 5-5 battler who could box if he wished but preferred to brawl in the trenches. Roach had fought for the ESPN belt seven months earlier, but dropped a 10-round decision to Louis Burke. His most recent bout was an eight-round no-contest against Efrain Nieves in Portland, Ore., exactly two months earlier, a result brought about after Nieves' head split open Roach's tender brows. Meanwhile, Cordova came into the bout on an up note as he decisioned the 12-1-1 Jimmy Jackson on the same date in Las Vegas.

Tempers boiled over at the morning weigh-in when Roach weighed three-quarters of a pound over the 130-pound limit while Cordova weighed a comfortable 126 ¾. Members of Cordova's camp shouted at Roach to "take it off, take it off," meaning the weight of course. While Roach willingly complied, members of his camp exchanged expletives with Cordova's team and some pushing and shoving ensued. Happily for the fans, the two fighters carried those hostilities into the ring.

Even though Roach owned the superior reach, trainer Eddie Futch wanted Roach to stand his ground and push Cordova back because he knew the New Mexican could not fight as well on the retreat. Meanwhile, the squat Cordova and his far lankier trainer Bob Foster had little choice strategically – it was full speed ahead.

The pair came out of their corners and immediately locked horns. Cordova landed a light left hook to the jaw while the taller, more angular Roach worked behind his jab. Following a clinch, Roach spun Cordova, then landed a good hook to the jaw. But the high-energy Cordova was in no mood to be pushed around and he appeared to relish the early exchanges. Cordova answered Roach's long right-left to the body with head-snapping uppercuts and the pair quickly established the terms of battle. There was a lot of physical contact as they pushed, shoved and bulled each other around the ring.

In the final minute, Roach darted out to long range and connected with a jab-cross-hook, then spun Cordova and whipped a right to the ribs. But Cordova struck back to the body and popped Roach with short rights over the top that sparked a rally by Roach. The bell sounded with Roach digging a right-left to the body and shoving Cordova away.

Roach began the second on the outside behind light jabs that were followed by rights to the body, but it didn't take long for Cordova to work his way inside and re-establish trench warfare. Roach continually spun Cordova off-balance to set up hard body punches. A big hook nailed Cordova in the midst of a wild exchange and Cordova was forced to hold on and muscle Roach to the ropes.

Surprisingly, Roach was proving he was at least Cordova's equal in physical strength as he traded evenly with the infighting specialist. Cordova was accustomed to dominating at close range, but when Roach began to get the better of the exchanges his frustration began to show. At one point, Cordova nestled his head under Roach's chin and lifted up, a blatant foul. An angry Roach responded by shoving Cordova to the corner pad and blasting him with a right cross to the jaw. The action was getting more chippy by the second, prompting Richard Steele to briefly lecture both men. Roach then punctuated a good round by gonging Cordova with a right at the bell.

The alley fight continued in the third as they tore into each other like two wildcats battling over a carcass. Roach pushed Cordova toward the corner, and after Cordova shoe-shined Roach's body he again lifted Roach's chin with his head. As Cordova spun him, Roach looked at Steele to complain, and he did so with a fresh cut over his left eye, no doubt a result of Cordova's headwork.

A snarling Roach smacked in a long right at ring center and Cordova responded with a right hand – as well as a head to the face. Roach hung on to regain his senses while Cordova whacked away and mushed his glove into Roach's grill. During a later exchange, Cordova again lifted Roach's chin with his head and an enraged Roach charged in with fists flying. Cordova nailed him with two rights that widened Roach's cut and a hook that made him grimace, but Roach fired back a right-left to the body. The anger was swelling in both men, and happily for the fans it took the form of scintillating, breathtaking action that lasted until the end of the round.

The first three rounds produced gritty, unglamorous physical warfare between two aggressors seeking to establish territorial dominance. Plenty of heads and elbows were employed and each man deftly spun the other into follow-up punches. Since each didn't possess a knockout punch, and because both had toughness to spare, a long punishing battle was guaranteed.

The bout shifted to long range in the fourth round and the shorter-armed Cordova's well-timed jabs tagged Roach time and again. A sweeping overhand right spun Roach's head, but Roach absorbed it well and fired right back. A triple jab sparked another firefight at close range, but Cordova, maligned as a face-first fighter with little defense, ducked and slipped many of the blows with surprising skill.

The fight had assumed a most unexpected pattern in terms of effectiveness. The taller Roach had his best moments on the inside while Cordova enjoyed his most effective round in the fourth due to his sharp jab and by tightening his usually leaky defense. Each was excelling in the other's anatomical specialty, yet they still produced thrilling back-and-forth action with just enough dirty stuff to push it toward an R-rating.

Cordova continued to surge in the fifth as a double jab snaked through and a right uppercut lifted Roach's head later in the round. Roach was falling into more clinches while Cordova remained the fresher and busier man. But Roach suddenly reversed the flow with 1:05 left in the round as a sizzling lead right stunned Cordova and had him holding on tight. After Steele broke them, they dug in their toes at ring center and ripped into each other with uncompromising fury – Roach to finish the job and Cordova to keep Roach from doing it. Only the round-ending bell had the power to stop them.

Cordova broke open an otherwise quiet sixth by landing a right that brought a heavier right by Roach that forced Cordova to seek the ropes' sanctuary. Cordova smothered Roach and returned to ring center, after which a triple jab propelled Roach toward the strands, where they spent the rest of the round pushing, shoving and trading. Cordova continued his surge in the seventh as he pelted the retreating Roach with jabs. Cordova countered a Roach jab with a solid three-punch salvo.

Though Roach was punching back at every opportunity, Cordova was getting the better of the action. Still, Cordova couldn't resist bending the rules, for he again lifted Roach's chin with his head. This time, Steele assessed a point penalty. Ironically, it was Cordova and his people who complained to the Nevada State Athletic Commission about Roach's headwork before the fight, and now it was he who was being punished on the scorecards – and appropriately so.

The grappling continued in the eighth as Roach draped his entire upper body on Cordova's back in the midst of a clinch, prompting Cordova to butt Roach in the stomach and Steele to issue a hard warning. Cordova tried to touch gloves with Roach, but Roach wasn't having any of it as he did not move a muscle.

With 1:13 remaining, in the midst of a toe-to-toe exchange, Roach's right-hook-right hurt Cordova, but Cordova continued to wade in fearlessly, slipping a right and answering with a clean right uppercut. The cut over Roach's left eye was no longer a factor, but blood was now coming out of the nose as yet another huge exchange ended the round.

Cordova began the ninth strongly by pushing Roach to the ropes and landing his best punch of the right – a right to the jaw. The iron-chinned Roach walked through it and landed a counter hook to spark another firefight. Roach again got the best of it with a series of hooks, and one of them snapped Cordova's head as he windmilled to the body. An overhand right by Cordova landed well but Roach's hook was even better. A right-left nailed Cordova coming in and a body flurry drove him back in the round's final seconds. Roach paid a price for his aggression as he walked back to the corner with more blood leaking from his left eye.

The already frantic pace escalated further in the 10th as both turned up the heat at close range. Cordova sprang up from a clinch and nailed Roach with a hook that drove him to the ropes. Cordova then poured on the pressure and by the second minute Roach appeared weaker. His punches lacked snap while Cordova's retained their zip and accuracy, and Roach was initiating more of the clinches. His fighting heart, however, overruled his flagging body by continuing to engage.

Roach started the 11th on the move, seeking to keep Cordova at bay with his superior reach. But Cordova wouldn't cooperate as he snapped off a four-punch salvo, all of which landed, followed by a one-two that brought a hearty reply from Roach. A big right to the face landed for Cordova and soon after Roach emerged with a nasty cut over the right eye. Roach continuously brushed the blood away, and Cordova drew strength from Roach's trouble. Roach drove a heavy right to Cordova's ribs, but Cordova continued to carry the upper hand as he got the better of the ensuing exchanges.

Sensing he was behind on the cards, Roach commenced the final round with a last-gasp push. A solid one-two landed and a jolting hook capped off a follow-up flurry, but Cordova waded in without ill effect. A whipping hook buckled Roach's knees, yet Roach refused to yield. The round was a microcosm of the fight, both good and bad, as they mauled, brawled and punched in search of the fight-deciding, judge-impressing finish. Each man pushed himself to the brink of exhaustion until the last second ticked off.

It was a close, hard-fought battle but even as they waited in the corners they still weren't sure the fight was indeed over because ESPN title rules included the possibility of a tie-breaking 13th round in the event of a draw. Futch was in the process of cutting off Roach's gloves when referee Steele intervened.

But in the end, there would be a decision and it would be split. Paul Smith saw Cordova a rather wide 117-111 winner while Harold Miller turned in a 115-113 vote in Roach's favor. Duane Ford cast the deciding vote, a razor-thin 114-113 for Cordova.

The verdict – and the fight itself – was well received, though many in the crowd were rooting for the popular Roach, who made his home in Las Vegas. It was the type of fight that elevated both fighters because they poured every ounce of themselves into the battle, and sometimes more than anyone had a right to ask. For Cordova, the bout made him a small-screen favorite while for Roach it showed those who made the deals that he was still a viable attraction worthy of bigger fights and the purses that came with them.

Epilogue: Cordova maintained a frenetic schedule for the next few years, and his body eventually yielded to his self-imposed never-say-die standards. Cordova fought three more times in 1984 with no victories to show for it. Two months after beating Roach, Cordova lost a 12-rounder to Ronnie Gary, then followed with two grueling draws with former featherweight title challenger Jorge "Rocky" Garcia. Cordova won his next five fights, including a 10-rounder over future IBF bantamweight champion Kelvin Seabrooks, before losing a majority 12 rounder to Joe Ruelaz in September 1985.

From that point forward, Cordova's career nose-dived and he soon became cannon fodder for up-and-comers. He lost to Steve Cruz (KO by 9), Lupe Miranda (L 10), Tony Lopez (L 10), Lester Ellis (KO by 10), Lupe Suarez (KO by 9) and Jaime "Rocky" Balboa (KO by 7, KO by 5). The 30-year-old Cordova's final fight took place April 21, 1992 at the Palace in Auburn Hills, Michigan, where Courtney Hooper stopped him in five rounds. In all, Cordova went 2-11-1 in his final 14 fights and retired with a record of 21-15-3 with nine KO.

Roach also kept up a busy pace as he knocked out Ruelaz in four rounds just seven weeks after losing to Cordova. He followed that with an eight round TKO of Richie Foster, but two months later he lost to Nieves for the second time. Over the next 19 months Roach fought 10 times, winning just four. Roach ran hot and cold in that period as he dropped a disputed majority decision to Bobby Chacon and was beaten by Greg Haugen (KO by 7), Hector Camacho (L 10), Andy Nance (KO by 10) and Darryl Tyson (L 12). He scored an impressive decision over Balboa, out-pointed Joey Olivera and stopped Martin Morado (KO 8) and Arnel Arrozal (KO 5). Roach's final fight took place October 24, 1986 at the Memorial Auditorium in Lowell, Mass., where David Riviello won a majority decision. At just age 26, Roach retired with a record of 39-13 with 15 KO.

Following his retirement, Roach became an assistant trainer under Futch and in the two decades since he has become one of boxing's best and most sought-after and successful seconds.

WARS OF ATTRITION

Total Punches Landed/Thrown

Round	1	2	3	4	5	6	7	8	9	10	11	12	Total
Cordova	32/66 48%	17/43 40%	28/77 36%	23/54 43%	26/51 51%	17/50 34%	21/68 31%	22/70 31%	20/67 30%	18/64 28%	24/72 33%	27/70 39%	275/752 37%
Roach	30/90 33%	19/68 28%	22/79 28%	15/47 32%	22/75 29%	11/53 21%	14/61 23%	27/59 46%	23/55 42%	24/58 41%	22/57 39%	22/66 33%	251/768 33%

Jabs Landed/Thrown

Round	1	2	3	4	5	6	7	8	9	10	11	12	Total
Cordova	5/11 45%	3/12 25%	3/5 60%	9/17 53%	5/11 45%	7/17 41%	3/13 23%	3/9 33%	1/10 10%	0/2 0%	1/4 25%	1/4 25%	41/115 36%
Roach	4/22 18%	4/27 15%	1/16 6%	4/16 25%	1/27 4%	2/18 11%	2/21 10%	1/4 25%	1/10 10%	1/6 17%	3/11 27%	1/13 8%	25/191 13%

Power Punches Landed/Thrown

Round	1	2	3	4	5	6	7	8	9	10	11	12	Total
Cordova	27/55 49%	14/31 45%	25/72 35%	14/37 38%	21/40 52%	10/33 30%	18/55 33%	19/61 31%	19/57 33%	18/62 29%	23/68 34%	26/66 39%	234/637 37%
Roach	26/68 38%	15/41 37%	21/63 33%	11/31 35%	21/48 44%	9/35 26%	12/40 30%	26/55 47%	22/45 49%	23/52 44%	19/46 41%	21/53 40%	226/577 39%

Tommy Cordova vs. Freddie Roach June 12, 1984, Las Vegas, Nevada

TALES FROM THE VAULT

Julio Cesar Chavez vs. Roger Mayweather II
May 13, 1989, Inglewood, California

Moments after Julio Cesar Chavez blew out Roger Mayweather in two rounds on July 7, 1985 in Las Vegas, no one – even perhaps Mayweather himself – ever dreamed a rematch would ever take place. And why should they? After Mayweather won the first round on all three scorecards and staggered Chavez with a scorching right cross to the chin, Chavez stormed back and scored three smashing knockdowns to force referee Richard Steele to wave off the fight. The victory was so impressive and overwhelming that Chavez was hailed as a superstar in the making while Mayweather was written off as a spent force.

But boxing has a way of rewriting scripts and over the next four years their respective paths would eventually lead back to one another. For Chavez, he would become one of the division's most outstanding champions, repelling the likes of Dwight Pratchett (W 12), Refugio Rojas (KO 7), Rocky Lockridge (W 12), Juan LaPorte (W 12) and Danilo Cabrera (W 12) in his nearly three-year reign. Chavez then certified his emerging greatness when he wore down and stopped Edwin Rosario to capture the WBC lightweight title, then knocked out tricky southpaw Rodolfo Aguilar in six rounds. He then concluded his brief stay at 135 by adding the WBA belt on a butt-induced 11 round technical decision win over friend and former sparring partner Jose Luis Ramirez.

With a slew of non-title fights mixed in with his championship exploits, Chavez's record swelled to 60-0 with 50 knockouts and his 26-year-old body commanded him to move five pounds upward in search of more lucrative game as well as a bigger slice of history.

As for Mayweather, he knew his days as a 130-pounder were over. He blamed the Chavez loss on his struggle to make the limit and he thought a move to lightweight would reinvigorate his career. The move had mixed results. While he defeated good names like Mario Martinez (W 10), Walter Sims (W 10), Oscar Bejines (KO 7) and Sammy Fuentes (KO 9), he also suffered setbacks to Freddie Pendeton (KO by 6) and Pernell Whitaker (L 12). Following the Whitaker loss, Mayweather decided to add five more pounds to his frame and the results could be seen in his muscular back and sturdier legs. In the end, those pounds made all the difference in the world and from it spawned a new life – and a new reputation.

Following victories over Frankie Davis and Mitchell Julien, Mayweather challenged Rene Arrendondo for the WBC super lightweight belt. "The Black Mamba" was motivated and sharp, and six rounds later he became the first former 130-pound champion to skip past lightweight and capture a 140-pound title. The knockout also spawned a new sobriquet: "The Mexican Assassin."

WARS OF ATTRITION

Starting with his win over Martinez, Mayweather would face and beat six successive Mexican opponents, the last five by knockout. Numbers five and six were a pair of title defenses against Mauricio Aceves (KO 3) and former lightweight sensation Rodolfo "Gato" Gonzalez (KO 12), and stuffed between them was a scintillating defense against perennial contender Harold Brazier (W 12). Following an impressive high-profile decision over Vinny Pazienza, the 28-year-old Mayweather was ready for a big money challenge, and that challenge came in the form of a old adversary – Chavez.

The fight was set for May 13, 1989 at the Forum in Inglewood, and the setting could not have been more perfect: "The Mexican Assassin" crossing swords with perhaps the greatest Mexican fighter of all before a rabid audience bent on vengeance. One was looking to make history while the other was seeking to make a point – that their first fight was a direct result of an enforced 13-pound weight loss in the weeks before the bout, not because of a superiority in skills.

The confluence of circumstances pointed toward a difficult fight for Chavez. The challenger was in the midst of a 195-day layoff, the longest of his career, and that hiatus was filled with distractions. He had financial hassles with promoters and felt the weight of expectations from media and a growing fan base that was poised to see him become the first Mexican to become a three-division champion. While in Los Angeles, Chavez hustled from neighborhood to neighborhood to build up the fight and nurture his image for the future.

Meanwhile, Mayweather was singularly focused on the task before him. The champion spent several weeks at manager Billy Baxter's 30-acre estate in Augusta, Georgia to get away from the distractions of his adopted hometown Las Vegas. It was the first training camp of his pro career, and the combination of added weight and the chance for revenge fueled Mayweather's hopes to reach peak form on fight night.

The weigh in produced two minor surprises. The first was that the naturally smaller Chavez made the 140-pound limit with no room to spare and the second was that Mayweather scaled a svelte 138 ¾.

Chavez's promotional push for "The Fury at the Forum" didn't produce a full house, but those who were there produced plenty of noise and enthusiasm. They chanted "Mexico!" for Chavez (60-0, 50 KO) and put forth good-natured boos when Mayweather (34-5, 23 KO) entered the ring wearing a black sombrero. As HBO blow-by-blow man Jim Lampley noted, Mayweather and the Mexican fans had a strange relationship: Although they boo him, they don't dislike him personally. They respected his skills and talent despite his penchant for beating their favorites.

Even though the 5-7 ½ Mayweather stood one-half inch taller than Chavez, his 73 ½ inch reach was a full seven inches longer – and he fully intended to use it.

The fight began with Mayweather working the jab and moving side to side while Chavez stalked steadily. Mayweather pulled away from a wide hook and snapped in a double jab. Chavez then connected with a light right over the top but Mayweather again trumped him with a double jab-right hand combo. As Mayweather dug in a pair of hooks to the ribs and a jab snapped back Chavez's head, the champion couldn't have conjured a better beginning.

Mayweather's tactics were readily apparent: He knew Chavez needed several rounds to get warmed up, and by staying on the move and utilizing his reach advantage he was able to take advantage of every opening Chavez's lunges produced while still remaining respectful of the Mexican's power. Instead of the quick-striking Black Mamba, Chavez saw an intelligent, tactical boxer-puncher. And what Mayweather saw was an inactive pursuer as the challenger unleashed just 31 blows in the opening round.

Mayweather worked steadily behind the jab in round two as Chavez started to pursue more purposefully. With a little more than a minute gone in the round, Chavez hit pay dirt as a solid hook buckled Mayweather's legs and had him reaching out for the top rope with his right glove. But the champion steadied himself and used his shoulders, elbows and upper body movement to blunt most of Chavez's follow-up assault. Mayweather even fake-wobbled all the way across the ring to further convince Chavez that the moment had passed and drove home the point moments later with a forceful counter right over the jab.

By firing back, Mayweather had surmounted his first critical physical and psychological hurdle. In their first fight, "The Black Mamba" dominated the opening round only to crumble under Chavez's first serious blows. Now, not only had he survived, he began to thrive as he connected with a sizzling jab-cross-hook combo and closed the round with a right that caught Chavez barreling in.

Referee Hank Elespuru was offended by one portion of Mayweather's tactical success – whenever Chavez got close enough to inflict damage, Mayweather clamped down on his opponent's arms and waited for the referee to break them. He issued warnings throughout the round, and as Mayweather walked toward his corner following the second, Elespuru issued a hard warning for holding.

In the opening seconds of the third, the pair fell into another clinch and as Chavez registered his frustration, Elespuru again cautioned Mayweather. Freed from the champion's long arms, Chavez leaped in with a hard, direct left to the chin that snapped Mayweather's head and followed with a series of accurate jabs. Chavez began to close the distance with his upper body movement, and one series of weaving tactics set up a solid hook to Mayweather's notorious chin.

Somewhat surprisingly, the jaw held up well and better yet for his fans, Mayweather fired back with gusto. One hook that landed slightly low brought a hard warning from Elespuru and a sweeping hook by Chavez brought loud cheers. Mayweather swiftly drove in a hook to the ribs and a right to the chin. By the end of the round, it was evident that Mayweather was determined to answer every Chavez assault with one of his own – and that victory wouldn't be easily earned by either man.

However, the road to victory for Mayweather was made more difficult when Elespuru informed Mayweather and corner man Jesse Reid that he had taken a point for the slightly low left that drew the warning but no formal announcement to the crowd or the judges.

With a measure of momentum in hand, Chavez revved up his pursuit in the fourth while Mayweather continued to keep his distance. After one clinch, Mayweather earned another warning for pushing off and Mayweather responded with a hard jab-cross-right uppercut salvo. Chavez then staggered the champ with a sweeping overhand right, but Mayweather struck back with another three-punch flurry.

Chavez now chased after the champion, leaping in with every punch as Mayweather landed several on-the-move jabs. When they clinched on the ropes, a frustrated Chavez blatantly raked Mayweather's face with the laces of his left glove, but instead of warning Chavez, Elespuru told Mayweather to quit holding.

If the message wasn't already clear to Team Mayweather, this incident graphically painted the picture: To leave the ring with the belt, they must not only get past Chavez, they also had to fend off the referee. A legal hook to the body by Mayweather prompted Elespuru to shout "low blow again!"

Emotions now were running high and the crowd was frenzied as the two boxers exchanged with relish. At one point Mayweather stepped back and yelled at Chavez, who shouted right back before the "Black Mamba" just missed with a goodnight right cross.

The rising tempers continued after the bell; Mayweather clamped down on Chavez's left glove as Elespuru stepped in to separate them and as Chavez expressed his exasperation, the referee forcefully separated the pair. Meanwhile, Reid leaped into the ring to make sure both fighters stayed separated.

Chavez's chief second Cristobal Rosas, knowing his man fought best with a quiet mind, sought to reassure his charge.

"Don't yell," he said through HBO interpreter Ruben Castillo. "Don't get upset. Just keep fighting your fight so you won't get tired."

In the other corner, Reid and Elespuru were engaged in an argument, perhaps about the third-round point deduction.

"He hit him low!" argued Elespuru.

"Yeah, but (Chavez) hit him in that round low," Reid yelled back.

"That doesn't make any difference," the referee replied. Then he told Mayweather, "quit your holding, all right?"

"Watch the low blows," Reid ordered.

Because of the dispute, Reid was late getting out of the corner to begin round five. Chavez started strongly, digging hard to the body while Mayweather's jabs carried a bit less snap. Mayweather cranked a low hook, but as Elespuru delivered yet another warning to the champion, Chavez nailed Mayweather with a jab and a low right to the body, which brought nary a word from the referee.

For the first time in the fight, Chavez began to resemble his best self. His unrelenting pressure and pinpoint hammers to the head and body started to have a visible effect on Mayweather. The champion spent longer stretches seeking out any rest he could get, which wasn't much. The fight's momentum, which was clearly Mayweather's at the start, was turning toward Chavez.

Reid, ever the astute second, immediately recognized this and tried to verbally turn the tide.

"What's happening is that what makes it look bad for the judges..." Reid began. But he stopped when it appeared Mayweather was more interested in drinking water than listening to him. Seeing this, he set his fighter's mind back on track. "...now listen to me, I'm trying to give you some good advice and I'm on your side...this is the man we want to win...when you're in the clinches with him and you're not throwing, he's winning points, even if he's missing you. He's trying to come over the top. You've got to start flurrying your punches like you did in the end. They don't have to be hard but you've got to start moving your hands inside." Moments later, Elespuru again warned Reid for departing the corner late.

As the bell rang for the sixth, Mayweather began to put what Reid said into practice as he moved with more fluidity and his jabs carried more power. But Chavez, freed from his early-round shackles, let his hands go and reached Mayweather with a right over the top. A right from Mayweather prompted Chavez to wiggle his hips, an unusual show of bravado that indicated the punch bothered him. Chavez quickly regained himself by looping in a right and driving him to the ropes with a follow-up right-hook combo. The fast pace began to tell on both men, though Mayweather seemed more affected by it as he initiated more clinches and his body appeared more flaccid. The crowd sensed Mayweather's predicament, and their chants of "Mexico!" projected their growing confidence that everything would be all right.

Chavez continued to apply the pressure in the seventh, driving Mayweather to a corner and belaboring him with lefts. The Mexican icon was more active as he pushed, pulled, bullied and asserted his will through the accumulation of punishment. Chavez also meshed in his underrated defensive skills, making Mayweather miss and making him pay with beautifully timed counters. While Mayweather did his best to hold his own, the battle was now being waged on Chavez's turf – a place where no man had yet bested him.

The heavy inside action again escalated tensions that manifested themselves after the seventh round bell. Chavez had Mayweather trapped in his own corner when he landed a late blow. Mayweather responded angrily and seeing this, Reid stormed into the ring, lowered his shoulder, grabbed Chavez around the waist and bulled him toward the middle of the ring as Elespuru held Mayweather. When Reid returned to the corner, someone in the crowd hurled a bag of ice toward him and more debris was thrown his way as Reid directed his fighter to punch and move.

Moments before the eighth round bell, Elespuru told Reid "you're out of the corner." He had seen enough of Reid, who had now twice charged into the ring to break up after-the-bell scuffles. The round began with paper cups, ice and other debris in the ring and, without his chief second in the corner, Mayweather appeared dispirited. Still "The Black Mamba" was a professional with a title on the line and he did the best he could under the circumstances.

Chavez, however, was fired up and poised to inflict serious damage. His punches carried more fury and soon he opened up a dangerous cut on the champion's left eyelid. With blood running into the eye, Mayweather reached down and cranked up several of the best rights he could throw. Despite three direct hits, Chavez merely stared back and beckoned him in. At this, Mayweather grabbed his trunks, hitched them down a notch, took a deep breath and yelled something. HBO analyst Larry Merchant surmised it to be something like *"damn, you can take a punch!"* But those howitzer-like rights did inflict damage, as Mayweather reopened an old cut near the bridge of Chavez's nose.

After trying to rattle Chavez physically, he tried to do the same mentally as he fired three hooks and a right off a mini-Ali Shuffle. Moments later, Elespuru stopped the action to have the ringside physician examine Mayweather's cut. The champion was sprayed with liquid from the volatile crowd as the doctor conducted his inspection, which concluded with allowing the fight to continue.

Knowing the fight was in danger of being stopped – and soon – Mayweather gunned in hard, energetic blows, but Chavez, discerning the champion's distress, fired right back. A huge right slammed against Chavez's jaw, but the Mexican walked right through it and continued to fight through the bell. A split second after the gong, Chavez landed a hook and Mayweather a small right. But here, temperatures were cooled considerably as Chavez waved his glove in apology and Mayweather stepped past Elespuru and hugged Chavez around the neck before walking to his corner.

With Reid gone, veteran second Miguel Diaz delivered instructions while the equally capable Eddie Aliano worked on the eyelid. But there was little they could say to help counteract the raging Chavez, who was fighting with the same verve and steely resolve he had during the late stages of the Rosario fight. Throughout the ninth and 10th, Chavez connected with withering, strength sapping accuracy. Ever the proud champion, Mayweather tried to retaliate but his tactics required more sustained energy than he had left.

In the end, Chavez's brutal mastery of boxing's physics and mathematics left Mayweather slumped in his corner between rounds 10 and 11. Seeing this, Elespuru approached Mayweather and asked, "do you want to quit?" Mayweather then hung his head, and his silent message told the referee everything he needed to know. The fight was waved off and for Chavez, history was his.

Chavez banged on his protective cup with both gloves as he was paraded around the ring, telling the world that this victory was produced by his valor more than anything else.

"It was a tough fight because it was not my night," Chavez said through Castillo. "Mayweather is a great champion and a great fighter and the fight was pretty even until now. I was psychologically defeated and down for this fight. All of my training was not concentrated on this fight. I had many, many, many problems psychologically. I didn't give even 50 percent. I promise that next fight, you will see the Julio Cesar Chavez of before."

A few minutes later, Mayweather would talk about his own physical problems.

"I got a bad cramp around the sixth or seventh round," he said. "They kept telling me to fight inside but I wanted to use my legs a little bit because I know I could outpoint him from the outside. He's really easy to hit, but he has a tremendous chin. (I got the cramps) because I had too many liquids today. I came in really light for the fight."

When asked whether he was satisfied by his performance, he replied "I'm not satisfied because I'm not a quitter. But I hit him with some tremendous shots that would have knocked out any other 140-pounder. He's not that great a puncher, he just wears you down. A guy like Meldrick Taylor will give him a lot of trouble."

Then, with a wry smile, he concluded by saying "he stopped the reign of 'The Mexican Assassin,' but I'll be back."

Epilogue: Mayweather was both right and wrong. Yes, he would be back as he fought 32 more times over the next decade, winning 25 and scoring 12 knockouts. His best wins came against Terrence Alli (W 10), Livingstone Bramble (DQ 5), Carl Griffith (W 10), Rod Sequenan (W 10), Patrick Byrd (W 10), Mike Mungin (W 10) and Carlos Miranda (KO 12). The Miranda victory came on a homecoming pay-per-view card that also featured his brother Jeff and a nephew who was destined for greatness – Floyd Mayweather Jr.

But he never wore another major world crown, though he made two attempts. On December 7, 1991 Rafael Pineda broke open a tensely fought match with a single blow in the ninth and captured the vacant IBF junior welterweight title. His second try came on June 25, 1995 against IBF king Kostya Tszyu in Newcastle, Australia, where the crafty Mayweather managed to last the distance before dropping a wide decision. Mayweather's final fight took place May 8, 1999 in Reno, Nevada, where the 38-year-old "Black Mamba" won a 10 round majority decision from Juan Francisco Mendez. Mayweather's final record is 59-13 with 35 KO.

Over the next 16 years, Chavez would become the greatest fighter Mexico has ever produced and arguably one of the top boxers pound-for-pound who ever lived. The Mayweather victory began a more than four-year reign that saw him amass 11 defenses and run his undefeated record to an incredible 87-0. The most famous – and most infamous – of those victories came against IBF champ Meldrick Taylor in a title unification showdown March 17, 1990. Entering the final round, Chavez was behind on two of the three scorecards when he scored a knockdown in the bout's final moments. Taylor regained his feet but because trainer Lou Duva's arrival distracted him, he didn't answer Steele when he twice asked, "are you OK?" The bout was stopped with just two seconds on the clock, igniting a firestorm that will forever rage in boxing lore.

Still, "J.C. Superstar" was the unquestioned best pound-for-pound boxer for several years, but that reign ended when he challenged WBC welterweight champion Pernell Whitaker September 10, 1993 in San Antonio. Though Whitaker appeared an easy winner, the bout was declared a draw. Chavez's unbeaten streak three fights later when Frankie Randall out-boxed and dropped the iron-jawed Mexican en route to a split decision victory.

Chavez regained the title in controversial fashion four months later when he won a butt-induced eight round technical decision and would defend his new title four more times before losing it on cuts in four rounds to Oscar de la Hoya on June 7, 1996. Chavez made two more bids to regain that belt, but was held to a draw by Miguel Angel Gonzalez in March 1998 and was dropped and stopped by Tszyu in July 2000. In between was a grudge rematch with De La Hoya for the WBC welterweight title, and after putting up a sterling battle he retired on the stool after eight rounds due to a severe cut inside the mouth.

Following a two-round KO over Terry Thomas, Chavez took a two-year hiatus. He then launched a multi-fight "farewell tour" in November 2003 that saw him avenge a previous loss to Willy Wise (KO 2), settle a score with Randall (W 10) and post a decision victory over Ivan Robinson (W 10). Chavez's final fight came in Phoenix, Arizona on September 17, 2005 when the 43-year-old retired on the stool after five rounds with Grover Wiley. Chavez's final record stands at 107-6-2 with 86 knockouts and he is a lock to be part of the International Boxing Hall of Fame's Class of 2011.

TALES FROM THE VAULT

Total Punches Landed/Thrown

Round	1	2	3	4	5	6	7	8	9	10	11	12	Total
Chavez													238/537
													44%
Mayweather													195/543
													36%

Jabs Landed/Thrown

Round	1	2	3	4	5	6	7	8	9	10	11	12	Total
Chavez													55/120
													46%
Mayweather													81/283
													29%

Power Punches Landed/Thrown

Round	1	2	3	4	5	6	7	8	9	10	11	12	Total
Chavez													183/417
													44%
Mayweather													114/260
													44%

* Fight originally done by CompuBox, but the original HTML files with complete round-by-round statistics no longer exist.

Julio Cesar Chavez vs. Roger Mayweather II May 13, 1989, Inglewood, California

★ Chapter 5 ★
UNDERCARD TREASURES

TALES FROM THE VAULT

John Tobin vs. Ferris Christian
June 15, 1989, New York, New York

When boxing's greatest fights are discussed, the conversation appropriately turns to the biggest names: Sugar Ray Robinson, Willie Pep, Muhammad Ali, Joe Louis, Roberto Duran, Henry Armstrong, and so on. They earned their place at the tip of the sport's mythical pyramid with sustained talent so brilliant that its images were forever burnished into the minds of all that witnessed them.

While the above names rest comfortably in their exalted places, millions of anonymous preliminary fighters can be found at the pyramid's wide base, flitting in and out of the sport without making much of an impact. They ply their trade with equal enthusiasm but without neither the fanfare nor the attentive audiences of their more blessed peers. Their paychecks sport two, perhaps three zeroes instead of the six and, in recent years, seven reserved for the elites. Worse yet, because they serve as the table setters for the ticket sellers, the audience forgets their exploits even before the fighters finish descending the ring steps. The details, if they are chronicled at all, are presented as agate-type afterthoughts.

But every so often two fighters travel far beyond their boundaries and create an extraordinary spectacle worthy of initial pleasant surprise and then of reflection years later. The names of the combatants made fade from memory, but the action they provided still create flickers and flashes in the mind. They are the kind of fights that move collectors to place an asterisk beside the names on the VHS tape label or a special notation on one's list such as "great fight" or "a real war."

This was the case when this scribe came across the fight between novice middleweights John Tobin and Ferris Christian, which took place at the Felt Forum inside Madison Square Garden. It was the opening bout of the MSG Network's telecast topped by a scheduled 12 rounder between world-rated Gino Gelormino and Anthony English, which was for Gelormino's WBC Continental Americas junior lightweight belt. Though English would score a huge upset by knocking out Gelormino in eight exciting rounds, they ended up being usurped by the upstarts.

Tobin-Christian was another chapter in an oft-told boxing story – the territorial rivalry. Tobin, 161, was from Roosevelt, New York while the 159-pound Christian hailed from the Bronx. And, like most preliminary fights, the specter of the unknown hung thickly. This was especially true of Christian, who was making his professional debut while Tobin sported a record of 1-2 with one knockout. Their respective physiques also foreshadowed another common story – puncher against boxer. The shorter Tobin's heavily muscled upper body was complimented by powerful tree-trunk legs while Christian had longer, smoother but still well-defined muscles and thinner, presumably more mobile, legs.

But when the opening bell sounded, any preconceptions one made about Christian flew out the window as he went straight at Tobin and launched the first punch, a left hook to the ear that knocked Tobin off balance. Tobin instantly answered with a right to the body and a hook that missed wildly over the top. Christian then connected with another hook and drove Tobin to the ropes with a flurry, but Tobin reversed their positions after landing a pair of hooks.

The terms of battle were immediately established: First, there would be no feeling-out period and second, the man who could give – and take – the most punishment would be the winner.

The two were in the process of exchanging furiously when Tobin's hook to the jaw buckled Christian's legs. Christian tried to hold on after absorbing a follow-up right to the forehead, but instead fell to the canvas on all fours when Tobin stepped away. A clear-eyed Christian rose to his feet at referee Arthur Mercante Jr.'s count of two and was so eager to resume the battle that he walked right into a lead right to the jaw that put him down again. This time, Christian's eyes were a bit glassy and his mouth hung open as if numbed by a situation that had the potential of spinning out of control. Only 41 seconds had elapsed, and though the three-knockdown rule was not in effect, it was very likely that the fight would end if Tobin floored him again. For Christian, his choice was simple: Fight or flight.

He chose to fight.

As Tobin rushed in for the kill, he was met with a furious and uninterrupted stream of wide looping punches. One of them, a hook, caught Tobin coming in and Tobin's upper body slumped forward. Yes, Tobin's thick legs were still firmly under him, but he had given Christian a telltale sign that something was amiss. Fueled by Tobin's pain, Christian escalated his attack by winging hard punches from both sides. Like Christian, Tobin chose to confront his situation head on and responded with even wider, looping blows. Even though Christian managed to slip many of Tobin's blows, this fight had little pretense of style or technique. This was an all-out brawl that tested each man's thirst for combat, will to survive and capacity to produce under severe conditions.

With every passing second, Christian's blows came slower and slower as the lactic acid in his muscles escalated to dangerous levels. Thus, Tobin's punches began to reach the target, but they no longer possessed the element of surprise that drove Christian to the canvas. Still, Tobin had the ability to hurt Christian, and with 25 seconds remaining in an extraordinarily chaotic opening round a flush right nearly produced the fight-ending third knockdown. This time, Christian kept himself upright and continued to blast away for the remainder of the round.

Christian began the second much as he did the first, by landing a good hook to the jaw that drove Tobin to the ropes. Tobin answered the only way he knew how – with heavy punches of his own. Neither man's shots had any forethought or strategic intent; they were throwing for the sake of throwing and the purpose behind each blow was singular and obvious: Inflicting as much pain within as short a time span as humanly possible.

Boxing has been described – and accurately so – as a "truth sport" because no other athletic endeavor can reveal an athlete's psyche so graphically. A fighter and his trainer can put together the best blueprint for battle, but at its core boxing is a sport of instinct. There is little time to contemplate one's situation when his head is snapping from side to side and his trunk is assaulted with heavy-handed hooks, crosses and uppercuts. It would have been easy for Christian to question his choice of profession – and to accept Tobin's superiority – after suffering two knockdowns in the first minute of his professional debut. But few fighters, even the most experienced of them, responded the way Christian did. Not only did he survive nearly two-and-a-half minutes without hitting the canvas a third time, he was the one pushing the pace at the end. Yet Christian's mind was clear enough to set his own stool upright after his corner man mishandled it reaching inside the ropes.

Midway through the second round, veteran trainer and MSG color analyst Gil Clancy marveled at Christian's bravery.

"It's a shame that this Christian has to fight a tough guy like Tobin in his first fight because he can be taught," he said. "Anybody who has shown the heart he has shown already in this fight can be taught to become a pretty good fighter." All great trainers know that desire is the fuel that propels a fighter's talent. They also know that a boxer with less ability but more character than his opponent often emerges victorious in wars of attrition. But if both fighters have the same will to win, all bets are off.

Tobin and Christian spent much of the round nailed to a small area near the ropes pounding away at one another with little pause. Christian chopped away like a lumberjack would at the base of a mighty oak, except that the oak-like Tobin chopped back with nearly equal fury. A little more than a minute into the second, Tobin showed small signs of wilting and Christian fed off his weakness by whipping in uppercuts with both hands. The strength was draining from Tobin's trunk-like legs and he tried to clinch several times, but he leaped out of his shell with hooks just often enough to keep Christian honest.

It was clear that Christian was gaining the upper hand and his new-found dominance was completed with eight seconds remaining in the round when a lead overhand right exploded off Tobin's cheek and deposited him face-first on the canvas. Seldom does a fighter rise from a face-first knockdown, but Tobin managed to haul himself upright on shaky legs at Mercante's count of five. Tobin was fortunate that the bell rang the instant Mercante allowed the fight to continue, for he had a vacant faraway look in his eyes and a stumbling gait as he walked to his corner. It was clear that he needed every second of the rest period to recover.

"What a fight, Sam," Clancy told blow-by-blow man Sam Rosen. "They're four-round fighters. Who would think these guys would meet each other? Two tough, tough guys that can fight."

Indeed they could. And there was even more in store.

Though Tobin was the one who had been battered and floored, he was the one who met Christian three-quarters of the way across the ring and threw the first punch, a left hook that just missed the target. But Christian's counter – also a left hook – sent Tobin wobbling into the ropes. Christian blasted away as he looked for the finisher. Tobin courageously tried to fight back but he seemed one good punch away from competitive extinction.

Christian trapped Tobin and the ropes and pounded every inch of available target without any regard to his own safety. "Knockout" was the only thing on his mind.

Meanwhile, Tobin was fighting back through the haze. As Christian fired away, Tobin flung a wild hook that landed heavily on Christian's jaw. Christian ignored the impact of that punch but a second hook a few moments later produced a surprising shock. After Christian secured a brief clinch, he pushed Tobin away and Tobin revealed his still vulnerable state by nearly stumbling to the canvas.

Christian moved in to resume the assault but Tobin somehow reset his tottering legs and wound up with a Hail Mary overhand right that detonated all over Christian's face. The stricken Christian somehow remained standing but it was clear he was mortally wounded Christian grabbed at Tobin tenuously as another overhand right caromed off Tobin's temple and a third connected with his ear. A slightly less winging hook nailed Christian, whose gas tank was now running low.

Yet another overhand right helped Tobin line up Christian, who was in the process of throwing his own right, for a monstrous left hook to the jaw. The effects of this punch did not manifest themselves for a very long split-second, but when they did, they were devastating.

Christin's upper body sagged backward – and nearly horizontally – between the top two strands of rope. As his grimacing head tilted upward, his arms instinctively shot straight out for a saving clinch that would never come. After Tobin landed a final winging right to the semi-conscious Christian's jaw, Mercante pulled Tobin away and began to administer a standing eight count. Christian tried to refocus, but his half-opened eyes and his upper body's involuntary weaving told Mercante everything he needed to know. At the count of three, Mercante stopped the count, wrapped his arms around Christian and began to remove the mouthpiece.

The fight was declared over at 1:35 of round three.

TALES FROM THE VAULT

It had been a remarkable seven-and-a-half minutes: Three knockdowns, countless changes in momentum and a dramatic, conclusive ending. Four-round fighters just getting their feet wet in the pro game aren't supposed to steal the show, but these did. No matter what these men would do in their careers, they can look back on this night and know that they expressed themselves athletically in a most extraordinary way. The record books will only say Tobin KO 3 Christian, but behind that single line of type was a story that was dying to be told.

Epilogue: Neither man came close to duplicating the level of performance they showed on this night, and soon they would exit the revolving door at the bottom of boxing's pyramid. Tobin fought only twice more – and would be knocked out in both. On January 29, 1990 he was knocked out in two rounds by future title challenger Tim Littles while the 5-0 Ron Morgan stopped Tobin in three the following August 19 in Harrah's Hotel and Casino in Atlantic City. Tobin retired with a record of 2-4 with two knockouts.

Christian bounced back nicely from the Tobin loss as he knocked out the 2-0 Donnie Leonardo in a single round on December 7, 1989. He followed that up with a six-round majority decision victory over Kelvin Prather on January 28, 1990 but his career would come to a sudden end on March 16, 1990 at Essex County College in Newark, N.J., where Joe Gatti stopped the 24-year-old Christian in one round. His final record stands at 2-2 with one knockout.

UNDERCARD TREASURES

Total Punches Landed/Thrown

Round	1	2	3	4	5	6	7	8	9	10	11	12	Total
Tobin	40/79	24/73	22/36										86/188
	51%	33%	61%										46%
Christian	37/97	51/102	20/47										108/246
	38%	50%	43%										44%

Jabs Landed/Thrown

Round	1	2	3	4	5	6	7	8	9	10	11	12	Total
Tobin	4/10	5/15	3/6										12/31
	40%	33%	50%										39%
Christian	1/10	0/3	0/0										1/13
	10%	0%	0%										8%

Power Punches Landed/Thrown

Round	1	2	3	4	5	6	7	8	9	10	11	12	Total
Tobin	36/69	19/58	19/30										74/157
	52%	33%	63%										47%
Christian	36/87	51/99	20/47										107/233
	41%	52%	43%										46%

John Tobin vs. Ferris Christian June 15, 1989, New York, New York

TALES FROM THE VAULT

Leland Hardy vs. Ike Padilla
March 30, 1989, New York, New York

One never knows when or where a classic fight will take place – the best we can do is an educated guess. Style matches such as Pacquiao-Morales, Chacon-Limon, Pryor-Arguello or Bowe-Holyfield carried the potential for greatness, but it wasn't until the fight ended that we knew the threshold had been crossed.

Most times, the greatest fights we'll ever see take place between two unknown club fighters who manage to steal a taste of immortality and burnish their names into the memories of those lucky enough to witness it. Such was the case for smallish heavyweights Leland Hardy and Ike Padilla, whose mini-Armageddon remains the most thrilling club fight this writer has ever seen.

Nine fights took place at the Felt Forum in New York City March 30, 1989. On a card that featured Renaldo Snipes, Merqui Sosa, Alex Stewart and Ricardo Cepeda, Hardy and Padilla were the ones the fans were buzzing about as they walked the streets outside Madison Square Garden after the fights had ended.

It wasn't that way when the two fighters entered the ring. Jose Antonio Martinez had just scored a two-round knockout over Mack Brown in a junior middleweight bout and the fans were settling in for another swing bout. Padilla (3-0, 3 KO) a native of Yonkers, was a former New York Golden Gloves champion who was in the first stages of a push he hoped would lead him down the same path as fellow MSG alum Cepeda, who would fight in the main event. If Padilla was exciting and successful, a world title chance might be in the offing 18 months or two years down the road. The Hardy fight was Padilla's first scheduled six-rounder.

Hardy (3-2-1, 2 KO) was just another guy Padilla had to fight in the progression toward that goal. The Philadelphian was now based in New York and though he had already tasted defeat, he still had the athlete's drive to create as much success as his situation would allow. After all, Freddie Pendleton overcame a 12-12-1 start to become IBF lightweight champion in the early 1990s and in the process became the patron saint of every fighter who wants to succeed without the corporate help reserved for Olympic champions or prospects with obvious, sensational talent.

When ring announcer Ed Derian announced house fighter Padilla, all he got was a smattering of polite applause but it was better than the stony indifference Hardy received.

That would change.

Padilla came out moving his upper body rhythmically from side to side while throwing jabs that fell short of the target. Hardy moved to his left in tight circles behind his high guard. Hardy's first jab snapped Padilla's head back and the New Yorker appeared slightly stunned. But Padilla, a puffed-up cruiserweight at 196, shook off the effects quickly.

After a brief feeling-out period, the two exchanged right-hand bombs – Padilla's sailed over Hardy's shoulder while Hardy's connected forcefully. Though the punch had much of Hardy's 197 pounds behind it, the thickly built Padilla absorbed the blow well. Hardy landed two more jabs as he circled away to set up his next attack. Padilla was still pushing the pace as he zipped two hooks to the body and popped in two jabs after missing two others. Padilla missed a left-right to the head but ripped a right uppercut to the ribs when Hardy left his elbows too high defending against Padilla's head blows.

Padilla was assuming early control of the fight as Hardy concentrated on throwing jabs and fending off Padilla's charges.

With 1:18 left in the round, both threw simultaneous hook-cross combinations and Padilla's right made Hardy stagger. Padilla pounced, digging rights and lefts to the body, but Hardy weathered the attack and proved it by crashing two good hooks to the jaw. Padilla's right eye already sported an abrasion and blood began to trickle from his mouth. Both men maintained a high work rate while searching for something that worked consistently. The round ended uneventfully with Padilla earning an edge.

The bell for round two sparked a series of electrifying events that would raise this bout from a humdrum anonymous undercard bout to something much more.

Padilla charged out of the corner and backed Hardy to the ropes with a one-two to the chin. A straight lead right to the jaw forced Hardy to retreat toward the corner pad and another one propelled Hardy to the canvas, his feet flying in the air as he landed near the corner. Up at two, Hardy appeared unhurt and his eyes refocused quickly as he took referee Wayne Kelly's mandatory eight-count.

Padilla raced in for the kill, throwing an almost uninterrupted stream of rights to the head and body. The left was merely a range finder as Padilla launched right after right. Hardy was trapped on the ropes, desperately trying to clinch while searching for an escape route but Padilla's whirlwind of punches and weaving upper body made him difficult to grab onto. After seconds that must have seemed like minutes, Hardy initiated a clinch and escaped from the neutral corner pad to ring center.

Padilla offered no respite as he mixed in hooks with his right hands. The New Yorker ripped a right to the ribs and sunk a searing hook to the liver, prompting Hardy to clinch again. In the few seconds he had while in the clinch, the hurt but clear-headed Hardy discovered the opening he needed to turn the tide. Two massive uppercuts landed flush and seriously rocked Padilla for the first time in the fight. Stung, Padilla fired back to the body and maneuvered Hardy to the ropes with a solid hook to the jaw. Hardy responded by snapping a right to the jaw as Padilla charged in, forcing Padilla to seek the refuge of a clinch.

For a man who was on the canvas just a minute before, Hardy had assembled an excellent comeback. With each passing second, the energy in his legs was regenerating and his blows regained their sharpness and power. Hardy popped the jab and landed a good straight right to the jaw while circling away nicely to his right. More of Padilla's punches landed on Hardy's arms and shoulders, but a few body blows still powered through.

With a minute to go, Padilla revved up his attack again as a right to the cheek caused Hardy to backpedal. Hardy kept his hands high in a protective shell, fielding as many of Padilla's blows as possible while he waited for a chance to strike back.

Sixteen seconds later, he did just that.

A torrid right uppercut to Padilla's jaw sparked a wild exchange of missed punches, after which Hardy exploded a left and a right between the eyes. A follow-up hook to the chin forced Padilla into full retreat. A home-run right uppercut missed and Padilla held on for dear life. While looking over Hardy's shoulder, Padilla shook his head "no" to tell his seconds he wasn't hurt.

It wasn't true.

A right cross-left hook combo hit the bull's eye and a crunching right uppercut landed with full impact. Padilla missed an overhand right, but it forced Hardy to take a half-step back. From there, Hardy landed a jab and a right to the temple that turned Padilla's legs to jelly. Another hook drove Padilla to the ropes and – in a delayed reaction – caused the New Yorker to drop to his right knee. Eighteen seconds remained in the round.

Up at five, Padilla told Kelly "I'm all right…I'm all right," shaking his head vigorously to emphasize the point – and also clear his head. Hardy charged forward, missing with a left-right but landing a gargantuan hook to the jaw that caused Padilla to stagger backward five feet toward the turnbuckle in Hardy's corner. Another hook at the bell left Padilla practically unconscious in a scene that best illustrated the phrase "saved by the bell."

Padilla's trainer Tommy Gallagher raced across the ring and squeezed a water-soaked sponge into his fighter's face and led him by the right arm back to the corner. Padilla plopped down on the stool, his mouth hanging open and his eyes struggling to focus as Gallagher furiously worked over him. Referee Kelly took a long, hard look at Padilla as he considered whether to stop the fight.

Whatever Gallagher did, it worked well enough to allow the fight to continue. By the time the third round bell sounded, Padilla appeared sturdier as he bounced on his toes. Hardy, however, was more than ready to put Padilla's resuscitation to the test.

Hardy fired a jackhammer jab to the face, and an overhand right to the temple buckled Padilla's legs. After another left-right landed flush, Padilla appeared ready to be taken. More blood poured from his mouth and it looked like the end was seconds away.

As Hardy raced in for the kill, Padilla launched a lead right, almost reflexively, that caromed off Hardy's jaw and – incredibly – floored him.

Seldom has the pendulum swung so violently from one fighter to the other – and back again. Just when the fans were preparing themselves mentally for a finish in one fighter's favor, the other man jolted them into a different reality. What began as just another preliminary fight evolved into something that defied description. It was becoming a point in time worthy of occupying a small corner of a fan's memory bank for a lifetime, a prospect unimaginable when Padilla and Hardy entered the ring a few minutes before.

The only question now was this – what would happen next?

Hardy arose at four, shaking his head in disbelief while the fans roared with a volume that rivaled those in MSG's big arena. Padilla, still badly hurt himself, flailed away inaccurately as Hardy struggled mightily to regain his equilibrium. Both men looked ready to fall and thoughts of a double knockout were racing through some heads. A Padilla right slid off Hardy's shoulder, but another one hit the target solidly. Another pair of rights drove Hardy to another set of strands and Padilla continued to empty his guns. Hardy whizzed a hook over Padilla's head and forced another clinch.

After Kelly separated them, Hardy snapped a jab as Padilla rushed in and a right to the ear sent Padilla off balance. Hardy then stepped in, planted his feet and drove a final, explosive right uppercut to the jaw that left Padilla spread-eagled on the canvas. Kelly ran in and immediately waved off the fight. As Padilla stared up at the ring lights through unseeing eyes, Kelly removed his mouthpiece.

The fight lasted seven minutes, twenty-two seconds, with both men going down in the second and third rounds. As the MSG Network's cameras scanned the crowd, most stood and cheered while others wore expressions of disbelief mixed with wonder.

Ever proud, Padilla wanted to get up but the ringside physicians kept him on his back for several more seconds. Once he assumed a sitting position on the canvas, the doctors occasionally pressed down on his shoulders to make sure he didn't attempt to stand until they determined Padilla had regained his senses.

"Wow, what a fight," MSG commentator Sam Rosen said. "Three rounds of banging, non-stop (action), both men going down twice and finally this bout was stopped. I wouldn't mind seeing a rematch of this one."

"Boy, you are a brave guy Sam," analyst Gil Clancy said. "If you tell each guy now that we're going to have a rematch, they'd kill you."

Epilogue: There would be no rematch, and neither man engaged in many more fights after this classic encounter. Boxrec.com does not have complete records on either man, so one can't be sure what happened afterward. According to the site, Padilla had only one more fight, a sixth-round knockout loss to James Holmes at the Felt Forum a little less than five months later. His record was 3-2 (3 KO).

Hardy went 2-2 in his final four fights, knocking out Anthony Hayes in one round at the Felt Forum three months later and stopping Elvin Evans three months after that at the Beacon Theatre in New York. Peter Wabuda stopped Hardy in three rounds January 3, 1990 at White Plains, New York and Ruslan Taramov scored a fourth round KO over Hardy April 12, 1990 at Korakuen Hall in Tokyo. His final record was 4-4-1 (4 KO).

UNDERCARD TREASURES

Total Punches Landed/Thrown

Round	1	2	3	4	5	6	7	8	9	10	11	12	Total
Hardy	22/55	21/56	11/27										54/138
	40%	38%	41%										39%
Padilla	26/87	40/86	10/36										76/209
	30%	47%	28%										36%

Jabs Landed/Thrown

Round	1	2	3	4	5	6	7	8	9	10	11	12	Total
Hardy	18/41	5/18	5/14										28/73
	44%	28%	36%										38%
Padilla	13/40	6/21	2/14										21/75
	32%	29%	14%										28%

Power Punches Landed/Thrown

Round	1	2	3	4	5	6	7	8	9	10	11	12	Total
Hardy	4/14	16/38	6/13										26/65
	29%	42%	46%										40%
Padilla	13/47	34/65	8/22										55/134
	28%	52%	36%										41%

Leland Hardy vs. Ike Padilla March 30, 1989, New York, New York

TALES FROM THE VAULT

Elvir Muriqi vs. Sam Ahmad
July 23, 2002, New Rochelle, New York

Every fighter who aspires to make a mark in the sport must go through a series of doors before he can lay eyes on the Promised Land. The first set of doors are wide and inviting as he races through a gauntlet of inferior opponents to establish his skills to the paying audience. After completing the string of showcase fights, narrower doors await as the prospect takes on journeymen, former contenders and other prospects in eight- and 10-round fights. Next up are former contenders, then fellow contenders and finally, a champion.

Once a fighter captures a title, his work is not yet done as every victory at the elite level brings him a step closer to the one entryway that ensures immortality – the Hall of Fame. Every fighter serves as the other's gatekeeper, and the pool of fighters occupying the next level grows ever smaller. In the short term, fighters fight for the money but in a larger sense they engage in combat to create – or defend – their place in the sport's pantheon.

On July 23, 2002 at New Rock City in Rochelle, New York, light heavyweight Elvir Muriqi (23-1, 13 KO) was ready to take another step in his journey. "The Kosovo Kid" had largely been successful in the early phases of his career, though he suffered one notable hiccup when he was disqualified in six rounds against Dan Sheehan two years earlier. But Muriqi received a second chance 14 weeks and three fights later and he made good by decisioning Sheehan in six rounds. Three months earlier, Muriqi stepped up the level of competition as he stopped the 9-4-3 Mike Coker just seconds into his first scheduled 10 rounder.

Standing in the way of Muriqi's progress was 35-year-old Sam Ahmad, who overcame a late start in the sport at age 29 to put together a 16-2-3 (7 KO) record, which included one no-contest. He had already collected several notable scalps, including Tyrone Frazier (W 4, W 6), John Scully (W 8) and Darren Whitley (W 8). He also inflicted the first blemish on Julian Letterlough's record two years before with 10-round draw. But Ahmad had fallen on hard times as he entered the Muriqi fight as he had lost two of his last three. The lone win, however, was a six-round decision over Muriqi's conqueror Sheehan, so for Muriqi the fight represented a point of progression – a win over Ahmad would further consolidate his revenge victory over Sheehan.

Also, as Muriqi's trainer Teddy Atlas said, an emotional test was at hand for his prospect.

"We're going to find out how mature my 23-year-old kid is after four years as a pro," Atlas told ESPN2's Mario Diaz. "Tonight, we're going to see if he can graduate. He's got to be steady and consistent. That guy over there is going to try to break him down emotionally as much as physically. My guy knows what to do. He has to be able to keep it together in his mind and do it round after round."

Atlas couldn't have known how right he would be. Before the night was over, Muriqi would endure a far sterner test than he or Atlas could have imagined.

The fight started well for Muriqi as a left-right to the body set up a good scoring hook to Ahmad's jaw. Another 45-degree hook landed for Muriqi, and he caught Ahmad with a cuffing right as he fell into a clinch. It was immediately apparent that the "Kosovo Kid" had the quicker hands, and his eight first-round knockouts proved he was a fast starter. The crowd picked up the chant of "MUR-EE-KEE" to reward his good beginning.

Forty-three seconds into the fight, everything changed.

Muriqi tried to grab Ahmad as he charged in, but he created an opening by leaving his left arm down. Ahmad threw a right-left to the body and went over the top with a crushing overhand right to the chin that sent Muriqi sprawling to the canvas and landing heavily onto the neutral corner pad. Embarrassed and hurt, Muriqi tried to push his unsteady body up with his left arm but was unsuccessful. His second attempt was better and he managed to get up by referee James Santa's count of four. Muriqi forcefully lifted his right arm and shook it to show both Santa and Atlas that he was fine.

His actions upon resuming the battle suggested otherwise as he immediately clinched to gain a few more precious seconds of recovery time. Three crucial parts of Muriqi's fistic constitution were being put to the test simultaneously: His recuperative powers, his survival skills and his presence of mind under fire. The fact he got up and continued to fight were two good signs.

At the 1:27 mark, Muriqi had an answer for Professor Ahmad in the form of a three-punch combination – a right to the chin, a southpaw left cross and a right to the ear that sent Ahmad on his ear. The pro-Muriqi crowd cheered and as Ahmad arose at four, many people thought the world was put back on its axis after a brief departure from its orbit.

Instead, Muriqi's head was nearly sent into orbit just four seconds later.

As Muriqi dipped to throw a hook to the body, Ahmad came over the top with a rocket of an overhand right that exploded off Muriqi's jaw. In a split-second, "The Kosovo Kid" was transformed from hunter to prey as his body collapsed and his head bounced off the canvas. On this night, Ahmad's overhand right was a formidable weapon for which Muriqi seemingly had no answers, and it was clearly the key by which Ahmad would be able to advance to the next door of his career. His entry into the next level seemed to be just a few seconds away as Muriqi struggled with the effects of his mighty blow.

Muriqi's fighting instincts were at war with his body as he tried to get up. His eyes were glassy and his legs were wobbly as he fell forward into the ropes. His arms reflexively shot out and Muriqi was able to catch himself. As he turned toward Santa at the count of seven, his wide-eyed expression betrayed his pain but the fact that he got up earned him the chance to fight on.

By arising from a punch that would have knocked most other men unconscious, Muriqi proved he had "heart." Under this severe trial by fire, Muriqi learned an important lesson about himself: No matter what else happened in this fight, he and Atlas would know that Muriqi possessed an extra reservoir of courage that would prove valuable in fights to come.

Survival was the only thought in Muriqi's mind as he clamped down on Ahmad. Pride was no longer an issue as he knew his body wasn't yet ready to absorb another blow of any kind. He hung on unashamedly as Ahmad dug rights to the body and furiously attempted to shake off his stricken opponent. Muriqi bulled Ahmad to the ropes and hooked both gloves on the upper strand to buy some more time.

As the clock ticked under 30 seconds, Muriqi's legs appeared stronger and he began to bounce and throw one-twos while grabbing Ahmad whenever he tried to press forward. Muriqi countered an Ahmad jab with a chopping right to the ear, which enabled him to force another clinch. The round closed with Ahmad landing two more overhand rights to the jaw and the still-buzzed Muriqi hanging on until the bell.

As he stumbled toward his corner, Muriqi again held up his right arm, both to show Atlas he was still fit to fight and to project his sense of triumph upon surviving the roughest three minutes of his career.

For such an immensely exciting round, the CompuBox numbers hardly reflected it. Muriqi landed 18 of 34 punches (47 percent) while Ahmad, who connected on just 14 of 42 blows, was able to produce two powerful knockdowns and seize control of the fight.

Muriqi began the second with a right to the body as Ahmad just missed with a home-run overhand right. Muriqi missed with a wide hook to the body, and as he threw long but inaccurate jabs his legs appeared somewhat steadier. But any thoughts of a revival were put on hold a mere 26 seconds into the round.

As Muriqi threw a one-two, the jab fell short, which created just enough of a crack for Ahmad to shoot a short, winging right to the point of the jaw. Though Muriqi fell heavily, he was up at two and his clear eyes were flashing with anger. He banged his gloves together and told Santa with conviction "I'm all right" when asked.

Ahmad raced in and landed an overhand right before Muriqi sloppily fell into a clinch. Muriqi's legs appeared stronger as he fired jabs and mixed in a hook to the body.

Just as it appeared the fog was about to lift, Ahmad's unleashed another thunderbolt counter right to dump Muriqi for the fourth time in the fight.

For Muriqi, Ahmad's right was a hammer of destruction, the ultimate trump card that would negate any good work he would do between knockdowns. Time and again, Ahmad would hit the jackpot by countering over Muriqi's right and as a result he stood at the precipice of victory. Ahmad had 74 more seconds to register the third – and probably final – knockdown of the round and given Muriqi's vulnerability to the right he literally was one punch away.

When the fight resumed, Ahmad went to the well once again but this time the overhand right missed. Muriqi got on his bicycle to bide some time, landing a light overhand right in the process.

Unbeknownst to Muriqi, fate was about to smile on him.

Muriqi fired a jab and an overhand right, and this time Ahmad's legs showed weakness. Encouraged, Muriqi landed another overhand right to the temple that had Ahmad holding on, and a third one-two sent Ahmad stumbling forward into another clinch. For the first time in the fight, Ahmad was clearly hurt and Muriqi, ignoring the fact that one stray bullet from Ahmad's right arm could end the fight, sought to press his advantage.

Muriqi ducked under an attempted Ahmad clinch to uncork a knee-buckling right uppercut. His adrenaline pumping, Muriqi fired an overhand right to the ear and buried a hook to the body before throwing Ahmad down to the canvas. Santa correctly ruled the tumble a push and the respite brought down the curtain on a breathtaking second round.

Despite being knocked down twice, Muriqi's stats far outstripped Ahmad's. Muriqi landed 25 of 45 punches (56 percent) while Ahmad was 12 of 31 (39 percent).

Muriqi began the third on the move behind a light jab with Ahmad looking to counter. Whenever Muriqi landed a punch he immediately nipped out of range, ever mindful of Ahmad's crippling counters. Meanwhile, Ahmad was still feeling the effects of Muriqi's late-round surge. His legs were unsteady and he wasn't able to put full weight on his punches because by doing so he would rock himself off balance.

Muriqi's jabs were now landing hard and flush, and Ahmad's punches had far less steam on them. Muriqi was fighting with a professional's composure and he appeared to be growing as a fighting man with every passing second. Two chopping overhand rights to the ear wobbled Ahmad's legs and as Muriqi bulled him to the ropes, a third overhand right further eroded Ahmad's foundation. After a right uppercut and a hook crashed in, Muriqi emptied his guns in pursuit of the final kill. An Ahmad hook-cross combination came dangerously close to landing flush, but Muriqi was no longer concerned with what was coming at him.

A chopping lead right to the ear sent Ahmad tumbling to the canvas with 51 seconds remaining in the round, and as Ahmad laid underneath the ropes with his eyes closed the fight appeared over. But Ahmad jumped up to beat Santa's count, showing that he, too, had fortitude.

A right to the ear forced Ahmad to grab Muriqi around the waist and take him down to the canvas with him. After Santa ruled the tumble a slip, Muriqi positioned himself in perfect range before cracking a right-left uppercut combination off Ahmad's jaw. Ahmad staggered toward the ropes and tried to hold on but Muriqi was not to be denied, landing a blizzard of blows that forced Santa to stop the fight with mere seconds remaining in the round. The triumphant Muriqi walked straight to Atlas to give him a big hug. After congratulating his warrior, Atlas, ever the teacher, first delivered a lecture to make sure the lessons were absorbed, then kissed him on the cheek and gave him an "atta-boy" swat on the behind.

Muriqi had closed the show in most dramatic fashion, landing 32 of his 44 power shots. But as well as Muriqi fought in the end, he was very fortunate to avoid disaster.

"I love ESPN, but I don't want to give them this good of a fight," Atlas told Diaz. "He went out there in his first big moment, and he made a lot of big mistakes – he pulled straight back, he dropped his hands and he stood there. He did stupid, stupid things and he almost paid the ultimate price for it. But having said that, he showed the heart of a lifetime by coming back and doing what he did. You wonder if a fighter has character and we found that out tonight."

Epilogue: Following the incredible war with Ahmad, Muriqi continued to walk though the doors laid before him while increasing the level of competition. Muriqi knocked out Mike Coker (KO 1) and Tiwon Taylor (KO 3) before stopping former title challenger James Crawford in four rounds. Muriqi struggled to a majority decision over Thomas Reid but followed up with a three-round KO over Charles Ward.

On October 2, 2004, Muriqi's momentum came to a screeching halt after Danny Santiago blasted him out in four rounds. Five months later, he blitzed the 10-59-3 Caseny Truesdale in 100 seconds only to stumble with a six-round split decision loss to Oleksandr Garashchenko April 30, 2005 at Madison Square Garden.

Three wins over Marlon Hayes (W 8), Ted Muller (W 8) and Derrick Reed (KO 1) in 2006 led to a crossroads encounter against Antonio Tarver in June 2007. The heavy underdog fought bravely against the former light heavyweight champ but fell just short as Tarver took a majority decision. Nevertheless, the Tarver fight raised Muriqi's profile considerably and after stopping Jameel Wilson in four rounds in January 2008 he received a crack at Clinton Woods' IBF light heavyweight belt on Valentine's Day 2009. Muriqi lost a lopsided 12 round nod but two months later he avenged the loss to Garashchenko with a 10-round decision in Serbia. In October 2009, Muriqi repeated his early win over Tiwon Taylor as he stopped him in two rounds. As of January 2010 his record is 37-5 (23 KO).

The Muriqi loss took virtually all of the steam out of Ahmad's career as opportunities for thirty-something fighters who had lost three of his last four were few and far between. Ahmad would fight only once more, a four-round stoppage to the 12-19-4 Ronald Boddie November 28, 2003 in Scanton, Pa. Ahmad's final record is 16-4-3 (7 KO).

TALES FROM THE VAULT

Total Punches Landed/Thrown

Round	1	2	3	4	5	6	7	8	9	10	11	12	Total
Muriqi													81/143
													57%
Ahmad													35/100
													35%

Jabs Landed/Thrown

Round	1	2	3	4	5	6	7	8	9	10	11	12	Total
Muriqi													23/49
													47%
Ahmad													12/46
													26%

Power Punches Landed/Thrown

Round	1	2	3	4	5	6	7	8	9	10	11	12	Total
Muriqi													58/94
													62%
Ahmad													23/54
													43%

* Fight originally compiled by CompuBox, but the original HTML files containing complete round-by-round statistics no longer exist.

Elvir Muriqi vs. Sam Ahmad July 23, 2002, New Rochelle, New York

UNDERCARD TREASURES

Brian Hallinan vs. Kenny Blackson
September 23, 1994, Upper Malboro, Maryland

One of the jobs of a promoter is to create an image in the ticket-buyers' mind that the fight they're selling will be an unforgettable spectacle that cannot be missed. The fighters assume intimidating poses and utter equally intimidating words about what they are going to do to the other man during a number of press conferences. Fight posters and commercials on TV and radio hyping the potential Armageddon are intended to heighten the mood. If everyone does the job right, a standing-room only crowd will buzz with anticipation and hundreds of thousands of pay-per-view homes will radiate that buzz worldwide.

But in the end, most fights never live up to the hype that precedes it. The reason why the 1985 war between Marvelous Marvin Hagler and Thomas Hearns is so revered is because it was one of the few fights in history that saw two Hall-of-Fame caliber fighters tear after one another in all-out combat. They put aside the niceties of boxing skill that accompanies most elite matches in favor of raw, uncompromising savagery. Both winner and loser were elevated and as a result the term "Hagler-Hearns" has become, along with "Zale-Graziano," "Ali-Frazier," and "Gatti-Anybody," synonyms for "great fight."

True greatness, however, can't be forced. All the promoting skills in the world can't make fighters rise above themselves and give absolutely everything for their art. That can only come from within and it's extremely rare when two boxers carry that mindset into the ring against one another. All the stars have to be aligned just right to make that happen and that might only come a few times a decade if we as boxing fans are lucky.

Veteran boxing observers will tell you that the best fights often involve two equally matched clubfighters who produce eight-digit efforts for their three-digit paychecks. For them, boxing is not a world of championship belts, lavish training camps and pay-per-view bonanzas but one of juggling full-time jobs, fulfilling family responsibilities and paycheck-to-paycheck survival. These men fight either out of financial necessity or to fulfill a burning desire to find out how far their talent can take them. To promoters, they are there to fill out the card and to fans they are diversions to keep them entertained while waiting for the main event but to these men, the fights are as real and important as anything in their lives. They may not have the skills of the big-name fighters, but their competitive juices are just as robust.

One never knows when a great fight will break out, and that certainly was the case on September 23, 1994 at the Show Place Arena in Upper Malboro, Md. There was a lot of weirdness surrounding this card. First, the original main event of Dana

Rosenblatt vs. Frankie Savannah was cancelled just hours before ESPN hit the airwaves because Rosenblatt was sent to the hospital after throwing up in the locker room. Apparently, Rosenblatt had changed his diet and his new diet didn't include enough fiber to counteract the adrenaline that comes with the internal excitement that comes with an impending fight. Thus, he got sick.

But if that wasn't enough, Keith Holmes, who was involved in the new main event against Andrew Council for the vacant USBA junior middleweight title, was arrested by FBI agents and U.S. Marshals the afternoon before the fight in connection with a May 2 drive-by shooting. Holmes was released after a $100,000 bond, but was to be extradited to Washington, D.C., in a few days. Holmes would win a 12-round decision over Council and his career would resume virtually uninterrupted six months later with a two-round knockout over Sam Wilson.

After Richard Frazier (yes, the man who would later challenge Roy Jones Jr.) won a six-round decision over Courtney Butler, Brian Hallinan and Kenny Blackston entered the ring to fight a four-round swing bout. The 25-year-old Hallinan was far more seasoned – his 71-9 amateur resume included two Pennsylvania Golden Gloves titles. As a pro, he carried a 6-0 (4 KO) record which included a win over the 5-0-1 Bobby Heath, and his last fight was a three round KO over Jeff Mann four weeks before.

The 26-year-old Blackston (2-1, 1 KO) of Baltimore didn't have much of an amateur career but after losing his pro debut to Michael Tidline El, Blackston won his next two fights. His most recent outing was a one-round victory over Alphonso Dyer three months before.

When the bell rang, the two boxers took about a half-second to feel one another out, then proceeded to tear into one another. Blackston fired hooks to the head and body while Hallinan worked rights over the top and underneath. Blackston's superior upper body strength forced Hallinan to the ropes, where an overhand right and a right uppercut ripped through the guard.

The fight's tone had been set in the bout's first 20 seconds as both men frenetically unleashed blows like a pair of lawn mower blades. Neither man's punches had much snap but the energy that drove them forward in turn energized a crowd that immediately knew they were watching something special.

Blackston countered a Hallinan hook with one of his own and a second bounced off the Pennsylvanian's forehead. A pair of follow-up hooks buckled Hallinan's knees and Blackston somehow turned up the heat even further in search of the early kill. He was working the hook overtime and he seemingly couldn't miss with it. An unofficial count had Blackston throwing 42 hooks in the first minute, and when he began mixing in overhand rights he put the undefeated Hallinan in a difficult spot.

It would have been prudent for Hallinan to hold on and collect himself. His face was already reddened from Blackston's blitz and he had already been stunned. But there are fights and situations that force a boxer to forego logic and simply go for it, and this was one of those times. Despite being pinned to the ropes, Hallinan kept pumping away as he used courage and tenacity to weather Blackston's incredible start.

The first clinch didn't come until midway through the round, but after referee Larry Barrett broke them they resumed their all-out attacks. Blackston jacked Hallinan's jaw with a jab, then moved into close quarters to resume the inside war. For the next minute the two men whacked one another incessantly, Blackston with the hook and Hallinan with the right.

A right-left to the jaw spun Hallinan's head with 36 seconds to go, but the Altoona resident stood his ground and fought back fiercely. Both launched simultaneous hooks that landed and Blackston drove Hallinan back with a huge right to the jaw and a hook that finally made Hallinan clinch. On the break, Hallinan defiantly shook his head "no" at Blackston and he backed up his bravado by whaling away with rights to the ribs, shoe-shining Blackston's flanks and punctuating a mind-blowingly exciting first round with a final right to the ear.

Seldom does a fight begin with intense bell-to-bell action that could take the breath away of even the most seasoned observers, but this one did. The punch-count this author conducted revealed Hallinan had landed 51 of his 121 punches, including 49 of 110 power punches, while Blackston connected on 48 of 116 blows, an incredible 84 of which were hooks. The two combined for just 14 jabs, with Hallinan throwing 11 of them and connecting on just two.

Refreshed by the one-minute rest, Blackston and Hallinan ripped away at each other in the second with Blackston's upper body strength proving superior as he bulled his opponent wherever he wished. Blackston showed a little more variety as he mixed in plenty of rights with his hooks.

But as the round progressed, the momentum began to shift from Blackston to Hallinan. During the infighting, Hallinan shifted into a southpaw stance and this tactic bore out several positive results. First, his right hooks were landing frequently and second, it allowed Hallinan to better defend Blackston's hooks.

As the seconds passed, Blackston started to slow down. His technique was more ragged and the blows that had such speed and snap in the first round were now pushed out and the punches that were so accurate now whizzed over Hallinan's head or were blocked by arms, shoulders and elbows. Two strong Hallinan rights forced a brief clinch and rights to the head and body caused Blackston to cringe as he fell forward to initiate another clinch. A double hook to the head and body took out some of the air out of Blackston and a right-right-left snapped the Baltimore boxer's head as he came in.

It was an immensely physical fight with lots of pulling, pushing, wrestling and especially punching. Hallinan was beginning to pull ahead, and like a marathon runner looking to put a rival away with a heart-breaking surge, Hallinan ended the second by popping Blackston with short straight shots while on the retreat.

Neither man landed a jab in the second, and Hallinan out-landed Blackston 49-28 and outthrew him 131 to 99. Blackston's battery was starting to run low while Hallinan's energy shone like a halogen as he was more efficient and his engine ran hotter for longer.

Still, Blackston jabbed with gusto and moved Hallinan back as the third began. Curiously, Hallinan came out of the corner as a right-hander and he took a double hook and overhand right as a result. But as soon as he shifted to the lefty stance, he landed his own double hook and an overhand right to the ear. Blackston pushed Hallinan to the ropes where they engaged in a rare clinch.

After Barrett separated them, Hallinan drove a right to the ribs and followed with a whipping double right to the body and head that sent Blackston crashing heavily on his left shoulder, bouncing off the canvas and leaving him spread-eagled on his back. It was a sudden, spectacular knockdown and as Blackston hit the canvas it was immediately clear the final two punches of the fight had been landed. When Barrett tolled "ten," Blackston was in a sitting position and was in no shape to get any further than that.

Hallinan fell to his knees and lifted his arms in thanksgiving, then ran over to the ropes to hug his trainers.

It was an incredibly hard-fought and hard-earned win and he was justifiably proud. ESPN usually didn't conduct interviews following swing bouts, but this one was so good that it couldn't pass without some sort of post-fight reaction.

"I hope the people back home are watching and I hope they realize that I'm not all talk," Hallinan told Al Bernstein. When Bernstein asked why Hallinan switched to southpaw, he revealed it was a tendency he had all his life but was told to suppress it by previous trainers.

"It started to come back naturally to me," he said. "When I was a kid I was ambidextrous but I favored my left hand. I was always told to stay away from the left hand and go right-handed. Now it's starting to creep back into me somehow and I'm not shutting it off anymore. I'm allowing it to take its course."

Hallinan admitted he was hurt several times in the fight but was able to overcome it through the power of hard work.

"I was on Queer Street a couple of times, no doubt about it," he said. "You train so intensely. When everybody else is out partying and drinking booze and having fun, you're in the gym. Friday night, Saturday night, everybody's out dancing and having a good time, you're in the gym."

As he was saying these words, there was no doubt he was feeling like he was missing out on the good times typical enjoyed by his fellow twenty-somethings. But on this day and on a national TV stage he showed that all the hard work was worth it.

Epilogue: Complete records for these fighters weren't available, but according to Boxrec.com Blackston would fight 13 more times over the next four years, winning 10 of them and four by knockout. He avenged one of the defeats by decisioning Jasper Goddard over eight rounds and his last listed fight took place February 10, 1998 when he decisioned Arturo Guillen over six rounds in Woodlawn, Md. His record stands at 12-5 (5 KO).

Hallinan followed the Blackston win with a four-round TKO over Horace Watterson five weeks later. Hallinan stepped up in class in his next fight when he took on the 14-1 Arthur Allen, but was stopped in two rounds. Hallinan rebounded nicely by beating the 10-0 Edward Ross over six rounds but two TKO losses to Darryl Ruffin (KO by 3) and Clarence White (KO by 4) ended Hallinan's career. The White fight, which took place August 16, 1996, left the 27-year-old Hallinan with a record of 9-3 (6 KO).

TALES FROM THE VAULT

Total Punches Landed/Thrown

Round	1	2	3	4	5	6	7	8	9	10	11	12	Total
Hallinan	51/121	49/131	6/18										106/270
	42%	37%	33%										39%
Blackston	48/116	28/99	8/30										84/245
	41%	28%	27%										34%

Jabs Landed/Thrown

Round	1	2	3	4	5	6	7	8	9	10	11	12	Total
Hallinan	2/11	0/10	0/2										2/23
	18%	0%	0%										9%
Blackston	1/3	0/7	0/9										1/19
	33%	0%	0%										5%

Power Punches Landed/Thrown

Round	1	2	3	4	5	6	7	8	9	10	11	12	Total
Hallinan	49/110	49/121	6/16										104/247
	45%	40%	38%										42%
Blackston	47/113	28/92	8/21										83/226
	42%	30%	38%										37%

Brian Hallinan vs. Kenny Blackson September 23, 1994, Upper Malboro, Maryland

UNDERCARD TREASURES

Tony Ridges vs. Roberto Cobos
April 21, 1995, Las Vegas, Nevada

When ESPN was still in its infancy in April 1980, it forged a partnership with Bob Arum's Top Rank to create "Top Rank Boxing." In the ensuing years, the series became one of the network's highest-rated programs and it served as a weekly platform for dozens of fighters who eventually became contenders and champions.

On April 21, 1995 at Arizona Charlie's in Las Vegas, ESPN was celebrating the 15th anniversary of "Top Rank Boxing" with the main event an attractive encounter between undefeated junior lightweights Julian Wheeler and Robert "Grandpa" Garcia for the NABF belt. While the fans settled into their seats to wait for Garcia-Wheeler, they were thoroughly entertained by a scheduled four-round appetizer that turned into its own main course.

Lightweights Tony Ridges and Roberto Cobos entered the ring a few minutes after cruiserweight John Kiser scored a six-round decision over Reggie Blackmon. Like the main event, Ridges-Cobos pitted boxer versus slugger and such matches usually are won by the one who can impose his style – and his will – on the other man. But as longtime fans are well aware, boxing is one of those sports where the word "usually" raises red flags.

The 24-year-old Ridges, 135, went into the Cobos contest on a three-fight winning streak after splitting his first four pro outings, including a four-round win over future contender James Crayton. His most recent outing was a one-round disqualification over Sean Green three months earlier, and while his 5-2 record included four knockouts, his mobility and hand speed was his stock and trade. A native of Anchorage, Alaska, Ridges moved to Las Vegas to give his career a jump-start.

At 23, Cobos, 135 ½, had far more professional experience as he sported a 15-1 (11 KO) record. The wade-in southpaw slugger began his career with four consecutive one-round knockouts and was 10-0 when he suffered his only defeat, a six-round decision to Ruben Nevarez. The El Paso, Texas, native rebounded nicely with five straight knockouts and was coming off an eight-round decision over Fernando Ligarte eight months earlier.

Perhaps the urge to shake off his ring rust could explain why Cobos raced out of his corner and initiated an uncompromising street fight. A left-right-right to the body was followed by a four-punch flurry to the body and two left crosses to the jaw that sent Ridges reeling to the ropes.

Less than 20 seconds into the fight, Ridges was already in danger of being blown out of the ring. Few fights ever begin in such whirlwind fashion and Cobos' opening attack prevented him from feeling his man out and assembling a plan of attack. Cobos' explosive start forced Ridges to act instinctively – and his instincts told him to strike back.

As Cobos barreled in, Ridges nailed him with a right cross that snapped the Texan's head back. Cobos walked through the blow and a big left cross set off an all-out body assault along the ropes. Ridges deflected many of the blows with his arms and elbows, but Cobos' superior upper body strength and smothering attack prevented Ridges from spinning his way back to ring center for several seconds. Once Ridges finally escaped, Cobos was still full of fire as he landed a left cross and a right to the body.

After Cobos' opening fury, the action slowed just enough to allow Ridges a chance to back away and use his boxing skills. But at that moment Ridges made an unusual choice – he was going to try and beat Cobos at his own game. Thus, instead of using the slight breather to turn the fight's flow his way, Ridges sought to turn the tables on Cobos.

Ridges commenced his chase by bowing his head forward and whaling away at the body. A right hook sunk deeply into Cobos' ribs and a right uppercut jerked the Texan's head skyward.

The terms of battle were now set: This was going to be a war for as long as it lasted.

The two men traded power shots freely on the inside with Cobos landing a four-punch flurry to the head and body and Ridges connecting with a right to the body, two hooks to the jaw and a snapping jab. The inside exchanges escalated toward a feverish crescendo as the seconds passed, with Ridges' whipping shots to the body gaining him a slight edge. As the round entered its final minute, the fight evolved into an all-or-nothing proposition, especially for Cobos because his intense first-minute assault left him somewhat winded and Ridges was showing no signs of slowing down. Though the tenor of the fight clearly favored the slugger Cobos, it was boxer-puncher Ridges who flourished as his harder, sharper blows shredded Cobos' defense.

But Cobos still had plenty of fight in him. After Ridges landed a jab-jab-cross-body hook combo, Cobos retaliated with a left cross and a right hook that shook Ridges briefly. Another right to the body, a right hook to the jaw and a left cross to the head connected sharply and another jolting left cross hit the target. A right-left combo at the bell capped a good comeback for Cobos after absorbing Ridges' withering mid-round assault.

And what an assault it was. In the first round, Ridges unleashed 125 punches and landed 46 of them for 37 percent accuracy, which was excellent for a volume-punching attack. Cobos, however, landed 52 of his 88 blows for an astonishing 59 percent.

Still, Ridges proved that he could slug with the slugger and as the second round began he came out with guns blazing to prevent Cobos from again seizing the early upper hand. Cobos was more than happy to oblige as they swapped full-blooded body shots.

It was the kind of unyielding toe-to-toe action that serves as the violent equivalent of the pre-fight staredown as both are designed to establish both physical and psychological advantage. In such a contest, the rules are simple. In the staredown, the man who makes the other look away is seen as the winner, and in all-out toe-to-toe wars the man who makes his opponent willingly break off the exchange is viewed the same way. One would have thought that the slugger Cobos would emerge victorious because his style was predicated on his ability to chop a man down punch for punch. But this time it was Ridges, the slick boxer, who made Cobos back away.

At that moment, Ridges had scored a psychological knockout over Cobos but in the physical realm there was still much work to do.

As Cobos retreated, Ridges fired a left-right to the body and a hurtful right uppercut to the jaw. With blood coming out of his mouth, Cobos caught the charging Ridges with a right-left. The pumped-up Ridges walked through the blows and fired away at Cobos' body like a man possessed. A ripping right to the ribs brought groans from the crowd and Cobos' body bent over ever so slightly. Cobos' resolve to fight remained strong as he snapped a long right-left that caught Ridges' cleanly.

Midway through the round, Ridges' five-punch flurry stunned Cobos, but the Texan roared back behind a right to the body and two jolting left crosses that had Ridges holding on. After the break, Ridges went back to Cobos' body, pounding rights and lefts to the flanks while nicely mixing in close-range shots to the head. It was a beautiful display of punch selection as Ridges' up-and-down combinations left Cobos wondering which part of his anatomy to defend. But Cobos was not about defense, and his answer to Ridges' well-executed offense was to stay with him punch for punch.

In the final minute, Ridges continued to nail Cobos with uppercuts but the Texan surged behind a double hook and two right-lefts. As the seconds ticked away, Ridges showed he had far more left in the tank by raking Cobos with combinations that seemingly had no end. By squaring his body to Ridges, Cobos presented an open target and Ridges took full advantage in the closing seconds with a searing right hook to the body and right uppercut to the jaw that caused Cobos' upper body to double over. Ridges pounced on his stricken opponent by unleashing a dizzying array of well-mixed combinations. A double hook to the body – and the bell – put an end to a nightmarish sequence for Cobos.

The stats confirmed what many already knew – it was a huge round for Ridges. The Alaska native landed 76 of his 125 blows for 61 percent. Cobos' drop-off in activity was apparent as his output dipped to 69 punches, but his 32 landed blows translated to a more than respectable 46 percent.

Cobos began the third round somewhat refreshed as he met Ridges at ring center and landed the first blow, a left cross to the jaw. All that did was trigger another bomb-throwing frenzy by Ridges and Cobos dug in his toes for another pivotal toe-to-toe exchange. Cobos fell to the canvas after a Ridges hook a few seconds into the round, but referee Kenny Bayless ruled it a slip. Unlike their second-round exchange, this one wasn't broken off willingly.

Cobos temporarily shifted the battle to long range as he landed a right-left, darted away, then connected with a right-left to the body. Ridges declined the invitation to box and instead whacked away at Cobos' ribs while mixing in a sharp uppercut to the jaw. Ridges bulled Cobos to the ropes and turned on the jets. Cobos' energy was melting away with every blow Ridges landed and it wasn't long before Cobos was fought into a standstill.

In all, 22 unanswered blows ripped through Cobos' defense, and a left hook to the body caused Cobos to fall to the canvas more from fatigue than anything else. After Cobos took a seven-count, Bayless asked him if he wanted to continue. Cobos nodded his assent, banged his gloves together and tapped Bayless' balled fists with his gloved ones in a "low-five" fashion to drive home his desire to continue fighting.

Sensing his prey was ripe for the taking, Ridges unleashed his killer instinct. Over the next 43 seconds, Ridges unleashed 44 blows and landed 29 of them, but most importantly Ridges didn't throw just for the sake of throwing. Every punch targeted specific areas for specific reasons and each one contributed to Cobos' demise. This latest attack was simply too much for Cobos to absorb and Bayless wisely stepped in at 2:14 of round three.

Ridges' trainer Eddie Mustafa Muhammad lifted his warrior in the air as the disappointed Cobos rested his head on the corner pad. He overcame his disappointment long enough to smile and warmly embrace the victor a few moments later. He, along with everyone else, recognized that not only did Ridges win, he did so with a spectacular display of will, strength and savvy beyond his young boxing years. And those body shots weren't bad either.

Epilogue: In the main event, Garcia defeated Wheeler by 12-round decision and nine fights later he won the vacant IBF junior lightweight title by outscoring Harold Warren over 12 rounds. Wheeler never won a major world title and ended his career in 2002 after losing a 12-round decision to the ill-fated Leavander Johnson in 2002.

Ridges returned to the ring just 11 days later and scored a four-round TKO over Manny Castillo. Following a six-round win over Francisco Rodriguez, he fought a pair of six-round draws with Joel Garcia and TKO'd Tito Tovar in four. The unbeaten streak was ended after Daniel Lujan scored a six-round decision in June 1996.

According to Boxrec.com, which indicated Ridges' record is incomplete, Ridges' final fight took place August 8, 1997 at the Orleans Hotel & Casino against Ahmed Santos, who scored a comprehensive 10-round decision. The 27-year-old Ridges retired with a 12-4-2 (8 KO) record.

Unlike Ridges, Cobos' complete record can be found on Boxrec.com, and according to the Web site, Cobos fought eight more times over the next two-and-a-half years, going 3-4-1 (1 KO). His first outing following the Ridges fight was a third-round TKO win over Enrique Baladez but from then on the wheels came off. In his next-to-last fight against Steve Quinonez, referee Mitch Halpern stopped the fight in the sixth round after Cobos turned his back and began walking toward his corner. Halpern interpreted it as a sign of surrender, but Cobos said he did so because he thought he heard the bell.

The final fight for the 25-year-old Cobos took place October 22, 1997 at Arizona Charlie's, the site of the Ridges fight, where he was stopped in nine rounds by Rafael Olvera. His final record is 19-6-1 (14 KO).

TALES FROM THE VAULT

Total Punches Landed/Thrown

Round	1	2	3	4	5	6	7	8	9	10	11	12	Total
Ridges	46/125	76/125	59/114										181/364
	37%	61%	52%										50%
Cobos	52/88	32/69	8/32										92/189
	59%	46%	25%										49%

* Fight originally done by CompuBox, but the original HTML files with complete round-by-round statistics for all categories no longer exist.

Tony Ridges vs. Roberto Cobos April 21, 1995, Las Vegas, Nevada

UNDERCARD TREASURES

Art Jimmerson vs. Lenny LaPaglia
July 14, 1988, New York, New York

For a fighter to achieve his greatest degree of success, he must possess complete mastery over mind and body. The benefits of a well-conditioned physique are obvious; after all, a boxer with superior speed, power and talent will emerge victorious most of the time.

But a well-conditioned psyche can be an even more devastating weapon. The mind is the engine that drives the body to execute its commands. A strong mind can force the body to do amazing feats in the face of adversity while a weaker mind would encourage it to shut down in a similar situation.

The relationship between mind and body is a purely individual one, and the way we react can change from fight to fight and even situation to situation. But more often than not, a strong mind is able to overcome a weak body while a weak mind can still impose its will over a strong body.

Sport often serves as the theater for these physical and psychological dramas, and boxing is the sport where the effects can be seen most graphically. Boxers are forced to react instinctively to a constantly shifting set of circumstances. During combat, there is little time to do much more than what comes naturally and the results can be memorable – both in good ways and bad.

One such example took place at the Felt Forum in New York City when Lenny LaPaglia and Art Jimmerson met in a 10-round light heavyweight bout. While the bout was incredibly action-packed, it also served as an example of how a formidable self-belief can overcome just about anything that can be dished out in the ring while also demonstrating how that self-belief can take its toll on the opponent.

LaPaglia entered the ring as a heavy favorite. The native of Melrose Park, Illinois was 31-5 with 29 knockouts and he was setting the foundation for a possible championship shot at 175. LaPaglia was best known as a middleweight and his ferocious, all-out approach helped him achieve a 20-0 (19 KO) start. The only "blemish" on LaPaglia's record came against Maurice Pitchford, who lost by four-round disqualification. On March 20, 1983, LaPaglia fought fellow unbeaten John Collins in a Chicago crossroads bout shown on NBC. Collins captured a 10-round decision, and LaPaglia would subsequently suffer two knockout losses to Danny Blake.

"The Rage" launched a comeback after 14 months away from the ring by beating Tony Golden over 10 rounds. For the next three years LaPaglia went 11-2 (10 KO), excelling against lower level opposition while running into roadblocks against better foes like the 27-3 Carlos Tite (L 10) and Doug DeWitt (L 10). LaPaglia's best win during this period was a 10-round split decision over Stacy McSwain. Also, LaPaglia gradually put on weight and by the time he met Jimmerson he was a full-fledged light heavyweight. He entered the Jimmerson bout on a four-fight win streak and was rated eighth by the IBF. His most recent outing came four months earlier when he scored a three-round TKO over Robert Folley, son of former heavyweight title challenger Zora Folley.

For Jimmerson (9-5, 2 KO), LaPaglia represented a steep step up in competition but he entered the fight full of confidence – and he wasn't afraid to show it. In the pre-fight press conference Jimmerson told LaPaglia that a severe beating awaited him, but if one looked at the fight on paper his rants were generally dismissed as typical pre-fight bluster. The St. Louis native who carried the nickname "Zorro" was seen as having little chance of upsetting LaPaglia. After all, if Manuel Murillo could stop Jimmerson in seven rounds, what chance could he have against LaPaglia?

The shorter Jimmerson saw only one option for victory: Walk straight into the buzzsaw and hope he would emerge from the other side. At the opening bell, Jimmerson marched out of the corner, dug his head into LaPaglia's shoulder and began firing away. LaPaglia was more than happy to reciprocate as he worked Jimmerson's body with thumping rights and lefts. As LaPaglia cranked a hook to the body, Jimmerson cracked him with a left hook to the jaw that forced LaPaglia back a couple of steps. LaPaglia whacked a right-left to the ribs after Jimmerson connected with his own right to the body.

The pace was hot from the start and it was surprising that Jimmerson was so willing to exchange with the heavier-handed LaPaglia. Not only that, Jimmerson used his lower center of gravity to maneuver LaPaglia around the ring. While both men freely attacked the body, Jimmerson also mixed in hooks and uppercuts to the head.

With 48 seconds remaining in the round, LaPaglia staggered Jimmerson with a hook to the jaw, but Jimmerson recovered quickly and continued to fire back. LaPaglia worked a three-punch combo, the last two of which sunk into Jimmerson's flanks, and followed with two more hammering hooks to the ribs. A LaPaglia hook pierced Jimmerson's liver and the St. Louis native was unable to conceal his pain.

LaPaglia chased after Jimmerson, whacking away at the body before a hook turned Jimmerson's legs to jelly. One of LaPaglia's hooks strayed low but when Jimmerson lodged a complaint, referee Fred Ucci said nothing. LaPaglia continued his steady attack for the rest of the round and capped it off with a hook to the jaw a full second after the bell.

In the second, Jimmerson worked the jab to set up a hard right to the side and pumped two right uppercuts to the jaw. The unhurt LaPaglia cranked two hooks to the body and followed with a right-left. The left landed below the belt and Jimmerson retaliated with a right to LaPaglia's hip.

"You're both hitting low," Ucci said. "I'm not gonna warn you anymore. Keep your punches up, both of you."

Just seconds after Ucci's caution, LaPaglia won an exchange of hooks and knocked Jimmerson to the ropes. Jimmerson landed a hook to the button as LaPaglia closed in, then worked his way in close to keep LaPaglia from generating maximum leverage.

Seldom does one see a fight where both boxers were so dedicated to infighting and body punching. Every second of every minute was a give-and-take toe-to-toe war in which every punch thrown set up the other's counterattack.

A missed right uppercut by LaPaglia enabled Jimmerson to land a hook to the jaw, which was followed by a right-left to the ribs and two right uppercuts. LaPaglia's street-fighter instinct commanded him to fight back immediately when hurt, and he retaliated with a short left uppercut to the jaw, a hook to the body, a hook to the jaw, another hook to the ribs and a right and left uppercut to the jaw. Every blow carried concussive power, the kind of power that asks the demanding questions of those who aspire to be the best they can be.

A searing hook to the liver lowered Jimmerson's hands, caused his upper body to sag and tested his resolve. He sucked in a deep breath as LaPaglia drove Jimmerson to the ropes and landed another hook to the ribs. A right uppercut and left hook spun Jimmerson's head and one had to wonder if he was about to fold his tent.

Instead of surrendering, Jimmerson dug in.

A winging left hook allowed him to escape the ropes, and a left-left-right set up a hard right to the ribs. He repeated the combination seconds later and ducked under a lazy LaPaglia hook. As an action-packed second round closed, LaPaglia grabbed the back of Jimmerson's head with his right glove while driving in four hooks, alternating between the head and body.

This maneuver might have provided a tiny glimpse into LaPaglia's mindset on this night. A spectacular early knockout would have done LaPaglia a world of good for two reasons: It would have once again certified his status as an exciting knockout puncher and it could have led to an elevation of his world ranking, which would have improved his chances for a title shot. But Jimmerson had not only stubbornly withstood his first threatening salvo, he fought back hard. So LaPaglia made him pay for his insolence by blatantly holding and hitting at the end of the second round.

The trench warfare continued in round three, with LaPaglia's punches the more powerful and Jimmerson's the more diversified. Jimmerson used the jab to set up his body punches while LaPaglia had no use for such niceties. Fifty seconds into the round, Jimmerson glided in behind a short hook to the jaw and moved LaPaglia back with a six-punch flurry. Jimmerson followed up with a right-left to the ribs and he jolted LaPaglia's head with a right uppercut.

Jimmerson used a triple jab to get a bead on LaPaglia before blasting him with a body shot. A crisp right-left to the head rattled LaPaglia and a right uppercut forced him to move back toward the ropes on unsteady legs. LaPaglia was hurt for the first time in the fight and it was here that the fans got another peek at LaPaglia's thought process.

The macho LaPaglia dropped his arms to the side and beckoned Jimmerson to hit him. Most fighters in this situation would hesitate to take the bait because "something for nothing" doesn't apply in boxing. They think that if they took advantage of the situation that something worse would be in store for them. In other words, the long-term benefits of self-preservation overrule the temptation to seize the short-term gain.

But Jimmerson didn't think about any of that as he blasted in a left-right-hook combination off LaPaglia's unprotected face. LaPaglia then raised his guard and spun off the ropes behind two light hooks. LaPaglia connected with a six-punch combination that ended with a left hook that made Jimmerson's legs quiver but Jimmerson pushed LaPaglia to the ropes and landed a right-left to the body and a left uppercut to the jaw. LaPaglia grabbed Jimmerson's right arm and popped him with a left hook, but Jimmerson retaliated with four hammering overhand rights that forced LaPaglia to release his grip and two left hooks that prompted LaPaglia to drop his guard again. As the bell rang, LaPaglia fired a four-punch salvo, and when Jimmerson complained by pointing his glove, LaPaglia nailed him with a hook.

LaPaglia's escalating frustration was approaching dangerous levels. He struck Jimmerson with his best punches but Jimmerson was not only staying upright he was firing back. Jimmerson might not have had LaPaglia's talent but he was brimming with mental strength. That mental strength fueled Jimmerson's resolve to absorb whatever LaPaglia dished out, and that in turn added to LaPaglia's duress.

LaPaglia, angry and bewildered as he was, was still a fighter at heart and because of that he continued to press forward in the fourth. After Jimmerson began the round by working both hands and bulling LaPaglia to the ropes, LaPaglia connected with a snappy right uppercut-left hook combination. LaPaglia followed up with two whistling hooks that made Jimmerson sag ever so slightly. Jimmerson landed a counter hook, but LaPaglia then drilled a crunching right.

Somehow, Jimmerson withstood the punch and managed a brief clinch. His will to win remained strong and he would not give LaPaglia the satisfaction of seeing him in a compromised state. Jimmerson worked his way in close and used the jab to set up a right to the ribs before clinching again. Because Jimmerson showed he could still fight back, LaPaglia stepped off the gas.

For LaPaglia, the quick KO he wanted was now off the boards and his disappointment began to show. With 1:20 remaining, LaPaglia listlessly backed to the ropes and adopted a rope-a-dope posture. Jimmerson took advantage by firing a right and two hooks. A buzzed LaPaglia again dropped his guard and Jimmerson made him pay by landing two flush hooks to the jaw. LaPaglia raised his guard and unleashed a flurry, but in the ensuing clinch he tucked his head underneath Jimmerson's and raised up. After Jimmerson landed another combination, LaPaglia dropped his arms and took eight unanswered punches. The round ended with a six-punch Jimmerson flurry and LaPaglia responded by hitting Jimmerson with a light hook a split second after the bell.

When LaPaglia chose to fight, he fought well but when he pouted he paid the price. His blows carried plenty of snap and power but Jimmerson's armor of willpower protected him from their effects. Jimmerson's competitiveness was breaking down LaPaglia mentally and the Illinois native was locked in a personal war. His tough-guy personality demanded that he must press forward but his frustration told him to find a way out of the situation, so he found himself alternating between the two approaches.

LaPaglia began the fifth by whaling away at Jimmerson's body, the punches coming in like boulders. Yet Jimmerson took them unflinchingly and continued to work his jab. LaPaglia soon retreated to a corner and dropped his arms, allowing Jimmerson to connect with a right-left to the body. LaPaglia didn't let the tactic last for long as he unleashed a five-punch salvo that forced Jimmerson to back off.

With 1:42 remaining, Jimmerson backed LaPaglia into his own corner and launched an overhand right that caught LaPaglia cleanly. LaPaglia lowered his gloves and Jimmerson nailed him with 12 consecutive blows. A pair of hooks spun LaPaglia's head violently and three consecutive rights to the chest sent him crumbling to the canvas. LaPaglia hung his head wearily and took several seconds to decide whether it was worth it to continue. At the count of seven, LaPaglia made his decision and by nine he was upright.

LaPaglia drilled in a flush hook to the jaw that made Jimmerson clinch and steal a deep breath while looking over LaPaglia's right shoulder. The hot pace was also taking a toll on Jimmerson.

Back at ring center, LaPaglia rattled off a hurtful seven-punch flurry capped off with a terrific overhand right. LaPaglia was digging deep within himself to produce a finish but Jimmerson was digging just as deep to fight back as he landed a strong counter hook. As LaPaglia blasted away, Jimmerson plowed straight ahead, willing to take whatever he had to in order to stay in the fight.

LaPaglia kept up his assault for a full minute and when he was finished he retreated to the ropes, dropped his guard and took two deep breaths. He had invested nearly all of his remaining energy into that attack and the fact that Jimmerson was still standing inflicted a mortal wound to his fighting spirit. LaPaglia summoned the energy to crank another hook to the body, but Jimmerson responded with a hook that drove LaPaglia to the ropes. As LaPaglia backed toward the strands, he lowered his guard yet again, allowing Jimmerson to drive five consecutive rights to the body. LaPaglia slumped to the floor for the second time in the round, and it looked as if he was finished.

Still, LaPaglia regained his feet at six, and by the time Ucci finished checking him over only six seconds remained in the round. LaPaglia ended the round well by landing two hooks and a right uppercut but right after the bell sounded, LaPaglia's frustration again bubbled to the surface as he popped Jimmerson with a hook to the jaw. Ucci immediately took the round away from LaPaglia, a round he wasn't going to win anyway because of the two knockdowns he suffered.

Jimmerson drew strength from LaPaglia's mental struggle with himself and he seized on every opening presented to him. His punches were quick, strong and thrown in combination and there was nothing LaPaglia could do to stop him. Jimmerson was having the best night of his young career, and the fact that it was coming against a top-10 contender gave him even more fuel to drive himself forward.

The emotional and spiritual contrast couldn't have been stronger. Jimmerson was fighting with supreme confidence, a confidence that created an invisible, but impenetrable, shield of invincibility. Meanwhile, LaPaglia was imprisoned inside a wall of negativity that threatened to send him into competitive free fall.

But LaPaglia remained a tough guy at heart and as the sixth began he made one final stand. Throughout his professional life LaPaglia had always depended on his enormous power to see him through and he knew that it would be his best chance to turn the tide. But on this night, Jimmerson was just too much. A right cross-left hook combo slammed against LaPaglia's face, and it was there that the final disintegration began. LaPaglia dropped his arms and allowed Jimmerson to land 13 unanswered punches to his unprotected frame. Then, feeling badly about his competitive faux pas, he fired back a few hard, but ultimately inconsequential, blows.

A minute into the round, LaPaglia, with his back to the ropes, landed an overhand right, but Jimmerson answered with a tremendous hook. That hook proved to be the final straw as waves of resignation enveloped him. LaPaglia dropped his arms for the final time and allowed "Zorro" to apply the finishing touches in the form of three consecutive rights to the solar plexus. LaPaglia fell through the second strand of ropes, and as he lay on the ring apron he looked up at Ucci and shook his head. He had had enough.

The fight was stopped at 1:12 of round six, and as Jimmerson celebrated his upset victory his body sent mixed signals. As he pumped his arms in the air, his face was awash in weariness and relief. He walked to a neutral corner, knelt down and offered thanks to God. That task completed, Jimmerson went to LaPaglia's corner and hugged his beaten adversary. The animosity they felt before the fight had disappeared.

When LaPaglia and Jimmerson entered the ring, the gulf in physical talent and accomplishments was wide. Much more often than not, the fighter with superior ability will emerge victorious. But there are those special nights when a fighter's resolve is so strong that it could conquer any obstacle that is placed in his path. For Art Jimmerson, July 14, 1988 was that special night. For Lenny LaPaglia, it was an emotional nightmare, but it would have been unfair to label him a quitter. He had fought too hard and too well to be saddled with that label. All he did was lose to the better man and he could take comfort that other – and better – nights lay ahead for him.

Epilogue: LaPaglia would enjoy further success, but only against limited opposition. Seven months after losing to Jimmerson, LaPaglia stepped up to cruiserweight and iced winless Nate Spears in one round. He followed that up with a third round KO over the 1-37-2 Terrence Wright two months later. Five weeks later LaPaglia upped the level of competition by fighting Bobby Arthurs, but LaPaglia ended up losing by fourth-round disqualification for excessive low blows.

LaPaglia won his next three fights by knockout, knocking out Darryl Fromm in five rounds to win a minor 175-pound belt, then belting out Andre Crowder (KO 1) and Rick Enis (KO 3) at cruiserweight. Three months after beating Enis, LaPaglia lost a Chicago turf war against Tony LaRosa by third round KO. LaPaglia's final fight took place March 31, 1995 in Detroit, and the 34-year-old fell victim to the legendary Thomas Hearns at 2:55 of round one. LaPaglia's final record is 36-9 (33 KO).

Jimmerson won his next two fights against Jerry Okorodudu (W 10) and Bill Lee (W 10) before stepping up in class against Jeff Harding. Jimmerson lost a 10-round decision to the future light heavyweight titlist and the same fate befell him in his next fight against another future champion in Dennis Andries. Jimmerson rebounded with victories over William Knorr (KO 1) and Randy Smith (W 10), but fell short of the mark against 1988 gold medalist Andrew Maynard (KO by 3).

Following the Maynard loss, Jimmerson sought to rebuild his career by fighting exclusively in St. Louis, and he would enjoy his greatest stretch of success. He won 15 consecutive fights, nine by knockout, to set up a match with Orlin Norris. Norris stopped Jimmerson in four rounds, and from then on his career nose-dived. Over the next eight years, Jimmerson would serve as a "name" opponent for a variety of up-and-comers. They included Brian LaSpada (DQ by 11), Torsten May (KO by 5), Vassiliy Jirov (KO by 2), Dale Brown (KO by 3), Adolpho Washington (KO by 3), Arthur Williams (KO by 1), Rich LaMontange (KO by 1) and Mike Rodgers (KO by 3). His final fight took place in Danville, Va., on Nov. 23, 2002 against Rydell Booker, who stopped the 39-year-old Jimmerson in two rounds.

TALES FROM THE VAULT

Total Punches Landed/Thrown

Round	1	2	3	4	5	6	7	8	9	10	11	12	Total
Jimmerson	33/55	44/77	46/77	44/68	34/62	21/26							222/365
	60%	57%	60%	65%	55%	81%							61%
LaPaglia	50/109	49/94	31/82	35/90	32/77	11/27							208/479
	46%	52%	38%	39%	42%	41%							43%

Jabs Landed/Thrown

Round	1	2	3	4	5	6	7	8	9	10	11	12	Total
Jimmerson	3/10	12/30	8/21	8/19	7/17	0/1							38/98
	30%	40%	38%	42%	41%	0%							39%
LaPaglia	0/8	3/13	0/10	1/13	1/9	0/1							5/54
	0%	23%	0%	8%	11%	0%							9%

Power Punches Landed/Thrown

Round	1	2	3	4	5	6	7	8	9	10	11	12	Total
Jimmerson	30/45	32/47	38/56	36/49	27/45	21/25							184/267
	67%	68%	68%	73%	60%	84%							69%
LaPaglia	50/101	46/81	31/72	34/77	31/68	11/26							203/425
	50%	57%	43%	44%	46%	42%							48%

Art Jimmerson vs. Lenny LaPaglia July 14, 1988, New York, New York

UNDERCARD TREASURES

Chris McInerney vs. Anterio Vines
July 5, 2005, Boston, Massachusetts

Boxing is a sport awash in pecking orders. Fighters of varying levels of experience are usually slotted into appropriately distanced fights. Beginning pros usually fight four- and six-round bouts and as they gain experience they are granted entry into eight- and 10-round fights. Those judged to have superior ability earn shots at regional, national, continental and finally world title contests lasting 12 rounds. Of course, boxing isn't that clear-cut, but that's the way the structure is supposed to work.

Then there are the pecking orders within a card. The preliminary fighters are supposed to serve as appetizers, warming up the crowd for the main event that's supposed to be the *piece de resistance*, the climax of the evening. But every once in a while, the undercard fighters produce a spectacle so unforgettable that they become the talk of the town – at least for that night.

That was the case when cruiserweights Chris McInerney and Anterio Vines crossed paths at The Roxy in Boston. Their four-round war packed far more fireworks than card-toppers Ian Gardner and Mohamed Said produced in their 10-rounder.

Entering the bout, however, the pecking order was firmly established. The 26-year-old McInerney, from nearby Stoughton, Massachusetts, was 3-0 with three knockouts. His first two bouts ended in first-round blowouts and his most recent effort – also at The Roxy – was a third round TKO of Joe Lorenzi on April 29. Meanwhile, Vines (4-5 with one knockout) was coming off two consecutive one-round knockout losses to prospects Curtis Stevens and Jonathan Banks. Though only 21 years of age, his hardened face made him appear years older.

Though the fight was not "fixed" by any means, the circumstances certainly were stacked in McInerney's favor; he was an undefeated local product fighting on familiar turf against a man with a losing record shipped in from Columbus, Ohio. Club fighters from the Midwest are notorious for their ability to make rising prospects look good and – on paper at least – there was little reason to believe anything would be different on this night.

The 6-3 McInerney towered over the 5-11 Vines as they received their final instructions and he sought to use his considerable physical advantages once the fight began. McInerney operated on the outside, using his jab to set up a chopping right while Vines used left-left-rights to try to get past McInerney's long arms. Vines pressured McInerney into the ropes, but McInerney immediately slid away to his right, reset his feet and shot a left hook through the guard.

Vines intelligently focused his attack on McInerney's long, lean body. While he didn't put his whole weight behind his shots, they were landing. One of those body punches set up a jolting jab that caught McInerney backing out, and the unhurt favorite responded with a long right to the jaw that stopped Vines in his tracks.

McInerney saw weakness in Vines after that punch, so he drove him back to the ropes with two looping rights and kept him there with a flurry of straight blows to the head and body. Vines covered up with hands held high, blocking and weaving his upper body away from most of McInerney's follow-up punches, before sliding away to his left and looking fully recovered.

With one minute remaining, Vines provided the first evidence that he was not going to be anyone's patsy. Vines leaped in with a sweeping hook and a clean right to the point of the jaw. McInerney was jolted, but he managed to escape from the ropes after landing a short right uppercut. Still, it was a worrisome sign for McInerney; he allowed Vines to get within punching range without making him pay a price. That, in turn, allowed Vines to build a reservoir of confidence.

McInerney caught the charging Vines with a crisp left-right combination, but Vines burrowed inside to work McInerney's body before catching him with a good hook. McInerney retaliated with several right uppercuts to the head and body that caught Vines cleanly. Then, as the bell sounded, McInerney drove Vines to a knee with a right to the temple.

That punch enabled McInerney to break open a close round, and the CompuBox statistics reflected it as McInerney landed 27 of his 65 punches (42 percent) while Vines connected on 22 of 70 (31 percent).

McInerney began the second round well as he kept Vines at a distance with his side-to-side movement and straight accurate punches. But Vines patiently looked for a way inside and found it when he maneuvered McInerney to the ropes and got in a right to the jaw and a left-right salvo to the ribs before McInerney clinched.

With a little less than a minute gone, McInerney asserted his dominance. After landing a right, he moved inside, nailing Vines with a left uppercut and flooring him with a perfectly thrown straight right to the face. As Vines knelt on the canvas, he pressed the thumb of his right glove into his eye and took every second of referee Kevin Hope's count. Rising at nine, Vines blinked badly as he turned away and walked toward a corner. Hope could have interpreted Vines' move as a sign of surrender but instead he told Vines to "look at me! Look at me!" Vines responded appropriately and Hope allowed the fight to continue.

Vines used his arms to block McInerney's follow-up assault and countered McInerney's jab with a snappy right-left-right over the top before clinching. Vines then nailed McInerney with a lead right, ducked under a right and connected with a hard hook to the side and a looping right to the neck.

Hope's decision to let the fight continue proved to be a turning point and Vines was taking full advantage. With every passing second the Columbus journeyman gained strength and confidence. Meanwhile, McInerney's technique was decaying and he was about to pay the price. Vines countered McInerney's lazy jab with a scorching left uppercut-right cross to the jaw, and the hometown favorite was badly wobbled. Vines jumped in with another left uppercut-right cross combo and zinged a hurtful hook to the side. McInerney backed toward the ropes, where Vines landed a whistling left-right and a ripping right uppercut that sent McInerney swaying to his right. The lanky McInerney took on the look of a wounded giraffe that was ripe for the kill.

But looks can be deceiving. As Vines moved in for that kill, McInerney landed a tremendous right to the face that shook Vines to his core. McInerney whaled way at the body before Vines finally managed a clinch. As the bell rang, Vines reached out with his right glove and gave McIneerney a low five, which the hometown man grudgingly accepted.

Vines had been on the verge of a huge upset, but his zeal to follow up almost cost him dearly. Though Vines had been dropped twice, he proved he could hurt McInerney – thus proving that he had a shot at winning the fight. But in order to do so, he had to walk the fine line of being aggressive without being *too* aggressive. And by allowing Vines to think he had a chance to win, he put himself in danger.

"Any time you allow somebody to get confidence, there could be a price to pay, especially if that somebody is a guy who's been losing and losing," ESPN2 analyst Teddy Atlas said. "All of a sudden, if you give him a little sniff of victory, and all of a sudden he can get intoxicated with that aroma. Vines was intoxicated with that aroma."

The two knockdowns put McInerney in a commanding position on the judges' scorecards, but Vines was still able to ask serious questions of the prospect. Despite the knockdown, Vines out-landed McInerney 20-18 and he connected on 48 percent of his blows. The hometown favorite was being tested and the nature of the exam escalated to a dangerous level in round three.

Thirty seconds into the third, McInerney made the mistake of being too relaxed in a clinch and Vines seized on his complacency. Vines whipped a right to the body that set up a clean, explosive hook to the jaw. A surprised McInerney fell straight back and tangled himself between the top two strands of rope before sliding to the canvas. After McInerney regained his feet at four, the underdog Vines rushed in and shoe-shined the body before ripping a mighty right uppercut to the jaw. McInerney was in desperate trouble as he sought the refuge of a clinch and he finally clamped down after fielding a vicious hook to the ribs and ducking under a wild right.

After they were separated, McInerney winged a lead right, but Vines slipped it and answered with a torrid right that caused McInerney to fall into the ropes. The stricken McInerney turned his body to the right and struggled to stay upright by wobbling crab-like for several steps. Referee Hope could have called it a knockdown because it was evident the ropes were the only thing keeping McInerney up. But Fate, and perhaps a friendly hometown atmosphere, worked in McInerney's favor.

Meanwhile, Vines continued to rake McInerney with powerful blows. A hook jolted McInerney's head and a second one that caused his legs to quake. The prospect was undergoing the kind of acid test that all up-and-comers must experience if they want to make a mark in the sport. A good fighter must not only be able to dish out punishment but bounce back from adversity not once, but time after time.

McInerney was standing, somewhat unsteadily, at a professional crossroads and he had just a split second to decide which fork he was going to take. His decision came in the form of a scintillating right cross that landed flush on Vines' jaw. The punch stunned Vines, but his adrenaline helped him respond with his own right.

The crowd at the Roxy was in an uproar as they witnessed the constantly shifting tide. ESPN2's blow-by-blow man Joe Tessitore perfectly captured their wonder when he said, "you never know what you're going to get; two guys that were sitting in the locker room that thought they had no chance of getting on TV tonight. Boy, did they come to live in the spotlight!"

As the round wound down, the torrid pace was starting to tell as they winged wild blows at one another. The precision of previous minutes had declined but the fighting spirit propelling the punches still burned brightly. As the bell rang, Vines whacked McInerney with a final looping hook to the neck that sent him stumbling drunkenly toward the ropes. Vines had returned to contention in a most convincing and dramatic way. After suffering a pair of 10-8 rounds, his pummeling of McInerney in round three could have easily been scored 10-7, and that put him in range of winning a decision. According to CompuBox, Vines out-landed McInereny by a brutally lopsided 24-5 margin.

Vines rode the momentum into round four behind two strong rights. McInerney connected with a side-winding, slapping right to the head and as they moved inside Vines was the one moving his hands. Vines pasted McInerney repeatedly with lead rights and he found success with occasional hooks to the body as the fight swung into the final minute.

After spending several long seconds in a clinch, Vines sprang up and stunned McInerney with a right uppercut to the jaw and a wide-angle left-right to the face. As the weary McInerney backed toward the ropes, he peeked at the scoreboard clock situated directly above the ring. Seeing that there were still 38 seconds remaining, his face creased into a slightly disappointed expression.

McInerney tried a four-punch flurry but Vines' two looping hooks put a stop to that. Vines countered a jab with a hook to the liver and as the final seconds tolled McInerney tried to steal the round with a last-ditch flurry that drove Vines across the ring and only the bell could make him stop. There were no congratulatory hugs from either man as they walked wearily to their respective corners. They were four-round fighters who put forth a championship effort and their reward was a resounding shower of cheers.

Vines had put together a more than admirable rally in the final two rounds as he out-landed McInerney 43-12. The statistics suggested Vines to be the superior fighter as he went 85 of 224 (38 percent) while the hometown man was 57 of 170 (34 percent). Still, considering the circumstances entering the fight, the fact that the fight would go to a decision was a surprise. And the fact that there was suspense surrounding that decision was a shock.

Ken Volovick saw the bout 38-37 for Vines while Gerry Mauer viewed it 37-36 for McInerney. Dan Mullen proved to be the decisive vote, and his 37-37 card put the finishing touches on that rarest of birds – a satisfying draw.

On most occasions, fighters from the Midwest – especially ones with losing records – are looked upon with skepticism and derision. But on this night Vines had done himself and his part of the country proud. He fought with courage, vigor and with a winner's commitment. The favored McInerney, in turn, may have suffered the first blemish on his previously perfect record but he also did himself proud by responding well to his unexpected adversity.

For McInerney and Vines, there are no delusions about becoming world champions and establishing lasting legacies. But for one night in June 2005 their collective courage helped them break through the pecking order in a most impressive and memorable way. The main event fighters – Gardner and Said – couldn't possibly top what McInerney and Vines produced, and that's no slight against them.

Andy Warhol says that everyone will have his 15 minutes of fame. Thankfully, few of us will ever expend 12 of them more violently than McInerney and Vines.

Epilogue: Vines fought just 24 days later, losing a six-round split decision to Anthony Russell in Brockton, Mass. Then he fought Rico Gaston to a six-round draw in Columbus, Ohio on August 19, 2005. Since then he has lost four consecutive fights, all by knockout or TKO. His most recent outing took place August 6, 2006 at Heinz Field in Pittsburgh, where he lost to the 14-0 Craig Cummings in three rounds. That proved to be the last fight of his career, and the 22-year-old Vines retired with a record of 4-10-2 with one knockout.

Conversely, McInerney didn't re-enter the ring for 13 months. His hiatus ended with a four-round decision victory over the 10-12 John Rainwater on June 17, 2006 and as of January 2010 he has gone 4-2 since. After beating Mike Bonislawski (W 6), Ricky Duffy (W 4), Vinnie Carita (KO 2) and Eric Starr (KO 5), he was upset by the 3-8 Gary Lavendar, who stopped McInerney in two rounds in June 2007. McInerney bounced back with a sixth-round TKO of Tim Flamos in December 2007 but Flamos turned the tables four months later with a third round TKO. McInerney's record stands 9-2-1 (6 KO).

TALES FROM THE VAULT

Total Punches Landed/Thrown

Round	1	2	3	4	5	6	7	8	9	10	11	12	Total
McInerney													57/170
													34%
Vines													85/224
													38%

Jabs Landed/Thrown

Round	1	2	3	4	5	6	7	8	9	10	11	12	Total
McInerney													14/61
													23%
Vines													27/86
													31%

Power Punches Landed/Thrown

Round	1	2	3	4	5	6	7	8	9	10	11	12	Total
McInerney													43/109
													39%
Vines													58/138
													42%

* Fight originally done by CompuBox, but the original HTML files with complete round-by-round statistics no longer exist.

Chris McInerney vs. Anterio Vines July 5, 2005, Boston, Massachusetts

UNDERCARD TREASURES

John Revish vs. Leo Lizarraga
April 2, 2004, Tucson, Arizona

Boxing has been described as an extension of life in general because the dramas that unfold in the squared circle mirror situations to which we all can relate. In our workplaces, we've all seen — or experienced — the passing of the torch from old lion to young lion, and sometimes that transition can get ugly. In the ring, that scenario often unfolds with brutal finality, and while the spectators hail the arrival of a new and fresh force they also feel pangs of sympathy for the vanquished.

Another life story often told in the ring is that of two aspiring pros seeking to make their way in the sport by having to go through the other. The winner earns the privilege of moving to the next step with his self-generated aura of invincibility intact while the other must pick up the pieces and begin again, this time with the scarlet letter of defeat — L — forever burnished on his record.

That was the tale that faced John Revish and Leo Lizarraga at the Desert Diamond Casino in Tucson, Arizona, where they met in a four-round welterweight bout that kicked off an ESPN "Friday Night Fights" telecast topped by Emanuel Augustus and Alex Trujillo. Revish was just 36 days removed from his professional debut, a one-round knockout over David Love in New Orleans while Lizarraga was a more seasoned 4-0 (3 KO), and his last victory was a two-round TKO over Robert Manore in Phoenix the previous December.

Another subplot surrounding this fight was that of hometown hero versus invading outsider, and on this night it was the 24-year-old Lizarraga, who resided in nearby Chandler, Arizona, who was the crowd favorite. It was a situation with which he was familiar, since he had never fought outside Arizona as a pro. The "outsider" was the 20-year-old Revish, a sophomore psychology major at Louisiana State University who toyed with the idea of walking onto the highly touted football program following a successful high school career. But now his athletic focus was on boxing in general — and on Lizarraga in particular.

The 5-8 Revish, 147, started the bout on the move behind his jab, but the one-inch taller Lizarraga, 146, beat him to the punch with a heavier jab and a follow-up hook that briefly knocked an off-balance Revish to the ropes. Revish pivoted away smartly, but his nervousness came to the surface as he shifted right, launched a hook and slipped to the canvas as he threw that hook. Revish scrambled to his feet, but as Revish launched another hook Lizarraga again demonstrated his quicker trigger by smashing a right cross-left hook combo. Lizarraga pushed Revish back with the jab and after Revish reset his feet he landed a right-left to the body and a right to the jaw.

But as Revish's right connected, Lizarraga exploded a hook that wobbled Revish and followed with a wicked right-left hook that put the visitor flat on his back.

Though Revish appeared to be faster, Lizarraga debunked that myth in the very first minute of battle. Boxing is just as much about timing as it is about raw physical gifts. Shorter fighters have out-jabbed much taller and long-armed men because they knew when to throw it. Such was the case when the 5-11 Mike Tyson fought the 6-5 Tony Tucker, and it was that jab that led "Iron Mike" out of early-fight difficulties en route to a title-unifying unanimous decision. Now, on a much smaller scale, the truism of timing again showed itself.

Revish immediately regained his feet, backed toward the farthest neutral corner and bounced lightly on his toes as referee Roger Yanez completed the mandatory eight-count. Sensing the end was near Lizarraga tore after Revish, backing him to the ropes with a left hook but missed wildly with another one as Revish retreated. Revish motored around the ring at full speed in both directions and flashed his hands in multi-punch bursts. But the intent of his punches was rooted more in survival than in scoring, and Lizarraga soon caught Revish with a straight right to the stomach. Lizarraga then whiffed on a home-run hook that brought an ominous "ooh" from the crowd.

Both men were fighting with anxiety – Revish's was that of a man trying mightily to hold off a rampaging adversary while Lizarraga's a wildness borne of a desire to put his opponent away impressively before a supportive crowd. Their mutual, but conflicting, goals produced sloppy but exciting action. Lizarraga missed with another huge hook, and as Revish grabbed his waist he uncorked a hard right to Revish's exposed ribs.

With 1:16 remaining, Revish ducked under a looping right and slid hard to his left to get out of the corner. As he was doing so, Lizarraga cut loose with an overhand hook to the head that sent Revish down for the second time, skidding several feet to a stop along the ropes. Again, Revish hastily regained his feet, turned his back and marched toward the farthest corner to put as much space between him and Lizarraga as possible. After completing the count, Yanez pointed a cautioning finger at Revish and told him, "protect yourself or I'm going to stop the fight, OK?" After nodding his assent, Yanez commanded "let's go."

Although the three-knockdown rule was not in effect, it is generally understood that referees will stop fights if a boxer is floored three times in a round because the upright boxer had demonstrated his superiority beyond a reasonable doubt. Rarely has a boxer come back from multiple knockdowns in a round, and those that do are accorded places in ring lore, especially if they do so in high-visibility championship contests. Diego Corrales immortalized himself by twice climbing off the deck to stop Jose Luis Castillo in their first fight, and that fantastic finish elevated their toe-to-toe slugfest to an exalted place on many historians' lists. Now, on a lowly undercard bout, Revish was in much the same situation, but his mindset was not one of executing a fantastic rally but of surviving the final minute without hitting the floor again.

Lizarraga went all out for the finish, but his punches mostly flew over Revish's head. Revish beat Lizarraga in an exchange of rights before sliding to his right around the perimeter of the ring. Revish tried to shoe shine a combination to the head, but Lizarraga blasted another pair of hooks to the jaw. The fight appeared to be moments from ending as Lizarraga lined up Revish for one final shot.

With Revish trapped on the ropes, Lizarraga deked with his left shoulder and launched a big looping right. But Revish saw it coming, and he bent his knees to duck underneath it. As Lizarraga commenced a hook to the body, Revish sprang up from his crouch with a dynamite hook that landed perfectly on the point of the chin and sent Lizarraga sprawling to the canvas. A badly dazed Lizarraga rolled onto his left side with a glazed look as Yanez administered the count. His spirit commanded him to rise, but Revish's punch had numbed Lizarraga's nerves to the point that they couldn't respond. Yanez counted "ten" and declared the fight over with just 20 seconds remaining in the opening round. As Revish celebrated with his corner, all Lizarraga could do was sit, shake his head and smile ruefully about what could have been.

It was an amazing turn of events. Up until that point Revish had only landed three power shots, but the fourth turned out to be all he needed to convert almost certain defeat into shocking triumph. According to ESPN analyst Teddy Atlas, the seeds of Lizarraga's defeat were sown when he chose to pursue Revish with no regard for strategy. He didn't set up any punches with the jab or work the body in a systematic way. Instead, the temerity of youth commanded him to adopt a buzzsaw attack with no rhyme or reason, and his wildness yielded the one opening Revish needed to instantaneously change his fortunes.

On this night, Revish invaded hostile territory and emerged with the spoils of victory, and in the process he shaped the story to a form that was more to his liking. Instead of the hometown hero bowling over the visitor, Revish crafted a tale of upset-minded upstart overcoming early adversity to post a spectacular one-punch knockout before a nationwide television audience.

Both men would go on to write other chapters in their careers, but on this night they authored a violently timeless masterpiece.

Epilogue: As it turned out, Lizarraga would only fight twice more – and neither fight resulted in victory. Nearly four months after losing to Revish, Lizarraga fought a four round draw with Jonathan Ochoa in Glendale, Ariz. The 24-year-old Lizarraga then fought his final pro fight on January 7, 2005 at Veteran's Memorial Coliseum in Phoenix, where he lost by three round disqualification to Juan Pablo Montes de Oca. His final record stands at 4-3-1 with three knockouts.

TALES FROM THE VAULT

Two months after stopping Lizarraga, Revish returned to the Desert Diamond Casino to fight Mikel Williams. Unfortunately for Revish, he wasn't as lucky as he registered a four round draw. The following month, Revish lost a four round majority decision to fellow unbeaten Jonathan Tubbs at Frontier Field in Rochester, New York. Revish then took nearly three years off from the sport and returned in June 2007 with a two round KO over Jerrick Stephens at the Youth Center in Cut Off, Louisiana. Revish won his next seven fights, five by knockout. That KO total includes his most recent outing in October 2009 when he stopped former fringe contender Thomas Davis in five rounds in Louisiana. As of January 2010, the 25-year-old Revish's record is 10-1-1 (8 KO).

Total Punches Landed/Thrown

Round	1	2	3	4	5	6	7	8	9	10	11	12	Total
Lizarraga	15/45												15/45
	33%												33%
Revish	6/28												6/28
	21%												21%

Jabs Landed/Thrown

Round	1	2	3	4	5	6	7	8	9	10	11	12	Total
Lizarraga	2/6												2/6
	33%												33%
Revish	2/7												2/7
	29%												29%

Power Punches Landed/Thrown

Round	1	2	3	4	5	6	7	8	9	10	11	12	Total
Lizarraga	13/39												13/39
	33%												33%
Revish	4/21												4/21
	19%												19%

John Revish vs. Leo Lizarraga April 2, 2004, Tucson, Arizona

TALES FROM THE VAULT

Derrick Roddy vs. Ricardo Kennedy
February 9, 1996, Atlantic City, New Jersey

During the 1990s, promoter Cedric Kushner put together a series of cards on cable and pay-per-view called "Heavyweight Explosion" on the theory that all-heavyweight cards would attract fans eager to see big men, big punches and big knockouts.

Investing one's chips in the heavyweight division is a high-risk, high-reward venture, and the "Heavyweight Explosion" cards included its share of duds. One fight that more than lived up to the billing took place when Derrick Roddy and Ricardo Kennedy met at the Tropworld Hotel and Casino in Atlantic City, N.J. in a scheduled 10 rounder that served as the main support to Ahmad Abdin and James Gaines.

On paper the bout served as a vehicle for the up-and-coming 26-year-old Kennedy; all of his 12 victories (against one loss and one draw) had come by knockout and 10 of those occurred in three rounds or less. Following the six-round draw against Ron Preston in December 1994, Kennedy had notched four straight knockouts against spotty competition. Nevertheless, the man known as "Explosive" was expected to personify his nickname against Roddy.

The 28-year-old Roddy had once been cast in Kennedy's role and at a well-muscled 6-6 and 230 pounds he certainly looked the part. More importantly, he translated his athletic ability to the ring as he rolled off 13 straight wins to begin his career, including 11 knockouts, against a string of "opponents." But when the Olathe, Kansas native stepped up against fellow prospect Daniel Dancuta in the "People's Choice One Night Heavyweight Tournament" in December 1993, he received a rude awakening as Dancuta put him to sleep in one round. From that point on, Roddy assumed the most dangerous of ring personas – the big puncher with the suspect chin that either takes you out or gets taken out.

In the nine fights since losing to Dancuta, Roddy had won four times, three by knockout, but three of his five losses were by KO. Just 27 days earlier, Roddy (17-6-1, 14 KO) won a wildly exciting four round shootout with Nelson Adams that saw Roddy pick himself off the floor once while scoring three knockdowns of Adams. During his losing streak, Roddy had ballooned to as high as 249½ in his two-round KO loss to John Ruiz, but for the Kennedy fight he was back down to 233. It was clear that he was primed for battle, and what a battle it would be.

Roddy took charge in the bout's opening seconds with a jab to the stomach as Kennedy whiffed on a right uppercut and a right over the top. Meanwhile, Roddy surveyed Kennedy from a distance as he circled slowly around the ring. Midway through the first minute, Roddy slid to his left along the ropes and stopped for an instant, just long enough for Kennedy to line up a powerful hook that clipped across Roddy's jaw. A surprised Roddy fell heavily to the canvas and the charged-up Tropworld crowd delighted at "Explosive's" instant detonation.

Kennedy slowly regained his feet at referee Frank Cappuccino's seven-count, and the charging Kennedy moved in behind a crunching right uppercut and a hook to the chest. As Roddy recoiled from the impact, Kennedy snapped a jolting jab to the jaw that prompted Roddy to latch on. Following the break Roddy recovered enough to resume his movement, but it didn't take long for Kennedy to strike again as a thudding right-left to the body and a heavy right to the ear buckled Roddy's legs. Roddy unsteadily traversed the ring in huge circles but the ring wasn't large enough to contain Kennedy, who ripped a right to the body, a pair of hooks to the jaw and a follow-up right uppercut.

Though Kennedy landed at will, he didn't go all out for the quick stoppage. He adopted a methodical, almost workmanlike approach that was unusual for a man accustomed to taking his opponents out early. The tactic worked well as Kennedy's right to the ear made Roddy slump into the ropes and two more rights to the ear forced another clinch. Roddy sneaked in a lead right as Kennedy moved in, but Kennedy walked through it and cranked a hook to the body, a right to the head, a hurtful hook and an overhand right that forced Roddy into all-out survival mode.

The lanky Roddy assumed a giraffe-like appearance as he raggedly moved about the ring, and with 37 seconds left in a harrowing first round Kennedy's chopping right sent Roddy into the ropes and three more rights caused him to squat toward the canvas. Though nothing but his feet touched the canvas, Cappuccino interpreted Roddy's move as a "time out" gesture and administered the state's first "squatting eight count."

When the action resumed Roddy attempted to catch Kennedy charging in with a right uppercut to the head but the Explosive One beat him to the trigger with an overhand right that persuaded Roddy to clinch away the final seconds.

Kennedy and Roddy had followed form in the first three minutes. The prospect successfully showcased his power game on a favorable – if not willing – target while Roddy's ability to ride out the assault ensured that the paying audience would see a more lengthy demonstration. Kennedy might have been able to take Roddy out had he opted for a full-throttled assault, but at 230 he was at his heaviest weight as a pro and he didn't want to risk exhaustion in the name of an eye-catching stoppage. That, he thought, would come in good time.

As for Roddy, his long-range boxing did him little good. Instead of keeping Kennedy at arm's length, he provided his rival optimum leverage on his powerful blows. Though three inches taller and the owner of a one-inch reach advantage, Roddy decided the safest place for him to be was at extremely close range. The move deprived Kennedy of the room he needed to get extension on his punches while it gave Roddy time to clear his head and break his opponent's momentum.

When the second round bell sounded Roddy put his plan into action as he ducked inside with a right to the body and kept his chest on Kennedy's until he was ready to make his move.

When he did, the results couldn't have been more devastating.

Roddy nipped outside and nailed a ducking Kennedy with a monstrous left uppercut and a pair of rights that sent Kennedy falling forward on all fours. The throng roared at this reality-snapping turn of events as Kennedy scrambled to his feet. Kennedy, though clearly stunned, continued to come forward and Roddy made him pay with a right to the ribs and a hook-cross combination that buckled Kennedy's legs. A right to the temple made the badly wobbled Kennedy fall into the ropes, where a pumped-up Roddy struck his wide-open opponent with a right to the jaw before Cappuccino administered his second count of the round.

Kennedy rested his arms across the top strands of rope and tried to shake out the cobwebs as Cappuccino tolled off the seconds. Kennedy tried to reverse the tide with a Pearl Harbor hook, but Roddy ducked it and instigated a wild mid-ring exchange. Roddy fired right after right as he drove Kennedy to the ropes, where he unleashed a tidal wave of lefts and rights. Kennedy forced Roddy to break off the exchange with a flush hook to the jaw that twisted Roddy's head and sent his mouthpiece flying across the ring.

It was the kind of punch that would have sent Roddy flying to the canvas just minutes earlier, but Roddy's adrenaline-flushed body was so into the moment that he walked through the blow and kept firing. An instant after Roddy took a half-step back, Cappuccino called a time out to have Roddy's mouthpiece rinsed and replaced.

For Kennedy, it was a most fortuitous break in the action and he took full advantage of the time-out to regain a semblance of awareness. When Cappuccino ordered the action to resume, a refreshed Kennedy ripped a pair of hooks to the jaw and a thumping right to the torso that drove Roddy to the ropes. A huge hook made Roddy's head swivel and a chopping right crashed through the guard. A right uppercut to the jaw and hook to the ear sent Roddy reeling to ring center.

As the second round entered its final minute, Kennedy was in the midst of a marvelous rally that forced Roddy to revisit recent demons. Suddenly, visions of round one were dancing in both men's heads as Kennedy pursued and Roddy prompted a clinch that would last several long seconds.

Once they were broken, the fight changed yet again.

Roddy ducked underneath Kennedy's hard jab and uncorked a pile-driving, off-the-floor right uppercut that sent Kennedy heavily to the canvas. Knowing he had executed a perfectly delivered punch, Roddy shot both arms upward and punched the air with his right glove as he marched triumphantly toward the neutral corner, convinced his night's work was over. Kennedy regained his feet at two, but he wobbled for several seconds before Cappuccino allowed the fight to continue.

However, in the excitement of the moment, it had slipped Cappuccino's mind that the three-knockdown rule was in effect and that he should have stopped the fight the moment Kennedy hit the floor. But it didn't matter as Roddy blasted a final right uppercut to send Kennedy to the canvas for the fourth – and final – time. Cappuccino immediately criss-crossed his arms and Kennedy, ever the fighter at heart, tried to plead his case. But it was to no avail as Roddy jumped on the ropes, hugged his corner men and basked in the crowd's plaudits.

By knocking out Kennedy in such spectacular fashion, he had crafted not only a comeback, but also a comeback within a comeback. He had overcome two first-round knockdowns to register four knockdowns in the second, but in doing so he had to survive a dangerous mini-rally from his opponent before he lowered the boom. In the end, Roddy was declared the TKO winner at 2:43 of round two, and in the process he had revitalized his career.

"I'm still hurt from the couple of knockdowns; I'm not going to deny it," Roddy candidly told commentators Arnie "Tokyo" Rosenthal and Kevin Kelley. "I just had to get myself back together. (My corner told me to) use the jab, set up with the jab because he was letting the jab come through and dropping his left hand coming over with the right hand."

As for the knockout punch, Roddy confirmed that victory was ensured by his very best.

"The best punch I got is my right uppercut," Roddy said. "I cannot predict the future, but I see myself getting better and better as time goes on."

In terms of heavyweight thunder, Roddy-Kennedy stole it from card-toppers Abdin and Gaines, who went the 10 round distance before Abdin won a unanimous nod.

Epilogue: Winners Roddy and Abdin met two months later in Bushkill, Pa., with Abdin stopping Roddy in the sixth. The Abdin fight sparked a steep career freefall as Roddy won just once in his final nine fights, a two round knockout of Dave Slaughter in January 1998. As for the rest, he fell victim to James Warring (L 10), Everett "Bigfoot" Martin (L 10), Derrick Banks (L 8), future heavyweight champion Vitali Klitschko (KO by 2), Cliff Couser (KO 2) and former cruiserweight champ Al Cole (KO by 3). The 31-year-old Roddy's final fight took place on January 30, 1999 at Atlantic City's Boardwalk Hall when Jeremy Williams scored four knockdowns before registering a first-round stoppage. Roddy's final record stands at 19-15 with 16 knockouts.

Just as Roddy's defeat to Abdin led to disaster, so did Kennedy's loss to Roddy as he dropped all but two of his final nine bouts – all of which ended by knockout. The two wins came in back-to-back fights against Joel Heinrich (KO 5) and Jack Johnson (KO 3) in a seven-week period in 1997 after a 10-round loss to Jeff Wooden two months after the Roddy bout. Kennedy's slide continued against Pele Reid (KO by 1),

TALES FROM THE VAULT

Larry Donald (KO by 5), Fernely Feliz (KO by 5), Vitali Klitschko (KO by 1) and Obed Sullivan (KO by 3).

The Sullivan defeat prompted Kennedy to retire from the sport, but he launched a one-fight comeback at age 36 on December 10, 2005 at the Turning Stone Casino in Verona, N.Y. against Derrick Brown. The comeback ended just 65 seconds after it began, and Kennedy retired with a record of 14-9-1 (14 KO).

UNDERCARD TREASURES

Total Punches Landed/Thrown

Round	1	2	3	4	5	6	7	8	9	10	11	12	Total
Roddy	3/11	16/51											19/62
	27%	31%											31%
Kennedy	20/53	14/37											34/90
	38%	38%											38%

Jabs Landed/Thrown

Round	1	2	3	4	5	6	7	8	9	10	11	12	Total
Roddy	1/4	3/9											4/13
	25%	33%											31%
Kennedy	1/14	3/10											4/24
	7%	30%											17%

Power Punches Landed/Thrown

Round	1	2	3	4	5	6	7	8	9	10	11	12	Total
Roddy	2/7	13/42											15/49
	29%	31%											31%
Kennedy	19/39	11/27											30/66
	49%	41%											45%

Derrick Roddy vs. Ricardo Kennedy February 9, 1996, Atlantic City, New Jersey

TALES FROM THE VAULT

Thomas Davis vs. Kendall Holt
June 18, 2004, Chicago, Illinois

Boxing is a sport that not only depends on physical skill and mental fortitude, it also relies on deception. The late Jose Torres said in his award-winning book "Sting Like a Bee" that pugilists succeed because of their ability to fool their opponents.

"Champions and good fighters are champions and good fighters because they can lie better than the others," Torres wrote. "A feint is an outright lie. You make believe you're going to hit your opponent in one place, he covers the spot and your punch lands on the other side. A left hook off the jab is a classy lie. You're converting an I into an L. Making openings is starting a conversation with a guy, so another guy (your other hand) can come and hit him with a baseball bat."

That ability to deceive extends to one's body type. One would think that a heavily muscled monster would be the biggest threat in the ring, but boxing history reveals this is not so. Some of history's most accomplished knockout artists sported physiques that would more likely inspire overconfident smirks than fear. Consider:

* Jimmy Wilde was just 5-2 ½ and weighed between 98 and 108 pounds, yet he produced 101 knockouts in 153 fights.

* Sandy Saddler stood 5-8 ½ and tipped the scales at 126 to 130 pounds, and his 103 knockouts in 162 fights proved his willowy body could generate ungodly power.

* Danny "Little Red" Lopez was just a half-inch shorter than Saddler and his pale, painfully thin offered no clue that he was a fistic powerhouse. Of his 42 victories 39 came by knockout, including six of his seven featherweight title defenses.

* Alexis Arguello was nicknamed "The Explosive Thin Man" because of his 5-10 frame and the ability to put 65 of his 90 opponents to sleep. And he was one of the few who carried his power with him through four weight classes, and had it not been for Aaron Pryor's own greatness he, not Thomas Hearns, would have been the first to win titles in four divisions.

The incongruity between body type and punching power extends to all levels of the sport, even to preliminary fighters, because of a simple thing called leverage. Height and reach are powerful advantages in boxing because they amplify a fighter's ability to hit his opponent without being hit himself, but a lean wiry boxer armed with proper technique can become a destroyer – no matter what the level of experience.

On June 18, 2004 at the DePaul Athletic Center in Chicago, welterweights Thomas Davis and Kendall Holt met in an eight round curtain opener on ESPN's "Friday Night Fights." Demetrius Hopkins and hometown hero Al "Speedy" Gonzalez topped the card, but the pyrotechnics produced by Davis and Holt made topping their fight an almost impossible task.

Holt, a native of Paterson, New Jersey, was a prospect on the rise. Blessed with fast hands, slick defensive moves and an excellent amateur foundation, Holt's knockout power was such that the nickname "Rated R" was hung on him. That power generated something unique to boxers with only 15 pro fights – national acclaim. Nearly three months earlier at the Miami's Miccosukee Resort, Holt fought Gilberto Reyes before ESPN's cameras. A little past two minutes into the fight Holt landed a massive hook to the jaw that propelled Reyes face first into the canvas, after which referee Jorge Alonso counted the badly dazed Reyes out. It was a knockout so breathtakingly spectacular that it was voted Sunday Night SportsCenter's "Play of the Week," an honor never before bestowed on a boxer.

Holt and his trainer happened to be watching the telecast, and they launched a celebration so loud and prolonged that the local police was summoned. When the officers were told why the pair was so overjoyed, they offered their congratulations and no charges were filed – though they were told to keep the noise down.

Holt (15-0, 11 KO) basked in his newfound notoriety, but soon it was time to get back to business and take another step in his professional journey. That next step took the form of the 6-2 Thomas Davis of Knoxville, Tenn., a 32-year-old who also boasted a good amateur career as he won the 1995 Armed Forces Championship. Unlike Holt, however, he had experienced defeat in the professional ring.

After running off eight consecutive wins, Davis suffered a draw to Victor McKinnis in June 2001 – as well as a broken knuckle on his right hand. The knuckle didn't heal properly because he waited until he secured a job – and the insurance that came with it – before seeking treatment. Once he got that treatment, he was able to resume punching freely with it but he waited nearly three years before re-entering the pro ranks. There, just two months earlier, Davis lost his first fight to slick 21-fight veteran Luis Collazo, a tough assignment for anyone much less an 8-0-1 prospect coming off such a long layoff. The recent defeat – combined with Holt's electrifying success last time out – painted a pretty picture for the 5-9 Holt and a grim one for Davis.

Davis began the fight by snaking out several long jabs, most of which fell short of the target while Holt surveyed behind a high guard. Holt immediately introduced himself to Davis by launching a whistling counter hook that brought oohs from the crowd and knocked Davis slightly off balance. Holt missed wildly with a follow-up hook and Davis took advantage by landing a long lead right to the ribs and leaping in behind a hook-cross combination.

Davis sought to consolidate his advantage by snapping out more jabs, but Holt put a stop to all that by unloading a hair-trigger lead right to the jaw that sent Davis stumbling forward into the neutral corner pad. Davis was unquestionably hurt and visions of another Holt demolition flashed through many minds.

"Don't go anywhere, Holt's looking to make SportsCenter again," cautioned blow-by-blow commentator Joe Tessitore as Holt pounded Davis along the ropes. Davis managed to spin away from the corner but Holt continued his hot pursuit with a hook to the jaw. Davis again veered to ring center and resumed shooting jabs to keep Holt at bay.

A few seconds of relative quiet was broken when Holt landed another gasp-inspiring hook. Davis replied with a hard jab, but Holt deftly slipped his follow-up shots by leaning away and using his left shoulder as a shield. Holt landed a jab to the stomach, slipped Davis' jab and connected with a thunderous counter right that had Davis covering up and retreating on unsteady legs. The crowd was reacting to every Holt explosion, fully believing they were seconds away from another spectacular early exit, and Holt fueled that hope by landing a right and a pair of hooks before Davis clinched and bulled Holt to another set of ropes.

Following the break, Holt again slipped Davis' jab and landed a hammering right over the top that made Davis grab. Holt bulldogged Davis to the ropes and pounded two rights to the ribs, after which Davis landed his own right to the side before clamping down.

As the round entered its final minute it was clear that both were looking to land their best punches. There wasn't much room for nuance or subtlety, for both men lived by the bomb – and also died by it. Holt wanted dearly to craft another "SportsCenter Moment" while Davis would have been content with earning Holt's respect.

Davis' attempted hook wrapped around Holt's head and Holt made him pay by turning over a short jolting hook as Davis grabbed on. Davis attempted to draw a bead on Holt but his blows lacked the necessary accuracy.

With 28 seconds left in a round dominated by Holt, all that had transpired would be transformed by a single blow.

Following a brief clinch, the pair returned to long range. Davis crouched forward and fired and jab to the chest before recoiling his upper body. From there, Davis deked a jab with his shoulder only to deliver a crushing right to the jaw at the exact moment Holt was loading up his own right. At the moment Davis' bomb landed Holt's right glove was at his belt line and as he crumbled to the canvas his upper body was splayed along the two lower strands of rope. Somehow, Holt arose at referee Tim Adams' count of five and Adams thoroughly assessed Holt's condition by commanding him to step forward, then back. Satisfied with the results, the fight was allowed to continue.

Davis, however, saw through Holt's charade, and his suspicions were confirmed when his right-left-right stiffened Holt's legs and a final right to the jaw sent him sprawling to the floor. With just one second remaining in an electrifying opening round, Adams stopped the contest.

The ring and the arena housing it vibrated with emotion. The crowd was a din and Davis rejoiced wildly over his rarest of accomplishments – a come-from-behind first round knockout. When Holt regained his senses, he was furious and disbelieving. But ESPN analyst Teddy Atlas knew this result was produced because of simple physics.

"I remember when I used to bring amateurs up; if I didn't know anything about the opponent, I'd look to see if he was tall and wiry," a pumped-up Atlas declared. "If he was tall and wiry, guess what? I'd avoid him because usually they could punch. And guess what? Davis can punch!"

Yes he could, and at least for one night Davis upheld the traditional foundation built by men like Wilde, Saddler, Lopez, Arguello and so many others who knew that boxing is not just about muscle but about what one does with the gifts he has.

Epilogue: In the years since this fight, Davis was unable to capitalize on his jolting victory over Holt. In his next outing three months later, Davis fell in nine rounds to Nurhan Suleymanoglu, prompting a nearly one year layoff. Things didn't get any better as he lost a decision to Oscar Diaz and suffered a three-round no contest to Richard Gutierrez after Gutierrez's head opened a severe cut over his right eye.

Despite his decay in form, Davis' tall-man power occasionally surfaced. In September 2006, Davis knocked Agustin Velez from the undefeated ranks via sixth round KO and stopped Richard Hall in the first round six weeks after a butt-induced technical draw against former title challenger Raul Frank. As of January 2010, the 37-year-old Davis is now in the midst of a streak that has seen him lose 12 of his last 13 fights. After losses to Joel Julio (KO by 7), Jose Valera (KO by 2) and James Moore (KO by 2), Davis returned to the victory stand with an eight round split decision over Chad Greenleaf. His nine most recent opponents – Henry Crawford, Luis Abregu, Nelson Linares and David Lemieux, Michael Jean Louis, Brad Soloman, Anthony Greenidge, John Revish and Fred Tukes – had a combined record of 112-5-5 and he lost to all of them. His record stands at 12-15-2 (7 KO).

Conversely, Holt rebounded tremendously from his defeat to Davis. Following a pair of victories over Roberto Ortega (W 6) and Juan Carlos Escobar (W 6), Holt knocked future lightweight champion David Diaz from the undefeated ranks with an eighth round TKO. Victories over Jaime Rangel (W 12), Vladimir Khodokovski (W 10), Isaac Hlatschwayo (W 12) and Mike Arnaoutis (W 12) propelled Holt to a title fight against WBO junior welterweight champion Ricardo Torres in Torres' back yard of Barranquilla, Colombia on September 1, 2007.

Holt appeared on his way to victory after decking Torres with a three-punch combination in the sixth round, but Torres emerged with a highly controversial 11th round stoppage loss after referee Genaro Rodriguez halted the action while Holt was in the midst of throwing a blow. Following the loss, Holt has become a hot-and-cold fighter stylistically as he either produced pulsating wars or sleep-inducing move-fests.

TALES FROM THE VAULT

He unimpressively out-pointed Ben Tackie en route to a 10-round majority decision that should have been unanimous on February 7, 2008 in Las Vegas, then scored an electrifying twice-off-the-floor one round knockout over Torres to seize the WBO title in July 2008. He notched one successful defense over Demetrius Hopkins (W 12) in December 2008 only to lose it in an unification fight with WBC champ Timothy Bradley in April 2009. As of January 2010, Holt's record is 25-3 (13 KO).

Total Punches Landed/Thrown

Round	1	2	3	4	5	6	7	8	9	10	11	12	Total
Davis	19/49												19/49
	39%												39%
Holt	16/38												16/38
	42%												42%

Jabs Landed/Thrown

Round	1	2	3	4	5	6	7	8	9	10	11	12	Total
Davis	10/27												10/27
	37%												37%
Holt	0/3												0/3
	0%												0%

Power Punches Landed/Thrown

Round	1	2	3	4	5	6	7	8	9	10	11	12	Total
Davis	9/22												9/22
	41%												41%
Holt	16/35												16/35
	46%												46%

Thomas Davis vs. Kendall Holt June 18, 2004, Chicago, Illinois

★ Chapter 6 ★
VENGEANCE IS MINE – GREAT GRUDGE FIGHTS

TALES FROM THE VAULT

Nigel Benn vs. Anthony Logan
October 26, 1988 London, England

To those who love boxing, fights can inspire all sorts of mental pictures. When I think of Sugar Ray Leonard-Wilfred Benitez, I see a pair of competitive white-coated scientists furiously trying to conjure a winning formula before the other does. Then there are matches like Carmen Basilio-Tony DeMarco, Matthew Saad Muhammad-Marvin Johnson and Jack Dempsey-Luis Firpo that burn snapshots of ferocious animals tearing into one another in scenes that would make viewers of the Discovery Channel squeamish.

When I think of Nigel Benn vs. Anthony Logan, only one image comes to my mind's eye: A throbbing, exposed nerve. This match of rising middleweight contenders that took place at Royal Albert Hall was filled with raw emotion, both in the ring and out. The result was one of the most explosive encounters ever seen in a British ring – or any ring for that matter.

Both men were edgy going into the match, which was for Benn's Commonwealth middleweight title. In a press conference held the week of the fight, Logan called Benn "a load of garbage" and the two engaged in several heated exchanges that nearly escalated into fisticuffs. Given both men's combative temperaments, it was no surprise that verbal haymakers would precede their physical encounter. All the better to sell tickets – and add petrol to an already raging fire.

The 24-year-old Benn was aptly called "The Dark Destroyer" as he tore through his opposition with a search-and-destroy mentality fostered by a rough childhood in Ilford, East London and his four years in the First Battalion of the Royal Regiment of Fusiliers. His time there included two tours of duty in Northern Ireland during the height of "The Troubles" and the experience further hardened an already hard man.

Benn was enjoying a perfect start to his boxing career – 18 fights, 18 wins and 18 knockouts, including 14 in the first two rounds. His fists detonated like nuclear bombs and his all-out pressure swallowed up adversaries much like the sport's biggest name at the time – heavyweight champion Mike Tyson.

Anthony Logan (16-1-1, 10 KO) was a native of Jamaica who moved to Hallandale, Florida to further his professional career. After a four-round draw to Armando Rodriguez in his second pro fight, Logan ran off 14 consecutive wins. Along the way he picked up the WBC Continental Americas middleweight title by decisioning the 47-18-19 Ramon Gaspar Abeldano. Seven weeks before his encounter with Benn, Logan lost that belt to David Noel by unanimous decision. Despite his excellent record, Logan entered the fight with Benn as the party of the second part, mere cannon fodder to further Benn's burgeoning career. But as Benn would find out the hard way, the 24-year-old Logan was no one's cannon fodder – he turned out to be the cannon.

An electric atmosphere permeated Royal Albert Hall as the two men awaited the opening bell. When it did, Benn came out storming, missing his first five swings but connecting with a hook to the body and a right to the temple that forced Logan to clamp down on Benn's arms. Benn broke free and continued to fire a steady stream of inaccurate bombs while Logan desperately sought to collect himself and find a way to slow down this tornado bent on blowing him away in the shortest time possible.

Benn bullied Logan to the ropes, but the Jamaican turned Benn around and landed a grazing right-left to the head. Benn spun him back with a right to the temple. After referee Larry O'Connell issued a warning to Logan for holding and hitting, the two resumed action at ring center at close range. Benn ripped a right to the ribs and rolled his upper body smartly away from Logan's retaliatory right-left. Benn zipped in a right uppercut to the jaw, but broke off the exchange after Logan responded with his own uppercut and hook to the head.

Benn missed a wild uppercut to the jaw, but a follow-up hook propelled Logan to the ropes and forced a clinch, which was quickly ended by another Benn right to the ribs after Logan rapped Benn's ear with a right hand. The fight was evolving into a series of short, intense skirmishes packed with powerful blows that required them to take short breaks after absorbing the other man's punishment.

After an extended clinch at ring center, Benn broke out and unleashed a short right hook-left hook combo that drove Logan back, and another short hook-uppercut cluster drove the Jamaican to the ropes. Logan countered with his best flurry of the fight – two compact hooks to the jaw, a right to the head, a right uppercut to the chin and another short hook before forcing a clinch.

Though the fight was less than two minutes old, the intense pace was beginning to tell. Not only were physical resources drained but mental ones as well. Benn exerted all-out, smothering pressure that couldn't be sustained for very long while Logan expended untold energy furiously fighting off a fistic avalanche. This was a fight that either had to end soon or else the participants would collapse from exhaustion.

After O'Connell separated the two men, Benn ripped a right uppercut to the jaw and charged in behind another right, but Logan smashed a left hook, a jab, a right hook, another right and a right uppercut-hook combo to Benn's head. Sparked into action, Benn missed a winging right-left to the jaw and clinched. Following the break, Logan, at long range for the first time, landed a quick right uppercut-left hook combination. As Logan took a half-step back, both launched simultaneous rights. Logan's got there first, exploding on the point of Benn's chin and driving the Britisher to the canvas.

Benn arose immediately, and though it appeared to be a clean knockdown, O'Connell called it a slip and wiped off Benn's gloves.

Neither man was fooled; Benn was decked legitimately and both boxers acted accordingly. Logan charged in wildly, looking to finish the job while Benn responded the only way he knew – firing hard punches to keep Logan off him and, more importantly, to exact revenge. As Benn bulled Logan to the ropes and winged a hook over Logan's head in the round's final seconds, the crowd was in a cacophonous frenzy, caught up in the energy of a fight whose action fulfilled every promise every promoter in history ever made about a fight. As the bell sounded to end an unforgettable first act, Benn shot a venomous look over his shoulder while Logan stood his ground, his right arm menacingly in the air and defiance oozing from every pore.

The first round had so much action that it only seemed to last ages, though it went the regulation three minutes. The break between rounds was another story – it clocked in at one minute forty-two seconds. It was the kind of fight that would make it easy for anyone, even the official timekeeper, to lose track. So much occurred in the round that the minds of those who witnessed it had to temporarily shut down to take it all in.

But there was more.

Logan landed three jabs as the second round opened while Benn stalked, ripping a right over the head but bullying Logan to the ropes with a solid hook to the jaw. A right to the temple knocked Benn off-balance but the Britisher roared back with hyperactive rights and lefts that were mostly blocked or slipped. Logan countered with a right hook to the head and another to the temple. Two more rights caromed off Benn's skull and now it was Logan who was barreling forward, working short smothering rights and lefts as Benn sought to stay at close range.

Logan pushed Benn off to get a little working room and scored with a terrific right uppercut to the tip of the jaw. Benn, undeterred, motored forward in search of the bomb that would polish off the stubborn Jamaican.

Yet it was Benn who was nearly finished.

Logan suddenly found the range with uppercuts, ripping a half-dozen of them as he whaled away frenetically. Several more powerful uppercuts crashed through, hurting Benn badly for the first time in the fight. But Benn, pure predator that he was, didn't possess a bag of tricks to help him survive another man's attack. There was no clinching or calculated upper body movement to fend off the blows. The only thing on Benn's mind was to find a way to get through the storm so he could launch his next wave of mayhem. His one-track mind, however, was now in danger of hurtling off the rails.

In all, Logan threw 22 punches in his flurry and every one of them was intended to put the hometown favorite away for good. Benn, stumbling now, winged a wild overhand right over Logan's head, and while the blow threw Benn off balance, it somehow positioned him perfectly for his next punch, an arcing, thunderous hook to the jaw that detonated with explosive force. Logan's head snapped violently to the side and he crashed to the floor, flat on his back. Logan struggled to rise but his body was in no shape to fully comply with his mind's commands. Somehow, he made it to his feet a split-second before O'Connell completed his count, but the referee wisely called off the contest.

Logan's corner protested in vain to a British Boxing Board of Control official about the stoppage as Benn exulted with his seconds. The raw emotions of combat couldn't be shut off easily, whether it was the fighters, seconds or fans. It was the kind of fight that seared itself into collective memories – and struck a raw – but welcome – nerve in all boxing fans.

Epilogue: Logan fought just five more times, going 3-2 (2 KO). Six weeks after the war with Benn, Logan returned to Royal Albert Hall to knock out Carlton Warren in two rounds. Only 11 days after that, he iced Gilbert Josamu in one round, setting up a showdown with the up-and-coming Chris Eubank, who decisioned Logan over eight rounds. Exactly one month after the Eubank loss, Logan was knocked out in one round by future WBA super middleweight champion Victor Cordoba. Logan ended his career against Edward Neblett March 25, 1990 at the friendly confines of Kingston, Jamaica. The homecoming ended happily for Logan as he won a convincing 12 round decision. His final record stands at 18-4-1 (13 KO).

Benn had many more chapters to write in his career. Six weeks after knocking out Logan, he took out Logan's conqueror David Noel in one round. Following two more knockouts to run his string to 22, Benn lost the commonwealth middleweight title to Michael Watson via six-round KO on May 21, 1989. Three fights later, Benn won the WBO middleweight title by stopping Doug DeWitt in eight and defended it with a wild one-rounder against Iran Barkley.

Three months after blitzing Barkley, Benn lost his WBO belt to Chris Eubank in nine dramatic rounds. Two fights later, Benn stopped up to super middleweight by decisioning Lenzie Morgan and the Briton would campaign in this division for the rest of his career.

On October 3, 1992, Benn stopped Mauro Galvano to win the WBC title. He defended three times against Nicky Piper (KO 11), Galvano (W 12) and Lou Gent (KO 4) before engaging rival Eubank in a highly anticipated rematch intended to unify the WBC and WBO belts. Though Benn appeared to have done enough to earn victory, the bout was judged a draw and both men kept their baubles.

As Benn matured physically, his style evolved with him. He no longer was the uncompromising slugger who had no need for finesse. Instead, he sharpened his skills and became a better-than-average boxer who could win a fight with his brain as well as with his brawn.

Benn defended his WBC belt five more times, beating Henry Wharton (W 12), Juan Jose Gimenez (W 12), Gerald McClellan in an unforgettable and tragic 10-round war of attrition, Vincenzo Nardiello (KO 8) and Danny Perez (KO 7). The "Dark

TALES FROM THE VAULT

Destroyer" shockingly lost the belt in his 10th defense against 40-year-old Thulane "Sugar Boy" Malinga via split decision, after which he proposed to his girlfriend Carolyne in the ring.

Benn finished his career with two stoppage losses to WBO super middleweight champion Steve Collins, neither of which ended conclusively. According to a subsequent article in Ring Magazine, the former wild child is now a born-again Christian who is looking to build a ministry in Spain. His final ring record is 42-5-1 (35 KO).

VENGEANCE IS MINE – GREAT GRUDGE FIGHTS

Total Punches Landed/Thrown

Round	1	2	3	4	5	6	7	8	9	10	11	12	Total
Benn	21/68	6/21											27/89
	31%	29%											30%
Logan	30/63	27/54											57/117
	48%	50%											49%

Jabs Landed/Thrown

Round	1	2	3	4	5	6	7	8	9	10	11	12	Total
Benn	0/0	0/0											0/0
	0%	0%											0%
Logan	1/7	1/7											2/14
	14%	14%											14%

Power Punches Landed/Thrown

Round	1	2	3	4	5	6	7	8	9	10	11	12	Total
Benn	21/68	6/21											27/89
	31%	29%											30%
Logan	29/56	26/47											55/103
	52%	55%											53%

Nigel Benn vs. Anthony Logan October 26, 1988 London, England

TALES FROM THE VAULT

Iran Barkley vs. Michael Olajide
March 6, 1988, New York, New York

From 1980 to 1987, the iron fists of Marvelous Marvin Hagler ruled the middleweight division. Through 12 title defenses, Hagler demonstrated beyond doubt he was a complete fighter as he seamlessly transitioned from boxer to slugger and southpaw to orthodox while never sacrificing the quality of his brilliant work.

Hagler fought with the intensity befitting someone whose constant companion was paranoia. He felt the "powers that be" never wanted him to become champion much less one of the greatest to have yet lived. He knew in his heart of hearts that politics, not his opponents' skills, would eventually seal his doom. On April 6, 1987, Hagler was convinced his premonition came true after Sugar Ray Leonard captured a split decision. A bitter Hagler never fought again while Leonard, feeling the rush of satisfaction that comes with toppling a great champion and proving the world wrong in the process, surrendered the WBC belt he won from Hagler and announced the fourth of what would become six retirements.

The ensuing vacuum triggered a feeding frenzy among the sanctioning bodies as well as the leading middleweights of the day. Two of them were Michael Olajide and Iran Barkley, who had already lost chances at vacant belts against Frank Tate and Sumbu Kalambay two weeks apart in October 1987. Despite the defeats, both Olajide (25-1, 17 KO) and Barkley (23-4, 14 KO) remained highly ranked on the basis of recent wins. After the loss to Tate, Olajide knocked out Franklin Owens in six rounds and beat Cecil Pettigrew via 10 round decision while Barkley escaped with a split decision over Sanderline Williams. Olajide and Barkley needed to make a big statement to convince the boxing world that they deserved another chance at glory, so they signed to meet each other at the Felt Forum in New York.

The Barkley-Olajide fight was aptly billed "Big Apple, Bad Blood," and not only did the styles offer an intriguing contrast, their life stories couldn't have been more different. Barkley was a native of the Bronx who was introduced to the sport by his sister Yvonne, a pro fighter with a respectable 10-2 record. A neighborhood bully tormented Barkley and Yvonne wanted to equip her brother with the ability to defend himself. Barkley developed his mean streak as a member of a street gang called The Black Spades, but he eventually returned to boxing and turned pro in 1982.

Barkley's early record was spotty as he suffered three losses in his first 12 fights to Osley Silas (L 6), Robbie Sims (KO by 6) and Eddie Hall (L 8). But Barkley found his stride as he won his next 13 bouts, including solid victories against Norberto Sabater (KO 2, KO 2), Randy Smith (W 10), Wilford Scypion (KO 8), Mike Tinley (W 12), James Kinchen (W 10) and Jorge Amparo (W 10) to earn his crack at Kalambay.

Olajide, on the other hand, was a one-man global village. Born in Liverpool, England to Nigerian parents, Olajide grew up in Vancouver, Canada before moving to New York City. When he wasn't exhibiting his dazzling skills in the ring, Olajide, who bore a strong resemblance to the "King of Pop" Michael Jackson, worked as a model.

Olajide fought 14 of his first 15 fights in Vancouver, with the one "away game" a nine-round knockout of Sakaraia Ve in Suva, Fiji Islands. On July 11, 1986, Olajide made a splash in his U.S. debut by beating Curtis Parker via 10-round split decision in Atlantic City and followed it with a unanimous nod over James "Hard Rock" Green three months later. From there, Olajide built the foundation for a title run with victories over Randy Smith (W 10), Knox Brown (KO 9), Ray Ray Gray (KO 10), Richard Burton (KO 4) and Don Lee (KO 9).

On May 10, 1987, a national TV audience saw Olajide pushed to the limit by Bermudan Troy Darrell, who overcame two first-round knockdowns to give Olajide a severe test before dropping a disputed decision. The hard-fought win earned Olajide his opportunity against Tate for the vacant IBF belt.

Barkley carried an additional handicap into the ring. During his bout with Williams 36 days before, he suffered a six-stitch gash over his left eye. Though Barkley was cleared by the New York Commission, the scar tissue was still tender and was just a couple of Olajide jabs away from ripping open. But Barkley's mouth was in perfect working order as he delivered a pre-fight quote for the ages: "This is a make-or-break fight. It'll make me and break him."

As Barkley and Olajide stood in opposite corners, the contrast in demeanor and personal style was starkly evident. Barkley, his hair closely cropped, wore basic black trunks with red lettering. A goatee framed one of the era's most intimidating scowls. His nickname was perfect: "The Blade."

Meanwhile, underneath Olajide's iridescent robe was matching gold sequined trunks and shoes. A magnificent mane of jheri curls adorned his head and his clean-shaven face was more likely to inspire jealousy than fear. His sobriquet, "The Silk," was also fitting.

Olajide opened the fight on the move, circling in both directions and staying far away from Barkley to burn off some nervous energy. Barkley briefly backed Olajide to the ropes and landed a solid right to the jaw, after which Olajide scampered back to ring center. Olajide used foot feints to disrupt Barkley's timing while "The Blade" stalked his prey, happy to land anywhere on Olajide's body. Olajide moved in to throw a hook that sailed over the ducking Barkley's head, after which "The Blade" countered with a glancing hook to the forehead. As the fight's initial seconds passed, Olajide's nervousness faded and the distance between them narrowed. Two sharp jabs speared Barkley's face and Barkley's counter right found nothing but air as Olajide darted away.

Midway through the round, Olajide fell off balance after swiftly retreating. Olajide backed into a neutral corner and sprung a trap on Barkley by landing a jab and throwing two hard hooks, the first of which connected solidly. The fight then settled into a rhythm of Olajide jabbing and Barkley pursuing, his shots missing the target but full of power.

With 20 seconds remaining, Barkley maneuvered Olajide near the ropes where his right-left-right combo was blocked. A solid uppercut found the mark, and Olajide motored away behind a double hook, the first of which landed. A few seconds later, Olajide again fired the double hook with the same result, but Barkley closed the opening round with a solid jab.

Barkley revved up his pursuit in round two, but Olajide's ability to slip, block and parry blows enabled him to avoid the brunt of "The Blade's" power. His confidence growing, Olajide began to play mind games as he faked a bolo with his right and popped in a jab, a move that brought a rueful smile from Barkley. His street fighter past bubbled up briefly in an ensuing clinch when he drove a heavy hook to Olajide's hip.

One minute in, Barkley caught Olajide with a hook to the ear. Olajide bounced off the ropes and slid to his left, but Barkley followed him with a chopping right to the jaw. Determined to stay off the ropes – where Barkley's power would be magnified – Olajide skittered to ring center, where his boxing skills would come to the fore. Olajide bounced a lead right off Barkley's dome and followed with a wide, glancing hook. Barkley snapped two inaccurate jabs as he continued his determined pursuit. Barkley countered a lead right by bending low, throwing a right-left that zipped over the ducking Olajide, and hitting the mark with a zinging hook to the jaw that forced an immediate clinch. All the while, the fighters were engaged in nonverbal combat. Olajide's eyes were wide open, his face a picture of intense concentration while Barkley's visage was angry and baleful.

With 56 seconds remaining, both men cranked up hooks. Barkley's got there first, and its force turned Olajide's legs to jelly. "The Silk's" mind commanded his body to stay upright, but his legs didn't receive the message as he first stumbled, then dropped to his knees near a neutral corner. His brain's message finally arrived a few seconds later, and when he arose at three Olajide appeared to have regained his composure.

Barkley stormed in behind winging hooks, and a heavy right crashed into Olajide's ribs. "The Silk" avoided most – but not all – of Barkley's blows with skillful upper body movement. Two more Barkley hooks ripped into Olajide's side and another to the head forced Olajide to escape to his right. Three more Barkley hooks slammed home, the third of which strayed low and drew a caution from referee Arthur Mercante Jr. As Barkley listened to the reprimand, Olajide brazenly beckoned Barkley in with his gloves. Barkley obliged, blasting in left and right uppercuts and ending the round with a slinging right to a ducking Olajide's forehead.

The Felt Forum crowd chanted "Barkley, Barkley" at the start of round three, and the object of their affection shot Olajide a small smile as if to say *"See? They're for me, not you."* The fight settled into a jabbing contest, which figured to benefit the quicker Olajide but in practice belonged to Barkley. Barkley built his reputation as a brawler, but at 6-1 with a 75-inch reach "The Blade" could also slice and dice with his heavy jab.

Meanwhile, Olajide's legs were playing tricks on him. A jab to the body and a quick hook sent Olajide off balance and he stumbled again after missing a lunging jab. Olajide's movement was jittery and unstable, but if he wanted to prevail, "The Silk" had no choice but to rely on those unsteady pins.

Olajide's outside packaging hardly conveyed an image of toughness, but as he tried to make the best of a bad situation against an opponent who would have liked nothing better than to knock his block off, Olajide showed a fighter's courage. As Barkley moved in, Olajide fired a chopping lead right that just missed the target, and Barkley stepped away nicely from an Olajide hook. "The Blade" fought with composure and intelligence, controlling Olajide with his jab and mixing in occasional power punches to keep him honest. Barkley punctuated an excellent round with three jabs and an overhand right to the jaw.

"The Blade" projected confidence as the fourth round opened, not only because of his success in the third but because the remnants of the cut above his left eye had not opened. He was convinced that he had Olajide's number and that it was only a matter of time before he would lower the boom. A lunging hook sent Olajide stumbling back and a right uppercut forced "The Silk" to clamp down on Barkley's arms. Olajide snapped a few jabs before falling into another clinch to clear his foggy head.

With one minute to go, the fog lifted in a most emphatic way.

Olajide missed with a jab and Barkley weaved in with a hook to the body and began to crank another hook to the head. But in doing so, Olajide spotted an opening and unleashed a hard reflexive hook to the chin that sent Barkley tumbling to the canvas on his behind. The crowd leaped to its feet at the surprising turn of events and Olajide, in an act of pure rapture mixed with anger, triumph and pride, raised his arms overhead and was reluctant to retreat to a neutral corner. As he walked toward the corner, he wore a big smile and banged his gloves together in celebration. Watching Barkley arise at three and skulk to the other corner to take Mercante's mandatory eight, Olajide taunted him by sticking his face out as if to say *"you just got decked by a 'pretty boy.' Take that, tough guy!"* Barkley, his pride stung, again wore a smiling sneer but he knew he had some work to do to regain control of the fight.

His confidence peaking, Olajide began slicing through Barkley's defense. A lead right glanced off the side of the head and a stabbing jab nicked "The Blade" between the eyes. After two more Olajide jabs hit the target, Barkley fired back a sneer. Olajide countered a missed Barkley jab with a quick right cross. Both launched hooks, and this time Olajide's landed on the forehead while Barkley's sailed by harmlessly. Another shorter, heavier hook connected as Barkley's wild swings found nothing but air. Two jabs and an overhand right punctuated a big round for "The Silk," and as they parted Barkley yapped at Olajide with a big smile laced with a heavy veneer of meanness. Barkley knew the score: He had not only lost the round, but also the momentum and he was clearly embarrassed by being dropped by a man he had dismissed as a sissy.

Olajide commenced the fifth smartly, pumping a jab that snaked in but two others fell short. Olajide ducked low to toss a lunging one-two to the body from long range.

Big mistake.

As Olajide moved in, Barkley whipped a crisp, perfectly timed hook to the temple that caught Olajide with his right foot in the air. Off-balance, Olajide struggled to stay upright, but instead he stumbled to the canvas and fell heavily on his right side, his legs splayed and his right arm laying awkwardly behind him. He slowly assumed a sitting position in the corner and arose by Mercante's count of seven.

Badly stunned, Olajide was still able to convince Mercante to let the fight continue. He stuck out his right arm and waved to Barkley, but "The Blade" was not fooled by Olajide's act of bravado. Barkley raced in behind a steady stream of home run hooks that Olajide blocked well, but it was clear "The Silk's" material was still frayed. Barkley then mixed in rights with his hooks and was hitting pay dirt, as well as Olajide's ribs and jaw. A fierce hook sent Olajide stumbling to the ropes and its impact caused Olajide to turn away at an angle. Another hook to the point of the chin snapped Olajide's head straight back, and it was clear the end was close at hand.

When a missed right uppercut caused Olajide to stumble away to his right, it was obvious his legs no longer had the strength to carry him safely away from the rampaging Barkley. That's when Mercante stepped between them and stopped the fight. The son of legendary referee Arthur Mercante Sr. first wrapped his arms around Barkley to stop him from inflicting further punishment while Olajide pleaded with him to let the fight continue. Fully realizing that this second loss represented a massive career setback, Olajide walked to his corner and laid his head on the corner pad in despair. Mercante rubbed his shoulder with his right hand and offered a few words of consolation and encouragement.

Meanwhile, Barkley wildly celebrated with his corner men, who held him aloft in triumph. He wore a wide smile that projected his relief, his sense of accomplishment and his sheer joy over the knowledge that he had just taken a huge step toward realizing his championship dream.

Barkley-Olajide was billed as "Big Apple, Bad Blood," and while the fight was in progress the emotional heat was more than evident. But with the contest over, competitive anger was replaced by shared respect as the two men embraced warmly. As Olajide whispered into Barkley's left ear, they were the picture of sportsmanship because each of them had just sampled the other's fighting heart and found it worthy.

VENGEANCE IS MINE – GREAT GRUDGE FIGHTS

The Big Apple was still there, but the bad blood was no more.

Epilogue: Though Olajide was three years younger than Barkley, his career ended up being much shorter. He fought just five more times, going 2-3 (2 KO). Six months after fighting Barkley, he knocked out Troy Watson in seven rounds at the Felt Forum but took off nine months before polishing off Kenny Lopez in four in Las Vegas. Olajide then lost his final three fights: a 10-round split decision to Dennis Milton, a lopsided 12-round decision to WBO super middleweight belt-holder Thomas Hearns and an eight-round TKO to Ralph Moncrief April 25, 1991 in Mobile, Ala. Olajide's final record was 27-5 (18 KO).

Meanwhile, Barkley would achieve his championship dream – three times over. Exactly three months after knocking out Olajide, "The Blade" shocked the boxing world by knocking out Hearns in three rounds to capture the WBC middleweight title. Cut badly and behind on points, Barkley unleashed an overhand right from nowhere that flattened the heavy favorite. "The Hit Man" got up, but Barkley's follow-up blows finished the job. When asked how he was able to overcome his injuries to emerge victorious, Barkley uttered the unforgettable phrase "I didn't have time to bleed."

Eight months later, Barkley, who was viewed as a sacrificial lamb to Hearns, fought 37-year-old Roberto Duran, who was viewed as big-name cannon fodder for Barkley. Like Barkley against Hearns, Duran summoned his A-game and captured a stirring split decision.

Consecutive losses to Michael Nunn and Nigel Benn seemingly placed Barkley into the "also-ran" category, but "The Blade" was nowhere near through. After beating Juan Hernandez (W 10) and Jesus Castaneda (KO 7), Barkley challenged Darrin Van Horn for the IBF super middleweight belt. Fighting with frightening intensity, Barkley steamrolled Van Horn in two rounds to capture his second belt. Incredibly, Barkley picked up his third world title just nine weeks later as he lifted Hearns' WBA light heavyweight belt via split decision. With the win, Barkley joined an ever-growing group of triple champions.

Barkley vacated the 175-pound belt in favor of the super middleweight belt, which he defended against James Toney February 13, 1993. Ten lopsided rounds later, Barkley was an ex-champion and would remain so for the rest of his career.

Barkley fought for a title one more time but lost by nine-round TKO to IBF light heavyweight king Henry Maske. After losing a majority eight-round decision to Rocky Gannon, Barkley moved up to heavyweight and saw success against limited opposition. The highlight of this phase of Barkley's career was a 10-round TKO over 41-year-old former WBA heavyweight champion Gerrie Coetzee June 8, 1997. Barkley would go a mere 1-7-1 (1 KO) in his final eight fights, including six consecutive defeats to end his career. Scaling 231 pounds, his final fight was a sixth round TKO loss to Keith McKnight July 31, 1999. The 39-year-old Barkley retired with a 43-19-1 (28 KO) record.

TALES FROM THE VAULT

Total Punches Landed/Thrown

Round	1	2	3	4	5	6	7	8	9	10	11	12	Total
Barkley	18/51	31/76	22/54	20/52	24/43								115/276
	35%	41%	41%	38%	56%								42%
Olajide	14/41	10/36	16/42	22/47	0/6								62/172
	34%	28%	38%	47%	0%								36%

Jabs Landed/Thrown

Round	1	2	3	4	5	6	7	8	9	10	11	12	Total
Barkley	9/23	7/22	16/34	7/25	1/3								40/107
	39%	32%	47%	28%	33%								37%
Olajide	11/32	8/22	15/35	12/31	0/4								46/124
	34%	36%	43%	39%	0%								37%

Power Punches Landed/Thrown

Round	1	2	3	4	5	6	7	8	9	10	11	12	Total
Barkley	9/28	24/54	6/20	13/27	23/40								75/169
	32%	44%	30%	48%	58%								44%
Olajide	3/9	2/14	1/7	10/16	0/2								16/48
	33%	14%	14%	62%	0%								33%

Iran Barkley vs. Michael Olajide March 6, 1988, New York, New York

Aaron Davis vs. Mark Breland
July 8, 1990, Reno, Nevada

The expectation game can be a brutal one. When a fighter demonstrates abilities far above the norm, the whispers of greatness turn into shouts and the hype machine shifts into overdrive. Then, when the fighter doesn't reach the heights demanded of him, the fall from grace is steep and destructive – no matter whether the degree of the fall is deserved or not.

This was particularly true of Mark Breland, whose spectacular amateur career inspired many to compare him to the fighter many consider the greatest of them all – Sugar Ray Robinson. And why not: Breland amassed a 110-1 record that included five consecutive New York Golden Gloves titles (the first fighter ever to do so), three amateur world titles and a gold medal in the 1984 Olympics. He was the most feared amateur of his time because of a right hand that produced dramatic knockouts in a sport where decisions are the norm.

Though Breland made good on the gold medal forecast, some felt he wasn't dominant enough in winning it. Still, he had top billing on the "Night of Gold" November 15, 1984 at Madison Square Garden, where six Olympic medalists made their professional debuts, many of them on ABC's prime time air. Breland solidly beat the 6-1 Dwain Williams over six rounds, but because he didn't score a dominating knockout some were left with a sour taste. After all, Robinson scored a two-round KO over Joe Echevarria in New York when he made his pro debut 44 years before, and the "next Robinson" failed to duplicate the feat.

The air of disappointment grew thicker when Breland failed to score a knockout in his next two fights against Marlon Palmer and Steve Little, but they quieted a bit when he polished off Vince Dunfee in two rounds in his fourth bout. When Breland stepped between the ropes, he was not only fighting the man across the ring but the ghost of Robinson and the overwhelming shadow it cast.

Breland knocked out 10 of his next 12 victims and went on to win the vacant WBA welterweight title by polishing off Harold Volbrecht in seven rounds. But Volbrecht enjoyed some good moments in that bout, and because Breland won a title vacated by linear champion Lloyd Honeyghan, the voices of dissent weren't silenced. After decisioning Juan Rondon in a non-title 10-rounder in Italy, Breland signed to defend against solid veteran Marlon Starling. A victory over Starling would have set things right in many people's eyes, but it was not to be as "The Magic Man" made Breland's title disappear in 11 rounds. The rematch 10 months later proved no better; though the fight was ruled a draw many believed Breland deserved to lose.

The Robinson comparisons ceased and Breland was left to reassemble the rubble.

But a funny thing happened on the road to redemption: Breland began to show the promise many saw in him. Four months after the Starling rematch, Breland dusted three consecutive opponents in a single round, the last of which was Seung Soon Lee for the WBA title vacated by Starling's successor Tomas Molinares. In his subsequent four defenses, Breland for the most part looked sharp and powerful against Rafael Pineda (KO 5), Mauro Martelli (KO 2), Fujio Ozaki (KO 4) and a badly faded Honeyghan (KO 3).

Because he no longer had to deal with the pressure of living up to the Robinson legend, Breland was free to showcase his considerable talent. At age 27 and in his physical prime, more sterling performances seemed likely.

Fresh off his destruction of Honeyghan, Breland signed to defend his title for the fifth time against fellow New Yorker Aaron Davis. Because Madison Square Garden was undergoing significant renovations, this New York turf war was moved to Harrah's Hotel and Casino in Reno, Nevada.

At age 23, Davis was making a considerable step up in competition. His best wins in his 29-0 (16 KO) record included a 10-round split decision over Horace Shufford, a 12-round nod over Luis Santana and a 10-round verdict over former WBA junior welterweight champion Gene Hatcher. Less than two months before fighting Breland, Davis struggled to a 10 round win over Curtis Summitt. Davis admitted he was caught looking ahead to Breland but the man billed as "Superman" promised he would be more powerful than a locomotive and make the giant leap needed to fly away with Breland's title.

As Davis awaited the first bell he bounced on his toes and made sure his left leg was slightly forward so he could immediately be in fighting position. Breland look relaxed as trainer Joe Fariello whispered last-minute advice outside the ropes over the champion's left shoulder.

Breland began the fight snapping jabs on the circling Davis, smartly using his five-inch height and seven-inch reach advantages. Because he moved forward behind the jab, Breland further magnified those edges and made life difficult for the young challenger.

With 1:38 remaining, Breland's dominance came to a sudden end as Davis fired a ferocious jab that caught Breland with his hands at chest level. The blow likely broke his nose and definitely buckled his legs. Breland grabbed Davis hard in a clinch and managed to hold on for nine seconds as the challenger unleashed two chopping lefts to the shoulder and a driving uppercut. After referee Mills Lane broke them, Breland threw a perfunctory jab and latched on again for another six seconds. As Breland sought the safety of repeated clinches, Davis worked hard to extricate himself, hurting Breland with a glancing left uppercut to the tip of the chin, a hard hook to the jaw, a hook to the stomach and a short left uppercut to the face.

As the round closed, Breland ripped a right uppercut at short range, but after landing he put his head down, tried to grab Davis' waist, stumbled forward several feet and fell to his knees. Upon resumption, Davis connected with two hooks to the jaw that drove Breland to the ropes, where the champion clinched the round away.

It was an exasperating start for Breland, who had tried for the past year to shake the images of the two Starling fights from the public's mind. In those bouts he floundered around the ring on disobedient legs, falling to the canvas after the slightest provocation. Davis was more than happy to take advantage of the situation but he couldn't do so because he chose to seek the one big bomb instead of building a foundation through combinations.

The fight may have been short on technique but it overflowed with competitive drive. In the final 10 seconds before the second round bell, Lane had to keep the fighters from prematurely resuming the action. Davis began well by landing two hard jabs and consolidated his advantage by mixing it to the head and body. Another jab sent Breland stumbling toward the ropes, touching his injured nose with his glove and forcing yet another clinch. As Davis connected with two more jabs, it was clear he had found a way to overcome Breland's anatomical attributes and exploit the champion's physical vulnerabilities. Every Davis blow made Breland's legs take on the appearance of a newborn colt. Yet while Breland's legs were shaky, his fighting heart was intact. He powered Davis to the ropes behind a sharp one-two and later slammed a hard hook to the ribs. Another left-right-hook volley sent Davis to the ropes, where two more hard hooks to the body followed.

Breland, with his left eye swelling underneath and blood covering his nose and mouth, closed the round strongly by landing his best right of the fight, causing Davis to fall into a clinch until the bell rang.

It is rare for a fight this young to evolve into a battle of attrition. Davis was breathing heavily due to a combination of nerves and his all-out effort to take Breland out in the first round while the champion struggled with a broken nose and failing legs. The sheen of physical skills had been stripped away with unusual dispatch, forcing both fighters to continue only with the force of will. All thoughts of a judge's decision were tossed aside as the boxing match turned into a legalized street fight. Both were fixated on hurting the other man with no regard for what they had to absorb to achieve their shared objective.

Still, both appeared fresher as the third began as each man's blows carried more speed and verve. Davis' jab connected more flush and with more impact but Breland's was more diversified as he used it to set up heftier blows. A strong left-right forced Davis back a step and the challenger's face began to lump up under the steady stream of Breland jabs, especially under the right eye. The challenger fared better in the final minute, looping in a lead right that forced a clinch and landing a strong hook to the cheek. A solid jab bounced off Breland's face but instead of clinching, the champion fired a solid right-left-right.

With 18 seconds remaining, however, the fight turned in a most violent way.

After Breland missed wildly with an awkward hook, Davis sent Breland stumbling to the ropes with a cuffing hook that landed more with the wrist than the glove. But a second hook cracked against the champion's face and a follow-up left-right sent Breland to the canvas. Up at two, Breland backed into the neutral corner. Blood was smeared all over his face and his mouth hung open, but he convinced Lane he was fit to continue. Fortunately for Breland, the bell sounded before Davis could launch another blow.

Between rounds, Fariello tried to encourage his charge by saying, "he's got a bad left eye. It's swollen shut….just stay with it, kid. Just stay there with him, all right? Stop the pulling out; stiff jab and a right hand on the way in."

Breland followed Fariello's counsel as the fourth began as he stood his ground and snapped hard jabs. Davis countered one of those jabs with a hook, but his follow-through wrapped around the back of Breland's head and the two wrestled to the floor. As the two exchanged jabs, it was clear Davis' was harder while Breland's was more frequent. They were also inflicting more damage, for the area around Davis' eye was not only swollen but also sported cuts above and below. Since the blood from the higher cut was dripping into the orbit, Lane asked the ring doctor to conduct an examination.

After the doctor cleared Davis for further combat, both men fought with more urgency. Davis feared his title challenge and undefeated record were in imminent danger while Breland wanted to preserve his title by any means necessary. Breland's face was not a pretty sight either as blood poured out of his nose and mouth, forcing him to gulp for air.

In the final minute, Breland landed his strongest hook of the fight, but Davis escaped the ropes and showed his bravado by rolling his gloves in a circular pattern. A huge hook that left Breland hanging on the ropes followed the showboat move, yet after the round ended, Davis tapped Breland on the arm to show his respect.

The swelling under Davis' left eye had become a blood-filled bubble and Lane had the physician conduct another exam, and the challenger again ratcheted up the aggression by throwing hard but inaccurate blows. Breland, however, was in his best form as he snapped jabs at the swelling and thumped rights to the body. He forced Davis to retreat the entire round, and though his legs still didn't look strong he smartly used his height and reach to dominate the round. As Davis took the blows he shook his head "no" but the ringside judges were probably saying "yes" when they marked their scorecards.

Breland continued to work the jab in the sixth but Davis, desperate to turn the tide, induced a clinch and hammered Breland with a left uppercut to the head, a hook to the ribs and two thundering hooks to the jaw as Breland hung on. One minute in,

Lane again asked for a check of the eye and as the physician wiped the blood Davis pleaded his case and won the right to continue. Davis cranked up his best hooks but they sailed harmlessly over Breland's head. The challenger smartly stayed on the inside, where Breland's long arms would be a hindrance. The infighting was often ugly and at one point Davis flung the champion to the canvas.

With 52 seconds to go, Davis slammed a right off Breland's cheek that caused the champ to take a knee. Because Davis helped Breland's fall it was not ruled a knockdown, but Breland was clearly hurt and Davis fired a strong jab and a looping right to the champion's broken nose. Breland retreated awkwardly and splayed himself against the ropes several times, and just like that the momentum had swung back the challenger's way.

Knowing this, Fariello appealed to Breland's pride between rounds.

"Let's find out if you're a champion now," the trainer said. "You're falling all over the place and it's all mental, Mark. It's all mental. You've got to pick it up, you understand? Let's see if you're a champion. You can *not* lose to this guy."

As another trainer chimed in with "he's more tired than you are," Fariello continued by saying, "He's shot, Mark. You've got to pick it up." Then kneeling and staring into Breland's eyes, he said, "Mark, listen to me: Don't give it up. I want you to give him a hard round this round. Go after him with your jab and fire your shots. Don't let him take the play and don't let him rough you up inside. It's all you, Mark, you've got to be a champion."

But it was Davis who tore out the corner behind wild hooks as the seventh began. Breland managed to return to ring center to snap his jabs and dig right uppercuts to the body when the action shifted inside.

"You really sense that both of these fighters are so close to the edge," ABC blow-by-blow man Dan Dierdorf observed. "Aaron Davis is so close for having that eye swell shut and stopping the fight and Mark Breland, I'm sorry, I still get the impression he's only one average shot on the chin away from going down and not getting up."

Throughout the first seven rounds, there was no letup in energy and intensity as both men expended their animosity. Breland ended a solid seventh by driving Davis to the ropes with a four-punch flurry and a searing hook to the liver.

Between rounds, the doctor again looked at Davis' eye and let the fight continue. Knowing that the next examination could be the last one, the challenger fought like a wild man as the eighth began. Davis shot out of the corner and landed a right-left to the body, and a second right-left sent Breland stumbling toward the ropes. A smashing hook snapped Breland's head straight back and a hook to the jaw forced the champion to clinch hard. Another searing hook caromed off Breland's head and Davis drove a vicious hook to the groin to get out of another clinch. Breland didn't complain and Lane didn't issue a warning.

In close quarters, Davis cranked a hook to the stomach, a left uppercut to the jaw and two whistling hooks. Another hook to the body and a looping hook to the ear connected as Breland broke the clinch. Somehow, the champion absorbed the punishment with aplomb and his durability would soon be rewarded.

After landing a hook to the ear and a solid jab, Breland's hook brushed against Davis' swollen right eye. The challenger's face showed distress as he raised his glove to protect it, and Breland jumped on the opening by shooting a left-left-right and a big hook to the jaw that drove a badly hurt Davis to the ropes. Breland fired a right to the body and a right uppercut to the chin that snapped Davis' head.

Breland, often criticized for his phlegmatic ring demeanor, unleashed all his weapons and all of a sudden it was Davis that had the look of a beaten fighter. A four-punch volley further weakened Davis, who spent several long seconds in a clinch. But Breland was also tired and he welcomed the brief respite. Both men had been hurt in the eighth and they were hurtling toward a competitive cliff. The only question was who would fall off first.

Between rounds Davis was encouraged by the brevity of the doctor's exam, for it indicated that the eye had not gotten appreciably worse. As the ninth began, blood poured out of Breland's nose and his left eye sported a small swelling – and this was the man who won the previous round. With a minute to go, Breland began to surge as a left-right backed Davis to a corner. The challenger drew in a deep breath, but sagged after absorbing a right to the body and a heavy right to the ear. It appeared Breland was finally asserting his dominance against this most stubborn challenger.

All that changed with 15 seconds remaining in the round. As Breland reached in to throw a right after his jab, Davis dipped to his left and uncorked a wild, looping overhand right that caught Breland coming in on the tip of his broken nose. He couldn't have been hit harder and Breland's weakened body couldn't withstand its effects.

Breland fell to one knee and collapsed flat on his back. Exhausted and damaged beyond description, Breland could only roll onto his right side before Lane tolled "ten" with a mere four seconds remaining in round nine. During the count, Davis walked two laps around the ring's perimeter and when it was declared over he jumped in the air and completed a somersault. He hugged trainer Billy Giles, then collapsed in a mixture of jubilation and exhaustion. At the time of the knockout, Davis led on two scorecards by one and three points while Breland was ahead by two on the third card.

"All losses are terrible," Breland said. "I take nothing away from him, he's a good fighter. He's just better than me tonight. I knew he could punch a little bit (with the jab) because he's a converted southpaw so the power hand is his left hand. I'll get in the gym and come back, maybe try to get a rematch. I'm not going to quit right now."

Before the fight, Davis openly and repeatedly questioned the former Olympian's fortitude but after experiencing Breland's talents first hand he expressed nothing but admiration.

"Mark is a great man," the new WBA welterweight champion said. "Mark had more heart than I expected him to and he did not quit because he didn't want to go back to New York a loser. But I'm coming back to New York a world champion…to the Bronx."

Epilogue: After winning the title from Breland, Davis notched a pair of non-title wins over Billy Durbin (KO 8) and Jorge Maysonet (W 10). His reign, however, was brief as Meldrick Taylor won his second divisional title by decision January 19, 1991. Davis competed for a title one more time, losing a majority decision to WBA junior middleweight champion Julio Cesar Vazquez in Monaco August 21, 1993. Davis won nine of his final 11 fights and ended his career on a six-fight win streak, the last of which took place July 23, 2002 when he captured a majority decision over Ross Thompson in New Rochelle, N.Y. The 35-year-old Davis retired with a record of 49-6 (31 KO).

Nine months after losing to Davis, Breland iced Ariel Conde in one round and followed with victories over Henry Anaya Jr. (W 10) and Julian Samaha (KO 1). But his momentum – and presumably his career – was halted after Jorge Vaca stopped him in six rounds.

Five years after the loss to Vaca, Breland launched a four-fight comeback that netted four wins. After decisioning Rick Haynes over 10 rounds March 21, 1997 in Jacksonville, Fla., the 33-year-old Breland never fought again, content he left the ring on his own terms instead of having another fighter force him out. Breland, who exited the ring with a 35-3-1 (25 KO), never reached the Robinsonesque heights predicted for him, but he earned a degree of validation by twice winning pieces of world titles, but more importantly conducting himself with class.

TALES FROM THE VAULT

Total Punches Landed/Thrown

Round	1	2	3	4	5	6	7	8	9	10	11	12	Total
Davis	20/38 53%	20/30 67%	21/38 55%	19/41 46%	13/37 35%	24/46 52%	21/44 48%	22/35 63%	12/29 41%				172/338 51%
Breland	18/50 36%	28/74 38%	30/70 43%	18/63 29%	26/70 37%	14/45 31%	22/65 34%	29/64 45%	11/52 21%				196/553 35%

Jabs Landed/Thrown

Round	1	2	3	4	5	6	7	8	9	10	11	12	Total
Davis	5/11 45%	14/20 70%	12/20 60%	9/21 43%	9/25 36%	6/11 55%	8/17 47%	1/2 50%	4/11 36%				68/138 49%
Breland	13/38 34%	16/40 40%	18/47 38%	14/46 30%	21/55 38%	6/27 22%	11/39 28%	5/21 24%	6/39 15%				110/352 31%

Power Punches Landed/Thrown

Round	1	2	3	4	5	6	7	8	9	10	11	12	Total
Davis	15/27 56%	6/10 60%	9/18 50%	10/20 50%	4/12 33%	18/35 51%	13/27 48%	21/33 64%	8/18 44%				104/200 52%
Breland	5/12 42%	12/34 35%	12/23 52%	4/17 24%	5/15 33%	8/18 44%	11/26 42%	24/43 56%	5/13 38%				86/201 43%

Aaron Davis vs. Mark Breland July 8, 1990, Reno, Nevada

Mark Kaylor vs. Errol Christie
November 5, 1985, London, England

The scene has played itself out many times before: Two people get into a street fight, only to be encouraged by a third party to settle their differences in a boxing ring. Usually this phenomenon takes place between a pair of ordinary citizens but when two highly regarded boxers are involved – especially when they happen to compete in the same weight class – the scent of big money tantalizingly hangs in the air.

In October 1985, middleweights Mark Kaylor (29-3, 24 KO) and Errol Christie (20-1, 19 KO) engaged in a very heated – and very public – brawl outside a gaming pub in London, and their fistfight inspired the powers-that-be to put together a 12-rounder for Wembley on November 5, 1985. The stakes were high – the winner would receive a chance at the British middleweight title, but more importantly to Kaylor and Christie, the winner would gain the upper hand in their personal war.

Their unscheduled tussle, and the subsequent media coverage, made the fight an easy sell and the fighters ended up splitting £82,500, a record for a non-title engagement. On fight night, a raucously pro-Kaylor crowd packed Wembley to see if their man from West Ham could give his opponent from Coventry his comeuppance.

The explosive atmosphere inside the arena was so incendiary that several security measures were instituted to prevent a potentially tragic turn. Police guarded every entrance to the building and more guards than usual were stationed around the barricaded ringside area. No alcohol was sold and the fanfare that accompanies most main events in England was kept to a minimum to keep territorial passions from being stirred further. Harry Gibbs, Great Britain's most experienced and respected referee, was chosen to control the match. There was enough tension as it was, and when the fighters entered the ring the chanting and cheers rose to a rousing crescendo.

As the introductions were read, Kaylor bounced on his toes and his laser-like glare bore into Christie. When his name was introduced, he took a couple of steps forward, raised his arms in the air and spun back toward his corner men. Christie was less animated, but no less intense.

Free to unleash their pent-up hostility, both men advanced quickly at the opening bell. Kaylor missed a lead left hook but connected with a close-in right to the jaw while Christie whizzed a home-run hook over Kaylor's head. Kaylor thumped a hook to the body after missing a right and Christie worked the jab well, landing three of them. Kaylor's eyes were aflame as he searched for an opening, and it took him just 20 seconds to find the one he wanted.

As Christie prepared to throw a jab, he dropped his glove to chest level and that hitch enabled Kaylor to snap over a right to the jaw that dumped Christie on his behind. The Kaylor partisans went wild as Christie regained his feet at two and walked unsteadily toward the ropes. Since there was no mandatory eight count, referee Gibbs immediately waved the two back together just six seconds after Christie hit the floor. Christie's only defeat was a 46-second blowout to Jose Seys and it appeared he might exceed even that mark of futility. Kaylor tore after Christie behind ripping hooks but Christie smothered his attack by moving inside.

Christie shifted to long range behind the jab and Kaylor, sensing his opponent had regained his equilibrium, decelerated his attack and concentrated on landing rights and lefts over the top but ended up wrestling on the inside. Christie landed a crisp jab, which set up a neat one-two to the face. After Kaylor connected with a lead hook to the solar plexus, Christie answered with another quick one-two and a counter hook to the body a few moments later.

After his terrible start, Christie fought with composure and his one-twos repeatedly sliced through Kaylor's defense. With 1:05 remaining in the round, one of those one-twos ripped through the guard and dropped Kaylor to his knees.

With the exchange of knockdowns, both men accomplished their first objective – getting their pound of flesh while wounding the other man's pride. Up at five, Christie charged in behind hooks and uppercuts while Kaylor initiated a brief clinch. Christie was throwing punches like a madman, but instead of using survival tactics Kaylor stubbornly stayed in range, ducking and blocking most of Christie's bombs. Kaylor wanted to show his opponent that he didn't need to hug and wrestle like Christie did earlier in the round. There were as many mind games being played as there were punches thrown and as the bell rang, Christie threw a left-right and Kaylor retaliated with a right clearly thrown after the bell.

It was a fiery first round that not only met but also exceeded the hype that normally surrounds a grudge fight. Both men hit the canvas and Christie already wore a badge of combat in the form of a cut left eye.

To protect the gash, Christie began the second on the move and landed a light left-right on the advancing Kaylor. They exchanged body hooks and a pair of Christie jabs set up a right that bounced off the temple. Kaylor's emotional intensity was obvious, but his ring work didn't reflect it as he let Christie dictate the pace with his smoother boxing skills. Christie used his quicker hands to connect with two jabs and a snappy one-two and another hard jab jerked Kaylor's head. In his anxiety to get to Christie, Kaylor was walking into punches and he was snorting through a nose that had undergone sinus surgery some time before.

After easily winning the second round, Christie continued to dictate the pace in the third, but as the seconds ticked by Kaylor began to do better work on the inside. Kaylor countered a Christie jab with a chopping right to the temple that prompted a clinch, and his hooks to the body were followed by several right uppercuts to the jaw.

Just as it appeared that Kaylor was regaining a foothold in the fight, Christie struck with a lightning lead right to the jaw that sent Kaylor on his back. This time, Kaylor took a full eight count and wasn't too proud to resort to clinching to survive. Up two-to-one in knockdowns, Christie moved inside and let the punches fly but Kaylor's well-timed clinches snuffed out any thoughts of a premature ending.

At ring center, Kaylor threw three swift jabs to set up a quick hook to the jaw, then moved inside and ripped Christie's body with both hands. The body blows in turn set up two solid hooks that snapped Christie's head and forced the Coventry man to start initiating the clinches.

With 12 seconds remaining, Kaylor countered a lazy jab to the shoulder with a sneaky right to the face and a driving hook to the body. Christie was desperately hurt as his upper body pitched forward and had he not fallen into a clinch his journey would have left him face first on the canvas. Just like Christie in round one, Kaylor overcame adversity to force his opponent into troubled waters.

The one-minute break did nothing to lift Christie's fog, and Kaylor cranked hooks to open the fourth. Kaylor was known for his tremendous hook, but it was a chopping right to the temple that buckled Christie's legs. Three more rights found the target and a fourth drove Christie to the ropes where Kaylor hammered him with a ceaseless flow of power shots. Christie appeared weary and clinched whenever the chance presented itself. Meanwhile, Kaylor sunk a hook to the ribs and a left uppercut to the jaw as Christie searched for an answer to his quandary.

The answer came in the form of fundamentals, for though he had a superlative knockout record Christie possessed good all-around skills. Despite being weary and hurt, Christie attempted to reassemble his offense by working behind the jab and concentrating on avoiding Kaylor's home-run hooks. As the seconds passed, Christie began landing more frequently. But great fights have an ebb and flow to them, and it shifts not only from round to round but moment to moment.

After Christie's boxing-oriented rally, Kaylor swung the momentum back his way with a stealthy right to the ear. As the bell rung, Kaylor rung Christie's bell with a crisp left uppercut-right hook to the jaw. His blood boiling, Kaylor unloaded another left-right as Gibbs moved in to separate them.

The obvious foul forced Gibbs to lay down the law, both to impose his authority but to also tamp down any retaliatory actions by Christie that might ignite the powder keg that was Wembley. Gibbs shoved Kaylor lightly and delivered a stern warning. Meanwhile, Christie wanted to settle the dispute himself and stood a few feet away from Kaylor and Gibbs, but Christie's second led him back across the ring to keep his fighter from incurring a penalty.

Kaylor sought to settle matters with his first punch of the fifth, a full-blooded right to the ear that caused Christie to hold on. Kaylor drove hooks to the body and head and two lead rights caromed off Christie's cranium. Rights to the head and body and a hook downstairs induced another clinch, and a right-left hit home for Kaylor. Christie held up well under the punishment as he attempted to regain control with stick-and-move tactics.

The fight's momentum was swinging in direct relation to the terms of battle – when the action moved inside, Kaylor's superior strength carried the day but when the two men fought at long range, Christie's sharper punching and maneuverability prevailed.

The combatants also invested a lot of physical and emotional energy in the first four-and-a-half rounds as they worked out their hostilities. One would think the action would eventually slow down, but their emotion-fueled adrenaline helped them sustain the hot pace. Still, Christie looked a bit ragged as he spun away from the ropes and Kaylor swarmed over him for the remainder of the round – and a little bit after. A split second after the bell, Kaylor snapped a left-right to the jaw and as Kaylor turned his back and walked toward his corner, Gibbs gave Kaylor a light backhanded slap to the neck to remind him who was the real boss in the ring. However, Gibbs showed restraint by not assessing Kaylor a point penalty.

In the sixth, Christie went back to boxing basics to regain his footing while the fiery Kaylor sought to press his advantage. Though Christie was landing his share of blows, they didn't have the impact of before and he had the look of a man who was fighting off a physical avalanche. A quick three-punch flurry stunned Christie but Christie bounced back with jabs and guts. A long right nailed Kaylor, but Kaylor countered with an aching hook to the ribs and a follow-up body flurry to end the round. This time, there were no round-ending theatrics from Kaylor, and it would not be a problem for the rest of the fight.

Christie worked the jab to open the seventh, setting up a sharp right-left and a strong right to the jaw. Another right cross twisted Kaylor's head awkwardly and, clearly hurt, fell forward into a clinch. Christie was energized by Kaylor's pain but Kaylor knew if he remained at close quarters, he eventually would break through with another fight-turning blow. A few seconds later, Kaylor's hunch worked to perfection as he ripped a three-punch combo that stunned Christie. An overhand right to the temple and a hook-right combo forced Christie to hold on, but when the fight shifted back to the outside a few moments later Christie's stinging right to the side of the head hurt Kaylor as the round closed.

The constant turns in momentum made predicting the result a perilous chore for those who had no money wagered and especially for those who did. The fight was seven rounds old and neither man had established a lasting control. Kaylor appeared to be the consistently stronger man, but Christie enjoyed more than his share of good moments. Time and again, the two men dug deeply to summon the energy to overcome their physical and mental fatigue.

It was almost inevitable that one man would step forward and claim his victory, and that step occurred late in the eighth. After an exchange of jabs, Kaylor smacked a counter right to the jaw and a follow-up hook that sent Christie heavily to the canvas in sections. As he turned over on his stomach, he nodded to his corner to let them know he was OK. But he clearly was not OK; though his face was bright and alert, his legs were dead and buried. He crawled toward his corner in the hopes he could use the ropes to haul himself upright, but he couldn't reach the strands in time. Gibbs counted him out at 2:35 of round eight and an overjoyed Kaylor skipped across the ring and mounted the ropes to revel as the crowd rapturously roared.

There was still the business of their grudge – did it still exist or did they beat it out of one another? After his brief celebration, the first thing Kaylor did was walk toward Christie's corner to give his valiant opponent a quiet word of encouragement, and a few moments later Christie's manager walked across the ring to kiss Kaylor's cheek. Christie himself, after being attended to by the ringside physician, arose and hugged Kaylor. It was clear their pitched battle enabled them to convert hatred into respect.

There is something about engaging another man in combat that enables him to form a bond that lasts a lifetime. More often than not, mortal enemies become friends because boxing allows them to get past the outer walls we all erect and access the contents of the competitive soul. Kaylor and Christie entered the ring as bitter rivals and the cauldron of their hatred created a potentially chaotic scene. In the end, however, all was forgiven and the animosity was washed away as the two men stood at center ring and held each other's arms aloft.

Boxing is often castigated as the red-light district of sports, but one of its unique virtues is that it can serve as a catalyst to settle differences that can't be resolved any other way. As Kaylor and Christie demonstrated, sometimes one has to wage war in order to secure a lasting peace.

Epilogue: Christie returned to the ring five months after losing to Kaylor, decisioning Hunter Clay over 10 rounds. Three more wins followed, including a decision win over former title challenger Sean Mannion. His next outing against Charlie Boston was a tumultuous affair as Christie climbed off the floor to deck Boston in the sixth only to be stopped in the eighth after suffering his fourth knockdown. Over the next three years, Christie went 8-4-1 (6 KO), and a three round KO loss to Michael Watson in 1990 effectively ended his career. The 30-year-old Christie fought once more 28 months after the Watson loss, with Trevor Ambrose knocking him out in two rounds on March 19, 1993 in Manchester. His final record is 32-8-1 (26 KO).

Even though he won the war against Christie, it would be more than eight months before Kaylor would return to the ring as he stopped Tony Cerda in six rounds. After climbing off the floor to knock out Tony Harrison in nine rounds, Kaylor challenged the 36-0 Herol Graham for the EBU middleweight title. A corner retirement following the eighth round ended his hopes of winning the belt.

Kaylor moved up to the light heavyweight division and found immediate success by scoring five consecutive knockouts. He challenged Tom Collins for the EBU belt but was stopped in the ninth with a single right to the jaw. Kaylor then dropped to the 168-pound class and after fighting Jerry Okorodudu to a 10-round draw, he lost a 12-round decision to EBU champ Mauro Galvano. He stopped future Thomas Hearns opponent Shannon Landberg (KO 6) and Roland Ericsson (KO 4) to set up a final shot at the EBU super middleweight belt against James Cook June 1, 1991 in York Hall, Bethnal Green, London. Kaylor, who had turned 30 just 22 days before, was TKO'd in six rounds and it would prove to be his final fight. His record stands at 40-7-1 (34 KO).

VENGEANCE IS MINE – GREAT GRUDGE FIGHTS

Total Punches Landed/Thrown

Round	1	2	3	4	5	6	7	8	9	10	11	12	Total
Kaylor	16/54	10/45	22/47	31/65	32/59	14/40	16/41	17/49					158/400
	30%	22%	47%	48%	54%	35%	39%	35%					40%
Christie	21/78	15/58	13/62	9/42	10/32	15/46	17/43	9/39					109/400
	27%	26%	21%	21%	31%	33%	40%	23%					27%

Jabs Landed/Thrown

Round	1	2	3	4	5	6	7	8	9	10	11	12	Total
Kaylor	0/7	1/6	2/6	0/0	0/2	2/10	4/15	4/16					13/62
	0%	17%	33%	0%	0%	20%	27%	25%					21%
Christie	9/35	6/36	4/27	5/21	8/22	10/26	8/24	5/28					55/219
	26%	17%	15%	24%	36%	38%	33%	18%					25%

Power Punches Landed/Thrown

Round	1	2	3	4	5	6	7	8	9	10	11	12	Total
Kaylor	16/47	9/39	20/41	31/65	32/57	12/30	12/26	13/33					145/338
	34%	23%	49%	48%	56%	40%	46%	39%					43%
Christie	12/43	9/22	9/35	4/21	2/10	5/20	9/19	4/11					54/181
	28%	41%	26%	19%	20%	25%	47%	36%					30%

Mark Kaylor vs. Errol Christie November 5, 1985, London, England

Rafael Orono vs. Chul Ho Kim II
November 28, 1982, Seoul, South Korea

Given the right circumstances, the desire to exact revenge can be a consuming force. When channeled correctly, dynamic events can be spawned while devastating — and even tragic — results can occur if it is pursued wildly and haphazardly.

In the larger arenas of life, Christians are advised to let God avenge their enemies instead of taking matters into their own hands. But in a sporting sense, there is no better arena to unleash pent-up anger than the one provided by boxing. The combination of one-on-one competition and the electricity generated by an enthusiastic crowd can produce an emotional explosion of nuclear proportions, and the cathartic feelings derived from successfully exorcising those demons can be just as powerful.

Rafael Orono was a swirling cauldron when he met WBC super flyweight champion Chul Ho Kim in Changchung Gymnasium in Seoul, South Korea. He was the personification of simultaneous anger, happiness and athletic focus as he awaited the opening bell, and the reasons for each state of mind were obvious.

First the anger: Orono was crowned the WBC's first super flyweight champion when he won a 15-round split decision over Seung Hoon Lee before his hometown fans in Caracas, Venezuela on February 2, 1980. On January 24, 1981 at the Plaza de Toros in San Cristobal, Venezuela, Orono made the fourth defense of the belt against the obscure Kim, who at the time was still two months away from his 20th birthday. Orono was coming off an impressive three-round blowout of the previously unbeaten Jovito Rengifo while Kim had rebounded from back-to-back blemishes to Yong Hwan Kim (L 10) and Kyung Ju Ha (D 10) with four consecutive victories over nondescript opponents within the friendly confines of South Korea. The Orono fight was the teenager's first outside Asia and through most of the first seven rounds the champion blunted the Korean's aggression with speed, movement and well-placed counters. Orono's dominance was such that even South Korean judge Hyun Sung Chung couldn't give his countryman a single round as his 80-75 scorecard was in line with those of referee Zack Clayton (80-72) and Angel C. Tovar (78-76).

Forty seconds into the ninth Kim rocked Orono's world in the worst of ways. As Orono backed to the ropes — a rare occurrence on this night — Kim landed a left-right-left to the body that made the champion suddenly turn away and slump to the canvas. The kneeling Orono, unable to catch his breath, could do no more than clutch his right side as Clayton counted him out. Twenty-five minutes of dominance was wiped out with a single combination to the breadbasket. But, as it turned out, Orono's agony was only beginning.

Orono and his manager Rafito Cedeno demanded a rematch, to which they were entitled due to the return-bout clause in the contract. But Kim's manager Ho-Yun Chun, knowing Orono would likely win a rematch even if it were held in South Korea, decided to make Orono wait…and wait…and wait some more.

Kim defended the belt against Jiro Watanabe (W 15), Willie Jensen (KO 13), Jackal Maruyama (KO 9), Koki Ishii (KO 8) and Raul Valdez (D 15) over the next 18 months to raise his stock in the boxing world. Meanwhile, Orono was left to seethe on the periphery of the title picture and he worked out his frustrations by maintaining an incredibly active schedule for a top contender. In a 16-month stretch, Orono fought 12 times and scored eight knockouts with his most impressive victories coming against former WBC junior flyweight champion Sun Jun Kim (W 10) and Oscar Bolivar (W 10). Though he decisioned both Kim and Bolivar the usually cautious Orono had adopted a far more aggressive style and the results were dramatic. Of the eight knockouts scored in his 12-fight stretch, five of them ended in either the first or second round. In the 14 fights he had before his first meeting with Kim, he had scored only one such KO.

The happiness for Orono (21-1 with 12 KO) came when WBC president Jose Sulaiman finally ordered Kim (19-2-1 with 9 KO) and Chun to honor the return-bout clause after keeping Orono in a holding pattern for 22 months. Kim and Chun's preferred course of action was a big-money unification rematch with Watanabe, who became WBA champion a year after losing to Kim and was 17 days removed from an impressive 12-round TKO over former two-time flyweight champion Shoji Oguma. In fact, Chun had flown in Watanabe and his manager Kiyoshi Yoshii to see Kim-Orono II as well as continue negotiations for Kim-Watanabe II.

Kim, 114 ½, began the fight bobbing and weaving to get inside the longer reach of Orono, 114 while the Venezuelan challenger tossed light range-finding jabs. Orono countered a light hook with a long, knifing left uppercut to the stomach and a jolting hook to the face that brought a concerned groan from the crowd. Another Orono hook landed on the ear and a rising left-right caught the onrushing Kim's chin. A sharp double hook to the body and head tagged Kim and a follow-up right lead from long range found the mark. Kim tried to bully Orono into the ropes behind two good rights to the body, but Orono smartly pivoted off his left foot and nailed Kim with a jolting left uppercut. After Orono avoided a lunging right to the body, Kim nipped back to long range and shook out his arms as if to loosen up a knot.

Orono was running on all cylinders as he landed a left to the temple and caught him coming in with another hook to the jaw. A lead right forced Kim to back away and two lead overhand rights pushed the champion off balance. A heavy right to the body capped off a dominant opening session for the challenger.

Kim and his camp quickly realized that this was a far different Orono than the one they defeated in San Cristobal. This was not the dancing master who depended solely on his mobility and quick hands. Now, Orono was willing to dig his toes into the canvas and let fly with all his might. Even the punches he missed were thrown with conviction, and, maddeningly enough, he remained as elusive as ever on defense.

Orono kept up the beat in round two, following his jabs with a right, then a hook-hook-cross that knocked Kim off balance. A hard jab snapped back the champ's head but moments later Kim managed to get inside with a right-left to the head and a right to the body that brought a disproportionate roar from a crowd eager to cheer anything Kim did. A cuffing hook backed Orono to the ropes, but the challenger drove Kim back to ring center with his own body hook. Orono followed a hard jab with a hook and a right to the short ribs.

After falling into a clinch – and as referee Rudy Ortega called for a break – Kim struck the back of Orono's head with a right, and the feisty Orono retaliated with a harder right to the jaw. The move brought a warning from Ortega but it also reaffirmed to Kim and his camp that Orono meant business and would do everything necessary to take back the crown he felt was his all along.

It was already apparent going in that Orono possessed the superior boxing technique, but the addition of well-channeled anger did wonders for the challenger's effectiveness as he continued to drive hard shots to all intended targets. Lead rights to the head and body sliced through Kim's defense while Orono used his legs to blunt the champion's charges. His jabs carried plenty of snap and enabled him to maintain his proper punching range while forcing Kim to lunge in time and again.

Kim was at a loss as to what to do. He lacked the height and reach to box Orono from the outside, but his attempts to get inside and work Orono's lean torso were smothered by harder, snappier punches thrown with purpose and precision. The only thing Kim could do is to do what he did best: Bob-and-weave his way inside, ratchet up the offense, and hope.

Orono opened the third throwing half-speed jabs to keep Kim at his preferred range, but Kim worked his way inside after slipping a wide hook and nailed Orono with a sweeping right that knocked the challenger off balance. An encouraged Kim rushed in but Orono cracked a right left to the body before twisting away. Kim hit the mark with a right to the body and a hook to the head, but Orono caught the charging Kim with a hook to the jaw while neatly ducking under Kim's right-left. Seeking a way to halt Kim's momentum, Orono returned to long range and began to shoot hooks. One whistling hook not only got Kim's attention but also halted his mini-rally as they returned to probing on the outside.

With 25 seconds to go, Kim absorbed a thumping hook to the body and decided to initiate a toe-to-toe exchange at close quarters, his best offering being a sharp right to the face. Orono responded with a left uppercut to the body, a right to the head, a left uppercut to the jaw and a right uppercut to the chin to force Kim to break off the exchange. Orono then chased after Kim, connecting on another right uppercut to the body to close the round.

Though Kim may have won this round (and Kim indicated as such by raising his right arm as he walked toward his corner) this sequence provided a valuable window into Orono's mindset. In the past, Orono might not have been willing to engage Kim in a slugfest but on this night he was willing to risk everything in order to achieve his objective. In addition to trading successfully with Kim, he then continued to pursue even after Kim voluntarily backed away.

Orono turned up the heat at the start of round four, closing the distance and letting his hands go. A hook to the jaw brought an ominous "ooh" from the crowd and a right uppercut to the body prompted Kim to back away and regroup. The champ tried to roughhouse Orono when he closed the gap, but Ortega swiftly warned him about grabbing the back of Orono's head, letting Kim know that he had little latitude while on the inside.

Orono got a telling clue to Kim's state of mind when Kim flinched noticeably from a feigned right uppercut. Still, Kim was willing to bull his way inside, and, after executing a dazzling series of bob-and-weave maneuvers, he landed his best combination of the fight. He nipped in behind Orono's left shoulder and connected with a lead right to the body, a hook to the head, a good one-two to the jaw and a right to the body. Orono responded with a hook, an overhand right to the head and a right that landed on Kim's belt line. Kim answered back with a one-two that produced a loud roar from a crowd that sensed Kim was about to get back on track.

Orono sensed that as well, so as the round began its final minute he shifted into an even higher gear by putting every ounce of power into each blow. A big lead right to the jaw and a whipping hook to the hip hit the mark and a follow-up hook strayed a bit low, drawing a warning from Ortega. But Orono wasn't concerned with niceties as he drove another heavy hook to the stomach following an overhand right up top. Orono swung a right to the ribs and slammed a hook to the jaw, after which Kim again was warned for holding behind the head. The challenger capped off an excellent down-the-stretch rally with a parting right uppercut to the chin.

Orono oozed confidence and the proof was his willingness to beat Kim at his own game. The Venezuelan had the height, reach and talent to outbox Kim and he proved as much in their San Cristobal fight. But it was another proposition entirely when such a fighter makes a conscious decision to go against his own nature and attack an opponent's strength. The fact that Orono was pulling it off had to have been a crushing psychological blow for Kim, but his champion's pride would not permit him to accept defeat without first giving himself a chance to turn the tide.

Orono began the fifth in a predatory mode as he pumped in punches that carried plenty of steam. The challenger wound up and delivered a Gavilan-like bolo to the body and Kim fell off balance after whiffing on a counter hook. Orono slammed home a one-two to the head after Kim reset his feet and just missed with a home run right uppercut.

One of the keys to Orono's success thus far was his ability to nail Kim with lead rights. This time he launched two of them; Kim managed to roll away from the first one but the second – launched while Kim was busy resetting his hands – exploded on his cheek, snapped his head and stiffened his legs. The impact was too much for Kim to take, so he turned away to his left toward the ropes and voluntarily fell to a kneeling position. Up at four, Kim turned toward Ortega with a pained expression.

For Orono, the moment for which he had waited 22 long months was finally at hand.

Orono chased Kim across the ring, his fists flailing wildly as the champion sought sanctuary near another set of ropes. Orono reset himself and then unleashed a left-right to the jaw that caused the champ to rebound off the ropes and then fall flat on his face. Kim groggily arose at five and glanced briefly away from Ortega to determine the location of the ropes. As Orono poured in punches, Kim looked almost helpless as he hunched forward at the waist. The challenger appeared to score knockdown number three after landing a hook to the short ribs, but Ortega called this tumble a slip. It looked like a hopeless cause for Kim as he still had 45 more seconds to survive.

Or did he?

The friendly hometown timekeeper rang the bell 42 seconds early, the instant Kim fell forward from a vicious hook to the side. Ortega waved off this knockdown and declared that the bell had saved Kim, after which he helped the champion to his feet and escorted him toward his corner. The timekeeper thought he might have been doing his countryman a favor, but all he did was delay the inevitable.

A ruthless Orono went back to work in round six, firing combinations at all targets. Kim was unable to do anything other than cover up along the ropes. A left uppercut lifted Kim's head and a chopping right to the temple brought it back down. A cuffing right to the ear sent Kim to his knees, after which Ortega walked to Orono and lifted his right glove.

For Orono, vengeance was finally his.

All three judges – Harry Gibbs, Mike Jacobs and Marcelo Bertini – scored the fight 50-44 for Orono. But for the new champion it wasn't about the points, it was about making a point. A point to himself – and especially a point to Kim.

"I proved I was the better man," a joyous, tearful Orono told Ring correspondent Joe Koizumi. "Kim's kayo over me was a fluke. I waited 22 months to meet him again."

"My mistake (was) going forward to counter Orono in round three," a disappointed Kim told Koizumi. "He was fast and powerful tonight."

Indeed he was. Orono was focused on regaining what he had lost in San Cristobal and he found his way back by digging deep within himself and imposing his will on a champion who couldn't have foreseen his change in strategy and temperament. For the first time in nearly two years, Orono had regained not only his title but also his peace of mind.

Epilogue: With his crown once again secured, Orono returned to Venezuela and continued his winning ways over the next 11 months as he steamrolled Pedro Romero in four rounds, decisioned mandatory challenger Raul Valdez and took out Orlando Maldonado in five. Orono returned to Asia one day short of a year after conquering Kim, this time going to Thailand to take on relative novice Payao Poontarat, who had won seven of his eight pro outings. The long, lean Poontarat scored a shocking split decision over Orono, winning eight of the 12 rounds on two cards.

Three 10-round decision wins set up a crack at WBA champ Khaosai Galaxy at Bangkok's famed Rajadamnern Stadium. The first four rounds were evenly contested, but the Thai powerhouse broke through in round five and scored a TKO. Over the next three years, Orono lost five more fights in a row, the last of which took place on August 13, 1988 in a bull ring in Cartegena against Daniel Blanco, who stopped the 30-year-old Orono in nine rounds. His final record is 32-8-1 with 16 KO.

Kim returned to the ring after an 11-month hiatus against Prayurasak Muangsurin at Taegu's Indoor Stadium. The comeback would prove to be very short-lived as Muangsurin won an upset 10-round decision, after which Kim announced his retirement. Even more surprisingly, the 22-year-old made his retirement stick, making him not only one of boxing's youngest champions but one of the youngest to leave the sport permanently. His record stands at 19-3-2 (9 KO).

TALES FROM THE VAULT

Total Punches Landed/Thrown

Round	1	2	3	4	5	6	7	8	9	10	11	12	Total
Orono	20/60	23/66	19/71	19/69	20/61	7/17							108/344
	33%	35%	27%	28%	33%	41%							31%
Kim	10/37	4/38	10/44	10/49	3/13	0/1							37/182
	27%	11%	23%	20%	23%	0%							20%

Jabs Landed/Thrown

Round	1	2	3	4	5	6	7	8	9	10	11	12	Total
Orono	2/25	7/36	3/39	5/30	2/21	0/2							19/153
	8%	19%	8%	17%	10%	0%							12%
Kim	0/8	0/10	2/17	1/13	1/4	0/0							4/52
	0%	0%	12%	8%	25%	0%							8%

Power Punches Landed/Thrown

Round	1	2	3	4	5	6	7	8	9	10	11	12	Total
Orono	18/35	16/30	16/32	14/39	18/40	7/15							89/191
	51%	53%	50%	36%	45%	47%							47%
Kim	10/29	4/28	8/27	9/36	2/9	0/1							33/130
	34%	14%	30%	25%	22%	0%							25%

Rafael Orono vs. Chul Ho Kim II November 28, 1982, Seoul, South Korea

Bruce Curry vs. Monroe Brooks
April 7, 1978, Los Angeles, California

Any veteran trainer will tell you that it is better to box with a relaxed body, a clear mind and an attitude of detachment. Focusing on the job at hand is crucial because a boxer distracted by intense emotions will most likely be carved up like a Christmas turkey and be sent spiraling toward certain defeat and humiliation due to the wildness borne of frustration.

But what would happen if both fighters entered the ring fueled by hatred triggered by shared experiences? What would occur if their fondest wish consisted of tearing apart the other man piece by piece before launching his head toward the Big Dipper?

When Bruce Curry (15-2, 9 KO) fought Monroe Brooks (37-3-2, 24 KO) on April 7, 1978 at the Olympic Auditorium in Los Angeles, the object wasn't just victory. It was their opportunity to inflict legalized violence on each other – and be paid for the privilege.

What madness could have occurred to transform a sporting event into a blood war? According to Jesse Reid, who was Curry's trainer and manager, it was a combination of competitive instincts – both in and out of the ring – a clash of personalities and a managerial situation that only stoked the fires.

At one time Thell Torrance and Henry Davis, who co-owned the Hoover Street Gym in Los Angeles, co-managed Brooks. But after Torrance returned from a trip to Mexico with Hedgemon Lewis, Davis unilaterally sold Brooks' contract to Jackie McCoy. Torrance learned of the news through TV reports and found them to be true after confronting Davis. Feeling betrayed, Torrance eventually severed ties with Davis.

Several years later, Brooks, who was still managed by McCoy, encouraged Curry to come out to California and join McCoy's stable. At first, the two were friends and they eventually shared an apartment. It was in this setting that the seeds of the feud were sown.

"They lived together in Los Angeles, near the Compton area, for nine months to a year," Reid recalled. "Monroe and Bruce sparred together and each thought they were better than the other. They also liked the same girl from Fort Worth. They always had a competitive edge with each other and there was a legitimate anger. Monroe eventually moved out when he made enough money to get his own place, but at the gym they were always at each other's throats."

The personal fury grew to the point that Curry could no longer stand having any ties to Brooks, including fighting under the same manager, so he went to Reid to change his situation.

"Curry wanted to get free of Henry Davis because he didn't want to be in the same stable as Monroe," Reid said. "Monroe had told Bruce to come out and sign with Jackie McCoy and Bruce ran into me knowing that I had fought for Jackie. Jackie thought Bruce wasn't the kind of kid he could work with, so Bruce, who read about me and what I had done for (light heavyweight contender) Jesse Burnett, begged me and kept asking me to become his manager. I got the price to where I thought it was fair, and for the first time in my life I bought a fighter's contract."

Both Curry and Brooks prospered in the years preceding their match. The 24-year-old Brooks maintained a busy schedule in 1978 as he had already recorded three bouts in the first three months. On January 19, he knocked out Mario Mendez in four rounds while he turned out Rafael Lopez's lights in three on February 22. Then on March 18, he halted Jose Gonzalez in two. Brooks was rated third in the world when he signed to meet Curry, and he was hoping the downward numerical string would continue, as that would mean he would stop Curry in one round.

The Curry bout was Brooks' second defense of the North American Boxing Federation junior welterweight title, a belt he won by knocking out Abe Perez in three rounds on December 1, 1977. That belt, along with his high rating, put him in prime position to secure a second world title shot. His first took place in Chiang Mai, Thailand on January 15, 1977 against WBC champ Saensak Muangsurin. Brooks blasted Muangsurin to the canvas in round three, but the champion rebounded strongly by decking Brooks in the 14th and 15th rounds before the bout was stopped with just 1:05 remaining.

Curry was equally active in 1978, though not as successful. On January 26, he traveled to Tokyo and knocked out Minoru Sugiya in three rounds and just nine days later – in Madison Square Garden more than 10,000 miles away – he lost a majority 10-round decision to Wilfred Benitez. The Benitez bout was a rematch of a highly disputed split decision loss that saw Curry score multiple knockdowns. Had New York's "rounds system" not been in effect Curry might have won the nod, but in the end the two Benitez fights were the only blemishes on Curry's ledger. Instead of brooding on the sidelines, Curry immediately returned to the winning column on March 18 by polishing off Luis Resto in two rounds.

The atmosphere inside the Olympic Auditorium vibrated with tension and excitement as the two men stepped between the ropes. The anticipation ran high because they knew that two explosive punchers armed with a white-hot hatred had the potential to produce unforgettable fireworks. Reid also knew this, and he told Curry that fighting with unchecked fury would interfere with the ultimate goal – victory.

"I told Bruce that anger will get the first guy beat," he said. "I told him he had to be under control for this fight. We knew Monroe would come after him, so I told Bruce to let him hyperventilate while you box him for the first four or five rounds. This was competitive for me also because Monroe's manager Jackie McCoy was my manager, and I was a young trainer coming up."

The fight began with the shorter Curry, 139 ¼, snapping out jabs while Brooks, 138 ½, threw jabs from a slightly hunched over stance. Curry connected with a solid right on top of the head and ducked under a chopping left-right. Curry appeared looser and fired his punches quickly and smoothly; conversely Brooks looked like a tightly coiled cobra anxious to strike at any moment.

Brooks cranked up a pair of hooks, but because he telegraphed them Curry nailed Brooks with an overhand right to the chin as he launched the second one. The prideful Brooks absorbed the blow unflinchingly and continued his pursuit. Curry landed a pair of glancing overhand rights and snapped in a jab. Brooks' hook to the ribs landed well, but Curry lashed back with a left that knocked Brooks' head straight back. The pair exchanged hooks but Curry followed his with a series of accurate jabs. As the round closed, Brooks connected with his best punch of the fight so far, a solid hook to the jaw. A split second after the bell rang, Brooks launched – and just missed – a second killer hook to the head.

Curry and Brooks decided to harness their competitive energy in different ways. Curry channeled his into sharper technique and finely honed reactions on defense while Brooks' emotions could be seen in every attempted blow. Each punch was thrown with the intent of inflicting severe pain; had Brooks had his way, he would have duplicated Jack Dempsey's performance against Jess Willard that saw him break the Kansas giant's jaw, ribs and cheekbone en route to scoring seven first-round knockdowns and a fourth-round stoppage.

Brooks began the second well as he landed a hook. But as he started to throw a second hook, Brooks left himself wide open and Curry made him pay with a compact counter hook that sent him flying to the canvas. Brooks hauled himself upright at referee John Thomas' count of three, but Curry got inside and cracked in an overhand right. Brooks cut loose with a winging hook that missed by a huge margin, and his desire to instantly make up for the knockdown transformed him into a wild man.

The follow through on one hook sent Brooks spinning to the canvas, and Curry stood over him with right hand cocked. Curry could have sneaked in a punch if he wanted to, but instead he allowed Thomas to pull him away. After Brooks regained his feet, Curry held up his gloves in "high ten" fashion and Brooks, somewhat surprisingly, accepted the gesture and tapped Curry's gloves. But that small sign of respect didn't stop either man from firing his hardest blows, and in fact the gesture settled down Brooks just enough for him to regain a semblance of his boxing self.

Curry snaked in a double jab-right cross combination followed by a solid hook while Brooks dove in behind a hook to the chest and beat Curry in an exchange of hooks. Curry nipped in and out, spraying in hard punches up and down Brooks' anatomy while Brooks drove in hard, but singular shots. The crowd roared as each man launched punches with full power, and as the round closed Brooks landed a hook, Curry popped in a straight right lead, Brooks connected with a hook that spun Curry sideways and concluded with a full-leverage left uppercut to the jaw.

Both men started the third boxing at long range, and Brooks was first to strike by catching a ducking Curry on the forehead with a left uppercut, a follow-up right to the jaw and won an exchange of hooks. Neither man was of a mind to hit singles and doubles to the gap; they not only wanted to hit home runs, they sought to rip grand slams with every punch. The difference was that Curry was more diversified offensively and defensively as he seized on every Brooks opening with hard, straight shots while also making Brooks miss by blocking, slipping and moving with a skill that belied his lesser pro experience.

Each fired in jabs to start the fourth, but it was Curry who doubled up. Neither man's jab was of the range-finding variety, they were thrown with purpose and carried hurting power. It didn't take long for the fight to return to its bomb-throwing template as they stood in front of each other and swapped heavy leather at close range, neither taking a step away from the other. Brooks stunned Curry with a close-in counter hook and followed with a hard right as Curry tried to strike back. Brooks' attack opened a cut over Curry's right eye, but instead of retreating to protect it he stormed back. Curry's overhand right brought a loud "oooh!" from the crowd – and a whipping right to the ribs from Brooks. A right uppercut-left hook salvo knocked Brooks off balance, but it was the blood around Curry's eye that prompted referee Thomas to halt the action.

The ringside physician allowed the action to continue, and Curry capitalized with a chopping right over a lazy jab and followed with a wide hook that wobbled Brooks. Curry rushed in with hands blazing, ignoring whatever blows Brooks managed to throw. A Brooks right to the body triggered a quick counter right-left, and Curry jacked Brooks' head with a jab. Brooks winged in a hook, after which Curry landed a right, and the round ended with a solid hook by Curry after taking a shoulder to the face from Brooks.

The hot-and-heavy action continued in the fifth, with Brooks pouring in power punches while Curry laid in wait, ready to pounce on every opening. As Brooks whiffed on a right, Curry stepped in with a short counter right that spun Brooks' upper body 90 degrees. The durable Brooks shook off the effects and kept charging in with little regard for Curry's power. At one point, Brooks barreled in with his face exposed, and Curry blasted in a lead right to the jaw. Brooks couldn't have been hit more any more impact, but he walked through it and continued to pursue and punch with fire in his eyes.

Because the action never decelerated, signs of a Curry weakness – stamina down the stretch – began to surface. Curry puffed heavily through his mouth and his guard dropped below chest level. He had invested a lot of energy in building his points lead and his body ordered him to take a breather. Brooks wouldn't permit it, and for the first time in the fight he began to dictate the terms of battle.

Brooks cracked a right to the body, pushed Curry off with his shoulder and drilled another right to the ribs. He bullied Curry to the ropes with a hook to the body, a right to the ribs and a hook to the head. Curry, now resting on the ropes, ducked under a right-left and unleashed a pair of stinging hooks. Brooks was undaunted, and he proved it in the final seconds by loading up and landing a huge hook followed by a second one moments later. Though Curry came in well under the 140-pound limit, getting there wasn't easy. And now, with Brooks weathering Curry's early assault only to come on stronger, there was talk around ringside that Curry had shot his bolt.

Curry opened the sixth on the move, biding his time and marshaling his energy, while Brooks was eager to expend his. Brooks fired a hook to the jaw, whiffed on one to the ribs but later connected on a pair of hooks to the head and body. Just as it appeared Brooks was going to consolidate his advantage, Curry instantly turned the fight his way when he nailed an off-balance Brooks with a right to the ear. Brooks sought to regain his equilibrium with a hook, but in doing so he left his head exposed. Curry stepped in the breech and connected with a big left that left Brooks' upper body splayed on the ropes.

Curry rushed in to finish the job behind a chopping right, but Brooks lashed out with his own flurry and the pair swapped power shots near the ropes. Most of their blows missed, but each one was intended to end the fight.

Though stunned, Brooks was so consumed with the thought of revenge that he sought to punch with Curry, not clinch. His persistence paid off when a body hook made Curry grimace and a hook to the face connected cleanly. Brooks slammed a right to Curry's ribs and ripped a left uppercut to the jaw, but during the assault Curry's mouthpiece dropped out and referee Thomas called time to have it rinsed and replaced.

It was a most fortuitous break for Curry, for Brooks was in the midst of his most sustained and effective rally. But when the action resumed, so did Brooks' surge as he won an exchange of rights. Curry, however, came out the winner when they traded hooks and a left hook-right cross combo backed Brooks away. Brooks doubled up with his hook but Curry answered with a flurry capped by a pair of sharp hooks. The crowd was frenzied as they ended the round with a savage exchange that lasted until the bell.

As weary as Curry seemed, the pace was also telling on Brooks, who at times fought with his guard down. Between rounds six and seven, Brooks was breathing deeply and had his arms draped on the ropes. Still, neither man was going to let a little thing called exhaustion get in the way of settling their mutual score.

Both fighters continued to fire hard in the seventh. Curry's punches were delivered quicker and with more fluidity while Brooks' swings carried plenty of pop. Brooks whipped in a hook over Curry's low guard but Curry struck back with a huge right cross-left hook combo that stunned Brooks and a follow-up cross-hook drove an unsteady Brooks backward. Brooks landed a double hook before falling inside, but pulled right back out behind another big hook. Curry answered with a hook, a right to the top of the head, an overhand right and a closing hook to the jaw.

Though Brooks was the one taking the punishment, he was the one coming forward, winging punches all the way. A hook and right landed well for Brooks, but a missed home run hook caused him to corkscrew his body wildly out of position. Curry pounced on the opening with a solid hook. Brooks absorbed it and bulled Curry toward the ropes and unleashed a storm of punches. It was truly caveman stuff as the fighters took turns hammering one another in a breathtaking exchange until the bell.

Between every round, the Olympic crowd gave Brooks and Curry a standing ovation. And why not; this was a fight that had everything a fan could want. This was no boxing match; it was a fight fueled by hatred, pride and courage and the winner would be the one who could summon up one final, fight-ending blow. A knockout was the only way this fight – and this feud – could end.

Curry appeared to gain a second wind in the eighth, and thanks to the work of Jake Shagrue, the cut around his right eye was no longer a factor. Brooks backed off and boxed more, putting more space between himself and Curry in an effort to regain enough strength for a big stretch drive. By using his height and reach, Brooks landed with improved precision. Yes, Curry was getting in his share of blows with his faster hands, but what course would the fight have taken had Brooks fought this way all along? Given the circumstances, however, a war was the only thing that made sense.

Midway through the ninth round, Brooks sought to catch Curry with a chopping right. But Curry slipped the punch, ducked inside, drew a bead with a right to the protective cup, planted his feet and uncoiled a short, crunching hook to the jaw just as Brooks cranked up his own wide hook. The massive blow to the point of the chin struck with perfect leverage and incredible swiftness, and Brooks fell to the floor just as swiftly. Brooks' head hit the canvas with a thud and his body formed the classic spread-eagle.

Few fighters would have the wherewithal – or the consciousness – to rise from such a fall, but somehow Brooks stumbled to his feet. His spirit was willing to fight until the bitter end, but his cloudy eyes and rubbery legs told a different story to Thomas, who immediately waved off the fight at 2:26 of round nine as Brooks fell backward into the ropes. At first, Brooks tried to argue, but as he pushed Thomas his legs gave way and he returned to the canvas.

Following a brief examination by the ringside physician, Brooks was helped to his feet and moments later a scene that no one could have envisioned before the fight played itself out – the two men were hugging and congratulating one another. Though still disappointed, the classy Brooks put his arm around Curry's shoulder and held up his left arm as he paraded his conqueror – who was now wearing the NABF title belt – around the ring.

"Monroe is a very experienced fighter and he's a good thinker, so I had to out-think him," Curry told CBS' Gil Clancy. "He was doing a lot of loading up and I was looking for a good counter punch, make him miss and get him with one of my good ones and I did. I proved myself and I deserve to get credit now when I fight. Right now, I want to fight Roberto Duran. This fight I was in good condition, but I think I was too anxious. I didn't overtrain but I was in good enough shape to put him out."

As Curry concluded his interview with Clancy, Brooks came up behind Curry, put his arm around him and patted him on the chest.

"(Curry) knocked me out, but Saensak Muangsurin didn't knock me out (despite the 15th round TKO). I predict that when Bruce fights him, he'd knock him out. Despite all the s**t we put on between the two of us, I have to confess, tonight he was the better man. Maybe the next time, I might be the better man but tonight he was the better man. I hope Bruce a lot of success in the future."

"Monroe, I thank you very much for the good compliment," Curry replied. "You were tough too, you were tough. You came out and you were loading up and I was trying to wait to counter punch and I caught you at the right time on the button."

"That's not it," Brooks replied. "If you catch a man, you catch him."

At least on this day, there was peace in the California valley.

Epilogue: Though Curry wanted to fight Duran after his knockout victory, it was Brooks who ended up fighting Duran. Following Brooks' knockout over Rafael Nunez, Duran vacated his lightweight title and stopped Brooks in eight rounds in a junior welterweight match December 8, 1978 at Madison Square Garden. Six months later, Brooks fought the 16-0-1 Ron Cummings to a draw over 10 rounds and talk of Brooks being washed up began to circulate. Brooks would prove the experts wrong as he ran off nine straight wins over the next two-plus years.

The resurgence landed him a crossroads fight with prospect Ronnie Shields at Dallas' Reunion Arena on May 8, 1982, with Shields winning a 10-round decision. Five months later he dropped a 10-rounder to recently deposed WBC junior welterweight king Saoul Mamby, a victory that earned Mamby a rematch with new champion Leroy Haley. The 30-year-old Brooks made one more return to the ring one year and five days after the Mamby defeat against Vilomar Fernandez on October 25, 1983 in Sacramento. The usually light-hitting Fernandez stopped Brooks in two rounds, and Brooks retired with a record of 48-8-4 with 33 knockouts.

After knocking out Brooks, Curry appeared to be a fighter on the rise. But his momentum was stopped cold as he lost his next two fights to Domingo Ayala (KO by 9) and Adolfo Viruet (L 10). Curry bounced back with decision wins over Wade Hinnant and Clinton McKenzie and followed with a two-round knockout of Willie Rodriguez to set up a confrontation with the surging Thomas Hearns on June 28, 1979 at Detroit's venerable Olympia Stadium. Though Curry opened a dangerous cut over Hearns' eye, Curry's all-out attack opened him up just enough for Hearns to blast him out in three thrilling rounds.

Curry rebounded with a pair of wins over Greg Stephens (W 10) and Jimmy Jackson (KO 7) but lost a bid to win the NABF welterweight belt when the 13-6 Greg Stephens stopped him in 11.

Curry continued his struggle upward, but a four-fight winning streak was halted by a seventh round TKO loss to Steve Hearon. But starting with a 10-round win over the 16-2 Mark Ibanez, Curry experienced a career renaissance. Wins over Edward Nuno (W 10) and Danny Favela (KO 8) set up a rematch with Shields for the USBA junior welterweight title and this time Curry captured a 12 round decision. Two fights later, on May 18, 1983, Curry won the WBC title by upsetting Haley. Curry made two defenses against Hidekazu Akai (KO 7) and Haley (W 12) before losing the belt by 10th round TKO to Billy Costello in a wild shootout. The 30-year-old Curry fought just once more, emerging from a two-year hiatus on April 29, 1986 to win a 10-round decision from Thomas Garcia in Arlington, Texas. Curry's final record stands at 35-8 with 17 knockouts.

Total Punches Landed/Thrown

Round	1	2	3	4	5	6	7	8	9	10	11	12	Total
Curry	20/61	28/71	14/57	32/75	16/55	31/77	38/89	24/72	5/35				208/592
	33%	39%	25%	43%	29%	40%	43%	33%	14%				35%
Brooks	12/41	10/43	9/46	25/59	23/45	26/55	26/61	17/48	10/27				158/425
	29%	23%	20%	42%	51%	47%	43%	35%	37%				37%

Jabs Landed/Thrown

Round	1	2	3	4	5	6	7	8	9	10	11	12	Total
Curry	10/40	4/31	10/41	10/35	5/26	2/25	8/25	5/37	1/26				55/286
	25%	13%	24%	29%	19%	8%	32%	14%	4%				19%
Brooks	5/21	1/20	2/28	8/25	5/13	3/7	8/30	13/41	8/22				53/207
	24%	5%	7%	32%	38%	43%	27%	32%	36%				26%

Power Punches Landed/Thrown

Round	1	2	3	4	5	6	7	8	9	10	11	12	Total
Curry	10/21	24/40	4/16	22/40	11/29	29/52	30/64	19/35	4/9				153/306
	48%	60%	25%	55%	38%	56%	47%	54%	44%				50%
Brooks	7/20	9/23	7/18	17/34	18/32	23/48	18/31	4/7	2/5				105/218
	35%	39%	39%	50%	56%	48%	58%	57%	40%				48%

Bruce Curry vs. Monroe Brooks April 7, 1978, Los Angeles, California

TALES FROM THE VAULT

Wilfredo Gomez vs. Derrick Holmes
August 22, 1980, Las Vegas, Nevada

Wilfredo Gomez is widely – and correctly – regarded as boxing 's greatest 122 pound champion. In his more than five-year reign he established an all-time record for consecutive title-fight knockouts with 17, a mark unlikely to be surpassed, and he did so with a devastating mixture of speed, skill and sock. Most of the time his opponents found themselves overmatched in terms of talent, with their only hope being that his battle with the scale would leave him too depleted to take care of the battle inside the ring. Unfortunately for his rivals at 122, that scenario never unfolded.

Gomez's dominance produced another potential enemy – complacency. The gulf between himself and his opponents was so wide that most experts wondered how he stayed motivated. Fighters such as Gomez needed goals beyond money to get his competitive juices flowing and push him toward prime performance, and most of the contenders couldn't offer him that. But when Gomez fought Derrick Holmes on August 22, 1980 at Caesars Palace in Las Vegas, the "Bazooka" had all the motivation he needed. The reason: Revenge.

In 1974, Gomez and Holmes met in an amateur tournament and the highly decorated Puerto Rican star was shockingly bombed out in a single round. It was one of only three defeats Gomez suffered in his 99-bout amateur career, which included gold medals in the 1974 Central American and Caribbean Games and the 1974 World Championships in Havana, Cuba. Gomez, who had lost a decision to Egypt's Mohamed Selim in the first round of matches in the 1972 Olympics, turned pro shortly after the World Championships because of financial necessity.

Now, six years later, they were fighting for a much bigger prize. At age 24, Gomez was considered among boxing's very best as he overcame a draw in his pro debut to register 29 consecutive knockout victories, including 11 since becoming WBC champion three years earlier to become his sport's new king of consecutive title-fight knockouts, surpassing Roberto Duran's mark of 10. Meanwhile, Holmes sported a 14-0-1 record, and his long, lanky build belied the 10 knockouts he had scored. Though he was a boxer by nature, he possessed dangerous pop in his right fist and he was not afraid to use it.

His past success against Gomez wasn't the only reason Holmes was confident, and in fact he had three more. First, he felt good about the bout's timing because he was set to celebrate his 25th birthday the following day. Second, he declared that if he dethroned Gomez, he would feel secure enough in his future to marry his longtime girlfriend Denise Harley. Finally, Gomez said that this would be his final fight at 122, which told Holmes – perhaps mistakenly – that Gomez's sights weren't fully trained on him, but on making weight and on his future as a featherweight. Gomez struggled terribly before tipping the scale at 121¾ while Holmes weighed a comfortable 120¼. The fight was part of NBC's short-lived revival of the "Friday Night Fights" series.

As the opening bell sounded, Gomez wanted to send a message that he meant business and he succeeded by immediately landing a left hook to the jaw. Holmes dropped his hands and shook his head "no" before missing with a pair of jabs. Gomez connected with another hook, but Holmes avoided taking the brunt because he pulled his head back in the nick of time.

Both men fought according to their builds in the early going as the lean, lanky Holmes stayed on the move and worked his jab to the head and body while Gomez stalked and studied. Holmes ducked under a lead right and responded with four quick jabs that set up a light right to the stomach. Holmes tried it again moments later, but this time Gomez deftly evaded every blow, showing off defensive skills not usually associated with prodigious punchers.

Gomez successfully leaped in with a right-left and Holmes answered with a pair of hard jabs, the last of which came after Holmes neatly ducked under a lazy hook. Several more jabs set up a fast right to the ribs. The challenger was boxing well, but he wisely resisted the temptation to go for the gusto early as he used his height, reach and mobility to create punching angles, pile up points and keep himself safe from Gomez's vaunted power.

Gomez flashed that power when a right to the ribs prompted Holmes to clinch and a lunging right-left caused Holmes to stumble back into the ropes. Gomez followed him, connecting with a right and pushing off slightly to create more punching room. But just as Gomez began to think about increasing the pressure, Holmes quickly proved to Gomez that he remained a dangerous proposition.

With a little more than a minute left in the round, Holmes followed two light jabs with a thudding right to the side of the head that stiffened Gomez's legs and caused his upper body to slump forward ever so slightly. Gomez tried to conceal his duress by dropping his guard and shrugging his shoulders but no one – least of all Holmes – was fooled. Gomez was in deep trouble, and Holmes took advantage moments later with another whistling right cross. Fortunately for Gomez, he was in good enough shape to shake off the bombs quickly enough to convince Holmes to let off the accelerator, and Gomez even ended the round with a short right and left hook to the face.

Both men started the second much as the first, except Holmes' jabs carried more snap. Gomez replied with a hook to the body and a right to the head that briefly knocked Holmes off balance. Gomez slipped a jab and nailed Holmes with a right to the jaw. As Holmes retreated to the ropes they both unleashed lead rights with Gomez's landing first and heavier. The champion then dropped his guard to chest level and tensed up as if he wanted to throw more bombs, but Holmes quelled the threat by landing a lead right and lunging toward close range. Holmes inched back and missed a sweeping hook but he then reset himself, poked out a range-finding jab and blasted Gomez with a hurtful right, his best punch of the fight so far.

But there would be more trouble for Gomez – much more.

Holmes got off his toes and began shooting rights to the body to lower Gomez's guard. The tactic worked as he deked a right to the ribs only to nail Gomez with a right to the jaw. Gomez drove Holmes toward the ropes by throwing a flurry to the body, but Holmes escaped and connected with a right to the head.

Holmes' confidence was growing by the second, and he showed it by abandoning his stick-and-move tactics and fearlessly engaging the powerful champion. His bold move paid big dividends with 20 seconds remaining when he threw two jabs to the head, faked a jab to the body and connected with an explosive right to the chin that buckled Gomez's legs and caused his upper body to slump. Surely memories of that nightmare in 1974 flashed in Gomez's mind as he tried to conjure a response.

Gomez was in desperate trouble, but he demonstrated championship instincts by fighting through the fog. He managed to grab Holmes, duck under a left hook, miss with a right over the top and connect with rights to the head and body. Holmes measured the champion with his left before just missing with a home run right.

The fight then took a head-scratching turn. The wild miss threw Holmes off balance and, with Gomez poised to take advantage, Holmes suddenly and voluntarily took a knee as the bell sounded. Though Holmes appeared stunned, it was Gomez who walked unsteadily to his corner. NBC analyst Ferdie Pacheco reported that Gomez appeared out on his feet and that his corner men spent the entire rest period working feverishly to revive him.

Despite the curious round-ending move, Holmes showed the world he was still capable of producing the magic that propelled him to victory in 1974. As Howard Cosell often said, there are horses for courses and styles for fighters. It didn't matter that one man entered the ring wearing the mantle of budding legend while the other languished in anonymity, for once combat began the past templates reasserted themselves. It's why Muhammad Ali had his Ken Norton, Jack Dempsey his Willie Meehan and Julio Cesar Chavez his Frankie Randall – and apparently Wilfredo Gomez his Derrick Holmes.

Holmes started the third strongly, smacking a jab to Gomez's face and nearly lifting him off the canvas with a left uppercut. Holmes moved his upper body side to side, whipped in a lead right and ducked under a Gomez hook. Holmes lunged in with a long right to the face that connected with impact, and suddenly Gomez was an open book for Holmes. Thoughts of a huge upset brewed in the crowd while Gomez struggled to find a way out of this troublesome thicket.

The confidence surged through Holmes, and he showed it by standing flat-footed and measuring Gomez with his left. Unfortunately for the challenger, it gave Gomez enough time to collect himself and find the answer he was seeking. After he slipped Holmes' jab, he sprang from his crouch and delivered a crushing right lead that sent Holmes falling forward to the canvas. It should have been counted as a knockdown, but referee Joey Curtis ruled otherwise and neither party objected to the call.

Holmes recovered well as he sneaked in a right to the face and a hook several seconds later, but Gomez struck back by flurrying to the body to set up a right-left hook combo to the head. Holmes' long right to the jaw prompted Gomez to lunge in behind a straight left that forced the challenger to clinch. Holmes' technique became more ragged with every passing second, and with a minute to go Gomez, who now sported a slight cut around his left eye, cashed in.

Gomez winged in a left that appeared to miss, but Holmes still crumbled to the canvas along the ropes and rolled on his back. This time, Curtis began a count, making up in some way for the knockdown he missed earlier in the round. Holmes arose at six, and Gomez powered in counter right-left over two missed Holmes jabs. As Holmes backed toward the ropes and covered up, Gomez connected with a swift left-right and a torrid pair of hooks that sent Holmes skittering away. Holmes missed with a wild right over Gomez's head and as the bell rung Gomez struck him with a final right-left.

Gomez's championship reign had been on the edge of extinction mere minutes earlier, but now he was in command as Holmes trudged to his corner.

A true knockout artist is at his most dangerous when he smells blood, and is even deadlier when the stakes are so personal. Any weariness he felt from the draining weight-making process and the hurtful blows he absorbed vanished, and he showed it by bouncing out of his corner at the sound of the fourth round bell and blasting Holmes to the canvas with an explosive hook to the jaw. With anger surging through his body, he dared Holmes with his right glove to get up as Curtis led him to the neutral corner. Holmes complied, albeit very slowly, at Curtis' count of eight.

Gomez blended savagery and science in his pursuit, mixing in shifty moves in both directions as he came forward to set up the perfect punching angle. Holmes tried to retaliate while on the retreat, but his blows no longer had threatening speed or snap. Gomez again flurried to Holmes' body – mostly with low blows – before flooring him for the second time with a right to the jaw, a right-left on the inside and a short hook. As Gomez backed away, he glared down at Holmes and begged him to get up with both gloves. Again, Holmes arose, this time at Curtis' count of five.

Though badly hurt, Holmes tried to fight back but to no avail. A sweeping, chopping right to the back of the ear produced the third knockdown, but since the three-knockdown rule was not in effect, Curtis was not obliged to automatically stop the bout. Up at five, Holmes was faced with the nearly impossible task of surviving 90 more seconds against arguably the best 122-pound puncher that ever walked the earth.

And worse yet, he was doing so with a broken jaw. According to Ring magazine, Holmes may have suffered the injury near the end of the second round, which might have explained why he had voluntarily taken a knee. One could also surmise that the massive right in round three that produced the "no knockdown" knockdown caused the break, but it didn't matter to Holmes when the fracture happened. All he was thinking about was survival.

A booming, full-bore right on the damaged mandible caused Holmes to back toward the ropes, turn his back and take a knee. Holmes' world was crumbling around him with dizzying speed: He had suffered a fourth knockdown of the round, his chances of winning a decision were destroyed, the crowd was booing at what they perceived was a lack of effort and his taunting opponent again stood over him. And there was still a minute left in the round.

Yet Holmes decided to fight on, this time getting up at three. Gomez slipped a jab, fired a lead right and connected on two more moments later. Holmes tried to throw a right but Gomez beat him to it and sent him spinning to the canvas for knockdown number five. Gomez looked over his shoulder and nodded his head in satisfaction before walking to the neutral corner, a place with which he was now intimately familiar.

With a justifiable 10-4 round staring him in the face, Holmes sat on the floor, his arms spread out over the second from bottom rope and seemed to be thinking whether getting up again was worth the trouble. He decided it was, arising at seven. He took a hook to the head, but managed to throw a whizzing right that threw him off balance. Gomez pursued, tagging him with a long right. As his round of horror neared its end, Holmes lunged in behind a right and clinched out the final seconds. As the bell sounded Gomez charged in menacingly and faked a hook-right before turning away.

With his dream plummeting into the abyss, Holmes tried his best to revive it early in the fifth. He threw the first two punches, a missed right-left, but smacked Gomez with a sizzling one-two that somehow carried the snap of the first three rounds. Fighting with extra energy and spunk, it was clear that Holmes was investing his final reserves into one last-ditch effort to hold off the avalanche. Meanwhile Gomez was biding his time and sizing up his prey, confident that he would soon produce the fight-ending combination.

A chopping right to the ducking Holmes' jaw caused Holmes to stumble away before regaining his balance along the ropes. A searing left-right-left-right crashed in and a big right to the broken jaw sent Holmes pitching forward for the sixth knockdown of the fight. By this time, the crowd was pleading with Curtis to stop the fight, and as Holmes arose at six his corner man was poised to throw the towel into the ring. But Curtis allowed the slaughter to continue, and Gomez gleefully raced in for the kill.

Gomez landed a right to the head and knocked Holmes back with a right-left. Gomez slipped the jab and connected with a perfectly delivered jab-cross-hook combo.

Another jab-right-hook smashed Holmes as he propped himself up on the ropes and a hook sent him careening to another set of ropes. Curtis was standing less than five feet from the action, yet he refused to step in.

A left uppercut sent Holmes scrambling away, but though his body was racked with incredible pain, his bravado remained intact as he threw in an Ali shuffle before Gomez closed in and continued his assault.

After absorbing yet another right, Holmes somehow plowed in a strong lead right that briefly stopped Gomez in his tracks. Any thoughts of a mind-blowing comeback evaporated when Gomez crashed in a right to the tip of the chin that sent Holmes, who was in the process of throwing his own hook, collapsing to the canvas. Holmes reclined on the floor, his elbows propping up his upper body, and chose to casually cross his feet. The fight, in effect, was over.

Holmes' corner stepped up to the ring apron, but Curtis wouldn't allow them to enter because he wanted to continue the count. Holmes did make it up, but at that juncture Curtis capped off a highly criticized performance by finally calling a halt at 2:29 of round five with Gomez's corner already parading their champion around the ring.

A physician who examined Holmes declared that the challenger had suffered the worst broken jaw he had ever seen, going as far as to say that tiny fragments of bone were falling inside Holmes' mouth every time Gomez struck him. How Holmes was able to function in that condition is beyond comprehension, but desire can carry an athlete past thresholds that even he could not have imagined.

The great thing about punching power is that it serves as the ultimate equalizer and the final word. It has the capacity to erase everything that had transpired and it replaces those images with a lasting aura of dominance. With Gomez in huge trouble and in danger of being knocked off his perch, he found a way to irrevocably turn the tide. That is, after all, the way of champions. And better still, it was the perfect way for Gomez to exorcise this ghost.

Epilogue: Holmes never regained the form that had him within a few punches of unseating the great Gomez, as he would only fight five more times before retiring at age 27. Holmes took nearly 15 months off to let his horribly broken jaw heal, and he returned to the winning track by stopping Jeff Roberts in two rounds. That was quickly followed by a 10 round victory over Kenny Mitchell less than two months later. But Holmes' drive for another title shot was irreparably harmed the following month when Franco Torregoza upset Holmes via eight round decision. Following an eight round nod over Donald Alston, Holmes would fight for the final time on September 15, 1982 in Madison Square Garden, where Paul DeVorce stopped him in three rounds. Holmes' final record is 17-3-1 with 11 knockouts.

Contrary to his pre-fight promise, Gomez defended his 122-pound throne once more before vacating, a third round KO over Jose Cervantes. Following a non-title three-round TKO over Raul Silva, Gomez met WBC featherweight champion Salvador Sanchez in a bout touted "Battle of the Little Giants." Many experts viewed Gomez as the favorite, but all that changed when Sanchez dropped the Puerto Rican star in the first round – breaking his cheekbone in the process. Though Gomez fought back valiantly throughout, Sanchez was too much for him and he registered an eighth round TKO.

Gomez then dropped back down to 122 and registered three more defenses against Juan "Kid" Meza (KO 6), Juan Antonio Lopez (KO 10) and an unforgettable war with Lupe Pintor (KO 14) before vacating the title for good. He went on to out-point Juan LaPorte to win the WBC featherweight title, only to lose it in his first defense via 11th round TKO to Azumah Nelson. Six months later, Gomez became a three-division champion when he won a highly controversial majority decision from WBC super featherweight champion Rocky Lockridge.

One year later, in his final appearance in a title fight, a brave but faded Gomez was hammered in nine rounds by mandatory challenger Alfredo Layne. Gomez fought twice more, this time as a lightweight, beating Mario Gonzalez in six rounds and Mario Salazar in two on July 19, 1989 in Hallendale, Florida. Gomez's final record stands at 44-3-1 with 42 knockouts, and he was inducted into the International Boxing Hall of Fame in 1995.

Total Punches Landed/Thrown

Round	1	2	3	4	5	6	7	8	9	10	11	12	Total
Gomez	14/35	12/48	29/74	27/53	36/72								118/282
	40%	25%	39%	51%	50%								42%
Holmes	22/66	17/77	11/54	9/44	10/47								69/288
	33%	22%	20%	20%	21%								24%

Jabs Landed/Thrown

Round	1	2	3	4	5	6	7	8	9	10	11	12	Total
Gomez	4/13	1/13	7/24	5/13	7/20								24/83
	31%	8%	29%	38%	35%								29%
Holmes	13/46	4/35	1/26	4/21	5/23								27/151
	28%	11%	4%	19%	22%								18%

Power Punches Landed/Thrown

Round	1	2	3	4	5	6	7	8	9	10	11	12	Total
Gomez	10/22	11/35	22/50	22/40	29/52								94/199
	45%	31%	44%	55%	56%								47%
Holmes	9/20	13/42	10/28	5/23	5/24								42/137
	45%	31%	36%	22%	21%								31%

Wilfredo Gomez vs. Derrick Holmes August 22, 1980, Las Vegas, Nevada

TALES FROM THE VAULT

Fernando Vargas vs. Ross Thompson
August 26, 2000, Las Vegas, Nevada

The act of striking another human being – even under the guise of athletic competition – is one fraught with emotion. It is not a natural activity, and most of us will go through life without having reason to hit or be hit. That said, we are still drawn by the prospect of seeing others exchange punches, and our desire to see it is heightened if the fight is fueled by passion, anger, vengeance or any combination thereof.

"Ferocious" Fernando Vargas was an athlete who possessed tremendous athletic ability amplified by a volcanic temper. As a 17-year-old amateur he was good enough to earn a spot on the 1996 Olympic team, and though he lost a debatable 8-7 decision to Romania's Marian Simion in the competition's second round, he was still talented enough to amass an excellent 100-5 record.

Once he turned pro in March 1997 he remained both precocious and "Ferocious" as he blasted out his first 14 opponents en route to winning the IBF junior middleweight title from Luis Ramon "Yory Boy" Campas in December 1998. Just days past his 21st birthday Vargas became the youngest champion in division history, but because he possessed charisma – that elusive inborn quality many called "it" – he had the potential of becoming a mainstream star. Successful defenses against Howard Clarke (KO 4), Raul Marquez (KO 11), Ronald "Winky" Wright" (W 12) and Ike Quartey (W 12) vaulted Vargas to the doorstep that would lead to that stardom – a unification showdown with WBA champion Felix Trinidad. The only man standing between Vargas and his big-money dream fight with Trinidad was IBF mandatory challenger Ross "The Boss" Thompson, who he met at the Mandalay Bay Resort and Casino in Las Vegas.

On paper, Vargas-Thompson was just another ho-hum showcase between a popular champion and a no-name challenger whose status as the number-one contender was questioned by most observers. The first point of contention was Thompson's inactivity – the Vargas bout was just his fourth in the last 34 months. The second was his level of opposition leading up to the fight as those four opponents – Leroy Owens, Thomas Cameron, Antonio Reese and Derrick Graham – were the very definition of obscurity. Finally, when Thompson did step up the quality of opposition, he lost. His three most notable opponents were Adrian Stone, James Page and Oba Carr – and they represented the defeats in his 24-3-1 (16 KO) record.

But in the days leading up to the fight, Thompson injected much-needed spice by firing a barrage of verbal bullets that struck the one place Vargas could not abide – his pride. He called Vargas "a bum" and "an ordinary fighter" who was "over-hyped." The hostility exploded at the press conference two days before the fight. While doing a television interview, Thompson was summoned to the dais. On his way, Thompson stopped behind Vargas, who apparently said something to him. Thompson responded by punching Vargas in the mouth and Vargas retaliated with a left hook that knocked Thompson off the dais. Once he recovered, Thompson went after Vargas again but his punch instead hit Vargas' promoter Gary Shaw. Both Vargas and Shaw suffered bloody lips and Thompson was asked by security to leave. The Nevada State Athletic Commission later fined Thompson $10,000.

Before departing, Thompson told the New York Times, "he's a bogus champion. All the reporters say I shouldn't be here. They haven't seen me fight. You have to understand that I have all this rage built up because of the disrespect put on me. I am going to win this world title."

Vargas, obviously, shared a different opinion.

"This guy is going to get punished before he gets knocked out," he told the Times. "I'm definitely going to carry him for a while. He's going to get hurt. He'll definitely get hurt."

Besides ambition and feelings of disrespect, Thompson had another source of inspiration. A member of a fighting family consisting of four brothers, he was the only one still active and he saw the Vargas fight as the fulfillment of a personal crusade. Two of the brothers were killed in separate incidents years earlier, and he told HBO's Larry Merchant that "we were all supposed to be champions" and that this fight was for them.

The odds makers, who have no room for sentiment, installed Vargas as a 30-1 favorite. But the pre-fight hostility invigorated an otherwise perfunctory exercise, and the cauldron of emotions extended to the moments after they entered the Mandalay Bay ring. As ring announcer Michael Buffer delivered his trademark phrase, the boxers taunted and gestured at one another and Vargas pulled away when referee Joe Cortez commanded them to touch gloves. Ever fair but firm, Cortez would not start the fight until Vargas reluctantly returned to complete the customary ritual.

Vargas started the fight quickly, rocking Thompson back several feet with his second attempted hook. After Thompson landed a jab to the stomach, Vargas drove him back again with a three-punch salvo. At long range, Thompson leaped in behind a strong hook and an overhand right that prompted Vargas to flash a rueful smirking smile. Thompson again lunged in with a left hook and a right to the body and missed with a long right and two jabs to the body moments later. Thompson's follow-up body jab and a leaping hook connected before yet another jumping hook-right-jab combo landed.

Thompson's tactics quickly became crystal-clear — standing at long range with his gloves at his waist, he used foot feints to draw Vargas out of position. If successful, Thompson then jumped in with quick yet looping punches that were both difficult to time and even tougher to counter.

Meanwhile, Vargas was surprisingly patient given his pre-fight fury. He did not race in recklessly and throw for the sake of throwing. His decade of experience in the amateur and pro game demanded that, and he realized that Thompson's tactics would take time to solve.

A short period of relative inactivity was broken with Thompson connected with a long hook to the body and missed a right to the head. Vargas ripped a counter right that forced Thompson to retreat to the ropes and the champion then ripped a five-punch flurry to the head and body. Thompson retaliated with a hook that whistled past Vargas' jaw but nevertheless prompted the champ to break off the exchange.

Back at ring center, Vargas smacked in a jab but Thompson did him one better with another leaping hook. Thompson tried another hook, but Vargas was ready with a right-left and a looping left uppercut to the body. In the round's closing moments, the first signs of Vargas' anger bubbled to the surface. An instant after Vargas landed a right, Thompson ducked inside and grabbed the champion's arm. Vargas swung his free left arm over the top and landed a pair of rabbit punches, prompting a warning from Cortez.

The second began with Thompson coming forward, landing a right to the ribs but whiffing on a hook-right-hook and a follow-up one-two. Thompson continued to jump in and out of range, but when Vargas tried it he was met with a solid hook. Vargas won an exchange of rights but Thompson connected with another lengthy right moments later. Vargas missed with a jab and Thompson replied with a wide swinging right-left to the head.

The fight's pace and geometry couldn't have suited Thompson better. After weighing in at 153 ½, Thompson entered the ring 30 hours later as a full-fledged light heavyweight at 173 and because he didn't have the foot speed to maintain constant movement he devised a fight plan that fulfilled his needs. Vargas, who put on 10 pounds after weighing 153, was more gifted by far but Thompson's tactics prevented him from drawing a bead. Thus the fight became one of brief herky-jerky skirmishes instead of crisp chain fighting. Both men were missing far more than they landed, but each punch carried plenty of venom. Still, Thompson's fight plan held down Vargas' offense as he threw just 64 punches in the first two rounds as opposed to the nearly 200 he unleashed in the final two rounds of the Quartey fight.

The third round saw both men flailing away, with Thompson getting in two hooks before falling into a clinch. In his mind, Vargas wanted to fight intelligently behind his jab before uncorking power shots, but the reality saw him ignoring the jab and missing more of his follow-up blows than usual because Thompson saw them coming. As the final minute began, Vargas broke through with a lead right but Thompson stopped the champion's surge by latching on and leaning forward. Frustrated, Vargas spun to the side and whacked Thompson with a pair of rabbit punches, prompting Cortez to take a point.

Vargas' anger had gotten the best of him in that sequence and he tried to make up for it by rushing in and landing a lead right, but Thompson managed to slip in a left hook that knocked the champion slightly off balance. For the first time in the bout, it appeared that Thompson's punch-and-grab tactics allowed him to gain a semblance of control.

However, a fight plan entirely based on unorthodoxy must be perfectly executed every second of every round, a tall order for anyone much less a heavy underdog against a talented young champion. With 28 seconds left in the round, Vargas provided a hefty dose of orthodoxy into the proceedings.

With startling speed, Vargas flashed a perfect left hook to the jaw and a follow-up right high on the head that sent Thompson tumbling to the floor. Thompson regained his feet immediately, but his eyes appeared slightly hazy as he took Cortez's mandatory count. Vargas charged in behind a right-left that drove Thompson to the ropes but Thompson clamped down on Vargas' glove and grappled with him in an effort to run out the clock. Vargas wrestled free and uncorked a six-punch flurry capped by a right and two hooks that floored Thompson at the bell.

The challenger arose at three, but because Thompson landed precisely where his ring stool would be, he nearly sat down without one underneath him as Cortez finished his count. Meanwhile, a pumped-up Vargas, uncertain whether the round had ended or whether Cortez stopped the fight, paced back and forth between the neutral corner and his own before finally sitting down midway through the rest period.

With stunning rapidity, Vargas had reversed the course of the contest and he was poised to act on his vengeance.

Vargas rushed out for the finish at the start of round four, but Thompson briefly stalled it with a clinch. Vargas broke free and continued his assault as Thompson tried to bob and weave from most of it. The two third-round knockdowns had taken much of the starch from the challenger and with Vargas so strong and surging with ferocity it appeared that it was a matter of when, not if, Vargas would end the fight.

Thirty-six seconds into the round, Vargas fired a quick hook-cross to the head – the same combination that produced the first knockdown – and the blows had the same effect as Thompson fell hard on his rump. With adrenaline pumping hard throughout his body and the heavily pro-Vargas crowd in full-volume rapture, the champion leaned over his prey, their heads inches apart, and screamed at him. Thompson's fury at Vargas' in-your-face gesture snapped him out of his haze and his face wrinkled menacingly before he arose at Cortez's count of four.

Unfortunately for Thompson, the physics of Vargas' punishment trumped his emotional desire to fire back. The challenger retreated to the ropes, and Vargas deftly created an opening by pulling down Thompson's left glove with his own. Through it, a snarling Vargas unloaded a venomous 11-punch flurry that moved Cortez to stop the fight at the 1:07 mark.

His revenge secured, Vargas proceeded to release his massive reserves of emotional energy. He leaped into head trainer Edwardo Garcia's arms and bellowed "who's a bum now? Who's a bum now?" in reference to Thompson's pre-fight rhetoric. He flashed the throat-slashing gesture several times and folded his arms in the classic menacing hip-hop pose. There were no handshakes or post-fight congratulations from either side in the ring because the emotional wounds were still too fresh.

"Ross Thompson said a lot of things that got me pretty pissed off outside the ring," Vargas told HBO's Larry Merchant. "But I've never lost my head inside the ring. I'm not saying outside the ring that I haven't, but inside the ring I've always been able to keep my cool. I know Ross Thompson's never been knocked out and never been down, and I think that shows what type of junior middleweight I am.

"He said I was nothing, he said I was no type of fighter, that I was a chump. I guess that this chump can fight a little bit," Vargas continued. "He disrespected me left and right and I showed what type of fighter I was. I had to show him that an Aztec warrior doesn't go down for anything, he goes out there and fights."

After leaving the ring, a humbled Thompson offered accolades for his conqueror.

"He's going to be one of the top fighters," Thompson told John Gregg of Boxingtimes.com. "His speed is much better than I thought he was. Fernando is a true warrior, a true champion."

The destruction of Thompson was the perfect lead-in for the showdown with Trinidad.

"I think I'm the best junior middleweight champion around and he thinks he's best," Vargas proclaimed after the fight. "There's only one way to find out. It will be like two lions fighting for two belts – his and mine."

Epilogue: Vargas got his mega-match with Trinidad on December 2, 2000 and the bout served as a microcosm for Vargas' talent and courage. Rising from two knockdowns in the opening minute, Vargas rallied to score his own knockdown in the fourth. The two traded bombs throughout, but Trinidad emerged victorious when three brutal knockdowns prompted Jay Nady to wave off the fight at 1:33 of the final round.

It could be argued that Vargas was never again the same fighter. Following two victories over Wilfredo Rivera (KO 6) and Jose Alfredo "Shibata" Flores (KO 7), Vargas secured his ultimate grudge match against WBC/WBA super welterweight champion Oscar de la Hoya. "The Golden Boy" broke open a close fight with a knockdown late in the 10th that led to an 11th round TKO.

Vargas, beset by an assortment of physical problems, nevertheless won his next four fights against Fitz Vanderpool (KO 6), Tony Marshall (KO 7), Raymond Joval (W 10) and Javier Castillejo (W 10) to earn a big-money match against Shane Mosley on February 25, 2006 at the Mandalay Bay. The first fight saw a surging Vargas lose by 10th round TKO due to a horribly swollen eye, but Mosley removed all controversy in the rematch five months later at the MGM Grand when a monstrous left hook led to a sixth round TKO.

Sixteen months later, the 29-year-old Vargas fought Ricardo Mayorga in another match fueled by mutual hatred and explosive emotion. Unlike the blood war with Thompson, Vargas ended up losing a majority decision, after which he announced his retirement. Should Vargas stick to his word, his final record is 26-5 (22 KO).

Thompson would fight just nine more times over the next four years, going 2-6-1 with one knockout. Ten months after the Vargas loss, Eric Mitchell stopped Thompson in the 12th. The lone knockout of the streak would follow nine months later, a one-round stoppage of Ron Johnston and the second victory, a six round decision over Sam Reese, followed fights with Aaron Davis (L 10), Jeff Lacy (W 12) and Shaun Creegan (D 6). Defeats to Levan Easley (KO by 1) and Antwun Echols (L 10) followed, future middleweight champion Kelly Pavlik scored an eight round decision victory that prompted a four-year hiatus. As of January 2010, Thompson's is 1-3 in his comeback, the most recent of which was a six-round unanimous decision loss to Daniel Sackey in October 2009, dropping Thompson's record to 27-14-2 (17 KO).

TALES FROM THE VAULT

Total Punches Landed/Thrown

Round	1	2	3	4	5	6	7	8	9	10	11	12	Total
Vargas													57/170
													34%
Thompson													85/224
													38%

Jabs Landed/Thrown

Round	1	2	3	4	5	6	7	8	9	10	11	12	Total
Vargas													14/61
													23%
Thompson													27/86
													31%

Power Punches Landed/Thrown

Round	1	2	3	4	5	6	7	8	9	10	11	12	Total
Vargas													43/109
													39%
Thompson													58/138
													42%

* Fight originally done by CompuBox, but the original HTML files with complete round-by-round statistics no longer exist.

Fernando Vargas vs. Ross Thompson August 26, 2000, Las Vegas, Nevada

Mike McCallum vs. Milton McCrory
April 19, 1987, Phoenix, Arizona

It was the spring of 1984 and Emanuel Steward had a decision to make. Two of his best fighters were in line for a bout with WBA junior middleweight champion Roberto Duran and each had a legitimate reason to fight him. His verdict would forever change the course of each man's career, and the situation he faced was a most unenviable one.

On the one glove was Thomas Hearns, the WBC super welterweight champion who at age 25 was at the absolute peak of his physical powers. "The Hit Man" (38-1, 32 KO) had won his last six fights since his lone loss, a 14th round TKO to Sugar Ray Leonard for the undisputed welterweight title, and he was fresh off a decision victory over Luigi Minchillo on February 11. It was the second successful defense of the 154-pound belt he won from Wilfred Benitez in December 1982 and he was itching for another big-money encounter. His freakishly tall 6-2 frame and 78-inch wingspan generated frightening power, the kind of power that keeps turnstiles turning and massive amounts of money flowing into the till. A title unification showdown with Duran would be a surefire winner at the box office because the bout would Hearns' iron fists against the fiery Duran's iron chin. From both an economic and athletic standpoint, Hearns-Duran made sense.

On the other glove was 27-year-old Mike McCallum, a 1976 Olympian from Jamaica who built a 21-0 (19 KO) record on body punching so savage that Hearns dubbed him "The Bodysnatcher" following a sparring session. Though his resume of opponents weren't as star-studded as Hearns' were, McCallum bowled over every foe set before him. His most notable victims were against 118-fight veteran Jimmy Heair (KO 2) and former WBA champ Ayub Kalule (KO 7). The Kalule bout vaulted McCallum into the world rankings and four additional victories over Tony Suero (KO 3), Jose Vallejo (KO 5), Manuel Jiminez (W 10) and Hasim Razzaq (KO 1) placed him as the mandatory challenger for Duran's title.

Duran had not made a defense since beating Davey Moore the previous June, though he lost a 15-round decision to world middleweight champion Marvelous Marvin Hagler in November. If the Panamanian wanted to keep his belt he had to fight McCallum – and soon. McCallum was ready and willing as the Razzaq fight had taken place on March 10, so the timeline was perfectly situated for McCallum to engage in a summer title shot against an aging icon. A victory, especially by knockout, over a living legend would serve as the ideal launching pad for the next phase of McCallum's career.

Those were the circumstances set before Steward, and in the end he chose to pursue the financial sure thing in Hearns-Duran instead of the speculative but calculated gamble that Duran-McCallum would have been.

An incensed McCallum immediately severed ties with Steward and signed with Main Events. Because the WBA stripped Duran for fighting Hearns instead of fulfilling his mandatory defense, McCallum was matched with number-two contender Sean Mannion for the vacant title on October 19, 1984 at Madison Square Garden on the undercard of Hagler's rematch with Mustafa Hamsho. McCallum thoroughly out-classed the Irish southpaw en route to a lopsided 15 round decision but his performance did nothing to increase his potential star power. Meanwhile, Hearns spectacularly stopped Duran in the second round with a right cross that still ranks among the hardest single punches ever thrown in the history of the sport. That performance heralded the return of "The Hit Man" and served as an immaculate prelude to a mega-match with Hagler.

While Hearns continued on his gold-plated road toward immortality, McCallum seethed about his lack of mainstream recognition as he knocked off challenger after challenger. McCallum topped Hearns by stopping Minchillo in the 13th round and he gained a small measure of revenge when he knocked out Kronk's David Braxton in eight rounds eight months later. That victory wasn't enough to completely salve the hard feelings against Steward because Braxton wasn't seen as one of the Kronkmaster's top-shelf stars. To get full satisfaction, he needed to blast out one of his big guns, and after defenses against Julian Jackson (KO 2) and Said Skouma (KO 9), McCallum got his chance when he signed to defend against Milton McCrory at the Pointe Resort in Phoenix, Arizona.

McCrory (31-1-1, 23 KO) was a former WBA welterweight champion in the midst of a mini-comeback after he was brutally stopped in two rounds by WBC counterpart Donald Curry on December 6, 1985. "The Ice Man" added weight to his 6-1 frame and won decisions from Keith Adams, Doug DeWitt and Jorge Amparo before stopping Rafael Corona in the first round six weeks before fighting McCallum. Likewise, McCallum (30-0, 27 KO) had tuned up for McCrory with his own first round KO over Leroy Hester in Kingston, Jamaica four weeks previously. The two fighters knew each other well as they had sparred several times at Kronk. However, both knew that there is a big difference between two teammates helping each other to get ready for fights and a fight between a champion hungry for recognition and revenge and a challenger eager to regain his lofty status in the sport's hierarchy.

Both fighters began the bout working their lefts from long range, but the straight-up McCrory was the first to build upon his jab by landing a long right and a solid hook to the jaw. At this point, McCrory backed up McCallum and a second hook made him retreat even further. McCallum slipped under a right and drove a hook to the side, but it was McCrory who dictated the pace and seized the initiative more often. A chopping right to the ear made McCallum's legs wiggle briefly and a right-left-right-left forced McCallum backward. The challenger took full advantage of McCallum's tendency to start slowly, and while the champion managed to land singular body shots with both hands from time to time, McCrory couldn't have dreamed a better start to his title challenge as he returned to his corner after the first three minutes.

McCallum's co-trainer George Benton also realized this, and he sought to give his charge a strategic kick-start.

"You've got to go forward with this guy," he said. "You've got to push him back with the jab. Jab at his chest, jab at his belly, jab at his head. Don't back away from this man; put pressure on him and make him back up."

McCallum, ever the good student, heeded Benton's advice as he stood his ground and sought to go punch for punch with McCrory. A pair of hooks sent the challenger stumbling off-balance across the ring before he awkwardly reached out for McCallum's shoulders. As McCallum advanced assertively behind hard jabs and hooks to the stomach, McCrory's punches looped instead of snapped toward the target.

Midway through the round McCrory tried to turn the tables by charging in behind windmilling blows, and though he won that exchange McCallum connected with two solid hooks that highlighted his superior infighting ability. A third hook landed moments later as McCrory flailed away with punches that had volume but little real power, but McCallum failed to consolidate his advantage by letting off the gas – a tactic for which he was heavily criticized against Mannion.

McCrory returned to jabbing busily in the third, but many of those jabs either fell short or fell victim to McCallum's excellent head movement. Conversely, McCallum's jabs were more powerful, precise and diversified. The evidence for that assessment was seen when McCrory pulled away from a successful exchange with a bloody nose, a nose that Steward later said was broken a week-and-a-half earlier. Though McCallum connected with a stiff counter right and a solid hook to the ribs in the final 30 seconds, the slower pace and the flow of the fight appeared to favor McCrory.

The bout may have lacked wildly dramatic ebbs and flows but it didn't lack for action as the pair engaged in an intense, well executed boxing match. Both fighters were operating from specific but divergent blueprints as McCrory sought to pile up points behind his long left while McCallum worked his punches up and down in the hopes of preparing his challenger for a late-round stoppage.

The fight took place within a tent with no air conditioning, and the combination of television lights and the body heat from the thousands of fans within sent the temperatures soaring toward 100 degrees. By the fourth, McCrory and McCallum were bathed in perspiration as they continued to probe for openings.

A long right-left from McCrory snapped McCallum's head midway through the fourth, and he furthered his advantage with a right to the body, a left hook to the jaw and a stinging right-left-left-right to the head. The salvo sparked McCallum into action with a right-left to the ribs, but at this point McCrory's hand speed and combination punching kept the champion on the retreat.

McCallum might have been losing the round, but he never lost his composure or his patience. Despite having scored plenty of early round knockouts, McCallum's style had always been predicated on long-term principles and he was willing to wait for the dividends. When McCrory threw combinations, McCallum made sure to sink a body shot or two into whatever holes McCrory exposed. In the midst of McCrory's best rally of the fight, McCallum knew his punches were inflicting damage and all the proof he needed could be seen on McCrory's face. More blood flowed from the challenger's nose, which caused him to paw at it with his gloves while breathing through a wide-open mouth.

For all his talent, McCrory never was able to adopt a stone-faced expression when he was in a difficult situation. In fact, ABC blow-by-blow man Jim Lampley said that McCrory sometimes had the look of "a frightened deer" when under pressure and now he was the very picture of duress as he dealt with his various injuries. McCallum may have been behind on points, but he was comforted by the fact that he had 11 more rounds to extract his pound of flesh.

Benton thought along those same lines between the fourth and fifth rounds as he instructed McCallum to slowly turn up the heat – and to do so while under control.

"Let me see you throw that straight right hard to the body," he said. "The body shots are killing him. Punch with authority; don't let your punches get sloppy and don't let yourself get sloppy. Get yourself together."

Benton's words didn't take immediate effect as McCallum's first punch was a winging hook to the body that missed badly while McCrory continued to move in both directions and throw tightly delivered blows with specific intent. At one point McCrory landed a long right to the face, then pivoted neatly to his right as McCallum dove in after him. The move made McCallum lightly bang his gloves together in frustration. McCallum ripped a hook to the body that brought a warning from Cortez, but in the next motion he blasted a hard jab off McCrory's broken nose. McCallum then ducked under a right and delivered a short counter right to the face that made McCrory briefly stumble. McCrory's nose leaked even more blood and the crimson began to smear all over his face as a hook forced him to backpedal.

The fight – which had been McCrory's up to this point – began to take a noticeable turn toward the champion, and confirmation came with 24 seconds remaining when he landed a good straight right, a right uppercut and a crunching hook during an exchange that saw McCrory miss wildly. A long straight right clanged off McCrory's face and McCallum capped off a solid final minute by winning an exchange of hooks.

McCallum continued to roll in the sixth as a heavy counter hook to the jaw brought oohs from the crowd and two more lefts connected to the head and body. McCallum ripped a jab to the body and two more to the head of the retreating McCrory. It was now McCallum who began and ended the exchanges, using his educated left to slowly dissect his quarry. McCallum smartly blended in occasional rights and right-lefts to the belly throughout the session and the champion capped off his best round yet when, with 10 seconds remaining, he landed two rights and a left to the body followed by a torrid hook as the bell sounded.

When McCrory dominated early, McCallum came back strongly and now a weakening McCrory was trying his best to stay in the fight. McCrory fired at McCallum at every opportunity, but he didn't have the firepower to keep the champion at a safe distance. A thumping right-left late in the seventh reverberated throughout the arena and a second right-left to the ribs coupled by a right-left uppercut to the jaw closed out another solid round for the champion.

McCrory tried to stem the tide early in the eighth with a stiff right to the face, but his follow-ups couldn't deter McCallum's inexorable advance. A right to the body followed by an overhand right to the jaw and a winging hook staggered McCrory and yet another overhand right nailed the challenger as he slid along the ropes. McCrory was in deep trouble for the first time in the contest and McCallum commenced what he hoped was a final definitive assault. His shoulders snapped violently as he unleashed a left uppercut to the head and a follow-up right-left-right. Three consecutive left uppercuts lifted McCrory's head, teeing it up for a tremendous overhand right-left hook combo.

McCrory bravely attempted to fight back because that was his only viable option. The champion's thudding body shots had robbed his legs of their spring, and all McCrory had left at his command were survival instincts fueled by a fierce fighting heart. One couldn't help but admire McCrory's courage as he continually drove himself forward in the face of McCallum's strafing attack. A right to the ear, a left uppercut to the jaw and a right-left to the face caused a stricken McCrory to stumble forward into McCallum as the round ended. The eighth was a rousing session that moved ringside analyst Alex Wallau to call it "one of the great rounds we've seen this year."

Between rounds referee Joe Cortez summoned the ringside physician to examine McCrory, who not only had a broken nose but now also had a nick above the left eye and a partially closed right eye. Cut man Ralph Citro applied Avitene, a medication used in open-heart surgery, to close the cut but it only provided a few seconds of relief as McCallum knocked it off with his first landed punch of the ninth round. The blood above the left eye flowed heavily and it forced McCrory to squint and bat at it with his glove. It was difficult enough for someone to fend off a skilled fighter like McCallum when completely healthy, but to do so when so badly injured was an untenable situation. Still, McCrory soldiered on as McCallum peppered away with short punches, and a piece of tape hanging from the challenger's glove prompted a time out.

Steward sagely wiped away the blood with a towel before working on the glove, causing Lou Duva, a man who has pulled off similar stunts to save his fighters over the years, to howl in protest. That sleight of hand aside, the fight started to take on an air of inevitability as McCallum stalked his man with assuredness, all the while driving lefts and rights to the pit of the stomach to further weaken his challenger. There was no quit in McCrory as he continued to trade shot for shot despite having every reason to feel discouraged and put upon, and only the bell interrupted his seemingly quixotic quest to reverse his fortunes.

The moment McCrory plopped on his stool, Citro administered to the challenger's injuries while Steward tended to the spiritual ones.

"You're ahead on points, you just got to move your legs," Steward implored. Then he drew upon past experience to amplify his point.

"(Like the fight with) Roger Stafford, move in and out with your legs," he said, referring to a fight when McCrory boxed his way to a decision victory after breaking his hand in the eighth round. "That's what we're talking about – leg boxing – not just standing in one spot."

"I'm trying," McCrory said. "I'm trying my best."

Indeed he was, but it wouldn't be enough. McCrory's spirit was willing but his flesh was weak as he started the 10th poking out a series of weak jabs. A jab to the body was enough to send McCrory to the ropes but the champion was taking his time as he allowed McCrory to escape and slowly circle away. A thumping right-left to the body was followed by a head-snapping jab that made McCrory totter back. A hook to the body moments later made the sound of a hammer on a hollow melon and it was evident that McCallum was biding his time, waiting for the perfect moment to launch his final assault.

With 1:20 to go, it began.

An overhand right drove McCrory to the ropes, triggering a vicious assault that ended with McCrory crumbling to the canvas. Though McCrory regained his feet immediately, it only took Cortez one look at the challenger's badly battered face to convince him to stop the contest at 2:20 of round 10.

As Cortez cradled McCrory's head, an exultant McCallum tended to a final piece of personal business. ABC's cameras didn't capture the event, but the announce team offered a vivid description.

"When the referee stopped the fight, Mike McCallum ran right over to Emanuel Steward and told him he had his revenge," Wallau said, referring to a shouted but unintelligble exclamation from the champion caught by the ringside microphone a few seconds earlier.

"(He) got right up in Steward's face," Lampley added. "It was a remarkable scene as McCallum wins a victory that he very, very badly wanted."

"The first couple of rounds, I wasn't getting off at all," McCallum told Wallau. "He was pasting me with that jab real good and throwing right hands that hit me a couple of times. But I was real cold; I couldn't get off. In the middle part I started getting myself together. Lou and George were telling me to stay right there, don't move, come back up, go to the body. Every time I hit him to the body he'd slow down or he'd flinch. It was beautiful."

A few minutes after the initial confrontation, McCallum and Steward spoke again, this time more amiably, but his post-fight comments indicated the bitter feelings had no subsided in the least.

When asked what he said to Steward immediately after the fight, he replied, "I said I am the champion of the world. Still the champ. I know he don't like that because it's very personal. He don't like losers and my revenge to Emanuel Steward is just keep winning. It's two defeats against the Kronk stable (Braxton and McCrory) and I'm still going strong."

McCallum stressed that he held no animosity for McCrory or with any of the fighters at Kronk, only against Steward. And when Wallau was asked about fighting Hearns to complete the triple play, McCallum was more than happy with that scenario. But before that fight could take place there was one significant roadblock to navigate – Donald Curry.

Epilogue: Three months after beating McCrory, McCallum smashed through the Curry roadblock with an electrifying hook to the jaw that left the former undisputed welterweight champion on his back for the 10 count. The victory dramatically lifted McCallum's profile in world boxing, but it was never compelling enough to draw Hearns into the ring. Soon after he defeated Curry, he vacated the WBA junior middleweight title to fight Sumbu Kalambay for the vacant WBA middleweight strap in March 1988. McCallum lost a close but unanimous decision but four fights later he secured a second crack at the WBA belt after Kalambay was stripped of it for fighting IBF king Michael Nunn. This time McCallum won by split decision over the much-avoided Herol Graham in May 1989.

McCallum defended the belt three times against Steve Collins (W 12), Michael Watson (KO 11) and Kalambay (W 12) while sprinkling non-title victories over Frank Minton (KO 4), Carlos Cruzat (W 10) and Nicky Walker (KO 5) to set up a supposed unification fight with IBF king James Toney. But McCallum was stripped of the WBA belt for accepting the bout with Toney and the 12-round draw left him title-less.

McCallum found new life in the light heavyweight division, and after three wins over Ramzi Hassan (W 10), Glenn Thomas (W 10) and Randall Yonker (KO 5), McCallum captured his third divisional title by beating WBC champion Jeff Harding (W 12) on July 23, 1994. He made one defense against Carl Jones (KO 7) before losing the belt in an upset to Fabrice Tiozzo (L 12). McCallum never again fought for a major world title and his 10-round victory over Ali Saidi would be his last one. After losing to Roy Jones in November 1996, the 40-year-old McCallum engaged in his final contest, a 12-round decision loss to Toney on February 22, 1997 at the Mohegan Sun in Uncasville, Connecticut. His complete record stands at 49-5-1 (36 KO) and he was inducted into the International Boxing Hall of Fame in 2003.

For McCrory, the McCallum fight represented his last opportunity to capture a world title. Six months after the loss, "The Ice Man" beat Herman Cavesuela to win the NABF middleweight title, a belt he never defended. After stopping Jerome Kelley in two rounds one month after beating Cavesuela, McCrory lost back-to-back fights to Lupe Aquino (L 12) and Joaquin Velazquez (KO by 7) that prompted a nearly two-year retirement. The 28-year-old McCrory launched a two-fight comeback that saw him beat Mike Sacchetti (W 10) and Robert Curry (KO 1). The Curry fight, which took place on April 6, 1991 at Honolulu's Aloha Stadium, took place on the undercard of Hearns' three-round TKO of Ken Atkin and proved to be McCrory's final bout. He retired with a record of 35-4-1 (25 KO).

VENGEANCE IS MINE – GREAT GRUDGE FIGHTS

Total Punches Landed/Thrown

Round	1	2	3	4	5	6	7	8	9	10	11	12	Total
McCallum	26/67	21/78	23/63	29/72	30/73	29/74	26/81	48/99	57/105	35/60			324/772
	39%	27%	37%	40%	41%	39%	32%	48%	54%	58%			42%
McCrory	24/95	30/99	12/91	29/93	13/76	9/60	16/72	17/77	18/81	7/45			175/789
	25%	30%	13%	31%	17%	15%	22%	22%	22%	16%			22%

Jabs Landed/Thrown

Round	1	2	3	4	5	6	7	8	9	10	11	12	Total
McCallum	14/40	5/30	10/37	13/33	14/41	20/48	12/50	8/32	13/27	14/26			123/364
	35%	17%	27%	39%	34%	42%	24%	25%	48%	54%			34%
McCrory	13/61	13/41	4/59	8/38	8/50	4/41	11/45	6/36	7/34	5/31			79/436
	21%	32%	7%	21%	16%	10%	24%	17%	21%	16%			18%

Power Punches Landed/Thrown

Round	1	2	3	4	5	6	7	8	9	10	11	12	Total
McCallum	12/27	16/48	13/26	16/39	16/32	9/26	14/31	40/67	44/78	21/34			201/408
	44%	33%	50%	41%	50%	35%	45%	60%	56%	62%			49%
McCrory	11/34	17/58	8/32	21/55	5/26	5/19	5/27	11/41	11/47	2/14			96/353
	32%	29%	25%	38%	19%	26%	19%	27%	23%	14%			27%

Mike McCallum vs. Milton McCrory April 19, 1987, Phoenix, Arizona

TALES FROM THE VAULT

Chris Eubank vs. Nigel Benn I
November 18, 1990, Birmingham, England

When two powerful personalities collide, no matter what the circumstance or venue, one of two things will happen. The first is that their combined talents will result in a sum that is greater than its parts, a collaboration so memorable that its legacy will far surpass the participants' physical time on earth (think John Lennon-Paul McCartney). The second, more unfortunate, result is that the animosity is so intense that it overpowers any urge to work toward the common good (think Don King and Bob Arum on most days, or congressional conservatives and liberals on all days).

Boxing can't exist without collaborations of some sort – after all, it takes two to fight – but unlike most real-life situations the sport actually feeds on conflict. If the public has reason to believe that the two combatants would like nothing better than to tear the other from limb to limb, all the better for everyone concerned. Such was the case on November 18, 1990 at the National Exhibition Centre in Birmingham, England when Nigel Benn put his WBO middleweight title on the line against Chris Eubank.

Both the 26-year-old Benn (27-1, 25 KO) and the 24-year-old Eubank (24-0, 14 KO) were a study in similarity and contrast. Each was Britons whose families had roots in the Caribbean – Benn from Barbados and Eubank from Jamaica. In their youths, they had multiple run-ins with the law, and boxing played a significant role in turning their lives around. Finally, both were intensely proud men who would rather die than submit to his opponents' will.

The differences, however, were stark. In the ring, Benn was a raging force of nature that possessed titanic power in both fists. After going 41-1 as an amateur, Benn turned pro and proceeded to live up to his nickname of "The Dark Destroyer" by knocking out his first 22 opponents, 19 of which fell in the first two rounds. Some foes couldn't even last a minute with the rampaging Benn; Ian Chantler went out in just 16 seconds while Leon Morris managed to stay 25 seconds.

The quintessential early Benn fight was his bout against Anthony Logan, a fight described by one observer as "The British Hagler-Hearns." Benn arose from a knockdown in the first round and was on the verge of being stopped in the second when he flattened Logan for the count with a sweeping off-the-floor hook to the jaw. Benn was a charismatic and emotionally charged warrior who stirred the fans' passions, and while he had an edge about him, he still became a fan favorite.

Conversely, Eubank was seen as a villain by most British fans and media. The man who dubbed himself "Simply the Best" was a careful, scientific boxer who fought only as hard as he needed to get the victory and nothing else. He didn't score his first knockout until his sixth bout and only had five in his first 14 fights, but in the 10 outings leading up to the Benn fight he experienced a massive power surge as he scored nine knockouts.

But the venom wasn't just inspired by his ring style, but also the way he behaved outside the ropes. His ring entrances were lavishly choreographed spectacles that ended with him leaping over the top rope and striking what he called the "peacock pose." Eubank consistently expressed his distaste for boxing, especially the business side of it, and that didn't sit well with either fans or with Benn, who radiated an unquenchable thirst for combat. He wore designer suits complete with monocle and gold-topped cane and indulged fully in the finer things in life – and he didn't hesitate to talk about them at length. He loved to philosophize on a wide range of subjects, even if his listeners preferred that he limited his prose to pugilistic matters.

His critics saw him as an eccentric snob and made fun of his lisping efforts to show off his vocabulary. His supporters viewed him as a badly misunderstood character that possessed – and acted on – deeply held convictions through his tireless efforts for charity. In their view, his perceived arrogance was really an unshakable self-belief based on hard work and results inside the ropes. Though he detested the business of boxing, he loved the science of it and the long journey one must take to achieve perfection in one's craft.

To describe Benn-Eubank as fire versus ice would be to understate the scope of their temperaments. A more accurate description would be a blowtorch versus a glacier, and the clash in personalities was on full display during the pre-fight press conferences. One famous episode occurred on ITV's "Midweek Sports Special" hosted by Nick Owen where Benn and Eubank sat next to one another along with Barry Hearn and Benn's manager Ambrose Mendy. Eubank sat with his back to a fuming Benn, who asked him why he would not look at him.

"I will look you in the eyes when I get you in the ring," Eubank replied. "When I finally do look in your eyes it will be when I am caning you."

Benn took every opportunity to express his burning – and genuine – hatred of Eubank, and Eubank admitted in his autobiography that it had an effect on him.

"Benn's approach was pure, venomous intimidation. And yes, it was terrifying; it felt very real," he wrote in "Chris Eubank: The Autobiography." "He was without doubt the most terrifying man I had ever met, still is."

But at the time, Eubank showed no signs of fear as he preened in his corner before the opening bell. On the other side of the ring Benn, his arms at his side, fired a heat-seeking glare as the 12,500 spectators crackled with excitement and anticipation. The first all British middleweight title fight established a record gate that exceeded 1 million pounds and the raucous crowd overwhelmingly was situated in "The Dark Destroyer's" corner.

Eubank threw the first punch, a fierce overhand right that just missed the ducking Benn, who connected with a hook to the body but missed the follow-up hook to the jaw. Eubank then skittered away as he missed a one-two and a right to the body. The combatants resembled tightly coiled springs eager to release their stored energy in the most explosive fashion possible, but each didn't know yet how to go about it.

Benn maneuvered Eubank to the ropes and landed a hook and overhand right following a missed right. Benn then skillfully weaved under Eubank's five-punch salvo and sprung forward with a hard jab as Eubank whiffed on a right. Benn advanced behind a cross-hook combo on the retreating Eubank, who again missed a swinging cross-hook combo before falling into an extended clinch.

Ironically it was the volatile Benn, not the cerebral Eubank, who was more composed in the early stages. His movements, both on offense and defense, were more fluid while Eubank's was stiff and inhibited. However, the clinch must have given him the time he needed to loosen up, for he broke away and landed his first good punch, a smacking lead right to the face. Moments later, Eubank unleashed a second one that made Benn's legs quiver ever so slightly.

Eubank smartly pivoted away from another Benn right, and suddenly the pace slowed to a level more suited to the thinking-man's challenger. Another Eubank right connected solidly and Benn was finding his foe a much tougher target as he glided around the ring. Two more lead rights and a hook tagged Benn, who loaded up with every punch only to find air as Eubank moved away. A frustrated Benn lifted Eubank on his shoulders after ducking a right-left, but the challenger stayed on course as he nailed Benn with yet another right lead. Benn connected with a hard jab as the round ended but Eubank landed one of his own a split second after the bell sounded. A furious Benn walked toward Eubank to confront him but referee Richard Steele jumped between them and guided Benn toward his corner.

Eubank, ever the psychological warrior, oozed confidence as he stood in his corner between rounds. He had good reason to feel that way, for after a cautious start he confirmed beyond doubt that he not only belonged in the ring with the most accomplished opponent of his pro career but that he had the tools to best him. Though he was a showman at heart, the realist in Eubank knew that he had to endure plenty of pain and punishment for the privilege of standing at his sport's pinnacle.

Both men threw and missed vigorously to start the second, but Benn broke the string of futility with a hook that ended an exchange and forced Eubank to back away. Eubank worked behind the jab but Benn came over the top with a solid right that brought a roar from the heavily pro-Benn crowd. Benn landed another right that made the skittish Eubank clinch and pull Benn down. Eubank then tried a five-punch flurry that Benn blocked with his arms, elbows and gloves, then it was Eubank's turn to show off his defensive skills as he rolled away from a big Benn right. Although each punch carried plenty of fury, they didn't possess world-class marksmanship.

As the two studied each other at long range, Eubank unleashed an eight-punch volley that included a one-two and a clanging right to the ear. Benn swiftly retaliated with a right to the body and an overhand right to the jaw moments later as the crowd chanted "NI-GEL! NI-GEL!" Both men planted to throw right hands but Benn's landed before Eubank could even pull the trigger. The blow snapped Eubank's head and bent his upper body back at an awkward angle, which told Benn all he needed to know about his rival's state. Benn cracked two more heavy rights as Eubank spun away.

Eubank knew he had to respond strongly if he wanted to convince Benn not to gun for the knockout, and he did so by keeping his hands moving, even if most of the blows missed the target. But he would top himself in a most dramatic way as the round began its final minute when a counter hook to the face and a right to the jaw turned the retreating Benn's legs to rubber. Another right sent Benn careening toward the ropes and Eubank stormed in with fists flying. He launched 14 unanswered blows highlighted by a right to the ribs, a hook-right combo and a final hook to the chin. At that, a clearly stung Benn roared out behind a pair of rights to the ear but Eubank spun him back to the ropes and fired seven more punches before Benn just missed with a ferocious uppercut an instant before the bell. At the sound of the gong, the pair stared at one another for a few long seconds before Steele again stepped between them.

Some grudge fights, like Terry Norris-Paul Vaden, never come close to matching the emotional heat outside the ring but after just two rounds everyone knew that Benn and Eubank had successfully translated their personal animosity into a pulsating passion play of skill and will. The contrasting styles and personalities produced a pleasingly explosive mix and the good news – at least for the fans – was that 10 more rounds were scheduled.

Benn still might have been stunned by Eubank's late-round assault but that didn't stop him from unloading fearsome looking bombs at the start of the third. Eubank coolly slipped and blocked must of them, but a left hook to the jaw and a left uppercut to the body broke through and made Eubank take a step back to collect himself. Benn then worked behind the jab and unloaded a hair-trigger overhand right-left hook over Eubank's jab that hurt the challenger badly. Eubank's torso pitched forward as he wrapped his arms around Benn's waist. Benn tore after his quarry but Eubank somehow landed a terrific right uppercut to the jaw in the midst of Benn's storm, which ended with Benn banging a solid hook to the ribs.

Each man winged hard punches even when the pace slowed, which didn't happen often. Eubank talked to Benn, who slammed a hard jab to the offending mouth and followed with a hook moments later. Eubank responded with a right to the body and a hook-right to the jaw and Benn answered that with a jab. Benn's face began to swell from Eubank's rights but, buoyed by his chanting fans, he remained the man who pressed the fight.

Eubank was quick to respond. A jolting jab snapped Benn's head and a beautifully delivered right uppercut rocked the champion. A second uppercut spurred Benn into action with a wicked overhand right. Eubank landed a right to the jaw that only stoked Benn's fire, which surged to the surface as he nodded his head, gestured with his gloves and uttered venomous words. Eubank correctly ignored the taunts and went about his work by snapping jabs and nailing Benn with an overhand right and a jolting hook that caught Benn coming out of his defensive tuck. Benn shook off the punch and delivered his own hurtful left to the face that buckled Eubank's knees. Benn followed with a strong right uppercut but Eubank ended the session with two more crunching rights to the jaw.

The two fighters' tense and taut faces wore expressions of intense concentration as the fourth round began, and it was Eubank who seized the initiative 35 seconds into the round with a ripping right to the jaw that sent sweat flying from Benn's head. Benn was struck with huge force, but the champion simply dropped his arms, nodded his head and slid to the ropes. Eubank wasn't fooled by Benn's show of bravado as he fired rights to the body and head as Benn bobbed and weaved. Benn lashed out with a smashing hook to the jaw that forced Eubank to break off the exchange, back away and slow the fight's pace to a crawl by standing motionless in front of Benn for four full seconds.

Eubank was fighting in sporadic clusters while a perpetually coiled Benn stalked, ever ready to unleash his firepower. That firepower would soon inflict horrific damage on Eubank.

A titanic right uppercut to the jaw ripped a massive cut on Eubank's tongue, and Eubank vividly described the effects of that blow in his autobiography years later.

"We were in a clinch and I had dropped my head on to his shoulder," Eubank wrote. "When you do that, your jawbone automatically opens. My jaw relaxed and my tongue slipped in between my bottom teeth and my top gumshield. At that exact second, Benn nudged me off his shoulder with a jolt and BOOM! He hit me with a mammoth right uppercut. The seismic impact guillotined my tongue with my own teeth, opening a deep, half-inch long laceration that immediately started bleeding heavily down my throat. I was drinking copious amounts of my own blood from that moment on."

The right uppercut and a hook to the short ribs sent Eubank stumbling to the ropes, where he immediately slapped on a clinch and caught a breather. A thunderous lead right deepened Eubank's duress but he recovered sufficiently enough to keep Benn from going all out for the KO. Instead Benn backed to the ropes, smiling and snarling as he evaded Eubank's blows. A right to the pit of the stomach forced Eubank to retreat but a snapping jab halted Benn's advance and enabled him to rest until the bell.

Despite the corner work of trainer Jimmy Tibbs and his assistants, the swelling below Benn's left eye continued to worsen and by the fifth it was nearly a slit. Eubank alternated between taking breathers and lashing out with one or two powerful shots to keep Benn occupied. A right landed directly on the eye and a follow-up left knocked Benn backward. Benn connected with a shotgun jab to the face but most of his blows were off target.

Meanwhile, Eubank's offerings were sharply delivered and painfully accurate. After a wild opening four rounds that accommodated Benn's chaotic ways, the fight now assumed a character that suited Eubank's approach. Though the challenger picked his shots with care, he still scored with definitiveness and searing precision. A piercing jab prompted Benn to bang his gloves together defiantly, but Eubank ignored the by-play and drove a long right, a strong one-two and an on-the-move jab to cap off a blueprint round.

Though the sixth began at a hot pace, the action soon slowed back down to Eubank's pace, allowing each man the opportunity to augment their physical assaults with plenty of hostile verbal and non-verbal flares aimed at each other's psyches.

A strong right stung Benn, who answered with a hook directly on Eubank's cup. The excruciating pain caused Eubank to drop to a knee as the crowd booed, mostly likely to chide Eubank for taking a time out instead of to protest Benn's foul. Eubank took a brief break, but Benn fired a second low left that forced Eubank to clamp on tightly as Benn hammered several rights to the ribs. Eubank darted out to long range and whipped four "in-your-face" jabs and followed with a chopping right to the ear, but Benn shook them off and continued to bang the body with rights. Eubank ended the round with a right directly on Benn's injured eye, which hadn't gotten much worse but was still nearly shut.

The pace picked up in the seventh, with Eubank stabbing Benn with jabs and the champion working hard on Eubank's body. With 49 seconds remaining, seconds after Benn unleashed another body barrage, Eubank connected with a tremendous one-two to the face that caught Benn coming in. A follow-up hook sent Benn wobbling to the ropes, but the ever-combative champion mugged at Eubank and dared him to hit him again – which Eubank did with a nine-punch fusillade. Benn smiled and yelled at Eubank to "come on!" as he danced around the perimeter. His eye had slammed shut, but he drove himself forward behind more thudding body shots – one of which strayed low and forced Eubank to turn his back and walk away in pain. Steele, who didn't see the offending punch, ordered Eubank to fight on and Benn whacked a right to the belt line and a glancing right uppercut to the jaw. A right to the ribs nearly doubled up Eubank in the closing seconds of another topsy-turvy round.

Encouraged by his late-round success, Benn charged out of the corner on stunningly springy legs and fired three hard jabs to the face to begin the eighth. Moments later,

Benn delivered a lightning bolt overhand right that landed high on Eubank's head and the challenger dropped to the floor. Eubank regained his feet instantly and yelled "Slip! Slip! Slip! Slip!" to Steele. As Steele administered the mandatory eight count, Eubank, resigned to the fact that the referee wouldn't change his call, nodded his head and told Steele he was fit to continue.

With a single punch, Benn had turned the fight and with his eye in a horrid state he knew the time had come to finish Eubank. A shotgun jab forced Eubank on his bicycle, but when he stopped and planted his feet he uncorked a pair of quick-fisted rights before returning to long range. A hurting left-right made Benn back away and gesture with his arms, and the crowd, sensing Benn was losing his chance, tried to lift his spirits by chanting "NI-GEL! NI-GEL!"

As the round began its final minute they stood at long range and rested. Benn broke the fistic silence with a long, flush lead right that exploded off Eubank's chin and a second right that glanced off the shoulder as Eubank leaned down. Eubank gestured that the punch was behind the head and Benn nodded at him. After Benn whipped in a right-left his corner pleaded with him to go for the kill but Benn hesitated, choosing instead to back away and feint with his gloves and shoulders. Eubank ended the stanza by landing a pair of one-twos that made Benn clinch the rest of the round away.

Entering the ninth round, the cards reflected the fight's constant ebb and flow. Judge Robert Balough had Eubank on top 76-75 but his peers John Stewart and Dalby Shirley had Benn up by the same score. Though the build-up of the fight suggested nothing but a knockout finish, the prospect of a decision began to enter many minds.

The action of the ninth round epitomized the bout's back-and-forth nature as each took turns seizing the initiative. Eubank continued to box while Benn remained eager to set up a fight-ending blow.

"This is the sort of fight that makes you an old man," ringside commentator Barry McGuigan observed. "There's only so many of these fights left in anybody, and let's not forget that Nigel Benn has had quite a few wars in the last few years."

Mere seconds after the former featherweight champion said those words they came to fruition. A searing jab-cross-hook sent Benn wobbling to the ropes on deadened legs and Eubank surged behind a 12-punch burst. The end was not yet at hand as Benn managed to clinch, but once Steele broke them Benn had nothing left with which to defend himself as Eubank crashed a huge right-left-right that caused Benn to slump into the ropes. That three-punch salvo had Benn in a nearly helpless state, and that prompted Steele to intervene at the 2:56 mark of round nine.

The realization of his dream had a profound effect on Eubank, who turned toward ring center, bellowed triumphantly, struck a pose mixed with pride and immense relief and dropped to both knees in thanksgiving. During the post-fight interview he proposed to his longtime girlfriend Karron, and he learned later that she was screaming "yes!" at the TV screen.

After a few minutes of recovery, Benn went over to Eubank and, at least for that moment, their shared rage turned to mutual admiration. It was another example of an enduring boxing truth: No matter how much one hates his opponent as a person, he can't help but give him his proper respect if he takes his best and still comes out the unquestioned winner.

Eubank may have received the victory in the record books, but on a larger scale both men emerged as winners because of the way they honored themselves during the course of combat. Because each man invested every part of himself into the fight, they produced a spectacle that will forever stand the test of time.

Epilogue: The two met again on October 9, 1993 at Manchester's Old Trafford Stadium and by this point both had captured belts at 168. Following the first fight, Eubank notched three defenses of the WBO middleweight belt against Dan Sherry (TW10), Gary Stretch (KO 6) and Michael Watson (W 12). He then captured the vacant WBO super middleweight title in a tragic rematch with Watson, who fell into a coma after suffering a 12th round TKO. Leading up to the rematch with Benn, he had defended his slice of the 168-pound belt seven times, all but one going to a decision.

After losing to Eubank, Benn racked up five straight wins to set up a match with WBC super middleweight champ Mauro Galvano, who he stopped in four rounds on cuts. Three defenses against Nicky Piper (KO 11), Galvano (W 12) and Lou Gent (KO 4) set up the second superbout with Eubank, which ended in an unsatisfying draw that many thought Benn deserved to win.

Eubank extended his reign to 14 defenses and his unbeaten streak to 43 fights before finally losing by decision to Steve Collins. Following two one-round knockouts over Bruno Godoy and Jose Ignacio Barruetabena, Eubank lost the rematch to Collins, this time by split decision. After two more tune-up wins, Eubank made one more attempt to win the WBO super middleweight title, this time against Joe Calzaghe for the vacant belt. Dropped in the opening seconds, Eubank lost a lopsided decision.

In the six months that followed, Eubank astonishingly put on 19 pounds of muscle and put forth two stirring challenges of WBO cruiserweight champion Carl Thompson, who defeated Eubank by a razor-thin unanimous decision and a 10th round TKO prompted by Eubank's swollen shut left eye. The 31-year-old Eubank retired following the July 18, 1998 rematch in Sheffield with a record of 45-5-2 (23 KO).

As tragedy had once touched Eubank in his rematch with Michael Watson, so it would be with Benn. Following successful defenses against Henry Wharton (W 12) and Juan Carlos Gimenez (W 12), Benn scored a riveting off-the-floor knockout of Gerald McClellan on February 25, 1995. But the joy of his upset victory was forever extinguished after McClellan suffered permanent brain injuries. Still, he soldiered on by scoring knockout wins over Vincenzo Nardiello and Danny Perez.

Like Eubank, Benn lost his last three bouts to Thulane "Sugar Boy" Malinga (L 12) and Steve Collins (KO by 4, KO by 6). The 32-year-old "Dark Destroyer" left the ring with a record of 42-5-1 (35 KO).

Total Punches Landed/Thrown

Round	1	2	3	4	5	6	7	8	9	10	11	12	Total
Eubank	22/64	25/76	19/57	15/54	17/47	15/36	13/45	14/43	22/59				162/481
	34%	33%	33%	28%	36%	42%	29%	33%	37%				34%
Benn	14/41	20/48	22/58	21/53	10/28	19/40	26/58	17/39	14/44				163/409
	34%	42%	38%	40%	36%	48%	45%	44%	32%				40%

Jabs Landed/Thrown

Round	1	2	3	4	5	6	7	8	9	10	11	12	Total
Eubank	8/21	2/16	6/18	6/21	11/27	10/23	6/24	7/27	11/32				67/209
	38%	12%	33%	29%	41%	43%	25%	26%	34%				32%
Benn	3/15	2/9	9/19	3/14	4/7	3/8	0/8	7/14	1/7				32/101
	20%	22%	47%	21%	57%	38%	0%	50%	14%				32%

Power Punches Landed/Thrown

Round	1	2	3	4	5	6	7	8	9	10	11	12	Total
Eubank	14/43	23/60	13/39	9/33	6/20	5/13	7/21	7/16	11/27				95/272
	33%	38%	33%	27%	30%	38%	33%	44%	41%				35%
Benn	11/26	18/39	13/39	18/39	6/21	16/32	26/50	10/25	13/37				131/308
	42%	46%	33%	46%	29%	50%	52%	40%	35%				43%

Chris Eubank vs. Nigel Benn I November 18, 1990, Birmingham, England

★ Chapter 7 ★
LITTLE BIG MEN

TALES FROM THE VAULT

Ricardo Lopez vs. Rosendo Alvarez II
November 13, 1998, Las Vegas, Nevada

For boxing's lighter men, the battle with the scale can be as fierce as the one inside the ring. Even so, the vast majority of championship weigh-ins are routine affairs that see every fighter scaling at or under the limit.

But every once in a while weigh-ins become much more than ceremonial, as the fiasco surrounding the weigh-in of Jose Luis Castillo and Diego Corrales the second time around proved. Though the in-ring action was as good – if not better – than the classic first fight, Castillo-Corrales II will always have a cloud hanging over it because of Castillo's inability (and some say unwillingness) to make 135.

The rematch between Ricardo Lopez and Rosendo Alvarez November 13, 1998 at the Hilton Hotel in Las Vegas, shares many parallels with the Castillo-Corrales rematch. Both fights were for a unified title, one man reported to the scales grossly overweight, the other fighter insisted on letting the bout proceed as scheduled and the fans were treated to a action-packed brawl.

By the time Lopez-Alvarez II took place, the 31-year-old Mexican (46-0-1, 35 KO) was approaching legendary status. Lopez had defended his WBC strawweight title 21 times since knocking out Hideyuki Ohashi in five rounds October 25, 1990. Though he carried immense power in both fists, Lopez was a supreme craftsman who kept his hands high at all times – even while awaiting the bell before each round. He moved fluidly in both directions, utilized subtle upper-body movement and almost always unleashed his bombs in combination. His skills were such that Lopez was a staple of Don King's pay-per-view undercards in the mid-1990s. Most experts not only considered him one of the sport's top pound-for-pound fighters, but also one of the most technically perfect fighters who ever lived.

The 28-year-old Alvarez, on the other hand, toiled in relative obscurity but those who saw him realized he represented a serious challenge to Lopez's dominance. He beat Chana Porpaoin by split decision in Thailand to win the WBA minimumweight title in 1995 and in his first defense, he scored a third-round KO over Kermin Guardia, who gave Lopez one of his tougher fights before dropping a decision 10 months before. Though Alvarez (24-0-1, 16 KO) was an aggressor who looked for the knockout, he went about his business scientifically by throwing sharp jabs and brutally effective combinations to the head and body.

A showdown between the world's best 108-pound fighters was inevitable, and the pair's first match on March 7, 1998 at the Plaza de Toros in Mexico City did not disappoint as long as it lasted. The ending was another story.

Alvarez dropped Lopez for the first time in his boxing career, amateur or pro, with an overhand right to the jaw in round two and they exchanged evenly until an accidental butt opened a large gash over Lopez's right eye. The cut was deemed too severe for Lopez to continue, and WBC rules dictated that Alvarez, the uncut fighter, be penalized a point. The deduction proved decisive as Tom Kaczmarek saw the fight 67-64 for Lopez, Samuel Conde voted 68-63 for Alvarez and Dalby Shirley's scorecard read 66-66, meaning Alvarez would have been ahead had the penalty not taken place. The technical draw allowed both fighters to retain their belts, but the superior fighter's identity remained a mystery. This was a rematch that *had* to be made.

November 13, 1998 fell on a Friday, and those who believed in bad omens were given plenty of ammunition. Christy Martin was scheduled to fight Sumya Anani on the undercard, but "The Coal Miner's Daughter" canceled at the last minute either due to sickness (Martin's story) or a dispute over money (Don King's story). If that wasn't bad enough, the events of the Lopez-Alvarez weigh-in the day before made things much worse.

Lopez, who never seemed to have trouble making the limit, weighed in at a trim 103 ½. Alvarez, for whom weigh-ins were always eventful, was 108 ¼ pounds – 3 ¼ pounds over the 105-pound limit. This surprising turn of events, which Alvarez blamed on a faulty hotel scale, had several effects:

* Alvarez was immediately stripped of his WBA minimumweight title.

* Had Alvarez won, Lopez would still be WBC champ, but the WBA belt he had just lost would remain vacant, so there was nothing for the Nicaraguan to gain except sporting pride, a paycheck and a possible third fight.

* Lopez would fight for only the newly vacated WBA strap. If victorious, the contest would not count as Lopez's 22nd WBC title defense because his opponent failed to make weight. This was a historically significant point because the Mexican could have been one step closer to equaling Joe Louis' landmark reign of 25 defenses.

Like Diego Corrales years later, Lopez had the option of canceling the fight. After all, at the 105-pound level a 3 ¼-pound weight advantage – and the edge in strength that comes with it – is almost overwhelming. But Lopez, like "Chico," didn't care. All "El Finito" wanted was the opportunity to conquer the man who troubled him so greatly eight months before. Lopez could have opted for a last-minute substitute, but "El Finito" insisted he wanted to fight no one but Alvarez. So Lopez agreed to a second weigh-in the afternoon of the fight with 115 pounds as the new standard. Lopez scaled 112 while Alvarez was 114. The fight, finally, was on.

Though the bout was no longer a unification match, a coin flip to determine the ring entrance order was still conducted. Lopez lost the toss and came out first while Alvarez, a champion no longer, got the champion's treatment. Once the fight began, however, both fought like champions.

Lopez began in typically classic form with his upper body hunched behind his high guard while Alvarez immediately assumed the aggressor's role. A sharp and focused "El Finito" used his long jab to establish distance while occasionally whipping hooks to the body. Alvarez initially tried to replicate the overhand right that decked Lopez but found that straighter rights to the chin worked better, landing a pair of them as the round neared an end.

Encouraged by his late-round success, Alvarez started the second brimming with confidence and initiated a series of bristling exchanges at ring center. Lopez tossed one-twos to the head and nicely mixed in bodywork, but his defensive maneuvers showed he learned an important lesson from the first fight. After finishing his combinations, Lopez immediately ducked his head and moved to the side instead of leaving it up in the air and making it vulnerable to Alvarez's counters. Lopez was putting everything behind his punches, but Alvarez, whose resistance may have been fortified by the extra weight, took everything in stride while continually marching forward and winging hard shots. Though highly competitive, Lopez clearly won the first two rounds.

Alvarez fared far better in rounds three and four as he accelerated his already fast pace. "El Buffalo" landed a hard hook late in the third. While Lopez was landing more punches, the abrasion around his left eye showed Alvarez was getting in his share. A right-left combination in the fourth connected flush and he was having better luck with his overhand rights. He also landed more than his share of low blows, drawing multiple cautions from referee Richard Steele.

Lopez sought to reassert control in the fifth by putting more power behind his punches, and a solid left-right caused Alvarez to mutter at Lopez underneath his breath. Both boxers were fighting at a high level as they skillfully merged their offensive firepower with sophisticated defensive maneuvers. Late in the fifth, an accidental butt opened a small vertical cut on the outside of Lopez's right eye and a point was deducted from Alvarez.

Alvarez charged out from his corner in the sixth and quickly backed Lopez to the ropes with three jabs and a right to the head. A snappy right in the final minute opened a more serious cut around the Mexican's left eye while Lopez raised a small swelling around Alvarez's right eye. The intensity stepped up a notch in the seventh as both unleashed power shots at ring center, but Alvarez won the round with his aggression and more effective punching.

The eighth saw both men slowing the pace to regroup for the home stretch. Lopez's white trunks were covered in his own blood but he showed no signs of weakening as he let fly dozens of blows. His superior technique controlled the ninth as Alvarez's punch rate eroded. Though Lopez won the 10th in similar fashion, the Nicaraguan inflicted further damage late in the round by opening another cut under the right eye. Lopez now sported cuts above and below both eyes and ringside physician Dr. Flip Homansky felt the need to check Lopez between rounds.

Smelling victory, Alvarez tore after Lopez in the 11th and his counter hooks worsened the cut under Lopez's right eye. Bloody and bruised, Lopez was experiencing the gut-check all dominant champions must pass to certify their greatness. To borrow from Sugar Ray Leonard, Lopez "brought it up from the gut" in the final minute as he peppered Alvarez with a six-punch combination and punctuated the rally with a right at the bell.

The two reluctantly touched gloves as the final round began, and Alvarez surged forward as he tried to pull off a knockout victory. Lopez was more than equal to the challenge, refusing to back away and beckoning Alvarez to engage him. Though the action was hardly one-sided, Lopez was the one who bit down harder in the fight's final 90 seconds. The preamble may have been troubled, but the bout itself proved to be one of 1998's best.

The scoring was appropriately close. Silvestre Abainza scored 115-113 for Alvarez but Jerry Roth and Larry O'Connell saw it 116-112 and 116-114 for Lopez, who added another belt to his collection.

"He is a very good and strong fighter and throws hard punches but he was stronger with more weight." Lopez told Showtime's Jim Gray through an interpreter. "He didn't want to make the weight, but I did what I had to do to beat him and I beat him."

"I think we were betrayed by the scale we were using," Alvarez said. "The other scale we were using coincidentally read the same weight as the first one, so we thought we were only one pound over. We didn't find out until the day before the weigh-in that we were five pounds over. Only God knows why I lost this fight, but it's OK, we'll go for the 108 pound title."

Epilogue: Alvarez eventually won the WBA junior flyweight title, but he did so on his second try. His first attempt against Beibis Mendoza for the vacant belt on August 12, 2000 ended in a seven-round disqualification loss due to excessive low blows but in the rematch seven months later Alvarez won his second divisional title via split decision. He would defend his new title three times, including a 12-round draw with IBF champ Victor Burgos in a unification bout December 13, 2003.

Since the bout with Lopez, "El Buffalo" won 13 of his final 16 fights, including 3-1 against Mendoza. Before his fourth fight with the Colombian October 2, 2004, Alvarez lost his *second* title to the scales as he weighed 3 ½ pounds over the junior flyweight limit. This time, however, Alvarez won a split decision so the belt remained vacant.

The 35-year-old Alvarez tried to win a third divisional crown when he took on WBC interim flyweight champion Jorge Arce in a grudge match on April 8, 2006 in Las Vegas. Arce's youth and power proved too much as "El Travieso" scored a sixth round KO. His final record reads 37-3-2 (24 KO).

TALES FROM THE VAULT

Lopez fought just three more times after the Alvarez rematch. He decisioned Will Grigsby to win the IBF junior flyweight belt Oct. 2, 1999 but a series of injuries kept Lopez on the shelf for 14 months. Following a third-round knockout against Ratanachai Sor Vorapin December 2, 2000, "El Finito" wrote the final chapter of his spectacular career by knocking out Zolani Petelo in eight rounds Sept. 29, 2001. Incidentally, Lopez-Petelo also represented the last match refereed by Hall of Famer Arthur Mercante. Lopez's final record reads 51-0-1(38 KO) and he joined Mercante in the International Boxing Hall of Fame in 2007 along with Roberto Duran and Pernell Whitaker.

Total Punches Landed/Thrown

Round	1	2	3	4	5	6	7	8	9	10	11	12	Total
Lopez	16/53	26/70	19/64	14/52	21/64	25/75	25/66	21/70	18/67	19/72	27/70	24/75	255/798
	30%	37%	30%	27%	33%	33%	38%	30%	27%	26%	39%	32%	32%
Alvarez	13/48	23/72	29/67	23/68	21/65	31/81	26/70	20/63	21/49	29/88	19/74	20/65	275/810
	27%	32%	43%	34%	32%	38%	37%	32%	43%	33%	26%	31%	34%

Jabs Landed/Thrown

Round	1	2	3	4	5	6	7	8	9	10	11	12	Total
Lopez	10/34	8/31	4/30	5/30	3/23	3/27	8/34	6/36	5/37	6/35	4/32	6/27	68/376
	29%	26%	13%	17%	13%	11%	24%	17%	14%	17%	12%	22%	18%
Alvarez	3/13	3/13	2/13	4/13	3/10	4/20	4/16	2/14	3/9	7/15	2/15	3/11	40/162
	23%	23%	15%	31%	30%	20%	25%	14%	33%	47%	13%	27%	25%

Power Punches Landed/Thrown

Round	1	2	3	4	5	6	7	8	9	10	11	12	Total
Lopez	6/19	18/39	15/34	9/22	18/41	22/48	17/32	15/34	13/30	13/37	23/38	18/48	187/422
	32%	46%	44%	41%	44%	46%	53%	44%	43%	35%	61%	38%	44%
Alvarez	10/35	20/59	27/54	19/55	18/55	27/61	22/54	18/49	18/40	22/73	17/59	17/54	235/648
	29%	34%	50%	35%	33%	44%	41%	37%	45%	30%	29%	31%	36%

Ricardo Lopez vs. Rosendo Alvarez II November 13, 1998, Las Vegas, Nevada

TALES FROM THE VAULT

Chan Hee Park vs. Guty Espadas
December 16, 1979, Pusan, South Korea

As the 1970s neared an end, the flyweight division was experiencing a changing of the guard. For most of the decade, names like Miguel Canto, Betulio Gonzalez, Guty Espadas and Shoji Oguma were fixtures in the title picture while Alfonso Lopez, Erbito Salavarria, Susumu Hanagata and Venice Borkorsor made occasional pit stops at the top of the division.

But for flyweights, life at the top is usually short-lived and 1979 proved to be a time of transition as new names took their places at the summit. Chan Hee Park shocked the boxing world by decisioning longtime WBC champ Canto March 18 in Seoul while Panamanian southpaw Luis Ibarra scored a 15-round win over Gonzalez for the WBA belt November 17 to end the Venezuelan's third and final championship reign. Other fresh faces like Tae Shik Kim, Peter Mathebula, Santos Laciar, and Antonio Avelar were poised to make their runs at the top, but members of the old guard weren't ready to yield their spots to the young guns just yet.

One of the most explosive "young gun vs. old guard" showdowns took place when Park (11-0-2, 4 KO) put his WBC title on the line against former WBA champion Espadas (31-3-5, 24 KO). The 22-year-old Korean was defending his title for the third time and was coming off a controversial draw against Canto, who many thought deserved the win. Espadas, who lost his belt to a resurgent Gonzalez following four successful defenses between 1976 and 1978, earned his chance at Park by knocking out Ruben Mancilla in three, Roberto Ruiz in seven and Jose Luis Cruz in six. Though a member of the "old guard," Espadas was still chronologically young as he would turn 25 in four days' time.

At 5-3 ½, Park was 3 ½ inches taller than Espadas and he possessed an impressive amateur background. The Korean won 123 of his 125 amateur fights and represented his country in the 1976 Olympics in Montreal. After defeating Abderrahim Najm of Morocco and Alican Ay of Turkey, Park lost a 3-2 decision to eventual gold medalist Jorge Hernandez of Cuba in the quarterfinal. After turning pro, Park took an accelerated route to a title shot, his first 10-rounder being a decision over Sang Il Chung in just his third pro fight.

Entering his title shot with Canto, Park wasn't seen as much of a threat because just 28 days earlier, he fought Siony Carupo to a 10-round draw. However, the Park who faced Canto was a revelation as his dazzling speed and footwork made Canto look like the 31-year-old, 65-fight veteran he was. The energetic Park built an overwhelming lead in the first 10 rounds and though Canto was able to rally in the last five, his lack of pop rendered him powerless to stop Park's drive to the championship.

Espadas, like Canto a native of Merida, Yucatan, earned his stripes in the professional ranks. He was 17 when he beat Chucho Loria over six rounds in his debut. His early record was dotted with five draws – the last of which was against perennial contender Willie "Birdlegs" Jensen in May 1976 – and a couple of losses to Pablito Jiminez (L 10) and Alberto Morales (L 10) in consecutive fights in October 1974 and March 1975.

Three fights after the draw to Jensen, Espadas challenged WBA champion Alfonso Lopez in Los Angeles October 2, 1976. Lopez knocked out Salavarria in 15 rounds to win the belt February 26, 1976 and decisioned Oguma April 21 to keep it. In a give-and-take battle, Espadas knocked Lopez out in 13 and proceeded to ruin the Panamanian as a world-class fighter as he went 15-15-2, including seven knockout losses, the rest of his career. Espadas packed plenty of power in his five-foot frame, especially with the left hook to the head and body. Though he was more than a year removed from his championship, he was still a considerable threat to Park's title.

The Changchung Gymnasium in Pusan was alive with excitement as Park and Espadas awaited the opening bell. The contrast in styles suggested an exciting fight was in the offing, but Park and Espadas ended up giving the boxing world one of the most intensely fought five minutes and forty two seconds in flyweight championship history.

Espadas immediately assumed the aggressor's role, throwing wide hooks at the circling Park, who snapped plenty of fast jabs. Just thirty-three seconds into the fight, Espadas took a short step forward, planted his left foot and slammed Park with a perfect lead hook to the jaw that dropped the champion on his behind and immediately silenced the raucous crowd. Park scrambled to his feet before a count could be given, and all of a sudden the Mexican already had a leg up on his effort to regain a title.

Instead of backing away to clear his head, Park came forward and exchanged with Espadas. A right to the body and a hook to the head landed flush and two more hooks connected as Espadas, looking to consolidate his advantage, pressed Park toward the ropes. His punches, however, were inaccurate. With Park's legs full of spring and his jabs landing crisply, it was clear his trip to the canvas had been a flash knockdown.

Espadas pulled Park into a clinch and dug three hooks to the body but the champion wrenched himself free and resumed his stick-and-move tactics. With nearly two minutes gone in the round, Park exploded a lead right-left hook combination off Espadas' jaw – the same combination that worked so effectively immediately after suffering his knockdown. The right-left landed again a few seconds later, and a follow-up overhand right sent Espadas to one knee and the crowd into an arm-waving, full-throated frenzy. Like Park, Espadas popped to his feet and skipped to a corner to shake some life into his legs.

After receiving the mandatory eight count, Park crashed a right off Espadas' chin and the Mexican responded with a lead right and two hooks. During a clinch, Park maneuvered Espadas to ring center and landed yet another right-left at close range that drove Espadas to the floor on his back. Again, Espadas arose quickly, but his legs weren't ready to function fully as he stumbled sideways along the ropes. He regained his balance only by hooking his left arm over the top strand. The crowd hollered at the top of its collective lungs as they sensed a stoppage was imminent but the round ended a few seconds after the pair was called back to action.

Park opened the second with a sharp jab to the chin while Espadas missed with a looping right. Park landed a lead hook solidly, but Espadas took the blow well and advanced behind inaccurate punches. Park's decided advantage in hand speed showed itself again as he landed a right-left and stepped away before Espadas could land a single hook. As Park connected with another overhand right, Espadas accidentally landed a hook low and Park retreated to a corner holding his groin. But the referee would have none of it and told the fighters to resume. Park dug two hooks to the body and Espadas countered with a swift hook to the jaw followed by a jab, another hook to the body and two hooks to the chin as Park backed away. Espadas landed two more jabs as Park chose to survey.

Park emerged from his temporary shell with a sharp jab and the right-left combination that had netted two knockdowns in the first. After yet another right-left, Park pulled away to complain of a low blow and again, no time out was granted. Another Park right-left connected and Espadas countered with a sharp jab to the chin. Espadas backed Park away with a right to the body, a left uppercut and a right to the ribs. Two more rights to the body landed for the Mexican but Park countered with his quicker jabs.

Park continued to work the right-left combination overtime while Espadas remained committed to a body attack. The Korean champion countered a missed Espadas hook with his own hook and then applied the finisher – a looping right and a pinpoint hook to the point of the chin – that caused Espadas to fall forward on his face.

Up at six, Espadas was wobbly and sported a long, deep gash over his left eye. The Mexican nodded to the referee and took a step forward to resume fighting. But the official waved off the fight, grabbed Espadas' left arm and led him to his corner. Park looked confused as his seconds lifted him in the air, but his hesitation turned to jubilation when the referee lifted his right arm to declare him the winner at 2:42 of round two. The overjoyed crowd chanted "Korea! Korea! Korea!" as their champion solidified his claim as the best flyweight in the world. It was also another victory for the young guns.

Epilogue: Seven weeks after the Espadas war, Park decisioned Arnel Arrozal to retain his title. Following a wide decision win over Alberto Morales April 12, 1980,

Park shockingly lost the WBC belt five weeks later to former champion Shoji Oguma after sinking to the canvas from a wicked body blow in the ninth round. But those in the know weren't so surprised. Both of Park's amateur losses came to southpaws, and the 29-year-old Oguma was one of the sport's cagiest left-handers.

Park earned a rematch with Oguma exactly five months later in Sendai, Japan following a six-round technical draw to Ver Libradilla on July 26. Park, bent on revenge, whipped himself into shape and even dared Oguma to test his abdominal muscles. But the Japanese emerged with a highly controversial split decision and a third fight had to be made to settle matters. Oguma won a well-received majority decision February 3, 1981 in Tokyo, and Park's days as a championship contender came to an end.

Park took 17 months off before scoring 10-round wins over Katsuyuki Ohashi and Rocky Pineda, but called it quits for good at age 25 after Wick Tengam knocked him out in four rounds December 12, 1982. His final record was 17-4-2 (6 KO).

Espadas returned to action eight months after the Park loss, beating Franco Torregoza over 10 rounds and knocking out Rodolfo Martinez (not the former bantamweight champion) in 10. But Espadas' run at another title was interrupted when future WBC flyweight champion Eleoncio Mercedes knocked him out in nine rounds.

The Mexican rebounded with four wins, including a 10-round decision over two-time 115-pound title challenger Raul Valdez, and he earned a crack at WBC junior bantamweight champion Payao Poontarat March 28, 1984 in Bangkok. Espadas decked Poontarat in the fifth and seventh rounds (the latter knockdown happening seconds after Espadas was dropped) but the Thai champ rallied to knock out the 29-year-old Mexican in the 10th. Espadas retired with a 37-8-5 (27 KO) record and he went on to help guide his son Guty Espadas Jr. to the WBC featherweight title in 2000.

TALES FROM THE VAULT

Total Punches Landed/Thrown

Round	1	2	3	4	5	6	7	8	9	10	11	12	Total
Park	25/86	37/82											62/168
	29%	45%											37%
Espadas	14/48	22/76											36/124
	29%	29%											29%

Jabs Landed/Thrown

Round	1	2	3	4	5	6	7	8	9	10	11	12	Total
Park	9/55	9/40											18/95
	16%	22%											19%
Espadas	2/14	8/29											10/43
	14%	28%											23%

Power Punches Landed/Thrown

Round	1	2	3	4	5	6	7	8	9	10	11	12	Total
Park	16/31	28/42											44/73
	52%	67%											60%
Espadas	12/34	14/47											26/81
	35%	30%											32%

Chan Hee Park vs. Guty Espadas December 16, 1979, Pusan, South Korea

Muangchai Kittikasem vs. Jung Koo Chang
May 18, 1991, Seoul, South Korea

Admit it – we've all done it. When playing basketball in the back yard, we imagine ourselves sinking a last-second shot to win the game. We fantasize about slamming a home run to bring our team back from the brink of defeat or running the length of the field for a game-saving touchdown.

As great as basketball, baseball and football are, no sport can match the drama of boxing. Where else can you see a 45-year-old George Foreman lose every second of every round against younger, faster Michael Moorer only to have "Big George" turn Moorer's world – and the entire sports world – upside down with a single right to the jaw? Where else can you see Jake LaMotta turn sure defeat into unforgettable victory by desperately rallying to stop Laurent Dauthuille with only 13 seconds left on the clock? With boxing, no victory is ever assured until the final bell rings and the result is announced.

Such was the case when WBC flyweight champion Muangchai Kittikasem met 108-pound legend Jung Koo Chang at the Olympic Gymnastics Hall in Seoul, South Korea. It was a tremendous war that saw a combined five knockdowns and one of the 112-pound division's most dramatic endings.

Coming into the fight, Kittikasem (14-1, 10 KO) was a 22-year-old youngster still looking to prove himself on the world stage. Though he won the WBC flyweight title after crushing the venerable Sot Chitalada in six rounds three months before, he was best known to American fans for his only defeat – a seven-round KO to Michael Carbajal the previous July in Carbajal's hometown of Phoenix. For that fight, Kittikasem went through a harrowing ordeal before barely making the 108-pound limit. Though he put up a more than credible effort, he didn't have enough in the tank to deal with a motivated, well-prepared Carbajal. His overwhelming effort against Chitalada proved Kittikasem no only was a talented fighter but also one of the world's hardest-hitting flyweights.

The 28-year-old Chang, on the other hand, sought to cap an already legendary career with a second world title. "The Korean Hawk" (38-3, 17 KO) was highly touted when he turned pro and he proved the experts correct by beating ex-champs Alfonso Lopez (KO 3) and Amado Ursua (W 10) to earn a title shot against WBC junior flyweight king Hilario Zapata in Chonju, South Korea, September 18, 1982. Zapata's second-half rally earned the Panamanian a disputed split decision, and a rematch was held seven months later in Seoul. Not long before the fight, Zapata was jailed for hitting his mother and the time away from training forced him to sweat off nearly

10 pounds in the days before the match. Bent on revenge, Chang feasted on the weight-drained Zapata before knocking him out in three one-sided rounds.

Over the next five years, Chang racked up 15 title defenses against, among others, future champions Chitalada, German Torres (three times) and Hideyuki Ohashi (twice) as well as Katsuo Tokashiki, a former WBA champion. Following the second win over Ohashi in Tokyo (Chang's only title fight outside of South Korea), the man considered the greatest fighter his boxing-rich country ever produced retired on top.

Severe financial problems forced Chang to return to the ring 14 months later. After a 10-round win over Armando Velasco in Pusan, Chang fought rising star Humberto "Chiquita" Gonzalez for his old belt. The 25-0 Gonzalez was too much for the veteran as he won a lopsided decision. Following an eight-round KO of Ric Siodora 10 months later, Chang received his first crack at the WBC flyweight title against old foe Chitalada, who was no longer the inexperienced kid he decisioned six years before. Still, the remnants of Chang pushed Chitalada to the limit before dropping a majority decision. His performance earned him this chance against Chitalada's conqueror Kittikasem.

As the heavily pro-Chang crowd cheered their hero's introduction, the relaxed challenger smiled and walked to Kittikasem's corner to touch gloves. Through the years, Chang had grown accustomed to the atmosphere surrounding a world title fight and he knew exactly what to do.

The two men felt each other out with Chang, 111 ¾, surveying the scene as he bobbed and weaved. Kittikasem, 111 ½, tossed out light jabs, landing one at a time. Midway through the round, Chang landed his first effective blows – a lead, looping overhand right to the head and a left to the solar plexus – before Kittikasem forced a clinch. While inside, Kittikasem landed an overhand right to the ear that caused Chang to stumble forward and push the Thai toward the ropes.

Over the years, Chang developed a reputation for being a dirty fighter but it was Kittikasem who hit Chang with an uppercut on the break, drawing a warning from referee Tony Perez. The champion continued his rough tactics by pushing Chang's head back with his open right glove, but Chang, knowing he had no right to cast stones, remained silent. Kittikasem neatly countered a missed Chang overhand right with three sharp jabs, two of which connected, and a right to the jaw. Chang ended the round with a hard, straight right to the chin and Kittikasem responded by popping Chang with a jab to the face a full second after the bell.

In the second, Kittikasem continued to probe Chang with the jab, but the Korean, sensing the previous round's foul tactics were designed to conceal nerves, tried some psychological warfare by waving his arms in a taunting manner. Kittikasem took the bait, hitting Chang with a hook on the break.

Chang was not the whirlwind of past years as he moved to and fro, looking to pick his spots. He landed a jab to the body, a stinging left-right to the chin and a hook to the body that inspired a roar from the crowd. After Kittikasem cracked Chang with a jab and a right uppercut, he again mushed the Korean's face with his open glove. Kittikasem's effective jabs raised a slight swelling over Chang's right eye, but he never followed up with combinations. Chang ended the second with a hard hook to the jaw and after the bell rang, Chang smirked as Kittikasem as he walked away.

Kittikasem began the third by popping Chang's injured eye with a jab but Chang pushed the champion to the ropes and landed a thudding right to the chin and a hook to the ribs before forcing a clinch. Chang appeared to have the slightly quicker hands while Kittikasem's blows had more steam. After being forced to the ropes again, Kittikasem spun off and landed several uppercuts.

The pace began to accelerate as the flyweights indulged in an extended test of strength. When Chang was at his best, he was a masterful infighter and he proved he could still maul with the best of them as he ripped a right to the body and a pair of hooks to the side as the round ended.

The champion started the fourth quickly, snapping a series of jabs to the face as Chang bounced lead rights off Kittikasem's jaw and bulling the champion toward the ropes.

Instead of staying there, Kittikasem smartly spun away and landed an uppercut to the chin. Chang tossed a left-right-hook combination, but Kittikasem countered with a heavy hook that staggered Chang. The Korean tried to mask the pain by mugging, but his eagerness to initiate a clinch revealed his true state. Kittikasem wasn't fooled as he sunk a right-left to the body and an uppercut to the pit of the stomach.

Chang tried the left-right-hook combo again, and just like before, Kittikasem slammed Chang with a searing counter hook that forced him to hold. Kittikasem ended his best round so far by landing a lead right and three thudding jabs to the face.

Sensing their man was in trouble, the crowd clapped rhythmically to encourage Chang but they also knew the fight was picking up after a relatively slow start. But they couldn't have known how much it was going to heat up in the fifth – and how quickly.

Seconds after the bell, Chang missed a lead right to the body but as he moved in, he landed a short hook to the jaw that dumped Kittikasem on his behind. Up immediately, Kittikasem tried to convince Perez he slipped, but the veteran referee would have none of it and continued the mandatory eight. The cagey Chang didn't rush in for the knockout, choosing to wait for his opening while bouncing lightly on his toes and moving his upper body from side to side.

A jab to the face landed well and he caught the champ with a lead right to the jaw and a left-right to the body. After landing a lead uppercut to the chin, Chang leaped in with a right to the body and a hook to the head that floored Kittikasem again. After Kittikasem arose at three, Chang had one minute 38 seconds to score the third knockdown that would give him his second championship, and this time he went all out by landing a right-left to the body and two uppercuts to the jaw. Chang dug hard to the ribs, but the naturally stronger Kittikasem slowly began to recover as the seconds ticked by. Kittikasem bounced a right off the ear that forced Chang to lean forward and clinch, but Chang ended his best round to date with a right and a light uppercut to the jaw. Though knocked down twice in the round, Kittikasem was so encouraged by his late-round success that he walked to the corner with his arms upraised.

By this time, both men figured out the tactics that worked for them. Chang cranked hooks to the body and bulled Kittikasem toward the ropes while the champ jabbed sharply and mixed in his own damaging hooks.

A jab-cross-hook combination landed effectively for Chang in the sixth while Kittikasem used his height and reach advantage well. When they were inside, Chang ruled while the long-range fighting belonged to Kittikasem. But Chang's persistence grated on Kittikasem and his frustration showed as he threw two punches after the sixth round bell.

The rap music that played between rounds reflected the fighters' hard-charging aggression. With the two fifth-round knockdowns, Chang enjoyed a significant lead on the scorecards. He demonstrated excellent hand speed and the bounce in his legs reminded many of a much younger Chang. Also, he exhibited more boxing skills than in his most recent efforts, which were clinics in mauling and brawling. Late in the seventh, Chang connected with two lefts and a right hook to the body before nipping out and nailing the champ with a lead overhand right. Kittikasem, for his part, continued to rip away at the body as he tried to establish the building blocks for a strong finish.

In the eighth, the two flyweights dug in their toes and engaged in the longest exchanges of the fight. Kittikasem continued to thump the body while Chang tossed speedy combinations. With a minute-and-a-half remaining Chang suddenly fell to the floor, and when he arose he demonstrated a sudden and inexplicable loss of energy. Fighting with his mouth open, Chang's shots were wider and less accurate. Sensing weakness, Kittikasem tore into Chang, banging shots to the body and pushing him in the clinches. Kittikasem drove a right to the body and followed with a right to the jaw.

With every punch the champ landed, Chang weakened more and more. It was as if all the verve of his youth was sucked out of his body and all Chang had left was the shell of his greatness. After tasting a final uppercut at the bell, Chang trudged to his corner with his mouth hanging open while Kittikasem looked composed and confident.

In the ninth, Chang came out on his bicycle with his arms at his side in an effort to collect himself. The Korean tossed a six-punch flurry that lacked steam, but Kittikasem countered with a lead right that had plenty of it. Chang was an easy target for the champion and his heavy blows continued to tear away at "The Korean Hawk's" carcass throughout the ninth and 10th.

Kittikasem was carving away Chang's lead on the scorecards while the crafty old war-horse was using every bit of knowledge to ride out the storm as he sought his second wind. Chang's mind remained sharp, but his body was betraying him. The Korean was merely fighting on courage and memory and the end seemed near as the fight entered the 11th.

Every great champion has the ability to draw on the talent that made him special, and Chang was no exception. The difference between a champion in his prime and one in his twilight is consistency. When he is young, the talent can be accessed every second of every round but when he gets older he can only summon flashes of it.

For Chang, that flash came in the 11th.

The Korean came out bouncing as the round began, but Kittikasem responded with a jab and a hook to the body. But Chang, reaching deep, shocked the crowd, Kittikasem and perhaps himself by landing a jab and a short inside right to the jaw that dropped the champion to his haunches. Kittikasem arose immediately and gritted his teeth in anger. He turned to the referee and stretched out his arms in a mixture of frustration and sheepishness as Chang regained the momentum on the scorecards. Chang rushed in for the kill, digging to the body and bulldogging Kittikasem to the ropes, but the Thai remained the sharper puncher as he snapped Chang's head with jabs and ripped hooks and rights to the body.

Confident he was going to win the 11th by a 10-8 score, Chang initiated a series of clinches to run out the clock because he knew he didn't have the gas to end matters before the bell sounded. The savvy crowd knew what Chang was doing and they cheered each time he induced a clinch. As the round ran down, Chang connected with a decent overhand right to the jaw.

Entering the 12th round, it was anyone's fight. Tom Kaczmarek had Kittikasem in front 104-102 while Rudy Jordan favored Chang 104-103. Chuck Giampa's card read 103-103. Both men needed the last round, but Kittikasem sensed he needed a big finish to secure a decision on his opponent's home turf.

Kittikasem started the final round going hard to the body while Chang continued to stall. Chang twice initiated clinches after tossing light flurries but Kittikasem's withering hooks were taking its toll on the older man. With a minute to go, it looked like Chang would beat the clock, but the champion had other ideas.

After Chang landed a good overhand right, he made a fatal mistake. He remained in a crouch for a split second too long, giving Kittikasem enough time to line up a rising hook to the jaw that froze Chang in the crouched position. A follow-up hook missed but the overhand right didn't, and the exhausted Chang fell spread-eagled to the canvas. Only 51 seconds remained in the fight.

Up at five, Chang staggered into the ropes yet convinced Perez he was OK to continue by nodding his head. A short inside hook to the jaw felled Chang again, and his head struck the second rope hard. Chang was on all fours, shaking his head and trying to summon the courage to rise again – which he did.

His legs were gone as he staggered forward into Perez. Chang's spirit was willing but his body could no longer comply. Perez held onto Chang and waved his right arm, stopping the fight with 24 seconds remaining in the final round. Chang was tantalizingly close to climbing the mountain once again, but Kittikasem was too young, too strong and too good for Chang this day.

Kittikasem knew how close he was to losing his title, and as his corner men lifted him in the air he wore a wide smile that exuded happiness as well as overwhelming relief. He lived out an athlete's ultimate fantasy by doing the one thing he needed to ensure victory. He sunk the big shot at the buzzer, he hit the game-winning homer and he certainly earned the game ball.

Epilogue: Kittikasem fought 13 more times following the Chang victory, winning 10 and losing three. After a 10-round non-title win over Jun "Lito" Gonzalez, he successfully defended the title against Alberto Jimenez (W 12) and Chitalada (KO 9). After two more non-title wins against Eddy Permaigui (W 10) and Tarman Garzim (W 10), Kittikasem was knocked out by Russian sensation Yuri Arbachakov (KO 8) in Tokyo June 23, 1992. Two knockout wins earned Kittikasem a rematch with Arbachakov, who stopped him in nine rounds March 20, 1993. The Arbachakov rematch was Kittikasem's last championship fight.

Kittikasem took 25 months off before returning with three quick knockout wins, then took another 33-month hiatus before being knocked out in four rounds by future 122-pound title challenger Shigeru Nakazato on Feb. 22, 1999. Kittikasem retired at age 30 with a 25-4 (17 KO) record.

The Kittikasem fight was Chang's final bout and he retired with a record of 38-4 (17 KO). After several years of waiting, Chang was enshrined in the International Boxing Hall of Fame's Class of 2010.

Total Punches Landed/Thrown

Round	1	2	3	4	5	6	7	8	9	10	11	12	Total
Kittikasem	10/34	11/42	19/47	25/63	19/64	34/71	23/60	37/98	36/68	36/80	24/75	24/57	298/759
	29%	26%	40%	40%	30%	48%	38%	38%	53%	45%	32%	42%	39%
Chang	3/20	8/35	12/38	13/42	21/67	24/64	30/80	20/83	15/59	18/75	12/53	6/34	182/650
	15%	23%	32%	31%	31%	38%	38%	24%	25%	24%	23%	18%	28%

Jabs Landed/Thrown

Round	1	2	3	4	5	6	7	8	9	10	11	12	Total
Kittikasem	4/17	6/25	5/15	8/20	3/11	19/35	7/20	0/5	3/12	15/35	7/23	7/13	84/231
	24%	24%	33%	40%	27%	54%	35%	0%	25%	43%	30%	54%	36%
Chang	0/7	3/19	2/11	3/14	3/12	8/21	8/28	0/2	3/13	2/19	3/7	2/8	37/161
	0%	16%	18%	21%	25%	38%	29%	0%	23%	11%	43%	25%	23%

Power Punches Landed/Thrown

Round	1	2	3	4	5	6	7	8	9	10	11	12	Total
Kittikasem	6/17	5/17	14/32	17/43	16/53	15/36	16/40	37/93	33/56	21/45	17/52	17/44	214/528
	35%	29%	44%	40%	30%	42%	40%	40%	59%	47%	33%	39%	41%
Chang	3/13	5/16	10/27	10/28	18/55	16/43	22/52	20/81	12/46	16/56	9/46	4/26	145/489
	23%	31%	37%	36%	33%	37%	42%	25%	26%	29%	20%	15%	30%

Muangchai Kittikasem vs. Jung Koo Chang May 18, 1991, Seoul, South Korea

TALES FROM THE VAULT

Sung Kil Moon vs. Nana Konadu I
January 20, 1990, Seoul, South Korea

The 115-pound weight class (known as junior bantamweight or super flyweight depending on the sanctioning body involved) was among the four weight classes created during the expansion of 1976-1980 which also saw the birth of junior flyweight, junior featherweight and cruiserweight. Though perceived by most as a way to generate more sanctioning fees, the "super flys" have produced its share of super fights.

Though it ended tragically, Robert Quiroga-Akeem Anifowoshe was one of the most action-packed fights of the 1990s. When one compiles a list of great 115-pound title scraps, one has to include Payao Poontarat-Guty Espadas, Katsuya Onizuka-Thanomsak Sithbaobay II, Khaosai Galaxy-Cobra Ari Blanca and Hyung Chul Lee-Katsuya Onizuka. But the first war between WBC titlist Nana Konadu and Sung Kil Moon may have been the best of them all. This fight had just about everything – knockdowns, boxing skills, hard punching, constant shifts of momentum and ceaseless bell-to-bell action.

The 25-year-old Konadu (18-0-1, 14 KO) was making his first defense a mere 74 days after dethroning longtime champ Gilberto Roman in Mexico City. Against Roman, Konadu was a revelation as he used his height and reach to outbox the supreme boxer and his power to score five knockdowns en route to a shockingly lopsided decision. The result was surprising only because Konadu seemed to come from nowhere to not only defeat, but also dominate, one of the division's greatest champions. Until the Roman fight, Konadu's best victories came against former IBF king Cesar Polanco (W 12) and former flyweight title challenger Stephen Muchoki (KO 12). The expectations surrounding Konadu were sky high in light of his performance against Roman as his blend of speed and power suggested bigger and better things were possible if he kept winning.

Unlike Konadu, Moon was a well-known commodity. The Korean was among his country's most decorated amateur fighters and turned pro under considerable fanfare in 1987 after advancing to the quarterfinals as a bantamweight in the 1984 Olympics. Though it took him nearly three years to turn pro, Moon made up for lost time by traversing one of history's quickest routes to a world title shot. Moon knocked out his first six opponents to earn a crack at Khaokor Galaxy's WBA bantamweight belt on August 14, 1988 in Bangkok. Moon and Galaxy traded evenly for six rounds before the Korean suffered a cut from an unintentional butt. The gash was deemed too severe for Moon to continue and because he led on all scorecards, Moon was declared the new champion.

Moon defended the title twice, dominating perennial challenger Edgar Monserrat (KO 7) and stopping Chiaki Kobayashi in five to set up a rematch in Bangkok with

Galaxy July 19, 1989. This time, the twin brother of 115-pound legend Khaosai Galaxy outclassed Moon, sweeping the scorecards and registering two knockdowns in the 11th round to regain the belt.

Once dethroned, titleholders usually try to reclaim their glory by moving up a weight class or two. Moon, however, chose to move *down* to 115 where his strength advantage would be magnified and the route to another title shot would be shorter. Moon weighed only 116 ¾ for the Galaxy rematch, so the drop in weight was hardly dramatic. Four months after losing to Galaxy, Moon – weighing 115 ¾ – polished off Romeo Opriasa in two rounds to set up the title shot with Konadu two months later.

The styles of Konadu and Moon figured to mesh well. Moon's straight-ahead style, wide clubbing punches and unyielding determination promised a formidable challenge to Konadu's well-rounded boxing skills and ability to win away from home. A high-action fight was anticipated, but no one at the World Trade Center in Seoul could have known they were about to witness one of the most explosive first rounds ever seen in championship competition.

Konadu opened the fight with hands high and bouncing up and down on his toes while Moon bobbed and weaved in search of openings. Both men forced a fast pace from the start, but neither was very accurate as Konadu pumped jabs and Moon threw wide punches to the head and body.

One minute into the fight, the fireworks began.

Moon missed with a lead right, but his follow-through positioned himself perfectly to fire a counter hook to the cheek that floored the Ghanaian champion. As Konadu arose at two, he shook his arms in frustration but took referee Tony Perez's count with composure. Moon missed with a home-run hook, and the unhurt Konadu countered with a right that staggered Moon slightly. Moon won an exchange of jabs and the Korean challenger countered a missed Konadu jab with a perfectly timed overhand right to the jaw that dropped Konadu for the second time.

Up at six, Konadu found himself in a precarious position: One more knockdown in the round would have ended his championship reign and he had 1:35 left to kill. If he ran away without offering any offense, the fight could be stopped anyway. If he stood and punched, Moon could score the decisive third knockdown in short order. There were many options, but few of them were promising.

Konadu's choice: Do his best and accept whatever happens.

After Perez finished his second count of the round, Moon barreled in to finish the job, but Konadu cranked a hook that landed with authority and a second hook to the temple backed Moon off a couple of steps. The overanxious Moon charged in wildly behind winging blows that Konadu slipped easily. Moon bulled Konadu to a corner, and in his haste to finish off his prey he ran into a short left to the button that dropped him to his knees. Up instantaneously, Moon had clearly suffered a flash knockdown but Konadu had taken his pound of flesh and was ready for more.

After Perez completed the mandatory eight against Moon, the Korean landed a cuffing right to the ear while a Konadu right whizzed past his chin. The champion pumped the jab incessantly and mixed in a strong lead right and a hook to the jaw. From time to time, the action looked ungainly as they swapped hard but inaccurate blows. As the bell sounded to end an unforgettable first round, the terms of battle were established: This would be no distance fight and the winner would have to endure a hellish test of character to achieve it.

Konadu opened the second strongly, his jabs solving the puzzle that was Moon's upper-body movement. His blows weren't hurting Moon, but they were scoring points. As Konadu leaned in with a right, Moon slammed a short right to the middle of the face. But as Moon charged in to follow up, Konadu connected with a crisp hook and retreated behind a series of jabs. Moon countered a jab with a lead right to the face, a hard jab and a follow-up right to the jaw. Moon drove a right to the body and landed two jabs to the face, after which he twice came over a Konadu jab to land a solid right.

A pattern was emerging: Since the jab was the foundation of Konadu's offense, Moon sought to time it and throw counters both under and over. Meanwhile, Moon's charges and wide punches offered Konadu many countering opportunities and the champion used snapping jabs followed by quick-fisted volleys to take advantage. It was high-speed, full-contact chess with Konadu throwing more and Moon connecting more forcefully.

Moon's technique wasn't pretty to watch, but his relentless pressure combined with a fierce inner drive forced Konadu to fight much harder than he intended.

The challenger was confident that his tactics would reap long-term benefits, for he knew no one could fight all-out for 36 minutes without exhausting himself. But while he waited for the champion to wind down, he knew the price of victory would be high and that he would have to dish out – and absorb – an extraordinary amount of punishment. Like Gene Fullmer before him, Moon's style might have appeared crude but there was a science that rested beneath the surface.

The pattern continued in the third as Moon relentlessly stalked and dug in occasional hooks while Konadu snapped jabs and tried to keep the fight at long distance with his legs. The scars of battle were beginning to show as swelling erupted underneath Konadu's right eye and a butt opened a vertical cut near the bridge of Moon's nose.

Feeling the blood running down his face, Moon accelerated his attack even more, and he scored a bulls-eye with a right to the forehead that decked Konadu for the third time in the fight.

After Konadu arose at three, Moon ripped a right to the body and a straight left to the jaw as the champ unsuccessfully tried to slip in a scorching lead right. Moon was swinging for the home run with every punch as he applied unrelenting and massive pressure. Konadu could no longer move laterally and the swelling underneath his right eye worsened considerably. Though Konadu continued to land jabs, they no longer had the same force but they did worsen Moon's cut. A double jab-right cross combination connected flush for Konadu as the round neared its end, but it was evident Moon had inflicted the greater damage.

Just as the fight appeared to be nearing an end, it turned again. Early in the fourth – after Moon whipped in a right to the body – Konadu snapped three sharp jabs, the third of which knocked an off-balance Moon to the floor. It was the fifth knockdown in slightly more than 10 minutes of action and no one knew where the thrill ride would make its final stop.

Up immediately, Moon resumed winging big rights as Konadu's pinpoint jabs stabbed Moon's cut. Moon slid under a jab to land a right to the body, a hook to the ear, a right to the jaw and a hard hook to the cheek that stunned the champion. Moon rushed in, throwing volleys of power shots and Konadu shifted into full retreat mode. But Konadu turned right back after several seconds of running to catch Moon with a sharp right-left-right to the jaw that pushed Moon toward the ropes. With 25 seconds remaining, Moon countered a triple jab with a solid hook that sent Konadu scurrying to the ropes and seeking the refuge of a clinch. Moon continued to rip hard shots, but Konadu recovered well enough to land two solid hooks. As another tumultuous round neared an end, Moon stunned the champion again with an overhand right and straight left to the head.

The pattern continued in rounds five and six as Moon nearly scored his fourth knockdown after his weapon of choice – a sneaky straight left following an overhand right – caromed off Konadu's jaw. Konadu continued to answer strongly, but even his best blows couldn't stop Moon's uncompromising advances. Meanwhile, the swelling underneath the champion's right eye was the size of a golf ball and the side of his head began to swell grotesquely. Late in the sixth, Konadu's rapid blows opened a gash over Moon's right eye. Despite the fact that both men's bodies were breaking apart like the fuselage of an airplane flying too fast, they still maintained their breakneck pace with no regard for the consequences.

Konadu managed to summon his best effort in round seven as he snapped hard one-twos while moving to his right to make sure Moon remained in his line of sight. Konadu timed Moon's rushes superbly and his blows caused the blood from Moon's vertical cut to flow more freely. Late in the round, Konadu raked Moon with blow after blow, backing him to the ropes and slowing his pursuit. It was, by far, the most dominant sequence by one man over the other in the fight.

The tide took another improbable turn in the eighth as Moon ratcheted up the pressure behind rights to the body and head that sent Konadu toward the ropes. The champion fought his way off with a steady stream of lightning combinations, but Moon pushed him back to the ropes with several rights to the ribs. As Moon whacked away at the body, Konadu escaped with a right-left-right and two more one-twos to the jaw.

The pace was simply inhuman, yet Moon looked so strong under Konadu's assaults that it appeared nothing could deter him. Moon was like a computer video game character that executed at such a high level that no human player could prevail because the computer simply *would not lose.*

The ringside physician checked Moon's cuts after the eighth round and deemed the challenger fit to continue. As Konadu continued to toss snappy combinations in the ninth, Moon put his head down and grinded away, determined to break the champion's will with no regard for what he had to take to accomplish his mission. But Konadu was not the "give-up" type, and his superior skill carried the majority of the round. Fittingly, the stanza ended with the fighters wildly bombing away.

As the bell for round 10 sounded, neither man moved from his stool as the fight was delayed several seconds. Moments later, Perez received word that the ringside physician was stopping the fight because Moon's cuts were too severe, but as Moon stood in his corner the injuries seemed to be no worse than in previous rounds. Nevertheless, the judges, not the fighters, would have the final say.

The decision was unanimous. Dalby Shirley saw the fight 86-84, Herbert Minn scored it 87-84 and Omar Minton's score was 86-82 for the winner – and new – champion Sung Kil Moon.

The Korean became the first and only fighter to capture two titles via butt-induced technical decision. The anti-climactic ending was highly unsatisfying to virtually everyone due to its suddenness, but as far as Sung Kil was concerned, he was simply – ahem – over the Moon.

Epilogue: Moon would prove to be a dominant champion, registering nine title defenses over the next three-plus years. Nearly four months after winning the title, Moon stopped Roman in nine rounds to further certify his credentials. He followed with wins over Kenji Matsumura (TD 5,), Konadu (KO 4), Ernesto Ford (KO 5), Torsak Pongsupa (KO 6), Armando Salazar (KO 8), former WBA bantamweight champion Greg Richardson (W 12), former two division champion Hilario Zapata (KO 1) and Carlos Salazar (W 12). On November 13, 1993, Moon lost the title by split decision to Jose Luis Bueno in Pohang, Korea. Moon, four months past his 30th birthday, never fought again, retiring with a 20-2 (15 KO) record.

Not surprisingly, Konadu had plenty more fights in him – 27 in all. After taking nine months off following the Moon bout, the Ghanaian polished off Diego Duran (KO 3) and Kevin Nwundidwe (KO 2) to earn a rematch with Moon. This time, Moon was dominant as he registered a fourth round TKO.

Over the next five years, Konadu took the long road back to a championship, winning 15 consecutive fights, scoring knockouts in 12 of them and racking up 10 of them in succession. The more impressive victories included Juan Polo Perez (W 12), Ruben Bastista (KO 2), Victor Rabanales (W 10) and Abraham Torres (KO 6). On January 28, 1996, Konadu won the WBA bantamweight title by coming off the canvas in the first round to knock out Veerapol Sahaprom in the second. It would be the Thai's only loss in the next nine years.

In a case of déjà vu, Konadu lost the title in his first defense via technical decision, this time to Thai Daorung Chuvatana after 10 rounds. A rematch was held eight months later with Konadu blasting out Chuvatana in seven rounds to regain the belt. An off-the-floor defense against Torres (KO 2) followed, and in a non-title fight three months later Konadu was an eight-round disqualification winner against Julio C. Alfaro.

Konadu lost the WBA title for the final time to Johnny Tapia in a close, but dull affair. The African warrior wound up his career with wins over Hector Acero Sanchez (W 10) and Amador Vasquez (KO 5) and a final loss to Daniel Seda (KO by 9). Konadu retired at age 37 with a 41-5-1 (32 KO) record.

TALES FROM THE VAULT

Total Punches Landed/Thrown

Round	1	2	3	4	5	6	7	8	9	10	11	12	Total
Moon	21/65	30/80	25/99	30/90	30/86	37/99	18/51	46/93	37/82				274/745
	32%	38%	25%	33%	35%	37%	35%	49%	45%				37%
Konadu	23/68	30/105	19/75	27/82	39/104	32/120	23/102	42/140	38/97				273/893
	34%	29%	25%	33%	38%	27%	23%	30%	39%				31%

Jabs Landed/Thrown

Round	1	2	3	4	5	6	7	8	9	10	11	12	Total
Moon	5/14	5/31	2/30	8/18	9/30	3/17	6/20	4/12	6/16				48/188
	36%	16%	7%	44%	30%	18%	30%	33%	38%				26%
Konadu	11/40	20/73	7/48	15/56	13/43	12/43	12/61	17/60	16/47				123/471
	28%	27%	15%	27%	30%	28%	20%	28%	34%				26%

Power Punches Landed/Thrown

Round	1	2	3	4	5	6	7	8	9	10	11	12	Total
Moon	16/51	25/49	23/69	22/72	21/56	34/82	12/31	42/81	31/66				226/557
	31%	51%	33%	31%	38%	41%	39%	52%	47%				41%
Konadu	12/28	10/32	12/27	12/26	26/61	20/77	11/41	25/80	22/50				150/422
	43%	31%	44%	46%	43%	26%	27%	31%	44%				36%

Sung Kil Moon vs. Nana Konadu I January 20, 1990, Seoul, South Korea

Fidel Bassa vs. Dave McAuley I
April 25, 1987, Belfast, Northern Ireland

In a strange way, boxing and books share similarities even though one is a physical pursuit and the other an intellectual one. To move the story forward, books are divided into chapters while fights use the division of rounds to tell its tale. Also, books are categorized by content – short stories, novels, nonfiction, etc. – and boxing can be partitioned the same way.

Some fights read like haikus – three-line, 17-syllable poems that can be read in a matter of seconds. Others, like the cancelled rubber match between Diego Corrales and Jose Luis Castillo, resemble farce. If one watches enough fights, an endless variety of labels can be affixed to what he sees, whether it is action thriller, mystery novel, poetry or outright fiction.

Some fights, however, rise to a higher level and are regarded as being among the greatest pieces of work ever produced. The "Thrilla in Manila" was high drama, with the main characters clearly defined and the story told in three distinctive parts before an unexpected twist brought the tale to an unforgettable close.

But there are classic books that are only known and appreciated by the cognoscenti, books that aren't automatically mentioned when the greatest works are discussed. The same phenomenon applies to boxing, and one such fight took place at the King's Hall in Belfast, Northern Ireland when WBA flyweight champion Fidel Bassa defended his belt against Irish hero Dave McAuley. It was a fight that pitted good versus evil (at least in the audience's mind) and featured more than its share of explosive plot twists. In the end, both combatants were elevated and the result was overshadowed by the raw courage and desire produced by victor and vanquished.

The 24-year-old Bassa dethroned Hilario Zapata under bizarre circumstances. During the eighth round of a fight held before thousands of Bassa partisans in Colombia, one of those spectators grabbed Zapata's leg and tried to pull him out of the ring while he was pinned in a corner. Zapata tried to fend off that fan when another struck him in the face. Instead of a disqualification victory, Zapata was given five minutes to recover and Bassa (17-0, 13 KO) went on to win a 15-round decision.

Bassa was a well-rounded boxer, able to move nimbly from side to side and pelt his opponents with well-placed and swift combinations. At just 5-2, it was difficult for a man his size to be a stick-and-move boxer, but his talent was such that he exited the ring the winner every time.

Bassa's first defense was against the 25-year-old McAuley (13-0, 8 KO), who won the vacant British flyweight title six months before by knocking out Joe Kelly in nine rounds in Glasgow. At 5-7 ½, McAuley was an extraordinarily tall flyweight, but while he had the equipment of a skillful boxer he had the soul of a warrior that craved confrontation. His zealousness sometimes got him into trouble as he was decked several times in early rounds. He may not have had a rock-hard jaw, but his reservoir of courage and fortitude ran deep and because of that he always found a way to emerge victorious. McAuley may have carried the nickname "Boy," but he fought like a real "Man."

Because of the political tensions that convulsed Northern Ireland, no national anthems were played. The only song sung was "When Irish Eyes Are Smiling," a tune that the last Irish flyweight champion Rinty Monaghan sang after every one of his fights. The audience at the King's Hall was in its full-throated glory and was ready to propel McAuley toward what they hoped would be a most glorious victory.

As the fight began, Bassa, an incredibly light 109 ¾, was on the move while McAuley, 111 ¾, stalked, his left hand moving quickly and rhythmically up and down. Bassa blocked McAuley's jabs while firing in two of his own. The champion lunged in with a right that missed but the follow-up hook snapped McAuley's head straight back.

Just forty-three seconds into the fight, Bassa countered a McAuley jab to the body with a powerful overhand right to the jaw that sent the challenger to his knees. A sheepish McAuley arose at two, and Bassa roared in behind a volley to the body that forced McAuley to hold on. Bassa continued to fire rights under and over in pursuit of a shocking early-round knockout. A torrid right to the temple caused McAuley to sag into the ropes but the Irishman temporarily staved off further damage by unleashing a pair of hooks. Undeterred, Bassa backed McAuley into the ropes and unloaded a torrent of blows. McAuley was in danger of being run out of the ring, and his problems worsened when he emerged with a severe cut over his right eye.

It was a nightmarish start for the Irishman, and Bassa was fighting with confidence and poise as he pot-shotted the challenger, who spent most of the round on the retreat. McAuley threw his trademark hooks not to land but to keep Bassa at bay and create a chance to settle down. He managed to ride out the final seconds of the first round, but if this trend continued much longer he would be lucky to see the fifth round, much less last 14 more.

"And that's a tragic three minutes for the British flyweight champion," intoned ringside commentator Harry Carpenter. "This is his first fight since becoming British champion and he couldn't have made a worse start. He dropped his left and he paid the penalty and he hasn't looked right since. He's been trying to get in the left hook – he's got a good left hook – and my word he does need it right now. But psychologically can be recover from this? It seems highly doubtful to me."

But as the second round was about to start, it was McAuley who was standing at ring center several seconds early and bouncing on his toes. The crowd sang "here we go, here we go, here we go" to spark their man and he answered them by landing a strong hook that caught Bassa coming in. It wasn't a hurtful punch, but it was an encouraging sign for a crowd that was hungry for any positive news. McAuley's jabs were starting to find the mark, but Bassa maintained his smooth boxing despite them.

A McAuley hook tenderized Bassa's ribs but the champion countered with a hook that forced McAuley back. Another McAuley hook under the elbow bent the champion over ever so slightly. McAuley snapped a hook to the body and a right to the jaw and another lead right caught Bassa charging in. After McAuley won an exchange of hooks, it appeared the challenger was warming to his task – and pulling himself past his early difficulties. Frustrated at McAuley's pluck, Bassa threw in a vicious head butt to close out an unexpectedly difficult second round.

McAuley again stood at ring center, but Bassa was still sitting in his corner with his legs extended outward a full 10 seconds after the third round bell sounded. It was obvious he couldn't hear the bell over the din of McAuley's fans. The champion – convinced his chance for the early knockout had passed – concentrated on piling up points. The surging McAuley missed with a winging right but his signature hook landed squarely on the jaw. Bassa dove inside to land a flurry of punches – and a head butt or two – while McAuley speared the champion's face with jabs and cranked hard hooks to the head and body.

It was clear that the Irishman was here to stay and because he had already overcome a bad beating in the first round he would prove to be a much tougher nut for Bassa to crack. The cut over the eye was under control and with every passing second McAuley was growing into his role of world title challenger, secure in the knowledge that he indeed belonged inside the ring with the best his division had to offer.

With 44 seconds left in the round, the fight took an extraordinary turn. McAuley winged a right that appeared to whiz over Bassa's head, but the champion fell to the canvas as if badly stricken. Up at two, Bassa wobbled around in a circle before facing referee Nick Morgan. His legs didn't look right at all as McAuley raced in behind a hook to the jaw. A cuffing hook to the face sent Bassa down a second time, but Morgan called this fall a slip. The champion's face wore a dazed look as Morgan wiped his gloves and his equilibrium appeared all but gone, but Bassa survived to the bell by staying close and firing blows to the body. After the bell sounded, Bassa's legs were so unsteady that his chief second raced across the ring and half-dragged his charge to the corner.

A close inspection of the replay revealed the source of Bassa's trouble: McAuley's head clipped Bassa's temple during his follow-through on the initial winging right. Though the boxers wore paper-thin six-ounce gloves, it was the impact of an unpadded head on a nerve center that took its toll on the champion.

Still, the challenger had come all the way back from his horrific start and Carpenter, who all but wrote off his chances after round one, now marveled "the champion is hurt and McAuley's now got a golden opportunity to become the world flyweight champion here in Belfast." The crowd sensed that as well as they spent the rest period yelling, chanting and cheering themselves into a vocal lather. They collectively floated on a wave of hope that their man was about to complete a most remarkable comeback.

Again, Bassa was late answering the bell for the fourth round, sitting placidly in his corner for five extra seconds. The rest period helped the champion, whose legs appeared strengthened as he circled the ring. McAuley, his spirits riding high, appeared steeled to do whatever it took to complete his mission. McAuley banged a hook to the jaw and a second one several seconds later connected well. Bassa stayed on his bicycle, throwing two- and three-punch flurries while fielding an occasional McAuley hook to the face. The men fought on even terms, which indicated a long, hard struggle was ahead.

As the fifth began, Bassa's chief second immediately lifted him off the stool and this tactic solved the champion's chronic tardiness for the rest of the fight. One minute into the round, McAuley leaped in with a sharp one-two followed by a short hook that caught Bassa perfectly on the point of the chin. The blow snapped Bassa's head but the champion absorbed the bomb well. After staggering forward briefly, he roared back with three powerful punches. Though they missed, they sent the message that he was still dangerous.

Bassa, again frustrated by the challenger's tenacity, rubbed his head against McAuley's cut eye, drawing a complaint from the challenger and a caution from Morgan. McAuley won an exchange of rights and was drawing even in the jabbing contest. But McAuley was now damaged around both eyes and his nose trickled blood as well. Nevertheless, the challenger was pushing the fight and stringing together better combinations. As the round concluded, Bassa connected with a winging overhand right but McAuley responded with a hook to the body and head.

Bassa started the sixth by landing a neat right-left to the jaw while ducking under McAuley's counters. Another hook following a missed right was on target. A right to the temple and a right uppercut to the jaw landed flush but the champion stumbled off balance after avoiding a McAuley hook. The right-left combination was working well against the challenger, so he rushed in to try it again. But this time, McAuley fired a short, straight left to the jaw that caught Bassa charging in and dropped him to a knee. Though it appeared to be a clean knockdown, Morgan ruled the fall a slip.

"If that's not a knockdown, I'm a Dutchman," declared the very British Carpenter.

McAuley stayed on the attack, nailing Bassa with a hook. A second hook nearly put the champion on the floor officially, but Bassa mounted a brave counterattack, bulling McAuley to the ropes with short punches on the inside that stemmed the Irishman's rally. Bassa punctuated his mini-rally with a strong right to the jaw as the bell sounded.

A minute into a quiet seventh, McAuley awakened the crowd with a right to the jaw and beat Bassa to the punch with a second right. A third right followed by a hook tagged the champion, but Bassa fielded the blows without too much concern. Bassa jumped in with a hook to the face that propelled McAuley back a step and all of a sudden the challenger appeared winded, drawing a deep breath while his body sagged during a clinch. McAuley expended a lot of energy in mounting his comeback and the effects of his exertion started to surface.

In the closing seconds of the round, the previously unmarked Bassa sustained a cut over his left eye after both men clashed heads while simultaneously ducking in. Angered, Bassa roughed up McAuley with his head, drawing a stern warning from Morgan. The Chicago referee grabbed Bassa's head by the temples and shook it vigorously to drive the message home. Meanwhile, crimson was spotted near McAuley's ear and his face was starting to become a mask of blood, bumps, bruises and abrasions. It was a portrait in pain but McAuley's desire to stand atop his personal Everest overrode everything else.

Between rounds, Morgan instructed the judges to take a point from Bassa for the late-round head butt, aiding the challenger's effort to get back into contention on the scorecards. With McAuley weakening, the math might be rendered moot.

The challenger arose from his stool slowly as the ninth began, as if the mere act was in itself a great effort. Bassa fired an overhand right to the jaw and cracked two hooks to the ribs. The champion maneuvered McAuley to the ropes and worked him over. The challenger's championship aspirations appeared lost.

Then, with shocking dispatch, those aspirations were found again.

McAuley, his back pinned to the ropes, uncorked a massive hook that caught Bassa as he was throwing his own right and the champion toppled to the floor. This time, there was no question of the knockdown's legitimacy and, remarkably, the Irishman had vaulted himself back into the fight. Up immediately, Bassa took the mandatory eight count. McAuley smacked Bassa with a wide hook to the jaw and three more crashed home. An overhand right connected flush and a hook that caught Bassa coming out of a clinch sent the champion stumbling back several steps.

A dream that looked dead seconds before was resurrected and McAuley summoned up all his reserves to transform it from one man's wish to historical fact. It was an incredible demonstration of competitive courage seldom seen in a sport where courage is a prerequisite.

McAuley continued the assault by blasting away at Bassa's body. Back at ring center, McAuley produced an overhand right, a left uppercut to the pit of the stomach, a cuffing hook to the ear and an explosive inside right to the jaw that decked Bassa for the second time in the round and the third time in the fight. The champion was driven hard to the floor this time and as he sat on the canvas he shook his head in dejection before arising at six.

One more knockdown was all McAuley needed to end the fight, but the effects of his previous beating inhibited his ability to line up Bassa for the finisher. The Colombian, exhibiting his own brand of championship bravery, bulled McAuley to the ropes and stayed inside the challenger's long arms. McAuley managed to land one last big right hand as the bell ended a ninth round for the ages.

"Would you believe it!" Carpenter exclaimed from ringside. "Look at this crowd, listen to this crowd...and come to think, listen to me because I'm going berserk, too. I've never seen anything like it in all my life! It's unbelievable! It goes one way and then the other and (color commentator) Herol (Graham) is laughing his head off...what on earth is coming next?"

What happened next was a huge right that put Bassa on rubbery legs in the opening seconds of the 10th and, true to form, Bassa intentionally and unashamedly rammed his head into McAuley's face. This time, however, Morgan declined to take another point. Bassa was again on the verge of defeat, but McAuley, tired as he was, couldn't find the key that would unlock the championship for him. McAuley swung hard but Bassa slipped most of the blows and was slowly reassembling himself. His legs regained their spring as he nipped in and out. Yet McAuley stubbornly drove himself forward, stinging Bassa with a head-snapping hook and an overhand right to the jaw before clinching.

All this, and five more rounds remained in the fight.

"McAuley is the new hero of Northern Ireland," Carpenter declared. "There were great days with (Barry) McGuigan but those days seem to be over, and a new era dawns and here's a man who is going to be a hero for the rest of his life for the people of Belfast."

Despite the growing collection of swellings, cuts and other assorted injuries to his face, McAuley seemed fresher as he answered the bell for the 11th. Bassa, too, appeared stronger than before, and given what both men suffered through it was nothing short of miraculous that they could stand, much less fight with such a high level of skill.

The action finally slowed a bit in the first part of the 12th, but midway through Bassa called upon an extra reservoir and drove McAuley to the ropes behind a relentless series of hooks and hurtful rights. A searing left uppercut jerked McAuley's head and the Irishman no longer had the strength to extricate himself from the ropes. Only a referee's break enabled the challenger to escape to ring center. With less than five seconds remaining in the round, with McAuley again languishing on the ropes, Bassa nailed the challenger with a whistling overhand right to the jaw that caused McAuley to sag and his knees to dip. McAuley's heart commanded him to stay upright and he rode out the storm until the bell saved him.

Breathing heavily in his corner, McAuley's face was a mess, and yet when one recalled that he easily could have been polished off in the first round, the fact that he made it to a 13th round was a monumental achievement. Before this day, McAuley had never gone past 10 rounds, and he never absorbed this kind of beating in the process. It was the kind of mental and physical test that certified one's fortitude for a lifetime, no matter what the ultimate result.

But amazingly, the fight nearly turned again early in the 13th when a desperation overhand right to the forehead caused Bassa's legs to give way in a delayed reaction. But Morgan ruled it a slip and Bassa again banged his head against McAuley's. An overhand right caused McAuley to wince noticeably and another one a few seconds later signaled the beginning of the end. The ropes kept McAuley upright and as he sought the refuge of a clinch the strength that had carried him this far was nearly gone.

With McAuley trapped on the ropes, unable to move, Bassa launched a pair of right hands. The first blasted against his cheek and the second caused McAuley's head to sickeningly roll on his shoulders.

The challenger fell to his knees, rolled onto his back and stared up at the ring lights, his reserves bone dry.

"Oh, isn't that sad?" exclaimed Carpenter. "I think he's over and I think he's out. I don't think he has any more to give and in fact Barney Eastwood has thrown the towel in from the corner. It's all over in the 13th round and the desperately sad sight of McAuley, who so nearly became flyweight champion of the world...and Bassa and his camp celebrate a truly amazing victory."

The final right-left to the head that caught McAuley on the way down was unnecessary, and Morgan declared the fight over at 1:45 of the 13th round. This chapter in boxing history had closed in most theatrical fashion.

Both men gave everything they had, and for the Colombian champion it was a tremendous demonstration of championship bravery. Any questions about his worthiness were settled beyond doubt, as few fights would ever present such a severe test. Bassa simply would not lose, no matter what his Irish challenger threw at him.

According to the judges' scorecards, Bassa's 13th round rally saved his title. Harmodio Cedeno had McAuley up 115-112 while Ove Oveson and York Van Nixon had the Irishman up 114-112. The championship was within McAuley's grasp and the quality of the fight demanded that a second volume be written.

Epilogue: Bassa and McAuley met 11 months and one day later at the King's Hall in Belfast but the rematch didn't live up to the epic original. Still, it was a closely contested match that saw the Colombian retain his title with a 114-113, 115-113 and 116-112 decision. Before that, Bassa recorded defenses against Hilario Zapata (D 15) and Felix Marti (W 12).

Bassa would only fight three more times after defeating McAuley in the rematch. After beating Ray Medel (W 12) and Julio Gudino (KO 6), Bassa lost a split decision to Venezuelan Jesus "Kiki" Rojas in Baranquilla September 30, 1989. The 26-year-old Colombian never fought again and retired with a record of 22-1-1 (15 KO).

TALES FROM THE VAULT

After losing to Bassa the first time, McAuley took more than seven months off to recover from his injuries. A 10-round decision over Roy Thompson set up the rematch with Bassa, but though he lost it the championship dream was only delayed. Three months after defeating Thompson, McAuley dethroned IBF flyweight champion Duke McKenzie by decision at Wembley June 7, 1989.

McAuley would have an eventful reign, winning a curious split decision over Filipino Dodie Boy Penalosa in a fight two judges saw as 120-109 and 119-113 for McAuley while the other had it 117-112 for Penalosa. After pitching a virtual shutout over Louis Curtis, McAuley was the beneficiary of a most unique decision against Rodolfo Blanco. Despite suffering four knockdowns, McAuley managed to capture a unanimous decision, with the Irishman winning by five and four points on two cards. The nature of the decision led the IBF to order a rematch, but not until after McAuley notched wins over Pedro Feliciano (W 12) and Jake Matlala (KO 10).

The rematch, held June 11, 1992 in Bilbao, Spain, was another close affair but Blanco lifted the title by 114-113, 114-113, 115-112 decision. Just four days short of his 31st birthday, McAuley retired from boxing, satisfied that he had become the hero of Belfast Harry Carpenter declared him to be more than five years before.

LITTLE BIG MEN

Total Punches Landed/Thrown

Round	1	2	3	4	5	6	7	8	9	10	11	12	13	Total
Bassa	23/73	18/64	11/59	11/39	9/42	16/53	13/45	12/49	20/68	15/56	11/38	24/76	10/31	193/693
	32%	28%	19%	28%	21%	30%	29%	24%	29%	27%	29%	32%	32%	28%
McAuley	7/25	20/45	10/34	13/40	11/45	16/42	7/27	5/29	34/73	13/52	8/45	18/69	3/15	165/541
	28%	44%	29%	32%	24%	38%	26%	17%	47%	25%	18%	26%	20%	30%

Jabs Landed/Thrown

Round	1	2	3	4	5	6	7	8	9	10	11	12	13	Total
Bassa	5/25	7/27	1/18	5/18	1/13	2/10	2/13	3/16	1/6	4/14	8/19	5/16	1/5	45/200
	20%	26%	6%	28%	8%	20%	15%	19%	17%	29%	42%	31%	20%	23%
McAuley	3/8	5/15	2/10	4/19	1/22	2/10	1/13	3/18	0/0	2/15	4/28	5/21	1/4	33/183
	38%	33%	20%	21%	5%	20%	8%	17%	0%	13%	14%	24%	25	18%

Power Punches Landed/Thrown

Round	1	2	3	4	5	6	7	8	9	10	11	12	13	Total
Bassa	18/48	11/37	10/41	6/21	8/29	14/43	11/32	9/33	19/62	11/42	3/19	19/60	9/26	148/493
	38%	30%	24%	28%	28%	33%	34%	27%	31%	26%	16%	32%	35%	30%
McAuley	4/17	15/30	8/24	9/21	10/23	14/32	6/14	2/11	34/73	11/37	4/17	13/48	2/11	132/358
	24%	50%	33%	43%	43%	44%	43%	18%	47%	30%	24%	27%	18%	37%

Fidel Bassa vs. Dave McAuley I April 25, 1987, Belfast, Northern Ireland

TALES FROM THE VAULT

Betulio Gonzalez vs. Martin Vargas
November 4, 1978, Maracay, Venezuela

Throughout the 1970s, the flyweight rankings were graced by some of the greatest names in division history. Masao Ohba of Japan was the 112-pound precursor to Salvador Sanchez as he racked up five defenses against excellent opposition before an automobile accident snuffed out his life at age 23. Then came Miguel Canto, who used his incredible Hall of Fame-caliber skills to carve out a four-plus year reign encompassing 14 defenses, a division record until Pongsaklek Wonjongkam surpassed it in June 2006 with a fourth round TKO of Everardo Morales.

Ohba and Canto headed a division dotted with talented fighters. Shoji Oguma was a tricky southpaw who briefly held the WBC title in 1973 before losing it to Canto in 1974. The body-punching specialist was a persistent sort as he received – and lost – five shots at regaining a share of the title before finally breaking through against Korean WBC titlist Chan Hee Park in 1980. Hard-hitting Mexican Guty Espadas held the WBA belt from 1976 to 1978, knocking out all four of his challengers. Since Espadas and Canto were born in Merida in the Yucatan Peninsula, a unification match would have been a natural but for whatever reason the fight was never made. Other notable names included Venice Borkhorsor, Erbito Salavarria and Franco Udella, who challenged for the WBC title before being crowned the first 108-pound champion in 1975.

Ohba, Canto, Oguma, Borkhorsor, Udella, Salavarria and Espadas all had one common name on their ledgers – Betulio Gonzalez. For most of the decade, the Venezuelan cutie served as the measuring stick by which all other flyweights gauged themselves, and more than a few times they were found wanting. In all, Gonzalez enjoyed three reigns between 1972 and 1979, joining Pone Kingpetch and Chartchai Chionoi as the only three-time 112-pound kings.

Gonzalez was Ohba's first title challenger, and though he provided stiff resistance the Japanese retained his WBA belt over 15 rounds. Canto and Gonzalez fought three times, with Betulio out-pointing the young Canto in their first fight in 1973 for the WBC belt but Canto won the second and third fights in hard-fought 15-round split decisions in 1975 and 1976. Gonzalez and Oguma fought four times, and three of those fights were for belts. Five months after Gonzalez out-scored Oguma over 10 in a non-title go, Oguma lifted the WBC belt after capturing a 15-rounder in October 1975. They met twice more in 1979 for the WBA title, drawing over 15 and Gonzalez knocking out Oguma in 12.

Borkorsor knocked Gonzalez out in 10 rounds to capture the WBC title, ending Gonzalez's first reign. But the Thai was unable to stay at 112 pounds for long, leaving for the bantamweights after decisioning Salavarria. Gonzalez stopped Udella in

10 rounds in the only defense of his second reign, but his 1971 bout with Salavarria provided arguably the most out-of-the-ring fireworks.

Predictably, the Venezuelan judge scored the bout for Gonzalez while the Filipino judge saw it for Salavarria. Referee Mills Lane scored it even, and the resulting draw set off a riot inside the Luis Aparicio Stadium in Maracaibo. Immediately after the fight, the Zulia State Commission announced that Gonzalez should be named champion because Salavarria had used an illegal substance. The commission confiscated a bottle from Salavarria's corner and forwarded it to the WBC. On December 29, 1971, five weeks after the fight, the WBC stripped Salavarria, citing use of a stimulant in his "sugar water." The WBC offered to award the title to Gonzalez, but he declined.

On November 4, 1978 Gonzalez (64-7-2, 41 KO) met Martin Vargas (47-4-3, 30 KO) for the WBA belt in the bullring in Maracay, Venezuela. This marked the first defense of Gonzalez's third reign, which began three months earlier when he captured a surprising majority decision over Espadas. At 28, Gonzalez was thought to be slightly past his peak but against the powerful Espadas he showed tremendous drive and durability by brawling with the brawler.

Now 29, Gonzalez was defending against the 23-year-old Vargas, who was bidding to become Chile's first world champion. He had failed in two previous attempts in 1977, losing 15-round decisions to Canto in fights that were held just 10 weeks apart, the first in Canto's hometown of Merida and the rematch in Vargas' hometown of Santiago. Vargas was a tremendously active fighter, and just one piece of evidence was that he scored a one-round KO over John Cajina only seven days after his first challenge of Canto. Coincidentally, Vargas came into the Gonzalez fight off a two-round KO of Cajina three months previously.

The styles figured to mesh well, as Vargas was a straight-ahead bomber and Gonzalez a cagey cutie with well-rounded boxing skills and very respectable pop in the right hand. The fight began true to form, with Gonzalez flicking jabs on the retreat and Vargas shuffling ahead behind harder, snappier jabs. After sizing each other up in the first minute, Vargas nailed Gonzalez with a right to the chin that forced the champion to the ropes, but Gonzalez spun out and resumed his smooth boxing. Vargas continued to charge ahead, landing a chopping right to the ear and a follow-up left-left-right. Another right glanced off the face and a shotgun jab popped Gonzalez's head back. Vargas trapped Gonzalez on the ropes and fired a left hook to the body and a looping right over the top. Gonzalez tried to escape, but Vargas drove him back to the corner pad with a missed hook and a right that landed on target.

With Gonzalez in a vulnerable position, the challenger began to rain in blows. He unleashed hooks to the body and one-twos to the head and it was obvious he was going for the big score then and there. A ripping hook appeared to stun Gonzalez, who up until then had deflected many of Vargas' bombs with his arms, elbows and savvy upper body movement. The champion's apparent distress sparked Vargas into accelerating his already furious assault, and only the bell put a stop to it.

Vargas' desire to win a title was fierce and the Canto fights taught him that he shouldn't try to box with a boxer. He wanted to seize the initiative early and force Gonzalez to fight at an uncomfortably fast pace in the hope that he could wear the older man out. At the same time, however, he had to make sure his own excitement didn't exhaust his energy supply.

Vargas continued to control the action in round two, landing stiff jabs and catching the champion with overhand rights. A left hook forced Gonzalez to retreat to his own corner pad and the challenger blasted away to the head and body. Gonzalez whiffed on a hook and Vargas bulled him back to the ropes behind three jabs. A left hook appeared to wobble Gonzalez, who at times beckoned Vargas forward by raising his gloves and pumping them in "come-on" fashion. Two right hands landed flush and Vargas followed with a left-right-hook combo and two more strong rights. Gonzalez landed a light counter hook and a jab snapped Vargas' head, but Vargas was in fistic heat as he slammed in another overhand right.

Gonzalez's concrete jaw held up well under the assault, but it was clear he was being dominated by the young challenger, who pumped in punch after punch without coming up for air. Another surprising twist was the stiffness and accuracy of Vargas' jab, which clearly made the power blows that followed far more effective. It was thought going in that Gonzalez owned the better jab, but Vargas was proving the experts wrong, at least for now.

Vargas kept up the beat in round three as his thudding jabs popped back Gonzalez's head and drove him toward the corner. This time, Gonzalez spun away. Four more solid jabs from Vargas set up a hook to the side of the head. The Chilean challenger was scoring often, but Gonzalez was playing it cool because he was spending more time in ring center and offering stiffer resistance, especially with his jab. Also, Gonzalez chose to stand between rounds to signal Vargas that his early fireworks had no effect on his stamina.

Gonzalez started the fourth appearing more engaged, landing a glancing hook and sliding away from two Vargas jabs. But Vargas continued to carry the fight and was moving forward with more vigor. A left-right-hook and two solid jabs tagged Gonzalez and another solid one-two connected, but Gonzalez was taking the blows without apparent effect. His anvil chin received another test when Vargas drove Gonzalez to the ropes with two solid jabs and unleashed another two-fisted attack to the head and body. This time however, Gonzalez fought back against the wild-swinging Chilean, nailing Vargas with a hook. Vargas retaliated with a left-left-right punctuated with a whistling hook to the jaw. Gonzalez tried to escape from the ropes but Vargas' superior upper body strength allowed him to bulldoze Gonzalez back into position. A hook to the body, a jolting jab, a sharp hook and a big right nailed the champion and a right uppercut-overhand right combo momentarily stunned Gonzalez. The champ fired back with two lefts and used his shoulder to create enough room to escape the ropes. A right and a wild hook whizzed by Gonzalez's chin, and the champ made him pay with a short inside hook to end another exciting round.

After all that, Gonzalez again stood between rounds. All the years he spent at the championship level had taught him how to avoid the brunt of most blows. After all, in his last outing he absorbed the best Guty Espadas could offer and Espadas was one of the hardest hitters in flyweight history – and while a solid puncher, Vargas was no Espadas.

Vargas continued to land Espadas-like hooks in the fifth and he followed two of them with a solid overhand right. Gonzalez was no longer waiting to retaliate as he landed his own hook, but Vargas walked through it and pounded in a hook, a jab, a right uppercut to the body and another searing hook. Vargas was feeling his oats as he danced on his toes in tight circles around Gonzalez, coupling his jabs with overhand rights and quick combinations. Every time Gonzalez retaliated, he unleashed an even more powerful response. His fast start had earned him a lead on the scorecards and he clearly had the momentum.

That all changed midway through round five.

A quick counter hook spun Vargas' body 90 degrees clockwise and his right leg slipped from underneath him. As Vargas stumbled toward the ropes, Gonzalez detonated two right hand bombs to the chin that had Vargas clearly hurt for the first time in the fight. The stricken Vargas bent his upper body at the waist and tried to weave underneath Gonzalez's punches, but after the challenger straightened up the energized Gonzalez pumped in piston-like lefts and rights. Like Gonzalez before him, Vargas moved his upper body and spun off the ropes by putting his left glove behind Gonzalez's head and pivoting hard to his left while pushing the champ into the ropes. With Gonzalez tangled in the ropes, Vargas leaped in and landed a tremendous right. But Gonzalez collected himself and landed a looping hook to the face at the bell.

Tellingly, Gonzalez accepted the stool.

Both men jabbed energetically to start the sixth and Vargas followed his jabs with winging power shots that Gonzalez slipped easily. Vargas persisted in throwing three- and four-punch combinations and a fair share still got through. A fierce right snapped Gonzalez's head, but the Venezuelan was leather-tough as he absorbed Vargas' best and landed occasional but sharp counters. The two flyweights had set a tremendous pace and it was difficult to fathom how they could maintain it for 15 rounds.

Gonzalez shifted gears in the seventh, standing more flat-footed and appearing eager to trade. The champ whacked a right to the body and speared Vargas' face with hard, driving jabs. Though Vargas was still working his jab, his pace had slowed dramatically and his guard was now at chest level. The Chilean wanted to score a blowout in the early rounds but Gonzalez was more than up to the challenge, and with nine more rounds scheduled Vargas knew he had to conserve his energy for the stretch run.

Gonzalez was not willing to play along. The champ opened the eighth with three piercing jabs and countered a Vargas right with a hook to the belly and another sharp jab. Vargas remained the unquestioned aggressor, but the fight had now become a boxing match where intelligence, skill and experience would rule the day. Gonzalez drove a right to the body and countered a Vargas jab with a harder, snappier jab. When Vargas drove Gonzalez to the ropes with a right to the body, he immediately darted away from the corner and skillfully operated at ring center for the rest of the round.

Gonzalez was all business in the ninth as he raced out of the corner and planted a right-hook combo and snapped a jab to the face. He darted inside to land a right-left to the body, nipped back out and drilled a one-two and a hook to the jaw. Vargas roared back with a left-left-right and a hook to the body, but little by little the fight was taking a serious turn. Vargas was the man on the back foot and because that was not his normal fighting mode he appeared uncomfortable and his form was ragged. Gonzalez, sensing the Chilean's decaying energy, decided to engage Vargas in a test of strength on the inside. But this was no normal test, for not only would Gonzalez gauge his challenger's physical tools, he would also examine his intellectual goods.

Gonzalez backed Vargas into the ropes, placed his head on his opponent's shoulder and went to work. Gonzalez drove a right and a left to the body and snapped a hook to the chin. Vargas looked to rest as he leaned heavily against the ropes with his chin down and his arms formed a vertical wall around his ribs and head. Vargas offered no resistance when Gonzalez popped his head with several jolting uppercuts. Following a right to the body, Vargas decided he had enough and tried to spin off the ropes. But Gonzalez blocked his escape route by shooting out his right arm, hooking his glove around Vargas' waist and pulling him back onto the ropes. After absorbing several more punches, Vargas tried to pivot off the ropes but Gonzalez used the same maneuver to block him a second time, then a third. Gonzalez had learned plenty of tricks during his 73-fight career and they were serving him well as he masterfully kept his quarry where he wanted him while Vargas couldn't figure out an escape route. Finally, referee Stanley Christodoulou put a stop to Gonzalez's tactics by separating them and warning Gonzalez about using his head as a pivot.

At ring center, Gonzalez continued to engage Vargas in close quarters. Vargas fired away but most of his blows whizzed harmlessly past the ducking champion, who bullied him to the ropes with his head. This prompted Christodoulou to separate them once again, and an angry Gonzalez waved his right arm derisively because he felt Christodoulou was interfering with his work. Vargas voluntarily retreated toward the ropes and Gonzalez whacked away with crisp shots under, over and around the Chilean's protective shell. When Vargas fought back, the Venezuelan favorite dodged the blows and drove hooks to the body and uppercuts to the jaw. It was a breathtaking display of ring generalship as the wily Gonzalez used his speed, strength and savvy to seize the momentum.

Vargas entered the ring with a discoloration around the right eye and Gonzalez's sharp blows had raised a grotesque swelling around it. Early in the 10th, Christodoulou escorted Vargas to the ringside physician for a brief examination. Though the area around the eye was badly darkened, the physician immediately ruled the injury didn't affect his vision and let the fight continue.

Fearing his third title challenge was nearing an end, Vargas stepped up the pressure and drove Gonzalez to the ropes with a flurry of body shots. A huge right snapped Gonzalez's head and a vicious hook connected several seconds later. Gonzalez darted inside to smother Vargas' assault, but the Chilean challenger blasted away with an overhand right. Vargas was scoring big in the short term but the punishment he absorbed soon had a telling effect. As the seconds ticked by Vargas' shots were missing their mark by nearly a foot and he found himself resting on Gonzalez's shoulder a few moments later. Gonzalez welcomed the respite, as it allowed him to catch his breath. As the round closed, Gonzalez caught a second wind and bulled Vargas to the ropes, using his forearms to pin Vargas whenever he tried to escape. Vargas fought back with two left uppercuts and a hook, but his efforts had the look of a last gasp. After the round-ending bell, Gonzalez marched to his corner while glaring at Vargas over his shoulder. He knew the end was near and he wanted to make sure Vargas knew it as well.

The Chilean still needed convincing as he began the 11th on the offense. He landed a heavy hook to the jaw and bulled Gonzalez to the ropes with a flurry punctuated by a solid one-two. Vargas was like a racecar running on fumes in that he wanted to leave everything on the track – win or lose – before being pushed back into the garage. Gonzalez waited out the assault and attacked with short snappy blows on the inside when Vargas finally decelerated. Vargas clamped down on Gonzalez's left arm to force a break, then nailed the champ with a right to the shoulder the instant he stepped back. But Gonzalez maneuvered the challenger back to the ropes and sunk punch after draining punch on all legal parts of Vargas' anatomy. Still, Vargas wasn't done as he somehow got on his toes and snapped in a hook and two rights.

When Vargas tried another lead right Gonzalez saw his chance.

Gonzalez missed with a counter right, but the follow-up left hook caromed off the side of Vargas' head. Vargas' neck muscles relaxed, tipping his head forward, and as the effects of the punch set in Vargas' body slumped and fell backward toward the canvas. After Vargas regained his feet at eight, Gonzalez raced in for the finish behind full-bore body punches designed to tenderize his ribs before consuming them whole. Vargas fought back fiercely but his punches sailed over Gonzalez's head. Vargas should have held on to survive, but his instincts told him to fight back no matter what the consequences. Vargas even got the better of the action in the final 15 seconds, but Gonzalez saw the big picture: The Chilean may be going down fighting, but he was about to go down just the same.

The champ was eager to get back to work in round 12, but it was Vargas who opened on his toes and worked the jab. But the movement was a mirage for his true state and Gonzalez proved that with his first two punches of the round, a right that missed and a hook that exploded off Vargas' jaw. Vargas hung in the air for a split-second before crumbling to his knees. The challenger was desperately exhausted as he rolled onto his back but incredibly he was up by Christodoulou's count of four.

When Vargas moved back to the corner pad, Gonzalez applied the final touches to his strategic masterpiece. He missed with a right uppercut and a left hook but the straight right splattered against Vargas' face. Vargas fell heavily to the canvas and his body was spread-eagled near the ropes. Vargas valiantly regained his feet by eight but his corner men had thrown in the orange-colored towel to ring center at the count of six and were already in the ring. Christodoulou couldn't see what the seconds were doing and after taking a long look at Vargas during the count he came to the same decision they did – the Chilean's courageous challenge had reached its end.

Gonzalez threw both arms in the air but he didn't have the energy to do much else. The "old man" of the flyweight division had once again repelled the challenge of a young gun with a combination of style and guile. He was there in the early 1970s when Ohba was the best and he was still on top at an age when most men his size had already seen their better days. And for Gonzalez, those better days would continue – at least for a while.

Epilogue: Three months after beating Vargas, Gonzalez traveled to Hamamatsu, Japan to face old foe Oguma for the third time. The 15-round draw spawned a fourth encounter five months later and this time Gonzalez put an exclamation point on his superiority by stopping Oguma in 12. Gonzalez lost the title in his next defense to Panamanian southpaw Luis Ibarra on November 17, 1979 in Maracay.

Gonzalez fought for a title twice more. WBA champion Juan Herrera stopped Gonzalez in seven rounds in December 1981 and against Herrera's successor Santos Laciar, the 32-year-old Gonzalez managed to turn back the clock against the prime Laciar, fighting well before losing a split decision. Gonzalez was inactive for two years after the Laciar loss, returning with a one-round knockout over Alberto Alger to set up a fight with Alberto Castro, who beat Gonzalez over 12 rounds. Gonzalez mounted another improbable comeback at age 38, dropping to junior flyweight and drawing with Juan Blanco for the vacant Venezuelan 108-pound belt. His final fight took place on November 28, 1988 when future champion Rodolfo Blanco stopped the 39-year-old Gonzalez in eight rounds. Gonzalez, whose name now appears on the International Boxing Hall of Fame ballot, retired with a record of 75-12-4 (50 KO).

Like Gonzalez, Vargas dropped down to junior flyweight after losing to Gonzalez. He won 13 consecutive fights, with future champions Rafael Pedroza (KO 4) and Joey Olivo (W 10) among his victims. On June 1, 1980, Vargas challenged dominant WBA junior flyweight champion Yoko Gushiken, but he proved not to be much of a challenge as he lost every round before being stopped in eight rounds. He never again challenged for a major title but he continued on winning far more than he lost. He maintained an extremely active schedule, fighting nine times in 1981 (7-2) and 10 times in 1982 (8-2) before beginning a three-year hiatus after a 3-1 start in 1983.

Vargas embarked on a six-fight comeback in 1986, and many observers believed he was done for good after Jaime Miranda took out Vargas in seven rounds on June 26, 1987. But incredibly, the 42-year-old Vargas returned to the ring after a 10-year layoff and scored seven consecutive knockouts over modest opposition. Vargas extended the win streak to nine before Joel Garcia stopped the 43-year-old Chilean hero in one round on July 31, 1998. Vargas retired with a record of 91-15-3 (63 KO).

TALES FROM THE VAULT

Total Punches Landed/Thrown

Round	1	2	3	4	5	6	7	8	9	10	11	12	Total
Gonzalez	6/18	17/36	16/31	14/37	21/50	16/25	16/29	17/35	42/65	28/48	28/50	3/8	224/432
	33%	47%	52%	38%	42%	64%	55%	49%	65%	58%	56%	38%	52%
Vargas	37/101	30/116	27/68	44/105	34/77	29/75	22/62	18/66	17/68	29/80	19/75	2/16	308/909
	37%	26%	40%	42%	44%	39%	35%	27%	25%	36%	25%	12%	34%

Jabs Landed/Thrown

Round	1	2	3	4	5	6	7	8	9	10	11	12	Total
Gonzalez	1/6	14/21	16/30	7/17	14/31	11/18	13/23	14/26	7/13	4/5	1/3	1/2	103/195
	17%	67%	53%	41%	45%	61%	57%	54%	54%	80%	33%	50%	53%
Vargas	11/48	16/67	21/56	19/51	22/54	17/52	18/50	13/49	6/16	4/11	4/26	2/12	153/492
	23%	24%	38%	37%	41%	33%	36%	27%	38%	36%	15%	17%	31%

Power Punches Landed/Thrown

Round	1	2	3	4	5	6	7	8	9	10	11	12	Total
Gonzalez	5/12	3/15	0/1	7/20	7/19	5/7	3/6	3/9	35/52	24/43	27/47	2/6	121/237
	42%	20%	0%	35%	37%	71%	50%	33%	67%	56%	57%	33%	51%
Vargas	26/53	14/49	6/12	25/54	12/23	12/23	4/12	5/17	11/52	25/69	15/49	0/4	155/417
	49%	29%	50%	46%	52%	52%	33%	29%	21%	36%	31%	0%	37%

Betulio Gonzalez vs. Martin Vargas November 4, 1978, Maracay, Venezuela

Amado Ursua vs. Hilario Zapata
February 6, 1982, Panama City, Panama

"Be who you are and say what you feel, because those who mind don't matter and those who matter don't mind."

– Dr. Seuss, U.S. author and illustrator (1904-1991)

* * *

The above quote reflects a simple yet profound wisdom that can be applied to many venues of our existence, whether it be carrying out the mundane tasks of daily life or stepping onto the sporting stage to showcase one's athletic gifts against another competitor. Another way to put this is, "being yourself is the easiest thing to be, but if you choose to stray from what you do best, you do so at your own peril."

During the early 1980s, WBC junior flyweight champion Hilario Zapata was one of boxing's most gifted defensive specialists. At 5-6 1/2, the Panamanian sported a frame that resembled that of a praying mantis, and the likeness grew even stronger when he maneuvered his rubber-like body away from his opponents' blows. His formidable array of defensive tricks baffled his opposition and rendered them virtually impotent as he pecked and poked his way to often-lopsided unanimous decisions.

His safety-first style stood in stark contrast to that of the great Panamanian champions of the past, especially the ferocious and heroic Roberto Duran. As a lightweight, Duran was a monster of legendary proportions as he wiped out 11 of his 12 title challengers over a nearly seven-year reign. Duran carried that ferocity up to 147, where he humbled American Olympic hero Sugar Ray Leonard with a level of intensity that personified the term "machismo."

Duran's shadow enveloped Panama's other champions and no one suffered more from the comparison than Zapata. He was the subject of criticism from the press because he often chose not to emulate Duran's fiery style. His fights were cerebral performances more suited to a symphony hall than a sports stadium and many of those who witnessed them behaved accordingly. As Zapata put round after round in the bank, the crowd buzzed quietly among themselves and cheered only after the decision in Zapata's favor was announced.

Zapata only needed to point at his record to quiet, if not silence, his critics. Less than 17 months after turning pro with a two-round TKO over Victor Lopez, Zapata captured the WBC junior flyweight belt from Japan's Shigeo Nakajima by unanimous decision – in Tokyo, no less. Over the next 23 months, Zapata registered eight defenses, with the best opponents being Nakajima (KO 11), German Torres (W 15), Joey

Olivo (KO 13) and former champion Netrnoi Sor Vorasingh (KO 10). By the time the 23-year-old Zapata signed to fight Mexican Amado Ursua on February 6, 1982 at the Gymnasio Nueva Panama in Panama City, he was starting to be recognized as one of his sport's finest champions.

Still, he felt the sting of criticism from his countrymen and on occasion he attempted to add more aggression to his game. The tactic worked wonders against Olivo, who at 5-9 was even taller than Zapata, and had gained enough attention in the U.S. media to entice ABC's cameras to Panama City to chronicle his title shot. The champ, however, sprung his stylistic surprise to great effect, both inside the ring and with the fans that roared their appreciation. In his most recent outing against Vorasingh three months earlier, Zapata battered the far slower Thai with punches from all angles en route to his third knockout in his last six fights.

The 25-year-old Ursua sported an unimpressive record of 27-9, but his 21 knockouts indicated he possessed unusual potency for a junior flyweight. The Mexican's pro career began with promise as he won his first 12 fights while scoring 10 knockouts. The last eight of those knockouts came in succession and he was on a roll by the time he met Jose Gallegos in June 1976. Gallegos shocked Ursua by winning a 10-round decision, and after scoring two knockouts over limited foes he again stepped up the level of opposition. The story was the same as he was stopped in consecutive fights against Rafael Gandarilla (KO by 9) and Jose Guzman (KO by 8).

Ursua, whose nickname was "Panterita" (little panther), won his next six fights (including a seventh round KO over former WBA flyweight champion Alfonso Lopez) but he kept slamming his head against the glass ceiling when he encountered higher-level foes. Future champions Olivo (L 12), Luis Ibarra (L 10), Lupe Madera (KO by 6) and Juan Herrera (KO by 8) as well as former victim Torres (KO by 6) not only took the measure of Ursua but ended up flourishing. It appeared that Ursua was fated to be a mid-level gatekeeper for those who aspired to be serious contenders. For him, however, a championship belt was seemingly beyond his grasp.

Less than two months after losing to Herrera, Ursua knocked out Arturo Tebaqui in four rounds and followed up by stopping Luis Fernando Hernandez in nine rounds two months after that. But Ursua really gained notice when he defeated Francisco Montiel (W 10) and old foe Torres (W 12) for the Mexican junior flyweight title. Ursua's reward would be a crack at Zapata (19-1, 8 KO).

As they received their final instructions, the five-inch difference in height was graphically apparent as Zapata towered over Ursua. But Ursua's sturdy build and muscular shoulders served as evidence of his significant edge in power. Ursua, 107, chose to survey Zapata, 108, in the fight's opening seconds, after which he lunged in with a right to the body and two winging hooks that Zapata easily avoided. Ursua ducked under a Zapata jab-right hook combo, but the champ's long but light left landed on

Ursua's forehead. Though Zapata was on his toes, he did not back up one step. Still, Ursua was unable to penetrate Zapata's high guard and his longer reach forced the challenger to lunge in with every punch, exposing him to the Panamanian's counters and giving the champion plenty of time to avoid them. Zapata stabbed a left cross into Ursua's face and he missed with two more moments later. The weaving Ursua worked his way inside behind a solid, but low, right to the body but his follow-up left hook whizzed over Zapata's head.

As Ursua ducked under a Zapata right hook, the champion landed a left to the ear and caught the Mexican barreling in with a right hook to the jaw. Unhurt, Ursua advanced behind three punches that missed the target. But the crowd, seeing the action heating up, began to buzz excitedly. The buzz grew louder when Zapata forced Ursua backward behind a left to the ear and a solid right to the body.

The flow of the fight was moving toward Zapata as his measured aggression presented Ursua with a formidable physical puzzle. By forcing the 5-1 ½ Ursua backward, Zapata took away Ursua's best opportunity to succeed. He surely couldn't outbox Zapata from long range and Ursua was too far away to unleash his power. From this posture, Ursua had no chance to be who he was.

Meanwhile, Zapata was becoming more comfortable with the assignment before him. He banged a wide right to the body and a right-left-right hook combo drove Ursua further back. At the same time, he deftly averted Ursua's two-punch reply by blocking the right to the body and ducking under the hook. The moves were executed instinctively and were completed while also maintaining his textbook guard. Zapata was exhibiting all of his talents in their full flower and his uncharacteristic aggression so far was paying big dividends, and he capped an impressive opening round with a left to the stomach.

Ursua began the second on a crab-like retreat, rolling his shoulders and bending his knees in search of that elusive angle of attack. Zapata snapped a jab into Ursua's face and a second one to his body before gliding away. Ursua missed a lunging jab and Zapata made him pay by catching him with a long left cross as he leaned away. Zapata parried a right to the body and tagged Ursua with a light left to the face.

The secret to Zapata's defensive wizardry was his sense of anticipation. His years of experience enabled him to spot clues to his opponent's next punch, and his lightning-quick reflexes allowed him to defend against the expected blow even before his opponent launched it. Because Zapata already covered up his vulnerable spot, he could shift his focus to his offensive counterattack. Triple champion Wilfred Benitez called himself "Radar" and "The Bible of Boxing" because he possessed similar gifts.

As Zapata moved forward to consolidate his advantage, he saw Ursua bend his knees and dip to his right. Zapata's experience told him that Ursua was about to launch a right to the body, so he dropped his left arm so his glove could parry the punch. But

Ursua crossed him up by changing the angle from a side winding right to the body to a swooping uppercut to the jaw that nailed Zapata flush. The champion's body slumped toward the canvas, and Ursua drove him to the floor with a follow-up left to the ear.

Zapata crashed heavily on his backside but was up at referee Ismael Quinones Falu's count of three. He stumbled slightly as he walked toward his corner, after which he shrugged his shoulders and stretched his neck muscles. When Falu allowed the fight to continue, Zapata's face was a mask of composure. Because Zapata was in excellent condition, he recovered quickly from the knockdown.

Ursua went for the kill but his wild swings found only air – and by a large margin. Zapata slipped a home run right, ducked a hook and pulled away from a right hook. Ursua missed with a right uppercut and Zapata countered with a right hook, and when Ursua whiffed on a winging hook Zapata stung him with a hard jab. The champion missed a left cross and barely avoided a dangerous looking right hook before landing a right to the cheek.

The boxing match was now a firefight and the quick blows presented an element of danger not usually seen in Zapata's fights. Ursua connected with a heavy left to the head but missed with a right because Zapata ducked it. Just as Ursua began to spring out of a crouch, Zapata landed his best punch of the fight – a crunching left cross that drove Ursua to the canvas. Just seconds after being on the floor, Zapata had turned the tables with an unlikely power surge.

Ursua leaped to his feet as soon as his behind hit the floor, but referee Falu did not issue a mandatory eight count as he did for Zapata. Instead, he wiped Ursua's gloves and allowed the fight to continue immediately, making it unclear as to whether he actually called Ursua's fall a knockdown.

Zapata acted as if it was as he drove Ursua back with a right-left and pelted him with an inside left to the face before darting out of range. Zapata banged a right uppercut to the body and beat Ursua to the punch again with a short left cross to the jaw that twisted the challenger's head. The crowd roared with each landed Zapata punch as the hometown champion sought a rare spectacular knockout.

As Ursua sought a clinch, Zapata cranked a right uppercut to the body and another to the face. A heavy left to the ear and a right to the face had Ursua in full retreat, staggering off balance toward the ropes. Zapata threw all caution aside and showed an unusual animalistic streak. His blood was in full boil as he banged more rights in the clinch and he strode in confidently as he prepared to apply the finishing touches.

Though Zapata clearly had the upper hand, he was entering perilous territory. He was indulging in a realm that was unfamiliar to him and went against the skill set that he spent years perfecting. Zapata was built to be a 15-round fighter that used subtle skills to bedazzle his opposition, not a toe-to-toe slugger bent on destruction. When one sails into uncharted waters, when one chooses not to "be who he is," he ends up paying a price. But Zapata believed the rewards far outweighed the risks, so he pressed forward.

As Zapata barreled in with hands unusually low, Ursua planted his feet and delivered a scorching right hook to the jaw that landed with full impact. Zapata's head twisted awkwardly and his legs sagged toward the canvas. But the champion managed to grab Ursua's waist and pull himself upright.

Ursua's blow would serve as a warning shot to Zapata, and to his credit the champ regained his equilibrium quickly. Ursua winged a wild right-left that Zapata avoided and a right uppercut-hook-hook combo missed as well. Zapata bought a few more seconds of recovery time by blatantly pushing down on Ursua's neck with his right elbow for several long seconds, a move that brought no warning from Falu. Zapata continued the dirty fighting as he landed a chopping left behind the ear. When Ursua backed away, he gestured at Zapata to complain about the foul. An angry Zapata lifted both gloves and as if to say, *"quit whining, you big baby; this is a fight!"*

Zapata was right about one thing: The boxing match had turned into a fight whose chaotic environment was not suited to Zapata's talents. Besides the all-out aggression, it was not like Zapata to taunt his opponents, so he was indulging in yet another unfamiliar realm.

Seconds after being teased by the champion, Ursua produced the perfect response.

The challenger dipped his knees, planted his feet and torched Zapata with a short explosive rising right to the jaw. The punch steamed past Zapata's low left and upon impact his body sagged toward the canvas. His head hit the floor hard and he was fully stretched out on his back, his eyes opened wide. At Falu's count of five he turned his body over and rolled to all fours and at seven he attempted to push himself up. But his arms weren't strong enough to finish the job, so he toppled forward again. Zapata finally managed to scramble to his feet, but he did so a split second after Falu counted him out at 2:47 of round two. As the referee wrapped his arms around the now former champion and led him to his corner, Zapata tottering legs confirmed he was in no shape to fight on.

Ursua was quickly surrounded by a scrum of reporters who wanted to chronicle his first words as champion. The Mexican journeyman had just pulled off a massive upset in the hometown of a dominant titleholder with a spectacular one-punch knockout. One look at his record told many that Ursua didn't have what it took to ascend his sport's highest mountain but he ended up standing at the summit because he stayed faithful to who he was and took advantage of Zapata's uncharacteristic boldness. He didn't care if some thought he was a caretaker champion, for all that mattered to him was the second word of that phrase – champion.

Epilogue: Ursua's reign as WBC junior flyweight champion lasted just 66 days as he dropped a majority decision to Tadashi Tomori in Tokyo. Three months later, Ursua lost a 10-rounder to future 108-pound legend Jung Koo Chang and was beaten in his next two outings by highly rated Candido Tellez (L 10) and Juan Manuel Rios (L 10). Ursua never again challenged for a belt and his pattern for uneven results continued apace. He went 6-8 in his final 14 fights, beating future title challenger Efren Pinto (KO 6) but losing to Juan Herrera (L 10), Dodie Boy Penalosa (L 10), Richard Clarke (L 10) and Luis Monzote (L 12), among others. His final recorded fight took place December 13, 1987 in Chungmu Gymnasium in Taegu, Korea when future two-division titlist Yul Woo Lee stopped him in five rounds. The 31-year-old Ursua's record was 34-21 (25 KO).

Just four months after losing to Ursua, Zapata regained the title after scoring a split decision over Tomori. He notched two defenses against Chang (W 15) and Tomori (KO 8) before signing to fight Chang again due to the close and controversial nature of that decision. Zapata, who served time in jail shortly before the bout, arrived in Korea in woeful condition and barely made the 108-pound limit. Chang swarmed over the weight-weakened Zapata and stopped him in three lopsided rounds. Things didn't get much better for Zapata in his next outing eight months later against bantamweight Harold Petty. In a bout marred by numerous Zapata fouls, the Panamanian was stopped in 10 rounds.

Zapata dropped back down to flyweight and won four fights to earn a shot at Santos Laciar's WBA belt. Laciar and Zapata fought 15 close but tedious rounds but the homestanding Argentine won a unanimous decision. Four fights later, Zapata became a two-division champion when he out-pointed Alonzo Strongbow for Laciar's vacated belt, and the Panamanian would enjoy a career renaissance. Zapata defended the WBA belt five times in 11 months before losing a controversial 15-round nod to Fidel Bassa in Barranquilla, Colombia. The rematch six months later in Panama City brought even more chaos as Zapata floored and clearly out-pointed Bassa only to have the fight declared a draw. Furious, the fans rioted, and though there was a strong case to make a third match it never took place.

Zapata fought once more for a title, but at age 34 he didn't have enough to hold off dominant WBC super flyweight champion Sung Kil Moon, who knocked Zapata out at 2:54 of round one. His final record reads 43-10-1 (14 KO).

Total Punches Landed/Thrown

Round	1	2	3	4	5	6	7	8	9	10	11	12	Total
Ursua	3/36	6/29											9/65
	8%	21%											14%
Zapata	7/45	15/38											22/83
	16%	39%											27%

Jabs Landed/Thrown

Round	1	2	3	4	5	6	7	8	9	10	11	12	Total
Ursua	0/6	0/2											0/8
	0%	0%											0%
Zapata	0/12	2/10											2/22
	0%	20%											9%

Power Punches Landed/Thrown

Round	1	2	3	4	5	6	7	8	9	10	11	12	Total
Ursua	3/30	6/27											9/57
	10%	22%											16%
Zapata	7/33	13/28											20/61
	21%	46%											33%

Amado Ursua vs. Hilario Zapata February 6, 1982, Panama City, Panama

TALES FROM THE VAULT

Masao Ohba vs. Chartchai Chionoi
January 2, 1973, Tokyo, Japan

Those who choose to fight for a living, no matter what level on the pyramid they occupy, are usually involved in the quest to improve their lot. The four-round fighter wants to ascend to the six-round level while the same could be said of six-round, eight-round and main-event boxers. The ultimate goal is always the same – a world title – but only a select few ever find themselves basking in that special glow of fulfillment.

Once fighters become champions, they are called to ascend a steeper and more treacherous mountain – one that if successfully scaled would lead them to a level of greatness that would live on long after their physical bodies have left this earth. Every time a champion turns back a challenger, he takes one step closer toward that summit. The conquering of a well-regarded challenger provides a high-risk shortcut, and the impressive disposing of said challenger speeds up the process even more.

Then there are fighters like Masao Ohba, who was on his way to becoming one of history's greatest flyweights before tragedy prevented him from completing his journey. But few fighters couldn't have asked for a better swan song than what Ohba produced when he fought Chartchai Chionoi on January 2, 1973 at Tokyo's Nihon University Auditorium.

Ohba achieved his professional summit at an extraordinarily early stage. He was just one day past his 21st birthday when he knocked out Thailand's Berkrerk Chartvanchai in 13 rounds to capture the WBA flyweight title, and over the next 21 months Obha put together an excellent reign while sprinkling in various non-title outings. He repelled the challenges of Betulio Gonzalez (W 15), Fernando Cabanella (W 15), former champion Susumu Hanagata (W 15) and Orlando Amores (KO 5) to establish credibility and stability to his reign. After disposing of Natalio Jimenez in a five-round non-title outing, Ohba signed to defend against the most experienced and dangerous challenger he had yet faced – Chartchai Chionoi.

The 31-year-old Chionoi is regarded as one of history's hardest hitting flyweights and he eventually converted that power into three title reigns. His first crack at a title occurred more than seven years and 53 fights into his career, mostly because he had lost 10 times along the way. Besides defeats to strong campaigners such as Mitsunori Seki (L 10), Ernesto Miranda (L 10), Hiroyuki Ebihara (L 12) and Bernardo Caraballo (L 10), Chionoi also lost to lesser lights Akira Oguchi (L 10), Singtong Por Tor (L 6) and Tsuyoshi Nakamura (L 10, L 12 in back-to-back fights).

But once Chionoi acquired his sea legs, he blasted a swath through the division and made his mark. Following a decision defeat to Hajime Taroura, Chionoi rolled off 15 consecutive victories, including a title-winning ninth-round KO over Walter McGowan, a seventh-round knockout in the rematch and a 13th round stoppage of Efren Torres, one of the most savage and punishing flyweight title fights ever staged. The Thai lost the belt to Torres (KO by 8) in the rematch 13 months later but regained it from Torres by unanimous decision in the rubber match 13 months after that before 40,000 fans at the National Stadium in Bangkok.

Chionoi's second reign was as short-lived as the first as Filipino Erbito Salavarria scored a second round KO in his first defense. Following a 10-round draw with Snappy Asano, Chionoi won five in a row (including a 10-rounder over Chartvanchai) to earn the chance against Ohba. With a victory, Chionoi would become the second man to earn a third flyweight title reign (countryman Pone Kingpetch was the first).

Plenty of eyebrows were raised at the weigh-in when Chionoi (57-14-2 with 35 KO) was a surprisingly light 109¼, nearly nine pounds fewer than in his most recent outing against Esteban Rangel (KO 2) 10 weeks earlier. Ohba (34-2-1 with 15 KO) was a more conventional 111 ¾.

Ohba began the fight on the move, carving tight circles around the stalking Chionoi behind fast jabs. Just 20 seconds into the fight, however, Chionoi proved the light body weight had no effect on his power as an overhand right to the ear sent the champ stumbling into the ropes, his body turning to the right as he was doing so. Another sweeping right just missed the target and Ohba escaped his crisis by pivoting to his left behind a cuffing hook.

Following a few seconds of probing jabs by both men, Chionoi wound up and blasted Ohba's cheek with an overhand right that sent him heavily to the canvas. Just 38 seconds had elapsed and already the champion was in a world of trouble. As he fell, Obha's right foot had folded awkwardly beneath his torso and he limped a few feet toward the farthest corner after arising at referee Yusaku Yoshida's count of five. As Yoshida commanded them back into battle, Ohba tried to shake some life back into his injured limb, and his duress gave Chionoi the green light to gun for the finish.

Chionoi's winging right and a follow-up one-two forced Ohba into the corner pad and the champion's legs were still wobbly after Chionoi spun him toward the champion's corner. A short hook to the button made Ohba shudder, and thoughts of the quick coronation of a once, and new, champion became very real.

But this situation was not new to Ohba, for he faced similar adversity against Amores in the first round of that fight. His resourcefulness got him through that crisis and he had every reason to believe his instincts would serve him well again. Those instincts, though, didn't include clinching, and even as he struggled to put weight on his right foot he fended off the charging Chionoi with sneaky rights, light one-twos and defensive maneuvers that made it difficult for the challenger to draw a bead.

A heavy right-left sent Ohba stumbling forward into Chionoi, bulling him into the ropes. Ohba earned a brief respite by ducking under a big hook and countering with a soft right. Chionoi ended the round in hot pursuit, but his KO swings only disturbed the air.

Chionoi was so eager to resume his assault that he walked to ring center several seconds before the second round bell, only to have Yoshida chase him back. Though Ohba was still reluctant to put full weight on his foot, he still attempted to execute his customary stick-and-move attack. When it became clear to Chionoi that Ohba was no longer in mortal danger, he let off the throttle and chose to engage in a jabbing contest, which was how he set up the first-round knockdown.

Ohba showed the first real signs of recovery 49 seconds into the round as he landed a hard right to the face that made Chionoi take a step back. Ohba soon adopted the role of cautious aggressor, and his precise jabs snapped back the challenger's head with regularity. Those jabs helped Ohba diversify his attack, for a right to the ribs connected solidly and he began to throw hooks off one successful double jab. Ohba absorbed yet another overhand right late in the round, but this time he took it without flinching.

The third was an impressive bounce-back round for Ohba, and he carried his newfound momentum early into the fourth as a left to the stomach and a right to the chin buckled Chionoi's legs. It was the first time the challenger showed Ohba he could be stunned, and for Ohba it marked an important psychological turning point. Ohba picked his spots wisely, landing a one-two to the face here, a counter hook over Chionoi's right to the body there and sprinkling in jabs in between. It was a recipe that Ohba had used time and again: Slowly breaking down opponents with skill, speed, savvy and, most importantly, patience. Though Chionoi showed signs of vulnerability, Ohba never pressed for the knockout. Instead, he approached his fights like families approach the concept of compound interest – they let the passage of time produce the big payoff in the end.

Meanwhile, Chionoi continued to work his left, jabbing with Ohba and occasionally turning them into hooks. Ohba may have been throwing more often, but Chionoi knew that his single-shot power could turn the fight at any moment. Still, a one-two in the final seconds made Chionoi seek a clinch, one of the few in the fight.

Ohba began the fifth working the jab furiously, quadrupling it at one point. His right foot no longer showed signs of duress as he moved in tight circles with more fluidity. He still had trouble avoiding Chionoi's looping right, but instead of wavering he came back with a left-left-right and a second right over the top moments later. Ohba's busy left also produced a noticeable swelling under the challenger's left eye, and his high cheekbones made the injury appear even more pronounced. Still, Chionoi continued to throw with full strength; even his jabs carried jolting power. Because Ohba's industriousness and command of range carried the day, the Thai was forced to operate within Ohba's rules of engagement.

With several good rounds behind him, Ohba's confidence surged. Midway through the sixth, he felt ornery enough to bull Chionoi to the ropes and pop him with a right-left-right before darting back to long range. He constantly stabbed Chionoi with jabs and followed with bouquets of hooks, crosses and uppercuts that carried more steam than at any juncture thus far.

As the fight neared the halfway point, Chionoi knew he had squandered a golden opportunity and he was determined to create a second chance. Choinoi found pay dirt early in the seventh in the form of a looping left to the chin that snapped Ohba's head straight back and forced him to retreat toward the ropes. Another snappy one-two connected as Ohba rolled his head away, and he followed moments later with a solid jab and heavy right to the ribs. Ohba was unfazed by Chionoi's rally as he continued to work steadily. A right over the top and a right uppercut to the jaw caught the challenger's attention and a left-left-right-left capped off a close, competitive round.

Chionoi continued to turn on the aggression in the eighth as he caromed a left hook off Ohba's head while Ohba picked away at Chionoi's defense by going under and over in unpredictable sequences. Chionoi landed a right to the solar plexus, but his wider punches also created countering opportunities for the champion.

Midway through the eighth, Chionoi made the mistake of throwing a lazy jab and Ohba seized on it by throwing a furious 12-punch flurry. That outburst was designed to gauge Chionoi's reaction – and Ohba saw telltale signs of weakness.

A right cross to the jaw prompted Chionoi to retreat weakly to the ropes, his left glove pawing at his eye. His body language oozed discouragement and the shark-like Ohba pounded in lightning-quick but feather-fisted combinations that threatened to overwhelm the challenger. The beating continued throughout the rest of the round, and it marked the most sustained dominance by either man so far.

However, Ohba still felt Chionoi was not yet ready to be taken out. He came into the ring expecting to go the distance and because he was scheduled to fight seven more rounds he saw the eighth as part of the tenderizing process. The champion was content to let the cumulative punishment sink in while marshaling his own strength for his next attack. Plus, he knew even a weakened Chionoi was still a risky proposition and he proved it as a hook made Ohba raise his glove and feel his jaw.

Midway through the ninth, a left-left-right sent Chionoi tottering away. Ohba sought to consolidate his advantage, but the challenger clamped on a well-timed clinch and came out of it with a hook to the jaw that forced the champ to retreat. Moments later, Chionoi landed a one-two to the face but Ohba had recovered sufficiently enough to engage the challenger in a hot exchange that lasted until the bell.

Chionoi sensed the fight's ebb and flow was turning in his direction and his feelings were confirmed as he began the 10th with strong hooks to the body and chin and a jarring jab to the jaw. Another hook crashed off Ohba's cheek but the champion remained composed as he ripped a one-two through Chionoi's guard and fired off a combination as the challenger languished on the ropes. A thumping right to the ribs forced Ohba to take a deep gulp of air but he responded with two heavy rights and a hook to the head.

Both men were digging deep to find the resources to achieve victory. Each man had proved they possessed championship-level physical skills, but, as is the case in most matches, it would be the man with championship-level will who would emerge victorious.

Seventy-six seconds into the 11th round, a lead right to the temple caused Chionoi's torso to bend horizontally and his unsteady legs to stumble toward the ropes. Ohba pursued, but Chionoi was able to slap on a clinch. A hurtful right further weakened Chionoi and though he fought back courageously one could sense something significant had been taken out of him. He was nearing the causeway from which only a Herculean effort could rescue him. Meanwhile, Ohba surged in a measured, patient way, content to further dress his quarry for the kill. The final five seconds of the round saw Ohba land three crushing rights to the jaw as Chionoi was propped up against the ropes. Though Ohba was in command, he too was tired as he heaved deeply with blood staining his mouthpiece. Ohba's rally was produced by resources only great champions possess, resources Chionoi once owned but were no longer in full flower.

Ohba tested Chionoi's sturdiness in the opening seconds of the 12th with a left-left-right-left but the challenger responded with a head-snapping left that told Ohba that he was not yet ready to yield. Still, Ohba fired his combinations with renewed purpose and added energy. He was like a cross-country skier who ruthlessly sought to dispose of his rival with a surge in the final few kilometers, but Chionoi's will once again welled up as he crashed two short hooks off the jaw. A third left coupled with an overhand right forced Ohba to clinch and suddenly the Thai was in the midst of a mini-rally.

It turned out to be an illusion, for when Ohba came out of that clinch he finally found the key to breaking Chionoi's spirit.

With 56 seconds remaining in the round, Ohba cracked a chopping right off the tip of Chionoi's chin that prompted the challenger to turn away and seek the sanctuary of the ropes. But the ropes would provide no safety as the champion rushed after him with an animalistic 34-punch assault that ended only after Chionoi fell to the canvas. Overcome by fury, Ohba smashed a final right to the jaw an instant after Chionoi hit the canvas and Yoshida moved in to pull him away.

As Yoshida administered the mandatory eight-count, Chionoi arose and looked over the ropes at the heavily pro-Ohba crowd, who was in mass hysteria. Yoshida ordered the fight to continue, but in reality the fight was over as Ohba belabored Chionoi with another 23-punch salvo that sent the challenger stumbling forward toward Ohba's corner and collapsing in a heap. Chionoi was an utterly spent force as he rested on the canvas and looked up at Yoshida, yet he arose again and prepared himself to absorb Ohba's next attack.

Only seven seconds remained in the round when Yoshida waved the fighters back to battle, and Ohba used every one as he drove Chionoi back to the corner post and blasted away with impunity. With Chionoi rendered helpless, Yoshida stepped in at exactly the 3:00 mark and declared Ohba the TKO winner. At the time of the stoppage, Ohba was ahead 53-48, 53-49 and 52-50 on the five-point must system.

At that moment, Ohba allowed his body to relax for the first time in nearly an hour. It was a long and difficult struggle for the 23-year-old, and his open-mouthed expression of triumph mixed with exhaustion revealed just how strenuous it was. Ohba had faced a challenger who had been at the mountaintop and was primed to regain his past glory, and he managed to take everything he could dish out before ultimately coming out on top. It was the ultimate test of a young champion's composure and competitive drive and the fact that he emerged victorious revealed everything fans ever needed to know about his potential place in boxing's giant pyramid. Only by beating the best can one become the best, and by beating Chionoi, Ohba proved beyond doubt that he would be a most difficult man to knock off the summit.

Epilogue: Just 22 days after this fight, Ohba was dead. He was driving his Corvette down a Tokyo expressway when he hit a truck going in the other direction. He had planned to vacate his 112-pound belt to go after the bantamweight title, but those plans were tragically cut short. His final record was 35-2-1 (16 KO).

Four months after losing to Ohba, Chionoi stopped Fritz Chervet in five rounds to win Ohba's vacated belt and finally joined Kingpetch as a three-time flyweight champ. He defended against Hanagata (W 15) and Chervet (W 15) before Hanagata brutally stopped Chionoi in six rounds to capture the belt. Chionoi fought twice more, beating Willie Asuncion over 10 rounds and losing to Rodolfo Francis via sixth round TKO. The 33-year-old Chionoi retired with a mark of 61-18-3 with 36 knockouts.

TALES FROM THE VAULT

Total Punches Landed/Thrown

Round	1	2	3	4	5	6	7	8	9	10	11	12	Total
Ohba	13/48	23/67	26/72	28/71	39/83	35/86	27/83	43/100	31/85	37/93	33/104	38/104	373/996
	27%	34%	36%	39%	47%	41%	33%	43%	36%	40%	32%	37%	37%
Chionoi	34/90	17/74	17/74	22/75	17/66	20/67	25/73	20/80	30/80	21/82	23/76	20/66	266/903
	38%	23%	23%	29%	26%	30%	34%	25%	38%	26%	30%	30%	29%

Jabs Landed/Thrown

Round	1	2	3	4	5	6	7	8	9	10	11	12	Total
Ohba	4/19	15/41	11/45	17/44	29/57	18/45	13/44	13/36	15/49	15/43	13/41	7/25	170/489
	21%	37%	24%	39%	51%	40%	30%	36%	31%	35%	32%	28%	35%
Chionoi	5/35	11/60	9/54	12/54	12/46	14/42	13/50	7/40	16/49	12/48	12/39	5/26	128/543
	14%	18%	17%	22%	26%	33%	26%	18%	33%	25%	31%	19%	24%

Power Punches Landed/Thrown

Round	1	2	3	4	5	6	7	8	9	10	11	12	Total
Ohba	9/29	8/26	15/27	11/27	10/26	17/41	14/39	30/64	16/36	22/50	20/63	31/79	203/507
	31%	31%	56%	41%	38%	41%	36%	47%	44%	44%	32%	39%	40%
Chionoi	29/55	6/14	8/20	10/21	5/20	6/25	12/23	13/40	14/31	9/34	11/37	15/40	138/360
	53%	43%	40%	48%	25%	24%	52%	32%	45%	26%	30%	38%	38%

Masao Ohba vs. Chartchai Chionoi January 2, 1973, Tokyo, Japan

Yuri Arbachakov vs. Muangchai Kittikasem I
June 23, 1992, Tokyo, Japan

All prospects that aspire to be great reach a point in time when they are confronted with their destiny. It is the moment when they must put into action everything they've ever learned and find out whether it is good enough to see them through or if it crumbles under pressure, self-imposed or otherwise.

During the era of eight undisputed world champions, these points came in waves and there was some margin for error because there was always a redemptive fight just around the corner. But during this age of glossy records borne of meticulous matchmaking, fighters are presented with an all-or-nothing scenario: Succeed, and become a champion with the potential to win fame and fortune. Fail, and be forced to wait two years – and perhaps longer – to get another chance. That is, *if* you get another chance.

Yuri Arbachakov was one of many fighters during the 1990s that had been confronted with this situation, but his had an added twist. When he signed to fight WBC flyweight champion Muangchai Kittikasem in Tokyo, he not only was fighting for his own success but he also was fighting for a place in his nation's history. For if he was successful, he would be the first Soviet-bloc fighter to win a professional boxing championship following the 1991 break-up.

The 25-year-old Arbachakov was a product of the highly successful Soviet amateur boxing program, winning both the European and World Championships as a flyweight en route to a 165-21 record. Upon turning pro in 1990, Arbachakov moved to Japan as part of Soviet Union president Mikhail Gorbachev's perestroika program, which was designed to restructure the nation's economic, political and social norms but unwittingly led to the nation's collapse and the end of the Cold War. Arbachakov began training at Tokyo's Kyoei Gym and was soon billed as "Yuri Ebihara," taking the surname of former flyweight champion Hiroyuki Ebihara.

Arbachakov began his pro career by knocking out Allan Tanaka in one round at Tokyo's Kokugikan on February 1, 1990. His sophisticated boxing style and wrecking-ball right cross quickly produced a stir at the world level, especially after he dusted former IBF flyweight champion Rolando Bohol in two rounds in just his sixth fight and polished off Takahiro Mizuno in one round to win the vacant Japanese title. Arbachakov's KO string eventually grew to 10 before Samanchai Chalermsri managed to last the 10-round distance. His final tune-up before his challenge of Kittikasem was a three-round KO of Suvatchai Chalermsri two months earlier.

In Kittikasem, Arbachakov (12-0, 11 KO) was facing a man two years younger chronologically but miles ahead of him in terms of world-class experience and quality of opposition. Kittikasem (20-1, 12 KO), whose birth name is Natawut Jataweemol, beat Tacy Macalos in just his seventh fight to win the IBF junior flyweight title and made three successful defenses over the next 11 months: Macalos (KO 7), Jeung Jae Lee (KO 3) and Abdi Pohan (W 12). With each passing month, the 108-pound limit was as formidable as his opponents, and by the time he met 1988 silver medalist Michael Carbajal on July 29, 1990 he needed several attempts before finally making it. His weakened condition, combined with Carbajal's immense talent, led to four knockdowns and a seven round KO loss.

Shorn of his crown, Kittikasem immediately moved up to flyweight, where he regained his knockout touch. He quickly disposed of Vic Galme (KO 1) and Welgie Leonora (KO 3) to earn a crack at longtime WBC flyweight champion Sot Chitalada in Ayuthaya, Thailand on February 15, 1991. Hungry for redemption, Kittikasem steamrolled the venerable champion before winning his second divisional title by sixth round KO.

Kittikasem proved to be a solid champion as he turned back three credible challengers. Against the comebacking Jung Koo Chang, Kittikasem roared back from three knockdowns to stop the South Korean legend with just 24 seconds left on the clock. Five months later – and two months after decisioning Lito Gonzaga in a non-title bout – Kittikasem won a majority decision from the 18-1-1 Alberto Jimenez. Then, on February 28, 1992 he sent Chitalada into retirement with a ninth round TKO. In the two months before fighting Arbachakov, Kittikasem scored a pair of 10-round non-title wins over Eddy Mermasugi and Tarman Garzim.

The normally aggressive Kittikasem began the fight on his toes and kept his distance from Arbachakov, who inched forward behind subtle head, shoulder and foot feints. Arbachakov connected with a jab to the belly while Kittikasem won an exchange of jabs because his landed more heavily. The two men intensely studied one another for openings that didn't immediately present themselves.

Fifty-five seconds into the fight, the challenger deked a jab with his shoulder then dropped a solid right to the temple before nipping away from Kittikasem's retaliatory right. Arbachakov exerted understated pressure by using his feet to cut off Kittikasem's potential escape routes. One could see right away that despite his relative inexperience as a pro, he was an extremely well-schooled fighter who knew how to dictate ring position using every tool at his disposal, not just with his swifter hands and sharper punches.

A sweeping hook caught Kittikasem moving to his right and moments later Arbachakov dove inside behind a long, fast right to the stomach. Like an offensive coordinator in football, Arbachakov was "spreading the field" by forcing Kittikasem to defend multiple spots, something that was impossible given the challenger's hand speed and intelligent punch selection. Arbachakov was a ring scientist who practiced thinking man's aggression, striking a perfect balance between caution and risk.

With 37 seconds remaining, both men launched rights with Arbachakov's catching Kittikasem coming in. The champion's follow-through on the missed right sent him stumbling across the ring toward the ropes where Arbachakov popped him with two hard jabs, one to the head and the other to the body. In the closing moments, Kittikasem tried a jab only to be nailed by a hair-trigger lead right to the temple that dropped him to all fours as the bell sounded. Kittikasem instantly regained his feet and walked unsteadily toward his corner.

Now knowing the formidable challenge before him, Kittikasem determinedly banged his gloves together and quickly rolled his head and neck to begin the second. Kittikasem still boxed at long range but he was no longer on the move, planting his feet firmly in favor of his calling card – power. As Kittikasem landed a right to the body Arbachakov was on his toes, nipping in and out in search of the perfect punching range. Each punch he threw was preceded with a cerebral series of moves and feints designed to open up Kittikasem's guard and when the challenger struck he did so with speed and accuracy.

As the second round continued, however, Kittikasem was getting a better lay of the land. Kittikasem caught Arbachakov with a looping right an instant after taking a hook and a pair of jabs snapped back the challenger's head. A jab-right to the body combo connected for the champ and Kittikasem answered a long right to the head with a solid hook and a home run overhand right that caught Arbachakov on the end of it. While Kittikasem was doing better, Arbachakov still finished the round better as a looping right to the temple sent Kittikasem badly off balance.

Arbachakov opened the third by maneuvering Kittikasem toward the ropes and connecting with a pair of jabs, one to the body and one to the head. But as the challenger pondered his next move, the champion struck – and struck hard.

Just 21 seconds into the round, Kittikasem followed a pair of light jabs with a booming right that caught Arbachakov – who was in the midst of a defensive maneuver – on the button. Arbachakov crashed hard on the canvas but arose immediately, stumbled to the neutral corner and rubbed his nose. As he took referee Jose Medina Solares' mandatory eight count, the challenger, ever the seeker of order, briefly patted down his hair with his glove to make sure nothing was out of place.

Though Kittikasem now had the upper hand, he remained respectful of his opponent's power while Arbachakov proceeded as if nothing had happened. His body language conveyed that he was still in command, not only of his own senses but also of the fight. His faith was quickly rewarded at the one-minute mark as Arbachakov came over a lazy jab with a hard cross to the ear that sent Kittikasem reeling toward the ropes. Arbachakov pursued vigorously, throwing a double hook to the head and body, an overhand right and a scorching one-two.

Arbachakov was like a super-modified 18-wheeler able to instantly shift strategic gears. He smoothly transitioned from offense to defense and back again, his deft defensive maneuvers dazzling the champ and his offense stunning him. After a few moments of fencing, Arbachakov drove a left uppercut to the jaw, pulled away from a hook and neatly slipped from a double jab-right cross combo.

But with 1:18 to go, Arbachakov switched back to offensive mode with devastating effect. A chopping right to the ear and a hook to the jaw sent Kittikasem into a near cartwheel before hitting the floor with his right elbow. Like his challenger before him, Kittikasem scrambled to his feet before a two-count could be rendered. Unlike Kittikasem, Arbachakov went for the kill. A chopping right buckled the champ's knees while a hook to the button and two more rights had Kittikasem ready to go. Kittikasem tried to come forward but Arbachakov carved him up with devastatingly precise counters: A one-two following a Kittikasem lunge, a one-two and a right uppercut following a wild right by Kittikasem; a hook to the body following another lunging right by the champ. Kittikasem was at a loss and because of that he was in danger of losing his belt then and there.

A torrid right uppercut sent a staggering Kittikasem reaching for the top rope and another huge right propelled the champ toward another set of ropes. Arbachakov struck Kittikasem at will, yet he stayed within himself, never forgetting the fundamentals that set up this golden opportunity. His own knockdown seemed ages ago as he capped off both his best – and his worst – round of the fight.

Arbachakov started round four by patiently working the left behind his feints, yet making Kittikasem bend to his strategic will by moving him back with almost subliminal aggression. Arbachakov picked the champion apart with surgical precision, instantaneously seizing on any opening Kittikasem gave him. Kittikasem tried a double hook to the body, but was met with a hard one-two and a snappy counter jab. Two jabs and a right pushed Kittikasem toward the ropes and two looping rights sent the champ on the run, even glancing behind him to locate another set of ropes. The round ended with Arbachakov zinging in a chopping right cross and a right uppercut to the jaw.

By keeping Kittikasem on his back foot, the champ couldn't generate the one thing that could turn the fight around – his one-punch power. The champ knew it as well and he tried to turn the tide in the fifth by making a concerted effort to come forward – whatever the cost.

Though Arbachakov continued to rake him with laser-quick punches, Kittikasem did better, landing a right to the ribs and knocking Arbachakov back with a right to the jaw. Arbachakov was now on the move, motoring smoothly in both directions as Kittikasem stalked. After Arbachakov weaved in behind a right to the body, he uncorked a heavy hook to the jaw that precipitated a test of strength in the trenches that lasted until the bell.

In round six, Kittikasem revved up his offense as he dug in his toes and winged hard shots. The champion wanted the battle fought on his terms – toe to toe – and Arbachakov was willing to accommodate him, but only to a point. He unleashed his hands in multiple-punch bursts, but he also retained enough defensive discipline to blunt the champion's counters. With 30 seconds left, Kittikasem put together two sharp jabs and several effective rights, but Arbachakov, as was the case throughout, conjured an even stronger response. A three-punch combo capped by a huge right hurt Kittikasem and a second right snapped back the champion's head in the closing seconds.

Knowing his championship was slipping away, Kittikasem cranked up the heat in the seventh as he burrowed forward behind rights to the head and body. Arbachakov, as usual, handled the situation calmly by moving nimbly side to side and surveying for openings. In the final minute, the pair planted their feet and traded powerful blows, but this time Kittikasem got the better of the action. It was the champion's best round in terms of sustained action, but his success was tempered when a heavy right to the temple stunned him in the closing moments.

With the fight nearing the two-thirds mark, it appeared the contest was trending toward one of attrition and conditioning. Each had taken the other's best punches and had recovered well from their respective knockdowns. The crowd, who wildly cheered Arbachakov's every success, had reason to believe the fight would go to a decision. But boxing is a sport when history can be made with lightning speed, even when the circumstances are pointing in a completely different direction.

Such was the case here.

Kittikasem continued to come forward in the eighth while Arbachakov peppered the champion with light flurries that poured over him like a waterfall. His punches landed with bedazzling accuracy, but the determined champion took them and bravely maintained his pursuit.

With 12 seconds remaining, Arbachakov snapped in a range-finding jab. Then, as Kittikasem cranked up an overhand right, Arbachakov stepped in and delivered a crushing right to the point of the chin that left Kittikasem flat on his face. The Thai fell in sections and didn't move a muscle as Solares completed the 10 count and removed his mouthpiece. At 2:59 of round eight, Arbachakov had elevated himself to a special place in boxing history, and he did so in spectacularly sudden fashion. The crowd roared its approval while those watching at ringside gazed in open-mouthed amazement. All that were present knew that this onetime prospect had been transformed into a champion, and perhaps a star that had the promise to shine for years to come.

Epilogue: Because their fight was so action-packed, the pair staged a rematch nine months later, this time in an outdoor stadium Lopburi, Thailand exactly five months after Arbachakov's successful first defense against Yun Un Chin. In another closely fought contest that saw the champion build a narrow lead on all three scorecards, Arbachakov scored a TKO in the ninth.

From there, the two men's careers took totally divergent paths. Kittikasem took a 25-month sabbatical, scoring three early knockout victories before returning to the sidelines. The 30-year-old Kittikasem again emerged after 33 months to take on prospect Shigeru Nakazato, who stopped Kittikasem in four rounds. His final record stands at 25-4 (17 KO).

Four months after beating Kittikasem for the second time, Arbachakov endured a formidable challenge from speedy switch-hitter Ysaias Zamudio before emerging with a unanimous decision. Following a non-title win over Hiroshi Kobayashi (KO 9), Arbachakov reeled off five defenses against future champion Hugo Soto (KO 8), Oscar Arcinega (W 12), Chatchai Sasakul (W 12), Raul Juarez (W 12) and Takato Toguchi (KO 9). Injuries kept Arbachakov from maintaining a more active schedule, and 15 months after beating Toguchi, his five-and-a-half year reign ended with a comprehensive decision loss to Sasakul on November 12, 1997 in Sapporo. The 30-year-old Arbachakov never returned, retiring with a record of 23-1 (16 KO).

Total Punches Landed/Thrown

Round	1	2	3	4	5	6	7	8	9	10	11	12	Total
Arbachakov	15/39	13/49	32/63	22/66	24/64	29/65	24/67	45/111					204/524
	38%	27%	51%	33%	38%	45%	36%	41%					39%
Kittikasem	8/35	15/52	9/50	13/46	22/63	17/66	17/63	20/62					121/437
	23%	29%	18%	28%	35%	26%	27%	32%					28%

Jabs Landed/Thrown

Round	1	2	3	4	5	6	7	8	9	10	11	12	Total
Arbachakov	10/30	6/37	8/25	12/42	6/36	16/36	9/33	22/61					89/300
	33%	16%	32%	29%	17%	44%	27%	36%					30%
Kittikasem	7/28	9/37	2/25	6/27	5/24	6/28	5/23	1/13					41/205
	25%	24%	8%	22%	21%	21%	22%	8%					20%

Power Punches Landed/Thrown

Round	1	2	3	4	5	6	7	8	9	10	11	12	Total
Arbachakov	5/9	7/12	24/38	10/24	18/28	13/29	15/34	23/50					115/224
	56%	58%	63%	42%	64%	45%	44%	46%					51%
Kittikasem	1/7	6/15	7/25	7/19	17/39	11/38	12/40	19/49					80/232
	14%	40%	28%	37%	44%	29%	30%	39%					34%

Yuri Arbachakov vs. Muangchai Kittikasem I June 23, 1992, Tokyo, Japan

TALES FROM THE VAULT

Mark Johnson vs. Leon Salazar
February 20, 1995, Inglewood, California

During the 1980s, Roger Mayweather rebuilt his career – and reshaped his reputation – by running a gauntlet of Mexican opponents in various California rings. Following his second round KO defeat to Julio Cesar Chavez, "The Black Mamba" became "The Mexican Assassin" after defeating six Mexican nationals in a period covering 15 fights and three-and-a-half years. In all, he defeated Mario Martinez (W 10), Oscar Bejines (KO 7), Sergio Zambrano (KO 6), Rene Arredondo to capture the WBC super lightweight title (KO 6), Mauricio Aceves (KO 3) and Rodolfo "Gato" Gonzalez (KO 12) before the run ended with a second loss to Chavez. By that time, Mayweather had built a love-hate relationship with the Mexican fans, teasing them by wearing a black sombrero to the ring and tossing it into the crowd.

But if one sought to find the ultimate "Latin Assassin," he needed to look no further than Mark "Too Sharp" Johnson during the 1990s. Because he campaigned in boxing's lightest weight divisions, his was a world dominated by Mexicans, Central Americans, South Americans and Asians, many of whom were hardened, battle-tested campaigners that demanded the same from their opposition if they were to survive. That was the gauntlet Johnson faced, and he was more than up for the challenge.

Beginning with a sensational 12 round split decision victory over Alberto Jimenez in May 1993 until he signed to fight Leon Salazar on February 20, 1995 at the Great Western Forum in Inglewood, Calif., Johnson had knocked off six Mexican nationals in a seven-fight period. Haitian Ancee Gideon, whom Johnson decisioned over 10 rounds in his hometown of Washington, D.C., was the one exception. Of those six victories, five of them took place at the Forum, as would this scheduled 12 rounder with Salazar. Since Salazar hailed from Panama City, Panama, he offered a slight change of pace in terms of nationality, but nothing in terms of intensity and competitiveness.

Besides his success with Latin fighters, a more important story line for Johnson was his struggle to receive a shot at a major title belt. The victory over Jimenez earned Johnson the Penta Continental flyweight championship, a regional belt designed to get a fighter a world ranking and a fast track toward a fight with one of the champions. Most fighters would earn that crack after a couple of successful defenses, but that would not be Johnson's fate.

The 5-3 southpaw was blessed with blazing hand and foot speed, excellent stamina and conditioning as well as above-average punching power. After losing his second pro fight – a four-rounder to Richie Wenton in Belfast, Northern Ireland – Johnson ran off 20 consecutive victories that included 13 knockouts, including a pair of three-rounders leading up to the fight with Salazar. That combination of skills represented a formidable threat to all the champions at 108 and 112 – including established stars Michael Carbajal, Humberto "Chiquita" Gonzalez and Yuri Arbachakov. Because Johnson was viewed as a high-risk low-reward option by the division's stars, Johnson had yet to secure the mega-match his talents merited. Thus, he was making the seventh defense of his regional title against Salazar despite being ranked second by the WBC.

The 26-year-old Salazar entered the Johnson fight with either a 20-4-1 (15 KO) record (according to the original Prime Ticket telecast) or an 18-6-1 (13 KO) mark (according to Boxrec.com). Nevertheless, Salazar had once been ranked as high as fifth in the world, earning a crack at IBF junior flyweight champion Carbajal in December 1990 after rolling up 14 consecutive wins following a 1-2-1 start. Salazar was stopped in four rounds, and since then he had gone 3-3, including three consecutive losses to Virgilio Chifundo (L 10), Robinson Cuesta (KO by 5) and Melchor Cob Castro (L 10) leading up to the Johnson fight. Given his recent lack of success, he was viewed as just another speed bump for Johnson.

It certainly looked that way in the opening seconds as Johnson stood his ground and blasted lightning-quick punches through Salazar's high guard. Seemingly every punch – whether it be a jab, hook, cross or body shot – was landing and the fight looked to become a showcase for Johnson's range of skills as Salazar backed away behind his high guard and absorbed everything Johnson dished out.

After taking a sizzling left uppercut to the jaw at the round's midway point, Salazar underwent a sudden change of attitude. He was taking a lathering from Johnson and he knew that if he didn't start fighting back it would be a short, painful and embarrassing evening. Suddenly, Salazar started coming forward and ripping with rights to the head and body, setting up a hook that lifted Johnson's head. After landing another pair of rights, Salazar made the decision to go toe-to-toe and take his chances. Given the quality of his opponent, Salazar knew he might still be in for a short and painful night, but at least he could leave the ring with his pride intact – and perhaps even a victory.

At the two-minute mark, Johnson was still outclassing Salazar, but the Panamanian was slowly building momentum. A double right to the head and body drove Johnson back and a follow-up right got a rise from the heavily Hispanic crowd as they sensed Salazar was going to give the "Latin Assassin" some stern opposition. A wicked right snapped Johnson's head, precipitating a ferocious slugfest at ring center that saw Salazar firing body blows and Johnson whaling away at the head until the round-ending bell.

The crowd was in a frenzy, and why not? It was boxing in its most raw form as the two men spent the final half of the round blasting away at one another. Johnson, with his multi-dimensional skills, could have blunted Salazar's aggression any time he wished but because he possessed the soul of a real fighter he chose to engage the Panamanian on his own macho terms. Plus, a spectacular knockout victory would give him ammunition in his quest to get that ever-elusive shot at the brass ring. Exciting fights equal big crowds and TV ratings, which in turn equals the ability to draw big enough money to attract champions.

Both men couldn't wait to return to battle as they left their stools five seconds early, but referee Larry Rozadilla blocked their paths with outstretched arms. When the bell for round two sounded, they planted themselves at ring center and let fly. Johnson crunched in a left cross and a left uppercut while Salazar answered with his own right to the face. Johnson landed a stiff left to the jaw and two long left crosses before Salazar dug a right to the stomach.

Johnson began to move a little more, but only to inch himself back to longer and better punching range. Salazar, whose 63-inch reach was three inches shorter than Johnson's, preferred trading in the trenches and he succeeded with a left-right to the ribs and a right uppercut smothered by Johnson's gloves. Salazar connected with a left hook to the ear but Johnson reflexively snapped his own right to the side of the head and a much harder right uppercut while backing away. Salazar fired a right uppercut to the body and the lightning-quick Johnson blasted a left cross-right uppercut-left cross combo. Johnson connected with three crisp left uppercuts before sliding to his right and uncorking a nasty right uppercut to the jaw.

Their intense and thrilling phone booth warfare was exciting to watch, but it was a battle plan that presented an element of danger for the more gifted Johnson. By staying inside and trading with a natural infighter, he risked getting nailed with a punch that could end his championship dreams in an eye blink.

Johnson nearly paid the ultimate price as Salazar landed a pinpoint lead right to the button that drove Johnson back and nearly floored him. Johnson retreated and stood there, frozen. Seeing his opportunity, Salazar leaped in and raked Johnson with a right to the body and a right-left hook to the face that made Johnson reach out to grab him. Salazar slipped underneath Johnson's grasp and pelted him with a right and a straight left that popped back Johnson's head. A right-left-right-left had Johnson tottering away before he managed to lock in a saving clinch.

Though Johnson tried to project an image of calm, no one, least of all Salazar, was deceived. Johnson was groggy and ripe for the taking, and it didn't help that he still had half of the round to survive. The situation before him demanded that he pull out every bit of skill and savvy to survive this onslaught. It was a test by fire that every fighter who aspires to become someone special must endure, but one never could have thought beforehand that this would be the fight – or the fighter – who would administer it. With incredible swiftness, the speed bump had turned into a giant road-blocking boulder.

Salazar again broke free from Johnson's clinch and ripped a half-dozen piledrivers to the head and body before delivering three consecutive rights to the jaw. By sheer instinct, Johnson landed a pair of rights, but Salazar steamed in more rights to the head and body that finally forced Johnson to get on his toes and move side to side before seeking a clinch. However, Johnson's attempt was weak and Salazar made him pay with two rights to the ribs and a scything right uppercut to the chin.

Without the resources to move – at least temporarily – Johnson moved inside in an effort to smother Salazar's blows, but the Panamanian kept pumping away with an unending series of rights. At this, Johnson's survival instincts commanded him to punch back and the result was an extended and breathtakingly savage exchange. The two fighters whacked away without pause for the remainder of the round, and as the crowd shouted in full-throated glee, Prime Ticket blow-by-blow commentator Tom Kelly compared the action to Zale-Graziano while younger analyst Rich Marotta likened it to Hagler-Hearns. Indeed, the action was *that* good.

Boxing is as much psychological as physical, and projecting an aura of strength is especially important during a moment of crisis. The second round, especially the final half of it, saw Johnson in a vulnerable state. Salazar, in turn, fed off that vulnerability and his subsequent success fueled his belief that victory was within his grasp. As the third round began, Johnson did his best to extinguish that hope.

Johnson was cool and collected as he tore in a right to the body and a right to the jaw before nipping to long range. Johnson then darted back in behind a left cross to the head and a right to the face that forced Salazar to the ropes. "Too Sharp" was sending an unmistakable message to Salazar through his actions: *"I am back and I am a man on a mission – a mission to destroy you."*

Slowly, but surely, that message began to take hold. A pained look creased Salazar's features as Johnson belabored him with sickle-like left uppercuts and thumping body shots along the ropes. A left cross nearly knocked out Salazar's mouthpiece, and Johnson responded by banging the body and driving Salazar back to the ropes. One could swear that Johnson was part Mexican as he blasted in body shot after body shot.

Now it was Salazar's turn to apply his survival instincts, and they fueled a fierce counterattack that carried plenty of spirit but lacked Johnson's superb accuracy. Meanwhile, Johnson took advantage of split-second openings with incredible precision, raking Salazar's anatomy with perfectly placed blows into tiny crevices. Salazar winced every time a body punch thundered in, but despite the pain he must have felt, he continued to fearlessly fire hooks and uppercuts from every conceivable angle.

It soon became apparent that something was wrong with Salazar's right hand, for while he freely threw it before he now kept it pinned to the side of his face. Still, he blasted away with the left as Johnson whipped in punches with both hands. A huge right uppercut lifted Salazar out of his crouch, and he suddenly looked disheveled. Blood was trickling out of his mouth and his trunks fell dangerously low around his protective cup. Johnson attacked his wounded quarry by lifting his head with a left uppercut and spinning it violently with a follow-up right.

As the round neared its end, Salazar went for broke as he lashed out with the right for the first time in quite a while. Four of them rocketed off Johnson's jaw as another terrific action round came to a close.

That final combination proved to be Salazar's last gasp. He made it to his corner with some difficulty, and after an examination by the ringside physician, Rozadilla stopped the contest. Though the official explanation was that Salazar suffered a broken right hand, Johnson's extraordinary bodywork also played a huge role in the Panamanian's decision. As Johnson offered his congratulations, the pain was written all over Salazar's face and slightly hunched over body.

It was an anti-climactic ending to a sensational fight that saw Johnson beat a courageous but ultimately outgunned Latin fighter at his own game. Moments after passing a momentous test, Johnson turned his attention to bigger and more lucrative game.

"This is my seventh time defending the title," Johnson told Prime Ticket's Fernando Paramo. "What else must I do to get a world title shot? I'm fighting opponents in the top 10, I'm looking good, what must I do? The WBC champion, the WBA champion, the IBF champion, one of you guys, give Mark Johnson a try. And if none of those guys give me a shot, I can make 108. Me and Chiquita at the L.A. Forum will be a great fight."

Epilogue: Johnson never got his showdown with Gonzalez at the Forum, nor did he get his superfights with Arbachakov or Carbajal. Johnson registered three more defenses of his Penta Continental title to become one of the very few fighters who racked up 10 successful defenses of a regional title. Johnson eventually gave up that belt to chase a world title shot, and after scoring three more knockouts he finally received his long-awaited chance against Colombian Francisco Tejedor for the vacant IBF title on May 4, 1996 at the Arrowhead Pond in Anaheim. Johnson finally became a champion when he blew away Tejedor just 95 seconds after the opening bell. Johnson was a busy champion, amassing seven defenses over the next three years before decisioning Ratanachi Sor Vorapin to grab the vacant IBF super flyweight title vacated by Johnny Tapia. Johnson defended that title twice before a jail sentence forced him to vacate it.

Johnson returned to the ring in June 2001 as a bantamweight, decisioning Sergio Perez in 10. Following a sixth round knockout of Arturo Valenzuela the following month, Johnson would lose for the first time in more than 10 years when Rafael Marquez scored a 10 round split decision that saw Johnson lose two points for holding, without which Johnson would have captured the split nod. Because of that controversy the pair were matched again four months later, but there would be no dispute this time as Marquez stopped Johnson in eight. Two months after decisioning Ricardo Medina over eight, Johnson won his third belt in two divisions by upsetting the unbeaten Fernando Montiel via majority decision. He followed with a defense over Luis Bolano (KO 4) and a non-title victory over Paulino Villalobos (W 10) before losing the belt by eighth round TKO to Ivan "Choko" Hernandez. Johnson's final fight took place on February 25, 2006 at the Mandalay Bay Resort and Casino in Las Vegas, where WBO super flyweight champion Jhonny Gonzalez stopped the 34-year-old Johnson in round eight. The bout was declared a non-title contest because Johnson weighed one-and-a-half pounds over the 118-pound limit. Johnson's final record stands at 44-5 with 28 knockouts.

Salazar fought on for three more years, serving as fodder for rising prospects and faded contenders alike. Salazar lost nine of his final 11 fights, with a 10 round draw over Emiliano Ferrer and a three-round KO over Juan Antonio Torres in back-to-back fights the only respites. Salazar lost his final seven fights, with a six-round KO loss to Gabriel Munoz on September 4, 1998 his final recorded fight before retiring at age 30.

TALES FROM THE VAULT

Total Punches Landed/Thrown

Round	1	2	3	4	5	6	7	8	9	10	11	12	Total
Johnson	50/109	43/92	56/117										149/318
	46%	47%	48%										47%
Salazar	29/83	51/105	22/86										102/274
	35%	39%	26%										37%

Jabs Landed/Thrown

Round	1	2	3	4	5	6	7	8	9	10	11	12	Total
Johnson	4/28	2/14	0/8										6/50
	14%	14%	0%										12%
Salazar	1/9	1/8	0/16										2/33
	11%	12%	0%										6%

Power Punches Landed/Thrown

Round	1	2	3	4	5	6	7	8	9	10	11	12	Total
Johnson	46/81	41/78	56/109										143/268
	57%	53%	51%										53%
Salazar	28/74	50/97	22/70										100/241

Mark Johnson vs. Leon Salazar February 20, 1995, Inglewood, California

★ Chapter 8 ★
SUDDEN AND VIOLENT ENDINGS

TALES FROM THE VAULT

Thomas Hearns vs. Juan Domingo Roldan
October 29, 1987, Las Vegas, Nevada

The pursuit of history has always provided a compelling story line for those who follow sports – and not just boxing. Who could forget the 1998 home run chase involving Mark McGwire and Sammy Sosa, Walter Payton surpassing Jim Brown's 12,312 career rushing yards (a record now owned by Emmitt Smith) or Tiger Woods winning four successive majors? The beat went on as Indianapolis Colts quarterback Peyton Manning broke Dan Marino's single-season record of 48 touchdown passes with number 49 in 2004, a mark subsequent broken by Tom Brady's 50 in 2007. Many celebrated sports achievements have come and gone, and the promise of more fantastic feats is just one of the reasons fans keep coming back for more.

From the time Hearns won his first belt as a 21-year-old, he envisioned the day where he would make his own mark in history. That day ended up being October 29, 1987 at the Hilton Hotel in Las Vegas when he destroyed Juan Domingo Roldan in four sensational rounds, an effort that not only earned "The Hit Man" the vacant WBC middleweight title but also his unprecedented fourth divisional crown. While several others have duplicated this feat since that seminal autumn evening, Hearns will always be remembered as the first.

Before Hearns earned a piece of ring immortality, three other legends tried and failed. Henry Armstrong, the only man to hold three undisputed titles simultaneously, tried to add to his collection on March 1, 1940, but a disputed draw to middleweight champion Ceferino Garcia – a fight many observers thought he won – denied him.

Alexis Arguello made two celebrated attempts to win his fourth belt against WBA junior welterweight king Aaron Pryor. Arguello's 14th-round knockout loss to Pryor on November 12, 1982 is regarded as one of the greatest fights in history, but the second fight 10 months later (a 10-round TKO win for "The Hawk") was a much better fight than many remember – another "Closet Classic" if you will.

Roberto Duran, who eventually won a fourth belt in 1989 after beating WBC middleweight champion Iran Barkley, made his first try in November 1983 against world middleweight champion Marvelous Marvin Hagler only to lose a narrow 15-round decision. Wilfred Benitez was in position to try for a fourth belt, but a loss to Mustafa Hamsho in a middleweight title eliminator put an emphatic end to the Puerto Rican's hopes.

"The Hit Man" won his first title in spectacular fashion before his hometown fans by crushing WBA welterweight champion Pipino Cuevas in two rounds at Detroit's Joe Louis Arena. Hearns' cerebral alter ego, "The Motor City Cobra," used his considerable skills to decision master boxer Benitez to capture the WBC 154-pound belt on December 3, 1982 in New Orleans.

Hearns' road to fistic glory encountered a considerable roadblock in the form of Hagler, who retained his world 160-pound title by spectacular third round KO on April 15, 1985. Following victories over James Shuler (KO 1), Mark Medal (KO 8) and Doug DeWitt (W 10), Hearns unleashed a full-frontal assault on his title chase. In his first bout as a light-heavyweight, Hearns joined the triple-crown club by battering WBC champion Dennis Andries over 10 rounds on March 7, 1987.

For that bout, Hearns was 173 ¾ pounds of spectacularly solid muscle. With the bout with Roldan – and the coveted fourth belt – on the horizon, Hearns was forced to deal with the prospect of melting off at least 13 ¾ pounds of muscle over the next seven months without sacrificing his strength.

Making weight was not the only problem confronting Hearns. The rugged Roldan was a formidable opponent with an intriguing life story.

This bear of a man's first ring encounter wasn't with a fellow boxer but with a fighting bear that was featured in a traveling circus. Roldan was able to avoid being floored for the three-minute match and won 100 pesos ($10) for his efforts. Shortly after his encounter with the wild kingdom he saw his first boxing show and when one of the fighters could not compete, Roldan filled in and fought to a four-round draw. Encouraged by his impromptu effort, Roldan decided to make boxing his vocation.

He was a hit from the start, earning the nickname "Martillo" (The Hammer) because of his enormous strength and punching power. Roldan hammered his way to a middleweight title eliminator against Frank "The Animal" Fletcher on the Hagler-Duran undercard. Roldan's emphatic six-round KO earned the Argentine a shot at "The Marvelous One" for the undisputed middleweight title March 30, 1984.

Roldan's swarming style troubled Hagler in the first three rounds and he scored a questionable – but official – knockdown in the bout's opening seconds (a blemish which was stricken from the record several years later at Hagler's request). "The Hammer's" looping power shots were thrown with startling speed and accuracy and the crowd began to sense a monumental upset was brewing. A Hagler uppercut to the face (some say a thumb, but replays were inconclusive) caused a grotesque eye swelling as well as an equally massive shrinking of his will to fight on. Following the 10th-round stoppage, a discouraged Roldan announced his retirement.

While visiting Las Vegas for the Hagler-Hearns showdown, Roldan bumped into Sugar Ray Leonard, who told him he was crazy to quit boxing after such a strong showing against the world's best pound-for-pound fighter. Encouraged by the superstar's words, Roldan returned to the ring as both a middleweight and light heavyweight. He won the South American 175-pound title by defeating Juan Carlos Gimenez and stopped former WBC light-heavyweight king J.B. Williamson.

Another impressive victory was a two-round stoppage of Carlos Herrera, who had stopped Benitez two weeks earlier and had challenged Maurice Hope for the WBC

154-pound belt a few years back. Ten straight wins led to Roldan's return to America on the undercard of Leonard-Hagler. His ninth-round stoppage of James Kinchen enabled Roldan to come full circle and gain a second chance at the middleweight title against Hearns.

Hearns and Roldan were fighting for the WBC title vacated by Leonard following his victory over Hagler. Hearns (44-2 with 37 KOs) successfully reduced himself to 159 ½ while Roldan (65-3-2 with 42 KOs) was 159 ¼. Given the styles and attitudes, a high-octane battle was predicted and that's exactly what the crowd at the Hilton's outdoor stadium received.

The opening bell saw Roldan fly out of his corner and unleash the wild, overhand blows that had been so successful against Hagler. Hearns handled the opening charge coolly and was ready with his answer. Two trademark overhand rights, his first effective blows of the fight, propelled Roldan to the canvas 57 seconds into the fight. Up at three, Roldan took referee Mills Lane's mandatory eight-count and though hurt, the South American stubbornly plowed forward.

This time Roldan's rights began landing, forcing Hearns to retreat and initiate repeated clinches. At one point, Hearns, his head underneath Roldan's armpit, straightened up and lifted Roldan several inches off the ground. An instant before the bell, Hearns scored with a lead right that decked Roldan a second time. Though the bell rang, Roldan still had to beat the count, which he did at six. Choosing to stand between rounds, Roldan sought to clear his head while his handlers worked feverishly to revive him.

Things didn't get any better for Roldan in the opening seconds of round two as Hearns landed a left hook that produced a third knockdown. With two-and-a-half minutes remaining, it was a good bet that Hearns would apply the finishing touches to his multi-title masterpiece.

Again up at three, Roldan didn't appear badly hurt this time and he continued to force a fast pace in the hopes of tiring Hearns out. The Argentine bull constantly pushed Hearns toward the ropes while seeking the equalizer that would turn the fight around. Hearns stayed on the back foot to establish the proper distance for his power shots while also using his superior hand speed to land combinations. As active as round two had been, it represented the "quietest" round of the bout.

The action picked up considerably in the third. Hearns opened the round circling and throwing the jab while Roldan continued his pressuring tactics. Forty seconds into the round, Roldan landed a solid right followed by a right-left-right that hurt Hearns. Sensing Hearns was in trouble, Roldan escalated his attack by landing two more thudding rights to the head. Hearns fired back, bloodying Roldan's nose, but Roldan unleashed another three-punch combination that kept the momentum flowing his way. Roldan landed a right that had Hearns grimacing and a big left near the end of the round punctuated Roldan's rally. The round's exertion took a clear toll on Hearns, who walked back to his corner and plopped on his stool, breathing heavily.

"Get out and box him a little bit more," trainer Emanuel Steward told Hearns. "You're going to run yourself out of gas because you're going too damn fast."

Hearns may have intended to heed Steward's advice, but Roldan had other ideas. For as frantic as the first three rounds had been, the fourth and final round proved to be even more so. Coming out of a clinch along the ropes in the opening seconds, Roldan threw two left hooks. The first one missed, but the second, which followed a missed right, landed squarely on Hearns' chin. "The Hit Man" was hit, and hit hard. Hearns' suspect legs wobbled and the American sought the relief of the ropes to stay upright.

As Roldan attacked, Hearns used excellent upper-body movement to avoid many of Roldan's follow-up blows. His head clearing within seconds, Hearns spun off the ropes and caught the charging Roldan with a vicious lead right to the forehead that turned the momentum instantly. Now it was Roldan who initiated the clinches, but his respite didn't last for long.

A few seconds later, Hearns applied the finisher – a single, concussive right to the jaw that left Roldan on his face, lying on the ubiquitous Budweiser logo at ring center. Roldan was motionless until the count of eight, upon which he rolled onto his back. As Lane tolled off the final two seconds, Hearns pumped his fist in the neutral corner, stomped his foot on the canvas and thrust both arms skyward as his corner men rushed the ring to congratulate their man.

The mixture of exultation and relief were evident in Hearns. He saw this accomplishment as his way of securing rematches with the two fighters that beat him.

"I'm so happy now that I don't know what to do," Hearns said. With Marvin Hagler nearby, he said, "I have done something that no other man has ever done. Even the two men that defeated me, Marvin Hagler and Ray Leonard, I know that they are looking at me now, they want to come back and do it again. There's got to be a way."

Epilogue: There wasn't a way, at least for a Hagler rematch. Disgusted with the sport after his loss to Leonard, The Marvelous One announced his retirement and made it stick. But Hearns got his second chance with Leonard in June 1989 and made the most of it, decking Sugar Ray in the third and 11th rounds. The draw decision was a shock, and even Leonard admitted Hearns deserved the decision.

Almost unbelievably, Hearns fought 20 more times over the next 19 years. Along the way he won the WBA light heavyweight title from Virgil Hill in 1991, lost it to Barkley in their rematch nine months later and supposedly ended his career with nine straight wins before losing to Uriah Grant via injury-marred second round TKO in 2000. But, like most of boxing's immortals, Hearns couldn't get boxing out of his blood. The 46-year-old Hearns launched a two-fight comeback that began with a ninth round TKO of John Long in July 2005 and ended with a 10th round TKO of Shannon Landberg in February 2006. Hearns' final record stands at 61-5-1 with 48 knockouts and is a lock to be enshrined in the International Boxing Hall of Fame in 2012 – provided he stays retired, that is.

After the fight with Hearns, Roldan would only fight three more times, beating Miguel Angel Maldonado (KO 6) and former middleweight champion Hugo Corro (KO 1) before losing his final match against Michael Nunn for the IBF middleweight title in November 1988. His final record is 67-4-2 with 44 KOs.

SUDDEN AND VIOLENT ENDINGS

Total Punches Landed/Thrown

Round	1	2	3	4	5	6	7	8	9	10	11	12	Total
Hearns	17/47	21/62	15/45	13/45									66/199
	36%	34%	33%	29%									33%
Roldan	25/75	16/64	25/82	11/45									77/266
	33%	25%	30%	24%									29%

Jabs Landed/Thrown

Round	1	2	3	4	5	6	7	8	9	10	11	12	Total
Hearns	3/17	8/35	9/25	2/19									22/96
	18%	23%	36%	11%									23%
Roldan	5/15	2/17	7/24	2/12									16/68
	33%	12%	29%	17%									24%

Power Punches Landed/Thrown

Round	1	2	3	4	5	6	7	8	9	10	11	12	Total
Hearns	14/30	13/27	6/20	11/26									44/103
	47%	48%	30%	42%									43%
Roldan	20/60	14/47	18/58	9/33									61/198
	33%	30%	31%	27%									31%

Thomas Hearns vs. Juan Domingo Roldan October 29, 1987, Las Vegas, Nevada

TALES FROM THE VAULT

Tommy Morrison vs. Donovan "Razor" Ruddock
June 10, 1995, Kansas City, Missouri

Why is the heavyweight division so popular? Why do fans and writers moan and groan so loudly when the division goes through the same doldrums every other weight class experiences? The vast majority of heavyweight fights are dull, clinch-filled affairs between men who either can't – or won't – get into proper condition. Most of boxing's greatest fights have taken place in weight classes far below heavyweight, and when it comes to action the big boys just can't keep pace with their smaller peers. Yet the division has maintained an iron grip on our collective consciousness, and one piece of evidence is the well-worn saying "as the heavyweight division goes, so goes boxing."

Why do fans stick with the heavyweights even after most of their fights leave them disappointed and frustrated? Here's why: When two strong, well-conditioned, predatory big men square off they can produce fireworks that leave fans breathless and wanting more. As consistently thrilling as the little guys are, they rarely produce the spectacular one-punch knockouts that burn themselves into our memories. In short, when heavyweights do it right, they can do it like no other.

When Tommy Morrison met Donovan "Razor" Ruddock, the fight was billed "Raw Power" for good reason. The 26-year-old Morrison (44-2-1, 38 KO) was a young, powerful slugger whose left hook left a long trail of inert bodies. Meanwhile, the left uppercut of the 31-year-old Ruddock (28-4-1, 20 KO) was so dynamic that it had its own name – "The Smash." After the iron-chinned Mike Tyson absorbed it for seven rounds in their first fight, he said in admiration "he hits like a mule kicks." His fourth-round knockout of former WBA champion Michael Dokes April 4, 1990 was one of the most chilling demonstrations of power ever seen in Madison Square Garden as "The Smash" left Dokes on the canvas for several minutes.

As terrific as they were from an offensive standpoint, they weren't invincible. After Morrison won his first 28 fights – 15 of which ended in the first round – "The Duke" earned a crack at Ray Mercer's WBO title October 18, 1991. Morrison started well as he used his superior hand speed to build an early lead. His eagerness to please the fans and his corner caused him to tire, which allowed Mercer the chance to regroup. The fight ended in the fifth after Mercer hit Morrison with a frightening series of unanswered punches that left "The Duke" virtually unconscious.

Morrison rebounded well, winning his next 10 fights. The fifth bout of that streak, against Joe Hipp in June 1992, offered a gut check like no other. Though he decked Hipp twice and broke the Native American's cheekbone, Morrison had to overcome two broken hands and a jaw fractured so severely the bone split in two to register a ninth round KO. Four fights later, Morrison decisioned George Foreman to win the vacant WBO belt and two months after a four-round blowout of Tim Tomashek, Morrison was poised to fight Lennox Lewis for the WBC title. All that separated Morrison from his date with destiny was former amateur star Michael Bentt. Instead, Bentt separated Morrison from his senses inside of one round.

Though Morrison would go 6-0-1 (5 KO) in his next seven fights, he was not a consistent performer. While he looked terrific at times, he also struggled. Against Ross Puritty, Morrison was decked in rounds six and 10 before earning a disputed draw. To his credit, Morrison stayed busy – the Ruddock fight was his fourth of 1995. He was impressive in victories against Ken Merritt (KO 1) and Marcellus Brown (KO 3) and his seven-round stoppage of Terry Anderson took place just five weeks before meeting Ruddock.

Ruddock began his career in 1982 with a fourth round KO of Wes Rowe – as a 183-pound cruiserweight. It wasn't until his ninth pro fight that the 6-3 Ruddock weighed over 200 pounds. The "Razor" also suffered early blemishes, drawing with the 7-20 Phil Brown in his fifth pro fight and losing to journeyman Dave Jaco on a corner retirement in the seventh five fights later. But Ruddock continued to grow as a man and a fighter, filling out to a solid 220 pounds. After winning a split decision from former WBA heavyweight champion Mike Weaver, Ruddock went on a tear, winning 11 in a row. His victims included James Broad (KO 1), James "Bonecrusher" Smith (KO 7), Dokes (KO 4) and Kimmuel Odum (KO 3) to earn a megabucks showdown with Tyson March 18, 1991 in Las Vegas.

The first fight was a raging slugfest. Ruddock was knocked down in the second and third but was able to carom more than a few power shots off Tyson's head and body. Referee Richard Steele controversially stopped the fight in the seventh after Ruddock staggered toward the ropes. The furor over Steele's decision spawned a return match 11 weeks later. The rematch was a brutal affair – Ruddock suffered knockdowns in the second and fourth rounds and lost a point in the eighth for hitting after the bell while Tyson was penalized in the fourth, ninth and 10th rounds for various fouls. Fighting through a broken jaw most of the fight, Ruddock dropped a 12-round decision.

Victories over Greg Page (KO 8) and Phil Jackson (KO 4) earned Ruddock a chance at Lennox Lewis in a WBC elimination contest on Halloween night 1992 in London. Lewis polished off Ruddock in two rounds before a raucous crowd hungry for a new heavyweight hero and when Riddick Bowe famously dumped the WBC belt in the trash can, Lewis was named the new belt-holder.

Unlike the active Morrison, Ruddock carried plenty of rust into the Municipal Auditorium in Kansas City. The Morrison fight was Ruddock's first in 16 months and only his second bout since the Lewis massacre. At 243, Ruddock was the heaviest of his career while Morrison weighed a ripped 227. Interestingly, the two fighters entered the arena from opposite ends simultaneously, with Morrison wearing a black robe with "TCB" (Taking Care of Business) accompanied with a lightning bolt on the back. Meanwhile, Ruddock sported a freshly shaved head and a look of pure menace.

The fight took place in an impossibly small 16-foot ring, ostensibly to benefit the hometown favorite Morrison but also one that also suited Ruddock.

When the opening bell rang, neither man had to take more than a couple of steps to be in the other's punching range. Morrison began the bout on the move while Ruddock stood tall and eyed Morrison intently in search of an opening. Both launched hooks that missed, but Morrison followed with a jab that popped Ruddock's head back.

It wouldn't take long for the fun to begin.

Fifty-two seconds into the fight, Ruddock landed his "Smash," and after taking a half-step back, "Razor" caught the advancing Morrison leaning in with a pulverizing right uppercut. The pro-Morrison crowd was stunned as they saw their man fall forward on his knees, but when he arose at two his eyes appeared clear. Ruddock maneuvered Morrison to the ropes and pinned him in the corner with another Smash, but Morrison spun out to ring center. Curiously, Ruddock didn't press his advantage, opting instead to survey for openings while Morrison began employing the lateral movement that worked so well against Foreman.

With 1:05 remaining, Morrison stepped inside, shot a right uppercut off Ruddock's jaw and pivoted away before "Razor" could respond. His upper body movement seemed to freeze Ruddock for the rest of the round but as the bell rang, Ruddock connected with a Smash and landed another as referee Ron Lipton leaped in to separate them.

Ruddock started the second quickly with a hook that drove Morrison to the neutral corner pad, but Morrison spun out and unleashed a quick four-punch combination – a blocked right-left to the body, a torrid right uppercut and a fierce hook to the head.

It was clear that Morrison had by far the faster hands and the superior fundamentals, but Ruddock's sheer size enabled the Jamaican/Canadian to cut off the ring and keep Morrison near the ropes. But Ruddock's accuracy wasn't there yet as he missed with a lunging hook as Morrison darted away and countered with a crisp jab. Morrison blocked a Ruddock hook to the body and answered with a wide hook as he pivoted away from the ropes.

With 54 seconds remaining, Morrison moved in close but Ruddock caught him with a short right uppercut to the jaw – the same blow that floored him in the first round. This time, "The Duke" absorbed the blow well and, confident he had adjusted to Ruddock's power, moved inside again. Borrowing a page from Tyson's playbook Morrison sunk a right to the body and followed with a scorching right uppercut to the jaw that buckled Ruddock's legs. His knees dipped toward the canvas, but his will kept him from falling. Instead, he stumbled toward the ropes and grabbed the top strand to stay upright. At this point, Lipton leaped in to administer a standing eight count because the ropes prevented a knockdown. Some of Morrison's fans were angry at

Lipton's timing, but the referee's interpretation of the rules was sound. Once the count was completed, Ruddock had 32 more seconds to survive.

Morrison continued to rip rights to the body and head that were a hair off target. Morrison connected with a right to the ribs and a left uppercut to the head, and Morrison closed a huge round with a right jab to the body and a left to the face.

The first two rounds vindicated the fight's billing of "Raw Power" and then some. Both had tasted the other man's best blows and had been knocked off their feet in the process. They fielded blows that would have discouraged other men from pressing forward, but Ruddock and Morrison weren't "other men" – they were fighters in every sense of the term.

Ruddock stood in the corner between rounds two and three to shake off the effects. Whatever he did must have worked because as the third round opened, Ruddock stormed out of the corner and cracked a Smash off Morrison's skull that could be heard above the considerable crowd noise. Yet Morrison came right back with his own hook that may have missed the target but sent a clear message: *"It's you or me and I'm ready to take all you can dish out to make sure it's me."*

Morrison ducked inside and landed two right uppercuts to the head while Ruddock concentrated on jabs. Going in, Morrison-Ruddock was viewed as a battle of left hookers but now they were utilizing other parts of their arsenals. Both were duly respectful of the other man's biggest weapon and each had the hook well defended. Morrison was often on the move, flicking jabs that fell short of the target but also kept the bigger man at bay.

Ruddock missed with a Smash but connected with a light right to the body. With 16 seconds remaining, Ruddock snapped in a hard jab but Morrison weaved in and connected with a light right to the body, a jab to the head and a right to the body that forced Ruddock to clinch. Morrison fought his way out with a mighty hook to the jaw. "The Duke" ducked back inside and nailed Ruddock with a jab and right uppercut to the body, but this time Ruddock broke free and landed a hook to the ribs as the bell sounded.

Ruddock tried the Smash again to open the fourth, but Morrison saw through the ploy and blocked it with his right glove. The Oklahoman moved inside to land a quick four-punch combination to the head and body.

The muscular Morrison was built for power but he also had underrated hand speed and boxing skills and it was clear he was far nimbler than Ruddock. At the same time, however, Morrison had to expend precious energy keeping Ruddock at arm's length and the effects began to tell. Midway through the round, Morrison's blows began to lose their snap and his movement appeared more ragged. Ruddock intelligently draped himself over Morrison's shoulders during the clinches to hasten Morrison's fatigue. Ruddock also relied on his jab, pumping in two of them as he backed Morrison to the ropes. A short left by Ruddock hit the button and three more jabs thudded in before "The Duke" was able to force an extended clinch.

In those 10 seconds, Morrison was able to summon a burst of strength that would bring about another violent pendulum swing. With 14 seconds remaining in the round, Morrison countered a Ruddock right uppercut with a massive hook, a right-left to the body and an overhand right to the jaw. Ruddock was clearly hurt and Morrison, suddenly energized, windmilled away. The brazen Ruddock looked at the crowd over Morrison's shoulder and opened his mouth wide to show everyone he wasn't hurt. No one was fooled, especially Morrison, and after the bell sounded Ruddock wisely sat on the stool.

This was a bout filled with high drama. Even when the fighters stared at one another while searching for openings, the potential for mayhem was always present. Both had already shown themselves capable of hurting the other man at any juncture and they also certified beyond doubt they could bounce back from adversity. Morrison was the faster and more technically sound fighter while Ruddock was stronger, more relaxed and dangerously heavy-handed.

Somewhat refreshed, Ruddock commenced the fifth by snapping jabs and driving Morrison to the ropes with a swift one-two. Ruddock then drove a hook below the belt that drew a warning from Lipton and gave Morrison a 37-second break to recover. Undeterred, Ruddock pushed "The Duke" to the ropes and hit the bull's eye with a Smash to the head that clearly rattled Morrison. Morrison retreated on unsteady legs as Ruddock caught him with another strong hook. After separating from a clinch, Ruddock beat Morrison to the punch with another hook and a straight right crashed home.

The concerned crowd chanted "Tom-mee!" to spark their man, but Ruddock continued to rain in powerful blows. A short lead right rocked Morrison and a hook forced a retreat. Two thumping jabs set the table for a right and two hooks that snapped Morrison's head as if it was on a swivel. Morrison managed to land two solid hooks as the bell, but it was clear that the fifth was Ruddock's most dominant round.

Ruddock snapped hard jabs as the sixth began and he methodically kept maneuvering Morrison toward the ropes. Though looking a bit ragged and worn, Morrison kept his poise as he moved to his left and landed an occasional jab. Ruddock wasn't pressing his advantage by tearing into Morrison, for he was aware that he needed to marshal his energy for the later rounds. After all, he went 19 rounds with Tyson and while he took a beating from "Iron Mike," stamina was never an issue. Ruddock knew the same couldn't be said of Morrison, so he knew he had plenty of time to wear out the Oklahoman before delivering the knockout drops.

Ruddock nailed Morrison with two hooks that caused him to stagger toward ring center. But as Ruddock moved in to deliver a right uppercut, Morrison sprung the trap and the effects couldn't have been more devastating.

Almost reflexively, Morrison unleashed a massive, pulverizing, gargantuan beauty of a counter hook that caught Ruddock on the point of the jaw. Ruddock's body spun nearly 180 degrees as he crashed to the canvas with concussive force. His body landed spread-eagled and it appeared that not only was Ruddock knocked out, he might have been more severely injured.

With one beautifully timed punch, Morrison captured the essence of why fans love heavyweight boxing so much – there are few things in this world that can provide a bigger thrill than a pure puncher landing a Sunday shot with full force.

But as extraordinary as Morrison's punch was, Ruddock's courage and resiliency was even more amazing. After absorbing one of the most devastating single shots in heavyweight history, Ruddock somehow managed to rise at the count of three and appeared fit to continue after Lipton finished the mandatory eight count. Ruddock forced a clinch as a still-tired Morrison whacked away at the body. Morrison pushed Ruddock to the ropes and landed a fusillade of one-twos to the head that prompted Lipton to apply a standing eight-count.

As Morrison moved in for the kill, Ruddock missed with a Smash but landed a good right uppercut. But Morrison was not to be denied because he knew that if he didn't get Ruddock now, he would fall victim to his own tiring body. In short – if one wants to mix gambling metaphors – Morrison had to go "all in" or else he would have crapped out.

Morrison surged ahead, windmilling to the head and body even as Ruddock tried to force a clinch. With seconds remaining in the round, Morrison set himself and delivered a five-punch combination that culminated with a straight left that snapped Ruddock's head grotesquely, prompting Lipton to leap in and stop the fight.

As Morrison lifted his arms in triumph and walked toward his corner, he was a picture of exhaustion as he barely acknowledged the back slaps and congratulatory hugs. He leaned over the ropes and took several deep breaths in order to collect himself. Meanwhile, the Kansas City fans waved their arms in the air and screamed themselves hoarse, not only because their hero had won the fight but because they had witnessed first-hand what heavyweight boxing *could* be but seldom is.

When Dave Bontempo asked Morrison about the hook that decked Ruddock, he revealed it was a product of keen observation in the face of a massive storm. When Ruddock was delivering his right uppercut, Morrison saw something in the Jamaican's delivery that tipped him off.

"As he was getting tired, he was raising his hip," Morrison said. "The punches that were coming up were slower. He was telegraphing them and I came over it."

Asked about his flagging stamina, he said, "I was hoping to hell there wouldn't be a next round. Tyson was right – he does punch like an effing mule. I take my hat off to him, he's a true warrior, but so are we. I'm back and I'm an improving fighter. The only thing that kept Tommy Morrison from improving in the last two years was himself. I've gotten myself away from all of the negative influences and I put myself right in the middle of my family, my church, my kid. For the first time, I'm happy on the inside and I am maturing in my professional career as well."

"He caught me with a good left hook and I went down," Ruddock told Bontempo. "But I had all my faculties when I was in the (neutral) corner. He thought he had me, but I thought he was going to punch himself out. He was dead tired. My hands were up and I was going to let himself punch out. While I was recovering behind my hands, I was waiting for the round to finish, but the referee stopped the fight. He punched pretty hard and I got a little careless because I thought I had him. I haven't been in the ring for over two years but all of my skills are still there. He just tagged me. But one thing you should know – when I come to fight, I come to fight."

Epilogue: Ruddock would continue to fight – 10 more times over the next six years – and won them all. It did, however, take 34 months for Ruddock to re-enter the ring after the Morrison fight as he knocked out Brian Yates in four rounds. During his comeback, Ruddock notched wins over Rodolfo Martin (KO 8), Tony DeRosa (KO 3), Anthony Willis (KO 6), Mike Sedillo (KO 8), Jose Ribalta (KO 1) and Harold Sconiers (W 10). In his final fight, Ruddock won the vacant Canadian title with a 10-round TKO over Egerton Marcus October 12, 2001 in Niagara Falls, New York. The 37-year-old Ruddock retired with a record of 37-5-1 (28 KO).

Though Morrison didn't know it at the time, the end of his career was close at hand. The sensational win over Ruddock earned Morrison the fight with Lewis that was derailed by his loss to Bentt. Though no major title was on the line, Lewis-Morrison was still a marquee heavyweight fight. Unfortunately for Morrison, Lewis was in top form as he registered a dominating six-round TKO.

In February 1996 Morrison announced he had tested HIV positive, and a three-fight $38.5 million deal with Don King that was to have concluded with a Tyson fight evaporated. Despite his health issues, Morrison managed to land three more fights over the next 12 years. First, he stopped Marcus Rhode on the undercard of George Foreman-Crawford Grimsley in November 1996. Then in February 2007 he convinced the West Virginia State Athletic Commission he was AIDS-free and after a rocky start he stopped John Castle in two rounds. Morrison's final fight took place at age 39 when he stopped Matt Weishaar in three rounds February 9, 2008 in Leon, Mexico on the undercard of Julio Cesar Chavez Jr.-Jose Celaya. His final record is 48-3-1 (42 KO).

SUDDEN AND VIOLENT ENDINGS

Total Punches Landed/Thrown

Round	1	2	3	4	5	6	7	8	9	10	11	12	Total
Morrison	12/43	19/60	13/39	30/66	10/34	26/61							110/303
	28%	32%	33%	45%	29%	43%							36%
Ruddock	7/28	6/23	11/28	12/34	23/41	6/21							65/175
	25%	26%	39%	35%	56%	29%							37%

Jabs Landed/Thrown

Round	1	2	3	4	5	6	7	8	9	10	11	12	Total
Morrison	4/26	3/28	3/20	3/23	3/24	7/17							23/138
	15%	11%	15%	13%	12%	41%							17%
Ruddock	2/16	4/14	7/19	6/17	6/14	2/13							27/93
	12%	29%	37%	35%	43%	15%							29%

Power Punches Landed/Thrown

Round	1	2	3	4	5	6	7	8	9	10	11	12	Total
Morrison	8/17	16/32	10/19	27/43	7/10	19/44							87/165
	47%	50%	53%	63%	70%	43%							53%
Ruddock	5/12	2/9	4/9	6/17	17/27	4/8							38/82
	42%	22%	44%	35%	63%	50%							46%

Tommy Morrison vs. Donovan "Razor" Ruddock June 10, 1995, Kansas City, Missouri

TALES FROM THE VAULT

Vincent Pettway vs. Simon Brown
April 29, 1995, Landover, Maryland

There's nothing like a good neighborhood brawl to get the juices flowing, both for the boxers and for the fans. When a fight pits local man versus local man, the stakes become personal. A world championship could be on the line but in many cases the real prize is the privilege of walking the local streets with one's head held high, secure in the knowledge that he successfully defended his town's honor – and the honor of those who root for him.

The battle between Vincent Pettway and Simon Brown at the U.S. Air Arena in Landover, Maryland was a good example of this phenomenon. Though Pettway (37-4-1 with one no-contest, 30 KO) was defending his IBF junior middleweight belt for the first time against two-division champion Brown (43-3, 31 KO), the geographical element added an extra layer of tension. Pettway was born in Baltimore and lived in Randallstown, Md., while Brown, though born in Jamaica, grew up in Washington, D.C. Because they share a home base, they had occasion to spar but up until this point their professional paths had never crossed.

The 31-year-old Brown had spent most of his career at welterweight, capturing the vacant IBF belt in 1988 by knocking out Tyrone Trice in 14 thrilling rounds. As champion, "Mantequilla" did his best to emulate his namesake Jose Napoles by racking up eight defenses of his IBF belt. Along the way, he also captured the WBC title by knocking out best friend Maurice Blocker in 10 rounds in 1991. A weight-drained Brown lost the WBC belt to the skillful James "Buddy" McGirt in his next outing but six fights later Brown shocked the boxing world by knocking out dominant WBC super welterweight champion Terry Norris in four rounds. The Norris conquest proved to be a high-water mark for Brown as he struggled to a majority decision against Troy Waters in his next fight just six weeks later and lost the title to Norris by lopsided unanimous decision four months after the Waters fight. Norris earned the shot at Pettway by scoring victories over Nestor Maciel (W 10) and Frank Newton (KO 2).

The 29-year old Pettway's championship road was a long one, requiring 10 years and 41 fights to secure his first shot at world honors. "The Ambassador" plied his trade in the Maryland/Atlantic City/Philadelphia corridor and he slowly gained notice with wins over Horace Shufford (W 10), Hugh Kearney (KO 2), Luis Santana (W 10) and James Hughes (KO 3). But he also lost fights to Javier Suazo (KO by 6) and back-to-back contests to Victor Davis (KO by 9) and Stephan Johnson (KO by 6). Following the losses, Pettway rebuilt his career with six consecutive wins and earned a chance at long-reigning IBF junior middleweight champion Gianfranco Rosi. Their first fight in

March 1994 ended in a six-round technical draw, but in the rematch six months later Pettway dominated en route to a fourth round knockout.

Like most good matches, Pettway-Brown offered many contrasts. Pettway was a polished boxer with one-punch knockout power who was also vulnerable to early-round knockdowns. Brown was a puncher with underrated boxing skills who wore down opponents with a potent body attack and a powerful left hook. The iron-jawed Brown had never been stopped or knocked out while Pettway lost all four of his fights by KO or TKO. Brown's championship-level experience was far superior as he won 11 of his 13 title fights. Pettway, meanwhile, was 1-0-1.

Respectful of Brown's power – and mindful of his own early-round difficulties – Pettway, 152¼, began the fight on the move while Brown, 154, sought to cut off the ring. Pettway threw occasional light one-twos and slipped underneath several Brown hooks. Midway through the round, the action shifted to close range and both men popped one another during an extended clinch. Pettway then broke away and connected with a triple jab. The champion weaved to his left and nailed Brown with a solid hook to the jaw, but Brown, true to form, absorbed it well. Pettway was off to a good start and he appeared to be the man in control as the first round neared an end.

But with 23 seconds left, that all changed.

After Pettway missed with a one-two, Brown landed a right uppercut to the body and a tremendous hook to the jaw that stiffened Pettway's legs. Pettway staggered sideways and desperately tried to grab Brown around the waist to keep from hitting the floor. But Brown shook him off and connected with a follow-up hook-right-hook that drove Pettway to the canvas heavily on his right side.

Up immediately, Pettway was badly dazed, tottering on unsteady legs. He dared not look at referee Ray Klingmeyer because one look into the fighter's eyes might have ended things right there, so Pettway kept his back to Klingmeyer until the count of seven. Once he turned around, Pettway's eyes remained wide but he managed to convince Klingmeyer he deserved a chance to continue. With only nine seconds left in the round, Brown raced in to finish the job but missed with a one-two, allowing Pettway to duck behind him and clinch the clock away.

Pettway's legs still weren't recovered as round two began, but he had no choice but to get on his bicycle to survive. The champ ducked under a Brown blow and clinched him from behind, buying him more valuable recovery time. Pettway scored with a hook to the body and a right-left to the head while avoiding a home run hook. Brown was hunting down his man and putting mustard behind every blow. Showing his experience, Brown took his time and his patience was rewarded as he tagged Pettway with a solid right to the backpedaling Pettway's jaw. Brown connected with a heavy hook while Pettway answered with a lighter hook to the face and a long right to the body.

Though nearly the same size anatomically, Brown's upper body was thicker and more powerful while Pettway's build was lean, lithe and flexible. The styles suited the body types as Brown chugged forward behind thudding punches and Pettway retreated behind crisp jabs and lively side-to-side movement. Late in the round, Pettway's jab consistently penetrated Brown's guard and a solid overhand right capped a nice rally. Brown's steady pressure won the round, but Pettway was successful in buying the time he needed to regain a foothold in the match.

Thus, Pettway was no longer in total survival mode in the third as he snapped two jabs and dug a hook to the body before he induced a clinch. Because Pettway's legs had regained strength, he was able to effectively dart in and out of Brown's punching range while landing his own sharp shots. Brown focused on working the body but he found it difficult to line up his elusive quarry. Pettway was boxing neatly and more confidently as a counter hook found Brown's jaw.

A few seconds later, Pettway's confidence would surge even higher as he countered a Brown jab by rocking back on his right leg and unleashing a hair-trigger right to the jaw that put Brown on his back with startling dispatch. Brown was ready to get up by Klingmeyer's count of five, but he wisely stayed on his haunches until eight. Upon rising, Brown demonstrated presence of mind by walking backwards toward the neutral corner to put even more distance between himself and Pettway.

Pettway had a full minute to polish off "Mantequilla," and he got off to a good start by landing a short hook-overhand right combo and a sharp jab to the face. Pettway ducked underneath a right and sprang up with a powerful hook to the chin. Another Pettway jab popped in and an overhand right made Brown's legs wobble. Brown was an easy target for Pettway, and the former two-time champ's wild looping punches offered plenty of prime counterpunching opportunities. Pettway fired in two lead rights to the jaw and a hurtful one-two drove Brown to the ropes as the round neared its end.

Pettway's masterful counter punching and blend of offense and defense helped him seize the momentum of a fight that had evolved into the wild give-and-take brawl with which he was familiar.

Because Brown was anxious to regain that momentum in round four, he fought with uncharacteristic wildness, winging many shots over the top. Still, he successfully cut off Pettway's escape routes and that allowed several hurtful punches to penetrate. A left uppercut had Pettway holding on while a heavy jab caught Pettway moving away and a right uppercut split Pettway's gloves. But Brown landed his share of blows as well as a right landed on the retreating Pettway and another one-two hit the target. Though Brown sometimes lunged in he was turning the fight his way as Pettway had done in the third, and the positive developments allowed Brown to rediscover his composure.

Brown picked up where he left off in the fifth, landing solid jabs to the face as Pettway continued to circle and toss light lefts. Brown lost his balance after missing a wild right, but as Pettway pressed in to take advantage, Brown uncorked a sneaky hook to the chest that stopped Pettway cold. As "The Ambassador" tried to negotiate recovery time in the clinch, Brown drilled two hooks to the jaw, a right to the body and another right to the temple. This time, Pettway absorbed the blows well and continued his swift lateral movement.

The bout, however, was about to take an ugly turn.

Pettway's follow-through on a right wrapped around the back of Brown's head at the moment Brown aimed a right to Pettway's body. The angle of the blow was changed, and instead of hitting the body Brown's punch landed on Pettway's protective cup. Pettway yelled as he doubled over, and Brown seized on the situation by nailing Pettway with a right that knocked out the mouthpiece, a left hook and a second right that drove Pettway through the ropes and onto the ring apron.

Because referee Klingmeyer didn't see the initial low blow, he proceeded to give Pettway a 10-count instead of the five-minute time-out he should have received. Somehow, the stricken Pettway managed to scramble back into the ring and regain his feet by Klingmeyer's count of nine, but "The Ambassador" was in no mood to be diplomatic. As Klingmeyer wiped his gloves, Pettway yelled "Low blow, man! Low blow!" Then, showing presence of mind, he alerted the referee that his mouthpiece needed to be replaced – enabling him to gain extra seconds of rest. After the mouthpiece was rinsed and reinserted, Pettway again spat out a parting "Low blow, man!" to drive home his point.

His sense of fairness violated, Pettway opted to exercise street justice on Brown by unleashing a blow squarely on Brown's protective cup. Pettway was fortunate he wasn't disqualified on the spot, but the fuming champion didn't feel like a lucky man. While Klingmeyer issued a warning to both fighters, Pettway angrily brushed away the referee's arm as he turned his back and walked toward a corner. Emotions were running high, and both fighters channeled their fury into every blow. Pettway threw his jab with extra gusto and Brown uncorked vicious hooks and rights to the body. The bell rang as both men were engaged in a heated exchange, and neither wanted to be the first to break it off. Pettway connected with a one-two as Brown turned away and Brown's trainer Aaron Snowell wrapped his arms around Pettway and pushed him away. Snowell then yelled at the referee because he failed to disqualify Pettway for his blatant foul earlier in the round.

The wall of composure that separates boxing from street fighting was obliterated and the U.S. Air Arena was perilously close to becoming a powder keg. Raw fury had taken over the fighters, their seconds and the booing crowd. The timekeeper had not stopped the clock while the chaos was going on, so there wasn't much idle time for anyone in the crowd to think about escalating the situation beyond booing.

The sixth began with Klingmeyer bringing both fighters to ring center to issue a stern command to keep it clean, and the boxers complied. Pettway fired hard jabs while Brown launched inaccurate hooks. As they clinched, they pumped in short, crackling blows – Brown with left uppercuts to the head and rights to the body and Pettway with rights to the head and body. The anger that had boiled over in the fifth was slowly dissipating and the bout reverted to a normal boxing mode.

As Brown ducked low to throw a body punch, his head slammed against Pettway's left eye, opening a small cut underneath the orbit. The butt's impact drove him into the ropes, where he was briefly tangled. Neither fighter reacted violently to the accidental foul, but one member of the crowd threw a wrapper into the ring.

Pettway caught the advancing Brown with a one-two and Brown missed with a winging hook. Then Pettway retreated a half step and peppered Brown with a left-left-right. Both men had well-earned reputations as big punchers capable of producing fireworks at any given moment, and in Pettway's case he carried the burden of being the recipient of those from time to time. In the days before the fight, the conventional wisdom was Brown had an edge because not only could he deliver a big punch, he also could take it better.

"The Ambassador," however, was about to turn conventional wisdom to conventional foolishness.

As Brown whiffed on an overhand right, Pettway dug in his toes and launched a pulverizing counter hook to the jaw that stiffened Brown's body and propelled him to the canvas like a mighty oak. Brown hit the floor and his head bounced off the canvas with a sickening thud. There was no question Brown was knocked out, but Klingmeyer administered a count to give Brown every chance to continue his challenge.

At Klingmeyer's count of seven, the unconscious Brown threw the first of what would be 11 jabs while still flat on his back in a chilling demonstration of his fighting instincts. Klingmeyer's 10-count ended at the 2:07 mark of round six, and when the fight was declared over Pettway and his handlers celebrated the biggest win of his career so far. He stopped the previously unstoppable and he did so in marvelous style.

Within a minute, Brown had regained consciousness and was sitting on a stool, but his eyes still struggled to focus on his surroundings. The fight-ending hook opened a cut over his right eye, but the medical personnel's quick work ensured that the cut was his most significant injury. At the time of the stoppage, Pettway trailed on two of the three scorecards, one by one point and the other by four points. Pettway led by one point on the third card.

The combat over and the hard feelings washed away by the exhilaration of victory, Pettway walked over to Brown's stool to embrace his valiant challenger. It was as resounding a knockout as any ever seen and Pettway more than earned the right to walk the streets of Randallstown, Maryland – and everywhere else – with pride.

Epilogue: Four months after stopping Brown, Pettway lost the IBF belt to Paul Vaden via 12th round TKO. Entering the final round, Pettway held a one-point lead on all scorecards. Pettway would challenge once more for a title, losing by eight round TKO to Vaden's successor, WBC/IBF champion Terry Norris. Over the next five years Pettway fought only six more times, winning the first five before losing his final fight by six round TKO to Luis Rosado in Baltimore on August 31, 2001. The 35-year-old Pettway retired with a 43-7-1 (32 KO).

Five months after losing to Pettway, Brown dropped a 10-rounder to Aaron Davis but earned a chance at WBO titleholder Lonnie Bradley following two wins over Mike Bryan (KO 1) and Glenwood Brown (W 10). Though Bradley dominated Brown over 12 rounds, it didn't represent the last time "Mantequilla" would challenge for a title. Three bouts later, he challenged Bernard Hopkins for the IBF belt and was stopped in seven rounds. The Hopkins loss was the first in what would become six consecutive defeats, the final of which was an eight-round decision to Omar Sheika at The Pit in Albuquerque, N.M. on January 8, 2000. At age 36, Brown retired with a record of 47-12 (34 KO).

TALES FROM THE VAULT

Total Punches Landed/Thrown

Round	1	2	3	4	5	6	7	8	9	10	11	12	Total
Pettway	13/41	16/46	23/60	8/34	12/53	9/27							81/261
	32%	35%	38%	24%	23%	33%							31%
Brown	14/39	18/48	14/43	15/47	16/49	4/20							81/246
	36%	38%	33%	32%	33%	20%							33%

Jabs Landed/Thrown

Round	1	2	3	4	5	6	7	8	9	10	11	12	Total
Pettway	5/23	5/26	4/20	6/24	4/27	2/15							26/135
	22%	19%	20%	25%	15%	13%							19%
Brown	5/9	7/26	4/16	5/22	2/14	2/10							25/97
	56%	27%	25%	23%	14%	20%							26%

Power Punches Landed/Thrown

Round	1	2	3	4	5	6	7	8	9	10	11	12	Total
Pettway	8/18	11/20	19/40	2/10	8/26	7/12							55/126
	44%	55%	48%	20%	31%	58%							44%
Brown	9/30	11/22	10/27	10/25	14/35	2/10							56/149
	30%	50%	37%	40%	40%	20%							38%

Vincent Pettway vs. Simon Brown April 29, 1995, Landover, Maryland

Derrick Jefferson vs. Maurice Harris
November 6, 1999, Atlantic City, New Jersey

When it comes to the state of boxing's health, size does matter. Throughout the sport's history, the presence of a heavyweight standard bearer has had a positive and direct effect on its standing with mainstream audiences. The names of Dempsey, Louis, Marciano, Ali and Holmes serve as historical lines of demarcation and their diverse personalities served as a reflection of their respective eras.

The era of split titles has blurred the lines somewhat. One could say the late 1980s belonged to Mike Tyson but ownership of the 1990s is somewhat murky. Did they belong to Evander Holyfield because his reigns spanned more years? Did they belong to Tyson because of his unmatched box office power? Or did they belong to Lennox Lewis because he ended up beating both Holyfield and Tyson?

The answer was still being determined in November 1999 as Lewis and Holyfield were scheduled to fight their rematch for the undisputed title following their scandalous draw in March. Meanwhile, there was plenty of activity among the contenders and on November 6, 1999, Atlantic City's Convention Hall played host to a doubleheader that promised to provide some clarity as to who would challenge the Lewis-Holyfield winner. The main event pitted Hasim Rahman and Oleg Maskaev while the appetizer matched hard-hitting Derrick Jefferson and slickster Maurice Harris.

Jefferson and Harris were a study in contrasts. At 6-5, 245 pounds, the 31-year-old Jefferson sported a powerful build and crunching one-punch KO ability. In his early 20s, Jefferson aspired toward a basketball career, but those dreams were shattered when an argument over a 25-cent piece of candy led to a bullet being fired into Jefferson's leg. Jefferson turned to amateur boxing at age 24 and he enjoyed success as he won a national title and registered wins over Michael Grant and Lawrence Clay-Bey. He turned pro at the advanced age of 27 and slugged his way to a 21-0-1 (17 KO) record, with his best previous victories being against Bert Cooper (KO 2) and Obed Sullivan (W 12). To his credit, "The D-Train" maintained an active schedule with the Harris fight being his fifth of 1999. His late introduction to the sport kept him from developing his full range of talents but the one ability he needed most – concussive one-punch power – could instantly make all things right in the end.

At 23, Harris was eight years younger but had three more years of professional experience. "Mo Bettah" was just 16 when he turned pro by losing a four-round decision to Joe Kenna and while still a teen-ager he fought – and lost to – Richard Frazier, Zuri Lawrence, Vaughn Bean and Dale Brown. Following the loss to Brown, Harris had a breakthrough when he decisioned the 18-0 David Izon over eight rounds. Though he would suffer two more losses to Dayton Wheeler and Gerald Nobles, he entered the

Jefferson fight winning nine of his last 10 fights, with the one loss a hotly disputed decision to forty-something Larry Holmes. Harris also received valuable seasoning by sparring more than 100 rounds with Lewis and participating in training camps with Roy Jones Jr.

Harris entered the fight full of confidence despite accepting it on only five days' notice. He felt Jefferson didn't present anything that he hadn't seen before and that his experience and intelligence would serve as antidotes to his opponent's size and strength.

At 6-4 and 211 pounds, the 16-9-2 Harris was long, lean and flexible and with nine knockouts (including six in the first round) he had respectable pop. But of the two, Jefferson was by far the bigger hitter shot for shot and Harris would need to dig deep into his bag of tricks to secure victory.

It didn't take long for Jefferson to force Harris into using them as he winged a home run hook moments after the opening bell. Harris whipped his upper body away from the blow and slipped to his left before leaping in behind a slapping hook to the face. Another light right-left to the face connected for Harris before he forced a clinch. Jefferson landed hooks to the ribs and chest as well as a quick left to the body and right to the head moments later.

Harris' quicker hands were evident as he rattled a right-left-right to Jefferson's head and a clean hook off the "D-Train's" jaw as the final minute began. Both men were fighting at a hard pace with Jefferson swinging heavy blows and Harris answering with movement and intelligence. Harris pulled away from a hard hook and motored to ring center, where he stung Jefferson with a hook to the jaw. His pride pricked, Jefferson steamed ahead behind a short right to the face. As the round closed, Jefferson caught Harris with a pair of hooks but "Mo Bettah" ducked away from four others. At round's end, Harris good-naturedly smiled at Jefferson at walked back to his corner knowing he was executing his game plan to the letter.

Harris' tactics were obvious – slip and slide, move and counter and hit and run – plus tie up whenever Jefferson moved into range. These tactics were a necessity for a 211-pound man operating in the land of 230-plus pound giants who not only possessed great size and power but also terrific athleticism. As one of those present-day giants, Jefferson's plan was also simple: Pound the body to take the zip out of Harris' legs and exert relentless physical and mental pressure before applying an explosive finisher. Both men would get the chance to execute their blueprints spectacularly in round two.

With 1:40 remaining in the round, Jefferson ducked underneath a Harris right and launched a hook at precisely the same moment Harris did. Though Harris' arrived first – and landed first – Jefferson's had so much leverage that it tore through Harris' defense and detonated with explosive effect. Harris fell heavily in the corner, but looked composed when he arose at Steve Smoger's count of eight.

Harris immediately went into survival mode by moving into close quarters. When Harris retreated toward the ropes, Jefferson smartly looked for openings to the body and he found them as he dug two heavy hooks to the ribs as Harris weaved his torso from side to side. Jefferson forced Harris off the ropes with a hook to the flanks and a right uppercut to the jaw, and another right uppercut-left hook combo dropped Harris a second time – this time on his face.

As Harris arose at seven, blood was dripping from his lower lip and he seemed moments away from a knockout defeat. Jefferson had nearly 40 seconds with which to work, so time was on his side. Jefferson barreled in for the finish, but Harris stepped in with a beautifully delivered hook to the jaw that dropped a shocked Jefferson to his knees.

It was an extraordinary turn of events. Just five seconds after they were called back into action, Harris managed to summon the power needed to deck a man 35 pounds heavier and with a boatload of momentum. Up at three, Jefferson tore after Harris and the two men spent the rest of the round exchanging heavy blows along the ropes while the crowd roared in appreciation. When the bell signaled the end of the round, the two men nodded and gave each other a high five before walking to their respective corners. This time, the gesture was motivated by genuine respect.

Harris started the third moving to his left and planting a left uppercut to Jefferson's jaw while Jefferson bored in behind a short hook. Coming out of a clinch, Jefferson pounded a left uppercut-right cross-left uppercut combo that prompted Harris to clamp on a "time-out" clinch. Jefferson was putting his entire weight behind every punch, which took away from his accuracy but also transmitted to Harris a constant sense of danger. Harris, however, was ignoring the message as he ripped short hooks to the body and head and followed with a stinging right-left and a double hook to the ribs. Jefferson's persistence paid off late in the round as he stepped in and drove a fierce right uppercut to the jaw that buckled Harris' knees and propelled his mouthpiece skyward. Energized by Harris' pain, Jefferson drove "Mo Bettah" to the ropes with a series of power shots, but Harris' deftly slipped them and the ensuing clinch prompted a pause to replace the mouthpiece that ran out the rest of the round.

Harris was by far the more polished boxer, but Jefferson's determination prevented him from being discouraged as blow after blow failed to penetrate Harris' defense. Despite suffering the knockdown late in the second round, he knew he could hurt Harris more often than Harris could hurt him. That knowledge kept him coming forward without pause – or fear.

With 1:16 remaining in the fourth, both launched simultaneous hooks with Harris aiming for the body and Jefferson the jaw. Both of them landed, but Jefferson's caused Harris' mouthpiece to fly out for the second consecutive round. Jefferson followed with an overhand right-right uppercut-hook combo but Harris replied with a short hook to the face. The hot pace was beginning to tell on both men and as a result they spent more of their time buying time in clinches. But that didn't happen often enough to compromise the quality of the contest, so the crowd held its collective tongue.

The fight was being waged within the brawling style that suited Jefferson. Harris would have preferred a contest of skills at long range but he was operating well within the boundaries Jefferson dictated. Harris was landing the cleaner, crisper shots but Jefferson's unyielding drive forced Harris to work much harder and much earlier than he would have liked.

Jefferson continued to press in round five and was rewarded by connecting with a strong hook. Harris tagged Jefferson with a long right, but Jefferson beat Harris to the punch with a quick hook that sent Harris scampering away to his right. Harris landed a trip-hammer right that caught Jefferson coming in, but "The D-Train" plowed through it unflinchingly and proceeded to work over Harris' body with sledgehammer blows. Harris wasn't as willing to trade with Jefferson as he was earlier, choosing to land one punch at a time before darting away. At the bell, Jefferson showed him why that was a smart move by blasting a hook to the stomach that made him wince and double over briefly.

Jefferson's brute strength slowly eroded Harris' mobility, and while Harris was the more accurate puncher it was Jefferson who was controlling the geometry of the ring as he forced his man to the ropes more and more. Midway through the sixth, Jefferson broke out of a clinch and fired a powerful right uppercut and a scything left hook that sent Harris to the ropes. Jefferson banged in a right over the top but Harris latched on and spun out to ring center. Harris snapped a jab and a jolting hook to the jaw before retreating to the ropes, where he curiously stood still for several seconds.

Jefferson saw that as his cue.

Jefferson leaped in with a hook to the jaw, a pile-driving right to the ribs and a nauseating hook to the liver that caused Harris to stumble forward and crash face-first to the canvas. Harris was aware of his surroundings as he glanced up at Smoger at five but remained on his stomach until seven before scrambling up at nine. But Harris was clearly hurt and tired as he advanced toward Jefferson with his hands at his side. Jefferson whacked a right-left to the body but Harris briefly blunted the attack by landing his own body hook.

Harris shouldered his way out of a clinch and missed with an overhand right, but rocked Jefferson to his core with a side-winding hook to the jaw that caused Jefferson to reach out with both arms for Harris' waist. Just like the second round, Harris was rebounding strongly from an earlier knockdown but now Jefferson was badly stunned and perhaps ripe for the taking.

But Jefferson reacted as he always did whenever Harris seized an advantage – he fired back.

As the two cranked simultaneous hooks, Jefferson's got there first – and with pulverizing results. The massive blow struck Harris' jaw perfectly and its aftereffects were frighteningly graphic. Harris' bloody mouthpiece shot from his mouth and his upper body pitched forward before he landed on his back with a resounding thud. The back of Harris' head slammed against the canvas and no count was necessary. Harris was out before he hit the ground and Smoger officially ended the bout at 2:52 of the sixth round.

It was the type of sensational ending that continually draws fans to the heavyweight division. They are the biggest men throwing the hardest punches that produce the most dramatic results. In most people's minds, bigger is better and at least on this night Derrick Jefferson proved them right.

Epilogue: Lennox Lewis won a 12-round decision to secure full ownership of the linear heavyweight title, and Oleg Maskaev confirmed himself as a top contender by knocking Hasim Rahman out of the ring in round eight after trailing early in the fight. In their rematch seven years later, Maskaev would again overcome an early deficit to stop Rahman, this time in the 12th round to win the WBC title.

Jefferson's time in the championship picture was brief as David Izon, Maskaev and Wladimir Klitschko scored knockout victories, with the Klitschko fight being for the WBO belt. Jefferson returned to the ring eight months later and began a five-fight winning streak with a one-round KO over Eric Curry. That string of success was broken in his most recent outing when DaVarryll Williamson stopped the 37-year-old Jefferson in two rounds on April 30, 2005. Jefferson's record reads 28-4-1 with 21 KO.

After losing to Jefferson, Harris' career assumed a hot-and-cold rhythm. Harris returned to the ring eight months after losing to Jefferson, scoring an eight-round decision over Bradley Rone. After scoring another eight-round win over Harold Sconiers, Harris challenged Chris Byrd for the USBA belt, but lost a comprehensive 12-round decision. Harris won just two of his next six fights, but one of those victories was a ninth round knockout over future WBO champion Sergei Lyakhovich, who entered the ring with a 16-0 record. That earned him a crack at the 23-1 Fres Oquendo, who stopped Harris in 10 rounds and prompted a nearly three-year retirement.

Harris packed on nearly 30 pounds during the hiatus and returned with an eight-round win over Franklin Edmonson in January 2006 but the hulking Tye Fields stopped Harris in four six months later. The final match for the 31-year-old Harris was a four round no contest against Rodney Wallace on November 17, 2007 at The Millennium Center in Winston-Salem, N.C., a bout that saw Harris weigh 260. Boxrec.com noted that the fight was originally considered a KO win for Harris but was taken away because Harris misrepresented himself to get the fight. His final record reads 20-14-2 (10 KO).

TALES FROM THE VAULT

Total Punches Landed/Thrown

Round	1	2	3	4	5	6	7	8	9	10	11	12	Total
Jefferson													98/302
													32%
Harris													79/167
													47%

* Fight originally done by CompuBox, but the original HTML files with complete round-by-round statistics for all categories no longer exist.

Derrick Jefferson vs. Maurice Harris November 6, 1999, Atlantic City, New Jersey

Paul Banke vs. Daniel Zaragoza II
April 23, 1990, Inglewood, California

The dream was about to come true for Paul Banke. He was fighting for a title at the Great Western Forum – located not far from his hometown of Quail Valley, California – and he was winning. Midway through the ninth round, a smashing right-left to the jaw had just floored WBC super bantamweight champion Daniel Zaragoza. After Zaragoza arose at six, Banke ripped open a third cut along the bridge of Zaragoza's nose to go with those around each of his eyes. He had the champion right where he wanted him and he appeared just nine minutes away from becoming the new champion. All he had to do was stay on the attack and the title was all but his.

But it was not to be. Thinking the fight was in the bag, Banke took his foot off the accelerator and began to coast. Instead of fighting with full fury and concentration, Banke showboated and taunted the champion at times and failed to follow up on his hard-earned advantage. The insults may have gotten under Zaragoza's skin, but the champion made him pay by outworking the 25-year-old Banke over the final three rounds and capturing a split decision. Upon hearing the verdict, Banke collapsed in disappointment and immediately left the ring to ponder what could have been – and whether he would get another opportunity.

After disposing of Jose Luis Soto (KO 2) and Lucilo Nolasco (W 10), Banke received word that Zaragoza and his people had granted him a rematch. The fight was to take place April 23, 1990 – 10 months after the first fight – and it again would be staged at the Great Western Forum.

Now 26, Banke (18-4, 11 KO) was no stranger to second chances. In fact, his very presence in the ring represented a new beginning. At various points in his life he struggled with addictions to alcohol and drugs but he said those days were behind him. Because he wanted people to see him as the drug-free person he had become, he billed himself as "The Real" Paul Banke. A southpaw who possessed the talent to box but preferred to bang, Banke was the embodiment of his local gym, "The All-Heart Boxing Club."

The 29-year-old Zaragoza (39-4-1, 19 KO) was making his sixth defense of the WBC title he won by stopping the comebacking Carlos Zarate in 10 rounds to fill the vacancy left by Jeff Fenech, who moved up to featherweight. Since beating Banke, Zaragoza notched two more defenses against Frankie Duarte (KO 10) and former WBA bantamweight champion Chan Yong Park (W 12) four months earlier. Like Banke, Zaragaoza was a southpaw, but unlike his younger challenger he invested full effort and attention every second of every round. Because he wasn't blessed with great speed or power, he focused on improving the things he could. His hard work produced results

— not only was he a 122-pound champion, he had also held the WBC bantamweight title, a belt he won after Freddie "Pebble" Jackson was disqualified for a blatantly intentional head butt in the seventh round. After losing the 118-pound belt to Miguel "Happy" Lora, Zaragoza moved up four pounds. His first fight at the new weight was a 10-round non-title loss to Fenech, but the Mexican entered the Banke rematch on a 13-fight unbeaten streak. The only blemish came in Zaragoza's first title defense when he fought a 12-round draw with Seung Hoon Lee.

Banke, 122, began this fight much like he did the first as he seized the role of aggressor and bulled Zaragoza, also 122, to the ropes. The champion pivoted away and landed a right to the body and a light right hook to the head. Zaragoza sought to keep his distance and catch Banke charging in, which he did with a left uppercut before initiating a clinch. Zaragoza was the more active fighter as he tossed two- and three-punch flurries while Banke continually moved forward and searched for openings. The challenger shoe-shined Zaragoza's body to set up a solid overhand left, but Zaragoza retaliated with an even stronger right that landed flush but failed to move Banke. The challenger backed Zaragoza to the ropes and worked the body, but one low right drew a complaint from Zaragoza and a caution from referee John Thomas. Banke knew that a body attack would be a major key to success, so he didn't let Thomas' warning rattle him. A right to the stomach set up a left cross that made Zaragoza immediately clinch.

As the round progressed, they exchanged quick-fisted blows and the effects were already becoming apparent. A tiny swelling erupted on the right side of Banke's jaw and the area around Zaragoza's right eye was reddening. Zaragoza was getting the better of the exchanges as he planted several straight lefts to the head. Zaragoza was putting everything behind his punches, as his grunting attested. Though Banke tagged the champ with a good left near the end of the round, Zaragoza's activity earned him the edge.

Banke had a better start in round two as he won an exchange of left crosses, connected with a nice right-left during a flurry on the ropes and drilled a right to the ribs at ring center. Banke was known as a boxer at the start of his career but he had always preferred to take the attack to his opponent, and Zaragoza's edges in height and reach gave him a good excuse to go toe to toe. At the end of the second, Zaragoza gave a nod of respect to Banke, for he knew that the opening pleasantries had ended and the real fighting was about to begin.

Banke confirmed Zaragoza's suspicions in the third as he answered a long left to the body with an overhand left to the jaw and a six-punch flurry under and over. Banke was letting the punches flow naturally, which resulted in a higher connect percentage. A right-right-left along the ropes snapped Zaragoza's head back, and the champion smartly circled away from the ropes, re-established punching range and launched a series of overhand lefts. A sharp right hook brought a nod of acknowledgment from Banke, whose nostrils were oozing blood. Banke knew he was most effective when Zaragoza's back was to the ropes, so the next time he got him there he started to whale away.

The two men were soon locked in a heated exchange and the Forum crowd was caught up in the action as they yelled, whooped, hollered and whistled their approval. The fight was turning into a brawl that suited Banke's stockier build, but both fighters' cores. Though Zaragoza operated best at arm's length, he couldn't resist a good brawl – even if it meant he suffered some damage himself. After the bell rang, Zaragoza stared at Banke, who nodded and walked to his corner while twirling his left fist in triumph.

Zaragoza suffered a cut on the corner of his left eye during the round and ringside physician Dr. Bernhard Schwartz was summoned. The slice was short in length but deep, yet because the blood was flowing away from the eyeball the fight was allowed to continue. Meanwhile, Banke was feeling good about the situation, even doing a bit of shadowboxing in the corner as he awaited the fourth round.

Banke sought to worsen the cut by tossing jabs and he used his superior hand speed to pop in combinations. Now it was Banke who was beating Zaragoza to the punch, and though the champ offered stiff resistance Banke won the stanza handily. Matters got worse for Zaragoza in the fifth when an accidental butt opened a dangerous cut on the eyelid. Both champion and challenger realized the dire situation immediately and both acted accordingly. Banke backed Zaragoza to the ropes whacked away while the champion fought his way off the strands and pelted Banke with long-armed combinations at ring center. Two strong hooks forced Zaragoza back to the ropes and the round ended with a thrilling and dramatic exchange that saw both men get in their best licks. Zaragoza appeared to stun Banke in the final 10 seconds with a heavy left, but the mounting crimson now posed a serious threat to Zaragoza's crown.

Dr. Schwartz again examined the eye between rounds.

"I think they can stop the bleeding," Thomas said.

"I want to see it though," he answered. "It's bleeding down the side right now, but if it (the blood) gets in the middle, call it and we'll stop it." All of this occurred as one of Zaragoza's corner men constantly pleaded for a butt ruling.

"The judges didn't see it and I didn't see it either," Thomas told the second. Thus, if the fight were stopped because of the cut, Zaragoza would lose by technical knockout.

Knowing his crown was in danger, Zaragoza started the sixth quickly by landing three big right uppercuts. Zaragoza was loading up another one when Banke countered over the top with a stinging left that made the champion grimace and retreat to the neutral corner. A left uppercut and overhand right nailed Zaragoza but the

Mexican fought off the ropes fiercely when Banke sought to follow up. Zaragoza's face was a blood-coated smear but he showed no signs of concern as he blasted two lefts off Banke's jaw. Banke backed off briefly before his overhand left smacked against the right eye cuts.

With 25 seconds remaining, Zaragoza picked up the pace and Banke went right with him, going punch for punch until the bell. After the bell rang, Zaragoza nodded at Banke, tapped his glove and rolled his own gloves as if to say *"now we're fighting like real men. Good job."*

The damage was mounting on both fighters. During an exchange late in the round, Zaragoza opened a cut over Banke's right eye while Zaragoza's left eye was swollen and discolored. Neither man let their injuries interfere with the ultimate goal as they went back at it in the seventh. Zaragoza dug hard rights to the breadbasket to set up a jolting left to the jaw and Banke forced the champion back with his own right to the stomach. With his back to the ropes, Zaragoza speared Banke with straight, long-armed blows to the head and body while Banke threw harder but less frequent shots. Banke was standing straight up and not particularly concerned with defense. Still, his punches created a thick hood of blood over Zaragoza's eyes. It was a gory sight, but Zaragoza kept firing away, showing a champion's grit and providing an object lesson to a man who desperately wanted to be a champion himself. At round's end, Zaragoza smiled and tapped his glove on Banke's shoulder, thoroughly enjoying the ferocious combat.

Banke was having a good time as well, and he stood at ring center for several seconds before the eighth round bell. Zaragoza was more than ready for him as he rattled Banke's head with a left uppercut and a left cross but because the Mexican was never a big puncher Banke continued to march forward. Despite having to brush away the blood every few seconds, Zaragoza out-worked Banke, who concentrated mostly on the champion's body. Banke rallied well over the final 30 seconds, yet it was clear that Zaragoza had seized both physical and mathematical command of the bout.

Entering the ninth round, Banke was behind by three, four and six points and it was obvious that he had to do something dramatic if he wanted to make his dream a reality. Though he had opened several cuts on Zaragoza's face, he had not broken the champion's will. In fact, the robust action drove Zaragoza to fight even harder. Despite his experience at the championship level, Zaragoza fought with the tenaciousness of a hungry young challenger and it would take a special effort by Banke to surmount it and achieve his goal.

The Great Western Forum crowd wanted to see that happen as they chanted for Banke to start the ninth round. Both men dug hard on the inside, and it was there that Banke received a sign of hope. A ripping left uppercut opened a gash under Zaragoza's right eye, and when the champion backed to the ropes Banke followed him in hot pursuit. Soon Zaragoza's mouth was hanging open and the swelling threatened to close the champion's left eye. His attack in the middle rounds racked his arms with fatigue, but because Zaragoza was a true fighting man he kept firing back. His blows, however, had an air of desperation and he occasionally dropped his arms to shake life into them.

Two chopping lefts and a searing right to the stomach made Zaragoza's body sag and Banke tore into the champion like a wild-eyed wolf on its stricken prey. But Zaragoza, hurt and weary as he was, fought back fiercely and the two were locked in a breathtaking exchange along the ropes.

With 1:06 remaining, Banke finally broke through. A huge left to the jaw sent Zaragoza slowly to the canvas and when he rolled on his back it appeared for a moment that the fight was over. But when the champion arose at Thomas' count of eight, he unleashed a robust "yeah!" to Thomas and "come on" to Banke as he waved in his opponent.

For Banke, the moment of redemption had arrived. Once again he was in the ninth round of a title fight and he had just scored a resounding knockdown. Last time, he let overconfidence get the better of him and because of that he paid a bitter price. Now he had the chance to wipe the slate clean and prove to the world – and to himself – that he had changed for the better.

Banke charged in and doubled over Zaragoza with a snappy right-left to the body, but like Rocky Balboa in his rematch with Clubber Lang in "Rocky III," Zaragoza beckoned his foe in and asked for more.

"If you're going to beat me, you'd better beat me in the right way," Zaragoza's actions said. *"If you're going to win my title, you're going to have to fight for it. So fight me!"*

With 12 seconds left in the round, Banke beat Zaragoza the right way. A smashing left nailed Zaragoza perfectly and the proud Mexican slumped to the canvas along the ropes, his body curling into a ball. Referee Thomas immediately stopped the fight with nine seconds remaining in round nine – representing a numerical as well as physical redemption for Banke.

Zaragoza quickly regained his feet and was the first to congratulate his conqueror. Banke accepted the former champion's gesture, then, overcome with emotion, rested his head on the shoulder of his corner man. Zaragoza, however, was in no mood for commiseration from his own people. He wanted a few moments to himself to reflect on what had just happened to him as well as wrap his mind around his new situation. He was offered comfort, but refused it; the only man he wanted to see was Banke. As he hugged him, he offered a few words of advice and encouragement. It would have been easy for Zaragoza to sulk and wallow in self-pity, but instead he comported himself like a real sportsman – and a real man.

"I fought him last year, and I fought a tough fight," Banke said to Prime Ticket's Ruben Castillo. "But I didn't fight my best performance. And tonight I didn't fight my best performance. A long time ago, before they fought for world titles, the gladiators, they didn't try to have a pretty style, they weren't trying to execute, they went in there to bang. You know what? I didn't care. Maybe I took too many head shots. I don't care. I wanted to bring this belt home."

In their two fights, Daniel Zaragoza taught Paul Banke what it meant to be a champion. More than anything else, Zaragoza showed Banke that one must get the job done first before basking in the victory, to be willing to suffer through anything to get the victory and to take an honorable defeat with grace. Zaragoza took Banke to the crossroads twice. The first time Banke made the wrong choice, but his actions the second time proved the hard lessons had been learned and applied. It was time for the two of them to part ways and proceed toward their separate destinies.

Epilogue: Nothing ever came easy for Banke, both in the ring and in life. Just shy of four months after beating Zaragoza, Banke traveled to Inchon, South Korea to fight the 14-0-1 Ki-Jun Lee. Fighting through cuts and swellings, Banke roared from behind to deck Lee once in the 11th and twice in the 12th to record a TKO with just 65 seconds remaining in the fight. Entering the final round, Banke led by two points on one card, trailed by one on the second and was even on the third.

On November 5, 1990 at the Great Western Forum, less than three months after the draining fight with Lee, Banke took on power-punching Argentine Pedro Decima. The back-to-back hard fights proved too much for even the resilient Banke as he lost every round before being stopped in the fourth following three knockdowns. Banke took nearly a year off before returning to the ring and decisioning Antonio Vasquez over 10 rounds.

Banke fought once more for the world title – and his opponent would be none other than Zaragoza, who had regained the title after beating Decima's conqueror Kiyoshi Hatanaka. This time, Zaragoza won a competitive but comfortable decision.

Banke would fight three more times, and lost them all. His final pro fight took place December 6, 1993 and the 29-year-old Banke fought listlessly in losing a 10-round decision to Juan Francisco Soto at the Great Western Forum. His final record was 21-9 (11 KO).

In July 1995, Banke served a brief stint in a Las Vegas jail for a traffic violation, and it was through Nevada's AIDS-testing of prisoners that Banke found out he was HIV-positive. On August 21, 1995 he was told he had full-blown AIDS, but showing the persistence that marked his ring career Banke has not succumbed to the disease.

Unlike Banke, Zaragoza had many more chapters to write in his career. He took nearly an entire year off following the Banke loss before returning with a 10-round victory over Moi Hernandez. He regained the WBC super bantamweight title in his next fight by beating Hatanaka at Nagoya's Rainbow Hall. After two successful defenses against Chun Huh (W 12) and Banke (W 12), Zaragoza lost the belt to Frenchman Thierry Jacob.

Zaragoza would remain a fixture on the championship scene throughout the rest of his career. He fought Jacob's successor Tracy Harris Patterson twice, the first being a draw and the second a cut-induced seven-round TKO loss. A six-fight winning streak earned Zaragoza another crack at the WBC super bantamweight belt, this time against Patterson's successor Hector Acero Sanchez. Despite scoring a knockdown and being the beneficiary of several point deductions, Zaragoza earned a head-scratching draw against Acero Sanchez. In the rematch five months later, Zaragoza, just a month shy of 38, became a three-time champion by capturing a split decision.

Over the next four fights, Zaragoza would put together an incredible run of success when, as the underdog, he beat Joichiro Tatsuyoshi (KO 11), Tsuyoshi Harada (KO 7), Wayne McCullough (W 12) and Tatsuyoshi again (W 12).

Finally, on September 6, 1997 in El Paso, Texas, the nearly 40-year-old Zaragoza met his match in 21-year-old Erik Morales – not that he made it easy for the youngster. At the time of the 11th round knockout, Zaragoza was ahead by one point on one card while trailing by one and three points on the other two. Zaragoza's Indian Summer run earned him enshrinement in the International Boxing Hall of Fame in 2004, and his final record stands at 55-8-3 (28 KO).

TALES FROM THE VAULT

Total Punches Landed/Thrown

Round	1	2	3	4	5	6	7	8	9	10	11	12	Total
Banke	32/103	26/84	45/121	30/86	52/114	42/106	29/82	35/89	58/113				349/898
	31%	31%	37%	35%	46%	40%	35%	39%	51%				39%
Zaragoza	33/98	33/91	45/130	41/119	52/133	50/134	48/134	40/118	30/118				372/1075
	34%	36%	35%	34%	39%	37%	36%	34%	25%				35%

Jabs Landed/Thrown

Round	1	2	3	4	5	6	7	8	9	10	11	12	Total
Banke	5/26	8/38	16/33	13/44	20/44	13/39	9/44	12/32	12/31				108/331
	19%	21%	48%	30%	45%	33%	20%	38%	39%				33%
Zaragoza	4/40	12/44	9/56	17/61	20/56	12/49	15/52	11/47	6/38				106/443
	10%	27%	16%	28%	36%	24%	29%	23%	16%				24%

Power Punches Landed/Thrown

Round	1	2	3	4	5	6	7	8	9	10	11	12	Total
Banke	27/77	18/46	29/88	17/42	32/70	29/67	20/38	23/57	46/82				241/567
	35%	39%	33%	40%	46%	43%	53%	40%	56%				43%
Zaragoza	29/58	21/47	36/74	24/58	32/77	38/85	33/82	29/71	24/80				266/632
	50%	45%	49%	41%	42%	45%	40%	41%	30%				42%

Paul Banke vs. Daniel Zaragoza II April 23, 1990, Inglewood, California

Prudencio Cardona vs. Antonio Avelar
March 20, 1982, Tampico, Mexico

Flyweights can't seem to get any respect. They work hard to squeeze their bodies down to the 112-pound limit and because of their small size they are capable of flashing breathtaking hand speed and unleashing combination after combination with minimal rest. As a result, far more often that not, they give fans the type of action-packed fights they crave.

Some of the greatest fighters in the history of the sport plied their trade here. Jimmy Wilde, known as "The Mighty Atom" because he often weighed around 100 pounds, scored a knockout for every pound he weighed and became the division's first champion in 1916 after he polished off Young Zulu Kid in 11 rounds. Argentine Pascual Perez stood only 4 feet 10 ½ inches but he was one of the division's giants as he reigned for nearly six years and registered nine defenses. At 5-1, Miguel Canto wasn't much bigger than Perez and he certainly didn't hit as hard as he knocked out only 15 men in 74 fights, but his dazzling defensive wizardry carried him to 14 defenses in a nearly five-year reign.

Sot Chitalada, Santos Laciar, Fidel Bassa and Hilario Zapata ruled the 1980s while Mark Johnson, Yuri Arbachakov and Saen Sor Ploenchit were among the best champions of the 1990s. In this decade, WBC champ Pongsaklek Wonjongkam reigned supreme with his division record 17 defenses while IBF champs Vic Darchinyan and Irene Pacheco as well as longtime WBO titlist Omar Narvaez put together quality reigns in the 2000s. Heck, even Manny Pacquiao, arguably the best pound-for-pound fighter in the sport, briefly held the WBC title in the late 1990s and in his time former WBC interim champ Jorge Arce was regarded as one of the sport's most exciting performers.

But in a nation where the credo of "bigger is better" always holds sway, the flyweights continue to languish in obscurity. Why? Because "Boxing's Little Giants" generally don't hit like giants. They don't produce the Tysonesque blows that inspire awestruck oohs and aahs from the spectators nor do their punches turn their opponents into unsensing masses of jelly that couldn't be roused even if the referee counts to 100. America is a nation that hungers for the spectacular, craves the charismatic and spends its time bemoaning the lack of heavyweight stars while the real stars are relegated to performing on undercards before embarrassingly small crowds.

But every once in a while, the little guys come up big and the results can be as awe-inspiring as those done by the big boys. One such case took place at the Estadio Tamaulipas Futbol in Tampico, Mexico when WBC champion Antonio Avelar took on Colombian challenger Prudencio Cardona.

Avelar, a native of Guadalajara, Mexico, was one of the division's true punchers as he blasted out 24 of his previous 29 victims. But his record also had eight losses, four of which came by knockout, so his life in the ring had a flair for the dramatic. Like many Mexicans, Avelar began his career very young as he beat Felipe Mayorga over four rounds four months short of his 17th birthday. Avelar won more than he lost, but following defeats to the 17-11 Juan Jose Guzman (KO by 7), future WBC junior flyweight champion Freddie Castillo (L 10, KO by 10) and future WBC flyweight champion Gabriel Bernal (L 10), Avelar was thought to be a hard-punching, but relatively safe, challenger. In fact, his first title shot against Canto occurred less than four months after his knockout loss to Castillo. Avelar ended up losing a 15-round decision to Canto, who would shockingly lose his title five weeks later to Chan Hee Park.

Though Avelar ended up losing to the Mexican legend, he benefited from the experience. The fight was not a blowout by any means and he gained confidence from the knowledge that he could compete with the very best in the division. From that point onward, Avelar became a terror. After avenging an earlier 10-round loss by decisioning Samuel Machorro, Avelar proceeded to knock out his next seven opponents. His victims included former WBA flyweight champion Alfonso Lopez (KO 5) and Alberto Morales (KO 10) to capture the North American Boxing Federation flyweight title. After destroying Rocky Mijares for the second time in the streak (KO 2), Avelar earned a crack at Shoji Oguma's WBC belt. The first six rounds were relatively even but early in the seventh Avelar knocked the crown off Oguma's head with a classic one-punch knockout. The 23-year-old Avelar, once considered a club fighter, was now a champion.

Avelar extended his knockout string to nine by traveling to Seoul, South Korea and polishing off former WBA titlist Tae Shik Kim (KO 2) in his first defense three months later. Now somewhat established as a champion, Avelar returned to his home country to defend against Cardona.

Meanwhile, the 30-year-old Cardona (30-6, 19 KO) entered the Castillo fight on a five-fight knockout streak of his own. The Colombian's most notable victim during that streak was Orlando Maldonado (KO 5), who lost by disqualification to Canto during the Mexican's ill fated drive toward a final championship shot. Like Avelar, Cardona's record was dotted with losses against men who either had big names or those who would acquire them in the future. Cardona was knocked out in three rounds by Betulio Gonzalez and lost 10-round decisions to future champions Luis Ibarra and Seung-Hoon Lee. Should Cardona win, he would join the select group of brothers to win world championships. Younger sibling Ricardo won the WBA junior featherweight title by knocking out Soo Hwan Hong in 12 rounds and racked up five defenses before Leo Randolph scored an off-the-floor 15th round knockout in May 1980.

Avelar-Cardona took place at an outdoor soccer stadium and the ring was bathed in bright sunshine. The dark blue ring mat was unusually thick and one could see the fighters' feet sink slightly into the canvas as they made their way around. Despite the two men's string of knockouts, Avelar was regarded by most to be the bigger puncher shot for shot, and the thick mat was designed to augment that advantage. Cardona, who weighed just 110 ½, had the same long and lean build as his brother Ricardo and he spent the moments before the opening bell bouncing lightly on his toes and doing some light shadowboxing. Avelar, who was right at the limit at 112, spent several long seconds kneeled in prayer. The opening bell snapped the champion out of his meditation, and finally the fight was on.

After the two fighters felt one another out, Cardona winged a wild hook from which Avelar easily leaned away. Avelar missed with a jab while Cardona fell short with hooks to the head and body, then whiffed on a left uppercut. Cardona barreled in behind a one-two that enabled him to land a short right and a cuffing hook before Avelar initiated the first clinch of the contest.

Though Cardona possessed a clear height and reach advantage, he assumed the role of aggressor. Because he was in the champion's home territory, he wisely decided to seize the initiative while Avelar opted to size up his man before launching his first assault.

Back at ring center, Cardona landed a jab to the stomach and a hook to the body several seconds later. Cardona deked an overhand right to get inside, but the challenger's head crashed into Avelar's just before he landed a cuffing hook to the ear. The grimacing Avelar immediately pulled away, clutching his left eye with his right glove and earning a very brief respite from referee Jimmy Rondeau. When the fight resumed, Cardona popped a jab into Avelar's face and just missed with a swooshing right to the jaw that forced the challenger off-balance into a southpaw stance. Instead of shifting back to orthodox, Cardona launched a glancing left cross to the face before shifting back to his more comfortable position.

Up to this point, Avelar had not done much beyond sizing up Cardona behind light jabs. But with the challenger taking the fight to him he felt he needed to strike back – and soon. He uncoiled from his crouch to land a hard jab to the face and a second jab brushed against Cardona's cheek. Cardona missed with a slashing hook before dancing out of range.

An exchange of jabs drew Cardona into close range, where he drove a right uppercut to the pit of the stomach. That triggered an energetic but inaccurate flurry capped by a strong right to the jaw. Avelar, with his back to the ropes, dug a short hook to the ribs and missed with a right uppercut as Cardona backed out of range.

As the round reached the halfway mark, the fight had the look of a lively feeling out process, scholarly but athletic. Cardona was ahead of the game as far as establishing range while Avelar was off to a typically slow start. It usually took the Mexican a couple of rounds to get warmed up but once he did he became a very dangerous proposition. But until then, Cardona sought to take advantage of every second at his disposal.

Avelar landed a light right to the jaw, and Cardona seized on the opening by landing a strong counter right that snapped the champion's head. The blow clearly stung Avelar and the challenger moved in with both hands blazing. Cardona sunk a heavy right-left to the body, missed a big uppercut and landed a right to the ear. A piercing jab snapped back Avelar's head and while the champ managed to duck under a big right, a cuffing hook knocked Avelar off balance.

Avelar was now badly hurt and he could no nothing more than weave his upper body from as many punches as he could. After Cardona landed another right to the temple, he connected with a huge hook that caught Avelar leaning away. Another right missed over the top, but it helped put Cardona in position to fire a knockout shot whose immense power defied the weight category of its origin.

A massive hook to the jaw twisted Avelar's head as he inched toward the ropes, and its effects first reverberated through Avelar's body, then deadened it. The instant after the punch landed, both of Avelar's arms dropped to the side, his upper body pitched forward, then fell in slow motion like freshly cut timber. He landed face-first with a resounding thud and not one muscle moved as Rondeau tolled the count. Every part of Avelar's body was flat on the canvas and both of his palms were turned upward. Meanwhile, Cardona stepped over Avelar's seemingly lifeless form and when he got to the neutral corner he spun and danced around, secure in the knowledge that he was mere seconds away from being crowned the new WBC flyweight champion.

The count was a mere formality and Rondeau officially declared the fight over just 2:04 after it began. Avelar's handlers rushed into the ring as one of them turned the now former champion onto his back. Cardona's handlers also rushed the ring to hoist the new champion into the air. The contrast of emotions was almost bizarre to watch. For one man, this was the highlight of his athletic life, a memory that would be savored for the rest of his days. For the other, there would be no memory of the exact moment he lost his championship but the after-effects would forever be felt in his heart and logged in the record books.

Seldom has a championship ever been won – and lost – so suddenly and dramatically. The fact that it happened in one of boxing's lightest weight classes made it even more unique and it proved beyond doubt that even the smallest of men can generate punches that boast heavyweight-sized results.

Epilogue: Cardona's reign as WBC champion lasted a little less than four months as he dropped a 15-round unanimous decision to former WBC junior flyweight champion Freddie Castillo. Cardona's loss to Castillo ignited a dizzying string of title changes as he was the first of seven men to lose the belt in his first defense. Over the next two years, the title passed from Cardona, Castillo, Eleoncio Mercedes, Charlie Magri, Frank

SUDDEN AND VIOLENT ENDINGS

Cedeno and Koji Kobayashi before Kobayashi's conqueror Gabriel Bernal managed one successful defense before losing to Sot Chitalada. Chitalada, incidentally, would hold the title for nearly four years.

After losing the belt to Castillo, Cardona went 4-0-1 to earn a crack at Santos Laciar's WBA belt on September 15, 1984 in Cordoba, Argentina. Laciar stopped Cardona in 10 rounds and it would mark the Colombian's final chance at a world title. From then on he lost far more than he won and he soon became a stepping stone for up-and-comers. His victorious opponents included future champions Juan Polo Perez (L 10, L 10), Raul Perez (L 10) and Orlando Canizales (KO by 6), title challenger Tommy Valoy (KO by 6) and future title challenger Pepillo Valdez (KO by 7). After losing to Valdez, Cardona stayed on the sidelines for two-and-a-half years. The 40-year-old Cardona took one more stab by taking on the 10-13-2 Darryl Pinckney on June 27, 1992 in Miami in a featherweight bout. Pinckney stopped Cardona in four rounds. It was the Colombian's 13th loss in his last 14 fights and his final record stands at 40-23-1 with 27 knockouts.

Avelar moved up to bantamweight following the loss to Cardona and he won 10 of his next 13 fights. He split two fights with Gilberto Roman (DQ 5, KO by 7), knocked out Freddie Castillo in four rounds and emerged victorious in an unforgettable eight-round slugfest with the young and powerful Wilfredo Vazquez to earn a shot at Miguel Lora's WBC 118-pound belt. The title shot took place 14 months after the debilitating war with Vazquez and it was no surprise when Lora stopped him in four rounds. It would prove to be Avelar's final bout and the 28-year-old Mexican retired with a record of 39-13-1 with 32 knockouts.

TALES FROM THE VAULT

Total Punches Landed/Thrown

Round	1	2	3	4	5	6	7	8	9	10	11	12	Total
Cardona	24/49												24/49
	49%												49%
Avelar	5/20												5/20
	25%												25%

Jabs Landed/Thrown

Round	1	2	3	4	5	6	7	8	9	10	11	12	Total
Cardona	4/8												4/8
	50%												50%
Avelar	2/11												2/11
	18%												18%

Power Punches Landed/Thrown

Round	1	2	3	4	5	6	7	8	9	10	11	12	Total
Cardona	20/41												20/41
	49%												49%
Avelar	3/9												3/9
	33%												33%

Prudencio Cardona vs. Antonio Avelar March 20, 1982, Tampico, Mexico

Julian Jackson vs. Herol Graham
November 24, 1990, Benalmadena, Spain

Of all the attributes a boxer needs to succeed, power is the one fans talk about most and the one that trainers, managers, promoters and TV executives covet above all others. A big punch is boxing's ultimate shortcut because it eases the path toward fame and fortune. The promise of witnessing a spectacular display of firepower draws bigger crowds, more press coverage and a freer flow of dollars into everyone's pockets. Plus, the fighter has to be attracted by the idea of earning the same paycheck while working fewer rounds.

For whatever reason, Julian Jackson was never able to achieve the worldwide acclaim his talents deserved. He certainly had the physical equipment to go all the way, both inside the ring and at the bank teller's window. His 5-10 ½ frame was muscular but not muscle-bound. At times his technique was of textbook quality as he maintained a high guard and executed well-delivered combinations to body and head. But what separated Jackson from everyone else was his unearthly power. He was the rarest of commodities – a pure one-punch knockout artist with both fists. He spoke of hitting men so hard that he felt his forearms vibrate and more than once he pointed his glove toward the ground even as his victim was still falling.

The inexperienced Jackson failed in his first title shot against WBA junior middleweight champion Mike McCallum in 1986 but three fights later he captured the belt McCallum eventually vacated by stopping In Chul Baek in three rounds. Jackson defended the belt three times against Buster Drayton (KO 3), Francisco DeJesus (KO 8) and Terry Norris (KO 2). The Drayton and Norris defenses were typically memorable as a single hook to the jaw felled Drayton while one concussive right blew Norris away. Jackson's star was about to soar when disaster struck in the form of a detached retina. The injury forced Jackson to cancel a defense against Troy Wortham and surrender the title.

Following successful surgery, Jackson returned to the ring as a middleweight 10 months after the Norris fight. "The Hawk" swooped down on John McClendon in two rounds and Wayne Powell in four to set up a fight with Sheffield, England's Herol Graham for the vacant WBC middleweight title. Because of the British Boxing Board of Control's ban against fighters who had suffered detached retinas, the November 24, 1990 bout was moved to the Torrequebrada Hotel and Casino in Benalmadena, Spain.

Graham (43-2, 26 KO) presented a formidable challenge. Though he carried the nickname "Bomber" – and his last nine victories had come by knockout – the southpaw Graham was known more for his speed and radar-like defensive skills. The 5-11 Graham's physique resembled that of a greyhound; he had a powerful upper body that featured long, loose muscles yet had thin legs that nevertheless obeyed his mind's every command. He used his uncommonly long 77-inch reach to keep his opponents at a safe distance and he used his snapping jab as a prologue to the harder punches that inevitably followed.

As an amateur he won the 1978 Senior ABA light middleweight title and turned pro shortly thereafter with a six round decision over Vivian Waite. Over the next eight-and-a-half years Graham built a 38-0 (21 KO) record, winning the British, Commonwealth and European light middleweight titles as well as the British and European middleweight belts. His most impressive victories during this time were a 10-round stoppage of former WBA junior middleweight champion Ayub Kalule and an eighth round TKO over Mark Kaylor. The 10-year winning streak (including his amateur days) ended with a razor-thin but unanimous decision to future WBA middleweight champion Sumbu Kalambay and four fights later he gave Mike McCallum one of his toughest fights before losing a split decision for the vacant WBA middleweight belt.

Despite the loss, Graham retained his high ranking and knockouts over Rod Douglas (KO 9) and Ismael Negron (KO 3) helped the Sheffield man stay in position for his second title chance against Jackson (41-1, 40 KO). At 30, Jackson was attempting to win his second divisional crown while the 31-year-old Graham was hungry to win his first before the sands of his prime years ran out.

A determined Graham seized the uncharacteristic role of aggressor as he planted his feet and drove Jackson toward the corner with a four-punch flurry. As Jackson slid to his left along the ropes, Graham connected with a right uppercut that pierced Jackson's guard. Jackson winged a dangerous-looking hook that just missed Graham's chin and the "Bomber" wisely retreated to ring center. A few seconds later Graham again surged forward and Jackson caught him with a hook that didn't land with full impact. Jackson was like a coiled spring as he maintained his high guard, but he didn't punch very often because he had trouble timing Graham's movement.

Meanwhile, Graham was off to a roaring start. He skillfully drew leads from Jackson and tagged him repeatedly with counters. He drove a swift right-left through Jackson's guard, then ducked under a wild overhand right to throw a three-punch combination that fell short but a follow-up left cross that didn't. As Jackson retreated toward the ropes, Graham connected with a tremendous right hook to the jaw. Stung, Jackson muscled his way off the ropes and whiffed on a big right. Graham peppered Jackson with a left-right-left and followed with a solid left to the face.

Graham was pushing the pace, yet he still befuddled Jackson with his highly advanced defensive prowess. It was the best of both worlds for Graham, who pelted Jackson with a left cross and a counter right-left as the round neared an end. Because Graham was the aggressor, Jackson couldn't generate his usual power and he didn't have the boxing skills to fight consistently and effectively on the retreat.

Frustrated by his slow start, Jackson started the second round quickly by landing a heavy right. But Graham avoided the brunt by leaning back, then sprung forward behind three long-armed punches. A few seconds later, Graham demonstrated his underrated power by smacking a loud left to the jaw that forced a stunned Jackson to back away. The blow landed squarely on Jackson's left eye and, blinking badly, he retreated to the ropes to cover up.

As Graham advanced, Jackson triggered a hook intended to catch Graham coming in but the top rope prevented Jackson from ever launching the punch. Graham leaned away from a wild right and suddenly the area below Jackson's left eye began to swell. Graham was countering beautifully and as Jackson stumbled across the ring after throwing a winging right over the top, "The Hawk" was being made to look like a novice. Jackson's punches lacked their usual speed and snap while Graham was totally on point.

The frustration was building inside Jackson as he barked at Graham after fielding two more left crosses. After Graham leaned away from a Jackson counter, "The Hawk" came off the ropes in a southpaw stance. This move usually confirms a fighter's bewilderment, but Jackson might have done this as a concession to his rapidly swelling eye. While he pumped a credible right jab, Jackson's bombs still couldn't find the elusive Graham.

The fortunes of each man couldn't have been more diametrically opposed. Graham looked every inch a champion yet wasn't extending himself in any way. For him, the fight wasn't much more difficult than a fairly intense sparring session. The deep breaths he took in the corner were purely voluntary and his face wore a composed expression. As for Jackson, he faced handicaps on three fronts: Physically (the swollen eye), strategically (he was being outmaneuvered in every way) and mathematically (he was two rounds down on all cards).

As round three began Jackson continued fighting as a southpaw while Graham shifted into his more customary boxing mode. He snapped out jabs and deftly averted Jackson's awkward swings. Jackson broke through with a strong right hook that made Graham clinch after their legs tangled. As Graham backed to the ropes Jackson lunged in behind a right-left, but Graham nailed Jackson with a tremendous left cross to the button that made "The Hawk's" legs shudder. Jackson held on as Graham spun him toward the ropes and pumped in several punches to the body. Graham continued his dominance at ring center, timing Jackson's rushes beautifully with his direct, precise punching while also dodging a disorganized four-punch flurry by Jackson.

The round closed with Jackson connecting with a right-left to the jaw and a parting right hook to the face. The bruising beneath Jackson's left eye darkened though the swelling itself hadn't gotten any larger. Still, referee Joe Cortez summoned the ringside physician to examine the eye, sending a clear message that the fight could be stopped

– and soon. In the other corner Graham was bright-eyed and completely unmarked, a man in total control of his domain. He entered the ring with a majority of the crowd on his side and it appeared that it wouldn't be long before they would cheer his coronation.

Jackson returned to the orthodox stance in round four but he could no longer mask his desperation. He lunged blindly with two left hooks while Graham darted behind him and pushed the off-balance Jackson to the canvas. Graham raised his arms overhead to induce a count from Cortez, but the veteran referee wasn't fooled as he simply wiped off Jackson's gloves.

The "Bomber" was known as one of the toughest men to hit cleanly on the chin as he wisely exercised caution before unleashing his blows. But against Jackson, Graham was experiencing an uncommon level of success and that success chipped away at Graham's mental defensive shield. With every passing second his fear of Jackson's power melted away and soon he was pursuing Jackson with unusual bravado. Two hefty left crosses forced Jackson back toward the corner pad and he tagged the retreating "Hawk" with a third left.

As Graham prepared to unleash a fourth left, Jackson saw his chance – and one chance was all he needed.

Graham's windup left a split-second opening and Jackson closed it with a sledgehammer of an overhand right. The blow first snapped Graham's head violently, then stiffened his entire body as he lost consciousness long before he hit the ground. Only Graham's deep breaths provided any indication of life and Cortez's 10-count was only a formality. At 1:13 of round four, an exultant but weary Jackson was declared the new WBC middleweight champion.

Jackson's immortal blow had proven beyond all doubt that he carried his ferocious power up to 160 and it would be five long minutes before Graham would regain consciousness. Jackson said after the fight that the final punch was produced from a blend of astute observation and unshakable faith.

"I knew I was behind, but I kept the pressure on him and I knew that sometime in the fight I would get my shot off," Jackson said. "I was timing him. While I was going back in the corner, I kept my eyes on him until he made that drop to deliver his left hook. He was open and I threw that right hook flush on the chin. I realized that I had to put the pressure on him because my eye was closing pretty fast. I knew I had to get him before the later rounds because I wouldn't have been able to see through this eye."

Considering he lost virtually every second of the fight before the shattering finale, Jackson was more than willing to give Graham his respect.

"He stunned me a few times but I had my faculties together," he said. "I was just waiting for that opportunity when I would land my shot. He moved pretty well and believe me, he surprised me when he stood in the middle of the ring. I expected him to move so he threw me off, and it took me a while to really get things together."

But when Jackson got things together, he did so with one of the most destructive single punches ever thrown in championship competition. It was the type of punch that makes fans want to see it again and again and in turn want to see Jackson perform again and again. It was simply a punch for the ages.

Epilogue: Graham returned 13 months later and successfully defended his British middleweight title with a sixth round stoppage of John Ashton. In March 1992, Graham attempted to exact revenge by lifting Kalambay's European title, but the African-turned-Italian retained the belt by decision. After Frank Grant stopped Graham in nine rounds for the British title, Graham announced his retirement.

But the 37-year-old Graham couldn't bear to leave the sport for good without making at least one more run at a title. Graham put together an unlikely winning streak as he beat Terry Ford (W 8), Craig Joseph (W 8), the 18-0 Chris Johnson (KO 8) and Vinny Pazienza (W 12) to earn a crack at Charles Brewer's IBF super middleweight title. The fight, which took place on March 28, 1998 at the Boardwalk Convention Center in Atlantic City, N.J., started well for Graham as he registered two knockdowns. But the gritty champion put together a tremendous rally and stopped the "Bomber" in round 10. Satisfied that he gave it his best shot, the 38-year-old Graham retired with a record of 48-6 (28 KO).

Jackson defended his new crown in typically splendid fashion as he iced Dennis Milton and Ismael Negron in one round and Ron Collins in five. But Jackson showed the first significant signs of slippage when Thomas Tate pushed him to the limit before losing a decision. Following a four-round non-title KO over Eddie Hall, Jackson defended against fellow mega-puncher Gerald McClellan, who stopped "The Hawk" in five rounds. Jackson earned a second shot at "The G-Man" one year and three victories later, but McClellan was simply too big and too powerful as the fight ended 83 seconds after it began.

The 34-year-old Jackson's skills were slipping dramatically, though he did manage to win one more belt. Jackson captured the WBC middleweight belt vacated by McClellan by crushing the previously unbeaten Agostino Cardamone in two rounds. Jackson lost the belt five months later when Quincy Taylor stopped him in nine. Jackson dropped back down to junior middleweight and won four bouts before Verno Phillips stopped Jackson in nine to pick up a fringe belt. The 37-year-old Jackson retired after being halted in nine rounds by Anthony Jones on May 24, 1998. Jackson's final record is 55-6 (49 KO) and he was inducted into the World Boxing Hall of Fame in 2006.

TALES FROM THE VAULT

Total Punches Landed/Thrown

Round	1	2	3	4	5	6	7	8	9	10	11	12	Total
Jackson	2/24	5/35	6/46	5/22									18/127
	8%	14%	13%	23%									14%
Graham	14/76	20/79	18/55	10/48									62/258
	18%	25%	33%	21%									24%

Jabs Landed/Thrown

Round	1	2	3	4	5	6	7	8	9	10	11	12	Total
Jackson	0/12	3/19	3/22	2/6									8/59
	0%	16%	14%	33%									14%
Graham	2/34	7/36	9/29	1/18									19/117
	6%	19%	31%	6%									16%

Power Punches Landed/Thrown

Round	1	2	3	4	5	6	7	8	9	10	11	12	Total
Jackson	2/12	2/16	3/24	3/16									10/68
	17%	12%	12%	19%									15%
Graham	12/42	13/43	9/26	9/30									43/141
	29%	30%	35%	30%									30%

Julian Jackson vs. Herol Graham November 24, 1990, Benalmadena, Spain

Alfonso Zamora vs. Alberto Sandoval
October 26, 1978, Inglewood, California

From 1964 to 1984, Don Chargin served as the matchmaker for the Olympic Auditorium in Los Angeles and he earned the nickname "War A Week" for the consistently high level of matches he put together. It certainly helped to have a talent pool consisting of all-action fighters like Danny "Little Red" Lopez, Ruben Olivares, Bobby Chacon, Mando Ramos, Pete Ranzany, Carlos Palomino, Jerry Quarry and countless others. But one of the most remarkably savage matches made during Chargin's tenure took place when former WBA bantamweight champion Alfonso Zamora fought Alberto "Superfly" Sandoval in a crossroads 10-round main event. It was a bout that had been postponed three times in a two-month period but once the pair stepped in the ring they made the wait more than worth it.

The 23-year-old Zamora (28-2, 28 KO) was on the comeback trail, engaging in his second fight since losing his title to Jorge Lujan on November 19, 1977 at the Sports Arena in Los Angeles. Lujan out-boxed the power-punching Mexican throughout and the fight's enduring image was a dispirited Zamora sitting on the canvas against a corner pad, staring up at referee John Thomas as he tolled the final seconds of his reign. It was an ignominious way to lose a championship and he took time off to ponder his future. Seven months later, he returned with a six round KO of Hector Medina in Mexico and the Sandoval fight represented his first serious attempt to regain his former status.

For Sandoval (28-1, 21 KO), the Zamora bout was his first major step up in competition. The speedy Californian spent much of his early career at 112 pounds and his skills were such that he earned the sobriquet "Superfly." Though his skill-set was mostly that of a boxer he carried an above-average punch as 11 of his 21 knockouts occurred within three rounds. His only loss was a four-round technical decision awarded to Eliseo Cosme due to a butt-induced cut, but Sandoval avenged it six weeks later via five-round KO. He earned his most noteworthy victory when he stopped Socrates Batoto in six rounds three fights before taking on Zamora.

Sandoval was a crowd favorite at the Olympic as this was his 21st appearance, but Zamora, fighting for the first time in this ring, had more than a few Mexican national supporters rooting for him. Sandoval, who would turn 23 once the clock struck midnight, was a 10-6 betting favorite at ringside and should be win, his next fight would be against Lujan. Sandoval, whose battles with the scale were often more difficult than the fights themselves, weighed a ready 118 ¾ while Zamora, about whom it was rumored that he was in poor shape, scaled 119 ¼. The Olympic was packed and 5,000 more stood outside the arena awaiting word of the result.

Both men exhibited lightning speed as the bout opened, moving in tight circles around one another. Sandoval fired range-finding jabs that fell short of the mark while Zamora lunged in with singular lead rights and dangerous-looking hooks. After the first minute, Sandoval began to land his jabs, sometimes doubling and even tripling them up. One of Zamora's hooks made Sandoval back up toward the ropes but Sandoval bounced right off and moved to his left.

Despite his well-deserved puncher's reputation, Zamora was hardly a plodder. He honed his excellent technical skills during an accomplished amateur career that was capped off by a silver medal in the 1972 Olympics in Munich. In many ways Zamora's style resembled that of Olivares, whose power overshadowed the skills that helped set up the knockout blows. Zamora knew how to cut off the ring and he used his feet to establish punching angles. He surveyed his opponents carefully before letting his punches go, just like Olivares had done years before. The crippling hooks and crosses had plenty of speed and snap and went straight to the target with devastating effect.

Those skills enabled Zamora to keep up with Sandoval as they spent most of the first round engaged in a high-speed boxing match. Both impressively blended offensive and defensive maneuvers to neutralize the other's attack. Sandoval might have earned a slight edge with two stinging jabs in the final five seconds, but others judged Zamora the winner on his aggressiveness. As the bell rang, the "Superfly" nodded to Zamora, not out of respect but with a pugnacity that said *"I'm right here and I'll stay here as long as I want, not as long as your power lets me."*

The nonplussed Zamora started round two well as he landed a lead right over Sandoval's quick jab, but Sandoval caught a moving Zamora with a left hook to the jaw that earned his attention. Sandoval's jab was connecting with more impact and a strong right helped amplify Sandoval's edge. With every passing second the intensity of the boxing escalated and it would be only a matter of time before one man or the other would introduce his power game.

Midway through the round, the expected fireworks erupted.

After Sandoval threw a double jab, Zamora planted his feet and delivered a howtizer right that shook Sandoval to his core. Sandoval's legs quaked violently but didn't collapse, and while he sought to get inside he didn't want to clinch. Within 25 seconds Sandoval had regained his equilibrium and after Zamora missed with an overhand right, Sandoval dug in a hook to the ribs and jolted Zamora with a short overhand right to the temple. Encouraged, Sandoval darted out and twice banged his gloves together to tell Zamora he was back in the fight and raring to go.

With 20 seconds left on the clock, Zamora again shook Sandoval with a lead right followed by a unique left uppercut-right uppercut-left uppercut combination. Sandoval somehow answered back, though his punches mostly found air as Zamora rolled away from most of them. The fight seemed to be following the pre-fight wisdom that said Zamora would dominate the early rounds with his power but if Sandoval could weather the early storm his superior boxing skills could prove decisive against Zamora's questionable stamina.

Early in the third Sandoval barreled in after missing with a wild right over the top and Zamora made him pay with a perfect right uppercut to the jaw. The dazed Sandoval lurched forward with saucer-like eyes and the shark-like Zamora unloaded with impunity, hammering Sandoval's ribs with hooks and snapping his head with several overhand rights. Sandoval refused to clinch, instead fending off whatever blows he could with his arms and fighting back gamely, if foolishly. Zamora's assault lasted a full 45 seconds and only his great courage kept him upright.

After a brief respite to catch his breath, Zamora almost dropped Sandoval with a hook. But as the clock rolled under one minute remaining Zamora began to tire and Sandoval somehow drew strength from it. Incredibly, an overhand right appeared to stun Zamora and a hard jab lashed the Mexican's face. Zamora took back the momentum with a powerful chopping cross and a smashing right-left nailed Sandoval with 15 seconds remaining. A right uppercut-right cross combo caused Sandoval to stumble back into the ropes, where his head got caught between the top two sets of ropes. Sandoval managed to last out the round but it was apparent that Zamora was in command.

Still, there was reason for Sandoval to be encouraged. He had just survived an extended and frightful beating from one of history's hardest punching bantamweights without hitting the canvas. In fact, he walked back to his corner with an almost inconceivable freshness.

A bright-eyed Sandoval began the fourth operating smoothly behind hard snapping jabs while Zamora's blows remained quick, thudding and accurate as they zeroed in on the Californian's head and body. Sandoval's resilience in the face of Zamora's powerhouse attack was amazing to watch, and even ringside commentator Jim Healy had to marvel.

"Sandoval is in simply awesome condition for this fight or he'd be long gone," he said. "Conditioning is what puts the strength in the legs when the brain *says 'you've been hit on the chin, go down'* and the legs say *'no!'*"

Zamora continued to put every ounce of strength behind every blow but Sandoval's heart continued to command him to fight back at every turn. He didn't possess Zamora's single-shot power but his superior quickness and marksmanship allowed him to produce an answer to every Zamora punch. Zamora was winning the fight big on the scorecards but Sandoval's sheer competitiveness made the fight a riveting spectacle. As the minutes passed, the relevance of another question gained importance: What would happen when Zamora's gas tank started to run low?

That answer began to emerge in the fifth round when Sandoval landed a popping hook to the chin at the end of a bristling exchange and a zipping overhand right drove

Zamora to the ropes. The right was Sandoval's best single punch of the fight so far, and his momentum got even stronger when another solid right bounced off Zamora's chin. The area underneath Zamora's right eye began to swell and a small cut was opened. His head was snapping back more dramatically whenever Sandoval landed and his own technique was more ragged.

A scorching hook-cross caused Zamora's right leg to buckle in a delayed reaction and he retreated to the ropes on very shaky legs. But Sandoval resisted the temptation to go for the knockout lest he be caught with another Zamora bomb. He went about his business like a professional, waiting for his chance to land another clean shot. That happened with less than 10 seconds remaining when he stunned Zamora with a right-hook-shotgun jab combo. After the bell sounded Zamora took a deep breath and walked slowly to his corner.

Sandoval continued to ride the wave of success in the opening seconds of round six as another shotgun jab rocked Zamora into the ropes. A few seconds later, a rocket-like right twisted Zamora's head awkwardly and sent him careening. Yet Sandoval remained cool and calculating, ever respectful of the power he has already tasted from Zamora.

But a man doesn't become world champion without resilience, and Zamora would prove he had plenty.

Zamora gained strength as he began to string together combinations at close range. The attack gathered steam as he pounded Sandoval with savage, powerful shots. A full-strength overhand right and left hook snapped Sandoval's head and soon Zamora was raking the Californian over the coals with his white-hot intensity. Another overhand right-left hook salvo stunned Sandoval and as Zamora hammered the Californian until the bell, one had to think Sandoval had squandered a golden opportunity by not going all out when he had the former champion hurt. Between rounds, Sandoval was breathing heavily while Zamora's second wind appeared to be coming at him in a rush.

The tide would turn again in the seventh as an early hook caused Zamora to lurch backward and a flush jab to the face backed him to the ropes. Then it flipped back several seconds later when the former champion stunned Sandoval with his own hook. Though tiring, Zamora somehow channeled the energy from his adoring fans and from the sight of Sandoval's distress into positive action. His punches ripped through Sandoval's defense but he was still in a vulnerable state. Zamora was knocked back a couple of steps by a single jab yet he forced himself past his own exhaustion to inflict even more damage to Sandoval. With blood seeping from his mouth and nose, Zamora showed the courage that many felt he lacked against Lujan and the results were a sight to behold.

Sandoval, too, pushed himself beyond previous limits and with 40 seconds remaining he rattled off a stinging left-left-right and a strong hook that made Zamora totter. Zamora roared back behind several monstrous body blows to keep Sandoval at bay, yet Sandoval was the one who put the exclamation point on the round as he stunned Zamora with two final hooks.

Buoyed by his strong finish, Sandoval began the eighth on inconceivably lively legs while snapping jabs into Zamora's face. He neatly ducked under an overhand right by Zamora and tagged him with a head-snapping right cross. The speedy boxer now was trading freely with the hard-hitting Zamora and was not getting the worst of it as another strong right and left hook had Zamora hanging on. Sandoval, as was his wont, didn't pursue the knockout despite probably being behind on points. The momentum had turned his way and he had reason to believe he still had enough late-round power to polish off the tiring Zamora.

After taking a breather, Zamora again revved up his body attack, belaboring Sandoval with a ceaseless succession of lefts and rights and seemingly gaining strength from every landed punch. It was as if a transfusion of energy were taking place, for Zamora was getting stronger at the same rate Sandoval was weakening.

With 13 seconds to go, Zamora sought to finish the round strong. He nailed Sandoval with an overhand right to the jaw and hooks to the body and head. The final punch of the three-punch salvo hit Sandoval on the tip of the chin, stiffening his legs instantly. As he tottered backward toward the ropes his body was thoroughly anesthesized but his inner will somehow kept him upright. Knowing that Sandoval was mortally stricken, Zamora rushed in with all guns blazing. Both men were in a race against time and physics: Could Sandoval last out the round and get the chance to recover in the corner and could Zamora polish him off fast enough to prevent it?

As an almost defenseless Sandoval struggled mightily to stay conscious, two final rights smashed against his head and his body fell to the left in sections along the ropes. As Zamora turned to run to a neutral corner, referee John Thomas grabbed Zamora's right arm and held it aloft. The clock read 2:59 of round eight when the fight was declared over and as Sandoval lay helplessly on the ground, there was no argument from anyone. For Zamora, the victory gave his career new life and for Sandoval it was a terrible way to celebrate an upcoming birthday.

Matchmaker Chargin certainly earned the nickname "War a Week" and on this night he might well have staged the war of the year.

Epilogue: Five months after losing to Zamora, Sandoval dropped a majority 10 round decision to Eddie Logan. Sandoval won the rematch by 10-round decision less than two months later and won subsequent decisions against Javier Flores, Juan Alvarez and Catalino Flores to earn a shot at Lupe Pintor's WBC bantamweight title on February 9, 1980 at the Forum in Inglewood, California. Though Sandoval fought bravely, Pintor was simply too good as he won nearly every round and stopped the "Superfly" in round 12. The 27-year-old Sandoval made one last stab at boxing as he took on

TALES FROM THE VAULT

Albert Davila at the Olympic Auditorium following a 31-month absence. Davila won a 10-round decision and Sandoval retired with a record of 32-5 (21 KO).

The road for Zamora would prove to be rocky for the rest of his career. Less than three months after beating Sandoval, Zamora struggled to a split decision win over Luis Rosario. Zamora then lost by five-round disqualification to Juan Alvarez and was defeated after a seven-round war with Eddie Logan. Two months after knocking out Melvin Johnson in three rounds, the 26-year-old Zamora was stopped in three rounds by Rigoberto Estrada at the Olympic Auditorium on September 19, 1980. Zamora's final record is 33-5 (32 KO).

SUDDEN AND VIOLENT ENDINGS

Total Punches Landed/Thrown

Round	1	2	3	4	5	6	7	8	9	10	11	12	Total
Zamora	7/31	22/67	48/97	25/63	15/53	40/86	42/91	26/57					225/545
	23%	33%	49%	40%	28%	47%	46%	46%					41%
Sandoval	11/59	17/71	15/70	13/65	22/67	13/64	22/78	18/57					131/531
	19%	24%	21%	20%	33%	20%	28%	32%					25%

Jabs Landed/Thrown

Round	1	2	3	4	5	6	7	8	9	10	11	12	Total
Zamora	1/10	1/9	4/6	2/10	3/13	3/9	5/15	5/8					24/80
	10%	11%	67%	20%	23%	33%	33%	62%					30%
Sandoval	9/50	8/39	8/36	10/41	10/38	5/31	12/43	7/33					69/311
	18%	21%	22%	24%	26%	16%	28%	21%					22%

Power Punches Landed/Thrown

Round	1	2	3	4	5	6	7	8	9	10	11	12	Total
Zamora	6/21	21/58	44/91	23/53	12/40	37/77	37/76	21/49					201/465
	29%	36%	48%	43%	30%	48%	49%	43%					43%
Sandoval	2/9	9/32	7/34	3/24	12/29	8/33	10/35	11/24					62/220
	22%	28%	21%	12%	41%	24%	29%	46%					28%

Alfonso Zamora vs. Alberto Sandoval October 26, 1978, Inglewood, California

TALES FROM THE VAULT

Julian Letterlough vs. Demetrius Jenkins
July 14, 2000, Hampton Beach, New Hampshire

Everyone loves a great comeback story. Scores of movies have depicted people who, by the sheer force of will, triumphed over difficult circumstances and made successful lives for themselves. The first "Rocky" movie is perhaps the finest example of this as a Philadelphia ham-and-egger made the most of his once-in-a-lifetime opportunity at the heavyweight championship by getting more out of himself than even he could have ever imagined. The story was told so compellingly that it earned the Oscar for Best Picture, which in turn vaulted its star, Sylvester Stallone, to his own highly successful movie career.

More than any other sport, boxing offers its participants an opportunity for redemption. A fighter with talent and desire can overcome the most humble of beginnings and propel himself toward fame, fortune and perhaps immortality. These redeeming qualities often extend to the bouts themselves, for a single punch can instantaneously reverse a fight's course and render moot everything that had transpired.

Such is the story of Julian Letterlough, who used boxing to become a small-screen action star in the early 2000s. Letterlough was born on Christmas Day in 1969 and as a child, he was nicknamed "Tyson" due to his slight facial resemblance and his penchant for getting into street fights. As the child grew into a man, he got into trouble with the law and was sentenced to seven years of hard time at the Pittsburgh State Penitentiary for assaulting a police officer. Letterlough found salvation in boxing while in prison and following his release he embarked in a professional career in October 1998. His odds of success were lengthened considerably by the fact he had not had a single amateur fight, but the thickly built Letterlough had the one ingredient that had the potential of trumping everything else – natural punching power.

Letterlough knocked out Byron Jones in two rounds in his professional debut and it wasn't long before he picked up the nickname "Mr. KO." Under the tutelage of veteran trainer "Slim" Jim Robinson (who guided Tim Witherspoon and Eddie Mustafa Muhammad among others), his opponents fell often and they often fell quickly. The 6-0 Dana Rucker was stopped in three rounds while useful veterans Napoleon Pitt, Eric Davis, Darryl Hollowell and Vinson Durham lost in three, three, six and two rounds respectively.

On April 9, 2000, Letterlough left the friendly confines of Pennsylvania to fight Troy Weaver (one of the triplet brothers of former WBA heavyweight champion Mike Weaver) for his WBO/NABO light heavyweight belt. It took Letterlough only 42 seconds to win his first belt. Two months later, he polished off the 8-0 Manny Rose to win the vacant Pennsylvania light heavyweight title and just five weeks later – on July 14,

2000 at The Casino Ballrom in Hampton Beach, New Hampshire, Letterlough (13-0, 13 KO) was signed to make his national TV debut against Demetrius Jenkins.

The 28-year-old Jenkins represented the first major test for Letterlough, now 30. Like Letterlough, Jenkins (18-4, 14 KO) enjoyed a fast start to his career as he bombed out seven of his first eight opponents but when he stepped up in class, Rocky Gannon blasted him out in one round. Jenkins was now a gatekeeper who succeeded against softer opponents while losing to better foes like Bryant Brannon (L 12), the 29-3 Billy Lewis (L 12) and Omar Sheika (KO by 3). Since the Sheika bout, Jenkins had won his last five fights, including victories over unbeatens Ali Supreme (W 4) and Pierre Karam (KO 6). Despite his recent success, it appeared that his biggest role was to gauge whether "Mr. KO" was worthy of taking his act to a larger stage.

The bout was scheduled for eight rounds to fit within ESPN's format, and the distance also suited Letterlough's prospect status. Though the Weaver and Rose fights were scheduled for 12 and 10 rounds respectively, Letterlough had not yet fought past six rounds while Jenkins had fought past eight rounds five times, including 12 twice.

It made for an interesting physical and style match; the stocky Letterlough was short on finesse but long on power (especially with the left hook) while the notoriously slow-starting 5-11 Jenkins was three inches taller and was armed with a few tricks up his sleeve.

Letterlough began the fight by landing a pair of hooks – one to the head and one to the ribs – while Jenkins kept his distance by staying on the move. Letterlough spent most of the first round diving in behind occasional hooks, one of which landed well as Jenkins was cranking up one of his own. Most of the round was quietly fought, but that certainly wouldn't be the case in round two.

Letterlough began the second working out of a crouch, using range-finding jabs to pave his way inside Jenkins' reach while Jenkins stayed on the move. But after Letterlough cornered Jenkins on the ropes, the bombs began detonating. With the flip of a mental switch, all caution fell away from Jenkins and suddenly he was eager to swap blows with the heavy-hitting Letterlough. At first, his looping shots whizzed over the ducking Letterlough, but a solid left-right by Jenkins caused "Mr. KO" to retreat. Instead of following up his advantage, Jenkins curiously backed all the way across the ring to the other set of ropes. Jenkins' move was soon revealed as a trap, for he caught the advancing Letterlough with a solid left uppercut to the jaw before deftly pivoting away.

Emboldened by his trickery, Jenkins tried it again and this time his right caught the ducking Letterlough on the back of the right shoulder. Still, Letterlough's legs crumbled and he fell to the canvas, after which referee Norm Villeaux began a mandatory eight count. Letterlough regained his feet instantly as the crowd booed the call, and neither man behaved as if a fight-changing event had occurred, for Letterlough continued his pursuit and Jenkins persisted in his sly countering games.

Jenkins soon found his magic potion in the form of a looping right hand that landed solidly as Letterlough charged in. After Letterlough responded with two hooks to the jaw, Jenkins spun away, pushed off Letterlough and landed two more overhand rights. Letterlough absorbed the bombs well and remained focused on hunting down Jenkins, rolling his shoulders and lashing out with power punches with a knockout artist's confidence. With five seconds remaining in the round, a short right to the jaw appeared to drop Letterlough heavily on his back, but this time Villeaux waved it off because Jenkins also used his shoulder to muscle him to the canvas.

Nevertheless, Jenkins was sure he had found his key to victory, especially since another chopping right sent Letterlough on his rump in sections mere seconds into the third. Up at two, a still shaky Letterlough charged in behind a wild overhand right that Jenkins ducked under and a cuffing right that allowed him to grab around Jenkins' waist and bull him to the ropes. Jenkins missed with two looping rights but a third clipped Letterlough's temple and stiffened his legs. A fired-up Jenkins fired in a right uppercut, a right to the head and another to the ribs, but the final right left enough of an opening for Letterlough to land a heavy hook that made Jenkins retreat instantly. A second hook further hastened Jenkins' retreat but as Letterlough tried to corner him on the ropes, Jenkins' right twisted Letterlough's neck and made him seek the safety of a clinch.

Neither man possessed educated jabs or subtle defensive skills. This fight may have been rude and crude, but it was definitely acceptable as they willingly and repeatedly tested the other's strength and durability. Letterlough received a glimmer of hope with 19 seconds to go when a hook to the body made Jenkins grimace and a looping right caught Jenkins' jaw moments later, but that hope faded as Jenkins responded with a trio of – what else – overhand rights as the round closed.

Told to use his jab, Letterlough began the fourth with a double jab that set up an overhand right to the temple. Jenkins was unhurt by the blow and he continued to work the overhand right. With 47 seconds remaining, Jenkins hit a bull's eye with the right and Letterlough couldn't hide his distress as his legs wavered and his upper body sagged subtly but perceptively. Jenkins jumped on him, driving a right uppercut between the gloves and an overhand right to the temple. Letterlough was badly stunned, but not enough for him to forget about his street-fighting instincts. As Jenkins sought to follow up, Letterlough fired a hook that landed below Jenkins' belt. The trade-off was a positive one for Letterlough – the move drew a caution from Villeaux but also forced Jenkins' to back off.

As the round closed, Letterlough attempted to set a trap for Jenkins. He backed to the ropes and beckoned his opponent in with his right glove. With Jenkins taking the bait, Letterlough unleashed a ripping hook that just missed the target.

Early in the fifth, Jenkins' chopping right brought a heavier right from Letterlough, sparking an exchange that ended with Letterlough staggering Jenkins with a hook to the jaw. Jenkins forced a clinch to gain a breather, but then stunned Letterlough with yet another overhand right. Jenkins went after the badly hurt Letterlough, who propped himself up on the ropes and winged his dependable left hook. As the two fighters swapped heavy leather, they began to resemble a pair of Wild West gunslingers shooting their best bullets in search of the next kill.

Letterlough again called Jenkins in with the glove, but this time he didn't take the bait as he chose to back away and allowed Letterlough to come off the ropes. The action slowed as each sought to recharge but the gun slinging resumed in the final 30 seconds. While both got in their share of licks, it was again Jenkins who got the better of the exchanges.

By the sixth, Letterlough was pushed into a strategic and mathematical corner. To this point Jenkins had dominated the action, though Letterlough had fired back often enough to make this a highly entertaining spectacle. Still, the two knockdowns gave Jenkins a large working margin on the scorecards and with five rounds left Letterlough had to sweep them – along with a knockdown or two – to give himself any hope of winning a decision. Thus, Letterlough decided to roll the dice and take the ultimate gamble – an all-out, full frontal assault that allowed little room for error.

Letterlough roared out of the corner and pushed Jenkins toward the ropes with a wild flurry of punches. Jenkins responded by going back to his bread-and-butter – the overhand right – but they lacked their earlier marksmanship. After Letterlough ducked underneath a very wild right, he made Jenkins pay a big price in the form of a scorching hook that spectacularly caught Jenkins as he threw his own hook. Jenkins' body turned as he followed through with the hook, after which he backed toward the ropes on shaky legs. Both men launched rights, but this time Letterlough's got through first and a follow-up hook to the temple broke off the exchange.

The two men exchanged rights – both of which landed – but Letterlough followed with a pair of hooks to the point of the chin. Jenkins responded with a right to the jaw, but then lost an exchange of rights and absorbed a cuffing right to the head.

The punches were coming fast and furious, but for the first time in the bout it was Letterlough who gained the upper hand as he doggedly walked through Jenkins' bombs to land even more of his own. As the round closed, a thudding right-left sent sweat flying off Jenkins' head and he capped off his best round with a shotgun jab to the jaw.

Letterlough landed another shotgun jab to open the seventh, one that drove Jenkins toward the ropes. Jenkins responded with a pair of on-the-move jabs, but Letterlough's two retaliatory jabs forced Jenkins to stumble briefly. Then the two took a slight breather and for a few long seconds they stared at one another like Rocky Balboa and Apollo Creed did in the final round of their first fight. Now, like then, the lull was excusable given the punishment dished out and absorbed. And like Balboa and Creed, Letterlough and Jenkins would soon end the respite with cinematic flair.

With the momentum suddenly going against him, Jenkins broke out a wrinkle early in the seventh as he turned southpaw. His right jabs were startlingly effective as he jerked back Letterlough's head from time to time. But tasting a big hook persuaded Jenkins to switch back to his natural stance, from where he connected with a right to the jaw and a right to the body. Letterlough responded with a lead right, a right to the body and a hook that narrowly whizzed past the target.

With a little more than a minute remaining, Jenkins moved toward the ropes and won an exchange of rights. And it was here that Jenkins committed a fatal error.

Boxing is not only about hitting the other man; it is about keeping from getting hit in return. It is a fighter's responsibility to have his gloves in proper position after he fires a punch. If he doesn't, he exposes himself to a potential fight-ending scenario. After Jenkins landed his right, the glove returned to chest level instead of near his chin while his left glove was well below his waist. With Jenkins propped up on the ropes and with both hands at his side, he was a sitting duck. And Letterlough, being the knockout artist he was, responded.

BOOM!

Letterlough uncorked a beauty of a hook that exploded on Jenkins' chin. All expression drained from Jenkins' face as his body slumped between the top strands of ropes. At 1:58 of round seven, Letterlough erased his deficit and was declared the TKO winner. As his handlers paraded him around the ring holding up his left glove, Letterlough looked as surprised as anyone over the sudden ending, but any surprise was quickly replaced with justifiable pride. He had passed his first real test as a professional fighter and for him, there would be more chances to add to his "Rocky" story. As for Jenkins, the chance to advance beyond a gatekeeper would have to wait for another day.

Epilogue: Three months after losing to Letterlough, Jenkins suffered a head-butt induced technical draw to Etianne Whitaker. An eight-round decision win over Eric Davis and an excellent third-round KO over the 15-1-3 Sam Ahmad earned him a chance at hot prospect Eric Harding. Unfortunately for Jenkins, Harding won a 10-round decision.

Over the next six years, Jenkins fought 10 more times, losing all but one. The victory came March 30, 2002 against the comebacking Frank Liles, whom he stopped in seven rounds, but the 36-year-old Jenkins is currently on a 10-fight losing streak, many of which came against a high level of opposition. His opponents included George Jones (L 10), Steve Cunningham (L 8), Clinton Woods (KO by 7), Syd Vanderpool (KO by 9), Manny Siaca (KO by 4) and Jaffa Ballogou (KO by 5). As of January 2010, his most recent fight took place January 31, 2009 against Darryl Cunningham in Royal Oak,

Michigan and the three-round TKO loss dropped the 38-year-old Jenkins' record to 21-17-1 (16 KO).

Letterlough fought a 10-round draw with Sam Ahmad in his next outing two months later, which was followed by a seven round KO of Max Heyman two months after that. But he cemented his place as an small-screen action star with a classic see-saw match with the undefeated Julio Cesar Gonzalez that saw Gonzalez dropped three times and Letterlough twice before Gonzalez won a hard-earned 12-round decision.

Letterlough earned his only world title opportunity three bouts later when he rose in weight to fight IBF cruiserweight champion Vassiliy Jirov on HBO on September 8, 2001. Though he fought with his typical bravery, the 29-0 Jirov had too much of everything for Letterlough, who suffered an eight-round TKO. From then on, Letterlough went go 4-3-2 (4 KO), but no matter whether he won or lost, he always gave it everything he had, which is all any boxing fan could want.

Letterlough's final fight took place October 1, 2004 when he stopped Eric Starr in two rounds in Reading, Pa. The 35-year-old Letterlough was intent on continuing his career but his story would take a tragic final turn. On July 8, 2005, Letterlough was shot in the back and killed after leaving a bar with his wife and was pronounced dead at the scene. His final record is 21-5-3 with 20 KO.

TALES FROM THE VAULT

Total Punches Landed/Thrown

Round	1	2	3	4	5	6	7	8	9	10	11	12	Total
Letterlough													98/386
													25%
Jenkins													89/310
													29%

Jabs Landed/Thrown

Round	1	2	3	4	5	6	7	8	9	10	11	12	Total
Letterlough													18/88
													20%
Jenkins													11/71
													15%

Power Punches Landed/Thrown

Round	1	2	3	4	5	6	7	8	9	10	11	12	Total
Letterlough													80/298
													27%
Jenkins													78/239
													33%

* Fight originally done by CompuBox, but the original HTML files with complete round-by-round statistics no longer exist.

Julian Letterlough vs. Demetrius Jenkins July 14, 2000, Hampton Beach, New Hampshire

Frank Liles vs. Tim Littles II
June 8, 1996, Newcastle, England

One of the best things about being a boxing fan is discussing with others how a certain fight will unfold. A well-matched contest offers many variables, both physical and psychological, but most times a well-informed observer can make a reasonable and fairly reliable guess as to how the battle will be waged. This is because fighters, like everyone else, have habits. Because most boxers fight in the same manner every time out, those who observe them have a template from which they can mentally mix their styles and produce a prediction.

Then there are fights that obliterate the mold. Who would have guessed Mike Tyson and James "Bonecrusher" Smith, a pair of explosive punchers, would produce one of the most mind-numbing heavyweight title contests on record? And on the other end of the spectrum, who would have thought that Frank Liles and Tim Littles would put forth the kind of slugfest they did on June 8, 1996 at the Telewest Arena in Newcastle, England?

Liles and Littles were fighting for the fifth time, and none of their previous efforts matched the sustained fury of this encounter. The pair met three times as amateurs with Liles winning each, the last of which took place in the semi-finals of the 1988 Olympic trials. But Littles (27-1, 18 KO) turned the tables in their only meeting as pros on July 7, 1992 in Hollywood, Calif., as he successfully defended his USBA super middleweight title and inflicting the only defeat on Liles' 28-1 (17 KO with one no-contest) record. That fight was a good, but not great, contest that saw Littles' harder punching trump Liles' boxing skills en route to a 116-112, 116-112, 117-111 decision that was a bit closer than the scores indicated. The template they created suggested an encounter dictated by boxing skills rather than a rough-and-tumble brawl highlighted by breathtaking displays of power.

"Styles make fights" is a truism that has been proved far more often than not, but at the same time one never can be sure what will take place when two well-conditioned athletes step between the ropes. This would certainly be the case with Liles-Littles II.

Much had changed since their first meeting four years earlier. Littles went on to defend his USBA belt against John Scully (W 12), Lenzie Morgan (W 12) and Armando Rodriguez (KO 1) to earn a shot at James Toney's IBF super middleweight title. In that bout, Littles opened a dangerous cut over Toney's eye, and "Lights Out," told that the bout would be stopped after the fourth round, wasted little time before turning out Littles' lights in dramatic fashion. Littles spent nearly a year away from boxing before returning with three knockout wins over Caseny Truesdale, Mike Belcher and Chris Sande.

Meanwhile, unlike the first fight, Liles entered the rematch as a defending champion. Liles bounced back from the Littles loss by stopping Merqui Sosa in the 12th round of a bout that saw the Dominican bomber penalized four points for various fouls. Two more victories over Cecil McKenzie (KO 8) and Mike Peak (W 8) earned Liles a title shot with WBA super middleweight king Steve Little in the unlikely venue of San Miguel, Argentina. Liles out-boxed Little over 12 rounds to win the title and in the 22 months since, he put together a solid championship reign with victories over former champ Michael Nunn (W 12), Frederic Seillier (KO 6) and Mauricio Amaral Costa (W 12). It isn't often that the loser of the first fight would enter the rematch as the man viewed as a fighter on the rise, but that's how Liles was seen by most of the experts sizing up the battle.

And what a battle it turned out to be, though it didn't look that way in the opening moments as the southpaw Liles worked the angles behind his right jab and Little plodded forward behind his own jab. Liles nailed a charging Littles with a right uppercut and followed up moments later with a left cross to the jaw. Meanwhile, a pumped-up Littles missed wildly with looping shots, one of which Liles ducked under and left him tangled in the ropes. After freeing himself, Littles settled down a bit and connected with an unusual combination, two consecutive right leads.

With 1:20 remaining in the round, Littles lunged in with a long lead right, and while the punch scored he left himself dangerously open. Liles capitalized with a crunching right uppercut that dramatically straightened Littles' body while stiffening his knees. Liles nipped out to long range, spun away from a looping hook and hammered Littles to the canvas with two right hooks and a left cross. Littles smartly took referee Mitch Halpern's mandatory eight on one knee before rising but the respite did him little good as Liles resumed his attack.

The champion drove Littles back with a tremendously accurate five-punch salvo and seemed to be on the verge of putting the challenger away when the bell sounded. According to Showtime's running clock, the gong went off 58 seconds early, and it couldn't have come at a better time for Littles, who walked toward the neutral corner before second Thell Torrance led him back to his stool. During the break, veteran second Luis Spada complained to Halpern about the timing error, but nothing could be done to rectify it. That moment of potential victory had forever disappeared into the ether, and all Liles could do was hope that another one would come his way.

Liles picked up where he left off at the start of the second, landing a left cross that buckled Littles' legs. Littles fired an arcing right hand that caught Liles flush in the face, and the champion made his condition seem even worse by staggering away after colliding knees with Littles at that same moment. Yet Littles was convinced he had wounded Liles, and he barreled in behind a right to the body that somehow wrapped around Liles' hip. Liles slipped to the canvas with a punching Littles falling on top of him.

When Littles regained his feet, he emerged with a gash on his left eyelid, adding another layer to his anxiety. Not only was he a challenger fighting far away from home, he was behind on points in what would likely be his final chance to win a world title – and now he sported a cut that could end that chance prematurely. Those fears were heightened a few moments later when Halpern asked the ringside physician to check the cut, with Littles constantly lobbying for an accidental head butt ruling to prevent a TKO loss. Halpern agreed, and the doctor offered his consent for the fight to continue following a brief examination.

Still, with all of these factors weighing on his mind, Littles pressed the issue, and the results were messy and at times blatantly illegal. Littles landed a hard right to Liles' groin and a follow-up rabbit punch, drawing a caution from Halpern. Liles fell into another clinch after missing with a left cross over the top, and Littles slammed him with a right to the back of the head and three hard, fast rights to the kidneys. Liles escaped and spread out his arms in exasperation, wondering why that sequence failed to draw a point penalty.

But Littles had more in store for him.

As they fell into another clinch, Littles tried two more rabbit punches to shake free, but those did not strike Liles with his full force. After separating, Littles bored in behind a looping left hook and a driving right to the protective cup, prompting Liles to grab again. Liles ripped in a right uppercut but Littles answered with an overhand right that backed the champion to the ropes. Littles ducked low and connected with a long right to the stomach and sprang up behind a left hook, a chopping right to the head and a hard right to the chest before Liles clinched again.

Littles, frustrated by Liles' consistent holding, was in a fighting fury and he acted on it by landing a right to the ear and three more to the back of the head that sent Liles to his knees in a neutral corner. At this point, Halpern deducted a point from Littles for an intentional foul and gave Liles extra time to recover.

A desperate Littles chased after Liles, landing a whipping right to the belly, but moments later Liles sent Littles tumbling hard to the canvas with a right hook. Up at four, Littles raced around the ring to show Halpern he was OK, but the bell sounded before another punch could be thrown.

For the second consecutive round the bell had saved Littles, who was now in the midst of a deep mathematical hole. The knockdowns he suffered in both rounds and the point penalty in round two likely placed him five points down, and the situation seemed to be spiraling out of control. Littles was an angry man as he walked towards his corner, gesturing furiously with his glove that he had been the victim of a butt.

Torrance knew that this was not the time to convey technical advice. Instead he tried to use a soothing tone to settle his man down and get his mind back on the task at hand.

"That's all right. Take your time," Torrance said. "Just get through the round. You're trying too hard."

Littles agreed, replying "I'm rushing myself."

"You hurt the man, Tim, just take your time," Torrance replied.

But thoughts of what he saw as injustice still flooded his mind as he asked Torrance to "tell the referee he's holding me, and they took the point." As Halpern came into his field of vision, Littles began to lobby: "Hey ref, you're gonna watch the holding, right? I was hitting because he was holding."

Convinced he wasn't going to get help from anyone outside of his own corner, Littles took matters into his own hands. Did he ever.

Littles began the third working from a crouch with the left arm extended, using it as a battering ram to get past Liles' long jab. The maneuver worked wonderfully as he first landed a right cross over the top, ducked under a right hook, then drove a right to the ribs, a right to the ear, a right to the back of the head and a final hammering right that sent Liles through the ropes.

Just like that, Littles had produced a violent shift in fortunes and the fired-up challenger raced around the ring in triumph before settling in a neutral corner. After Liles rose at Halpern's count of four, Littles barreled in and ripped in several rights before executing a classic hip-toss to free himself from Liles' grip.

"I'm not going to warn you again," Halpern told Littles. "I'm not messing around here." Littles wanted so badly to win the fight – and he was so frustrated by Liles' clinching – that he temporarily suspended his knowledge of the rules. Littles was dancing on the edge of disqualification, and that possibility became even more real when he blasted a right below the belt. As Halpern issued yet another warning, Littles angrily gestured with both gloves that Liles was pushing him down while he punched, causing otherwise legal punches to stray low.

Littles bullied Liles to the ropes and connected with a right to the ribs and a hook to the jaw that forced Liles to hold and push Littles across the ring. As the round passed the midway point, Littles was in command as he rocked Liles into the corner post with an overhand right. When Liles clinched again, Littles pushed Liles off and the champion voluntarily took a time-out knee. A looping right sent Liles to the other corner post and Liles again held.

Liles' tactics were obvious: By repeatedly clinching he was not only buying time to clear his own head, but he also was breaking up Littles' attack into bite-sized pieces as opposed to a long string of hurting punches. Like a cold capsule that releases medicine a little bit at a time, Liles was making sure Littles could only dish out small doses of punishment. The ploy worked as Liles eventually found his way out of imminent danger. The action eventually settled into a more sedate pattern as Liles backed away at long range while Littles bobbed and weaved after him.

With 30 seconds remaining in a tumultuous third, Liles hit Littles with a left cross-right hook, after which Littles slammed home a short right cross that moved Liles to clamp down yet again.

Following the break, Littles advanced, ducked under a left cross and prepared to throw a right. Unfortunately for Littles, he bobbed up right into the path of a crushing right hook to the jaw. It was a punch Littles never saw coming, and he fell forward on his face. Somehow Littles managed to rise at Halpern's count of seven, but because he stumbled forward toward the corner pad the referee had no choice but to wave off the fight. Just two seconds remained on the clock, but it was unquestionably the correct move.

When Showtime's Ferdie Pacheco asked about Littles' fouling tactics, he replied that he knew they were coming.

"I anticipated it because he fought me that way," Liles said. "He always fought determined against me. I anticipated a tough battle and that's why I said it wasn't going to go six rounds."

As for the knockout punch, Liles said he was playing to his strength all along.

"I basically really wasn't throwing a jab, but that's how I set everybody up with my hook," he said. "My hook is my biggest shot. He walked right into it and it was a brick. Anytime I hit anybody like that I just step over them."

In a final reference to avenging his only pro loss, Liles declared, "I owed him one…I owed him one."

Epilogue: Liles would reign for another three years, beating Segundo Mercado (KO 5), Jaffa Ballogou (W 12) and Andrej Shkalikov (W 12) before Byron Mitchell ended Liles' nearly five-year reign with a come-from-behind 11th round TKO. The 37-year-old Liles fought just once more after that, as he emerged from a nearly three-year retirement to fight Demetrius Jenkins, who stopped Liles in seven rounds on March 30, 2002 at the Sovreign Center in Reading, Pa.

Liles' final record stands at 32-3 (19 KO with one no-contest).

After losing to Liles, Littles retired from the sport and made it stick for more than six years. But Littles – one day after turning 38 – couldn't resist climbing back into the ring one more time, and his opponent was the well-regarded Derrick Harmon. On November 3, 2002 at the Table Mountain Casino in Friant, Calif., Harmon stopped Littles via the three-knockdown rule in round two. Littles' final record is 27-3 with 18 knockouts.

TALES FROM THE VAULT

Total Punches Landed/Thrown

Round	1	2	3	4	5	6	7	8	9	10	11	12	Total
Liles	12/33	7/34	4/25										23/92
	36%	21%	16%										25%
Littles	3/46	13/78	12/54										28/178
	7%	17%	22%										16%

Jabs Landed/Thrown

Round	1	2	3	4	5	6	7	8	9	10	11	12	Total
Liles	1/12	1/12	0/7										2/31
	8%	8%	0%										6%
Littles	1/31	1/41	0/22										2/94
	3%	2%	0%										2%

Power Punches Landed/Thrown

Round	1	2	3	4	5	6	7	8	9	10	11	12	Total
Liles	11/21	6/22	4/18										21/61
	52%	27%	22%										34%
Littles	2/15	12/37	12/32										26/84
	13%	32%	38%										31%

Frank Liles vs. Tim Littles II June 8, 1996, Newcastle, England

★ Chapter 9 ★
UPSETS AND UNPREDICTABILITY – A WALK ON THE WILD SIDE

TALES FROM THE VAULT

Antwun Echols vs. Charles Brewer
May 19, 2001, Uncasville, Connecticut

Self-preservation is the most powerful of human instincts. Amazing things can happen when one is forced into a situation where there is no room for compromise. In life, the actions that follow might determine whether one lives or dies. In the less serious arena of sports, the viability of an athlete's career may hang in the balance.

When "Fight Doctor" Ferdie Pacheco was NBC's boxing consultant in the 1980s, he coined a phrase that perfectly described such situations in boxing – "crossroads fights." All fighters eventually come to a point in their careers when they stand at the cliff's edge – if they win, they will take a giant step toward the promised land of championships, fame and financial security. But if they lose, they will experience a career tailspin from which escape is improbable and most likely impossible.

That was the situation on May 19, 2001 at the Mohegan Sun Casino in Uncasville, Connecticut when Antwun Echols met Charles Brewer. The fact they were fighting for the vacant NABA 168-pound title was immaterial because the real prize was their fistic survival.

Antwun Echols (24-4-1, 23 KO) had his first test of resolve following his first pro fight, which he lost by first round TKO to Anthony Ivory. Echols couldn't have asked for a worse start to a career, but the man known as "Kid Dynamite" picked himself up and dusted off his next 13 opponents, only one of which lasted more than four rounds. Echols then lost a 12-round majority decision to Chris Johnson, but rebounded nicely by going 9-0-1 in his next 10 bouts, all of the victories achieved by knockout and the draw coming against future WBC super middleweight champion Eric Lucas.

His run of success earned him a chance at IBF middleweight champion Bernard Hopkins, and though he lost by a wide unanimous decision he showed enough flashes of his potential to keep his name at the forefront of the division. After losing to "The Executioner," Echols avenged his pro debut loss by decisioning Ivory over 10 rounds and knocking out Lionel Ortiz in seven rounds to put himself in position to fight Hopkins again.

This time, it was Hopkins who had to overcome severe adversity. The Philadelphian separated his left shoulder in the sixth round after Echols body-slammed him, an act that prompted a two-point deduction and a potential disqualification. Hopkins, however, chose to fight on rather than win by DQ. The champion knocked Echols down in the seventh en route to a 10th round TKO.

With prospects of a third middleweight title opportunity a long shot at best, Echols found himself at a professional fork in the road. It had been six months since his second loss to Hopkins. His previous trainer was no longer in the corner and Dan Birmingham was brought in to add more skills to his already prodigious power. He also stepped up in weight class and he did not want to take the scenic route to a title opportunity. His first fight at the new weight would be against none other than Charles Brewer.

Unlike Echols, Brewer (36-7, 26 KO) had already stood atop boxing's summit. He won the vacant IBF 168-pound belt by knocking out Gary Ballard in five rounds June 21, 1997. He successfully defended the belt three times, outscoring Joey DeGrandis while stopping Herol Graham (KO 10) and Antoine Byrd (KO 3). The Byrd fight took place in Leipzig, Germany, which gained Brewer valuable exposure and set the table for his next defense against national favorite Sven Ottke.

The Ottke-Brewer fight took place October 24, 1998 in Dusseldorf and after 12 closely contested rounds, Ottke became the new champion by a razor-thin split decision. Many thought Brewer had done enough to win, so Brewer earned a chance to regain the belt after polishing off Carlton Holland and Reggie Strickland in two rounds each. The rematch occurred September 2, 2000 in Magdeburg, Germany and Ottke again prevailed by split decision.

Brewer decided to remain in the 168-pound class since he was so well established. Three months after the second Ottke loss, Brewer iced Esteban Cervantes in one round to set the stage for the fight with Echols. A victory would provide powerful ammunition for another chance at a belt, perhaps not against Ottke, but against WBO champion Joe Calzaghe, WBC king Eric Lucas or WBA titlist Byron Mitchell. A defeat would force Brewer to take a long and winding road back to contention and at age 31, Brewer didn't have time to waste.

Several questions surrounded Echols-Brewer: How would Echols handle someone with Brewer's considerable strength? Did he have the chin to absorb a strong super middleweight's punch? Would Brewer, who suffered knockdowns early in fights, be able to stand up to Echols' power? Was Brewer past his prime or did he possess enough in the tank to make another title run?

When two punchers collide, one of two things happen – a dull fight because both men are too respectful of the other's power, or a memorable fireworks display that boxing fans dream about but seldom see.

At first, it looked like it was going to be Option 1 as both fighters tossed sharp jabs while moving around each other in tight circles at ring center. But the niceties didn't last long. Just 66 seconds into the fight, Echols maneuvered Brewer into the ropes with a blocked one-two but Brewer countered with a strong hook to the jaw that Echols took well.

Back at ring center, Echols threw another flurry that backed Brewer to the ropes but this time he followed up with a sharp left uppercut and a right cross that snapped Brewer's head. Brewer smartly spun away from the strands, but Echols made sure he took a flush jab to the face as payment for the privilege.

In the final minute, Brewer assumed the aggressor's role, landing a one-two and catching Echols with a long right. Two more one-twos connected, and the second pair buckled Echols' legs. Echols complained to referee Michael Ortega that the second right landed on the back of the head but after Ortega opted not to issue a warning, an angered Echols went on the attack. Two blocked jabs set up a right to the body, a hook to the jaw line and a grazing right, but Brewer countered with a pushed right hand that knocked Echols off balance. After the bell sounded, Echols stuck out his tongue at Brewer, who responded to the insolent gesture with indifference.

Brewer snapped the jab as the second round opened, keeping the shorter Echols at bay, but Echols leaped in with a blocked one-two and a snappy hook to the chin that forced Brewer to the ropes. At close quarters in ring center, Brewer landed two hooks to the ribs and a third hook caught Echols coming out. Echols mugged at Brewer and shook his right arm awkwardly at his side to show him the punch didn't bother him.

Brewer knew better, and he showed him in the best possible way that he wasn't fooled. A classic one-two rocketed off Echols' face and floored him heavily. As he arose at six, he complained to Ortega, perhaps thinking he had been hit on the break but everyone else knew the blows were legal – and devastating.

"The Hatchet" raced after Echols, eager to chop his man down. He connected with a solid right to the jaw and his left hook landed on the armpit. A left hook drove Echols to the ropes, where he awkwardly forced a clinch. After Ortega broke them, Brewer exploded with two 45-degree hooks to the jaw that decked Echols in his own corner. Left on all fours, Echols scrambled to his feet at the count of six. This time, his eyes were glassier, and with 1:13 left in the round he had a lot of work left to do if he wanted to make it back to his corner.

Brewer swung indiscriminately in his haste to polish off Echols yet many of the blows that landed did so with breathtaking force. Brewer connected with a long right to the ear and dug hard to the body with both hands as Echols forced another clinch. As wildly as Brewer pursued, Echols was equally wild going backward, tossing out jabs to keep Brewer at a safer distance. Echols fought through the haze surprisingly well as he slipped more blows than anyone had a right to expect. But he didn't evade all of them, as Brewer snapped two searing rights to the face that prompted Ortega to take a long look and consider stopping the fight.

Though it appeared Echols would last out the round, Brewer unloaded two long left uppercuts to the jaw that sent Echols to the deck for a third time in the round. Only three seconds remained on the clock and because the three-knockdown rule wasn't in effect, Ortega continued the count after the bell. Somehow, Echols composed himself quickly enough to convince Ortega he could fight on.

Echols let out a deep breath as he made his way back to the corner on slightly buzzed legs and plopped on the stool. As the doctor looked into his eyes, Echols told him "I'm all right."

"Listen, you gotta punch," Birmingham told Echols. "This guy is on a roll now, so we're going to have to punch to keep him off of you. Stiff jabs…stab him with the jab. Then you gotta come back with the right hand and a hook. Don't just jab and stick and move. You're gonna have to hold your own and punch with this guy. It's OK, you've weathered the storm."

But Brewer had plenty more storm for Echols when the bell rang for round three. Winging punches with no regard for defense, Brewer was in pure search-and-destroy mode to see how well Echols had recovered from his second-round beating. Echols passed the test, moving well from side to side and slipping punches better so Brewer retreated from hyperactive mode to slower, but steady, pressure.

As Brewer set himself to throw a wide hook, Echols showed the world why his nickname was "Kid Dynamite." Echols beat him to the punch with a short, explosive right to the head that couldn't have landed more flush. A badly stricken Brewer wobbled to the ropes, and in a flash Echols was on him, connecting with a right to the temple. A third right snapped Brewer's head violently, his mouthpiece hanging precariously on his lips.

Then things got weird.

As Echols began to throw a wide left hook, Ortega stepped between the boxers to render an eight-count because he determined Brewer would have gone down had it not been for the ropes. Because the action was so violent, Ortega had to move in forcefully and his arm accidentally pushed Echols to the canvas – face down. Ortega called time to allow Echols to regain his feet. Once Echols was safely in the neutral corner, Ortega completed his eight-count against Brewer. The unexpected break allowed Brewer 18 seconds to regain his senses.

The two threw simultaneous hooks, with Brewer's landing on the button, but the adrenaline-fueled Echols fired back with a right to the temple and a hook to the jaw that forced Brewer a half-step back.

With 1:58 left, Echols slipped underneath a Brewer jab and unleashed a ferocious roundhouse right to the jaw that landed with mammoth force. Brewer stumbled around in a semi-conscious haze, yet he somehow forced a clinch. Off the break, Echols snapped off four powerful blows that connected with sickening impact – a long left uppercut, a longer right to the jaw, a hook to the chin and a right to the forehead. Ortega had seen enough and stopped the fight at the 1:21 mark of round three.

The crowd was stunned, then angered by what they saw as a premature stoppage. The question that weighed heavily on their minds was this: Why would Ortega stop the fight so quickly after Brewer was hurt when he let the fight go on much longer when Brewer had Echols in deep trouble?

"When Echols was in trouble, he got up all three times," Ortega told Showtime's Tim Smith. "I checked his eyes, he looked very good and I thought he was still in the fight. When Brewer went into the corner here, he looked to me like he was hurt. He almost lost his mouthpiece and he was basically saved by the ropes so I called that as a knockdown. He got hit three or four times in a row and he was still wobbly. There is no (standing) eight count in the ABC rules. Basically he knew where the ropes were behind him; he took several shots right to the head and it looked to me that he wasn't protecting himself. Even when I jumped in to stop the fight, he was still wobbly and off-balance. Putting up your hands is one thing but defending yourself is another."

Brewer, aghast and angry at the stoppage, had a vastly different view.

"My head is very clear," he told Smith with a fury that made his voice rise an octave above normal at times. "All of a sudden, he doesn't want to give me a count and then he calls the fight off. What the hell is that? I wasn't in a whole lot of trouble; I was in the process of clearing my head and getting back into the fight. I was nowhere near out of it. To have this happen on my home turf is a disgrace to boxing."

Asked about the possibility of a rematch, a bitter Brewer said "I don't think he wants to do it again to tell you the truth, because I will tear his a** up."

"I got on my feet (in the second round) so that proves the point that I was all right," a considerably calmer Echols said to Smith. "I came back to knock him out, which is what a true champion does. If you don't respond, you're hurt. I had him hurt out there and I thought the referee was going to stop it, so I continued to hit him with hooks and overhand rights. I thought it was (stopped correctly) because I am too strong for Charles right now."

On the subject of a second fight with Brewer, he declared "there will be no rematch because I have nothing to prove. We had our fight and I knocked him out. We want Calzaghe because I feel I deserve it."

Epilogue: Ironically, it would be Brewer, not Echols, that got a shot at Calzaghe, losing a wide decision six months after Brewer won the vacant NABF belt by beating Fernando Zuniga. Following the loss to the Welshman, Brewer posted three solid wins over Scott Pemberton (KO 6), Etienne Whitaker (W 10) and Freeman Barr (KO 5) before being knocked out in nine rounds by Mario Veit for the interim WBO title. Brewer's last fight took place April 15, 2005 in Copenhagen against Lolenga Mock who knocked out the 34-year-old Brewer in 10 rounds. Brewer's final record is 40-11 (28 KO).

As of January 2010, the 38-year-old Echols remains active. Seven months after beating Brewer, Echols won by five-round disqualification over the 16-0 Lawrence

Chapman, who was chased for excessive holding. Echols then outscored the difficult Kabary Salem over 12 rounds and knocked out Oscar Bravo (KO 1) and Richard Grant (KO 3) to earn a chance at the IBF super middleweight title, which was vacated after Sven Ottke was elevated to "super champion." His third chance at a world title wasn't the charm as he dropped a 12-round decision to Anthony Mundine.

Again forced to regroup, Echols defeated Ross Thompson (W 10) and Jameel Wilson (KO 7). But the Wilson win was to be his last, for he has gone 0-7-3 in his last 10 fights. The most recent defeat was a sixth round corner retirement against Angel Hernandez in August 2009, dropping Echols' record to 31-12-4 (27 KO).

TALES FROM THE VAULT

Total Punches Landed/Thrown

Round	1	2	3	4	5	6	7	8	9	10	11	12	Total
Echols	10/76	5/36	16/33										31/145
	13%	14%	48%										21%
Brewer	15/61	34/80	2/10										51/151
	25%	42%	20%										34%

Jabs Landed/Thrown

Round	1	2	3	4	5	6	7	8	9	10	11	12	Total
Echols	5/53	3/26	1/9										9/88
	9%	12%	11%										10%
Brewer	6/39	2/12	0/1										8/52
	15%	17%	0%										15%

Power Punches Landed/Thrown

Round	1	2	3	4	5	6	7	8	9	10	11	12	Total
Echols	5/23	2/10	15/24										22/57
	22%	20%	62%										39%
Brewer	9/22	32/68	2/9										43/99
	41%	47%	22%										43%

Antwun Echols vs. Charles Brewer May 19, 2001, Uncasville, Connecticut

Merqui Sosa vs. Prince Charles Williams I
January 13, 1995, Atlantic City, New Jersey

Boxing's appeal has many layers. Those with a seasoned eye can spot the nuances that allowed Pernell Whitaker to slip his opponent's punch while positioning his body to launch a well-timed counter. Others can appreciate how Buddy McGirt used his educated feet and sharp blows to systematically break down opponents or marvel at Julio Cesar Chavez's ability to the southpaw riddle that was Hector Camacho.

But make no mistake, boxing's popularity lies in its brutality. Fighters blessed with punching power can seize the public's imagination like no other group of athletes. If they also have charisma, the potential flow of cash could become a tidal wave. If anyone doubts, just ask Manny Pacquiao and Floyd Mayweather Jr.

Sometimes, however, a boxing match can become too brutal even for those who are hardened to the game's violence. Such was the case on January 13, 1995 at Bally's Park Place in Atlantic City when Merqui Sosa met Prince Charles Williams for the vacant NABF light heavyweight belt. Over the course of seven rounds, Sosa and Williams inflicted such tremendous damage that the fight was stopped to ensure their future well being.

Entering the fight, both men's boxing futures hung in the balance. Sosa (24-4-1, 20 KO) began his career as a middleweight and made significant noise on the New York circuit with his heavy-handed knockouts. Sosa won his first 18 fights, 14 by knockout, to earn a crack at fellow unbeaten James Toney. Despite being dropped in the third round, Sosa fought Toney well enough to lose a 12-round split decision. Following the loss to Toney, Sosa rose to super middleweight and found success over Tyrone Frazier (KO 10). His next two outings against Tony Thornton and Steve Little were less so as he lost a split decision to the "Punching Postman" and drew over eight rounds to the future WBA super middleweight champion.

From that point forward, Sosa's career was up-and-down as he beat lower-level opposition but failed against top-tier opponents. He beat Willie Kemp and Lenzie Morgan but lost to Frank Liles and WBA super middleweight titlist Michael Nunn. Sosa fought only twice in 1994, beating Philip Morefield (KO 3) and Robert Curry (KO 4) to set up the crossroads fight with Williams. At 29, Sosa was at the tail end of what would probably be his prime years and time was running out on his championship dreams.

The 32-year-old Williams (36-6-2, 27 KO) had been a pro for 17 years and was a fixture on the light heavyweight scene for more than a decade. Unlike many fighters who eventually captured a championship, Williams not only lost his pro debut to Henry Bunch Bey (L 4) but also drew in his second outing to Michael Hardin (D 4). At 15, Williams was a boy fighting men and as he matured the results followed suit.

In his next 15 fights, Williams continued to learn on the job, winning most but losing some as well to Jeff Lampkin (KO by 6) and Reggie Gross (KO by 1). Another draw to Hardin (D 6) also marred his record and when he entered the ring against former two-time light heavyweight champion Marvin Johnson November 8, 1984, Williams was seen as a stepping stone. Though he lost a 10-round decision to "Pops," the fight proved to be a valuable learning experience. It would be nine years before he lost another fight and in that time he won the IBF title from Bobby Czyz and racked up eight defenses in a five-year reign before being dethroned by Henry Maske.

Williams was on the comeback trail but the road he took leading up to the Sosa fight was rocky. Following the Maske defeat, Williams won three fights to set up a match with IBF super middleweight champion Toney. Hoping to wear down the naturally smaller man, Williams chose to engage Toney on the inside. For a while, it worked. But in the 12th a sizzling overhand right put Williams down and out. The image of Williams' body splayed on the canvas was the last memory boxing fans had before the fight with Sosa and many observers wondered whether "Prince Charles" still had the tools to become a king again.

Sosa also wanted to know the answer and he sought it quickly by charging out of the corner behind two overhand rights and a clanging right to the ribs. Williams latched on and drove in body shots as the two men pushed against each other in ring center. Forty seconds into the fight, Williams suffered the fight's first injury, a cut over the left eye that referee Ron Lipton ruled as coming from a punch.

Neither fighter believed a feeling-out period was necessary and the pace was red hot. Williams said before the fight that he wanted to engage Sosa at long range but the Dominican's fast start put a stop to that. Sosa and Williams often fought along the ropes and they took turns spinning one another onto the strands and whaling away with multitudes of hooks and uppercuts. In one sequence, Williams turned Sosa into the ropes to land an overhand right, a hook to the body and a fierce right uppercut to the jaw. After Williams hammered two more hooks to the body, Sosa took one step to his right and forced Williams onto the ropes. But Sosa added a wrinkle as he moved laterally to keep Williams' body directly in front of him, all the while bombing away at all parts of "Prince Charles'" anatomy.

It was a give-and-take war at close quarters, and neither was particularly concerned about saving his strength for the later rounds. All that was on their minds was surviving until the next moment while letting the future take care of itself. By the third minute of round one, it was clear that this fight had the makings of a classic – for as long as it lasted.

Though Williams spent most of his time with his back on the ropes, he was doing plenty of good work with his right uppercut, the primary weapon in his title-winning victory over Czyz seven years earlier. Sosa worked hard throughout and his full-frontal assault projected an image of dominance.

As round two began, Sosa again rocketed from the corner to land an overhand right, and again Williams bulled Sosa to the ropes with hooks to the body and a sharp hook to the jaw. A scintillating right uppercut banged against Sosa's face, and "Prince Charles" was digging into Sosa like a starving lion tears into a T-bone. A big right by Sosa worsened Williams' cut and he was finding the range with his hook, which broke through three times despite Williams' high guard.

Referee Lipton, meanwhile, allowed the fighters to work on the inside as he stayed close enough to the action to step in whenever necessary. But because Sosa and Williams were fighting at such a high level, Lipton's intervention was deemed unnecessary and the veteran referee was seasoned enough to let well enough alone. As the round closed, an off-balance Williams fell to the canvas when his overhand right whizzed over Sosa's head. The break was one of the few incurred during another torrid round.

Sosa winged a hook as round three began, but by this time Williams was wise to the ploy as he ducked underneath it and slammed three hooks to the body. Williams mauled Sosa to the ropes behind a right uppercut, but Sosa answered with several nice right-lefts to the head. With 1:58 left, Williams' right uppercut made Sosa's knocked-knees dip slightly but Sosa quickly recovered with two left uppercuts to the jaw and a right-left to the body. Williams ripped the ribs and a right uppercut-left uppercut combo swiveled Sosa's head and backed him to the ropes. After another warning for butts against both men, Williams surged, whaling away with powerful blows with both hands and imposing his natural light heavyweight strength. A left uppercut-overhand right combination connected flush, but Sosa tagged Williams between punches with a sharp hook to the jaw. Williams answered with an even better right to the chin.

Despite the punishment already absorbed, the fight maintained its rock-em, sock-em persona. With every blow, Sosa-Williams was working its way up the mythical pyramid of great fights. The pinnacle was still in the distance, but by the end of round three it had already ascended farther than most.

Round three was another scintillating statistical frame as Sosa landed 41 of 80 punches (51 percent) and Williams connected on 25 of 60 attempts for 42 percent. With men these big and powerful, the high connect rates inflicted visible physical damage. The blood from Williams' cut smeared his face and splotched Sosa's trunks. Swelling erupted underneath both of Sosa's eyes, yet he was the one who continued to push a hard pace. Perhaps his fuel was personal – a couple of days before the fight his wife bore Sosa's first child, a daughter named Scandinavia. As has been proven many times before, there's nothing like family responsibility to drive a man toward greatness and the financial security that comes with it.

Sosa fired a right to the body to start round four, but Williams picked up the beat as he pumped both hands to Sosa's head and body. The two men continued to push and pull on one another while exchanging volleys of strong, sharp punches. Two snappy hooks peppered Williams and while Sosa was doing a better job of keeping his opponent's back on the ropes, Sosa successfully drove in uppercut after uppercut. Williams countered a wild Sosa hook with a short right to the ear that sent Sosa off balance.

The fight's momentum began to shift in the final minute of round four when two hooks and a torrid right uppercut slammed home for Sosa. Williams, who had been enjoying a good round, started to show signs of weakness as he chose to rest more while close range and no longer tried to match Sosa punch for punch. The fight's tremendous pace – and Sosa's precise power punching – eroded Williams' ability to fight at long range. Sosa ended the round by bouncing uppercuts off Williams' chin, and, almost unbelievably given the torrid pace thus far, Sosa stepped on the gas and surged ahead.

Williams was not yet ready to concede as two right uppercuts sliced through Sosa's guard as round five began. Those uppercuts gave Williams the room to spin off the ropes and a third uppercut clearly hurt Sosa as his knees dipped toward the canvas. His iron will, however, kept Sosa upright. The swelling underneath Sosa's eyes worsened, but there was nothing wrong with his arms as he regained the momentum with two strong hooks to the jaw. Williams' punching form appeared more ragged but he, too, fought through his fatigue. Only a loose piece of tape on Williams' left glove interrupted the action, and referee Lipton called for one of his seconds to cut it away.

Sosa seemed to benefit from the brief rest as he cracked Williams with a right and drove him to the ropes with a volley of body shots. A huge hook caromed off Williams' jaw with 17 seconds remaining in the round, but Williams, though clearly tired, summoned an excellent hook and right uppercut at the bell.

As the sixth commenced, Sosa threw Williams a curve by dancing out of his corner behind long, quick jabs. The move was intended to further erode Williams' confidence, for Sosa wanted to prove that the fierce chest-to-chest combat had no effect on his stamina. But the ploy only lasted for a minute, after which the two resumed their infighting clinic for the rest of the round. Sosa kept Williams pinned to the ropes, but "Prince Charles" proved that one could score effectively while in a seemingly disadvantageous position.

Between the sixth and seventh rounds, ringside physician Dr. Frank B. Doggett visited Sosa's corner to check on his facial swelling, but after a brief examination he deemed Sosa fit to continue.

Sosa started the seventh at long range as Williams bobbed and weaved with hands high. Williams cracked a hook at short range that twisted Sosa's head, but Sosa absorbed the blow well, proving beyond doubt that he could absorb a legitimate light heavyweight's best punch. Second by second, Williams' fatigue mounted as he hung on to Sosa for longer stretches in their rare clinches. Sosa, meanwhile, kept blasting away at Williams, and he found it easier to maneuver him around the ring. It was obvious that Williams had hit a wall and he was fighting two formidable opponents – Sosa and his own exhaustion.

In the final minute, Sosa returned to long range, convinced he could do whatever he wanted. He invested even more energy into every punch and exerted relentless pressure in the hope that Williams' resolve would finally crumble.

After the round-ending bell, Lipton asked Dr. Doggett to examine Sosa, whose eyes were nearly swollen shut. As famed cut man Ralph Citro tended to Sosa, Dr. Doggett tapped Sosa's right cheek to point out his area of concern. Then he walked to Williams' corner to assess the condition of his cut.

Just before the beginning of round eight, the fight was stopped. Sosa, convinced he had outlasted Williams, bounded to the ropes and raised his arms in celebration. After all, he had just enjoyed his most dominant round and he appeared to have far more energy in the tank. But Dr. Doggett ruled that *both* men were too damaged to continue and though Sosa held a 69-63, 69-64 and 69-64 lead on the scorecards, the fight was ruled a technical draw.

Williams, though clearly fatigued in the seventh, felt he still had more to give.

"I'm very disappointed the fight was stopped because I feel I was coming on and that I would stop him in another round or two," Williams said. "(Sosa's) eye was almost closed and I was beginning to have my way."

Despite the fact that he would have won under most other circumstances, Sosa was extraordinarily sportsmanlike.

"I give a lot of credit to Charles because I was in great, great shape," he said. "I think in the next round I would have stopped the guy because I feel strong. But he is a great champion. No matter if they say it was a draw, I feel that I won."

"It was a grueling fight, a battle of attrition and to be eminently fair so that neither fighter would have an unfair advantage, I had the doctor periodically check them when I deemed it necessary," Lipton told ESPN's Dave Bontempo when asked to explain the ruling. "I also felt that, along with the three judges, that the initial cut early in the bout was from a clean punch. Both fighters had eye injuries – we periodically checked it – and as the bout regressed to the point where the injury was severe the doctor ruled that both fighters were unable to continue because of the severity of the eye cuts. The way the supervisor had explained the rules of the NABF title beforehand, the proper decision was that it was a draw. It's a rarity in boxing when both fighters are unable to continue, but you never know what is going to happen in boxing."

True, but one aspect of Sosa-Williams I had become a virtual lock: Sosa-Williams II.

Epilogue: The rematch was indeed made, five months after the original. Their second fight lived up to the first as they again traded brutal inside punches, and unlike the

TALES FROM THE VAULT

first match it went on to a definitive – and scary – conclusion. Williams was declared a TKO loser in round 10, after which he was carried off on a stretcher. Sosa, overcome with emotion, was in tears during the post-fight interview as his concern for Williams overrode any elation over his victory.

Williams recovered and was able to fight one more time. On March 24, 1996, Williams scored a two-round knockout over Chris Vernon in Nice, France, raising his final record to 37-7-3 (28 KO).

Sosa fought 14 more times, going 9-5 (6 KO) over the next five years. The second win over Williams vaulted Sosa into championship contention and after polishing off Benito Fernandez in three rounds, Sosa earned a fight with IBF super middleweight champion Roy Jones Jr., who did not put the title on the line. Jones was simply too fast and too talented for Sosa as the fight was stopped in the second round.

Sosa won his next six fights, the biggest of which was a 10-round decision over future IBF light heavyweight champion Glen Johnson. After beating Johnson, Sosa lost back-to-back fights to Kenny Bowman (L 12) and Ray Berry before beating Eric Holland over 10 rounds. Sosa lost an NABF title bout to Thomas Tate and was stopped in two rounds by James "The Harlem Hammer" Butler, but, like Williams, Sosa ended his career as a winner. On June 16, 2000 in Reno, the 34-year-old Sosa stopped former title challenger Segundo Mercado in six rounds. The victory raised his record to 34-9-2 (27 KO).

UPSETS AND UNPREDICTABILITY – A WALK ON THE WILD SIDE

Total Punches Landed/Thrown

Round	1	2	3	4	5	6	7	8	9	10	11	12	Total
Sosa	33/91	28/76	41/80	40/77	55/93	42/84	36/69						275/570
	36%	37%	51%	52%	59%	50%	52%						48%
Williams	31/63	31/70	25/60	25/55	26/71	18/41	16/38						172/398
	49%	44%	42%	45%	37%	44%	42%						43%

Jabs Landed/Thrown

Round	1	2	3	4	5	6	7	8	9	10	11	12	Total
Sosa	0/4	0/1	1/6	0/0	2/3	7/16	4/11						14/41
	0%	0%	17%	0%	67%	44%	36%						34%
Williams	4/7	5/13	1/10	2/8	2/15	3/11	2/11						19/75
	57%	38%	10%	25%	13%	27%	18%						25%

Power Punches Landed/Thrown

Round	1	2	3	4	5	6	7	8	9	10	11	12	Total
Sosa	33/87	28/75	40/74	40/77	53/90	35/68	32/58						261/529
	38%	37%	54%	52%	59%	51%	55%						49%
Williams	27/56	26/57	24/50	23/47	24/56	15/30	14/27						153/323
	48%	46%	48%	49%	43%	50%	52%						47%

* Fight originally done by CompuBox, but the original HTML files with complete round-by-round statistics no longer exist. With no final totals shown after the fight, and with the files lost, the author performed his own count to compile these statistics.

Merqui Sosa vs. Prince Charles Williams I January 13, 1995, Atlantic City, New Jersey

TALES FROM THE VAULT

Joel Casamayor vs Diego Corrales I
October 4, 2003, Las Vegas, Nevada

EDITOR'S NOTE: *This piece was originally written in October 2006, just a few days before Casamayor and Corrales met in their rubber match in Las Vegas. At the time I thought it would be interesting to break from the usual format and tie in a fight from the past to an upcoming event so for this book I chose to preserve my perspectives of the time.*

* * *

On Saturday, Joel Casamayor and Diego Corrales will resolve their competitive dispute once and for all when they meet for the third time at the Mandalay Bay Events Center in Las Vegas. The fight may be for Corrales' WBC lightweight title but for them this fight is for an even bigger prize – the right to proclaim himself the superior fighter. The contrast between the skillful Casamayor and the explosive Corrales is obvious, and the history between them in and out of the ring adds even more drama to an already exciting story line.

This rubber match wouldn't be the attraction that it is had it not been for their tremendous first encounter, which took place October 4, 2003 at the very same Mandalay Bay, only this time it served as the main supporting bout on the James Toney-Evander Holyfield pay-per-view. Both men had reached a critical point in their respective comebacks where they had to prove that they were worthy of a fight with Acelino Freitas, considered by many the best 130-pounder in the world.

Freitas earned that distinction by defeating Casamayor by a split decision marred by foul-induced point deductions against the Cuban. Casamayor (29-1, 18 KO) had won three fights since then, and his most recent outing was a razor-thin 10-round decision over the intriguing up-and-comer Nate Campbell eight months previously. Because he struggled mightily at times against the Floridian, there were whispers that the 32-year-old Casamayor was on the decline but his camp countered by saying Casamayor took the Campbell fight on just two-and-a-half weeks notice and consequently wasn't totally primed for the challenge Campbell presented.

There would be no such excuses for the Corrales fight. The bout was billed as an IBF junior lightweight title eliminator, meaning the winner would likely get the next title shot. He also received excellent sparring from top lightweight Juan Lazcano, who was preparing for a fight with former lightweight champion Stevie Johnston. Finally, his turbulent personal life had reached a more serene point as he had recently converted to Christianity and was baptized before 2,000 onlookers three weeks before the Corrales fight.

For Corrales (37-1, 31 KO), this was the first big step in his comeback following a 14-month prison stint for domestic abuse, which transpired following a 10th round TKO loss to Floyd Mayweather Jr. in 2001. After his release he engaged in four bouts, the most recent of which was a third round KO over Damien Fuller 13 weeks before. Based on his name recognition and superior performance during his comeback, Corrales had risen to the number-four spot in the IBF, earning him a crack at the number-three rated Casamayor. Like Casamayor, Corrales received excellent sparring from world-class slickster Cory Spinks.

Corrales and Casamayor couldn't have been more different physically and stylistically. At 5-10 ½, Corrales was extremely tall for a 130-pounder and against Casamayor he would enjoy a 3 ½-inch height advantage. But Casamayor's 69-inch reach was just one inch shorter than Corrales' and his multi-layered ring craft stood in stark contrast to Corrales' uncompromising, take-no-prisoners aggression. To win, Casamayor had to use his superior mobility to stay away from the ropes and set up his pinpoint counters while Corrales needed to cut off the ring and whack away at the body to drain the strength from Casamayor's springy legs. His warrior mentality was obvious to everyone as he wore camouflage trunks and an intense, stone-faced expression while Casamayor's visage transmitted serenity and composure.

As expected, Casamayor began the fight moving swiftly in both directions before smoothly flowing inside with a left to the belly. Corrales concentrated on trapping Casamayor along the ropes, and when he successfully maneuvered him there he landed a solid hook that prompted an immediate clinch. Corrales applied steady pressure to Casamayor, but the Cuban's defense was more than equal to the task as he slipped underneath a left-left-right and capitalized with a right-left to the body and a harder left to the ribs.

Casamayor focused his offense on Corrales' long, lean torso but was more than willing to shift his attack to the head when the opportunity presented itself. He pelted Corrales with a counter left to the jaw, but Corrales answered a few moments later with a hook to the face that appeared to startle – but not hurt – the Cuban. For the most part, however, Casamayor controlled the round with his thoughtful movement and his crisp, precise counters.

Casamayor's trainer Joe Goossen was more than pleased with his charge following the first round.

"Very good, verrrrry good," he said. "You're seeing everything and that's what I love. You're using your feints; you're using your smarts."

He was also using his head – and not only for thinking. A butt late in the round opened a cut over Corrales' left eye, and since it was located directly over the orbit the blood could have affected Corrales' vision enough to justify a stoppage. But cut man

Ruben Gomez was able to keep the blood flow under control. What he couldn't control was Casamayor's fouling.

Casamayor began the second quickly as he landed a solid left cross to the jaw but he also attempted to sneak in an uppercut while holding the back of Corrales' head, an infraction that drew a caution from referee Tony Weeks. The 1992 Olympic gold medalist was a master of boxing's darker arts and his vast experience in the amateur and pro ranks have taught him just how far he could go before drawing warnings. He didn't always get away with it as point deductions cost him a victory over Freitas and as a result his reputation preceded him. In the clinches against Corrales, Casamayor subtly rubbed his head against the cut in an effort to open it up further and kept a close eye on where Weeks was at all times. Most of the time, however, "El Cepillo" operated at long range, moving skillfully side to side and making himself a difficult target for Corrales to line up. Corrales briefly trapped Casamayor on the ropes and ripped a left to the body, but Casamayor spun out of danger.

Casamayor caught Corrales with a solid lead cross to the face while Corrales whiffed on a home run hook. The Cuban made him pay for that miss by smacking home another left cross. As the round proceeded, Corrales had some success with jabs and singular hooks but wasn't unable to land anything with significant power. A final right-left near the bell enabled Casamayor to put another round in the bank.

Casamayor's movement served two specific purposes. First, Casamayor knew that Mayweather benefited greatly from lateral movement to set up the punches that floored Corrales five times – and the power of those punches were magnified because "Pretty Boy" caught Corrales coming in. Second, it forced "Chico" to constantly reset his feet and prevented him from generating his fight-ending power.

Corrales' trainer Kenny Adams knew this and tried his best to turn the tide between rounds.

"You're not letting your hands go," Adams said. "You're looking for one little shot for him. You've got to use that stick, OK? Utilize the jab, then turn the hook off the jab and drop the right hand. The right hand is right there but you're waiting too long to get there. Quit resetting! Don't reset!"

Corrales did his best to follow instructions in the third as he continued to pursue behind more jabs, but those jabs failed to reach the elusive Casamayor.

His troubles worsened 25 seconds into the round.

Casamayor ducked underneath a hook and weaved his way inside Corrales' reach. With a subtle movement of the head, he created just enough space to nail Corrales with a tremendous left cross to the button. Corrales fell to the canvas on his rump and he wore a chagrined expression as he arose at two. He walked to the farthest neutral corner and smiled ruefully as he took the remainder of Weeks' mandatory eight-count.

No longer the cautious boxer, Casamayor reached in with a left cross but was met with a sharp Corrales hook. The Cuban walked through the blow and buckled Corrales' knees with another huge cross to the jaw. In his haste to finish off Corrales, Casamayor again reached behind the neck and drove two left uppercuts into Corrales' immobilized head. The uncharacteristically blatant foul prompted Weeks to deduct a point from Casamayor, neutralizing the mathematical advantage the earlier knockdown produced. Angered – and still convinced that Corrales was still buzzed – Casamayor got off his bicycle and looked to exchange with "Chico." But at 128 ½ pounds Corrales was in superb physical condition and that enabled him to regain himself quickly, so Casamayor wisely returned to his stick-and-move tactics.

Corrales still had problems reaching Casamayor, especially with the left, while Casamayor repeatedly connected to the head and body with his powerful left. Corrales remained steadfast and patient, believing his constant pressure would eventually pay dividends. To get what he wanted, however, he had to march through plenty of enemy fire, much like the soldier image he portrayed with his camouflage trunks. That payoff would have to wait as Casamayor polished off another round by rattling off a right-left-left combo and a snappy left cross to the neck.

Corrales seemed frustrated as he shook his head and smiled wanly as he approached his stool. He still believed in his chances of victory, but he also believed it wasn't going to be easy. Adams also had faith in his man as he told Corrales "you're finding yourself," as he sat on the stool. Along with the encouragement, he had a change in tactics.

"Don't try to play games with him," Adams said. "Now, we're going to move the opposite way – move away from the left hand. In other words, I want you to move back to the left. But at the same time you're going to try and turn the hook and right hand out. Bring the right hand back up; you're dropping the right hand, you hear?"

Corrales knew he was keeping his left too low but old habits are tough to shake off, especially in the heat of battle. And "Chico" would pay an immediate price.

Casamayor was back on the move in the fourth, but this time the motion was used to set a trap. Casamayor took a short step to his left and used a foot feint to establish position. Then he planted his feet and drove a huge, crackling left to the jaw that stiffened Corrales' legs and sent him reeling to the canvas near Casamayor's corner. Corrales was caught with his left hand at chest level, enabling Casamayor to step in and take advantage.

The bewildered Corrales was up at four, but he received a few extra seconds of rest because the overanxious Casamayor had strayed from the neutral corner before Weeks completed his eight-count. Casamayor was convinced Corrales was seriously hurt this time, so he barreled inside and let his hands go. Two left crosses nailed Corrales, who did his best to hold on. A looping left to the jaw and a longer left a few moments later added to Corrales' woes. He was sure that victory was just a few punches away, so he tossed aside his previous caution and went for the kill.

But no matter how troubled Corrales was, his ever-present punching power served as the ultimate wild card that could deliver him from danger at any point of a fight. With 1:58 remaining in the round – and less than 45 seconds after he was on the floor – Corrales pulled out that wild card.

As Casamayor charged in behind another long left, Corrales stepped in and cracked him with a gorgeous short hook to the jaw that dropped Casamayor like a shot. With a shocked look on his face, "El Cepillo" fell backward and hit the canvas hard. Thankfully for Casamayor, it was a flash knockdown and he wore a composed look as he arose at four. The sudden knockdown served as a fresh reminder of why he adopted such a cautious approach at the beginning, and he intelligently returned to those tactics when the action resumed.

Hungry for the knockout, Corrales chased after Casamayor, but the Cuban deftly ducked under the blows and motored side to side before initiating a clinch. Corrales tagged Casamayor with two more inside lefts before Casamayor clinched and rubbed his head underneath Corrales' chin. With 30 seconds remaining, a quick hook-right combo stunned Casamayor badly and "El Cepillo" limited the damage by falling into another clinch. Corrales was still whiffing on many of his hooks, but his relentless pressure was beginning to take effect as Casamayor wasn't moving as swiftly. For the rest of the round, Casamayor had the look of a man growing somewhat weaker while Corrales suddenly resembled a powerhouse. A knot erupted on the right side of Casamayor's head near the temple, and the swelling was a physical representation of the shifting tide.

But like Corrales, Casamayor was a resilient sort and the rest between the fourth and fifth rounds did him a world of good. His legs appeared stronger and his punches stiffer as a solid left and a right-left-left combo found the mark. A looping left cross forced Corrales to seek the sanctuary of a clinch and a few moments later another searing left buckled Corrales' legs. A right jab to the body and a cross to the head powered through and a right jab snapped Corrales' head. Meanwhile, Corrales had stopped trying to cut off the ring. Instead he was standing upright at ring center, in perfect range for Casamayor's blows. Though Casamayor was landing crisply, Corrales didn't seem to be in imminent danger of falling. He was just absorbing Casamayor's measured attack without much retaliation.

As the seconds passed, Casamayor became the pursuer while Corrales sought to box more. The marks of battle were evident as the knot on Casamayor's head was somewhat larger while a swelling erupted around Corrales' mouth and blood came out of "Chico's" nose.

Casamayor turned up the pressure in the sixth as he walked to Corrales behind hard, snapping jabs and a straight left to the body. Corrales answered with a quick cuffing hook but Casamayor retaliated with a left to the jaw and a straight right-left to the belly. A jolting jab rocked back Corrales' head and suddenly the swelling on the right side of Corrales' face grew noticeably larger. His face was misshapen and bloated, and his strength seemed to be waning as he chose to follow Casamayor around the ring instead of trying to cut the ring short.

With 48 seconds remaining, a jolting left smacked against Corrales' face and a follow-up right forced "Chico" to retreat. Blood was gushing out of his mouth by the time another right-left crashed home. Still, Corrales was a warrior at heart and he sensed his chance at victory was slipping away – so he made the decision to fight his way out of trouble.

Two huge hooks nailed Casamayor, who stepped away awkwardly. By this time, the crowd was cheering wildly for Corrales who had become the underdog in their eyes. Corrales turned up the heat but Casamayor danced away the rest of the round and avoided any more serious trouble.

It was a typical display of courage and resolve on Corrales' part, and that was what made what happened in the next few seconds as difficult to swallow as the blood that Corrales was surely ingesting.

Dr. Margaret Goodman, the chief ringside physician, saw the thick blood Corrales had spat out and advised Weeks to stop the fight between rounds six and seven.

"Give me one round! Give me one round!" Corrales pleaded. But Dr. Goodman was unswayed. The strong left hand Casamayor landed in the final minute produced two dangerous cuts inside the mouth, and one of the cuts went through the entire lip. The volume of blood was such that choking was a very real and dangerous possibility.

As adamant as Dr. Goodman was medically, Corrales was just as convinced he could fight on. Angry and distraught, he stalked the ring and refused initial treatment for his injuries. The crowd, seeing Corrales' brave rally in the final minute, voiced its displeasure because they thought the stoppage prevented Corrales from staging a dramatic comeback – a comeback they felt cheated out of seeing. When Casamayor approached Corrales to congratulate him, "Chico" had one thing on his mind – a rematch. Three times he asked Casamayor to commit to an immediate rematch, but Casamayor gave him no such assurances. For now, however, a rematch would have to wait until Corrales was sufficiently healed.

"He had two really bad lacerations through his mouth and he was bleeding profusely," Dr. Goodman told Showtime's Jim Gray. "That makes you in danger of swallowing blood and you could aspirate very (easily). It was very dangerous to allow that to continue. It's a tough call (to make because) he's a great fighter, a great champion; it's certainly nothing I wanted to do."

"I'm a fighter, that is what I'm here to do and this is part of the job," Corrales said of his willingness to continue. "I had him hurt and I probably would have finished him off this round. He was hurt real bad. I hurt him all through the fight and I was definitely still in the fight. A little blood, a little cut, I'm not gonna die from this."

Corrales revealed that the sharp left Casamayor landed in the final minute of the round produced the fight-stopping injury.

"As soon as he hit me, the mouthpiece went through my lip," Corrales said. "I knew it instantly, as soon as he hit me, BANG, a gob of blood just gushed out of my mouth. The mouthpiece split and I don't know if I had my lip underneath the mouthpiece or how I did it. I don't think there are many people who are as scrappy, as gutty and willing to go through the kind of stuff I'm willing to go through. Pain? I'm in the pain business…how could you stop this fight? Why not let this fight go on? If I'm gutting it out, if he's gutting it out, if we're both gutting it out, who cares?"

"Every time he was hitting him, he hurt him," said translator Luis DeCubas. "If he didn't get him now, he'd get him later on. It would be no problem."

"I was in great shape and I recuperated right away," Casamayor said through DeCubas. "I knew that if I boxed him the knockout would come. I shouldn't have traded with the guy. I knew that the game plan was to box in the first five or six rounds and then from there we'll start picking him apart."

When asked if he would give Corrales a rematch, Casamayor was less than enthusiastic.

"No," he said. "He was one of the 10 best pound-for-pound fighters in the world right now and that's the reason we took the Corrales fight. Freitas hasn't been fighting anybody and now we can give him the opportunity because the fans know who is the best 130-pounder in the world pound-for-pound."

Epilogue: Casamayor may have won this fight, but Corrales ended up getting what he wanted. Casamayor never got his rematch with Freitas but Corrales received an immediate rematch with Casamayor five months later. In an interesting twist, Goossen left Casamayor to work with Corrales and his boxing-oriented blueprint helped "Chico" earn an early points lead and survive a 10th round knockdown to earn a disputed split decision.

From there they went their separate ways. After Casamayor beat Daniel Seda over 10 rounds, he received a shot against WBC lightweight champion Jose Luis Castillo. Though he boxed smartly throughout, two of the three judges preferred Castillo's aggression, allowing the Mexican to retain his title. In June 2004, Casamayor fought a draw with Almazbek "Kid Diamond" Raiymkulov that many thought he deserved to win. The Raiymkulov fight was Casamayor's only outing of 2005, but he returned the following year with solid wins over Antonio Ramirez (KO 5) and Lamont Pearson (KO 9) to earn the rubber match with Corrales. Casamayor, now 35, sports a record of 33-3-1 (21 KO).

For Corrales, the two Casamayor fights were just the beginning of a formidable fistic gauntlet that has transformed him into one of the sport's most beloved warriors. Five months after beating Casamayor in their rematch, Corrales stepped up in weight and challenged WBO lightweight champion Acelino Freitas. Outboxed throughout most of the early rounds, Corrales scored knockdowns in the eighth and ninth rounds before a third – and final – knockdown in the 10th prompted Freitas to surrender. Nine months later, Corrales and Castillo would produce one of the most thrilling finishes in boxing history as "Chico" overcame two knockdowns in the 10th only to rally and stop Castillo at the 2:06 mark. Five months after their classic first encounter, Castillo and Corrales met again but Castillo was unable to make the 135-pound limit. Ever the warrior, Corrales put the fans and the sport ahead of his own interests and fought anyway. Corrales paid the price for his courage as a scorching left hook took him out in the fourth round. The two were scheduled to fight a third time but the fight was cancelled due to Castillo's continued inability to make 135. Thus, the rubber match with Casamayor represents Corrales' first outing since October 8, 2005. The 29-year-old Corrales' record is 40-3 with 33 knockouts.

Postscript: Casamayor wouldn't fight again for another year, winning a hotly disputed split decision over Jose Armando Santa Cruz. The Cuban expatriate redeemed himself in many eyes when he scored an off-the-floor 10th round TKO over the Gatti-esque Australian Michael Katsidis in March 2008 but six months later he lost the title of linear lightweight champion to Juan Manuel Marquez, who stopped Casamayor in the 11th.

The 38-year-old Casamayor remains active, and as of January 2010 his most recent fight was an eight-round decision victory over Jason Davis in November 2009 that raised his record to 37-4-1 with 22 knockouts.

Beset by weight issues, Corrales fought just once more – this time at welterweight against Joshua Clottey in Springfield, Mo., on April 7, 2007. Corrales looked dreadful in losing a 10-round decision to the Ghanaian, who went on to capture the vacant IBF belt from Zab Judah three fights later. Exactly one month after the Clottey fight seemingly signaled the end of his boxing career, a motorcycle accident fueled by alcohol consumption signaled the end of his time on earth. One of boxing's most dynamic warriors was dead at age 29.

TALES FROM THE VAULT

Total Punches Landed/Thrown

Round	1	2	3	4	5	6	7	8	9	10	11	12	Total
Casamayor	10/27	10/29	15/40	21/48	23/47	21/50							100/241
	37%	34%	38%	44%	49%	42%							41%
Corrales	8/46	14/50	12/43	19/46	7/30	11/49							71/264
	17%	28%	28%	41%	23%	22%							27%

Jabs Landed/Thrown

Round	1	2	3	4	5	6	7	8	9	10	11	12	Total
Casamayor	4/13	2/7	6/15	7/20	12/24	11/26							42/105
	31%	29%	40%	35%	50%	42%							40%
Corrales	4/23	3/23	2/15	0/2	3/13	3/23							15/99
	17%	13%	13%	0%	23%	13%							15%

Power Punches Landed/Thrown

Round	1	2	3	4	5	6	7	8	9	10	11	12	Total
Casamayor	6/14	8/22	9/25	14/28	11/23	10/24							58/136
	43%	36%	36%	50%	48%	42%							43%
Corrales	4/23	11/27	10/28	19/44	4/17	8/26							56/165
	17%	41%	36%	43%	24%	31%							34%

Joel Casamayor vs Diego Corrales I October 4, 2003, Las Vegas, Nevada

UPSETS AND UNPREDICTABILITY – A WALK ON THE WILD SIDE

Juan Coggi vs. Eder Gonzalez I
December 17, 1993, San Miguel, Argentina

Home field advantage. Teams in every sport spend the entire regular season fighting to secure it, and the very best of them have it throughout the entire playoffs as a reward for their success. It's a result of human nature; for some reason we are much more comfortable performing in front of people who want us to succeed and who are willing to do their part to make it happen.

The feeling of belonging and support give us the extra push we need to achieve the main objective – winning the game while pleasing the audiences both at the stadium and watching on television. The "away" team, on the other hand, must adopt an unnatural mindset; they must find pleasure in playing spoiler and draw strength from the booing that accompanies their success. When they do a good job, they must generate the immediate positive feedback among themselves and be content to wait until they return home to receive it from their fans.

Boxing may be a one-on-one sport in the ring, but the concept of home field advantage is just as strong. The size of the ring and the canvas surface is often tailored to the house fighter's strengths and the term "hometown decision" is firmly in the sport's lexicon. But even boxing has its limits and those limits were crossed in a most outrageous way when when Argentine Juan Coggi defended his WBA junior welterweight title against Colombian Eder Gonzalez at the Club Defensores de Villa Lujan in San Miguel, Tucuman, Argentina. The events that occurred were so blatantly one-sided that one in-ring participant ended up being banned for life.

But first, a bit of background: Coggi (64-2-2, 30 KO) had been a fixture on the 140-pound landscape since July 4, 1987 when he shockingly knocked out the 48-0 Patrizio Oliva in three rounds to win the WBA title. In the four defenses that followed, Coggi proved himself a quality performer as he defeated the 47-1 Sang Ho Lee (KO 2), Harold Brazier (W 12), Akinobu Hiranaka (W 12) and Jose Luis Ramirez (W 12). The first three fights took place in Italy with the fourth in France, so Coggi proved he could win away from home. But Coggi made one road trip too many as he lost a majority decision to Loreto Garza on neutral ground in Nice, France, August 17, 1990.

Coggi won his next 13 fights to earn a shot at his old belt against Morris East January 12, 1993 – this time in Buenos Aires. "Latigo" was dominant in scoring an eight-round stoppage over the inexperienced East, winning virtually every round on all scorecards. In his second reign, Coggi proved to be an active champion as he won a non-title third-round KO of Domingo Martinez just 41 days later and successfully defended against Joe Rivera (KO 7), Hiroyuki Yoshino (KO 5), Jose Rafael Barboza

(W 12) and Guillermo Cruz (KO 10). The defense against Gonzalez would be his fifth of 1993 and his ninth over two reigns.

Though Gonzalez (21-2-2, 15 KO) was rated number four in the WBA, he was a mystery to many observers. The only recognizable name on his ledger was Amancio Castro, who knocked Gonzalez out in 12 rounds for the WBC Fecarbox welterweight title on December 15, 1989. Since then, Gonzalez won eight of his nine fights, with the one loss coming by sixth round KO to Edwin Murillo. Gonzalez avenged the defeat in his next fight one year and 12 days later via third-round KO and he tuned up for the Coggi fight by icing the 0-8 Juan Lebron in two rounds four months earlier.

Gonzalez immediately assumed the role of aggressor as he used foot and shoulder feints to maneuver Coggi to the ropes. Coggi retreated with his hands high, elbows tucked in and upper body leaning back slightly as he looked for chances to counter. The first was quiet and studious as both men gathered reconnaissance. Late in the round, Gonzalez countered a lunging Coggi left to the body with a reflexive lead right that caught the champ on the cheek. It was a dangerous-looking blow that fell just short of perfection, but it also planted a seed in Gonzalez's mind.

Both men continued to probe with jabs and feints early in the second with Coggi concentrating on landing his powerful left to Gonzalez's body. The lull was typical of Coggi's fights; for he was willing to wait several rounds for the chance to unleash his potent left cross. The crowd knew this, so they didn't get on their champion for the slow action.

Coggi rewarded their patience by leaping in with a long, hard left cross to the jaw that snapped Gonzalez's head back and forced him to retreat to the corner pad while hopping on his right foot. Gonzalez was clearly hurt and Coggi jumped on him, mixing his blows nicely between head and body. Gonzalez forced Coggi back by bulling with the shoulder and throwing a long right but Coggi drove him back to the ropes with two more stinging lefts.

A right hook to the jaw dropped Gonzalez heavily to his knees 1:15 into the round and Gonzalez wore a pained and perplexed expression as he arose at the count of four.

Coggi appeared to be seconds away from a convincing victory. Had Coggi scored that victory, boxing would have been spared untold embarrassment, for the events of the next several minutes would rank among the most exciting yet maddeningly bizarre sequences ever witnessed in championship competition.

After referee Isidro Rodriguez, who was working his 63rd championship contest, completed the count Gonzalez backed toward the corner pad and Coggi inched his way forward to set up the finisher. But like the spider with the fly, Gonzalez had a surprise in store as he launched a monstrous lead right that exploded off Coggi's jaw. The effects of the blow rippled through the champion's body in a most dramatic way. His upper body pitched forward and his arms dropped to the side before falling backward as if descending through water. Finally, his stiffened frame crashed to the floor with a resounding thud. As he lay on the canvas, Coggi's eyes were wide but unseeing as he struggled to get his legs under him. The champion's reign was in mortal danger of ending then and there – after all, most fighters hit with such a bomb rarely muster enough energy to lift their heads much less regain their feet.

Somehow, Coggi pulled himself up. Though 14 seconds had elapsed in real time, all Coggi had to do was get up by Rodriguez's count of 10, which he did. Still, he was in terrible shape as he hopped on his right leg and struggled to regain his equilibrium. After Rodriguez wiped his gloves, Coggi wobbled to the corner pad and Gonzalez jumped in with a series of smothering punches. Gonzalez landed a chopping right to the side of the head and two left hooks to the jaw caused Coggi's upper body to fall into Rodriguez.

As Coggi fell into the ropes on stiffened legs, Rodriguez wrapped his arms around the Argentine favorite. Normally this gesture signaled the end of the fight, but for reasons only known to Rodriguez, he wasn't stopping the fight, *he was helping Coggi to stay upright!* Rodriguez steadied the champion by pinioning him to the corner with his upper body while holding the upper strand of ropes with each hand.

Meanwhile, a rapturously happy Gonzalez was in the neutral corner hugging his corner man in celebration of his apparent upset victory. But Team Gonzalez had to immediately switch gears after Rodriguez let go of Coggi, walked to their corner and informed them the fight was continuing. Forty-six seconds remained in the round, plenty of time to apply the finishing touches to a champion who was struggling just to remain conscious.

By now the scene was mass confusion as another player joined the fray. With 42 seconds on the clock, Coggi's adviser Luis Spada jumped onto the ring apron outside the ropes to get Coggi's attention. Fighting through his mental fog, Coggi turned and staggered into the corner. When Coggi turned toward ring center, Spada hooked two fingers around Coggi's trunks from behind to stabilize his champion and yelled several instructions into his ear. Spada's act normally would have prompted an immediate disqualification, but Rodriguez didn't know what to do to reverse a situation that was quickly spiraling out of control.

More time ticked off and nothing was happening. Gonzalez was in his corner bouncing on his toes waiting for Rodriguez's next command while the groggy Coggi sought to adjust a mouthpiece that was about to fall to the canvas. Finally, with 27 seconds left in the round, Rodriguez signaled the fight to continue – with Spada still on the ring apron holding up his fighter. With Coggi unable to move he was a sitting duck for Gonzalez, who wound up and blasted his wide-open target with an overhand right to the jaw. Had Spada not been where he was, Coggi surely would have fallen to the canvas. But Spada was there to wrap his right arm around Coggi's chest to keep him from collapsing.

After landing that titanic right, Gonzalez then backed off a step and Rodriguez stepped in the breech. Gonzalez walked to his corner believing the fight was over because he had just smashed a defenseless opponent, but the referee indicated the round had ended. There were two problems with Rodriguez's action here – no bell could be heard above the din and had there been a bell, it would have rung 20 seconds early.

Given Coggi's wretched condition following the knockdown, it is safe to say that had it unfolded without interruption on another day and in virtually any other spot around the world, Eder Gonzalez would have been declared the new champion, either by clean TKO or by disqualification. But on this day and in this place, the strong odor of home cooking permeated the hearts, minds and actions of those who had a direct bearing on this contest.

Spada and his assistants took full advantage of the situation as they worked feverishly over Coggi. As the champ took several deep breaths, Coggi stood up for a few seconds to test his legs only to sit back down. Coggi pulled away as Spada waved what appeared to be smelling salts under Coggi's nose.

The arena was in an uproar as the third round began with Gonzalez rushing in to finish the job. The Colombian's huge right caused Coggi to stagger back several feet to his corner and a second right sent him skittering to his right before falling into another corner pad. Coggi was absolutely helpless as Gonzalez blasted away with both hands. Coggi managed to grab Gonzalez after the challenger launched 25 unanswered blows. After Rodriguez broke them, Coggi wobbled to yet another corner and looked to ride out the storm by adopting a rope-a-dope defense. A right uppercut and left uppercut split Coggi's guard and a right sank into the ribs before Coggi locked in a clinch.

Fifty seconds into the round, Gonzalez began to get arm weary and soon he was leaning on Coggi along the ropes. But after the break, another scorching right wobbled Coggi to the ropes and a somewhat re-energized Gonzalez continued his assault. Though Coggi clearly remained in survival mode, he started to fight back as he countered Gonzalez's wide swings with a series of short uppercuts. After another break that saw Rodriguez push Gonzalez back more than halfway across the ring (instead of the regulation one step), Coggi thought about following him out but decided to stay put in the corner. Gonzalez nailed him with yet another right to the jaw that prompted Coggi to clinch, and his legs had not regained their strength as he tottered toward his fourth set of ropes in the round. But Coggi's ring sense was in full working order; after both men tumbled to the canvas following a sloppy clinch, Coggi glanced over his shoulder and spotted the ropes before backing into them. Just as Gonzalez whacked Coggi with a long right to the jaw, the bell sounded. While the third round must have seemed interminably long for Coggi, the bell had rung a full 28 seconds early.

It was yet another break for the home team, and the boxing match began to take on the air of a scene straight out of the WWE's past where one wrestler repeatedly is denied the victory due to slow counts, double-teaming from "managers" and a blatant disregard for the rules. In the scripted world of "sports entertainment," these actions are not only accepted but they also add to the drama. But boxing, for the most part, had overcome its era of fixed fights to the point where events like these would be considered a monstrously inexcusable violation of justice.

The tilted events began to have a positive effect on Coggi, who seemed steadier as he answered the bell for round four. His legs were planted firmly underneath him as he lashed out with two quick jabs and landed a right hook. Gonzalez landed a right to the jaw, but Coggi took it much better. Convinced Coggi was no longer vulnerable, Gonzalez retreated to long range.

For Coggi, the crisis had finally ended and he could shift his focus to launching a comeback. Though the events surrounding rounds two and three provided an extraordinary assist, Coggi's recuperative powers were still something to behold. As Gonzalez laid back and boxed, Coggi shot a big left to the jaw that sent the challenger staggering to the ropes. As Gonzalez languished, Coggi hooked his right arm around Gonzalez's left arm and blatantly held and hit with nine consecutive lefts to the head and body. Rodriguez, continuing to show his pro-Coggi stripes, said nothing. The timekeeper, seeing Coggi doing a little better, ended the fourth round only 15 seconds early.

Gonzalez had every reason to be furious, but he and his people took everything with remarkable calm. Gonzalez stood near ring center, more than ready to resume the action for round five. The reason for his eagerness was immediately apparent 10 seconds into the round when he floored Coggi with a quick overhand right to the jaw. Though it appeared to be a clean knockdown, Rodriguez ordered Coggi to his feet, wiped off his gloves and wiped out the extra point Gonzalez should have earned. Still, Coggi got to his feet quickly and neither Gonzalez nor his corner lodged any protest.

Gonzalez stepped in behind another long right – which he still was landing at will – but because he felt secure with his apparent early lead he didn't press for the knockout. Coggi drove Gonzalez to the ropes with a left cross and countered a right uppercut with another strong left. Coggi darted inside and drove 17 hold-and-hit uppercuts with nary a word from Rodriguez, whose performance had already descended into farce. The same could be said for the timekeeper, who let the round go an extra three seconds to allow Coggi to get in a few bonus fouls.

Incredibly, Spada issued a complaint to Rodriguez about Gonzalez's work with his head but Rodriguez dismissed Spada with a wave of the hand. It should have been apparent to Spada that Rodriguez had already done quite enough to assist his man, but human nature dictates that once someone gets an inch they'll want a mile.

Gonzalez drove Coggi back with a stiff jab to start the sixth, but Coggi recovered and engaged the challenger in a jabbing contest. One of Coggi's jabs set up a whipping left to the jaw, and another left late in the round propelled Gonzalez to the ropes, where

Coggi proceeded to throw 11 more hold-and-hit uppercuts before Rodriguez finally separated them.

Gonzalez again tagged Coggi with a hard jab to kick off the seventh, and the crowd sought to rally their man by amping up the volume and clapping in rhythm. Coggi's left eye was swollen and both cheeks were reddened. Gonzalez, for his part, was completely unmarked.

Coggi had a tendency to lull his opponents to sleep, then shock them with the power of his hair-trigger left cross. For this reason one of Coggi's nicknames was "The Whip," and the champion was successful in slowing the fight's pace to a crawl as the round proceeded. Gonzalez helped by biding his time, but he did manage to back Coggi into a corner behind a pair of rights.

Then, with 1:06 gone in the seventh, the moment for which Coggi had been waiting happened.

A straight left to the jaw landed on Gonzalez with stunning impact and he was forced to back into the corner Coggi had just vacated. A flurry of punches highlighted by four lefts sent Gonzalez stumbling forward to his knees, and a few members of the overjoyed crowd tossed papers into the air near the ring.

Gonzalez stumbled forward after rising to his feet at Rodriguez's count of four and looked in terrible shape as he tried to steady himself. Meanwhile, as Coggi stood in the neutral corner, a man in a gray suit spoke into Coggi's right ear while standing on the apron, another clear violation that should have resulted in a disqualification loss for Coggi. But any concept of order or fairness had long been thrown out on its ear, and with Fate's man so close to victory, there was no way that the rule of law would ever be applied now.

Like Coggi before him, Gonzalez tried to adjust his mouthpiece as Rodriguez asked if he wanted to continue. The mouthpiece dropped to the floor, which should have earned Gonzalez a brief time out to have it replaced and rinsed, but, predictably, Rodriguez did no such thing.

After receiving advice from the man in the gray suit, Coggi raced out of the corner without waiting for Rodriguez to formally wave him in. The champion blasted two lefts, a right hook and a final left before Gonzalez's corner man raced through the ropes, broke up the two fighters, and wrapped his arms around his fighter. At 2:26 of the seventh round, the only result that would have been permitted officially went into the books.

Coggi turned his back and leaped skyward in triumph while a multitude of corner men and supporters poured into the ring to celebrate what was an extraordinary – but wholly illegal – comeback.

The final insult came when the scorecards were revealed. All three judges had Coggi ahead – Luis Pabon saw the bout 58-56, Jesus Celis scored it 57-55 and Jose Campos somehow viewed the bout 59-58, meaning he saw more even rounds than for either boxer. So one can safely assume if Coggi was not going to win by knockout, he would win it on the scorecards.

But in retrospect, that shouldn't be much of a surprise. After all, that's what home field advantage is all about.

Epilogue: Coggi said after the fight that he remembered nothing from the second round forward and Spada said, in classic understated fashion, that his fighter was "lucky" to escape with his title. Referee Rodriguez was banned for life by the WBA, who ordered Coggi and Gonzalez to meet in an immediate rematch.

The bout took place March 18, 1994 at the MGM Grand in Las Vegas and once again circumstances conspired against Gonzalez. This time, visa problems complicated Gonzalez's trip from Madrid, Spain, where he was based at the time. Gonzalez spent 20 hours in the air and didn't land in Las Vegas until 9 p.m. the night before the fight. Gonzalez reportedly weighed in at 10 p.m. and remained awake after midnight to undergo the required medical exams.

Showtime analyst Dr. Ferdie Pacheco reported that Gonzalez was seen sleeping in his dressing room shortly before the fight yet with 1:10 remaining in the first round Gonzalez decked Coggi with a right to the jaw. Gonzalez continued to rake Coggi with rights in round two and opened a cut around Coggi's left eye with his first right of the third round. But like the first fight, Coggi roared back from behind – this time with no help from anyone – and floored Gonzalez with a pulverizing left with 1:45 left in the round. Gonzalez arose at three, and Coggi worked him over with heavy rights and lefts. A head-snapping right hook drove Gonzalez to his knees, at which point Gonzalez's corner threw in the towel. In Nevada, however, that didn't signal an automatic stoppage. Coggi's corner men ascended the apron to get Steele's attention, but the referee disregarded the towel and continued the count. With blood pouring from Gonzalez's lower lip, Steele stopped the fight at the 2:01 mark and Coggi was declared the winner and still champion.

Gonzalez fought only three more times, losing each one. On May 16, 1997 in Barranquilla, Colombia, the 29-1-1 Hugo Pineda stopped the 32-year-old Gonzalez in two rounds. Gonzalez subsequently retired and his final record stands at 22-8-1 (15 KO).

Coggi had plenty more chapters to write in his career. After polishing off Mario Morales (KO 3) in a non-title affair, Coggi lost the title by decision to Frankie Randall. Three fights later, Coggi and Randall met again on January 13, 1996 and once again controversy met Coggi. Coggi scored a questionable knockdown in round three and a clash of heads sent Coggi down and out in the fifth. The butt did not open a cut on Coggi, but it left him in a heap in the corner. Coggi was unable to continue after being given five minutes to recover and the WBA's accidental foul rule dictated that the scorecards would determine the winner since the incident occurred after the third round. Several minutes after Coggi was wheeled from the ring on a stretcher, he regained the title by five-round technical decision since he held a one-point lead on each scorecard.

The two would fight again seven months later – in Argentina – and Randall regained the belt via unanimous decision. Coggi would never again fight for a major belt, and his final bout took place May 29, 1999 in Bari, Italy where he lost a unanimous decision to Michele Piccirillo. The 37-year-old Coggi retired with a record of 75-5-2 with 44 KO.

UPSETS AND UNPREDICTABILITY – A WALK ON THE WILD SIDE

Total Punches Landed/Thrown

Round	1	2	3	4	5	6	7	8	9	10	11	12	Total
Coggi	1/18	6/20	11/31	11/41	13/45	11/41	15/32						68/228
	6%	30%	35%	27%	29%	27%	47%						30%
Gonzalez	4/23	16/34	35/69	11/23	9/22	7/29	5/24						87/224
	17%	47%	51%	48%	41%	24%	21%						39%

Jabs Landed/Thrown

Round	1	2	3	4	5	6	7	8	9	10	11	12	Total
Coggi	1/11	1/7	0/1	0/13	3/13	4/26	4/13						13/84
	9%	14%	0%	0%	23%	15%	31%						15%
Gonzalez	3/18	3/8	2/8	4/10	1/5	1/11	1/15						15/75
	17%	38%	25%	40%	20%	9%	7%						20%

Power Punches Landed/Thrown

Round	1	2	3	4	5	6	7	8	9	10	11	12	Total
Coggi	0/7	5/13	11/30	11/28	10/32	7/15	11/19						55/144
	0%	38%	37%	39%	31%	47%	58%						38%
Gonzalez	1/5	13/26	33/61	7/13	8/17	6/18	4/9						72/149
	20%	50%	54%	54%	47%	33%	44%						48%

Juan Coggi vs. Eder Gonzalez I December 17, 1993, San Miguel, Argentina

TALES FROM THE VAULT

Vilomar Fernandez vs. Alexis Arguello I
July 26, 1978, New York, New York

Greatness has always been an elusive quality. Even if one is blessed with the raw physical talent, achieving it requires much more than just looking good in the ring. First, one must have the desire to hone his talents in the gym and on the road, doing all of the grunt work day after day and year after year until everything he needs to do becomes second nature. Then, after doing all of the prep work, he must translate it into positive action inside the ropes as he mows down a gauntlet of his most challenging rivals. If he is successful enough times, he won't have to say a word about how great he is; his legacy will do all of the talking for him. For the best of the best, greatness is a goal for which to strive and the ultimate rewards are riches, fame and an impact that will last long after his physical body has left this earth.

But for others, if they are fortunate, greatness can emerge for one glorious night where everything they've ever learned comes pouring out in waves of excellence and execution. On more than one occasion, we've seen journeyman athletes produce feats so amazing that we say to ourselves "where did *that* come from, and why couldn't he have done it all along?"

On those nights, everything seems so easy that one feels as close to invincible as a mortal human being can be. Every shot goes in, every putt falls, every pass is completed and every swing produces spectacularly successful results. But that feeling – best described as being "in the zone" – departs as quickly as it arrived and one is left to wonder when, or if, it will ever return.

When Alexis Arguello and Vilomar Fernandez fought at Madison Square Garden's main arena on July 26, 1978, most experts believed Arguello was in for a fairly easy workout. Arguello was the reigning WBC super featherweight champion and at age 26 he was nearing the peak of his powers. And what powers they were; in 59 victories Arguello had scored 49 knockouts and since winning the belt from Alfredo Escalera in January, "The Explosive Thin Man" had already registered two defenses against Rey Tam (KO 5) in April and a 115-second destruction of Diego Alcala 53 days earlier. Experts rated Arguello as one of the two or three best fighters pound-for-pound and serious talk had begun about a showdown with undisputed lightweight champion Roberto Duran. The Fernandez fight, a non-title 10 rounder, represented Arguello's first step toward an eventual fight with the mighty "Manos de Piedra" and it was intended to prove the Nicaraguan's prowess against a full-blown lightweight.

Fernandez, a native of the Dominican Republic fighting out of the Bronx, was a fleet-footed stylist who carried a modest record of 21-6-3 (7 KO) into the ring against Arguello. Four months younger than Arguello, he was a man who possessed good, but not spectacular credentials. He was best known for his gritty challenge against WBA champ Duran 18 months earlier, a fight that saw Fernandez frustrate Duran with his stick-and-move tactics before Duran knocked him out in the 13th. As his record indicated, Fernandez was a hot-and-cold performer. He held good wins against fellow Duran victim Ray Lampkin (W 10), Frankie Otero (W 10, W 10), Antonio Amaya (W 10) and Ray Lunny III (W 10) but he also suffered consecutive losses to Walter Seeley (L 10), Edwin Viruet (L 10) and Ezequiel "Cocoa" Sanchez (L 12). Thirteen months earlier, Arguello polished off Sanchez in four rounds in the very same MSG ring where he was about to fight Fernandez.

Because the vast majority of Fernandez's fights took place in the New York area, he became a fan favorite. Though he was a shifty boxer, Fernandez was by no means boring because underneath the flash he possessed a feisty combative spirit. Still, Fernandez didn't enter the Arguello fight on a good note as he fought a 10-round draw against Larry Stanton four months earlier. Given that information, it's no surprise that many experts expected Arguello, 135 ¼, to blow out the 134 ¾-pound Fernandez in two or three rounds and provide a good case to put together the Duran fight as quickly as possible.

Moments after the first bell sounded, a charging Fernandez landed a straight right to the body and fired a wild hook over Arguello's head that sent him off-balance. The sneak attack sent an immediate message to Arguello that Fernandez was fighting for more than a paycheck; he was fighting to win.

As the two fighters sized each other up, the difference in size was graphic as the 5-10 Arguello towered over the 5-6 Fernandez. But equally graphic was the difference in mobility and speed. Arguello stood erect in a classic boxing pose, rolling his shoulders and probing for openings with the jab with feet firmly planted on the canvas. Fernandez, however, moved smoothly, mostly to his left but sometimes doing a fancy skip-step as he darted to his right, then back left.

Arguello tried a jab and Fernandez triggered an overhand right that just missed the target. After snapping in a jab, Arguello countered a Fernandez jab with a left uppercut to the stomach and a right over the top. Fernandez countered Arguello's jab by landing two quick body hooks, then zipping out of range before Arguello could react.

Though the normally slow-starting Arguello pressed the action, he seemed bothered by Fernandez's quickness as he found himself uncharacteristically lunging in with several of his power shots. Arguello thumped a left-right to the body in the final 30 seconds but Fernandez immediately tagged Arguello with his own hook before sliding off and bopping away the rest of the round.

Fernandez knew he had to treat Arguello as a ticking bomb that could explode the moment he made a mistake. Because of Arguello's height and reach advantages, Fernandez was forced to adopt guerrilla warfare tactics to snip Arguello's wires one by one.

His plan was to use his speed to dart inside Arguello's long arms, land quick two- or three-punch flurries and then dash out of range before Arguello's receipt could reach him. Without the power to hurt Arguello, Fernandez had to keep up the beat for the entire 10 rounds while hoping to score enough eye-catching blows in each round to earn the favor of referee Arthur Mercante Sr. and judges Artie Aidala and Sam Iron. In short, Fernandez had to pitch a perfect game and anything less wouldn't do.

Arguello turned up the pressure in round two, chasing Fernandez to the ropes. But the Dominican speedster fired a left-right to the body and landed an overhand right to the jaw that brought a roar from a crowd who appreciated the risks Fernandez was willing to take. Fernandez soon was pulling out every trick he ever learned to score points against Arguello. For instance, Fernandez dashed inside Arguello's reach from the right side and landed a direct short hook between Arguello's gloves before sliding out. He leaped in behind two hooks and fired a one-two to the body. Then, after Arguello landed hard hooks to the body and head that sent Fernandez toward the ropes, Fernandez cleverly blocked and slipped Arguello's ensuing six-punch flurry by keeping his hands high, his elbows tucked in and expertly weaving his upper body at just the right moment. Later, Fernandez tagged Arguello with a bizarre side winding left-right to the jaw and followed with three more slapping hooks to the jaw. He shoe-shined Arguello's body with four punches and zipped out of range before the Nicaraguan could pull the trigger.

As the round wound down, Fernandez realized he was in the midst of the fight of his life. He was breathing deeply "in the zone" before a crowd that wildly cheered his every move. His confidence soaring, Fernandez did a show-off shuffle step that set up a solid hook to the body. Fernandez was running on all cylinders as he continually befuddled one of the best fighters in the business. Meanwhile, Arguello kept poking out the left, not necessarily to score but to keep this little water bag in one place long enough to line up a big shot. Fernandez wouldn't cooperate as he always managed to find an escape route with almost ridiculous ease. As the second round bell rang, a frustrated Arguello raised his right glove with a mixture of disappointment and derision.

Fernandez seized the initiative at the start of round three by nailing Arguello with a lead right to the jaw, zipping to his left, blocking an Arguello right and tossing a five-punch flurry before resuming his stick-and-move tactics. Arguello missed over the top with a right and Fernandez countered with a hook to the top of the head and a right-left to the chin a few seconds later. Arguello dug in a couple of rights at close range, but Fernandez escaped and dropped in an overhand right that brought a roar from the crowd. Though the gentlemanly Arguello was generally well liked, Fernandez's surprising performance convinced them to invest their loyalty in the underdog.

An accidental low blow brought a Fernandez complaint to Mercante and an apology from Arguello, but Fernandez made him pay with a swinging left to the chin. After

Arguello missed over the top, Fernandez ducked underneath and effortlessly glided to his right. Normally, a defensive boxer who is constantly on the move would draw boos but the savvy MSG crowd knew this was the only way Fernandez could compete with Arguello. As each minute passed, they realized that Fernandez was weaving a fistic masterpiece as he skillfully blended his defensive wizardry with blows that came from unimaginable angles.

Arguello-Fernandez was evolving into a battle between the boxing textbook versus something completely different – and different was winning. For all of his gifts, Arguello was being exposed as painfully slow of foot and Fernandez's above-average speed only served to magnify it. Up to this point, Fernandez's mobility rendered Arguello's offense impotent for two reasons. First, Arguello was a marksman who threw punches only to land them and because Fernandez refused to stay in one spot for very long Arguello was unable to draw a bead, even with his jab. And second, because Fernandez chose to move to his right as well as to his left, Arguello had to constantly reset his feet. Thus, Arguello had no time to dig his toes into the canvas and generate any power on his punches. At points, Arguello was made to look foolish by a man who was perfectly executing a brilliantly conceived fight plan. It was as if Fernandez had been injected with a dose of Willie Pep's DNA.

Fernandez continued to confound Arguello in the fourth and before the fifth Arguello's trainer Al Silvani was seen talking intently into his charge's ear, urging him to pick up the pace. Ever the picture-book fighter, Arguello tried to jump-start his offense behind the jab, but Fernandez showed no signs of slowing down despite continually moving at full speed for the entire fight. With a little more than a minute remaining, Fernandez threw a triple jab, made Arguello miss with a hook, then nailed him with as hard a right as he could throw before sliding away to his own right. It was Fernandez's best punch of the fight, but his lack of power was proved beyond doubt as Arguello absorbed the blow unflinchingly.

Just before the bell sounded, Fernandez uncorked a final overhand right to the jaw and as he walked to the corner he was as calm as he could be. He had the bearing of a man who had been here before but in truth he had not been. Fernandez had performed well in spots against Duran, but there was never the sense that he could actually topple the great "Hands of Stone." But here, against another elite fighter, Fernandez was not only winning he was dominating.

Up to this point, Fernandez was having everything his own way and it was clear that he had passed the first test of whether his skills could match up with Arguello's – at least on this night. But the Dominican had yet to face the exam that would determine if he could pull off the improbable: What would happen when Arguello finally reached him?

Early in round six, "The Explosive Thin Man" finally began to detonate. After fielding yet another right lead, Arguello bounced a right off Fernandez's jaw and as Fernandez retreated to the ropes Arguello turned on the jets. Two left hooks and a right to the body connected on the retreating Fernandez. A hard right hit the target and Arguello caught Fernandez coming out with a hook. Another hook nailed the circling Fernandez and a right to the ear and two more hooks wobbled Fernandez ever so slightly.

It was the first real crisis of the fight for Fernandez and though he was still on the move his form was more ragged. After Fernandez missed with a wild hook, Arguello countered with a crisp right, a thumping hook to the body and a chopping right to the chin. Fernandez responded with a right to the jaw but Arguello retaliated with a right to the head, a hook to the body and another right to the jaw as the round neared an end. Arguello was finally landing the blows that had flattened so many previous opponents, and though his surge arrived much later than expected he apparently had found his way back into the fight. Fernandez had provided a thrill in the early rounds, but many at this point had to think that Arguello's class would rule the day – however belatedly.

Fernandez, however, didn't think that. The minute's rest had done him a world of good and as the seventh began the spring in his legs and the sharpness in his blows had returned as he speared Arguello with two jabs. For whatever reason, Arguello wasn't able to turn up the pressure after his sixth-round success and the fight returned to the early pattern of Fernandez moving and Arguello stalking. In the final 30 seconds, Fernandez shoe-shined Arguello's body before landing a light left uppercut and hook to the face. After Fernandez pelted Arguello with a lead right to the chin, a short hook and a popping right, the bell rang and the crowd wildly cheered Fernandez's comeback.

Fernandez had managed to get past the crisis and for the first time the possibility of a massive upset seemed very real. As Arguello stood in his corner and tried to shake some life in his arms, he knew he had only nine minutes to turn the tide and save his showdown with Duran. But Fernandez remained on point as he used every inch of the MSG ring to dip, slip and dodge while rattling Arguello's head with occasional blows.

Midway through the round, as Fernandez danced at long range, Arguello's frustration finally bubbled to the surface. He spread out his arms as if to say *"when are you going to fight me?"* Fernandez wisely didn't take the bait and continued to stick and move. Later, Arguello faked a bolo punch with his right arm and the crowd booed his uncharacteristic showboat move. Unwilling to be topped in any category, Fernandez shuffled his legs and rolled his arms and upper body in exaggerated fashion as if to mock Arguello's mocking of him. Then he delivered the final insult as he popped Arguello with two on-the-move hooks, ducked under an Arguello right and forced a clinch. Though Arguello induced an inside exchange in the final 30 seconds, he wasn't able to damage Fernandez in any discernable way and Fernandez punctuated another jaw-dropping round with two crackling rights.

The brilliance had returned for Fernandez, and Arguello's exasperation continued to mount in the ninth as he stood in front of Fernandez with his left arm dangling at his side. It was a testament to Fernandez's incandescence on this night that Arguello, who always won his fights on skills alone, would resort to psychological warfare to suck in an opponent. Soon, Arguello returned to normal fighting mode and tried a heavy right to the jaw. Fernandez ducked under, escaped to ring center and flashed four lefts to the jaw. At the bell, Arguello held out his right glove in a gesture of respect. Fernandez tapped it in high-five fashion and the two men walked to their respective corners.

Desperate to turn the tide, Arguello cranked up the heat in the 10th but in the early portions of the round the still-fresh Fernandez remained an elusive target. Arguello briefly trapped him on the ropes but his flurry found only arms, elbows and air as Fernandez slid to his right.

Midway through the round, Arguello got one final opportunity to reverse all that had occurred to this point. The two traded simultaneous hooks and while both of them landed, Arguello's was far heavier and a stunned Fernandez skittered away. Seeing his chance, Arguello threw all caution aside and unleashed his entire arsenal as Fernandez languished on the ropes. Fernandez absorbed the barrage and managed to escape by landing two body shots and dashing to his right. As the fight entered the final minute, Arguello snapped off a five-punch flurry and blasted Fernandez with his trademark right to the jaw.

It was now a race against time and mathematics, both of which were working against Arguello. An air of high drama hung thickly as Arguello pushed hard to apply the finisher. With 15 seconds remaining, Arguello cracked a vicious right that twisted Fernandez's head. Instead of cowering, Fernandez fought back just as viciously behind a four-punch volley to the body and a final three-punch salvo shortly before the final bell.

When the gong sounded and Mercante stepped between them, Fernandez hopped in the air while staring at a dejected Arguello, showing that he still had plenty left in the tank. The frenzied crowd wildly celebrated a fight that on paper looked to be a mismatch but turned into something much more. Arguello smiled and congratulated Fernandez as they awaited the verdict.

Referee Mercante awarded both boxers five rounds, which brought boos from the crowd. But the boos turned into rapturous cheers when it was announced that judges Aidala and Iron scored the bout 5-4-1 and 6-4 for the majority decision winner Vilomar Fernandez.

The loss snapped a 25-fight winning streak that spanned four years, two divisional championships and eight title fights while also derailing any immediate plans for a fight with Duran, who unified the belts by beating WBC titlist Esteban DeJesus six months earlier. For Fernandez, the fight was not only a revelation, it stamped him as a legitimate contender for lightweight honors. No matter what the future would hold for Fernandez, he could at least remember July 26, 1978 as the day when true greatness touched him on the shoulder and allowed him to produce of the most dazzling displays of "The Sweet Science" of this, or any other, decade.

Epilogue: Four months after beating Arguello, Fernandez won a 10-round decision over Isidro Perez to set up a crossroads fight with the 11-0 Howard Davis Jr. Though Davis won a hard-fought 12-round decision, climbing off the floor in round two to do so, both men received title shots in their next outings. Davis lost a 15-rounder to WBC champion Jim Watt while Fernandez met the same fate against WBA king Hilmer Kenty. Fernandez's time as a top contender ended in his next fight as he was vaporized in two rounds by rising star Rodolfo "Gato" Gonzalez.

After scoring three wins over Elwood Campbell (W 8), David Abella (KO 5) and Arseneo Green (W 10), Fernandez crossed swords with Arguello for a second time on February 26, 1983 in San Antonio's Freeman Coliseum. This was Arguello's first outing after his unsuccessful first challenge for Aaron Pryor's WBA 140-pound title and this time "The Explosive Thin Man" won an easy 10-round decision over a slower 30-year-old Fernandez. The Dominican would fight four more times, winning three over Monroe Brooks (KO 2), Angel Cruz (W 10) and Billy Parks (W 10) before ending his career with a 10-round split-decision loss to Ricky Young on June 28, 1985. The 33-year-old Fernandez retired with a mark of 30-11-2 with nine knockouts.

Arguello's loss to Fernandez wiped away any incentive for Duran to stay at 135 and he soon vacated the titles to move up to welterweight. Watt and Ernesto Espana grabbed the belts while Arguello returned to 130 to defend his own title. Over the next two years, Arguello notched six title defenses before making another assault on 135, which began with an eighth-round stoppage of Cornelius Boza-Edwards. After struggling to a 10-round split decision over future champion Jose Luis Ramirez, Arguello polished off Robert Vazquez in three rounds, then out-pointed Watt over 15 rounds to capture his third divisional crown.

Arguello defended the WBC lightweight belt four times against Ray Mancini (KO 14), Roberto Elizondo (KO 7), James "Bubba" Buscheme (KO 6) and Andy Ganigan (KO 5) before moving up to 140 to pursue a then-unprecedented fourth divisional title. A resounding one-punch KO over Kevin Rooney in two set the stage for his classic first encounter with WBA junior welterweight champion Aaron Pryor, which he lost in 14 rounds. A revenge victory over Fernandez and a third round KO over former lightweight titlist Claude Noel (KO 3) set up the second fight with Pryor. Floored in the first and fourth rounds, Arguello rallied in the middle rounds before a point penalty halted his momentum. When Arguello was decked a third time in the 10th, he sat on the canvas to wait out the 10-count and announced his retirement immediately after the bout.

Two years later, Arguello returned to the ring and saw some success, knocking out Pat Jefferson (KO 5) and Billy Costello (KO 4) to establish his credentials for a possible shot at WBA junior welterweight champion Patrizio Oliva. But doctors advised Arguello to retire after spotting an abnormality with his heart, and Arguello heeded their word. He was enshrined in the International Boxing Hall of Fame in 1992, and it appeared the final chapter of his life in boxing had been written.

Needing closure – and money – a 42-year-old Arguello donned the gloves again, joining Ray Leonard, Azumah Nelson and Jeff Fenech as the only Hall of Fame enshrinees to emerge from retirement to box again. Though his physique was as trim as ever, his body betrayed him. Arguello suffered a broken hand en route to a majority decision win over Jorge Palomares and he ended his career on January 21, 1995 in Las Vegas when he lost a 10-round decision to Scott Walker, a tall, mobile southpaw. Arguello hung up the gloves for good with a record of 82-8 (65 KO).

TALES FROM THE VAULT

Total Punches Landed/Thrown

Round	1	2	3	4	5	6	7	8	9	10	11	12	Total
Fernandez	11/27	20/43	15/30	11/37	15/36	7/22	23/57	12/30	12/28	16/47			142/357
	41%	47%	50%	30%	42%	32%	40%	40%	43%	34%			40%
Arguello	9/43	11/63	11/57	3/37	7/59	21/70	9/43	11/55	6/40	24/86			112/553
	21%	17%	19%	8%	12%	30%	21%	20%	15%	28%			20%

Jabs Landed/Thrown

Round	1	2	3	4	5	6	7	8	9	10	11	12	Total
Fernandez	1/7	0/5	0/4	2/16	3/15	1/7	4/17	4/11	3/11	3/14			21/107
	14%	0%	0%	12%	20%	14%	24%	36%	27%	21%			20%
Arguello	2/24	0/29	1/28	1/28	1/36	1/12	3/22	1/17	1/22	2/22			13/240
	8%	0%	4%	4%	3%	8%	14%	6%	5%	9%			5%

Power Punches Landed/Thrown

Round	1	2	3	4	5	6	7	8	9	10	11	12	Total
Fernandez	10/20	20/38	15/26	9/21	12/21	6/15	19/40	8/19	9/17	13/33			121/250
	50%	53%	58%	43%	57%	40%	48%	42%	53%	39%			48%
Arguello	7/19	11/34	10/29	2/9	6/23	20/58	6/21	10/38	5/18	22/64			99/313
	37%	32%	34%	22%	26%	34%	29%	26%	28%	34%			32%

Vilomar Fernandez vs. Alexis Arguello I July 26, 1978, New York, New York

Kelvin Seabrooks vs. Thierry Jacob
July 4, 1987, Calais, France

Matthew Saad Muhammad is one of the most celebrated of light heavyweight champions because of his perseverance. Time after time for year after year Saad Muhammad would be taken to the brink of competitive extinction only to suddenly turn the tables on his overconfident opponents and leave them wondering what truck had just hit them. Saad Muhammad was boxing's equivalent of Harry Houdini as his great escapes in the ring earned him his rightful place in Halls of Fame that spread from Canastota to California.

But Saad Muhammad isn't the only fighter gifted with the ability to instantly turn adversity into ascension. Kelvin Seabrooks' entire athletic life was the epitome of surmounting long odds to become greater than the fates destined for him.

For most of his career, Seabrooks served as fodder for fighters perceived to be potential stars. He often fought on short notice and in the home areas of his more favored foes, circumstances that managers of prospects wouldn't dare attempt. Seabroooks' 22-13 (17 KO) record showed the scars of his overly ambitious and dangerous early life as a pro. In his sixth pro fight he lost an eight-round decision to the 10-0 Jerome Coffee and his next bout was a decision loss to the 10-2-1 Kenny Mitchell, his first scheduled 10 rounder. Losses to Carmelo Negron (KO by 7), Myron Taylor (L 10), Gaby Canizales (L 12), Pat Cowdell (KO by 5), Calvin Grove (L 10), Tommy Cordova (L 10) and Harold Petty (L 12) also dotted his record. But there was a flip side to Seabrooks' travails as he picked up valuable firsthand experience against some of the most talented young fighters in the world, and he possessed enough raw ability to spring the occasional upset. He inflicted the first two losses on the formerly undefeated Lane Killian's record (KO 5 and KO 6) and he shocked the 15-1-1 Ray Minus in three rounds.

Exactly four months after a sixth-round stoppage loss to Yogi Buchanan, Seabrooks traveled to Australia to fight recent title challenger Freddie Jackson. Jackson had suffered a recent disqualification defeat to Daniel Zaragoza for the vacant WBC bantamweight title and his management saw Seabrooks as a good steppingstone back to title contention. Instead, Seabrooks crushed Jackson in two rounds and, following a one-round KO over Tony Reyes in Charlotte, decisioned the 14-0-1 Louis Curtis (a 1976 Olympian) over 12 rounds to capture the USBA bantamweight title. That victory earned him a world ranking and a crack at the vacant IBF title against Colombian Miguel Maturana – in Cartagena. But the veteran road warrior was unconcerned and he proved it beyond doubt by crushing Maturana in five rounds. In the midst of his mediocrity, Seabrooks dug deep within himself and pulled out a higher level of performance, and he now had a championship belt to match his championship courage.

Seabrooks began this most unlikely title reign by following a familiar scenario: Traveling to an undefeated challenger's home country to put everything he had worked for at severe risk. On this day, Seabrooks was fighting southpaw Thierry Jacob in Calais and Seabrooks was worldly enough to realize the situation before him: By the end of the day, Jacob *should* be the new world champion, and it was Seabrooks' task to make sure Jacob's "happy ending" didn't happen. The only good omen Seabrooks could bring to the ring was that the bout was taking place on America's Independence Day.

Jacob entered this title shot with a glossy record, but with little substance behind it. Besides beating a very young Vincenzo Bellcastro, Jacob piled up victories against a succession of obscure European opponents. But if his promoters had their way, July 4, 1987 would be his coronation day and he would be crowned before thousands of his adoring countrymen.

The crowd was doing its part to pump up Jacob as they loudly chanted "Thierry! Thierry! Thierry!" as both men prepared to begin combat. But they received a mighty shock less than 15 seconds after the opening bell when Seabrooks landed a right-left-right to the jaw that sent Jacob heavily to the canvas. To their relief, Jacob regained his feet at three and as he stepped sprightly toward a corner he convinced everyone – including the referee and Seabrooks – that he had suffered a flash knockdown.

Still, Seabrooks jumped on the opportunity for an early finish as he fired a succession of right leads that fell short of the mark while Jacob alternated between moving, jabbing and clinching as he sought to further clear his head. Jacob won an exchange of lefts and he backed Seabrooks away with a long left cross to the face.

All was going well for Seabrooks – perhaps too well. Certain fighters are built for domination while others, like Seabrooks, were meant to struggle before securing that treasured victory. Somehow, he must have known he was going to encounter rough weather before leaving this ring; the only mystery was when he would face his first hurdle.

It didn't take long for that hurdle to show up.

As Seabrooks followed Jacob to the ropes, he prepared to throw a wide hook. But Jacob beat him to the punch with his own left that smacked squarely on the jaw and the champion was sent flying across the ring before hitting the canvas. Like Jacob before him, Seabrooks leapt to his feet and calmly took the mandatory eight count. Seeing his chance, Jacob rushed in behind three big lefts that had the champion in full retreat and seeking the safety of a clinch. Another cluster of lefts had Seabrooks wobbling all over the ring and he hit the canvas for the second time with 16 seconds remaining in a thrilling opening round. Again, Seabrooks was on his feet within two seconds and by the time the count was completed, Jacob didn't have a chance to sufficiently follow up. Where once the crowd was pondering their hero's quick demise, they were now on their feet screaming at the top of their lungs.

In a way, Seabrooks had Jacob right where he wanted him. The champion was accustomed to wild starts and early knockdowns while Jacob was used to dominating in more controlled settings. The Frenchman's intent was to outbox Seabrooks over 12 rounds, but all that changed the moment he put the champion on the deck. Through his own vulnerability, Seabrooks was able to suck Jacob into the type of firefight that best suited his abilities. It was an extremely dangerous way to operate, but if it was good enough for Houdini, it was good enough for Seabrooks.

Jacob continued his surge in the second with a huge left to the jaw, but this time Seabrooks took the punch well. No matter how thoroughly he warmed up in the dressing room, Seabrooks still required several minutes of actual combat to get his engine running at full speed and for his jaw to be properly fortified.

Seabrooks swung wildly at Jacob, missing most but connecting some, but the more precise Jacob struck back with a combination that drove the champion across the ring. Seabrooks recovered instantly and fired back a right to the chin that jerked Jacob's head straight back. The two men traded violently in a savage game of give and take with never a moment's peace. Three big lefts capped by a flurry pushed Seabrooks toward his own corner, but somehow he survived and fought back with a four-punch flurry. They unleashed power punches so numerous they were difficult to follow, and the crowd was getting more than its money's worth as each man put the other through a trial by fire.

Seabrooks possessed an unshakable faith in his ability to come out on top in heavy exchanges. Jacob, for his part, knew that he would lose in the long run if he continued to trade with Seabrooks so he began the third in a boxing mode as he went side to side behind swift jabs. Seabrooks worked his right-lefts overtime, though most of his blows were wildly off target.

A big left forced Seabrooks to retreat and another one connected several seconds later. Jacob dug a heavy hook to the body and a straight trip-hammer right caught Seabrooks as he began his hook and caused him to wobble into the ropes. All thoughts of careful boxing again vanished as Jacob rushed Seabrooks and bombed away. His bravado did not serve him well at this juncture, for sometime during the ensuing exchange Jacob suffered a long and deep cut above his right eye.

Jacob started the fourth at long range to protect the cut, but Seabrooks popped the challenger's head back with a lead right. Jacob then retaliated with two strong lefts to the chin. As much as Jacob's brain commanded him to box, his fighting spirit urged him to go for the gusto. A right uppercut hurt Seabrooks briefly but he instantly waded forward and fired an array of powerful punches to induce an exchange that lasted until the bell.

Seabrooks' trainer urged his charge to lower his target, saying "you're missing everything up top. He's going underneath everything you're throwing."

Jacob again boxed at the start of the fifth and Seabrooks chose to wait him out because he knew the instant a hard punch landed he would get the type of fight he wanted. Surely enough, that punch came in the form of a big left to the jaw that backed Seabrooks to the ropes. Jacob followed with guns blazing and Seabrooks fired back in the hopes of landing something – anything – on his challenger. Jacob was winning the rounds, but Seabrooks was always in the fight as he exerted heavy pressure and induced exchange after exchange. An overhand right slammed against Jacob's chin and pushed him back toward the ropes, but the Frenchman instantly spun away and threw a four-punch flurry to stem Seabrooks' surge. Jacob's cut had not gotten appreciably worse and his aggression and combinations had to serve him well on the judges' scorecards.

Jacob continued to box at long range in the sixth and resisted the urge to pursue Seabrooks even after stinging him with a right-left to the chin. Seabrooks wasn't doing much other than slowly stalking Jacob behind his high guard and surveying the landscape. Two more right-lefts from Jacob sparked the crowd into a chant of "Allez! Allez!" (Go! Go!) A huge left uppercut rocked Seabrooks' head back and a follow-up left cross-straight right drove Seabrooks to his knees in the closing seconds of the round. Seabrooks arose instantly from his third knockdown and tried to convince referee Paul Venti that his fall was the result of a slip by scooting his feet on the canvas. But Venti wasn't fooled as he administered the mandatory eight count. The bell rang upon completion of the count and as Jacob walked toward his corner, he hugged the champion both in joy of his succession and in appreciation of Seabrooks' toughness.

Jacob continued his rally in the seventh as he blasted in a left cross while ducking underneath Seabrooks' counters. As the round proceeded Jacob speared Seabrooks seemingly at will with long lefts, but after absorbing two more Seabrooks lashed out with two lead rights that drove Jacob back across the ring. For Jacob, it was a fresh reminder that the champion, no matter how vulnerable he looked, was always dangerous. He was a master of digging himself out of holes that would bury most other fighters and to him, Jacob was just the latest person who was trying to keep him in his place. This struggle for Seabrooks would be personified by the events of the tumultuous eighth.

Seabrooks began the round by bulling the challenger to the ropes, but Jacob managed to plow in a left cross with his back on the strands. Seabrooks retaliated with a splendid seven-punch salvo that forced Jacob to hold. It was his best effort in several rounds and he tried to sustain it by driving Jacob to another set of ropes with a right to the body. However, Jacob managed to escape with a four-punch flurry capped by a strong left uppercut. Both men worked strongly at close range and the already heavy pace picked up even more when Jacob stunned the champion with a sterling 14-punch attack that forced Seabrooks into retreat.

As Jacob sought to follow up, Seabrooks lost his footing and partially entangled himself in the ropes. Though Seabrooks instantly righted himself, Jacob went all out for the knockout as he cracked a succession of full-force left uppercuts off the champion's jaw and ignored all of Seabrooks' less accurate counters. Another huge cross blasted through and Seabrooks couldn't conceal his duress as his upper body slumped slightly.

The champion was absorbing a frightening amount of punishment but Seabrooks, like Saad Muhammad before him, was gifted with the ability to maintain presence of mind through the most severe storms. As the charging Jacob followed a stumbling Seabrooks along the ropes, Seabrooks somehow produced a monstrous hair-trigger lead right to the jaw. Jacob was badly hurt as he reached out for the top rope with his right glove while dropping his left arm to waist level. The pendulum had swung instantly and violently toward Seabrooks and Jacob desperately bought time by sidestepping the champion's charge and throwing him into another set of ropes, and Venti's subsequent warning gave him even more recovery time.

Jacob was visibly tiring as his windmilling blows lacked the speed and snap that he had even a minute earlier while Seabrooks was amazingly fresh. With 16 seconds remaining, a torrid Seabrooks right uppercut caused Jacob to drop his guard and retreat to the ropes on unsteady legs. Another right thudded against Jacob's temple and a flush hook to the jaw turned Jacob's head grotesquely. Jacob was almost defenseless as yet another right propelled him to the ropes. The French crowd that had been yelling excitedly just minutes earlier was buzzing in anxiety and horror at this theatrical turn of events.

As the ninth opened, Jacob shifted into survival mode as he tried to retreat on legs reluctant to obey his brain. Convinced his moment was at hand, Seabrooks rained down blows that had Jacob weaving from corner to corner. Jacob proved his resourcefulness by landing enough right-lefts to convince Seabrooks to take his foot off the pedal – at least for now.

The crowd tried to lift their man further by singing and chanting and he responded by fighting out of his fog behind jabs and one-twos. A six-punch flurry caught Seabrooks, who turned Jacob to the ropes and landed four punches to the head and body. The final blow of the flurry, a thudding hook to the ribs, weakened Jacob considerably as he grimaced and gestured to his corner that something was terribly wrong. Seabrooks remained incredibly composed as he clinically sunk a straight right to the breadbasket, but Jacob also demonstrated a fighter's courage as he closed the round with two left crosses.

Jacob had expended an extraordinary amount of energy throughout the fight, no doubt fueled by fighting for a title in front of a screaming, supportive throng. But his adrenaline supply was ebbing fast and he appeared utterly spent as he shook his head while walking back to the corner and plopped on his stool. While in the corner, much attention was devoted to the cut above Jacob's right eye, which had grown to nearly an inch in length but was not bleeding heavily. Many sets of fingers pried at the cut and Jacob's chief second – his father Jacques – called for referee Venti to come to the corner.

Seeing his son's exhaustion, he formulated a plan. He suspected Thierry was well ahead on the scorecards, and he would eventually be proven correct as judges Torben Seeman Hansen, Jim Traylor and Sheila Harmon saw Jacob as a 88-81, 88-82 and 89-82 winner. If the fight were stopped because of the cut, which he believed was caused by an intentional butt, the scorecards would determine the winner.

At first, the plan did not seem to take hold as Seabrooks was lifted into the air in celebration as the fight was stopped between rounds. Jacob congratulated his opponent and he was soon held aloft and accepted the plaudits his brave – but unsuccessful – challenge deserved. But while all this was going on, an argument raged between a member of the French commission – who believed Jacob should be declared the winner due to the head butt rule – and an IBF representative. The IBF official said the cut was produced by a legal punch and was widened by another legal blow in the fourth and that those decisions were made at the referee's discretion. Plus, he said that the doctor – not referee Venti – stopped the fight due to the cut, and because the cut was produced by legal blows the result would be a 10th round TKO for Seabrooks.

As the argument raged, Jacob was again raised onto his handlers' shoulders to rev up the crowd, which was growing more angry and confused. Suddenly, a large bottle of champagne was handed to Jacob and he was spraying it in celebration. Moments later, the reason for his jubilation was announced: The TKO in favor of Seabrooks was changed to a technical decision for Jacob – who was then declared the new champion.

Confusion reigned supreme as Jacob rejoiced and Seabrooks left the ring amid debris thrown by the fans. The identity of the true titleholder remained a mystery. The French federation declared the bout a "no contest" until IBF President Bob Lee decreed that Seabrooks was the winner and still champion.

The chaos surrounding the result was typical of Seabrooks' entire life as a professional boxer. Everything he earned in the squared circle never came easily and it usually was achieved against prohibitive odds. Still, he persevered with his usual aplomb and though the ultimate result was delayed, he was able to leave France with his title – and his dignity – intact.

It was a great escape with which Matthew Saad Muhammad – and Harry Houdini for that matter – would have been proud.

Epilogue: Seabrooks again hit the road – this time to Italy – to defend his title against Ernie Cataluna four months after the Jacob fight. In another wild brawl, Seabrooks emerged with a fourth round TKO and he followed up by returning to France three months after that to knock out Fernando Beltran in two. Seabrooks' championship train came to a final stop on July 9, 1988 in Atlantic City when Orlando Canizales stopped him in the 15th. Seabrooks earned a rematch with Canizales after stopping Dwayne "Bobo" Brooks in four rounds, but fell in 11 rounds after another typically brave showing.

From then on, Seabrooks returned to being a steppingstone, winning just one of his final eight fights, the last five being by TKO. His final bout was a two-round defeat to Jimmi Bredahl in Copenhagen, Denmark on March 17, 1995. Seabrooks, just one week past his 32nd birthday, retired with a 27-22 (22 KO) record.

Jacob thought he had become a champion the night he fought Seabrooks, but Lee's decree put a halt to that proposition. It would take 19 more fights over the next four-plus before Jacob finally ascended a throne. Along the way, he was stopped by Fabrice Benichou for the vacant EBU title and knocked out in six rounds by IBF titlist Jose Sanabria. But like Seabrooks, Jacob eventually persevered. He decisioned Duke McKenzie over 12 rounds to win the EBU belt and four fights later he scored a unanimous decision over Daniel Zaragoza to capture the WBC belt. His reign as champion didn't last long as Tracy Harris Patterson blasted him out in two rounds three months later.

Jacob received two more successive cracks at a belt, but Wilfredo Vazquez proved himself the superior fighter as he scored TKOs in the eighth and 10th rounds. Eleven months after the second Vazquez defeat, on May 20, 1994, the 29-year-old Jacob ended his career in Coquelles, France by decisioning Edgar Orlando Ballen over eight rounds. He retired with a record of 39-6 with 20 KO.

TALES FROM THE VAULT

Total Punches Landed/Thrown

Round	1	2	3	4	5	6	7	8	9	10	11	12	Total
Seabrooks	11/47	13/67	15/69	13/71	9/48	2/18	13/46	24/84	23/69				123/519
	23%	19%	22%	18%	19%	11%	28%	29%	33%				24%
Jacob	26/82	46/138	27/86	31/93	24/81	13/56	16/67	50/116	25/61				258/780
	32%	33%	31%	33%	30%	23%	24%	43%	41%				33%

Jabs Landed/Thrown

Round	1	2	3	4	5	6	7	8	9	10	11	12	Total
Seabrooks	3/19	0/11	2/15	2/17	0/7	0/8	0/2	0/3	1/6				8/88
	16%	0%	13%	12%	0%	0%	0%	0%	17%				9%
Jacob	5/35	7/55	4/35	1/36	5/36	3/31	2/19	2/21	3/22				32/290
	14%	13%	11%	3%	14%	10%	11%	10%	14%				11%

Power Punches Landed/Thrown

Round	1	2	3	4	5	6	7	8	9	10	11	12	Total
Seabrooks	8/28	13/56	13/54	11/54	9/41	2/10	13/44	24/81	22/63				115/431
	29%	23%	24%	20%	22%	20%	30%	30%	35%				27%
Jacob	21/47	39/83	23/51	30/57	19/45	10/25	14/48	48/95	22/39				226/490
	45%	47%	45%	53%	42%	40%	29%	51%	56%				46%

Kelvin Seabrooks vs. Thierry Jacob July 4, 1987, Calais, France

Frankie Duarte vs. Alberto Davila II
June 27, 1987, Inglewood, California

Rematches occupy a long and storied place in boxing lore. Many times matches spawn far more questions than answers and the only way many of them can be resolved is by pairing them a second time – and sometimes a third or fourth time.

On other occasions, circumstances demand that a second fight take place long after the first had happened, and this was what occurred when bantamweights Frankie Duarte and Albert Davila clashed on June 27, 1987 at the Forum in Inglewood, California. Normally, one would have thought their first fight – a dominating fifth round TKO by Davila at the Olympic – would have emphatically settled the issue. But the stories surrounding this second fight were hardly normal.

First was the time element – their initial bout took place 10 years and 20 days earlier when the 22-year-olds were jockeying for position for a title shot against either WBC bantamweight champion Carlos Zarate or his WBA counterpart Alfonso Zamora. Since Davila's victory, much had happened to both men. For Davila, his adventures took place inside the ring as he failed in title shots against Zarate, Jorge Lujan and Lupe Pintor before finally capturing the WBC belt vacated by Pintor with a 12th round TKO of Kiko Bejines. Davila's jubilation turned to tribulation as Bejines subsequently died of his injuries. Davila defended his belt just once against Enrique Sanchez before being forced to surrender it due to the effects of a back injury that prevented him from putting it on the line in a timely manner.

Since returning to the ring in August 1985 after a 14-month hiatus, Davila tried to regain the WBC title against the gifted Colombian Miguel "Happy" Lora. Their fight, held before 50,000 in Baranquilla, Colombia in November 1986, saw Lora win a comprehensive decision, but Davila still entered the Duarte rematch as the Colombian's mandatory challenger. A win over Duarte could set the stage for a second crack at Lora, a shot at IBF king Kelvin Seabrooks or perhaps a chance at the winner between newly-crowned WBA champ Chan Yong Park and Wilfredo Vazquez, who were scheduled to fight in the fall.

In contrast, Duarte's troubles occurred outside the ring – and his wounds were mostly self-inflicted. Shortly after the loss to Davila, Duarte descended into a nightmare of alcohol and drugs. Still, he managed to win four consecutive fights, including the California featherweight title from Francisco Flores. But he suffered a frightful beating from future WBC super featherweight champion Rolando Navarrete over 10 rounds and following another 10-round loss to Neptali Alamag in Honolulu he eventually quit the ring.

Over the next 39 months, Duarte subjected his body and his family ties to tremendous abuse, but while he wasn't bingeing, he was searching for his place in life without boxing. One time he attended a welding class and some of his classmates recognized him and recalled how they used to chant his name. Back then, the chants provided fuel for Duarte's fire, but the fighter's precipitous descent only inspired disillusionment from his classmates – and himself.

Once Duarte reached bottom, he was pushed into the most important decision of his life – either fight back or die. Knowing Duarte's fortitude, it was no surprise that he chose to live. He quit drugs cold turkey and one day he walked into Ten Goose Gym, which was headed by trainer Joe Goossen. At first, Duarte worked out just to drop excess weight (the onetime bantamweight now weighed 138) but as the pounds melted off some of his old skills began to resurface. When he made his return against Luis Hernandez on May 30, 1984 (a seven-round TKO win), he weighed a svelte 122 but while he resembled his old self physically he was definitely not the same fighter as before.

He was better.

Yes, he was still a slow starter but the punishment he absorbed in the early rounds wasn't nearly as severe. His defensive skills improved under Goossen and his offense produced the victories of old. The first big test of his comeback came on April 9, 1985 when he fought undefeated WBA bantamweight champion Richie Sandoval in a 10-round non-title go. Duarte gave as good as he got before dropping a split decision. Heartened by his tremendous showing against a reigning champion, Duarte continued to progress. He went 4-0-1 in his next five fights, with a two-round head-butt induced technical draw to top contender Freddie Jackson being the only blemish.

Following a stirring nine-round TKO over Jesus Salud for the NABF title, Duarte earned a crack at WBA bantamweight king Bernardo Pinango on February 3, 1987 at the Forum. Pinango had defeated Sandoval's conqueror Gaby Canizales eight months earlier and he entered the fight as the favorite. Despite scoring a knockdown in the 12th and being the beneficiary of three penalty points, Duarte somehow lost the decision by one, two and five points. Crushed by what many saw as a robbery, Duarte was left to begin again and the fact that Davila once again was the man who stood between him and a title shot just added to the fight's "full circle" flavor.

Duarte-Davila II was for Duarte's NABF belt and at 117 ½, Duarte (42-7-1, 32 KO) was at his lightest weight in a decade. Davila (53-8-1, 25 KO) scaled 118. Both men appeared in the prime physical condition befitting such an important contest.

Duarte came out of his corner with his shoulders hunched forward and his chin tucked into his chest while Davila fired several range-finding jabs. A masterful boxer, Davila's quicker jabs were delivered fluidly while Duarte's stiffer jabs had the pop of those thrown straight from the shoulder. After an initial feeling-out period, the action began to pick up midway through the round as Duarte landed a good inside hook and

Davila tossed quick-fisted clusters in unpredictable sequences. His double jabs landed squarely on Duarte's nose while Duarte's light one-two sparked cheers from his supporters. But it was Davila's jabs and his still-effective defensive skills that carried the round.

Duarte picked up the pace in the second by landing two clean lead rights to the jaw and a solid one-two forced Davila to take a backward step. Davila bounced a crisp lead right off Duarte's jaw and soon the two bantamweights were swapping fast, sharp blows while still maintaining a high level of technique. Seconds after Duarte connected on a left-right, Davila replied with a crunching counter right to the jaw, a hook to the body and a pinpoint jab. Davila's superior hand speed enabled him to beat Duarte to the punch time after time, but it was Duarte who drew first blood as he opened a small cut over Davila's left eye.

The intense boxing became even more so in the third as they executed every punch in the book with a level of skill that could only be explained by their experience. They spent much of their time in the center of the ring rotating around one another in tight circles. They very rarely clinched and at 32 they maintained a pace that would have made their 22-year-old selves proud. The action gradually moved into the trenches – Duarte's turf – but Davila's quick hands enabled him to maintain the edge.

A left followed by two rights shook Duarte with 30 seconds remaining but Duarte furiously fired a quick combo capped by a scorching hook to the jaw that rocked Davila's head back. The crowd was in an enthusiastic uproar as the two fighters not only met, but also far exceeded, the already high expectations this neighborhood showdown generated.

Things got even more exciting one minute into the fourth when Davila planted his left foot and turned his jab into a jarring hook that found the point of Duarte's chin and sent the Ventura resident crashing to the canvas. It was only the second knockdown of Duarte's long career and the first since Davila turned the trick in their first fight. Duarte immediately regained his feet with a look of disgust on his face, a face that now sported a welt under the right eye.

Knowing he was not a one-shot knockout artist, Davila wisely chose not to gun for the early knockout but instead banked on his precision. He was fighting with the supreme timing of his prime and a sharp left uppercut to the chin highlighted that fact. But Duarte was still very much in the fight as he tore at Davila with combinations at every opportunity, though his punches lacked his rival's speed and snap. In the final 15 seconds, Duarte summoned a fresh supply of adrenaline as he unleashed nearly 30 punches as the blood began trickling down his cheek.

Davila continued to work effectively in the fifth but Duarte slowly began turning the fight with body shots that forced Davila to reset. The infighting heightened the risk of unintentional head butts, and one caused Davila to complain to referee Lou Filippo, but no warning was given. Duarte continued to pick up steam as he marched forward behind quick combinations. While Davila still occasionally tagged Duarte with quick hooks, they weren't coming as frequently. Duarte invested a lot of himself into his rally and his exertion was made clear when he stole a deep breath coming out of a clinch. Still, the fact that he had just won his first round had to have fortified his resolve.

Sensing a turn in momentum, the Duarte fans began chanting "Frankie! Frankie!" to give their man a further jolt of energy and he responded by reopening the cut over Davila's eye and firing a flurry highlighted by two rights. A triple right uppercut sparked another Duarte salvo and suddenly Duarte appeared to be the fresher man. His punches were snappier than in previous rounds and Davila looked more concerned about the cut than about Duarte.

Davila went back to basics in the seventh as he worked Duarte's swelling with sharp jabs. But Davila's rally was short-lived as Duarte again forced a give-and-take battle on the inside.

With a minute remaining the fight took a pivotal turn. With both men leaning forward, the tops of their heads rubbed against one another and the clash created a horrible cut around the left eye that caused blood to cascade down Davila's cheek and onto his chest. Both men maintained a hard pace as Duarte sought to take advantage of his sudden good fortune and Davila tried to keep his opponent at arm's length.

As Davila walked to his corner, he lodged a brief complaint to Filippo to let him know that a butt caused the cut. Under a recently passed rule in California, the break between rounds was extended to give the doctor ample time to examine the cut while also giving the corner the time they need to administer treatment.

"Let it go for a while," Dr. Bernhardt Schwartz told Filippo. "But if it gets worse, tell me."

Duarte's chance to snatch victory was as plain as the blood on Davila's face and he came out throwing a long series of rights. Soon, thick dark crimson covered everything on his face from the left eye down and Duarte made it worse by popping in short shots on the inside. A tremendous right made Davila back away, and though Davila retained the sharpness of previous rounds it was Duarte's work rate that enabled him to win his third consecutive round. The last five seconds saw both fighters blasting away with furious flurries that belied both their relatively advanced ages and the punishment they had absorbed.

Davila's cut man John Montes Sr. worked hard to stem the bleeding but no matter how much treatment he administered, it couldn't be stopped. Had it not been such a meaningful fight for both men it would have been halted at the end of round seven, but Davila had fought so well that he deserved every benefit of the doubt – and Duarte in turn merited every opportunity to produce a conclusive finish.

Davila speared Duarte's face with jabs to start the ninth, snapping his head back and keeping far enough away to give the medicine a chance to take hold. But for Davila it was a race against time, physics and the willingness of those in charge to let the fight continue – and all three were in ever shrinking supply. Davila's face was such a gory sight that it made Duarte's lumping face look good by comparison.

The ringside physicians allowed the fight to continue into the 10th, and Davila was battling bravely through a number of deficits. But Duarte was in the midst of his trademark late surge and he appeared to cut deeply into Davila's early lead – no pun intended. But just as the fight was about to head into a dramatic homestretch, it was over.

During the fight's most sustained exchange, Filippo stepped in, formed the traditional signal for "time out" and escorted a disheartened Davila to his corner. Dr. Schwartz examined the cut and, after a brief consultation, the cut was deemed too dangerous. As Filippo walked over to Duarte and raised his right arm, a dejected Davila hung his head and walked toward the neutral corner. Though Duarte was announced as the TKO victor at the 2:09 mark, the real fight was just about to begin.

When the scene shifted to a lower floor at the Forum, Davila and his corner people issued a complaint to Marty Denkin, the assistant executive officer for the California State Athletic Commission. They said Davila's fight-ending cut was the result of a head butt and Denkin himself indicated as much at the end of the seventh round. Filippo, however, did not see the butt and because of that he didn't feel it necessary to consult the judges.

Denkin said California rules dictated that the referee poll the judges and Denkin made it known that he himself had talked to the judges – and each said they saw a butt. If Filippo had consulted the judges and if even one of them had seen a butt, that would have been the official ruling.

Denkin also said that the NABF didn't have a rule addressing this situation, but part of the agreement between California and the NABF stipulated that the state's regulations would be applied in situations the NABF rules didn't cover. So Denkin recommended that the commission reverse the result to a technical decision for Davila since he was ahead 87-83, 87-83 and 87-84 on the scorecards.

"I was worried about the cut, but I have a good cut man in John Montes," Davila told Prime Ticket broadcaster Rich Marotta after the fight. "I feel like the winner now and I feel I should have gotten all the glory there on national TV because I felt I won the fight. The cut was caused by a head butt, and being ahead I felt I should have won the fight. I honestly feel he doesn't feel in his heart that he won the fight, and I felt I got cheated out of it."

"I was really enthused right after the fight because I felt I was coming on," Duarte countered. "I felt, even though I was down in the fourth, by the 10th I felt I had everything in control so I had nothing but good feelings because I thought in the next couple of rounds I would definitely win those. Maybe then I would need a knockdown just to get the decision or possibly stop him.

"When I went to the press conference – not worrying about the scoring; I was the winner you know – I heard I was behind on points by a pretty good margin and then I got really crushed. I said 'awwww, man!' It took my wind away from me knowing that he was ahead on points."

When asked if he felt like it was a hollow victory, he said "yes, because I was unable to get to my best rounds. It was so typical of my fights: I would lose the early rounds and I come back after the guy wears down, then I completely take over. I was disappointed that the fans didn't get to see me at my best. People are coming up to me every day and tell me 'did you hear about this or that?' and I tell them 'don't tell me nothing about it. On the 17th when they give the decision, well, then, tell me about it.'"

Epilogue: The battle outside the ring raged for some time and it wasn't until July 17 that the issue was settled – sort of. The six-member California State Athletic Commission split 3-3, but because a seventh member was absent no determination was made and Duarte kept the title.

Despite Duarte being declared the winner, Davila got the first title shot. Following victories over Juan Jose Estrada (a three-round technical decision) and Gil Contreras (W 12), Davila received his rematch with Lora. Though Lora won a wide decision, the match was clouded by controversy as a bottle filled with sugar water was confiscated from Lora's corner midway through a fight that saw the champion tiring. Despite the apparent evidence, the WBC retained Lora as champion and Davila, just nine days short of his 33rd birthday, never fought again. He retired with a record of 56-10 (26 KO).

Duarte took one year and two days off before returning to the ring with a seventh round TKO of Ron Cisneros. A pair of 10-round decisions over Miguel Juarez and Jorge Ortega followed, and on August 31, 1989 Duarte received his long-awaited second shot at a title against WBC super bantamweight champion Daniel Zaragoza at the Forum. Just four days short of his 35th birthday, Duarte was too slow for the razor-sharp southpaw and after losing every round on two scorecards the fight was stopped in the 10th round. Duarte retired immediately after the fight, saying with a wry smile that he "needed to get a job." His record stands at 47-8-1 (34 KO).

UPSETS AND UNPREDICTABILITY – A WALK ON THE WILD SIDE

Total Punches Landed/Thrown

Round	1	2	3	4	5	6	7	8	9	10	11	12	Total
Duarte	21/66	40/112	50/120	42/136	33/124	47/144	36/143	40/157	35/113	36/109			380/1224
	32%	36%	42%	31%	27%	33%	25%	25%	31%	33%			31%
Davila	28/80	47/103	45/105	51/107	40/102	44/106	38/108	51/121	44/100	30/78			418/1010
	35%	46%	43%	48%	39%	42%	35%	42%	38%	38%			41%

Jabs Landed/Thrown

Round	1	2	3	4	5	6	7	8	9	10	11	12	Total
Duarte	12/43	13/48	12/45	7/33	8/39	11/43	8/49	7/37	10/41	7/29			95/407
	28%	27%	27%	21%	21%	26%	16%	19%	24%	24%			23%
Davila	18/56	22/54	24/61	25/56	18/57	19/56	26/64	15/48	30/70	13/38			210/560
	32%	41%	39%	45%	32%	34%	41%	31%	43%	34%			38%

Power Punches Landed/Thrown

Round	1	2	3	4	5	6	7	8	9	10	11	12	Total
Duarte	9/23	27/64	38/75	35/103	25/85	36/101	28/94	33/120	25/72	29/80			285/817
	39%	42%	51%	34%	29%	36%	30%	28%	35%	36%			35%
Davila	10/24	25/49	21/44	26/51	22/45	25/50	12/44	36/73	14/30	17/40			208/450
	42%	51%	48%	51%	49%	50%	27%	49%	47%	42%			46%

Frankie Duarte vs. Alberto Davila II June 27, 1987, Inglewood, California

TALES FROM THE VAULT

Freddie Pendleton vs. Tony Lopez
August 12, 1995, Las Vegas, Nevada

In most other sports, the playoffs represent the culmination of a team's season. The competitive intensity picks up game by game and round by round because of the shadow of finality that is always present: Win and move on, lose and go home.

For boxers, especially those at the highest levels, every fight has multiple levels of finality. First, the contest itself can end at any moment, for he or she is always a referee's count of 10 away from being eliminated. And second, the ultimate result has a direct effect on his standing in the sport. A victory can vault a fighter toward a big-money crack at a championship while a defeat relegates him to smaller cable shows and pushes his title chase back as many as two years – and that's the fate of someone who entered the bout just one step away from glory. For those who are farther away, a win means a step up the ladder while a defeat could signal the end of his life in the ring.

The pressure to perform in every single fight is immense, and in that sense boxing is a never-ending series of playoff situations. This constant shuffling of the deck is a key ingredient to boxing's ability to create unforgettable moments of drama.

On August 12, 1995 at the MGM Grand in Las Vegas, Freddie Pendleton and Tony Lopez found themselves at a career crossroads. The 32-year-old Pendleton (38-20-4 with 26 KO) was 18 months removed from his reign as IBF lightweight champion, which ended via decision following a brutal slugfest with rising star Rafael Ruelas. A 10-round loss to the 28-1 Giovanni Parisi made some observers think that the game had passed "Fearless Freddie" by, but he rebounded with three straight wins to vault himself back into the title picture. His most recent outing was a 10-round TKO over Darryl Tyson to win the USBA junior welterweight title four months earlier, and owning that regional belt meant a spot in the world rankings. For Pendleton, beating the charismatic Lopez – a champion at both junior lightweight and lightweight – would give him a mighty push toward another title shot.

For Lopez, also 32, the situation was more desperate. In his last fight nine months earlier, WBC super lightweight champion Julio Cesar Chavez stopped Lopez in 10 rounds, and the final rounds weren't good ones for "The Tiger" as Chavez methodically wore down his brave challenger. Lopez got the shot at the Mexican icon courtesy of a three-bout winning streak after he lost the WBA lightweight title to Dingaan Thobela and the highlight of that streak was a 10-round TKO over former IBF king Greg Haugen. Entering the Pendleton fight, Lopez had no such career capital at his disposal, so for him a victory was particularly paramount.

Pendleton, 140, always started his fights with a home run punch, usually an overhand right. On February 12, 1988 this tactic worked to perfection as fellow contender

Sammy Fuentes was polished off in just 15 seconds. From that point forward, it became a Pendleton trademark and such was the case this night against Lopez as he unleashed a huge hook. Though Lopez, 140, easily ducked under the punch, Pendleton had succeeded in sending a message of aggressive intent. But it was Lopez who was coming forward, forcing Pendleton to the ropes with a good left hook a few moments after countering a jab with an overhand right to the jaw.

Pendleton possessed edges in speed and power entering the fight and a little more than a minute into the round he exploited them to the fullest. Two quick jabs set up a booming overhand right that slammed off Lopez's ear. Upon impact, Lopez's legs quaked as if electricity was surging through them before they collapsed underneath him. Lopez fell hard to the canvas but he handled the crisis with a veteran's professionalism as he calmly took Mitch Halpern's eight count to collect himself before rising.

Meanwhile, Pendleton drew strength from Lopez's trouble and he went all out to cash in. He landed two strong hooks and a heavy right as Lopez propped himself on the ropes, then unleashed a 10-punch salvo before Lopez could manage a clinch. Pendleton continued his hot pursuit but Lopez slipped and deflected most of the blows before clamping on well-timed clinches. The moment it appeared that Lopez had fought his way out of the storm, Pendleton dragged him right back in. Another chopping right that grazed the temple caved in Lopez's legs and he fell for the second time. Again, Lopez coolly arose at four and surprisingly it was he that landed the first punch – a lead right – when the fight resumed. And again Pendleton pressed hard for the finish, missing most of his follow-up blows, though a hook in the final seconds broke through.

Chief second Al Bonanni tried to calm his warrior down between rounds, telling him "all I want you to do is stay short with those punches." It was good advice because his over-anxiousness might have prevented him from getting that much-desired quick stoppage.

Lopez began the second well as he drove Pendleton back with a right-left to the chin. But "Fearless Freddie" enjoyed an even better start as a short classic one-two decked Lopez for the third time. Lopez was up at Halpern's count of four but he would be down again seconds later, this time from a scorching hook to the jaw. Lopez shook his head in frustration as he got up at three. Though he appeared to be perfectly fine, his body could not withstand Pendleton's firepower. While the three-knockdown rule was not in effect, it was very likely that Halpern would stop the fight should Lopez go down again in this round. And this round had more than two minutes remaining.

Pendleton put the pedal to the metal as he rushed in behind a lead right and a hook to the body, but after seeing Lopez take the blows better, he throttled down his offense and began to work behind the jab. In this high-stakes game, Pendleton held all the cards. By dropping Lopez four times he had already demonstrated his superior power and because he established a huge cushion on the scorecards, the most likely way he would lose was by knockout. As the man who spent most of his career at lighter weights, it was unlikely that Lopez could produce the thunderbolt he needed.

Or could he?

After the second round ended quietly, Pendleton began the third in much the same fashion as he continually beat Lopez to the punch with his quicker, more potent blows. But Lopez would dramatically turn the tables a few moments after he leaped in behind a right-left that forced Pendleton toward the ropes. As Pendleton spun away, Lopez's one-two sent a shocked Pendleton to the floor. The crowd erupted at this turn of events, and in an instant a potential blowout was transformed into a seesaw struggle for survival.

Pendleton scurried to his feet and, anxious to turn the fight back his way, loaded up on every punch.

Meanwhile, Lopez was almost serene as he sized up the situation, landing an overhand right and a looping hook to the chin that caught a wide-eyed Pendleton. Lopez picked his spots like a true pro – a quick left here, a snappy one-two there, a leaping right-left-hook combo here and a well-timed clinch there – and he was making it all work. All the while, Lopez was building momentum and it was having its effect on the formerly dominant Pendleton. A pinpoint right to the jaw wobbled Pendleton and for the first time in the fight it was he who sought the safety of a clinch.

With mind-blowing dispatch, the fight was taking on the look of Aesop's fable "The Tortoise and the Hare." Pendleton, the hare, had benefited from a fast start but because Lopez had shown so much resourcefulness, he was now starting to flourish. The most famous line from the fable was "slow and steady wins the race" – and the question of the moment was this: could Lopez actually win this race?

Desperate to regain lost ground, Pendleton pelted Lopez with a triple jab to start the fourth, but Lopez's thumping hook to the body made him take a step back. While Pendleton was the faster fighter, he still had a reservoir of power at his disposal and he used it, pun intended, fearlessly. A pretty jab-right uppercut-left hook combo buckled Lopez's legs and had him hanging on. But even as Lopez sought the security of a clinch he nailed Pendleton with a hefty left-right that brought a cringing "ohhhh" from the crowd. Pendleton continued to load up and let go with no real concern as to whether his blows landed while the ring wise Lopez tried to ride out the storms that seemed to come in waves.

Moments after Halpern warned an overanxious Pendleton about hitting on the break, Pendleton planted his feet and unloaded a monstrous hook to the jaw. But instead of falling, Lopez incredibly crashed his own right to the jaw. Still, Pendleton roared after the "Tiger" and closed the round with yet another right to the head.

Pendleton may have had a huge lead on the scorecards, but the fight was still up for grabs due to the wildly unpredictable shifts in momentum. Despite his shaky start, Lopez proved his toughness by surviving and coming back with his own offensive. Other fighters who enjoyed quick starts such as Pendleton had against Lopez would have become discouraged when his opponent fought back, but the Fearless One's strong self-belief immunized him from any such feelings. After all, this was a man who overcame a 12-12-4 start to become IBF lightweight champion.

The fifth was a slightly slower round as both realized that a longer fight was not only a possibility but also a probability. Still, Pendleton rubberized Lopez's legs with a terrific double hook but Lopez hung on by borrowing a page from Archie Moore's play book as he used the "armadillo" defense – crossing his arms in front of him while hunching forward and rolling his upper body while firing rights over the top. One of those rights made Pendleton's legs dip, after which he spent the rest of the round circling away. Because Lopez outworked Pendleton over the last half of the round, he regained a modicum of momentum.

The pattern of the fifth continued in the sixth as Lopez lobbed in bombs that penetrated Pendleton's guard from all sides. He was particularly effective with hooks to the body followed by rights over the top while simultaneously blunting most of Pendleton's blows. With each passing second, this tortoise methodically broke down the hare with thudding, unglamorous shots. Lopez was enjoying his best, most consistent round as Pendleton had slowed just enough to be within the "Tiger's" range. A short right to the side of the head tagged Pendleton and a harder right nailed him several seconds later, but Pendleton reminded Lopez of the danger before him as he landed a crisp right as the bell sounded. Lopez's success in the sixth extended to the seventh as his ground game continued to thwart Pendleton's high-flying offense. A right to the jaw sent Pendleton to the ropes on somewhat unsteady legs and a jab-right-hook combo connected cleanly enough for Pendleton to seek a clinch. Lopez shook him off with a right that forced Pendleton to gallop toward ring center. Lopez tried to pursue his stricken quarry, but instead he fell into a clinch.

Back at ring center – and at close range – Lopez got the better of the exchanges and for the first time a look of concern crossed Pendleton's features. He had used plenty of gas in trying to put Lopez away and like the hare he was he was seeing his tortoise gaining ground. His worries were compounded after two heavy rights visibly shook Pendleton and a third closed Lopez's best round yet.

Entering the eighth, Pendleton still retained a lead on the strength of his four early knockdowns but it was clear his dominance was a thing of the past. There were still five rounds to be fought and given the flow of the fight it was conceivable that Lopez could still win a decision if he ran the table. Should Lopez pull it off, it would greatly advance his title hopes because of the storybook nature of his comeback. Conversely, Pendleton's career would suffer a significant setback, for few fighters ever built such a huge early advantage only to lose. It would have been the kind of defeat that would have been difficult to shake off mentally – and even tougher to shake off professionally. Instead of Lopez, who entered the fight perhaps one loss away from being a steppingstone for up-and-comers, it might be Pendleton who would wear that yoke.

Just as it was good news for Lopez that there were five rounds to build on his rally, it was good news for Pendleton that there were five rounds left to change his fate.

Did he ever.

A split-second after Lopez scored with a lunging hook, Pendleton missed with an equally lunging right. As an off-balance Lopez fell forward, Pendleton reset his feet and plowed in a crushing right to the point of the chin that snapped Lopez's head violently and instantly put Lopez in huge trouble. On numbed legs, Lopez staggered forward and managed to grab Pendleton around the waist. Following the break, Pendleton smashed an overhand right to the temple that set up a one-two that deepened Lopez's peril. Lopez tried to buy time by moving forward and grabbing Pendleton, but "Fearless Freddie" shook him off and delivered a final right to the ear. As Lopez stumbled across the ring, Halpern stepped in, grabbed Lopez and waved off the fight 43 seconds into the eighth round.

The stoppage was not well received. Lopez wore a disgusted expression and the MGM Grand crowd loudly voiced their displeasure at the sudden stoppage. It was a controversial end to what had been a thrilling and tumultuous fight, but that didn't matter to Pendleton and his celebrating corner men.

In the famous fable, slow and steady may have won the race. But then again, Aesop's hare didn't have a great right paw.

Epilogue: Due to the controversial ending, neither man's standing in the sport suffered. Seven months after losing to Pendleton, Lopez was given a crack at Charles Murray's NABF junior welterweight title in Murray's hometown of Rochester, N.Y. After losing a 12-round decision, Lopez managed to rebuild his career with five straight wins, including a three-round knockout of the 20-2-4 Jaime Ocegueda to win the WBO/NABO junior welterweight belt. But on February 20, 1999, four days short of his 36th birthday, Lopez lost the belt to Hector Quiroz by first-round knockout. Lopez never fought again and he retired with a record of 50-8-1 with 34 knockouts.

Five months after beating Lopez, Pendleton took out Ralph Southerland in one round and four months after that, Pendleton found himself across the ring from young, powerful IBF welterweight champion Felix Trinidad. Youth and strength would prevail as "Tito" bombed out Pendleton in five rounds.

Pendleton received two more opportunities to win major titles, failing both times. IBF junior welterweight king Vince Phillips stopped Pendleton in 10 while WBA welterweight champ James Page stopped him in 11. The final fight for the 38-year-old Pendleton took place October 27, 2001 at the M.E.N. Arena in Manchester, the home base of WBU junior welterweight champ Ricky Hatton. The 25-0 "Hit Man" blasted out Pendleton in two rounds, and "Fearless Freddie" retired with a record of 47-26-5 with 34 knockouts.

UPSETS AND UNPREDICTABILITY – A WALK ON THE WILD SIDE

Total Punches Landed/Thrown

Round	1	2	3	4	5	6	7	8	9	10	11	12	Total
Pendleton	24/89	13/68	12/60	25/93	21/60	21/66	10/53	6/18					132/507
	27%	19%	20%	27%	35%	32%	19%	33%					26%
Lopez	7/19	13/33	25/59	11/35	24/57	23/52	22/60	2/6					127/321
	37%	39%	42%	31%	42%	44%	37%	33%					40%

Jabs Landed/Thrown

Round	1	2	3	4	5	6	7	8	9	10	11	12	Total
Pendleton	9/45	7/51	4/30	7/55	10/34	9/38	4/27	2/10					52/290
	20%	14%	13%	13%	29%	24%	15%	20%					18%
Lopez	1/3	6/13	6/21	4/9	5/22	5/16	2/7	1/2					30/93
	33%	46%	29%	44%	23%	31%	29%	50%					32%

Power Punches Landed/Thrown

Round	1	2	3	4	5	6	7	8	9	10	11	12	Total
Pendleton	15/44	6/17	8/30	18/38	11/26	12/28	6/26	4/8					80/217
	34%	35%	27%	47%	42%	43%	23%	50%					37%
Lopez	6/16	7/20	19/38	7/26	19/35	18/36	20/53	1/4					97/228
	38%	35%	50%	27%	54%	50%	38%	25%					43%

Freddie Pendleton vs. Tony Lopez August 12, 1995, Las Vegas, Nevada

TALES FROM THE VAULT

Paul Whittaker vs. Don Lee
June 19, 1989, Metairie, Louisiana

People find sports attractive for a variety of reasons. They provide action, competition, inspiration and amusement while also offering a microcosm of the human experience. We all can relate to the joys of victory and the disappointments of defeat because we've already experienced them on a smaller scale. We also form connections with certain individuals whose backgrounds and personalities strike a chord within ourselves.

Boxing is the most personal of sports because of its intense one-on-one nature. During the course of combat we can observe how a fighter carries himself over a wide range of situations. Many times what we see provides a reflection of a person's character: When he faces adverse situations, does he summon the courage to attack them head-on or does he look for an escape hatch? How does he deal with frustration? When things are going well, does he symbolically put his foot on his opponent's throat and finish the job or is he content to coast to a decision victory? If he has an opponent one punch away from doom, does he have the cold-blooded viciousness to pull the trigger or does he show mercy? Patterns develop over time, and the answers to those questions determine how fighters are perceived by fans and remembered by historians.

Then there are those situations for which no one can possibly prepare. Emotions that are usually kept in check can erupt with startling unpredictability and the resulting chaos can even spread into the audience. The smoldering, but healthy, cauldron of tension encouraged by boxing can instantly be transformed to a dangerous, life-threatening inferno. The riots sparked by the events of the first bout between Riddick Bowe and Andrew Golota is just one example of how perilous the emotional line boxing walks can be.

When Paul Whittaker challenged NABF super middleweight champion "Dangerous" Don Lee June 29, 1989 in Metairie, Louisiana, nobody could have anticipated just how dangerous the environment would get. It was a fight that had everything a fan – and a psychologist – could want.

Lee had the physique and record to back up his nickname. At 6-2, he was a long, lean southpaw armed with a 76-inch reach and a dynamite left cross. His 27 knockouts in 31 victories showed he could hit, but because all four of his losses came by knockout, he showed he could also be hit. Three of those losses, however, came to contenders Michael Olajide, Michael Watson and Jeff Harding, and Lee entered the Whittaker fight on a four fight win streak capped by a 12-round decision over Sanderline Williams to capture the vacant NABF belt.

While Lee was the champion, the presence of Whittaker (22-2 with 17 KO) was what attracted an enthusiastic full house to Metairie's Landmark Hotel. The native of

Metairie began his pro career with 17 consecutive knockouts, 13 of which occurred in the first two rounds. The knockout frequency, of course, throttled down when the competition was stepped up, but he still had good wins over Barry Audia (W 10), Lee Sanders (KO 6) and Mike Sacchetti (W 10). His only two losses came to Wilfred Benitez (L 10) and Matthew Hilton (KO by 4), but he entered the Lee fight off a solid 10-round win over Knox Brown three months earlier.

The thickly built Whittaker stood a full five inches shorter and he had the additional deficit of never having faced a southpaw as a pro. Conversely, Lee felt the pressure of defending his belt in his opponent's hometown before a hostile audience, and a defeat would deal a mortal blow to his title hopes.

Lee began the fight working jabs and one-twos while Whittaker bulled his way inside behind lead rights to the head and body – and a well-placed head or two. Once in close range, Whittaker deftly locked Lee's left arm while working over the body with a succession of quick hooks.

With one minute remaining, a moment after landing a right to the body, Whittaker connected with a looping lead right that sent Lee crashing to the canvas and the crowd onto its feet. Up at five, it was clear that Lee's historically questionable chin would again play a factor and Whittaker rushed in to finish the job. After absorbing a head butt underneath the jaw, Lee proceeded to do a good job smothering Whittaker by locking down an arm and laying his upper body on his opponent's shoulders for the rest of the round.

Lee's chief second Delanis Hammond sought to reassure his charge.

"That was a flash knockdown, OK?" he said. "You were standing around a little too much. I don't want you in that corner on the ropes. Don't aim at his head, now aim at his chest. If you miss with the left hand, come back with the right hand, understand? Keep him on the end of what you're throwing."

Lee started the second throwing easily timed half-speed jabs, and Whittaker took advantage by landing another looping right that floored Lee for a seven count. Again, Lee survived by smothering the shorter Whittaker, who depended entirely on singular bombs because he was too anxious to string together combinations.

Lee was searching for an answer to counteract the rampaging Whittaker. Lee briefly switched to the orthodox stance, but was jolted back to lefty by yet another right to the jaw. Then, in the late stages of the round, an answer showed itself. He caught Whittaker coming in with a flurry that included a solid left uppercut. The blow stunned Whittaker and Lee connected with a second one a few moments later.

Between rounds, Whittaker's trainer/manager Les Bonano noticed that his charge breathing far heavier than the action suggested. Bonano saw that the tide was beginning to turn for Lee despite being down four points.

"Calm down," he said. "You see, you're nervous. You're not right. You sparred better than you're doing right now. I want you to relax."

Though Lee still threw jabs that lacked snap, his left uppercuts carried full power – and he was hitting the target again and again. A left uppercut-jab-left uppercut-right combo drove Whittaker back and had him holding on for the first time early in the third. After shaking Whittaker loose, Lee smacked a left cross that sent Whittaker stumbling off balance. Whittaker's face was red and a swelling and cut kept his left eye company. Two more left uppercuts smashed through and a left cross to the face snapped back Whittaker's head.

Fueled by adrenaline, Lee let his hands go like a threshing machine and he landed with dizzying rapidity. Whittaker desperately sought to get inside Lee's long arms, charging behind looping punches and one stray head to the chest. Whittaker bulled Lee to the ropes with a right to the torso, but Lee slammed in a pair of snappy left uppercuts. The cut on Whittaker's face grew deeper and larger and the blood seemed to energize both men as they traded fiercely along the ropes. A left cross hurt Whittaker, who broke off the exchange with a grimace on his face. A brilliant comeback round for Lee closed with a whistling left uppercut-right hook-left uppercut to the face.

Seeing his warrior badly hurt and stumbling on weakened legs, Bonano broke out the verbal whip.

"Get that f*****g look off your face," Bonano said to a discouraged Whittaker. "God d**n it, you're in a war with this guy. But if you want to win it, you gotta go take it. You're losing your concentration. You're got to make up your mind and deny it in your mind. You've got to be inside and I don't want to see that look on your face. I want you to say, '*I want to get this m**********r.*' I want you to bang him but you've got to get close enough so he can't hurt you."

A rejuvenated Lee bounced out of his corner in the fourth and snapped three jabs before delivering yet another left uppercut. A second one landed during a flurry and Whittaker stumbled back before crumbling to the canvas. A pumped-up Lee then got in three light punches to the head before stepping away. Whatever hurt Whittaker may have felt was replaced with anger as he jumped to his feet and glared at Lee. Though the crowd booed loudly at the obvious foul, referee Lucien Joubert did not issue a warning.

Whittaker sought to crowd Lee, and, still furious over the foul, he put a little more mustard on his bullying tactics by putting his head underneath Lee's chin and hitting him on the break. A lead overhand right snapped Lee's head and he followed up with a right uppercut and a looping left to the ear. Lee responded with his pet punch, the left uppercut, and the two tore at one another with both hands at close range.

Whittaker stepped away from one exchange with a nasty cut at the corner of the right eye and the blood clearly bothered him as he blinked and repeatedly wiped it away with his glove. Another left uppercut wobbled Whittaker, but Lee wasn't able to follow up as both engaged in gratuitous grappling and mauling. As the round closed, the right side of Whittaker's face was a bloody mess.

The wrestling continued into the fifth, but Lee's left uppercuts continued to pierce Whittaker's face and his peppering flurries on the inside kept Whittaker busy on defense. Another big left cross drove Whittaker back several feet and it became clear that the local hero could not fight effectively while on the retreat. Still, Whittaker had a firm grip on his warrior's heart as he beckoned Lee to "come on" after fielding a right-left to the body. Lee responded by doing just that: Belting him with a left cross to the face, stabbing him with jabs and whipping in even harder punches with more accuracy.

The crowd looked to pick up Whittaker's spirits by chanting "Paul! Paul! Paul!" but it was doing little good as Lee kept up the pressure. Soon the hot pace slackened slightly and they fell into several clinches to recharge their batteries.

With 17 seconds left in the round, Lee connected with a powerful left uppercut that prompted Whittaker to voluntarily take a knee. Lee then unleashed two punches – a right and a left – on the fallen Whittaker. This was the second time Lee hit Whittaker while he was down. Once can be chalked up to an overabundance of emotion. Twice signals more sinister motives. Referee Joubert glared at Lee as he ordered him to a neutral corner, then proceeded to issue a point penalty after administering the mandatory eight count.

"I can't understand how a veteran of over 30 fights can lose his head that way when he's winning the fight," observed SportsChannel America analyst Wally Matthews. Neither could anyone else in the arena.

Lee went for the finish in the sixth with short combinations while Whittaker held on for survival. He continually gunned in left uppercuts in search of the one that would put the Louisiana lad away. A long solid, left cross capped off a flurry and drove Whittaker to the ropes. Joubert warned Lee for holding behind the head as he lined up Whittaker for another left uppercut.

Whittaker was in a bad state. His face was bloody and his legs were wobbly. The two knockdowns he scored in the first two rounds seemed like a distant memory. His competitive drive was the only thing keeping him on his feet and that was what commanded him to lash out with wild, inaccurate blows.

With 1:13 to go, with Whittaker stumbling forward, Lee stepped back and drilled in a left uppercut, a right hand and a huge left cross that sent Whittaker to the floor for the second time in the round. And for the second time in the round – and the third time in the contest – Lee struck the fallen Whittaker with a chopping left to the face. An enraged Whittaker tried to hit Lee with a backhanded right, but the punch ended up hitting Joubert in the stomach as he pulled Lee away.

"Lee hits him again!" Matthews yelled, his voice cracking in exasperation. "This is crazy and he should be disqualified!"

The scene inside the arena was spiraling into chaos. Whittaker jumped to his feet, popped out his mouthpiece and glared at Lee with a mixture of rage and bewilderment. Bonano climbed into the ring to protest to Joubert while the crowd hurled programs, plastic cups and crumpled pieces of paper into the ring. Ringsiders reached under the ropes to remove the bigger items as the fighters continued the contest.

"There's so much debris in the ring it's not safe," Matthews declared. "I don't know what they're doing in this state. The referee has no control of this fight. The commission has no control of it. These men are fighting with papers and cups in the ring. I've never seen anything like this!"

Meanwhile, Lee was whaling away at Whittaker, who was bent over nearly double along the ropes. A final right hook sent Whittaker slumping to the canvas with 11 seconds remaining. For all intents and purposes, that should have been the crowning moment for Lee as he had just scored what would have been a fight-ending third knockdown of the round. But for the third time in the round – and an incredible fourth time in the fight – Lee stood over Whittaker, took aim and planted a left cross to the head.

All hell proceeded to break loose, both in the ring and out. Bonano stood on the ring apron as Whittaker walked disgustedly toward him. More debris, beer spray and cascades of boos showered the ring and someone in the crowd even tried to throw a chair into the squared circle. As the scene spiraled out of control, Bonano shifted his focus from his own anger to crowd control as he walked into the ring and gestured for the throng to stop.

"The ring is so littered with paper cups, it looks like a parking lot after a tailgate party," Matthews declared as the incensed crowd chanted obscenities.

The bell had sounded amid this tumult and Joubert, his shirt stained with blood and other liquids hurled by the crowd, calmly walked to each of the judges and collected their scorecards. He then leaned over to consult with NABF representative Duane Ford. Shortly thereafter, the fight was stopped and Whittaker was declared the new champion, which turned the anger into full-throated cheers.

"We have a rule on continual dirty fouling which is flagrant," Ford told Matthews afterward. "The referee took three points and came over and said 'can we disqualify him?' I said 'if it's your decision, you're well within it.' He disqualified him."

When Whittaker was asked if it was satisfying to win the belt in this manner, he said, "yes it is, because I felt he was being a little unfair there. He was holding behind my head and hitting me with that left uppercut he throws. That's one of his best punches. Then he hits me four or five times when I was on the ground, some good clean shots that I wasn't even expecting. I thought the referee would be in there. I mean, fight fair, let's go. We have 12 rounds to go. What happened, happened and I'm the champion now."

While Whittaker basked in his triumph, Lee was left to explain the inexplicable.

"It wasn't emotion, it was a flow of punches," Lee said. "We trained to do a lot of series of punches, and before I could run the series of punches off Paul would go down and I had to catch myself to keep from hitting him as I stopped. It was too late, the guy was down on the floor already."

Then he shifted to three other excuses: Lack of motivation, lack of vision and his opponent's fouling.

"Paul did everything to win and I had nothing to win," Lee said. "I come here to his hometown, so it was a thing where I tried to execute and I didn't know the guy was down until the referee stepped in. I feel the disqualification was unjustified because the referee should have taken total command of stepping right in between Paul Whittaker and myself and pushed us completely back and pulled us apart. I was told not to break and let the referee do his job and that's what I did. For the first couple of rounds, he intentionally hit me low, but I kept to my main strategy. I don't think I would get a fair shake because I was coming to his hometown and I knew he had the edge on me."

Lee tried to conjure up a suitable explanation for his actions, but one thing was painfully clear: For one night in a boxing ring in Metairie, Lee had lost all reason. Hitting an opponent not once, not twice, but four times while he is on the canvas, each time appearing as if it was premeditated, defies all logic. The negative energy created by Lee's acts rippled throughout the arena, pushing the crowd's anger far beyond the bounds of decorum. This toxic and perilous situation was diffused when cooler, sober heads rendered the only sensible decision that could have been made.

Passions run deep in boxing and sometimes one's passion for victory can overrun a person's common sense. But in the end, order was restored and justice had prevailed.

Epilogue: The 29-year-old Lee would fight just once more as a professional as he won a 10-round decision over Keith McMurray in his adopted hometown of Milwaukee on November 13, 1989. He retired with a record of 32-5-2 with 27 knockouts.

As for Whittaker, he would fight only four more times over the next 17 months. He successfully defended his NABF title by ninth round KO over Nicky Walker to earn a shot at WBA super middleweight champion Christophe Tiozzo in Arles, France on July 20, 1990. The 26-0 Tiozzo won virtually every round before stopping Whittaker in eight rounds.

Whittaker returned to the ring quickly, scoring a one-round KO over Charlie Brooks less than two months after the Tiozzo defeat. Whittaker then followed up with an NABF title defense against Randall Yonker in Mobile, Ala., on November 13, 1990, but Whittaker was stopped in four rounds. He then retired with a record of 26-4 (21 KO).

TALES FROM THE VAULT

Total Punches Landed/Thrown

Round	1	2	3	4	5	6	7	8	9	10	11	12	Total
Whittaker	18/45	23/56	14/58	11/44	13/31	14/43							93/277
	40%	41%	24%	25%	42%	33%							34%
Lee	12/77	16/88	35/126	28/113	34/105	40/102							165/611
	16%	18%	28%	25%	32%	39%							27%

Jabs Landed/Thrown

Round	1	2	3	4	5	6	7	8	9	10	11	12	Total
Whittaker	2/10	5/16	6/19	2/11	2/8	2/3							19/67
	20%	31%	32%	18%	25%	67%							28%
Lee	6/48	6/48	4/40	7/44	13/43	9/30							45/253
	12%	12%	10%	16%	30%	30%							18%

Power Punches Landed/Thrown

Round	1	2	3	4	5	6	7	8	9	10	11	12	Total
Whittaker	16/35	18/40	8/39	9/33	11/23	12/40							74/210
	46%	45%	21%	27%	48%	30%							35%
Lee	6/29	10/40	31/86	21/69	21/62	31/72							120/358
	21%	25%	36%	30%	34%	43%							34%

Paul Whittaker vs. Don Lee June 19, 1989, Metairie, Louisiana

UPSETS AND UNPREDICTABILITY – A WALK ON THE WILD SIDE

Lee Roy Murphy vs. Chisanda Mutti
October 19, 1985, Monte Carlo, Monaco

No one can be sure what will happen when two boxers climb inside the ropes and do battle. While the object of the sport – victory – is ever constant, the route getting there can assume a nearly limitless number of forms. Even casual observers have seen the usual fare – decisions and knockouts – while more seasoned viewers have seen disqualifications, corner retirements, Fan Man interruptions and much more.

But few fights have ever produced an ending the likes of what happened on October 19, 1985 in Louis II Stadium in Monte Carlo when IBF cruiserweight champion Lee Roy Murphy defended his belt against Chisanda Mutti. It was a conclusion that stretched the bounds of reality and overshadowed what remains one of the greatest fights in divisional history.

The 27-year-old Murphy (22-0, 19 KO) was defending the belt he won via 14th round TKO of Marvin Camel for the second time while the 21-4-2 (15 KO) Mutti, 28, was making his first attempt at world honors. These were two men who had followed divergent paths to get to this point. Murphy was a decorated amateur who amassed a 157-17 record, winning the 1979 Golden Gloves at light heavyweight and earning a spot on the 1980 Olympic Team. But any dreams of gold were snuffed out when President Jimmy Carter ordered a boycott of the Moscow games to protest the Soviet Union's invasion of Afghanistan. This action prevented him – as well as teammates Richard Sandoval, Jackie Beard, Bernard Taylor, Joe Manley, Johnny Bumphus, Donald Curry, James Shuler, Charles Carter and James Broad – from showcasing their skills before a worldwide audience. They were also denied the opportunity to turn pro with the same network TV fanfare and financial reward bestowed upon members of the legendary 1976 American squad.

Instead, Murphy was relegated to building up his record around his hometown of Chicago. While he initially campaigned as a light heavyweight, the cruiserweight division promised a quicker route to a title shot. That career path paid off marvelously when he stopped Camel, and he solidified his claim to divisional supremacy by stopping Young Joe Louis (KO 12) in his first defense.

Mutti, a native of Zambia, had to come up the hard way, both in life and in boxing. Mutti was knocked out in nine rounds by Frank Lucas in his pro debut, and, depending on which source one consults, he lost a 15 round decision to top middleweight contender Tony Sibson in either his fourth or 16th pro fight. While he bowled over lesser competition, he was hot and cold when he stepped up. He lost a pair of fights to Lotte Mwale (KO by 13, L 12) but fought future cruiserweight champion Jeff Lampkin to a 10 round draw and defeated Jerry Celestine (KO 5) and future title challenger Tom

Collins (W 8). He also entered the Murphy fight on a three-bout winning streak, with the victory over Collins being his most recent effort.

Murphy, 190, took the fight to the challenger early, backing him up with sharp right-lefts over Mutti's long jabs while also successfully cutting the distance between himself and the 188-pound challenger. He landed by far the harder and more accurate blows because he was able to slip underneath and effectively fire out of his crouch. Later in the round, Murphy's jab came into play as three of them snapped back the Zambian's head. Despite Mutti's strong one-two in the final minute, the first stanza clearly belonged to the champion.

The pattern continued in the opening moments of the second, but Mutti then served notice that he wouldn't be an easy mark as a snappy jab-hook-cross combo made Murphy grimace and back away. A left uppercut followed by a chopping right to the jaw buckled the champion's legs and a second right drove Murphy to the ropes. A hook-right forced Murphy to cover up, and Mutti blasted away with both hands. But instead of gunning for the knockout, Mutti methodically and purposefully picked his spots, showing the composure of an aspiring champion. Mutti smartly jabbed to the stomach to set up three overhand rights to the jaw, and after Murphy escaped from the ropes, Mutti bombed a hook to the ribs, a right to the jaw and a double hook to the head.

Murphy powered his way back to ring center and tried to launch a counterattack but his swings only disturbed the air as Mutti dashed away. Late in the round the pair exchanged hard jabs but just as the first round belonged to Murphy, the second was unquestionably Mutti's. At the bell, Murphy extended his glove in respect but Mutti slapped at it only grudgingly.

Told by his corner to "give him no room," Murphy came forward and found pay dirt with two jabs, a right and a cuffing hook in the opening moments of the third. Murphy also found the range with his jab as it regularly bounced off Mutti's face. But the challenger soon maneuvered Murphy to the ropes and cracked an overhand right along with another one a few seconds later at ring center. Each man mightily tried to impose the successful strategies employed in the first two rounds and the result was a fast-paced battle saturated with clean power punches set up by solid fundamentals. It was a fight that had something for both the connoisseur and the caveman that resides in every boxing fan, and with each passing second the pace and action gradually escalated past the norms of big men.

The normally staid crowd was riveted by the back-and-forth action as they continually buzzed and cheered whatever big punches found the target. An overhand right lead by Mutti got a rousing reaction and a second one snapped Murphy's head back. As Murphy rested on the ropes, Mutti dug hooks to the head and body and ripped a right to the side of the face. Murphy temporarily held him off with a right uppercut-left hook combination, but Mutti poked in a pair of jabs and followed them with a solid hook. A long overhand right nailed Murphy, igniting a fusillade of punches as Murphy leaned against the ropes. But Murphy still had enough of a response within him to convince the challenger to throttle down his attack for the final moments of the round.

Murphy began the fifth strongly as he jabbed repeatedly to Mutti's stomach and followed with a long right to the body. As he was doing so, however, Mutti made him pay with a stiff hook to the jaw. Despite the punishment he absorbed early in the fight, Murphy withstood it with oak-like solidity, and he sought to further prove his durability by dancing on his toes and firing hard jabs.

As Murphy retreated to the ropes, Mutti nailed him with an overhand right but Murphy fought his way out of trouble with more stiff jabs to the belly. A wicked right and a follow-up hook pushed Murphy to the ropes but this time the champion gave as good as he got instead of letting Mutti tee off on him.

Still, Mutti was more than capable of dishing out punishment for as long as Murphy wanted to take it. Three hooks and a right caught Murphy and another right-left-right rattled his head. A one-two to the jaw buckled Murphy's knees moments later, after which he cranked hooks and rights to the head and body. Murphy proved rawhide tough as he continued to work behind his jab, landing enough of them to convince Mutti he was not yet ready to be taken.

The pair picked up the pace in the sixth, but Mutti again got the better of it as a pair of solid rights had him wavering to the safety of the ropes. Mutti tore into the champion for several harrowing moments but Murphy's stubbornness enabled him to endure and weather the wave. With the surge passed, Mutti was content to pick away with well-chosen bombs as Murphy tried to roll away and block the blows while punching just enough to keep Mutti honest. Late in the round they moved to ring center to exchange on the inside but a rippling right prompted the champ to again move to the ropes for the balance of the session.

Murphy, sensing he was falling far behind on the scorecards, ratcheted up the aggression in the seventh as he plowed inside behind two rights to the ribs and snapping jabs when he darted to long range. Encouraged by his success, Murphy switched gears by going on his toes and gunning a right-left to the jaw and a light overhand right. The nonplussed Mutti took everything in stride and kept finding opportunities for his jabs and singular rights again and again. But any thoughts of a Murphy rally turned instantly with a pair of spring-loaded lead rights and a hook-right uppercut combo.

The champ repeated his pattern of going to the ropes whenever he found himself in difficulty, but this time Mutti continued to rip away with a wide array of punches to every available open spot. Murphy eventually worked his way off the ropes and pushed forward, catching Mutti with a long lead right and wobbling Mutti slightly with a hook to the jaw. Mutti kept up the pressure by connecting with a right-left-right shortly before the bell.

The crowd heartily applauded the action, and why not? For a division originally created to accommodate too-fat light heavys and too-small heavyweights, this fight represented the best of both worlds – the power of the big boys and the speed of the smaller men. Both combatants were intent on inflicting damage in the eighth and both succeeded as they teed off on each other and continually traded the momentum. Neither man made much of an effort to evade the incoming bombs as they concentrated on loading up and letting the bullets scatter wherever they may.

But as evenly contested as the eighth was, that's how lopsided the ninth was. A sweeping hook stunned Murphy and made his body sway dangerously to the side. A follow-up nine-punch barrage persuaded Mutti that his time to become a champion had arrived and he pursued the crown like a hungry lion does with his choice of prey. With Murphy teetering on the ropes, Mutti unloaded 23 unanswered blows before the champion could conjure a reply.

Soon, the accumulated punishment became too much for even the stout hearted Murphy to bear without a break. A triple hook followed by a one-two staggered Murphy and caused him to turn away toward the ropes. Two cuffing hooks finally sent the champ crashing hard to the canvas, and Murphy, trying to regain his bearings on all fours, slowly rose at referee Larry Hazzard's count of eight. A monstrous right and two hooks spun Murphy's head and another chopping right found the temple. Murphy attempted to bull his way inside but the thicket of punches was too much to penetrate at first. Only when Mutti slowed his attack did Murphy secure a saving but clumsy clinch.

Mutti again drove Murphy back with a four-punch flurry and it appeared the champ was running on fumes. A right and two hooks slammed home and a follow-up seven-punch salvo had him on the edge of extinction. It was by far the most convincing round by either man, and thoughts of a title change ran rampant.

Murphy knew he was in mortal danger of losing his crown, but he had enough resourcefulness to go back to what worked in the past. As the 10th opened, Murphy returned to jabbing to the body to soften up his foe, and just like before the ploy worked. Mutti, though a bit winded from his gigantic effort in the ninth, plowed forward and nailed Murphy with big punches. A huge right sent Murphy backing across the ring, but the champ recovered quickly with several jabs, a sharp cross and a right uppercut-left hook combo.

Neither man knew it at the time, but a big turning point was at hand as Murphy's tenacity was about to pay off in a dramatic way.

An overhand right and a cuffing hook sent Mutti falling into the ropes, and suddenly Mutti had the look of a wooden fighter. Though he was still firing away, his punches lacked their earlier precision and he no longer made the effort to execute defensive moves. Somehow, although Mutti had dished out far more punishment, the grueling pace had more of an effect on him than on Murphy.

Murphy started the 11th jabbing to the belly, which set up a jolting left-right-hook to the jaw that sent Mutti staggering across the ring. Mutti was tiring and Murphy knew it, but the challenger still had enough in the tank to stand and trade at ring center, and he was only slightly getting the worst of it. Mutti tried to breathe new life in his legs by bouncing up and down but a huge hook and a right cross did more to lift the challenger's spirits.

With startling speed Mutti had reclaimed a measure of momentum as he landed two jabs, three hooks, two rights, a left uppercut and a final right. But just like before, Murphy waited for Mutti to wind down before launching his own counterattack. And what an attack it would be.

It began with a counter right cross and a right uppercut and it ended with Mutti on the floor from a combination punch-trip. Hazzard counted the fall as a knockdown and Mutti made it to his feet by eight. Murphy went for it all and had Mutti all but out along the ropes. Mutti leaned way back on the ropes and summoned the will not only to stay on his feet, but also to fire back.

Murphy was too strong for Mutti to hold off for long. A one-two and a double right snapped Mutti's head after which the champion moved in for the kill. Mutti again turned the tables when a hook and a right to the temple made Murphy slump into the ropes. Both men stood on the precipice of victory and defeat simultaneously, each just a punch or two away from ending the fight, and as the bell rang Mutti had trouble finding his corner while Murphy trudged toward his. With four rounds remaining, this already action-packed bout was building toward a dramatic crescendo.

Murphy began the 12th by getting into Mutti's chest but Mutti retreated to long range and just missed with a weary right to the head. Mutti's blows lacked steam, but his heart continued to propel him forward. Murphy answered a Mutti right with his own right and moved back toward the corner pad in the challenger's corner. As Mutti closed in, Murphy landed a scorching right uppercut, after which they exchanged a pair of hooks and crosses.

Each was playing a dangerous game of "can you top this" as they traded at a furious pace while never straying far from the corner. A cuffing right threw Mutti off balance and a pair of jabs popped into Mutti's face.

And then it happened – one of the strangest yet most exciting ends ever seen in championship annals.

Mutti leaped at Murphy with a left and delivered a concussive right to the jaw. At that precise moment Murphy curled a side-winding right that caught Mutti perfectly on the point of the chin. Upon impact, Murphy's body slumped into the corner pad while Mutti's fell forward and then behind Murphy. The weight of Mutti's body pushed Murphy to the right and Mutti tried to keep himself upright by reaching out for Murphy. Instead both men fell to the floor along the ropes with Mutti landing atop Murphy before sliding to the floor.

In short, both men had just scored a legitimate knockdown of the other and found themselves a 10 count away from a double knockout.

Hazzard positioned himself between both men and began to count. Midway through, he used both hands to toll the count over each man while also moving his head side to side to keep tabs on both men's progress. Murphy got to his feet at seven and stood in Mutti's corner, after which Hazzard turned his attention to Mutti, who was still on all fours. But the challenger could rise no further and at the moment Hazzard reached "ten," he waved the fight over with an appropriately dramatic flourish. At 1:53 of round 12, Murphy had retained his championship just seconds after suffering his own knockdown. And Murphy needed this miracle, for he trailed by three, four and four points on the scorecards entering the 12th round.

The movie "Rocky II" saw Rocky Balboa win the heavyweight title from Apollo Creed in this very same manner, and at the time critics blasted Sylvester Stallone's screenplay for what they saw as an unrealistic and overly melodramatic conclusion. And now, half a world and half a decade later, this incredible scenario played itself out in actual championship competition, with the only difference being that the champion kept his crown instead of losing it.

The wonders of boxing, no matter how long the sport is permitted to exist, will never cease, and Murphy-Mutti is just another example of just how right that is.

Epilogue: Exactly six months after stopping Mutti, Murphy broke open an even fight with Dorcey Gaymon to win via ninth round KO. Six months later, the Murphy magic ran out as Rickey Parkey stopped him in round 10. Murphy never again fought for a title, and he retired at age 40 after launching a two-fight comeback in 1998 that saw him notch a pair of wins. His record stands at 30-4 with 23 knockouts.

Mutti's stirring challenge of Murphy earned him a fight with rising star Evander Holyfield five months later, but "The Real Deal" dispatched Mutti in three rounds. Mutti qualified for a shot at Parkey's IBF crown by knocking out Dave Russell in 11 rounds to win the Commonwealth title, and though Mutti again mounted a stiff challenge Parkey won in the 12th. Mutti went 1-3 in his next four fights before ending his career with a 12 round draw with Joseph Poto on July 1, 1989 at age 32. His career record is 23-9-3 with 17 knockouts.

UPSETS AND UNPREDICTABILITY – A WALK ON THE WILD SIDE

Total Punches Landed/Thrown

Round	1	2	3	4	5	6	7	8	9	10	11	12	Total
Murphy	26/67	14/67	32/88	13/64	24/64	14/50	28/67	21/62	9/36	32/57	35/69	21/44	269/735
	39%	21%	36%	20%	38%	28%	42%	34%	25%	56%	51%	48%	37%
Mutti	16/50	33/71	29/78	30/74	37/64	42/82	27/73	26/68	48/101	38/69	26/75	17/45	369/850
	32%	46%	37%	41%	58%	51%	37%	38%	48%	55%	35%	38%	43%

Jabs Landed/Thrown

Round	1	2	3	4	5	6	7	8	9	10	11	12	Total
Murphy	16/45	8/45	16/53	8/45	19/48	4/25	14/34	8/38	3/16	19/35	9/21	6/15	130/420
	36%	18%	30%	18%	40%	16%	41%	21%	19%	54%	43%	40%	31%
Mutti	7/29	11/30	11/41	11/40	18/37	14/32	8/41	8/32	7/22	21/44	4/16	4/13	124/377
	24%	37%	27%	28%	49%	44%	20%	25%	32%	48%	25%	31%	33%

Power Punches Landed/Thrown

Round	1	2	3	4	5	6	7	8	9	10	11	12	Total
Murphy	10/22	6/22	16/35	5/19	5/16	10/25	14/33	13/24	6/20	13/22	26/48	15/29	139/315
	45%	27%	46%	26%	31%	40%	42%	54%	30%	59%	54%	52%	44%
Mutti	9/21	22/41	18/37	19/34	19/27	28/50	19/32	18/36	41/79	17/25	22/59	13/32	245/473
	43%	54%	49%	56%	70%	56%	59%	50%	52%	68%	37%	41%	52%

Lee Roy Murphy vs. Chisanda Mutti October 19, 1985, Monte Carlo, Monaco

★ Chapter 10 ★
BACK FROM THE BRINK – GREAT COMEBACKS

TALES FROM THE VAULT

Danny Lopez vs. Juan Malvarez
September 15, 1978, New Orleans, Louisiana

Over the course of history, a number of boxers have earned the label "television fighter." They came in all shapes, sizes and styles. For instance, Chuck Davey was a slick southpaw whose boxing skills and long unbeaten streak drew in the men while his good looks and college education attracted the ladies. Aggressors like Ralph "Tiger" Jones and Bob Satterfield were consistent crowd-pleasers while Gaspar Ortega and Chico Vejar could be counted on to provide longer, entertaining fights that would allow more commercials to be shown.

Some of them achieved true greatness – Sugar Ray Robinson, Carmen Basilio, Emile Griffith, Willie Pep, Kid Gavilan, Sandy Saddler and many more made boxing one of the most popular sports in America during the 1950s and 1960s. In the 1970s and 1980s, Roberto Duran, Carlos Zarate, Ray Mancini, Bobby Czyz, Frank "The Animal" Fletcher, Marvin Johnson and Matthew Saad Muhammad were among those who provided many thrilling moments. In recent years warriors like Arturo Gatti, Micky Ward, Ray Oliveira, Kevin Pompey and Manny Pacquiao have proudly continued the tradition.

Perhaps the greatest "television fighter" of them all was Danny "Little Red" Lopez, whose fights often turned into full-blown melodramas in which he overcame early beatings to score sudden, spectacular knockouts. He often walked into the ring wearing a colorful Indian headdress in honor of his mother's heritage, but his powerhouse ring style was pure Mexican like his father. His soft-spoken, humble personality stood in sharp contrast to his ferocity inside the ropes. In an era in which fights were regularly seen on ABC, NBC and CBS, the Lopez name guaranteed terrific fights – and huge ratings.

The greatest example of the Lopez legend occurred September 15, 1978 when Lopez defended his WBC featherweight title against Juan Malvarez on the undercard to the rematch between Muhammad Ali and Leon Spinks. More than 63,000 fans packed the Superdome to watch Ali become the first man to gain a share of the heavyweight title three times. But while they waited for the main event, Lopez gave them an extraordinary appetizer.

The 26-year-old Lopez (37-3, 35 KO) was making his fourth defense of the WBC featherweight title he won from David "Poison" Kotey in Kotey's native Ghana. Lopez was enjoying a successful 1978 as he scored two six-round knockouts over Kotey on the undercard of Spinks-Ali I February 15 and Brazilian Jose DePaula April 23. At 125 ¼ pounds, Lopez's weight was the second lightest of his reign to date (he was 125 against Jose Torres September 13, 1977.)

Malvarez (43-7-6, 22 KO) was a blank slate to American fans but to South Americans he was very familiar. The title shot against Lopez was Malvarez's 10th fight of 1978. The good news was that he was 8-0-1 entering the Lopez fight, but the bad news was that the 10-round draw against Ramon Reyes in San Juan, Argentina took place just six weeks previously. Not many people thought Malvarez would be "the one" to end Lopez's reign, but "Little Red's" defensive vulnerabilities ensured that the Argentine would get in his licks.

The shorter Malvarez, respectful of Lopez's power, came out on the move, circling nicely in both directions while Lopez stalked and tossed out jabs to establish distance. Malvarez popped Lopez with a quick hook and a double jab, the second of which landed squarely. The Argentine exploited his speed advantage by firing a jab and nipping away before Lopez could even react. The challenger had found a comfortable rhythm while the notoriously slow-starting Lopez struggled to find his range.

Only thirty-seven seconds into the fight, Lopez's troubles worsened. A three-punch combination – a lead right, a left hook and a right to the ear – dumped Lopez on his right side and sent shock waves through the crowd. "Little Red," having been in this position many times before, was composed as he arose at the count of two and glared across the ring. Lopez shook his head in disappointment as Italian referee Marcelo Bertini tolled the mandatory eight count, but if anyone was qualified to handle the situation Lopez was. But it wouldn't be easy.

Malvarez landed a hook to the jaw and another hook-right hand combination a few seconds later. The Argentine knew he wasn't a knockout fighter, so he smartly went back to the stick-and-move tactics that produced the knockdown. Lopez continued to walk down Malvarez, but his blows continued to fall short of his constantly moving target.

Lopez maneuvered Malvarez to the ropes, but the challenger landed a solid hook and cleverly spun out to his right to extricate himself from Lopez's trap. Lopez landed a decent lead right but Malvarez countered with a sharper left-right.

Malvarez was having a dream-like first round as he continually caught the champion coming in time and again. His confidence rising, Malvarez threw a four-punch combination with the third – a left hook – landing solidly. Another left hook-right-hand combo smacked against Lopez's jaw and yet another hook drove Lopez to the ropes. Lopez was an open book for Malvarez, but the Argentine resisted the temptation to trade with Lopez and retreated to ring center.

Backing to the ropes, Malvarez induced a jab from Lopez and quickly snapped off a left hook-right cross combination that clearly stung the champion. Lopez remained dogged in his pursuit, catching the bobbing and weaving Malvarez with a cuffing hook and a decent right as Malvarez rolled away. The South American ended perhaps the greatest round he ever fought with a right-left-right to the chin.

"Try to stay in close to him," trainer Bennie Georgino told Lopez as he furiously massaged his shoulders and applied Vaseline to his fighter's unmarked face. "Keep your chin down because he's going to go for broke."

Malvarez began the second on his bicycle, looking to duplicate his first-round success. He missed a lead left hook but the second half of a double-jab landed well to the body. A right uppercut glanced off Lopez's face but a follow-up left hook-right cross landed forcefully and knocked the champion off balance. The crowd roared, convinced that Malvarez had the right stuff to spring a monumental upset on one of boxing's biggest stages.

The Argentine seemed convinced as well, leaping in to consolidate his advantage. But Lopez fired a shot across the bow with a lead right that barely missed the target. Malvarez leaped in a second time, missing with another lead hook before nipping out again. But when the Argentine tried the move a third straight time, Lopez was ready with his reply.

"Little Red" fired a solid right that knocked Malvarez back a step. Foolishly, Malvarez leaped in again, this time behind a lead right uppercut. After landing a light jab, Lopez unleashed a single, concussive, perfectly timed howitzer of a right hand that caught Malvarez coming in and separated him from his senses. The follow-up left-right was unnecessary as Malvarez crumpled to the canvas. The Argentine rolled onto his stomach, rubbing his nose repeatedly with his gloves. As Bertini completed the 10-count, Malvarez was on all fours and he would remain on the canvas for two full minutes.

"I sure didn't expect him to come out quickly," Lopez told Howard Cosell. "He really surprised me when he dropped me with a couple of good combinations in the first round. I kept my cool and I started to watch my hands, keeping them up a little bit to keep from getting hit, and I finally got in a good shot on him which paid off."

The fight lasted just three minutes forty-four seconds and Lopez lost all but the final 10. That's why boxing – and warriors like Danny "Little Red" Lopez – make for great television. In this age of reality TV, there is no more real sport than the sweet science.

Epilogue: Lopez returned to the ring just 37 days after belting out Malvarez, scoring a fourth-round disqualification win over Fel Clemente. Three more defenses followed against Roberto Castanon (KO 2), Mike Ayala (KO 15 in Ring Magazine's 1979 Fight of the Year) and Jose Caba (KO 3) before Lopez was dethroned by Salvador Sanchez (KO by 13). After losing the rematch to Sanchez in 14 rounds June 21, 1980, the 28-year-old Lopez retired at the suggestion of Georgino. Lopez went on to work for a number of construction companies and tried his hand at acting and training fighters. But nothing could substitute for the thrill of combat so at age 39, Lopez returned to the ring to see if he still had it. As it turned out, he didn't – club fighter Jorge Rodriguez stopped Lopez in two rounds and the former ring great retired for good with a record of 42-6 (39 KO).

Malvarez fought 36 more times over the next five years, going 27-4-5 (16 KO). Malvarez won the Argentine featherweight title with an 11th round KO of Julio Alegre less than two months after fighting Lopez. Seven fights later, he added the South American featherweight belt from fellow Lopez victim Jose DePaula. Following six more wins, Malvarez received a second shot at a world title against WBA champion Eusebio Pedroza, but the great Panamanian stopped him in nine rounds. It was Malvarez's final chance at world honors, though he continued to defend his Argentine and South American titles. Mario Miranda KO'd Malvarez in one round for the WBC Continental Americas featherweight belt and drew with Fernando Sosa June 4, 1982. In a rematch with Sosa, Malvarez lost the Argentine featherweight title but he ended his career with a six-round knockout of former WBA junior featherweight champion Sergio Palma on June 4, 1983. Malvarez's record is 70-12-11 (42 KO).

TALES FROM THE VAULT

Total Punches Landed/Thrown

Round	1	2	3	4	5	6	7	8	9	10	11	12	Total
Lopez	16/75	6/16											22/91
	21%	38%											24%
Malvarez	35/68	4/11											39/79
	51%	36%											49%

Jabs Landed/Thrown

Round	1	2	3	4	5	6	7	8	9	10	11	12	Total
Lopez	9/34	3/8											12/42
	26%	38%											29%
Malvarez	3/10	2/4											5/14
	30%	50%											36%

Power Punches Landed/Thrown

Round	1	2	3	4	5	6	7	8	9	10	11	12	Total
Lopez	7/41	3/8											10/49
	17%	38%											20%
Malvarez	32/58	2/7											34/65
	55%	29%											52%

Danny Lopez vs. Juan Malvarez September 15, 1978, New Orleans, Louisiana

Rafael "Bazooka" Limon vs. Rolando Navarrete I
May 29, 1982, Las Vegas, Nevada

From the time he won the WBC junior lightweight title from Alfredo Escalera January 28, 1978 to his final title defense April 7, 1980, Alexis Arguello ruled the division with an artist's touch and a wrecking ball's destruction. The unquestioned best 130-pounder in the world scored seven knockouts in eight defenses, with only Arturo Leon able to last the full 15 rounds. Once Arguello vacated the belt to pursue the lightweight title following an eight-round non-title win over Cornelius Boza-Edwards, a wildly wonderful scramble for dominance ensued.

Three of Arguello's title-fight victims – Bobby Chacon, Rafael "Bazooka" Limon and Rolando Navarrete – joined Boza-Edwards to form the nucleus of an unforgettable round robin. Over the next three years, this quartet of warriors produced four title changes, two consecutive Fights of the Year and a lifetime's worth of thrills.

Limon got the ball rolling by knocking out Idelfonso Bethelmy in the 15th to win the vacant belt December 11, 1980. Less than three months later, "Bazooka" lost the title to Boza-Edwards in a savage, foul-filled 15 round war. The England-based Ugandan successfully defended against Chacon with a 14th round TKO but was shockingly dethroned by Navarrete via one-punch KO in five rounds. Navarrete, in turn, barely held onto the belt by overcoming a fifth-round knockdown to knock out Chung Il Choi in 11 rounds.

Navarrete's second title defense against Limon took place on May 29, 1982 at the Aladdin Hotel in Las Vegas. The 25-year-old Navarrete (42-9-3, 22 KO) and the 28-year-old Limon (45-11-2, 33 KO) were mirror images in many ways – both were southpaw sluggers who had little use for ring science and technique. Back-alley brawls were more their style, but Navarrete had the quicker hands and straighter punches while Limon's extraordinary stamina and unshakable will were his biggest assets.

A few months before this fight, Navarrete was involved in an automobile accident that totaled his car, but luckily he was unscathed. In fact, his training was going so well that he had to stop sparring for four days to maintain his peak for the fight. At 129 ¾, Navarrete weighed a few pebbles below the junior lightweight limit.

Limon, who had a history of lax training habits, was in tremendous condition for this fight. A few days before the match, Limon's physician, Dr. Ismael del Morel, said the Mexican was in the best shape of his career. The evidence: Limon weighed in at a svelte 128 ¼.

Limon and Navarrete opened the fight with probing jabs, but it didn't take long before they started getting down to business. Both men whacked away at the body, but Navarrete's shots were slightly quicker and more accurate. With a minute left, Limon leaped in with an overhand left to the head and a wide right to the pit of the stomach, but Limon's big windup enabled the champion to counter with his specialty – a right hook to the chin. The blow sent the off-balance Mexican reeling toward the ropes, but he didn't appear badly hurt. As the round closed, Navarrete ripped a left to the body and a right hook to the jaw that caught Limon rolling away. Limon, always disdainful toward opponents, stuck out his chin and mugged while the Filipino replied with a counter smirk.

"Hey, cut that out," said referee Joey Curtis. Asking Limon not to taunt opponents is like ordering Shaquille O'Neal not to dunk – doing so would take away their best weapon. Psychological warfare was an integral part of Limon's strategy. The leather-tough Mexican didn't win fights with technical skills, flowing combinations or one-punch power. Instead, he wore down his opponents physically with withering body blows and mentally by belittling them after their punches caromed off his iron jaw. He wasn't a pretty fighter, but more often than not he got the job done.

Navarrete, for his part, needed to modify his style to counteract Limon's assets. Normally a slam-bang aggressor, the Filipino showed off his counter punching abilities in round two. Early in the round, Limon ripped a right to the body but Navarrete responded with a reflexive right hook to the jaw. Limon tried it again 20 seconds later and Navarrete not only caught him with a harder right hook, a follow-up straight left backed Limon off. When "Bazooka" whipped in a left to the stomach, Navarrete stepped inside and jolted Limon with a six-inch right hook to the face. The Filipino was countering beautifully, and Limon knew he had to change the flow of the fight if he wanted to regain his title.

With less than a minute remaining in the round, Limon initiated a long toe-to-toe exchange at ring center that satisfied his taste for raw combat. After Navarrete landed a left uppercut to the jaw, Limon twice stuck out his tongue as well as two jabs and a left-right to the body. Though Limon carried the last 60 seconds, it wasn't enough to overcome Navarrete's fine work in the first two minutes.

Feeling the momentum shifting his way, Limon opened the fourth with a wide right hook to the jaw and cranked hard body shots, but Navarrete answered with a left-right to the body, a follow-up hook to the ribs and a right hook to the jaw. A knifing left to the side backed Limon to the ropes, and Navarrete jumped in with a right hook-left cross that caused Limon to duck low and desperately grab at Navarrete's waist. As he forced a clinch, Limon stole a few seconds to clear his head. After Curtis broke them, Limon circled away and unleashed another series of body blows – and twice stuck out his tongue after he finished a volley. The "tongue lashings" convinced Navarrete to return to counter punching mode.

Navarrete was landing one hard punch at a time while Limon was throwing clusters of power shots – and working on the Filipino's mind.

The champion began the fifth bouncing lightly on his toes, then exaggerating it to taunt Limon. Navarrete was entering dangerous territory, for he was not one to tease his opponents. He was entering Limon's world now – just like one doesn't hook with a hooker, one shouldn't taunt with a taunter. Limon caromed a left off Navarrete's forehead and connected with a snappy jab, though Navarrete continued to shuffle away Ali-style. Surprisingly, Navarrete sneaked in a short right to the forehead and a right-left to the face coming out of the shuffle that forced Limon backward. A follow-up left to the temple and a right to the jaw sent Limon into full retreat.

Then, Limon stopped, glared, extended his arms and turned his gloved palms upward to beckon Navarrete to come forward. The champion complied, making Limon pay for his insolence by landing a jolting hook on the ribs and a solid shot on the psyche. The battle was as much psychological as physical and two solid right hooks from Navarrete in the closing seconds allowed the champion to put another round in the bank.

The flow of the fight wasn't going Limon's way as Navarrete continually clocked him with harder, sharper counters. He was even holding his own in the taunting department and nobody out-taunts "Bazooka" Limon. When he tried to box on the retreat, Navarrete took advantage of Limon's lack of fundamentals by belting him time and again. When he brawled, Navarrete was more than his equal. Limon seemed hesitant to take his usual chances because he knew a harder counter blow would be coming his way. He was having his style taken away from him and he had to find some way to solve the puzzle that was Rolando Navarrete.

His answer: Do what he does best – throw caution to the wind and whatever happens, happens.

Limon began the seventh firing hard, landing a right hook, a jab and a fusillade of body blows that pushed Navarrete back. The champion ripped in a low right and pushed Limon to the ropes with another right to the ribs. Navarrete whipped in three more body blows and a right hook to the jaw that jarred Limon's head. A follow-up right-left crashed home for Navarrete and he won an exchange of big lefts because his was released slightly quicker. Limon drove Navarrete back with an overhand left to the temple and Navarrete responded with three low blows, which drew a verbal caution from Curtis. With 20 seconds left, Limon ripped two rights to the body and a right hook to the jaw, but Navarrete again beat Limon to the punch when they launched simultaneous lefts as the round closed.

The fight began to turn Limon's way with a minute remaining in the eighth when a chopping left to the temple stunned the champion. Limon cranked a terrific right to the body, a right uppercut to the jaw and a chopping left to the ear that hurt Navarrete badly for the first time in the fight. Limon wailed away, but instead of holding, Navarrete slugged with Limon, landing a good chopping left to the jaw. Blood began to trickle out of the champ's mouth and Limon continued to pour on the pressure until the round-ending bell.

Curiously, Limon chose not to press his advantage as round nine started, Navarrete landed a chopping right hook to the chin and won yet another exchange of simultaneous hooks. Stung into action, Limon unleashed another barrage of body blows, leaving himself open for a lead left cross to the jaw. At ring center, Limon landed a chopping left to the jaw and staggered Navarrete with a one-two to the point of the chin. Navarrete was so hurt he was frozen into position and Limon took advantage by firing off a long string of wide, powerful blows. The brave Navarrete refused to clinch, and he cleared his head enough to land a scorching right hook that caught Limon coming in. It was a similar blow to the one that netted Navarrete the title from Boza-Edwards but Limon responded with an even better left cross that caught Navarrete in mid-punch.

Both fighters were dishing out brutal punishment and it was inevitable that the action would decelerate. Limon was clear-eyed but weary while Navarrete was both tired and troubled. The fight was slowly evolving into Limon's specialty – a man-sized war of attrition where intangibles such as pride, courage and toughness would determine the victor instead of speed, strength and talent. But Navarrete, a gritty, proud man who loved being champion, would not go willingly.

Navarrete picked up steam as the 10th wore on, landing a good left and a snappy right hook to the jaw that sent water flying off Limon's head. His legs seemed stronger and his blows thrown with more conviction while Limon appeared to be recharging his batteries. Navarrete strung together a nice three-punch combination – a left and two rights to the body immediately followed by another right hook to the jaw as Limon backed away. Two more right hooks punctuated a good bounce-back round for the champion.

Limon, somewhat refreshed from his three-minute respite, started the 11th firing to Navarrete's body, but the champion took the blows well. An upward arcing right and a left hook to the jaw drove Limon to the ropes, but the challenger spun out smartly to ring center to resume his attack. Each man had a reply for the other's volleys but Navarrete's blows were sharper and crisper. Limon, however, enjoyed an edge in the round's final 20 seconds after he drove Navarrete to the ropes and cranked off more blockbusters to the body.

It was amazing that neither man was significantly marked by the brutal punishment each dished out. The fact that they fought a virtually foul-free fight was nothing short of miraculous to veteran boxing observers. Limon always relished a good, hard fight and perhaps his remaining within the rules was his way of showing respect.

Entering the 12th round of the scheduled 15-round bout, Navarrete was pulling away on the scorecards. Dave Moretti had the champion leading 106-104 while Tomotsu Tomihara and Anselmo Escobedo also saw it for Navarrete 107-103 and 107-104 respectively. Earlier in the year, the WBC announced it would cut its championship contests from 15 rounds to 12 for safety reasons.

The 12th was anything but safe for Limon and Navarrete.

The former champion began the 12th sharply, landing thudding jabs and maneuvering Navarrete toward the ropes. At the one-minute mark, both men decided to trade punch-for-punch on the inside to see who was better. Navarrete already proved he was the better boxer, but he wanted complete victory over a man who prided himself on his grit. They tore into each other, whacking away at whatever target was available and at some that were not. As formidable as Navarrete was, he was tempting fate when he decided to play the old "Saturday Night Live" game "Quien Es Mas Macho?" with Limon.

Navarrete was on the verge of winning his battle of attrition with Limon when, with 14 seconds remaining in the round, Limon landed a left uppercut that caught the ducking Navarrete on the point of the jaw. Another left uppercut landed flush and a right hook drove the champion to the ropes. The energy drained out of Navarrete's body as Limon drove a right to the body, a right hook to the jaw and a chopping left to the head. Navarrete's hands dropped below his waist and he was an open target as he leaned forward at the waist. A final, neck-wrenching left uppercut put Navarrete on his back. Incredibly, Navarrete got to one knee at the count of nine, but the Filipino was unable to beat Curtis' count. Because the bell couldn't save a fighter, the bout ended at 3:08 of round 12.

Limon celebrated in his corner as his handlers lifted him in the air, a wide smile creasing his usually stoic visage. He raised in arms in triumph as he became only the third man to regain a portion of the 130-pound title (Johnny Dundee and Samuel Serrano were the others). But making history didn't matter to a blood-and-guts warrior like Limon – all he wanted was to make good money and give a good show while doing it. After all, Rafael "Bazooka" Limon epitomized the term "prizefighter."

Epilogue: On December 23, 1988, Limon and Navarrete met a second time as junior welterweights in Manila. Predictably, this bout came nowhere near to matching their first encounter – Navarrete decked Limon in the second round en route to a 10-round decision victory.

Meanwhile, the WBC junior lightweight title merry-go-round continued. After Limon retained the title by scoring a come-from-behind seven-round KO of Chung Il Choi, he lost the belt to Chacon in one of history's greatest fights. Chacon's 15-round KO was voted Ring magazine's 1982 Fight of the Year and Chacon's next outing, a 12-round barn-burner against Boza-Edwards six months later was Ring's Fight of the Year for 1983.

Then things got complicated. To get a shot at Limon's title, Chacon signed a promotional deal with Don King saying that should Chacon win, he would next defend against rising star Hector Camacho. After Chacon captured the belt, he sought a rematch with Boza-Edwards, the WBC's number-one contender. Chacon defeated Boza-Edwards in May, but the WBC stripped Chacon for not honoring the contract with King, meaning Chacon became the first champion ever stripped for defending the belt against that sanctioning body's mandatory contender.

Three months after Chacon beat Boza-Edwards, Camacho knocked out Limon in five rounds to win the vacant belt. Following one defense against Rafael Solis (KO 5), Camacho vacated the title to move up to 135. On September 13, 1984, number-two contender Julio Cesar Chavez knocked out mandatory challenger Mario Martinez in eight rounds to win the title and finally bring stability to that championship.

After losing to Limon, Navarrete won his next four fights by knockout before suffering a five-round KO loss to Martinez, earning Martinez the chance to fight Chavez for the belt vacated by Camacho. After the loss, Navarrete took a four-year sabbatical from the sport before returning with a second round KO over Elmer Leonardo. Navarrete ran off seven more wins, five by KO, before being knocked out in six rounds by Tae Jin Moon. From there, Navarrete lost four of his final five fights before retiring for good at age 34 in 1991. His record is 54-15-3 (31 KO).

Limon's decline was longer and more precipitous than Navarrete's. Three years after losing to Camacho, Limon returned to the ring to take on 31-3-3 Oscar Bejines, a tough assignment for anyone, much less someone with three years worth of ring rust. After losing the first three rounds, a frustrated Limon quit during the fourth. From then on, he served as cannon fodder for younger, stronger fighters, including a 60-0 Chavez, who knocked him out in seven rounds.

Limon won just two of his final 11 fights, and the most noteworthy moment of his post-championship career took place when he fought Sharmba Mitchell March 8, 1990 on USA Network. Limon, whose fighting skills were long gone, resorted to clowning throughout most of the fight and during a clinch he pulled down Mitchell's trunks. Thankfully, Mitchell was wearing underwear. Mitchell (14-0, 6 KO) left the ring with an eight-round decision win but lost a bit of his dignity.

The 40-year-old Limon ended his career with a seven-round TKO loss to John Armijo Sept. 7, 1994 in Huntington Park, Calif. His final record is 52-23-2 (39 KO).

BACK FROM THE BRINK – GREAT COMEBACKS

Total Punches Landed/Thrown

Round	1	2	3	4	5	6	7	8	9	10	11	12	Total
Limon	12/38	30/79	20/56	22/63	12/43	17/62	39/79	43/100	37/80	24/54	21/50	39/69	316/773
	32%	38%	36%	35%	28%	27%	49%	43%	46%	44%	42%	57%	41%
Navarrete	10/52	15/43	13/40	15/41	12/35	10/28	40/84	27/67	32/78	18/45	29/67	28/62	249/642
	19%	35%	32%	37%	34%	36%	48%	40%	41%	40%	43%	45%	39%

Jabs Landed/Thrown

Round	1	2	3	4	5	6	7	8	9	10	11	12	Total
Limon	3/20	12/48	12/36	7/33	7/28	10/48	14/27	13/37	10/28	14/36	9/21	13/22	124/384
	15%	25%	33%	21%	25%	21%	52%	35%	36%	39%	43%	59%	32%
Navarrete	2/28	2/17	2/15	0/6	1/7	2/10	5/19	3/14	3/21	3/10	2/7	2/7	27/161
	7%	12%	13%	0%	14%	20%	26%	21%	14%	30%	29%	29%	17%

Power Punches Landed/Thrown

Round	1	2	3	4	5	6	7	8	9	10	11	12	Total
Limon	9/18	18/31	8/20	15/30	5/15	7/14	25/52	30/63	27/52	10/18	12/29	26/47	192/389
	50%	58%	40%	50%	33%	50%	48%	48%	52%	56%	41%	55%	49%
Navarrete	8/24	13/26	11/25	15/35	11/28	8/18	35/65	24/53	29/57	15/35	27/60	26/55	222/481
	33%	50%	44%	43%	39%	44%	54%	45%	51%	43%	45%	47%	46%

Rafael "Bazooka" Limon vs. Rolando Navarrete I May 29, 1982, Las Vegas, Nevada

TALES FROM THE VAULT

Danny Williams vs. Mark Potter
October 21, 2000, London, England

Every fighter who steps between the ropes must possess a certain level of courage; otherwise they would never have stuck with the sport. But all fighters aren't created equal — some are blessed with more physical talent while others make up for their shortcomings with mental fortitude that wears out opponents just as effectively as a hook to the liver. More than a few times, a boxer endowed with determination and grit overcomes obstacles that would have conquered others to emerge with a memorable victory.

Some boxers, however, manage to go beyond the reasonable limits of human endurance to acquire that valuable "W." British heavyweight Danny Williams was one such fighter, and his bout with Mark Potter on October 21, 2000 at the Conference Centre in London produced one of the most mind-blowing examples of fortitude ever seen in the ring.

Williams was a rising heavyweight in 2000, winning 21 of his first 22 fights with 17 knockouts. The "Brixton Bomber" turned pro in 1995 with a second-round knockout of Vance Idiens and scored 12 knockouts in his first 15 fights before losing a 12-round decision to Julius Francis for the British and Commonwealth heavyweight titles. Two fights and eight months later, Williams captured the vacant Commonwealth belt by polishing off Henry Senior in two rounds.

The fight with Potter represented Williams' first defense of the belt as well as an opportunity to capture the vacant British title. In the past, Williams had problems with his weight, scaling as high as 260 for his fight with Senior. But for Potter, Williams weighed 253 and looked in reasonable condition.

Potter was born in Rush Green, England and made his home in Walthamstow in South London. A bruising, aggressive fighter, Potter raced to seven consecutive wins to start his career but lost an eight-rounder to Antoine Palatis in Pont-Aldemer, France. After scoring four more victories, Potter lost a eight-rounder to Keith Long but won the vacant British Southern Area heavyweight title by knocking out Danny Watts in six rounds seven months before this fight with Williams.

The last match for both men took place on the same card at York Hall 29 days earlier, with Potter decisioning Luke Simpkin over six rounds and Williams knocking out American Quinn Navarre in six frames. That card was headlined by Glen "The Road Warrior" Johnson, who stopped Toks Owoh in six rounds and Ricky "The Hit Man" Hatton's five-round stoppage of Giuseppe Lauri. Williams entered the ring with much more experience, both in terms of opposition and scheduled distances. The bout was Potter's first 12-rounder and his second fight slated for 10 rounds or more while Williams had engaged in six bouts set for 10 rounds or longer.

But when it comes to neighborhood matches, all that matters is whether East London (Williams) or South London (Potter) would prevail. As the two large men stood in a ring that looked tiny by their presence, the crowd was ready to see some action.

Did they ever get it.

A split-second after the opening bell rang, the fired-up Potter set the tone by landing a lead right to the head. Potter dug two hooks to the body while Williams countered with a hook. A mere seven seconds into the fight, Potter landed a left-right to the jaw that sent Williams to the canvas. John Coyle, one of the most respected referees in the country, did not rule it a knockdown because Williams' legs appeared to slip out from underneath him a fraction after the punches landed.

Potter said before the fight that "I will break Danny Williams' heart" and as he steamed ahead he was intent on making good on his words. He whipped in rights and lefts to the body as Williams calmly fended them off. Williams, on the move, landed a snappy hook and dug another to the body, but Potter countered with his own hook and a one-two to the head.

Midway through the round, following a break, Potter snapped off a jab, two cuffing hooks and a solid right to the jaw. Williams responded with hook that landed low and a flush jab that forced Potter back a half step. Potter drove a hook to the body and backed Williams to the ropes, where a clinch ensued.

Williams was fighting in bursts while Potter maintained a fast tempo, always pushing and pulling in the clinches while firing off short punches whenever he could. Potter ended an excellent first round by landing a right uppercut that neatly split Williams' guard and a right-left to the stomach.

Potter came out jabbing in the second round, landing three of them. Williams countered with a solid jab and a grazing right that caused Potter to fall to one knee. It was a stunning case of deja vu in reverse – the first round saw a knockdown that wasn't called a knockdown seven seconds in while the second stanza started with a knockdown six seconds in. This time, Coyle applied a mandatory eight-count to Potter, though replays showed Williams' punch grazed Potter's shoulder and knocked him off balance.

Up at two, Potter complained that Williams' blow landed on the back of the head, but Coyle would have none of it and completed the count. Angered, Potter charged in behind clusters of shots to the body while driving Williams to the ropes. Despite a 19-pound weight disadvantage, the 234-pound Potter's low center of gravity enabled him to maneuver Williams with relative ease.

Forty-five seconds into the round, Williams landed a hook below the belt and Potter fell to the canvas, clutching his groin. Coyle called for time and allowed Potter to recover. While on his knees, Potter took a few deep breaths and was ready to continue after a 30-second break. This time, as Potter charged in, Williams accelerated his punch count and a couple of rights landed cleanly. Potter bulled Williams to the ropes and bought time in a clinch.

Another Williams hook strayed low and while he tried to apologize, Coyle still took a point away. Undeterred, Williams continued to dig lefts to the body at close range as blood seeped from Potter's nose. Potter began to breathe heavily as the strain of bullying the 253-pound Williams started to show.

Williams and Potter exchanged jabs to start the third but Williams followed with a long right that just missed the target. That punch dislocated Williams' right shoulder and as the Brixton man circled the ring, his arm hung awkwardly at his side and a knot could be seen at the top of the shoulder blade. But Williams didn't panic or show signs of distress – he initiated a clinch and tested the shoulder by rolling it. Williams then implemented a pattern of survival: Throw a jab, then clinch until the referee separated them, all the while running time off the clock in an effort to get back to the corner.

Potter didn't seem aware anything was amiss as he continued to press ahead, though he was landing more hooks because Williams was no longer able to protect the entire right side of his body. Williams concealed his trouble so well that it took a full minute for the ringside commentators to notice Williams' injury. Once they did, they compassionately called for Williams to end matters voluntarily.

"Anyone else would have just walked to the side, what a show of courage from this man," Jim Watt said. "Williams should just walk to the side. This is a show of courage he could do without because if he gets knocked out here no one else would listen to the excuses later. He's unfit to box. If that shoulder is gone he's unfit to box and he should just walk to the side and declare this over because nobody would hold anything against him."

But Williams chose not to yield and he bravely landed a hook to the head and another to the chest before initiating another clinch to give him time to work out his problem. Somehow, Williams got through the rest of the round and incredibly, by the time he got to the corner his shoulder appeared to be fully restored. The knot was gone and as his corner tested the range of motion by pulling his glove so that it would touch the opposite shoulder, he did so without pain. As he stood in the corner awaiting the fourth round bell, he was able to lift his arm into the proper defensive position.

Potter was still forcing the pace, but his blows lacked the zip of previous rounds. Williams continued to bide his time in the clinches as he tested the shoulder by throwing short rights to the ribs and attempting overhand rights to the head. Second by second, Williams assured himself that his arsenal was fully reassembled.

Breaking out of a clinch, Williams threw another low hook to the body that floored Potter, and this time Coyle deducted two points. After being penalized his second and third points of the fight, Williams sprung into action, landing with a snappy jab and overhand right to the jaw. A ripping right uppercut caught Potter well and proved beyond doubt that the right shoulder was in good working order.

Potter leaned heavily on Williams, whose back was on the corner pad but Williams broke away and fired jabs as Potter steadily motored forward, digging hard blows to the head and body as the round ended.

The pattern continued in the fifth as Potter bustled forward, clearly the busier man. Williams was picking up the pace, aware he needed to rally if he was to be competitive on the scorecards in case the fight went the distance. Throughout the fight, Williams neglected his jab and Potter took advantage by barreling in without fear of retaliation.

A ripping uppercut to the jaw jolted Williams' head and two more buckled his legs. Williams countered with a torrid hook and the action picked up considerably. Potter dug a right-left to the body then launched another hook to the body, a hook to the head and a right cross to the jaw. A Williams right uppercut jerked Potter's head upward and Williams extricated himself from the ropes and returned to ring center. Williams landed an overhand right to the ear but stumbled backwards from the force of the blow. The sportsmanlike Potter didn't take advantage of Williams' vulnerability, instead letting him regain his balance while he stood at ring center. The crowd appreciated his gallantry, but Williams did not. When Potter extended his left glove in the traditional "let's touch gloves" gesture, Williams shook his head "no."

Potter chugged forward and Williams, showing full confidence in his shoulder, landed a flush right uppercut to the jaw. Potter responded with an uppercut and a double hook to the head and body. A lead right sent Williams stumbling to the ropes. Potter was bulldozing Williams around the ring and was doing a good job of staying at close range to smother Williams' long-armed bombs. The underdog Potter was demonstrating the best form of his career by far and as he connected with a final right to the jaw he banked yet another round in his favor.

Twenty-five seconds into the sixth, an old problem for Williams resurfaced. Firing an overhand right that whizzed over Potter's head, Williams' shoulder popped out again. Unlike the first time, when he hid the injury well, the pain was so intense that Williams made his situation clear to everyone – including Potter. Williams grimaced as he stiffly held his arm away from his body and retreated in an almost crab-like fashion. He made no pretense of trying to lift his arm into defensive position. Potter fired away, but Williams weaved his upper body from side to side and avoided the brunt of the attack.

Williams somehow fended off Potter by throwing sharp jabs out of a crouching position. Potter, curiously, didn't swarm Williams. Perhaps he thought Williams was playing possum and, respectful of Williams' power, kept his cool. Meanwhile, many of Williams' jabs were landing flush and he was able to keep Potter at bay.

The courage demonstrated by Williams was remarkable. Fighting through enormous pain and unable to defend his right side, Williams could have easily given up. Instead, his first impulse was to fight on and make the best of a desperate situation against a man who arguably won every round and was enjoying the best night of his career. Time was also running out for Williams because the ringside doctors and corner men surely would not allow him to continue in that condition.

With 55 seconds left in the round, a dramatic fight turned into one for the ages.

As Potter moved in to launch another right hand, Williams uncorked a perfectly timed left uppercut to the jaw that felled Potter like a giant oak to a lumberjack's blade. The astonished crowd cheered wildly at this almost unthinkable turn of events. Potter was flat on his back at ring center but courageously regained his feet by Coyle's count of nine, with blood pouring out of both nostrils.

Williams rushed in behind a left that missed over Potter's head but a second one hit the button and Potter fell again. Twenty-six seconds remained in the round as Potter arose at nine. Williams landed a cuffing hook to the head but it was enough to floor Potter for the third and final time. Incredibly, Williams pulled off a miraculous victory just 21 seconds from what would have been his final round of action. In short, sudden death was transformed into sudden victory.

Williams triumphantly stormed around the ring, shouting, "Yes! Yes!" But with the fight over and victory secured, the adrenaline faded and the reality of his situation hit Williams with crushing force. He fell to his knees in agony and as the doctors attempted to manipulate the shoulder, Williams groaned as wave after wave of intense pain reverberated throughout his body. A few minutes later, Williams walked out of the ring sporting a makeshift sling and, more importantly, one of the most hard-earned and courageous victories ever seen.

Epilogue: Potter took six months off before returning with an eight-round decision over Michael Murray. Eleven weeks after that, Potter was stopped in seven by Alex Vassilev for the vacant WBU International title after falling three times in the round. Potter launched a successful mini-comeback by winning his next six fights, five by knockout, to earn a British title elimination bout against Michael Sprott March 18, 2003 in Berkshire, England. Three rounds later, Potter was knocked out and he never fought again. At age 28, Potter retired with a 21-5 (13 KO) record.

Eight months of rehab followed the Potter victory and Williams proved his shoulder was fully healed as he blitzed Kali Meehan in 32 seconds. Following wins over Julius Francis (KO 4), Shawn Robinson (KO 2), Michael Sprott (KO 7), and Keith Long (W 12), Williams earned an EBU title shot against the 16-0 Sinan Samil Sam, who stopped Williams in six rounds on the three-knockdown rule.

Six weeks after fighting Sam, Williams split two fights with Sprott, knocking him out in five then losing a 115-114 decision four months later. Two more knockout wins over Ratko Draskovic (KO 1) and Nigou Augustin (KO 3) earned Williams a fight with Mike Tyson.

In a bout that strangely resembled Williams' fight with Potter, Tyson injured his knee during the first round but continued to fight on. However, no miracles were in store for the badly faded "Iron Mike" as Williams rallied to register a shocking four-round stoppage and earned a chance at WBC champion Vitali Klitschko. "Dr. Ironfist" unloaded his iron fists all over Williams, decking the Brixton man four times before finishing him off in eight.

Williams took a seven-month sabbatical before returning with a three-round knockout over Zoltan Petranyi to earn a fight with Audley Harrison for the vacant Commonwealth title. Williams decked the heavily hyped 2000 Olympic champion in the 10th round en route to a 12-round split decision victory, after which he won the Commonwealth title from previously undefeated Matt Skelton by split nod and stopped Adnan Serin in three rounds. Then Skelton and Harrison avenged their defeats by scoring back-to-back wins over Williams but "The Brixton Bomber" won the British title by stopping Scott Gammer in nine rounds on March 2, 2007. A four-round no-contest to Oleg Platov was followed by wins over Marcus McGee (W 6), Konstantin Airich (KO 7) and John McDermott (W 12) and an eighth round TKO loss to Albert Sosnowski.

The 36-year-old Williams continued to campaign in 2009, retaining the British title with a split decision over John McDermott in May. In October, Williams took part in the "Prizefighter" tournament and suffered two first-round knockdowns against Carl Baker en route to losing a three round decision. As of January 2010, his record stands at 41-8 with 31 knockouts.

TALES FROM THE VAULT

Total Punches Landed/Thrown

Round	1	2	3	4	5	6	7	8	9	10	11	12	Total
Williams	10/27	18/47	6/29	11/38	12/32	7/32							64/205
	37%	38%	21%	29%	38%	22%							31%
Potter	33/103	22/72	28/70	30/84	19/59	15/46							147/434
	32%	31%	40%	36%	32%	33%							34%

Jabs Landed/Thrown

Round	1	2	3	4	5	6	7	8	9	10	11	12	Total
Williams	1/1	2/6	0/18	4/13	2/13	5/21							14/72
	100%	33%	0%	31%	15%	24%							19%
Potter	2/11	1/9	2/6	5/12	2/11	3/12							15/61
	18%	11%	33%	42%	18%	25%							25%

Power Punches Landed/Thrown

Round	1	2	3	4	5	6	7	8	9	10	11	12	Total
Williams	9/26	16/41	6/11	7/25	10/19	2/11							50/133
	35%	39%	55%	28%	53%	18%							38%
Potter	31/92	21/63	26/64	25/72	17/48	12/34							132/373
	34%	33%	41%	35%	35%	35%							35%

Danny Williams vs. Mark Potter October 21, 2000, London, England

BACK FROM THE BRINK – GREAT COMEBACKS

Jim Watt vs. Charlie Nash
March 14, 1980, Glasgow, Scotland

Variety, they say, is the spice of life and boxing is just one of the places this truism can be applied. Fighters' styles assume all sorts of forms – some are slick boxers who employ deft sleight of hand while others are mad bombers who blast their opponents into submission. As with most things, the majority of fighters find themselves occupying various degrees of middle ground. Such was the case with Jim Watt and Charlie Nash, who fought for Watt's WBC lightweight title March 14, 1980 in Glasgow's Kelvin Hall.

Like styles, entire career paths can take on a character of their own. Some, like Mike Tyson and Wilfred Benitez, amazed many with their precocity while George Foreman and Archie Moore gave the rest of the world's geriatrics reason for eternal hope.

Watt's career fell somewhere between the two extremes, though his more closely followed Moore and Foreman than Benitez and Tyson. Given his methodical ring style and placid temperament during fights, it would have been difficult to imagine Watt as a streaking young comet that gave the world a spectacular, but brief, thrill. Instead, Watt traveled the long, hard road that builds character as well as a deep appreciation for the accomplishments that would follow.

Make no mistake, Watt had a chance to be that comet. As a 15-2 fighter, the 24-year-old found himself standing across the ring from former lightweight champion Ken Buchanan in a bout for the British lightweight title January 29, 1973 in Glasgow. Eight months earlier, he won the belt by knocking out Tony Riley in 12 rounds and Buchanan (who two fights earlier was dethroned by Roberto Duran) was Watt's first internationally known opponent. Watt fought bravely and well, but Buchanan's toolbox was still full enough to capture a 15-round decision as well as Watt's title.

After the Buchanan fight, Watt wandered a bit, still winning more than losing but not putting everything together. He won his next five fights but lost a 10-rounder to Anthony Morodi in Johannesburg. He captured the vacant British lightweight title by beating Johnny Cheshire and decisioned Billy Waith over 10 rounds but then he lost a 15 rounder for the vacant Commonwealth title to Jonathan Dale and a 12-rounder to Andre Holyk.

Following a three-round TKO loss to Johnny Claydon, Watt was 28 and nearing the end of what would normally be considered his peak years. But somehow, he found that certain something that allowed him to raise his game to a new level and the wave of success would continue for virtually the rest of his career.

After knocking out Franco Diana in six rounds, he avenged his losses to Claydon (KO 10) and Holyk (KO 1) – and the Holyk win also earned him the European lightweight title. Victories over Jeronimo Lucas (KO 10), Perico Fernandez (W 15), Billy Vivian (W 8) and Antonio Guinaldo (KO 5) led up to a chance at the WBC lightweight title vacated by Duran.

All things considered, the title bout with Alfredo Pitalua was a one-and-done deal for Watt. A second chance was unlikely given his age. But Watt came through as he became a world champion four months shy of 31, winning the belt by 12th round TKO.

Watt's oft-detoured road had reached a golden fork that promised a string of healthy paydays but it came with one big catch – he had to keep winning.

His first defense was successful as he knocked out Robert Vazquez in nine rounds. The next assignment for Watt (35-7, 25 KO) was an optional defense against Northern Ireland's Nash. Optional defenses are seen as easier because the choice of opposition lies with the champion's brain trust, who of course would pick someone they feel their man can beat.

Nash had other ideas. A fellow southpaw, the 28-year-old Nash was coming off the biggest win of his career – retaining his European lightweight title with a 12-round decision over Buchanan three months earlier. Unlike Watt, Nash (21-1, 7 KO) started his career quickly, beating Ray Ross over 10 rounds for the vacant Northern Ireland lightweight title – in his pro debut, no less. Though quick-fisted, Nash was not a hard hitter as he scored only four knockouts while going 13-0. Eight fights and 18 months after winning a final eliminator for the British lightweight title, Nash stopped Claydon in 12 rounds to win the belt. That fight was called off because Nash was 10 points ahead on the referee's scorecard – a "mercy rule" stoppage so to speak.

He never defended the title, but he kept winning as he avenged an earlier loss to Adolfo Osses by stopping him in three rounds in his next outing. Impressive performances against Americans Willie Rodriguez (W 10) and Jerome Artis (W 8) were among the victories that led up to the Buchanan fight that vaulted Nash to this opportunity.

A crowd of approximately 6,000 jammed Kelvin Hall to see what was billed as the first all-British world title fight since September 1949. The pre-fight buildup featured much needling, as Nash repeatedly accused Watt of ducking him for years. A proud man, Watt fired back verbally and was more than eager to prove himself the superior fighter. Nash received a healthy ovation as he was introduced, but the reception for the hometown hero was nothing short of thunderous.

The quick-starting Nash began the fight on the move, occasionally burrowing inside with bursts of rights and lefts. Watt, with hands held high, snapped hard and accurate jabs to Nash's face while using nifty upper-body movement to avoid must of Nash's punches. The Scot was a natural right-hander who fought as a southpaw, so his jabs were much more powerful than the typical lefty.

As Watt ducked to slip a jab, Nash caught the champion with a sharp right uppercut to the jaw, then tossed a right jab to the body and a straight left to the head. Gradually, Nash gained confidence as he out-hustled the normally slow-starting Watt. Nash tagged Watt with a straight left coming in and another left whipped Watt's head to the side. Nash peppered the champ with combinations from the outside that weren't especially accurate, but kept his opponent busy on defense.

With 1:20 left in the opening round, Nash, backing to the ropes after taking a Watt jab, bent at the knees to deliver a right uppercut that missed. But his next two punches – a crisp left to the jaw and an explosive right hook – shockingly drove the champion to the seat of his pants.

Watt arose so quickly that referee Sid Nathan never administered a count, and the Scot didn't appear badly hurt. Nash charged in anyway and Watt induced a clinch after the challenger's blows whizzed over his head. After the break, Nash hit the bull's eye with another left cross, a leaping right uppercut to the jaw and two chopping lefts to the ear before digging hard at Watt's body. Another sharp right-left penetrated Watt's defense, and Nash was on a roll.

Or was he? While Nash was scoring well, his blows didn't carry enough steam to hurt Watt seriously. The champion absorbed Nash's attack with typical stoicism, always chugging forward behind his thudding jab. In the final minute, an accidental butt opened a cut over Nash's left eye and Watt spent the rest of the round spearing the challenger's face with jab after jab. Still, Nash had to be buoyed by this tremendous start to a world championship challenge.

Between rounds, Nash's corner did an excellent job of closing the gash, and it was not a factor for the rest of the fight.

The jabbing contest resumed in the second with Watt getting the better of it. Watt jumped in with a cuffing right hook as Nash bustled to the body. A short right hook drove Watt to the ropes, but Watt bounced off nicely. Watt ducked under a Nash right hook and connected with a chopping left to the ear. A few seconds later, Watt countered a winging right-left with a right hook to the point of the chin.

After an unsettled start, Watt had found his rhythm and the full range of his fundamentals were put on full and graphic display. Watt's heavy jab was like a metronome as it repeatedly crashed against Nash's face and he occasionally worked in well-timed left crosses and right hooks to the head and body. Watt had pulled himself together brilliantly and Nash seemed an open book to him. Watt smartly blocked and dodged Nash's quick-fisted flurries and retaliated with sharp counters. It wasn't flashy stuff, but for those who like solid, sound boxing technique, it was a joy to watch. In short, Watt fought as a seasoned and mature 32-year-old should.

Watt's jab continued to penetrate as the third round began, but Nash was getting in his licks as well. He landed a right-left to the head as he rushed forward and beat

Watt to the punch with his jab. Nash's fans chanted "Charrrrr-lieeeee, Charrrrr-lieeeee" and were feeling a little better about their man's chances. But Watt put a stop to that by landing a sizzling left to the jaw and snapping a flush right to the chin. Nash, standing tall before Watt, was thinking offense only, but his blows lacked accuracy because Watt was so solid defensively.

As the round closed, Watt's supporters serenaded the champion by inserting Watt's name into familiar songs. The Glasgow crowd had always been a source of strength for Watt and he responded by giving them his best.

Knowing he had lost the previous two rounds soundly, Nash started quickly in round four as he landed a solid one-two and pushed the champion back with a pair of right-lefts. A cluster of body shots induced a clinch from Watt, but Nash broke free and landed a nifty right hook to the chin. Nash tried to follow up, but Watt moved his upper body just enough to avoid the brunt of Nash's attack.

Though not hurt badly, Watt backed away to regroup. One thing about Watt – give him time to think and he'll find a way to hurt you. In a few seconds' time, Watt would administer a lesson in brutality.

Watt smacked a tremendous left off Nash's jaw and Nash took Watt with him as he fell to the canvas. Nathan began his count at six after showing Watt the neutral corner where he wanted the champion to stand. Straying from character, Watt was wild as he bullied Nash to the ropes. A big right hook smashed Nash and another snapped the Irishman's head straight back. Nash fought back bravely, but his blows missed their target. A straight left rocketed off Nash's jaw and the challenger fell to the canvas for the second time in the round.

On all fours, Nash struggled up by Nathan's count of nine. Desperate to survive, Nash retreated swiftly and reached Watt with a jab. He had more than a minute to go before he could return to the safety of his corner, and with Watt raging after him his chances of doing so were virtually nil. Finally, Watt drew a bead with a jab and finished the fight with a final left to the jaw. Nash arose at seven, but Nathan saw enough and stopped the contest.

Watt lifted his arms in triumph, a stoic look still on his face. But when he saw manager Terry Lawless, Watt unleashed his raw joy as he pumped his arms, yelled "yeah!," leaped into his arms and gave him a giant bear hug. He blew kisses to the crowd and he reveled in the ring with a variety of well-wishers. Finally, Watt spotted Nash, with whom he traded barbs before the fight and blows during it. The competition over and awash with victory, Watt let his previously felt bad feelings go as he lifted Nash's left arm and paraded with him around the ring.

For Watt, the victory allowed him the privilege of driving a few more miles down the golden championship road. For Nash, his step backward left him with a flat.

Epilogue: Just six weeks after his loss to Watt, Nash got back on the horse, bombing out Pedro Acosta Nunez in seven rounds and retained the EBU belt by decisioning Francisco Leon over 12 rounds. Nash then fell on hard times, going 2-3 in his final five fights. He was decked three times en route to a sixth-round KO loss to Joey Gibilisco to lose the European belt, but rebounded nicely with wins over George Metcalf (KO 2) and Frank McCord (W 8). Nash was stopped in his final two fights, first by Tony Willis (KO by 3) and by 17-0 German Rene Weller (KO by 5) in Cologne March 4, 1983. His final record is 25-5 (9 KO).

Watt continued the Indian summer of his career with a pair of scintillating upsets, the first being a lopsided 15-round decision over 1976 U.S. gold medalist Howard Davis Jr. June 7, 1980 in Ibrox Park in Glasgow. In a fight of substance over style, Watt shrugged off Davis' flashy attacks and methodically pulled away on the scorecards to hand the American his first professional loss.

Watt's run continued the following November as he scored a controversial 12th round stoppage of Sean O'Grady. Trailing on the cards and sporting several cuts on his face, Watt caught a big break in the 10th when a butt opened a monstrous vertical cut on O'Grady's forehead. The blood eventually covered O'Grady's entire face and the fight had to be stopped. O'Grady's camp, as well as many fans, alleged Watt deliberately butted the American in a desperate attempt to save his championship. Replays, however, did not support that contention.

On June 20, 1981, Watt's career came to an emphatic end as he dropped a comprehensive 15-round decision to Alexis Arguello, who won his third divisional title. Watt, one month short of 33, retired with a record of 38-8 (27 KO).

TALES FROM THE VAULT

Total Punches Landed/Thrown

Round	1	2	3	4	5	6	7	8	9	10	11	12	Total
Watt	21/59	34/77	35/68	15/40									105/244
	36%	44%	51%	38%									43%
Nash	29/92	27/86	17/83	17/43									90/304
	32%	31%	20%	40%									30%

Jabs Landed/Thrown

Round	1	2	3	4	5	6	7	8	9	10	11	12	Total
Watt	16/45	20/48	24/48	4/12									64/153
	36%	42%	50%	33%									42%
Nash	10/45	15/43	10/54	9/21									44/163
	22%	35%	19%	43%									27%

Power Punches Landed/Thrown

Round	1	2	3	4	5	6	7	8	9	10	11	12	Total
Watt	5/14	14/29	11/20	11/28									41/91
	36%	48%	55%	39%									45%
Nash	19/47	12/43	7/29	8/22									46/141
	40%	28%	24%	36%									33%

Jim Watt vs. Charlie Nash March 14, 1980, Glasgow, Scotland

Kennedy McKinney vs. Junior Jones
December 19, 1997, New York, New York

Imagine this: Two world-class fighters engage in a high-energy, back-and-forth war that had multiple knockdowns and a thrilling, come-from-behind, one-punch knockout victory – at Madison Square Garden, no less.

Most times, this scenario would describe not only the Fight of the Year but also possibly the Fight of the Decade. Yet the extraordinary scrap between Kennedy McKinney and Junior Jones wasn't even the best fight that took place inside MSG on December 19, 1997. That honor belonged to Naseem Hamed-Kevin Kelly – a four-round, six-knockdown free-for-all that will forever be remembered as one of the greatest fights ever staged at "The Mecca of Boxing." But make no mistake: Hamed-Kelley *had* to be that good to upstage McKinney-Jones.

Such is the fate of the Closet Classic.

Had it not been for the American debut of British sensation Hamed, McKinney-Jones would have been a worthy main event attraction. McKinney, a gold medalist in the 1988 Olympics, was a former IBF junior featherweight titlist who possessed one of the deadliest right hands in the game. At age 31, McKinney was viewed as a fighter who had seen his best days, especially after he suffered five knockdowns in his 12th round TKO loss to Marco Antonio Barrera in one of 1996's most brutal fights. McKinney (32-3-1, 18 KO) rebounded well from that defeat, beating Hector Acero Sanchez (W 12) and Luigi Camputaro (KO 5) to put himself one victory away from another title opportunity.

Jones, who celebrated his 27th birthday the night of the McKinney bout, was a smaller version of Thomas Hearns with his wide shoulders, pipe-cleaner legs and overwhelming offensive skills. Those skills carried him to the WBA bantamweight title, which he won by decisioning Jorge Eliecer Julio. Six months later, in his second defense, a weight-drained Jones shockingly lost the belt to John Michael Johnson by 11th round TKO and his slide continued two fights later when he was stopped in three rounds by the 18-18-2 Darryl Pinckney.

Though Jones won his next nine fights, he was still a prohibitive underdog against the 43-0 Barrera on November 22, 1996 when they clashed for the Mexican's WBO junior featherweight belt. Five rounds later, Barrera was no longer undefeated and Jones had regained a place among the sport's elite. A rematch was held five months later, with Jones earning a close but unanimous decision. During that fight, Jones suffered an injury to his right hand that required surgery and a 245-day layoff, the longest of his career. The McKinney fight was Jones' first chance to test the repaired hand in official competition. Despite their differing paths, McKinney and Jones essentially had the same style – textbook fighters who relied on solid jabs, straight right hands and sensational offensive firepower.

During the final instructions, an insolent McKinney bounced on his toes with his back turned completely to Jones, who nevertheless stared at the back of McKinney's head. When asked by referee Wayne Kelly to touch gloves, McKinney slowly spun around and nonchalantly touched Jones' glove while never looking his opponent in the eye.

Once the fight started, McKinney saw plenty of Jones.

"Poison" started quickly, popping a stiff jab into McKinney's face as "The King" tossed out half-speed jabs intended more to keep Jones at long range than to score. Encouraged by his initial success, Jones mixed in hard jabs to the body while assuming the aggressor's role.

As they fell into the first clinch 44 seconds into the fight, a butt opened a gash under Jones' right eye. As Jones missed with a looping right, his arm hooked around the back of McKinney's head and the follow-through forced McKinney's head into his own. In a way, Jones butted open his own eye.

Jones recoiled in pain and grimaced to show referee Kelly something was wrong. He felt for blood with his right glove and a look of disappointment briefly creased his face when he saw the crimson. Still, McKinney seemed a half step behind and Jones pushed him to the ropes and landed a right to the body and a one-two to the head.

At the two-minute mark, the older McKinney began to warm to his task. Two jabs struck Jones' cut and he dug several rights to the body in the clinches. A strong right found Jones' temple as the Brooklynite hung on. Jones countered with a good hook in close but missed with another hook as McKinney spun away, allowing "The King" to land another overhand right to the ear.

The inside fighting was rough, but as the round closed they created just enough distance to blast away at each other. Jones landed a right to the body and a hook to the chin while McKinney retaliated with a solid hook to the ribs. The combative Jones fired right back with a right-left-right, another right to the body and a parting hook to the belly. The round was largely ruled by Jones' aggression, but the round-ending slugfest suggested the best was yet to come.

"I need that jab more," trainer Tommy Brooks told Jones between rounds. "Don't load up. Box, box this guy man. He'll run right into it."

But Jones was in no mood to box – he wanted to put on a show for his hometown fans as well as the worldwide media. A spectacular knockout victory over McKinney would have made him the next logical opponent for the winner of Hamed-Kelley and Jones would have benefited no matter how the main event turned out. Jones-Kelley would have been an attractive brawl between two New Yorkers – a natural for Madison

Square Garden's big arena. If Hamed won, Jones would be in line to make the biggest payday of his career.

Fueled by his success in the first, Jones roared out of the corner and fired a sizzling jab through McKinney's guard. When McKinney clinched, Jones shook him off and blasted away with powerful volleys to the head and body that drove McKinney back. A right to the jaw caused McKinney to stumble back a step, and Jones pursued eagerly, his wide eyes burning with intensity. McKinney, for his part, stood up well under the punishment and his durability persuaded Jones to slightly decelerate his attack.

Jones used his broad shoulders to drive McKinney to the ropes, where he fired a right uppercut and a cuffing hook. McKinney, after missing a couple of punches over Jones' head, cranked a short hook to the eye bone that caused Jones to immediately retreat to ring center. Jones unleashed an overhand right-left hook combo but McKinney answered with three short, chopping rights to Jones' ear.

While he remained on the losing end of things, McKinney was building a solid foundation for later in the fight. Jones was no longer moving forward and McKinney was doing a better job of judging the perfect range for his two bread-and-butter punches: the jab and his potent right cross. Because Jones ignored his own boxing skills by choosing to brawl, he gave McKinney his best chance of winning.

Realizing this, Jones began to box from longer range in the final minute and the move paid immediate dividends. Three snappy jabs and a pretty one-two landed flush and Jones consolidated his advantage by connecting with two more jabs and a chopping right. Another right caused McKinney's legs to shake slightly and seeing this, Jones peppered McKinney with a dizzying array of power punches that drove McKinney to the ropes before "The King" clamped down. McKinney chopped in a good right, but Jones continued to win the exchanges with his sharper combinations.

Jones won the first two rounds cleanly, but HBO analyst Larry Merchant saw a trend that could prove poisonous to "Poison." "Jones is fighting at a very, very fast pace," Merchant said. "If McKinney can weather it, he believes that Jones has a stamina problem and McKinney is hitting him with some heavy stuff."

The CompuBox numbers confirmed Merchant's opinion. In the second round, Jones launched 100 punches and landed 48 of them, including 36 of 64 power shots. McKinney, however, was also doing excellent work as he landed 31 of his 58 punches for 53 percent accuracy. Jones was carrying the fight, but at what cost down the road?

In the meantime, Jones continued to fight with vim and vigor in the third, going so far as to lift McKinney a few inches off the ground while in a clinch. Jones was busy with the jab while McKinney sought to land his blows in between Jones' flurries. Jones fought frenetically while McKinney was as calm and composed as a man in his situation could be, sneaking in quality punches from time to time.

The action sometimes turned awkward as both occasionally struggled to find their timing and range. Coming out of one of the resulting clinches, Jones winged a right-left to the body, a tremendous right hook to the temple, a second one to the ear, a short hook to the jaw and a right uppercut to the chest that caused McKinney to crumple to the canvas. McKinney stayed on his haunches until the count of eight, assuring his corner and Kelly that he was fine. The blood on his mouthpiece and the little shake of the head to clear the cobwebs suggested his declaration wasn't entirely truthful, but it was truthful enough to let the fight continue.

Like Hearns, Jones had a finely honed killer instinct. He climbed all over McKinney, firing quick-fisted blows that broke through McKinney's high guard. A screaming hook made McKinney's knees dip and two more right uppercuts jerked his head violently. But also like Hearns, Jones sometimes was overanxious when trying to finish his man and as the round clock ticked under the 30-second mark Jones began to slow down. McKinney hung tough through Jones' torrent of blows, and he occasionally landed uppercuts as he waited out Jones. McKinney landed a solid counter right and an exchange of rights left both men slightly wobbly. The round ended with a rousing toe-to-toe rally that thrilled the MSG crowd. Jones was winning all the rounds, but McKinney's heart and durability made a lopsided fight wildly entertaining.

Round three was statistically brutal. Jones launched 105 punches, and his 51 connects exceeded McKinney's total punch output of 47. It was a bad round for McKinney and he knew it. If he wanted to continue the fight, he had to first convince everyone he was still fit to fight. As he sat down on the stool and had water poured over his head, he told trainer Kenny Adams "I'm all right. I'm all right." A few seconds later, the ringside physician asked how he was doing. McKinney turned his head, looked directly into his eyes and fired a snappy "I feel fine." But the damage has been done as he spat out thin ribbons of blood into the bucket.

"Kennedy McKinney may be the one who was starting a trucking company, but it was Junior Jones who hit like a truck in that round," the astute Merchant observed. "But it seems to me Jones has to learn to pace himself a little bit. He was just a little too reckless with his energy. He's fighting at a furious pace and if McKinney can survive this next round or two, he can still be a danger."

As the fourth round commenced, Jones probed with jabs while crouched slightly. His mouth was open, and though he was not yet gasping for air, he did not possess the same verve as before. McKinney snapped a lead right to Jones' chin and a long one-two to the chin forced Jones to circle away. Jones no longer was the pursuer who snapped off dangerous combinations; instead, he spent his time circling to the right and catching his breath in clinches he initiated. A strong right caught Jones on the chin and the pace had finally slowed to a pace fit for a "King."

Midway through the round at ring center, both men launched simultaneous rights, with McKinney's landing first and hardest. As Jones backed away, his right knee buckled. But Jones' instinct told him to fight, not run, so he attempted to regroup by firing a lunging jab. McKinney took a step forward, lined up his shot and fired his signature right cross to Jones' temple. The impact was sudden and unmistakable. Jones fell forward and tried to grab McKinney's waist, but as McKinney stepped away Jones crumbled to the canvas on all fours.

Showing incredible presence of mind, Jones looked up at Kelly, reached out with his right hand and claimed his fall to the canvas was a slip. Kelly bought the fable and wiped Jones' gloves without administering a count. The move may have saved him a point on the scorecards, but it also proved to be the worst thing he could have done for himself. As far as his chin was concerned, McKinney had scored a legitimate knockdown. His foggy brain and unsteady legs agreed and they could have used the eight-second respite a mandatory count would have provided. Plus, a full minute remained in the round.

The veteran McKinney took his time, marshaling his energy and sizing up the situation. McKinney pumped in two jabs, the second one forcing Jones to the ropes. Jones' right arm instinctive reached for the top strand because his legs no longer had the strength to carry him unassisted.

With 36 seconds remaining, near a neutral corner, both launched right hands. Jones' landed lightly on McKinney's face, but the impact of McKinney's left Jones on his face. "Poison" fell to the canvas as if he had been shot. Up at eight, Jones told Kelly "I'm all right," but his body told another story. His torso swayed slightly and his legs were quaking underneath him. As he tried to step toward McKinney, his legs turned to rubble and he fell again, his spirit willing but his body no long able to comply. Kelly stopped the contest at the 2:39 mark of round four.

Just like that, McKinney, who was all but out in the third round, had revived his career. In his moment of triumph, his thoughts turned to a group of people that always needs guidance and hope. "Hey, to all you young kids out there: Hard work pays off," he said, looking directly into HBO's camera. "Work hard and God will give it to you." A great right hand doesn't hurt either.

When asked by Merchant his thoughts on the punch that decked him, he said he was "surprised. I never thought in a million years he'd be able to knock me down, but he caught me with a good shot. Barrera knocked me down five or six times, but you saw I kept getting up. I have resilience. I'll go down, but it's hard to keep the old man down."

McKinney said he drew inspiration from one of Jones' past fights.

"I saw him when he fought Darryl Pinckney," he said. "He started to hit Pinckney and then he got relaxed and he dropped his hands. Then Pinckney came over and caught him. (It was) the same thing with me. When he knocked me down, I thought *'uh oh, he's gonna relax now because he thinks he has me.'* And that's what he did: he relaxed. He thought he had me, but hey, this right hand is no joke."

It sure wasn't.

Epilogue: Fittingly, both McKinney and Jones fought for titles in their next outings – after an appropriately long rest. Both, however, lost to dominating champions. Jones received the first opportunity nine months after the McKinney fight against WBC super bantamweight champion Erik Morales in Morales' hometown of Tijuana. Four rounds later, Jones was another notch on "El Terrible's" growing list of victims.

McKinney stayed out of the ring for 11 months before challenging WBC featherweight king Luisito Espinosa, who scored an unexpectedly easy two-round KO in Indio, California.

The Jones fight turned out to be McKinney's last hurrah as a world class fighter. He would fight just five more times after his failed challenge of Espinosa, going 3-2 with no knockouts. After splitting two fights with Mario Diaz (W 10) and Jorge Antonio Paredes (L 10), McKinney took a 29-month sabbatical. "The King" returned with six-round wins over Gene Vassar and Joseph Figueroa, but 10 months later, on April 4, 2003 in Uncasville, Conn., the 37-year-old McKinney ended his career by dropping a six-rounder to Greg Torres. His final record is 36-6-1 (19 KO).

Jones fought eight more times following the Morales defeat, enjoying more success than McKinney. He won a 12-round decision over former IBF featherweight champion Tom "Boom Boom" Johnson for a fringe 130-pound belt. Seven weeks later, he knocked out Richard Evatt in 11 rounds to capture another fringe belt at featherweight and scored a 10-round majority decision over another former champion Tracy Harris Patterson seven months after that. His modest win streak earned Jones a shot at Paul Ingle's IBF featherweight title. Jones started well, but the British fighter's pluck – and Jones' stamina issues – led to an 11th round TKO. It would be Jones' last world title opportunity.

Jones returned to the ring a year later, beating Manuel Sepeda (W 10), Mike Juarez (KO 7) and Johnny Walker (W 10). Any dreams of late-career glory ended on December 6, 2002 when the 31-year-old Jones lost a lopsided 10-round decision to Ivan Alvarez at the Silverdome in Pontiac, Mich. Jones ended his career with a record of 50-6 (28 KO).

BACK FROM THE BRINK – GREAT COMEBACKS

Total Punches Landed/Thrown

Round	1	2	3	4	5	6	7	8	9	10	11	12	Total
McKinney													78/200
													39%
Jones													130/301
													43%

Jabs Landed/Thrown

Round	1	2	3	4	5	6	7	8	9	10	11	12	Total
McKinney													22/88
													25%
Jones													33/122
													27%

Power Punches Landed/Thrown

Round	1	2	3	4	5	6	7	8	9	10	11	12	Total
McKinney													56/112
													50%
Jones													97/179
													54%

* Fight originally done by CompuBox, but the original HTML files with complete round-by-round statistics no longer exist.

Kennedy McKinney vs. Junior Jones December 19, 1997, New York, New York

TALES FROM THE VAULT

Kevin Kelley vs. Derrick Gainer I
June 15, 1996, Jacksonville, Florida

In order for fighters to become noticed – and ultimately remembered – they must find a way to rise above the teeming masses of mediocrity. Ray Robinson and Willie Pep did so by showcasing their transcendent skills against multiple generations of peers. Rocky Graziano blazed his way into millions of memories by blasting through opponents with an unending stream of powerful rights, then parlaying his charisma into a successful television career.

Arturo Gatti became one of his generation's most beloved warriors by rescuing himself from places that would have swallowed up virtually everyone else. His thrilling one-punch knockout over Wilson Rodriguez launched not only a career but also a legacy. As the years progressed, Gatti's legend has grown to the point where he rendered himself bulletproof at the box office. No matter whether he won or lost, his meritorious service to the sport guaranteed him a spot on HBO's big-money stage as well as an adoring throng to watch him perform his brutal magic. Despite his nine losses during an era when one defeat could destroy a fighter's marketability, more than a few observers believe Gatti's fistic journey will end with enshrinement in the International Boxing Hall of Fame.

Kevin Kelley's career merged elements of all the above. "The Flushing Flash" was a skillful southpaw who not only had boxing ability but also one-punch power. He also possessed a giant fighting heart that pulled him through gut-check fights against Troy Dorsey and Tomas Rivera, among others. Finally, he was blessed with the gift of gab, which came in handy in several ways. As a rising featherweight prospect, he used it to promote himself and establish a strong following in the media capital of the world. After confirming his credentials inside the ring he used it to secure color commentary jobs outside the ring, and received generally good reviews.

Most importantly, however, Kelley's mouth ended up writing checks many fighters would cash for years to come when he convinced HBO to take a chance on the little guys. Though he lost his WBC featherweight title to Alejandro Gonzalez in his HBO debut, the fight itself was so dramatic that "The Network of Champions" launched the "Boxing After Dark" series to showcase the talents of boxing's Little Big Men. This move greatly enhanced the careers of Marco Antonio Barrera, Erik Morales and Manny Pacquiao just to name a few, and their exposure to American audiences will virtually guarantee them spots in the Hall of Fame. While it is unlikely that Kelley will have a plaque on the museum's walls, he definitely qualifies as one of the sport's great trailblazers.

On June 15, 1996 at the Jacksonville Coliseum, the 28-year-old Kelley (43-1-2, 30 KO) sought to take another step toward regaining his lost status by taking on Florida's

Derrick "Smoke" Gainer (17-3, 10 KO). Though Kelley-Gainer was the main support to Roy Jones' defense against Eric Lucas, Gainer was looking to get out from under "Superman's" cape by knocking off his best opponent to date. Some observers criticized Gainer for riding Jones' coattails to secure HBO air time, but for the 23-year-old it represented a chance to quiet the nay-sayers and prove his worth on the world class level.

Well aware of this, the usually cautious Gainer, 126, roared out of the corner with two overhand lefts to the ear. But Gainer's aggression only lasted long enough to establish he was willing to fight if necessary, and the bout quickly assumed the more expected pattern of Gainer boxing and the 124 ½-pound Kelley stalking. Another solid left cross hit Kelley's face, but the New Yorker did a good job of keeping Gainer near the ropes by cutting off his escape routes. Kelley wasn't doing much offensively and Gainer moved side to side and flicked jabs to keep Kelley at long range. Kelley landed a long left to the body, but Gainer smartly countered with a right hook before spinning out to ring center.

Though the statistics said the 5-9 Gainer had a two-inch height advantage and a one-inch reach edge, the Floridian looked much taller and long-armed. Kelley struggled to find a way inside without lunging in and exposing himself to Gainer's counters. This inhibited Kelley's offense, and Gainer ended a good opening round by landing a sharp jab to the body. In the first round, Gainer landed 15 of his 40 punches (38 percent) while Kelley's output was an anemic 6 of 27 (22 percent).

Kelley sought to rectify the problem in round two by working the jab to Gainer's head and body and bulling him to the ropes with a left to the body, a left to the head and a missed overhand right. Gainer saw through the tactic and slipped away to ring center. Kelley popped a light overhand left to the face and two left-left-rights backed Gainer to the ropes, but this time Kelley pinned him there by ripping both hands to the body while mixing overhand lefts over the top. Gainer fought his way out behind a right hook to the ear and a left cross to the jaw that brought cheers from the pro-Gainer crowd. They cheered even more when he followed with a right-left to the jaw and a right to the body that drove Kelley to the ropes. Kelley retaliated with an overhand left to the face and Gainer countered with a strong right hook.

The boxing match was turning into a fight.

Gainer landed a right to the body and a right-left to the head and followed with a snappy cross to the jaw a few seconds later. Another left cross caused Kelley's knees to dip slightly and Gainer closed the round with a right-left followed by a jaw-jacking jab to the face.

Gainer continued his hit-and-run tactics in the third as Kelley tried to get closer by landing occasional shots to the body. A little left to the eye raised a small swelling over Kelley's eye and another left landed in the same spot a few seconds later. Gainer caught a ducking Kelley with a right uppercut and a sneaky left cross smacked against the eye. Two jabs connected sharply and an overhand left sent Kelley to the canvas, but referee Frank Santore ruled the fall a slip. But both fighters reacted as if the slip were a knockdown and Gainer turned up the heat, drilling a left to the forehead and driving Kelley to the ropes with a left to the stomach.

With 20 seconds left in the round, both launched lefts. Gainer's was triggered first but it sailed over Kelley's shoulder. Kelley's, though launched later, hit the target with tremendous force and caused Gainer to crumple to the canvas. Kelley briefly stood over Gainer with arms upraised before Santore pointed him toward a neutral corner. Gainer regained his feet at seven but there wasn't enough time for another punch to be thrown.

Round three presented an interesting scoring challenge. Gainer dominated most of the round but Kelley scored a knockdown in the final seconds. Some judges would have scored the round 10-9 for Kelley because a knockdown usually produces a two-point swing. Had it not been for the knockdown, Gainer would have won the round 10-9, but the knockdown turned a Gainer 10-9 round into a 10-9 Kelley round. Others, like HBO's "Unofficial Official" Harold Lederman, credibly scored the round 10-10 to give Gainer due credit for dominating the round while not penalizing him too heavily for his defensive lapse.

Gainer wasn't thinking about the scoring as he stood in the corner awaiting round four. His sheepish smile was proof he was replaying the knockdown in his mind, but when the bell rang his face hardened into one of intense concentration. Curiously, Kelley didn't jump on Gainer but chose to stay at long range. "Smoke" obliged by spearing Kelley with his long-armed punches and whenever Kelley managed to get close he smartly clamped down on his arms and waited for Santore to separate them.

With 16 seconds remaining in the round, the course of the fight took a dramatic turn.

Kelley ducked low to crank a right to the body and Gainer caught him with a right hook to the swollen eye. Kelley recoiled in pain and covered up as Gainer unleashed an avalanche of blows. Kelley voluntarily took a knee to regain his composure. After he arose, the right eye was a mess as there was swelling above and below.

Between rounds, Kelley and trainer Phil Borgia told Santore that a thumb caused the injury but replays were inconclusive. What was conclusive was that Kelley was in a world of trouble.

"Look at me!" Borgia yelled. "We've trained to fight with no eyes. You've got one eye and that means you have to work that right side even more on the slip. You got me?"

"Got you," Kelley answered.

"It don't mean a thing kid," Borgia said.

The trainer wanted his fighter to force Gainer to move toward Kelley's good eye, and both Borgia and Kelley had experience in this area. Kelley fought well for several rounds against Gonzalez with a swollen orbit and against Rivera, Kelley came back from two knockdowns and a horrible swelling to score an eighth-round knockout in a bout ESPN's Al Bernstein called the most dramatic comeback within a fight he had ever seen. So if anyone was equipped to handle this situation, Kelley was.

Knowing he had to get things done quickly, Kelley bolted out of the corner and tore after Gainer. Just 20 seconds into the round, Kelley uncorked a tremendous straight left to the jaw that propelled Gainer to the canvas. Up at four, Gainer told Santore "I'm all right," but his legs said, *"we're not."* As soon as the action resumed, Gainer wisely draped himself all over Kelley while Kelley twice popped him in the clinches with lefts to the face. Kelley drove Gainer back to the ropes and fought like a wild man, with every blow intended to end the fight immediately. Santore looked closely at Gainer, but Gainer saved himself by bouncing off the ropes and unleashing a four-punch flurry.

Then Gainer found a potential key to victory.

"Smoke" began moving to the left – toward Kelley's blind side – and smacked several straight lefts squarely on the wounded eye. Kelley continued to lunge in and Gainer's legs steadily regained strength as he motored around the ring. Gainer's mind wasn't focused on consolidating his strategic advantage; he just wanted to get back to the corner and clear his head. He figured the swollen eye would still be there to exploit in later rounds – if the doctor didn't stop the fight first.

Kelley's cutman Al Gavin worked on the injured eye but there was little even he could do as he lightly worked the Enswell over the upper and lower swellings. Borgia, meanwhile, sought to encourage his fighter.

"Look at what you did with one eye," Borgia marveled. "You need to pick it up here on the inside. He's running. He ain't going to win the (WBU) title running. Increase the jab and work your knees."

Then he leaned in close and said in a growling whisper "…and work your 'turn-overs.' He's there when you're on the inside. You trust me?"

Kelley trusted him implicitly, but Gainer's long-range tactics made it difficult for "The Flushing Flash" to follow through. At the one-minute mark, Kelley maneuvered Gainer to the ropes and worked the body with a right before the two men tangled and forced a break.

"Kelley's playing the wrong game," HBO analyst George Foreman observed. "He's waiting and waiting and waiting. Believe me, that's Gainer's game. He's just got to throw punches, keeping punching all the time." As Foreman was saying this, Kelley followed the advice to a tee as he trapped Gainer and the ropes and let his hands go at close range. But Gainer spun off the ropes and slashed a hurtful left to the eye that blunted Kelley's attack. Another long left to the injured orbit snuffed out Kelley's rally, and Gainer spent the rest of the round at long range, smartly using the jab to keep Kelley at arm's length while seeking further opportunities to exploit the eye.

Boxing is a sport with little room for strategic mercy. If an opponent is badly cut, fighters are taught to go after it. If a rib is broken, one must put aside his humanity and attack the injury. Some, like former heavyweight champion Floyd Patterson, refused to operate that way. If a fighter was cut, he shifted his attack to the body. In his second career, Foreman often asked referees to spare outmatched opponents extended beatings. But Gainer was among the legion that followed the sport's brutal code and he had no qualms about going after Kelley's eye. The ends, after all, justified the means.

Meanwhile, Borgia urged Kelley to free himself from his psychological shackles.

"You have got to be on this man's a**, damn it!" he said. "Do you understand me? You can't be outside because he's going to hit you with punches you can't see. Work your way in with the jab and let it go!"

But Gainer was working his plan too well, and his formula for victory was set — move to the left, pop Kelley with punches on the blind side and wait for the referee or doctor to stop the fight. He nipped in and out and stabbed Kelley with long jabs, short flurries and sharp left crosses. The swelling was growing to grotesque proportions, but there was little Kelley could do to stop Gainer's momentum. The only way for him to win was for Gainer to make a mistake.

With victory a real possibility, Gainer's confidence soared. He landed several four-punch salvos and another heavy left landed flush on the injured eye. Gainer wanted to be more than just Roy Jones' tag-along and he was moments away from establishing himself as a title threat before thousands of cheering fellow Floridians on American boxing's biggest television stage. For Gainer, life seemed very, very good.

As the ringside physician examined Kelley's eye, the fighter let out a groan. "I'm letting him go," he said after prying open the swelling. "Can you see out of the other eye," the doctor asked. "I can see," Kelley responded. With the right eye slammed shut, it would have been reasonable for the doctor to stop the fight but the physician chose to give the fighter a chance to bail himself out of a tight spot. Kelley received a double blessing of sorts – a Florida doctor that chose not to stop the fight in the home fighter's favor, and one with an "old-school" attitude.

Kelley began the eighth by bulling Gainer to the ropes with a right-left to the body and an overhand left as Gainer freed himself. Another light jab backed Gainer to the strands and Kelley worked him over at close range. Gainer was no longer on the bicycle and Kelley had successfully maneuvered his opponent into a position where he could do his best work.

Gainer fired two quick four-punch flurries in an effort to escape the ropes, but Kelley refused to retreat. Kelley continued to muscle Gainer against the ropes but took a crisp left to the face for his trouble. Kelley worked Gainer's body relentlessly while Gainer flashed his hand speed until he finally escaped to ring center.

While there, Gainer snapped a flurry that included three lefts to Kelley's eye. Kelley, clearly hurt, retreated to the ropes with hands held high. With victory at hand, Gainer turned up the aggression and let his fists fly. Kelley popped in occasional body punches, but Gainer's dominance was clear. Even when the action shifted away from the ropes, Gainer chose to stay at close range in an effort to extend his rally. A three-punch salvo connected and an overhand left to the eye hit home.

With 56 seconds remaining in the round, "The Flushing Flash" produced a lightning bolt that left Gainer's dreams up in smoke.

As both men launched left crosses, Gainer's again was triggered first but Kelley's landed with crushing force. As Kelley threw his overhand left, his feet shifted into a right-handed stance – thus the term "turnover." The shift enabled Kelley to gain even more momentum and power, and it was enough to extricate Kelley from another perilous situation.

At regular speed, the exchange was difficult to see due to its speed and suddenness. The impact of Kelley's shot sent Gainer flat on his back and at the count of seven, Santore stopped the fight because it was clear Gainer wouldn't be able to rise by the 10-count. At 2:16 of the eighth round, "The Flushing Flash" once again became "Captain Comeback."

"We were working on switching over, so I saw Gainer's right hand being down," Kelley told HBO's Larry Merchant. "So what I did was I came over the top and I switched…bang…left hand. I turned righty. We call that punch 'the crunch' because my habit is that I turn righty when I throw it over the top."

Kelley banked on Gainer's confidence becoming an Achilles' heel.

"The eye gave him a false sense of courage," he said. "When he saw the eye swelling, he saw that he actually had my title and he had me beat. The one thing you don't sleep on is a champion and today I answered a lot of questions. I never told Phil that I was going to stop fighting. I had two closed eyes against Alejandro Gonzalez. I'm used to it and I've fought like it before. That's what makes champions. I think Gainer learned a lesson also in that he fought a man with a closed eye. I have to give Gainer credit – he's a very, very good fighter. And I'm going to tell you something: In another year or two, he can be champ of the world."

"Kevin caught me with a good shot," a reflective and composed Gainer told Merchant. "I was winning the fight but I got a little careless. If you get careless, then you get caught, and if you get caught you get knocked out. I was moving and I dropped my hand and he switched off and caught me with a shot. He didn't extinguish 'Smoke' Gainer. I'll be back."

Epilogue: Gainer indeed would be back. On July 18, 1998 Gainer and Kelley fought again and this time the Floridian won a unanimous 10-round decision. In fact, the Kelley rematch was just the seventh victory in what would become a 16-fight winning streak that earned him a chance at Diego Corrales' IBF 130-pound title. Fighting outside his natural weight class, Gainer fell to the bigger, stronger, harder-hitting man in three rounds. But Gainer belatedly fulfilled Kelley's prediction for him three fights later when he stopped WBA featherweight champion Freddie Norwood in the 11th round on September 9, 2000. Gainer notched three defenses against Victor Polo (W 12), Daniel Seda (TD 2 due to a Gainer cut produced by a butt) and Oscar Leon (W 12) before dropping the belt in seven rounds to Juan Manuel Marquez. He would receive another title shot, however, this time against WBA champion Chris John April 22, 2005 in Jakarta, Indonesia. Gainer ended up being a step slower than the quick-fisted John and dropped a decision. Gainer won his final two fights, the last being a 10-round split decision over Carlos Navarro July 14, 2007 in Biloxi, Miss. His final record reads 41-7-1 (24 KO)

After the first Gainer victory, Kelley continued to roll by beating Edwin Santana (W 12), Jesus Salud (W 12) and Orlando Fernandez (KO 10) to earn a big-money fight against British-Yemeni sensation Prince Naseem Hamed at Madison Square Garden December 19, 1997. Hamed and Kelley put on an unforgettable spectacle as they combined for six knockdowns before Kelley was stopped in four rounds. Two fights later, Kelley lost the rematch to Gainer.

In the ensuing years, Kelley has scored several good wins (Hector Velasquez, Frankie Archuleta, Humberto Jose Reyes, and Juan Carlos Ramirez among others) while failing against others (Erik Morales, Marco Antonio Barrera and Bobby Pacquiao). As of January 2010 Kelley's most recent outing was a two round TKO loss to the 20-1 Vicente Escobedo in May 2009, dropping the 42-year-old Kelley's record to 60-10-2 with 39 knockouts.

BACK FROM THE BRINK – GREAT COMEBACKS

Total Punches Landed/Thrown

Round	1	2	3	4	5	6	7	8	9	10	11	12	Total
Kelley													104/274
													38%
Gainer													156/366
													43%

Jabs Landed/Thrown

Round	1	2	3	4	5	6	7	8	9	10	11	12	Total
Kelley													19/77
													25%
Gainer													37/154
													24%

Power Punches Landed/Thrown

Round	1	2	3	4	5	6	7	8	9	10	11	12	Total
Kelley													85/197
													43%
Gainer													119/212
													56%

* Fight originally done by CompuBox, but the original HTML files with complete round-by-round statistics no longer exist.

Kevin Kelley vs. Derrick Gainer I June 15, 1996, Jacksonville, Florida

TALES FROM THE VAULT

Joichiro Tatsuyoshi vs. Sirimongkol Singwancha
November 12, 1997, Osaka, Japan

The art of the comeback is something that is widely attempted but rarely acquired. Attaining a championship belt is difficult enough, but regaining it – not once, but twice – is a feat achieved by relatively few. History is replete with examples of deposed champions whose pride pushes them to take their quest one step too far. But those who take the risk and succeed are rewarded with a special brand of immortality.

When someone reaches the summit of his chosen sport multiple times it almost always prompts a wave of good feelings, especially if several years have passed between reigns. More often than not the athlete had to endure more than his share of adversity on his road back to the top, whether it be a career-threatening injury or a personal vice that had to be conquered before the journey could even begin. Usually, the culminating victory is preceded by a series of smaller ones that help make achieving the goal even sweeter.

Joichiro Tatsuyoshi is someone who knows all about this. The success that accompanied his early career seemed all too easy. At age 21 – and in only his eighth professional bout – Tatsuyoshi captured the WBC bantamweight title by stopping Greg Richardson in 10 rounds. No Japanese fighter had ever gained a championship in fewer bouts, and the future seemed bright for the outspoken man who fancied himself as the bad boy of Japanese boxing. He wasn't above taunting his opponents and his rebellious streak struck a chord with younger Japanese fans that felt trapped by their nation's societal constraints. Tatsuyoshi's admirers bestowed him the nickname of "Joe" after the hero of Japan's most popular boxing comic story and biographies about him flew off the shelves. Whenever he fought, Tatsuyoshi fed off the energy of his boisterous followers and produced brawl after breathtaking brawl.

Tatsuyoshi's troubles began shortly after stopping Richardson as doctors discovered a ruptured retina in his left eye. A year would pass before he made his first title defense against Victor Rabanales, who dominated Tatsuyoshi before stopping him in nine rounds. After the Rabanales fight, it was determined that the retina had detached and the Japanese Boxing Commission ordered Tatsuyoshi to retire. Following successful surgery, Tatsuyoshi challenged the JBC's policy by saying he was fully recovered and capable of continuing his career.

The JBC was caught in a philosophical and financial quandary. On the one hand, it wanted to safeguard fighters who had suffered retinal injuries but the immensely popular Tatsuyoshi was Japan's biggest draw and remained a big player on the world stage. The JBC crafted a compromise: Tatsuyoshi won the right to compete in Japan, but only in world championship fights.

Tatsuyoshi regained the WBC "interim" title after beating Rabanales by split decision but lost the chance to recapture the "full" title after breaking his hand in the first round en route to a majority decision defeat to Yasuei Yakushiji. Following two wins over Noe Santillana and Geronimo Cardoz in Las Vegas, Tatsuyoshi failed in two attempts to lift Daniel Zaragoza's WBC super bantamweight title, the first by 11th round TKO and the second by a unanimous decision. Tatsuyoshi appeared to have run out of chances after the second Zaragoza loss and a lackluster 10-round decision win over Ricardo Medina suggested Tatsuyoshi was a fading force.

But "Joe" remained a big-money attraction and on November 22, 1997 he received one last crack at a world title, this time against WBC bantamweight champion Sirimongkol Singwancha in Tatsuyoshi's hometown of Osaka. Like Tatsuyoshi, his route to the title was a short one as he knocked out Jose Luis Bueno in five rounds to capture the "interim" belt in his 13th pro fight. At 19, Singwancha was one of history's youngest champions regardless of division and his three subsequent title defenses against Jesus Sarabia (W 12), Javier Campanario (KO 4) and Rabanales (W 12) suggested a long reign was possible. At 5-8 with a 72-inch reach, the now 20-year-old Singwancha was a towering physical presence and his prime years were well ahead of him.

Osaka's Castle Hall was packed with rabid Tatsuyoshi fans and as the first bell sounded, they let out a loud roar of anticipation. Tatsuyoshi began the fight moving nimbly around Singwancha, but it was the champ who set the tone with hard, sharp jabs that threatened to break open Tatsuyoshi's well-worn scar tissue around the eyes. Tatsuyoshi rolled his upper body from side to side, but Singwancha's precise jabs continued to hit the mark and he soon followed with chopping rights and hooks.

Unhurt, Tatsuyoshi was using his superior mobility to dart in and out in search of his perfect punching range. Late in the round, Tatsuyoshi slipped Singwancha's jab to land his own jab, then used the same maneuver to twice tag the champ with a solid right-left hook combo. Another right to the ear backed up Singwancha and the crowd went wild, thinking the champion had been hurt. But the Thai ended the round well with a hook to the nose and two piercing jabs that made the challenger grimace.

Singwancha went back to the jab in round two, but Tatsuyoshi's slick upper body movement proved to be an effective defense. Tatsuyoshi slipped underneath a jab to land a hook to the body and pulled off the maneuver again a few seconds later. The young champion appeared one-dimensional as he relied heavily on the jab to set up occasional power shots while Tatsuyoshi's style was richer and more diversified, both on offense and defense. When Singwancha jabbed, Tatsuyoshi answered with two of his own. Occasionally he hooked off the jab or slid off to the side to create a punching angle. At other times, he shuffled his feet forward before jabbing to throw off Singwancha's rhythm, then bounced the jabs off the champ's chin.

Late in the second, Tatsuyoshi brought out another weapon in his arsenal – psychology. After ducking underneath a blow, he danced away, dropped his hands and tauntingly shrugged his shoulders up and down. He teased Singwancha by staying just out of punching range with his arms at his side, and the crowd loved the challenger's show of bravado. But Singwancha answered the taunts by smacking two hard jabs off the face and landing a light right-hook combo as the round closed.

Tatsuyoshi turned up the pressure in round three as he countered a jab with a leaping right-left to the face. Singwancha launched a counter right that whizzed past Tatsuyoshi's chin, but a left-left-right didn't miss. Singwancha was starting to time Tatsuyoshi's movement better as he nailed the challenger with a looping right as Tatsuyoshi moved to his left. Singwancha dug a right uppercut to the body and connected with a strong jab. In the final 12 seconds, Singwancha leaped in with a lead right to the jaw and a right-left popped Tatsuyoshi's head back, but the challenger answered with a hurtful hook to the stomach that had the champ holding on tightly until the bell.

That sequence enabled Tatsuyoshi to establish an important psychological foothold – he showed he could hurt Singwancha but the champion had yet to show he could seriously hurt Tatsuyoshi. Emboldened by his success, Tatsuyoshi started round four by backing the champ to the ropes and blasting him with a right-left to the jaw. A second right to the face stunned Singwancha and that provided the cue for Tatsuyoshi to launch every weapon in his arsenal.

The challenger darted in with a one-two and powered through a lead right to the jaw. He dug a hook to the body and countered a missed right uppercut with a solid hook to the jaw. A one-two set up a three-punch combo that rattled Singwancha's head. He walked through a solid right-left to land a snappy jab-left uppercut-right uppercut combo and won an exchange of rights. Tatsuyoshi was nothing short of brilliant as he shrugged off Singwancha's blows and pelted the champ with well-timed counters. In the final 15 seconds, Tatsuyoshi slammed in two lead rights and a follow-up barrage sent the champion stumbling toward the ropes. It was the first clear sign of vulnerability by the champion, and Tatsuyoshi sought to drive that point home when the bell rang. Instead of walking back to his corner, Tatsuyoshi bumped shoulders with the champion and stood defiantly at ring center as Singwancha was escorted to his corner.

It was a huge round for Tatsuyoshi and the hometown crowd played no small part in it. Every blow was greeted with full-throated rapture and it was clear Tatsuyoshi was feeding off their energy. Tatsuyoshi was revved up and feeling sky-high as he stood in his corner and led the cheers as he awaited the fifth-round bell. He was convinced he was just moments away from becoming a three-time bantamweight champion.

Tatsuyoshi jumped all over Singwancha, landing a lightning-quick left-left-right-hook to the body combo and a lead right sent water spraying from the champion's head. A right-left uppercut combo banged through and it was clear Tatsuyoshi was going all out for the knockout. Had he been a stiffer puncher Singwancha would have been put away long before, but the champion was big, strong and tough to chop down.

When the action moved inside, Singwancha began landing the harder blows and slowly turning the tide in his favor. A right to the ear sent Tatsuyoshi stumbling forward a step and a hook landed flush on the jaw. The Japanese challenger had drained himself in his knockout quest and was looking weary. A heavy right to the side of the head hurt Tatsuyoshi and the fans had to wonder if their hero had shot his bolt.

They didn't have to wonder long.

Tatsuyoshi tapped his inner reservoir to hurt Singwancha with close-range combinations that nearly doubled over the champ. Seeing Singwancha's weakness, Tatsuyoshi blasted away with blinding combinations. Singwancha managed to secure a clinch and as he straightened up and took a deep breath, his eyes were wide with surprise. Just a few moments before, the challenger was tired and vulnerable and now he was strafing him with quick and accurate clusters.

With 29 seconds left in the round, a textbook one-two sent Singwancha heavily to the canvas near his own corner. In one motion, Singwancha rolled over and up to his feet at the count of two. Meanwhile, Tatsuyoshi retreated to the neutral corner with his right arm upraised, acknowledging the ear-splitting roars that reverberated throughout Castle Hall. When referee Richard Steele called them back together, the two men traded furious blows whose purposes were diametrically opposed – Tatsuyoshi sought to put the champ away while Singwancha fought for survival. As the bell sounded to end a riveting round, almost everyone in the house knew that Tatsuyoshi had successfully turned back the clock and that it would take a formidable effort to deny what he felt was his destiny.

Tatsuyoshi started the sixth on fire, driving a hook to the body and unloaded a series of blistering combinations. Singwancha weathered the storm and nailed Tatsuyoshi with a tremendous right cross that clearly hurt the challenger. Tatsuyoshi ducked inside to clear his head, but Singwancha landed a chopping right to the side of the head and a flush jab. But Tatsuyoshi knew this was his last, best chance to regain a title, so he sucked it up and matched Singwancha punch for punch in an intense exchange. Singwancha tagged the charging challenger with a left uppercut and right cross and two thumping jabs found the mark. Tatsuyoshi's chopping right twisted Singwancha's head awkwardly and he followed with a right-left to the head and a tremendous hook to the body. When Singwancha didn't respond immediately, Tatsuyoshi rattled off a six-punch combo.

The battle shifted inside and the two men took turns dishing out tremendous punishment. Singwancha fired a pair of one-twos to the jaw and a right to the head and hook to the body stunned the challenger. A right cross caromed off Tatsuyoshi's unprotected jaw, but the Japanese roared back by winning an exchange of hooks and connecting with a parting jab as an extraordinary sixth round closed. Both men were clearly winded as they plopped on their respective stools.

Both men exchanged freely in close quarters as the seventh began with Singwancha gaining an edge by using his upper body strength to push Tatsuyoshi toward the ropes while continuing to throw punches. Tatsuyoshi retreated inch by inch, not because he wanted to but because Singwancha forced him to do so.

For the first time in the fight, Singwancha strung together combinations and he had Tatsuyoshi's head snapping back time and again. The boisterous crowd grew quieter as they sensed their man was in trouble. Singwancha cracked two hooks to the jaw and a solid left drove Tatsuyoshi across the ring. As they milled on the inside, Singwancha landed a chopping right to the ear but missed with a wild left hook.

That miss would prove crucial.

Showing presence of mind and incredible timing, Tatsuyoshi shifted his body slightly, lined up Singwancha with the left and exploded a right cross off the jaw and a hook to the belly that turned the tide in a most violent way. The body shot drove Singwancha to his knees and as he struggled to his feet at the count of eight the end looked near. It was a massive turnaround and Tatsuyoshi sought to take full advantage by racing across the ring and firing off a 16-punch flurry that had Singwancha careening around the ring. Referee Steele, seeing Singwancha was helpless, stepped between the fighters and stopped the bout at 1:54 of the seventh round.

His journey completed, Tatsuyoshi leaped in the air and fell to his knees in celebration. His corner swarmed around the new champion and the fans enveloped him in a resounding wall of sound. Meanwhile, the heartbroken Singwancha sat in his corner and wept. He had given everything he had in defense of his championship and his reward was seeing another man walk away with the belt. That realization hit him harder than any of Tatsuyoshi's blows.

For Tatsuyoshi, victory meant history – he became the first fighter to capture a share of the bantamweight title three times, and he did so against three different champions. For Singwancha it was his most disappointing day as a pro but at 20 the future still carried promise. His story still had many more chapters to be written but on this day, he served as a supporting character to another man's greatest moment as a professional. Unlike the fictional Japanese super hero "Joe," Tatsuyoshi's comeback story was very real.

Epilogue: Tatsuyoshi returned to the ring five months later and scored a 12-round decision over Jose Rafael Sosa. His next defense against the undefeated Paulie Ayala was stopped after six rounds due to an unintentional headbutt and Tatsuyoshi retained the belt because he was ahead on all three scorecards at the time of the stoppage.

The Ayala victory would prove to be his last as a champion. Veerapol Sahaprom stopped Tatsuyoshi in six rounds to win the belt and the Thai won the rematch eight months later in the seventh. Tatsuyoshi quit the ring for three years before returning for two fights. After stopping Saen Sor Ploenchit in six rounds, the 33-year-old Tatsuyoshi ostensibly ended his career with a 10-round decision over Julio Cesar Avila on September 26, 2003. But Tatsuyoshi wasn't done with the ring, for he launched a badly received comeback at age 38 by stopping novice fighter Phalangchai Chuwatana in two rounds. Then, on March 8, 2009 at the famed Rajadamnern Stadium in Bangkok, Sakai Jockygym TKO'd the shadow of "Joe" in seven rounds. As of January 2010, Tatsuyoshi's record stands at 20-7-1 (14 KO).

Singwancha took the long, slow road to redemption, winning 23 consecutive fights over the next five years to earn a shot at the vacant WBC super featherweight title. The Thai made good on his opportunity, knocking out Kengo Nagashina in two rounds to become a two-division champion. After a non-title KO win over Richard Cabillo, Singwancha scored a lopsided decision over Yong Soo Choi to retain the title. The Thai stopped Anthony Tshehla in six rounds in a non-title bout, but lost the championship by decision to Jesus Chavez on August 15, 2003.

Since losing the title to Chavez, Singwancha has remained active. As of January 2010, he is riding a 20-fight winning streak, and one of his victories included a seven-round TKO win over former "Contender" star Michael Clark on May 14, 2005. His most recent outing, a two-round KO of Mohammed Saleh in August 2009 in Nakhon Ratchasima, Thailand, raised the 32-year-old's record to an impressive 63-2 (37 KO).

TALES FROM THE VAULT

Total Punches Landed/Thrown

Round	1	2	3	4	5	6	7	8	9	10	11	12	Total
Tatsuyoshi	33/61 54%	13/54 24%	16/61 26%	57/103 55%	71/123 58%	48/104 46%	26/48 54%						264/554 48%
Singwancha	32/92 35%	26/65 40%	27/84 32%	25/81 31%	30/76 39%	46/99 46%	35/62 56%						221/559 40%

Jabs Landed/Thrown

Round	1	2	3	4	5	6	7	8	9	10	11	12	Total
Tatsuyoshi	24/47 51%	8/36 22%	8/37 22%	16/35 46%	4/19 21%	8/14 57%	4/15 27%						72/203 35%
Singwancha	25/64 39%	20/46 43%	14/49 29%	18/41 44%	3/10 30%	10/24 42%	13/19 68%						103/253 41%

Power Punches Landed/Thrown

Round	1	2	3	4	5	6	7	8	9	10	11	12	Total
Tatsuyoshi	9/14 64%	5/18 28%	8/24 33%	41/68 60%	67/104 64%	40/90 44%	22/33 67%						192/351 55%
Singwancha	7/28 25%	6/19 32%	13/35 37%	7/40 18%	27/66 41%	36/75 48%	22/43 51%						118/306 39%

Joichiro Tatsuyoshi vs. Sirimongkol Singwancha November 12, 1997, Osaka, Japan

John Mugabi vs. James "Hard Rock" Green
February 19, 1984, Tampa, Florida

When a fighter is being groomed for greatness, the early portion of his career is carefully choreographed. The skillful manager chooses opponents who are good enough to offer the prospect a stylistic problem to solve yet not be talented enough to win. Ideally, the level of competition is raised slightly in every bout and by the time he is ready to make the big step, he will be fully equipped to handle any situation that comes before him.

John "The Beast" Mugabi certainly qualified as a prospect. Following an amateur career that culminated with a silver medal in the 1980 Olympics for his native Uganda, Mugabi began his pro career with a first-round knockout of Oemer Karadenis December 5, 1980 in Cologne, Germany. A first-round knockout in his pro debut is hardly unusual for prospects; in fact it's the desired result. After all, the potential star must demonstrate his superiority to make the case for bigger and better fights down the road.

When the knockout streak stretches to four or five fights, some mild notice is generated but when it reaches double-digits, eyebrows start arching upward. For Mugabi, that 10th knockout came against Curtis Taylor in March 1982, and it was the eighth fight that ended in the first or second round. At this point, Mugabi's competition was raised and he passed the test with flying colors as he iced respected journeyman Curtis Ramsey in one round.

From then on, the budding legend of "The Beast" grew exponentially and he was greatly helped by the expertise of Mickey Duff, who he met shortly after he moved to London following his pro debut. After eight fights he moved to Tampa, Florida and his knockout string quickly caught the eyes of NBC executives.

Doug Demmings, who went eight rounds with Marvelous Marvin Hagler and the full 10 with Alan Minter, became knockout victim number 13 when he fell in five. Former junior middleweight title challenger Gary Guiden never fought again after becoming Mugabi's 15th notch. Former WBA junior middleweight champion Eddie Gazo lasted only one round to become number 18 and tough Curtis Parker became Mugabi's eighth first-round knockout victim and 19th overall. By the time he met James "Hard Rock" Green on February 19, 1984 at the Hyatt Regency in Tampa, the 24-year-old Mugabi was on the cusp of a title shot as he was rated second by the WBC and eighth by the WBA at 154 pounds.

The 25-year-old Green (18-3, 11 KO) represented a step up in competition for Mugabi as the New Jersey resident was rated number seven in the WBA and 13th by the WBC. But the 5-5 fireplug had fallen on hard times as he went 2-2 in his last four bouts. One of those losses, a sixth round TKO to Frank "The Animal" Fletcher on October 16, 1982, was particularly disillusioning. Green dominated Fletcher over the first four rounds, but in the fourth a cut was opened over the right eye. The cut worsened in the fifth and in the sixth, Green threw the first punch but then stopped fighting completely because the blood rendered him helpless. Over the final 70 seconds, Fletcher unleashed 94 unanswered blows and referee Frank Cappuccino had no choice but to stop the fight.

Questions about Green's fighting spirit swirled, and matters didn't get much better as he lost a 12-round decision to David Braxton three fights later. Green entered the Mugabi match off a two-round knockout win over Bobby West two months before, but because of the two losses he was viewed as a pit stop for the Mugabi championship express.

Both men weighed in at 154 pounds and the battle plans were crystal clear. For Mugabi, it was simple – overpower Green like he did his previous 19 opponents. For Green, the plan was more complex. First, he had to find a way to neutralize Mugabi's six-inch reach advantage, and do so without getting nailed with one of Mugabi's bombs. Second, he needed to get "The Beast" into the later rounds as none of his fights had lasted more than six rounds. A tired Mugabi would be a vulnerable Mugabi. Finally, he had to hit Mugabi hard enough to earn respect and thus inhibit his offensive firepower.

Green started the fight by ducking under Mugabi's jab, bullying him to the ropes and popping him with a short hook that sent water flying from the Ugandan's head. Mugabi winged rights and lefts with full power but Green skillfully dodged them and landed a right-left hook to the head and hooks to the head and body. Green wasn't hurting Mugabi, but he was scoring points. More importantly, it was he, not Mugabi, who dictated the terms of battle.

A Mugabi jab and right to the body connected well but all it did was trigger a Green salvo to the body punctuated by a jolting hook to the jaw. Green countered a Mugabi left uppercut with hooks to the body and face. Green ended the round by ducking under four Mugabi hooks and answering with his own precise hook.

In terms of execution, it was a dream round for Green; he not only survived the first round but he dominated it with skill and intelligence. Still, Green had to duplicate this success nine more times to ensure victory because even if "Hard Rock" fought perfectly for nine rounds, two minutes and 49 seconds, Mugabi could render all his efforts moot with one mighty blow.

Mugabi knew that to land that one blow he had to try something other than plowing over his smaller foe. So he began to tap the experience gleaned from his amateur days by working behind the jab and establishing longer punching range. His tactics paid dividends as he caught Green coming in with a hook, his first big scoring blow of the bout. Green also benefited psychologically as he absorbed the punch well and pelted Mugabi with a hook, a right to the body and another hook to the jaw. Green countered a missed jab with a quick left-right to the body as well as a right to the ribs and hook to the jaw. "Hard Rock" ended an excellent second round by getting the better of an extended exchange at close quarters which was punctuated with a jolting right to the jaw.

A split second after the bell rang, a frustrated Mugabi tagged Green with a hook. Green tried to retaliate, but referee Joe Cortez held him back. The ringside physician paid a visit to Mugabi's corner to examine his eye, which caught an accidental thumb sometime during the previous round.

Green was executing beautifully. He moved in and out of range as he pleased and his shots continually shredded Mugabi's defense. He successfully walked the tightrope that big punchers dictate to their opponents – doing enough on offense to impress the judges while still respectful of his opponent's power. The plan was to take Mugabi into the later rounds and win a decision but there soon would be reason for Green to raise his expectations.

With 1:40 left in the third, Green popped out of his crouch and nailed Mugabi with a quick jolting right. A few seconds later, another counter right twisted Mugabi's head awkwardly and had him seeking the refuge of a clinch. But Green shrugged him off and nailed him with a huge hook to the jaw that put him in deep trouble for the first time in his professional life. A right to the ear drove Mugabi towards the corner and he desperately reached out with both arms to grab Green's head.

Since Mugabi had always been the attacker, he never had to sharpen his survival skills and Green took full advantage by battering Mugabi with every punch in the book. The pro-Mugabi crowd shrieked in shock as their man soaked up tremendous punishment. A monsoon's worth of blows rained down on the African, and had Green been a more powerful puncher he surely would have finished the job then and there. But because Green was not blessed in that way, he eventually ran out of steam and he ended up burrowing inside to recharge his batteries for the remainder of the round. Needless to say, Mugabi was grateful for the respite.

When the bell ending the third sounded, Green took a deep breath, looked out into the hostile audience and shrugged his shoulders as if to say *"well, I did the best I could but I just couldn't knock him out."* Meanwhile, the ringside physician and Cortez took a close look at the battered Mugabi and seriously thought about stopping the fight. But manager Mickey Duff repeatedly and forcefully assured them his fighter was fit to continue. Eventually, they relented and the fight was allowed to proceed.

Both men were in recovery mode as the fourth round started but Mugabi broke the cycle by landing a hard right to the jaw, his best blow of the bout so far. As was his habit, Mugabi went for the kill but Green wasn't yet ready to be taken as he skillfully dipped and slipped Mugabi's quick-fisted follow-ups. Another hard right stunned Green along the ropes but again "Hard Rock" escaped further damage, even going as far as to taunt "The Beast" by dancing around the ring and beckoning him with his right glove.

But Mugabi was doing better as he pot shotted the charging Green with rights. Mugabi drove a right to the ribs and Green, still weary from his third-round exertion, sought to rest in a clinch. When the bell rung, he wearily backed into the ropes with a slight wobble in his knees. Upon seeing this, Mugabi realized two things – first, Green was a tough nut; and second, that nut was showing the first signs of cracking. To finish the job, Mugabi had to practice something he didn't need to before – patience.

Mugabi began the fifth at long range, surveying Green for openings. It didn't take him long to find a good one as he uncorked a massive hook that hit Green flush. But Green only grimaced, shook his head and nailed Mugabi with his own right, sparking a fierce mid-ring exchange.

The lessons were coming at Mugabi from all directions. In the third, he was given a pop quiz on how to survive when badly hurt. Then he was forced to abandon his familiar all-out style in favor of a more conservative attack – all this while operating with an eye affected by an accidental thumb. Now he was given another problem to solve: What does a big puncher do when an opponent takes away his most formidable weapon? Many end up losing their poise, then the fight. The wiser ones continue to plug away, secure in the knowledge that the knockout blow can manifest itself at any moment while at the same time piling up enough points to capture a decision.

For Green, this fight was an opportunity to take a giant step toward redemption but for Mugabi it represented a symbolic purification through competitive fire. It offered Mugabi the chance to smooth the rough edges of his style and leave the ring a more complete fighter. It was up to Mugabi to choose his path; would he treat it as a short-term crisis to escape or would he allow himself to explore other options and arm himself with valuable experience that he would need in bigger fights down the road?

The answer began to emerge in the sixth as Mugabi worked his jab at long range, and it set up a right uppercut to the body and a left hook that sprayed water from Green's head. Two more hooks glanced off Green's jaw a few seconds later. Mugabi was on his toes, using his height and reach advantages to good effect. He no longer was a one-dimensional bomber who said of every opponent "I knock him out." Instead he was growing up before thousands of eyes in the arena and millions around the nation. Green helped the process along by not pressuring Mugabi as he had in earlier rounds. Green's troubles multiplied late in the round when a stray thumb hit his left eye. Green held his glove to his eye and winced noticeably for the rest of the round.

The eye swelled between rounds and manager Lou Duva told Green to spend the next round on his bicycle to allow himself to recover. The new-and-improved Mugabi pursued Green calmly and fired long-range jabs. A solid right smacked against the swelling and a follow-up jab snapped Green's head back. By the two-minute mark, Green's eye was nearly slammed shut but he managed to land three crisp hooks before the bell.

Between rounds seven and eight, Green told Duva he had triple vision, prompting the old-school trainer to say, "hit the one in the middle." Quitting was not an option for either fighter or trainer.

A chopping right stunned Green in the eighth, but the American responded the way he always did – by charging forward and striking back. Green bulldogged Mugabi to the ropes like a linebacker hitting a blocking sled, but when the game switched back to boxing from football at ring center, it was Mugabi who was in charge as he snapped jabs at the injured eye. In the final minute, Mugabi nailed Green with four consecutive overhand rights while Green shoe-shined Mugabi's body. Another left-right from Mugabi connected cleanly, and the rest of the round saw the action decelerate to nearly a crawl.

Duff felt much better about his fighter's prospects after the eighth because he believed Mugabi had finally seized control.

"All you must do now is don't do anything stupid," Duff said. "Keep your hands up nicely and you must go forward, John. Come forward with the jab and your hands up and you won't get hurt." Mugabi followed his advice to the letter during the first half of the ninth but a rejuvenated Green started to engage Mugabi more and landed a good lead right to the temple. Later, Mugabi caught Green coming in with a hook but "Hard Rock" unleashed two good rights to steal a slower-moving ninth.

As the fight entered the 10th, Mugabi had made up significant ground on the scorecards and the momentum had clearly swung his way. Even though he had never fought past six rounds before this day, Mugabi had plenty of bounce in his legs and snap on his blows. Green, for his part, showed the courage many felt he didn't have by continuing to fight hard despite a closed left eye. With his face a bloody mess, Green had the temerity to taunt "The Beast" as he backpedaled around the ring. Mugabi saw this as a sign of weakness and he plowed forward, going all out for the knockout.

Mugabi trapped Green in his own corner and pounded away with eight unanswered blows that culminated with a jolting jab to the head. At this point, referee Cortez had seen enough and called a halt. Duva jumped into the ring to complain about what he felt was a premature stoppage but Green offered no protest. Instead he immediately bounded to center ring and embraced the back of Mugabi, who was busy hugging corner man George Francis. Mugabi had gotten the best of both worlds in this fight; he not only got a gut check, he was also able to keep his knockout string alive.

"This was a tough fight for me," Mugabi told NBC's Dr. Ferdie Pacheco. "It was the toughest I've had in my life. He is a tough guy."

"In the second round, he caught a thumb, an accidental thumb, and I'm beginning to believe in the thumbless gloves," Duff added. "He caught a thumb and he couldn't see. The third round was very crucial because he had to get over the round and gradually, for his eye, focus back. Outside of that, he was never really in trouble except he was in with a man who was fighting for his life."

Duff fully realized the challenges his man had overcome, and he predicted this experience would serve him well in the future.

"We've proved now we've overcome adversity in a fight," Duff said. "Mr. Hearns (the WBC champion at the time), we await your pleasure. I'm going to phone the WBC tomorrow and make sure they act responsibly because he is well overdue to make a mandatory defense."

"He had a thumb in his eye in the third or fourth round," a calmer Duva told Dr. Pacheco. "He started complaining about double and triple vision so I had to give him the old adage 'hit the guy in the middle.' He started picking it up and he started to get a little cute and used the ring a little bit. I would have rather he kept right on top of the guy. I thought he hurt him every time he hit him. He had him hurt on numerous occasions."

He concluded the interview by asking the question that was on more than a few people's minds: "Wouldn't this make for a hell of a rematch?"

Epilogue: There would be no rematch, and the fortunes of each man took opposite directions. Green would fight 12 more times over the next 12 years, winning only four. After the Mugabi loss, Green took nine months off before posting wins against Gary Coates (KO 6) and Jake Torrance (KO 6). Those victories set up an over-the-weight bout with world welterweight champion Donald Curry, who was testing the 154-pound waters. The bout was stopped after two rounds and from then on Green would serve as a "name" for up-and-comers like Robert Hines (D 10), Kevin Watts (L 10) and Michael Olajide (L 10). Following the Olajide loss, Green spent eight years away from the sport and his return began well as he knocked out Victor Davis in four rounds. But losses to Bryant Brannon (KO by 10) and John David Jackson (L 8) sandwiched a four-round retirement victory over Tyrone Haywood, the final win of Green's career. The 37-year-old Green took one final stab at glory by taking on Otis Grant for the NABF middleweight title on January 15, 1996 at the Landmark Inn in Woodbridge, N.J. But a 12th round TKO loss convinced Green that the time to bow out had arrived. Green's final record is 22-10-2 (15 KO).

Mugabi continued to march toward a title shot as he scored five knockouts over Wilbert "Vampire" Johnson, Frank "The Animal" Fltecher, Nino Gonzalez, Earl Hargrove and Bill Bradley. Though he had scored 26 consecutive knockouts to start his career, he still entered the ring a considerable underdog against legendary middleweight champion Marvelous Marvin Hagler. Boxing with composure and skill, Mugabi gave

Hagler all he could handle before exhaustion – and Hagler's fists – caved him in midway through round 11.

Mugabi's stirring performance against Hagler raised his stock in the boxing world, and in his next fight he fought Duane Thomas for the vacant WBC super welterweight title nine months after the Hagler defeat. Thomas shocked the boxing world – and Mugabi – by stopping the Ugandan in round three after a blow (some say a thumb) shattered Mugabi's orbital bone.

Mugabi remained out of the ring for two years and appeared to regain his knockout touch by stopping his next eight opponents. The string of success earned him a title shot against newly crowned WBC super welterweight champion Rene Jacquot, who stunningly lifted the belt from Curry in his most recent outing. Mugabi captured the belt after Jacquot broke his ankle while slipping to the canvas, forcing the stoppage in round one.

Mugabi was finally a champion and he celebrated with a pair of non-title one-round knockouts over Ricky Stackhouse and Carlos Antunes Fonseca. His first title defense came against the formidable Terry Norris, who was stopped by Julian Jackson in a previous title challenge. Norris, hungry for redemption, attacked Mugabi from the opening bell and registered a knockout two minutes and fifty-seven seconds later.

Mugabi would fight for a belt once more, losing by first round KO to WBO champ Gerald McClellan three fights and 20 months after the Norris defeat. Mugabi took a five-year break from the sport after the McClellan bout, moving to Australia and re-launching his career in 1996 with a 10-round decision over Peter Kinsella. Three fights later he won the vacant Australian super middleweight title by decisioning Jamie Wallace over 12 rounds. He never defended that belt.

After going 1-2-1 in his next four fights, Mugabi – two months shy of his 39th birthday – ended his career by losing a 12-round decision to the 19-0-1 Glen Kelly on January 16, 1999 in Sydney. His record stands at 42-7-1 (39 KO).

TALES FROM THE VAULT

Total Punches Landed/Thrown

Round	1	2	3	4	5	6	7	8	9	10	11	12	Total
Mugabi	15/88	16/71	18/69	32/99	20/53	21/76	13/34	32/59	20/60	24/50			211/659
	17%	23%	26%	32%	38%	28%	38%	54%	33%	48%			32%
Green	28/65	27/56	58/99	15/41	25/57	23/53	8/18	18/47	42/79	4/13			248/528
	43%	48%	59%	37%	44%	43%	44%	38%	53%	31%			47%

Jabs Landed/Thrown

Round	1	2	3	4	5	6	7	8	9	10	11	12	Total
Mugabi	5/31	4/30	4/18	7/28	6/15	6/20	6/21	17/29	7/27	6/15			68/234
	16%	13%	22%	25%	40%	30%	29%	59%	26%	40%			29%
Green	1/6	1/16	3/7	2/6	3/11	1/10	1/3	1/11	2/10	1/4			16/84
	17%	6%	43%	33%	27%	10%	33%	9%	20%	25%			19%

Power Punches Landed/Thrown

Round	1	2	3	4	5	6	7	8	9	10	11	12	Total
Mugabi	10/57	12/41	14/51	25/71	14/38	15/56	7/13	15/30	13/33	18/35			143/425
	18%	29%	27%	35%	37%	27%	54%	50%	39%	51%			34%
Green	27/59	26/40	55/92	13/35	22/46	22/43	7/15	17/36	40/69	3/9			232/444
	46%	65%	60%	37%	48%	51%	47%	47%	58%	33%			52%

John Mugabi vs. James "Hard Rock" Green February 19, 1984, Tampa, Florida

Rolando Navarrete vs. Chung Il Choi
January 16, 1982, Manila, Philippines

When Rolando Navarrete met Cornelius Boza-Edwards for the WBC super featherweight title on August 29, 1981 in Viareggio, Italy, he was cast in the role of stand-in. Sure, the 23-year-old Filipino boasted a fine resume. He had experience (50 fights in a career that began three days after his 16th birthday), as well as a crowd-pleasing aggressive style. His one other title challenge, a fifth-round TKO loss to then-WBC champ Alexis Arguello, was aired by ABC so Navarrete was a familiar face to American audiences.

But Navarrete wasn't supposed to perform on this big stage – at least not yet. The man from whom Boza-Edwards won the title, Rafael "Bazooka" Limon, was supposed to fight on this night but illness forced him to the sideline. So the eighth-ranked Navarrete, who was preparing to fight Gerald Hayes, was asked to step in. Boza-Edwards vs. Navarrete promised to provide quality entertainment but most expected the leading man to emerge with his star intact.

But Navarrete carried his own script into the ring and decided to become a scene-stealer. Midway through the fourth round, the Filipino southpaw floored the champ with a ferocious right-left and he decked the champ a second time with his "money punch" – a potent right hook. The champ survived, but not for long as another pulverizing right hook put him down for the 10-count at 1:41 of the fifth.

The stand-in was now the star and on January 16, 1982 Navarrete (40-8-3, 18 KO) was the man of the hour as he put his new title on the line before 30,000 of his countrymen at Rizal Memorial Stadium in Malate, Metro Manila, Philippines. The supporting actor on this day was South Korean up-and-comer Chung Il Choi, a former Asian Amateur Games champion who was a confirmed knockout artist. His 13-0 record boasted 12 knockouts, with eight of them coming against Filipinos. His most notable wins came in three consecutive fights between October 1980 and April 1981 against Rod Sequenan (KO 8), Rey Tam (KO 3) and Nene Jun (KO 5). But Navarrete also had success against Tam (KO 4) and Jun (W 12, W 12), who were fresher fighters when he beat them. Still, Choi entered the title shot with five consecutive knockouts, including a one-round blowout of Erning Grafe in his most recent outing.

The pair spent several long minutes in the ring being gloved up, introduced and posed for photographers but it didn't take them long to warm up once the bell rang. The 5-8 ½ Choi, 130, immediately assumed the role of aggressor against the 5-6 Navarrete, also 130, launching a lead right that whizzed past the champ's jaw. Though Choi had the physical equipment to stick and move, he chose to plant his feet and engage the champ, who calmly operated behind high-held gloves.

Choi began the action at the 44-second mark when his cracking hook and strong right backed the champ to the ropes, but Navarrete slid away, returned to ring center and continued to size up the challenger. Choi, however, was in no mood to study so he fired off a seven-punch flurry, but the champion's skillful upper-body movement enabled him to slip every blow. A few seconds later Choi launched another four-punch salvo and again Navarrete dodged every bullet. But the pugnacious Choi persisted and this time his effort was rewarded as a stinging right-left reached Navarrete and a follow-up right forced the champ to back away. Choi then attacked viciously, driving Navarrete across the ring with a six-punch volley. Navarrete was not seriously hurt as he returned to ring center and hit Choi with a right hook to the body and a counter left to the ribs after Choi missed a right-left-right.

A strong right-left-right to the jaw wobbled Navarrete 1:47 into the round and the challenger raced in like a school of starving piranhas as he launched a piston-like 15-punch flurry that drove the Filipino to his own corner pad. Navarrete banged a short left cross to the jaw, but the raging Choi ignored it and unleashed another eight-punch volley. A follow-up right-left missed the target, but another right-left-right propelled the champ back to the ropes. Navarrete fought off the strands with two lefts to the jaw and they spent the rest of the round recharging their batteries at ring center.

The first round proved beyond doubt that Choi loved the bright lights and wanted more than anything to become the leading man. He took the fight to the champion and he didn't care that he was doing so before a crowd that would have loved nothing more than to see him fall flat on his face. Instead, he was in a mood to upstage the star and seize the glory.

A minute into the second round, Choi landed a left-left-right but moments later Navarrete would show the challenger just what he was up against. Navarrete countered a wild Choi right with a short left to the chin that wobbled the challenger. Navarrete was in hot pursuit and he wound up a big left to the body. But Choi was ready for him and he caught the champ with a huge counter hook to the jaw. Though Navarrete appeared to take the blow well, Choi saw weakness and took the initiative by firing a right-left-right-left. Navarrete banged a right-left to the body that temporarily backed off the challenger, but Choi persisted behind a light left-left-right-left followed by a right-left.

Then came Choi's first real test. Navarrete nailed Choi with his "money punch," the big right hook, and followed it with a left. Other men, including Boza-Edwards, had fallen from similar blows but here Choi was up to the task. Sure, he wobbled, but he also fired back as he dug a right to the body and a light left to the forehead before circling away. Choi tagged the champion with a hook coming in and a dangerous looking right-left zinged past Navarrete's chin. Navarrete nailed Choi with a lead left cross to the jaw, but all it did was spark a short but fierce exchange along the ropes. A solid right hook slammed against Choi's temple as the round ended, and the challenger walked to his corner with a moderate but persistent flow of blood from his nostrils.

Choi continued his aggression in the third, faking a left and driving a right to the body while the follow-up hook just missed. Choi tried the move again a few seconds later and this time it worked brilliantly. The straight right to the ribs hurt Navarrete badly and he tottered to the ropes. Choi fired away with 15 straight blows, but the champ's arms and elbows deflected most of them. The crisis passed relatively quickly, and Navarrete turned Choi toward the ropes and popped him with a left to the head and right to the body before returning to the center of the ring. A straight left to the eye made Navarrete wince, but the Filipino countered a follow-up lead right with a solid left uppercut to the body.

Choi burned lots of energy in the early stages by bouncing on his toes, continually feinting with his left and projecting an anxiousness to get going even during the bout's quieter moments. Conversely, Navarrete was the picture of composure as he weaved his upper body and maintained a relaxed posture. His experience told him that this bout was scheduled for 15 rounds and that he had plenty of time to wear down his eager, but relatively green, challenger. But in the meantime Choi made life difficult. Late in the round, a right followed by a right-left triggered yet another piston-like seven-punch flurry. As he sat in the corner, the blood from Choi's nose was under control and he was comforted by the fast start that enabled him to seize an early lead on the scorecards.

Choi stood at ring center several seconds before the fourth-round bell, and American referee Chuck Hassett had to keep Choi at bay by extending his right arm. But when the bell sounded Choi was on his toes and circling the ring. Navarrete slipped a right and drove a heavy left to the stomach but missed a pair of straight lefts a few seconds later. The chaos of the first three rounds was a thing of the past and the fight settled into a more deliberate pace. That suited Navarrete just fine because now he was given a chance to catch his breath and plot his strategy.

Choi caught Navarrete coming in with a 45-degree hook but Navarrete answered with a right hook to the jaw and a clean counter left a few moments later. Choi still fired occasional right-left-rights, but they missed the target — sometimes by a wide margin. A right hook to the body by Navarrete drew a caution from Hassett, but that didn't stop the champ from landing a heavy left to the stomach a few seconds later. As the round neared a close, Choi stopped bouncing, planted his feet and began to throw lead rights. Two of them landed particularly well and his follow-up seven-punch flurry ended what had been the fight's quietest round thus far.

Choi continued to box in the fifth, his jabs designed more to keep Navarrete at bay than to score. The champ maintained his high guard, and while he picked off many of the blows he wasn't doing a lot on offense. Choi had tried to bowl over Navarrete like he did his previous 13 opponents but now he was fighting at a more sedate pace because he knew the champ was made of far sterner stuff. Navarrete's cuffing right hook set up a strong straight left that made Choi back up, and he followed with a straight left to the head and a right hook to the body. Choi missed over the top with two rights and Navarrete drove a hard left and right to the body. It was evident that Navarrete was enjoying his best sequence of the fight, and as Choi stumbled off balance following a wild left, the champ was ready to consolidate his advantage.

Choi, however, had other ideas.

As Navarrete pressed ahead, Choi caught him with a short right uppercut to the jaw and a follow-up right hook appeared to stun the champ. A fired-up Choi unleashed a torrent of blows but the still composed Navarrete clipped Choi with a right that halted his progress momentarily. A right-left-right caused Navarrete's upper body to pitch forward and he appeared ready to go down, but when Choi rushed in Navarrete fired a fierce left-right to the body that slowed the attack slightly.

Though Navarrete was putting up a brave front, the earlier right hook had made him vulnerable and Choi was ready to cash in. A long right clipped the champ's jaw and it was followed by a right-left, a lead right and another right-left uppercut-right. A strong right-left to the jaw wobbled Navarrete again and a final lead right sent the champion to the canvas. Navarrete immediately rolled over and crawled to the ropes, where he hauled himself up at two. Navarrete had hit the ground with 24 seconds remaining in the round, but the bell rang and instant after Hassett completed his mandatory eight-count. The bell had sounded 10 seconds early, preventing Choi from following up his advantage. Despite this, Choi's corner lodged no protest at the time.

Though Choi didn't go for the KO as the sixth began, he fought with verve at long-range as the left in a right-left combo snapped Navarrete's head. Choi worked the lead right overtime while a serene Navarrete sought to recover behind his high guard. Choi had his formula for success – lead rights that set up multi-punch combinations – and was working it to the utmost. Navarrete, who sought to recover behind his high guard, didn't have an answer for Choi's long-armed aggression and things didn't get better as a heavy left sent him stumbling into the ropes with less than 10 seconds remaining in the round. Navarrete's light left-right to the body didn't prevent Choi from putting yet another round in the bank.

Choi was in clear command of the fight but he had a big decision to make – should he go for the knockout and risk exhaustion or should he step off the gas and save enough energy to fight the remaining nine rounds should he need to? Choi had gone past five rounds only twice in his career and his three most recent fights went a total of 11 rounds, so the challenger had considerable doubts about his stamina. Navarrete had no such concerns as he had traversed 10 or more rounds 23 times, including 12 rounds seven times. Though just 13 months older, the 24-year-old Navarrete was light years ahead in terms of experience and ring intelligence. While Choi was piling up the points, Navarrete was hoping his best moments would come in the near future.

Choi made his decision at the start of round seven – he went on his bicycle – and Navarrete began to show signs of life a little less than two minutes into the round. Choi feinted a right hook and Navarrete leaped in with a right hook and two clean lefts to the jaw. But instead of firing back with gusto whenever he was hit hard, as he had in earlier rounds, Choi held back. That told Navarrete everything he needed to know, that the worst had passed and there was still a long way to go.

Near the end of the round, Navarrete countered a Choi right with a long left over the top that snapped the challenger's head. When the bell sounded, Navarrete stared at Choi, then turned toward his corner and walked back with first his right arm in the air, then pumped both arms just before he sat down. He knew he had turned a corner and that his time to shine was on the horizon.

The eighth round began quietly, with Choi on the retreat and Navarrete chugging forward. The pace of the fight had slowed dramatically, but every passing second meant a quiet momentum was building for the champ. He had survived Choi's adrenaline-fueled bolt and not only was he still standing, he was still strong. He began driving forward with body punches but remained respectful of Choi's power. Unlike the early rounds, Navarrete had an immediate response when Choi punched and he even danced lightly on his toes. He brimmed with energy and punched well off the bounce. A right to the body and a left to the jaw forced Choi to retreat and another flurry forced the challenger back further. When Choi responded, he lacked his earlier marksmanship. The South Korean showed no signs of fatigue, but his effectiveness was clearly compromised as he let the champion take the lead.

Late in the round, Choi had had enough and unleashed a flurry that hit only air. After a cuffing right to the ear by Navarrete, the bell sounded. A split-second later Choi landed a right, and Navarrete hung around for a few seconds and patted him on the behind to let him know he had taken note of Choi's transgression – and to let him know he was the one in control.

As the ninth round bell sounded, Navarrete raised his left arm to the crowd to inform them that everything was under control and that it was only a matter of time before he would put away this troublesome neophyte. But Choi proved he wasn't through as a lead right caused Navarrete to blink briefly and grab for his left eye. A second right hit the target, and the challenger decided this was the perfect time to rev up his dormant engine. Navarrete was ready for Choi's surge and he drove him to the ropes with several body punches. Choi responded with a pair of stinging rights and a right-left, but Navarrete was not going to let the challenger regain control so easily as he concentrated on ripping Choi's long, lean torso. The bodywork set up two strong right hooks to the face as the round ended, and Navarrete again walked to the corner with arms upraised.

Choi continued to press in the 10th, doubling and tripling up on his jab but falling short of the mark. Navarrete countered a lead right with a hefty right hook and rushed in behind a long left cross to the jaw. He countered another Choi right with a left uppercut to the body and the effects of his sustained bodywork began to surface. Choi had begun to slow down and his bursts were coming fewer and farther between. And he still had five-plus more rounds to go.

Calculating that he didn't have enough left to last the distance, Choi decided to make one final drive for championship glory – and it produced results. A strong right knocked Navarrete back a step and two more rights got the champ's attention, but little else. But a follow-up right-left-right made Navarrete totter on unsteady legs. Navarrette answered with a body blow but this sequence represented Choi's best chance in several rounds to reel in the championship belt. He fired away with his piston-like blows and it appeared the fight was about to turn once again.

It did, but not in the way Choi thought.

As Choi pumped away, Navarrete blasted through Choi's guard with an explosive left. Choi backed away and Navarrete cashed in with his "money punch" right hook. The blow landed flush and Choi crumbled to the canvas on his stomach. The challenger rolled onto his back and slowly regained his feet at seven. Eighteen seconds remained in the round and Navarrete proceeded to use every one of them. The champion missed with a home run right hook but a second one caught Choi coming in. A split second after the bell, Choi caught Navarrete with a right to the back of the head that made the champion's legs dip for an instant, but Navarrete regained his balance when referee Hassett stepped between them.

Choi knew he was in desperate straits and Navarrete correctly felt he had the situation well in hand. Choi launched a final assault, lashing out with straight rights and lefts. But in the end it was all in vain as a right hook to the jaw caused the valiant challenger to slump to the floor, his knees and elbows flat on the canvas. Choi was the very picture of exhaustion as he took a couple of deep breaths and rolled on his back. He managed to regain his feet, but only a split-second after Hassett's count of 10. At 1:35 of round 11, Rolando Navarrete had officially repelled a most dangerous challenge to his championship, and the physical and emotional stress of doing so hit Navarrete harder than Choi ever could. The Filipino hero collapsed to the ground and stayed there for several long moments as his handlers and supporters surrounded him.

A similar scene had occurred following another famous championship fight held in Manila – "The Thrilla in Manila" between Muhammad Ali and his valiant challenger Joe Frazier. An exhausted Ali sat down in the middle of the ring as his supporters surrounded him. Like Ali and Frazier, Navarrete and Choi had given everything in producing an extraordinary championship contest. The previously obscure Choi stamped himself as a dangerous challenger of the future while the one-time stand-in Navarrete proved beyond doubt that he was deserving of his star status.

For Navarrete, his championship play had been extended for at least one more act.

Epilogue: As it turned out, Navarrette's role as a champion ended in his next fight. Four months after the war with Choi, Navarrete lost the belt in a classic war with Rafael "Bazooka" Limon, who roared from behind to score a 12th round TKO. Navarrete would win his next four fights by knockout but a fifth-round TKO loss to rising Mexican Mario "Azabache" Martinez on June 23, 1984 prompted Navarrete to take a nearly four-year sabbatical from the sport.

Navarrete returned with a two-round TKO of Elmer Leonardo on May 6, 1988 and the win streak eventually stretched to eight fights. But the Filipino's title drive ended on October 13, 1989 in Araneta Coliseum – the site of the "Thrilla in Manila" – when Tae Jin Moon stopped him in six rounds. Including the loss to Moon, Navarrete lost five of his final six fights. The final fight took place on July 31, 1991 at Araneta Coliseum, with the 34-year-old Navarrete being stopped in six rounds by William Magahin. His final record stands at 54-15-3 (31 KO).

Surprisingly, Choi would only fight twice more. A six-round KO of Fel Salvador on June 20, 1982 set up a fight with Navarrete's successor Limon for the WBC title three months later at the Olympic Auditorium in Los Angeles. Again, Choi started strongly as his whipping combinations built a tremendous lead on the scorecards. After six rounds, Choi led 60-54 on one card and 60-55 on the others, but like Navarrete before him Limon rallied strongly and stopped Choi at 2:33 of the seventh. The 24-year-old Choi never fought again and his final record stands at 14-2 (13 KO).

TALES FROM THE VAULT

Total Punches Landed/Thrown

Round	1	2	3	4	5	6	7	8	9	10	11	12	Total
Navarrete	7/32	12/36	13/33	9/35	13/28	10/42	8/21	16/45	18/39	15/40	15/30		136/381
	22%	33%	39%	26%	46%	24%	38%	36%	46%	38%	50%		36%
Choi	19/93	22/70	16/66	18/61	28/72	21/70	4/17	12/45	13/40	20/65	12/40		185/639
	20%	31%	24%	30%	39%	30%	24%	27%	32%	31%	30%		29%

Jabs Landed/Thrown

Round	1	2	3	4	5	6	7	8	9	10	11	12	Total
Navarrete	1/7	0/6	2/10	1/6	1/3	0/7	0/3	0/3	2/5	1/3	1/4		9/57
	14%	0%	20%	17%	33%	0%	0%	0%	40%	33%	25%		16%
Choi	5/35	8/33	3/26	2/21	8/27	4/23	2/7	2/15	3/13	8/29	2/10		47/239
	14%	24%	12%	10%	30%	17%	29%	13%	23%	28%	20%		20%

Power Punches Landed/Thrown

Round	1	2	3	4	5	6	7	8	9	10	11	12	Total
Navarrete	6/25	12/30	11/23	8/29	12/25	10/35	8/18	16/42	16/34	14/37	14/26		127/324
	24%	40%	48%	28%	48%	29%	44%	38%	47%	38%	54%		39%
Choi	14/58	14/37	13/40	16/40	20/45	17/47	2/10	10/30	10/27	12/36	10/30		138/400
	24%	38%	32%	40%	44%	36%	20%	33%	37%	33%	33%		34%

Rolando Navarrete vs. Chung Il Choi January 16, 1982, Manila, Philippines

Pernell Whitaker vs. Diosbelys Hurtado
January 24, 1997, Atlantic City, New Jersey

When a historian gauges a great fighter's worth he asks several questions. How did his physical skills measure up to those of his peers? Was he so dominant over his opponents that he could rightly lay claim to an era as opposed to a small slice of time? How did he perform against his best opponents? Finally, does he possess that special brand of fortitude and resourcefulness needed to bail himself out of adverse situations?

By the time Pernell Whitaker signed to meet Diosbelys Hurtado on January 24, 1997 at the Convention Center in Atlantic City, he was considered by most measures a great fighter. At his peak, he was regarded as one of history's greatest defensive masters and was one of a select few to have won belts in four weight divisions. He had registered eight defenses of the IBF lightweight title he won from Greg Haugen in February 1989 and before moving up to 140 in 1992 he managed to become the first undisputed 135-pound champion since Roberto Duran. Whitaker proceeded to win the IBF junior welterweight title from Rafael Pineda, the WBC welterweight title from James "Buddy" McGirt and the WBA junior middleweight belt from Julio Cesar Vazquez.

Despite his accomplishments, one aspect of Whitaker's resume remained unresolved – how would he react if he found himself in a desperate situation? Whitaker's polished skills enabled him to breeze through even the best of his opponents, and though his record read 39-1-1 (16 KO), an excellent case could be made that he should have been 41-0. The split decision defeat to Jose Luis Ramirez in March 1988 is regarded as one of the most scandalous verdicts of the 1980s while his draw to Julio Cesar Chavez in 1993 ranks with the very worst of the 1990s.

Early in his career, many observers thought Roger Mayweather would serve as a good barometer of Whitaker's worth, and though "The Black Mamba" scored a ninth-round knockdown Whitaker won a rather easy decision. After Whitaker virtually shut out Ramirez in their August 1989 rematch, future Hall of Famer Azumah Nelson presented the next great threat to Whitaker's reign. The Ghanaian, who was attempting to win his third divisional championship, applied heavy pressure throughout but Whitaker was never in any true danger as he sliced and diced his way to a decision. Even the 87-0 Chavez, the consensus pound-for-pound best at the time, wasn't able to ruffle Whitaker's feathers. There was uneasiness among experts about Whitaker's fistic profile because while Whitaker impressed, he was never pressed.

When Whitaker stepped between the ropes against Hurtado, there was a groundswell of opinion that the 33-year-old's skills were beginning to sour. He spent his entire 1996 campaign dealing with tall, strong Puerto Rican Wilfredo Rivera, who pushed Whitaker to a split decision in their first fight in April and a close unanimous decision in September. While insiders thought Hurtado was a somewhat dangerous choice, he wasn't considered dangerous enough to keep Main Events from committing Whitaker to a superfight with Oscar de la Hoya 10 weeks down the road. In fact, De La Hoya was in the audience to check out his opponent as well as help HBO hype the showdown.

As for Hurtado, he had already faced his share of adversity though in the ring he was 20-0 with 13 knockouts. Because he was Cuba's top amateur at his weight, he had the chance to see the world beyond Fidel Castro – and he began to doubt Castro's Communist propaganda. In Cuba, he lived in a home without electricity, running water or television while the countries he visited had those amenities and much more. So in November 1994, following a tournament meet in Connecticut, he contacted a Cuban exile and arranged a meeting at the hotel where he and the rest of the team were staying. He waited until everyone was asleep before he exited the room, stepped onto an elevator, met his contact and walked out into a strange – but free – new world. Hurtado was one of six Cuban boxers to defect, and they settled in Miami to form the nucleus of "Team Freedom." Hurtado was the first member of the group to receive a title shot, and as he entered the Convention Center ring to face by far the most accomplished opponent of his young pro career, he wore a look of quiet confidence.

The gulf in experience was staggering. In Hurtado's 20-fight pro career he had fought a total of 81 rounds. Whitaker's experience in championship fights alone – 214 rounds – more than tripled Hurtado's entire professional life. But Hurtado had advantages as well. At 5-11 he was five inches taller and his 74-inch wingspan was a full nine inches longer than that of the champion.

He also had the element of surprise, and that was apparent mere moments after the first bell sounded.

Hurtado threw a jab to the body that prompted Whitaker to drop both gloves to chest level. Seeing the opening, Hurtado cracked a right to Whitaker's exposed jaw – and down went the champion. Just five seconds into the fight, before anyone had a chance to settle in, the heavily favored champion with a superfight on the horizon had fallen heavily onto the seat of his pants. It was quite a concept to wrap one's mind around, but Whitaker immediately jumped to his feet and took referee Arthur Mercante Jr.'s mandatory eight count with a wide, wry smile on his face. Though the knockdown was clearly of the flash variety, it sent a powerful message that Hurtado was intent on ruining the party scheduled for April 12.

When the fighters were brought back together, Hurtado proceeded to unveil his strategy. He used his lively legs to motor around the ring from side to side while constantly throwing lead rights and swift unpredictable combinations. It was a blueprint that had been used before by Poli Diaz five-and-a-half years earlier, but unlike the shorter Diaz Hurtado had the physical equipment to maximize it. By doing so, he forced Whitaker to assume the uncomfortable role of aggressor and the man regarded as one of the great defensive masters of all time was reduced to chasing his opponent and firing lefts that fell far short of the mark.

Another part of Hurtado's strategy was to unsettle the control-oriented champion by using foul tactics. After Hurtado landed a left uppercut to the jaw, Whitaker fell into a clinch, where the Cuban then whacked the back of Whitaker's head. The move drew a strong response from Mercante, but it had its intended effect. After Hurtado missed with a five-punch flurry, Whitaker nailed Hurtado with a hook to the jaw after Mercante called for a break, drawing a warning as well.

Nothing was going right for the champion and he was clearly frustrated. Whitaker had made a living frustrating other fighters with his highly evolved defensive prowess and now the shoe was on the other foot. It was a startling role reversal: Whitaker was in with a younger, faster, harder-hitting opponent who was stronger at the weight and now he served as the plodding foil who was subject to his opponent's will. This fight was supposed to serve as Whitaker's showcase for the big money fight with De La Hoya, but Hurtado's formidable opening sequence turned the event into a struggle for survival.

It was going to be a long, difficult night for Whitaker and he was none too pleased. After the first round bell sounded, a smirking Whitaker made sure to walk into Hurtado's path and bump shoulders with him. Hurtado, who unlike Whitaker was intensely focused on the task before him, ignored the gesture and calmly made his way back to the corner.

Hurtado was back on his bicycle in the second, and Whitaker attempted to cut off the escape routes behind his jab. As the challenger threw a right-left, Whitaker caught him with a solid left cross that made him take a couple of jittery steps backward. The Cuban quickly recovered and continued to apply the game plan. His multi-punch flurries mostly missed the target, but it kept Whitaker at a safer distance. The psychological warfare also continued as Whitaker pulled out an old trick by spinning behind Hurtado and patting him twice on the behind. The edgy Hurtado retaliated by firing a jab to the face over Mercante's shoulder. As Mercante warned Whitaker, the champion looked down at the floor and shrugged his shoulders as if to say, "what else am I going to do?"

Hurtado dove in behind a right and his head nearly clashed with Whitaker's, drawing a complaint from the champion and a warning from Mercante. It was abundantly clear that the son of Hall of Fame referee Arthur Mercante Sr. was going to earn his money this night.

Still, Hurtado was fighting a brilliantly awkward fight. He punched in flurries, clinched at opportune times and caught Whitaker with blows that normally would have deflected off the champion's defensive shell. His head and shoulder feints short-circuited Whitaker's defensive pattern, forcing him to totally rewire his style on the fly.

"(Hurtado is fighting) like a jazz musician at a rock concert," HBO color commentator George Foreman said. Hurtado was forcing the 33-year-old Whitaker to work every second of every round, and he had to do so without his considerable bag of tricks. In order to win and get a chance to cash in against "The Golden Boy," Whitaker had to transform himself from a slickster who benefited from the mistakes of others into a fighter who had to force the action and break another man's will.

Meanwhile, Hurtado was feeling great and as he awaited the start of the third round he leaped off his stool and bounded into the air like a human pogo stick. His plan was working to perfection and was already three points up on most scorecards. In the third, Whitaker, resigned to his stylistic fate, tried to make the best of his situation by turning up the pressure and punching with Hurtado whenever the challenger unleashed a flurry. Whitaker was totally committed to being the aggressor and he waded in with little regard for what was coming back at him. The confident Hurtado did a little "Ali shuffle," which drew boos from the crowd, and moments later Whitaker hit Hurtado with a solid left as the Cuban spun away. Whitaker enjoyed a better third round and was starting to acclimate to his new situation.

Trainer Ronnie Shields attempted to further clarify the revised game plan between rounds three and four.

"You've got to keep the pressure on him," he said. "Feint with the guy and your hands have got to be high. And look, snap that jab! You can't just lay a jab out there. Feint him and throw a head hook. Fast punches, forget the power, fast punches, all right?"

In the fourth, Hurtado combined his hit-and-run tactics with guerrilla warfare. He countered a Whitaker jab by launching a wild four-punch flurry that extricated him from the ropes and drove Whitaker back to ring center. But late in the round, Whitaker found a glimmer of hope as he nailed Hurtado with a heavy right to the hip that made the challenger yell. As the bell round, Hurtado drove a low left to the thigh that doubled Whitaker over. Mercante told him that the next low blow would bring a point penalty.

Whitaker's corner, however, had reason to be encouraged. "Sweet Pete" had just won his first round and his late-round body shot proved to be a revelation.

"I've been watching him," Lou Duva said. "Every time you hit him to the body he picks his legs up. You gotta go to the body with this guy!"

But in the fifth, Hurtado's movement didn't give Whitaker much of a chance to attack the ribs. While on the ropes, Hurtado weaved his body left, then right before unleashing a huge right that nearly drove Whitaker to his knees. But the champion saved himself by grabbing Hurtado around the waist and hauling himself back upright. Moments later, Hurtado whacked a right to the ribs and briefly doubled Whitaker over and pivoted away to ring center by placing his right hand between Whitaker's arms and spinning in a tight circle. He might not have had as much championship experience, but his deep amateur background taught him much about the ways of the ring.

Whitaker was growing more frustrated with his situation and that angst manifested itself in increasingly obvious ways. After bulling Hurtado to the ropes, he grabbed the Cuban's left thigh and lifted it in the air while banging a short right to the ribs. Moments later, Whitaker fired an intentionally low left to Hurtado's protective cup.

Halfway through the round, Whitaker landed a clean left cross to the jaw, his best punch of the fight so far. But Hurtado was unhurt and he proved it by clanging a right off Whitaker's temple. Whitaker sneaked in another low left, and Hurtado countered a missed right-left with a wild windmilling six-punch flurry. A decent left pushed Hurtado toward the ropes, but the challenger landed a right-left to the body, with the right straying low.

The fight was dissolving into a foul-fest and after Hurtado pushed down on Whitaker's neck with his left arm while whacking him with a right to the back, Mercante's patience reached its end. The New York referee assessed a point penalty, potentially erasing the advantage he gained with the first-round knockdown. Hurtado tried to make up for it by firing a five-punch flurry, then an 11-punch burst before ending the round with a chopping right as Whitaker came in.

The dirty fighting continued midway through the sixth as Whitaker sunk a left to the hip that forced Hurtado to his knees. He wore a rueful smile as he waited out the 20-second timeout, but things were about to get worse for Whitaker.

With 1:12 remaining, Hurtado backed toward the ropes and as Whitaker advanced, Hurtado fired a quick left to the cheek that dropped Whitaker to a knee. Whitaker grabbed the sides of his head and shouted an agonized "no!" as Mercante pointed Hurtado to a neutral corner and began administering his second eight-count. Whitaker knew that the knockdown added another brick to his growing mathematical burden. Still, the only thing that was hurt was his pride so Hurtado continued to stick and move for the rest of the round. As the bell sounded, Whitaker complained to Mercante about a perceived foul while Hurtado walked to his corner with his right arm in the air.

De La Hoya wore a grim expression as he arose from his seat and put on the HBO headset. With Whitaker falling further behind on the scorecards, he feared his April date with "Sweet Pete" was in severe jeopardy.

"I'm stilling crossing my fingers," De La Hoya said with more hope than conviction. "I'm kinda shaky now, but I think Whitaker will do well. He's having trouble with him, but he'll come on in the later rounds."

The instant after De La Hoya spoke those words, Hurtado nailed Whitaker with a right to the jaw. The two knockdowns were of the flash variety, but this time Whitaker was legitimately hurt. He sought to collect himself while in a clinch as his personal hole grew ever deeper.

De La Hoya and everyone else who wanted the April fight to happen were sweating bullets because they knew Whitaker's history. Whitaker always built huge leads in the early and middle rounds then took advantage of his opponents' mistakes as they tried to turn the fight in the late rounds. Now it was Whitaker's turn to bail himself out, and because he had never scored a knockout past the sixth round the prospects of a fight-saving rally were dim at best. To close the gap on the scorecards, Whitaker would need some help from Hurtado.

With 1:44 remaining in the seventh, Whitaker got some. A moment after blasting Whitaker with a right Hurtado spun behind the champion and landed a rabbit punch, drawing his second point deduction from Mercante. Whitaker held out his arms, willing to accept Hurtado's apology. But an angry Hurtado was in no mood to do so as he popped Whitaker with a quick right to the body and left to the jaw. Whitaker turned to Mercante for help, but the referee judged that Hurtado simply took advantage of an opening Whitaker gave him.

Then Whitaker received a stronger sign of hope. A solid left landed on Hurtado's jaw and a second chopping left appeared to stun the Cuban. In the ensuing clinch, Hurtado raised his eyebrows in surprise. As the round closed, Whitaker slammed home a looping left, a right and a parting left that forced Hurtado to hold on. The late-round rally showed Whitaker he could hurt Hurtado, and both men found themselves at an important crossroads. For Whitaker, the task was obvious but Hurtado also had to answer an important question: Now that the adrenaline of being a title challenger had worn off, did he have the poise to catch a second wind and snuff out a desperate champion's rally?

The eighth round saw Whitaker fight with more confidence, and Hurtado didn't retaliate after Whitaker landed a strong left to the face and a hurtful left to the body. Hurtado caught Whitaker with a right as the champion barreled in and whaled away with blows that caught Whitaker's arms. But Whitaker was timing Hurtado's rushes better and took advantage of the openings Hurtado's misses provided. It appeared Whitaker had found a formula to prevail, and his corner knew as much.

"You're not fighting on heart, you're fighting on experience," Shields told Whitaker between rounds.

Though Whitaker had closed the gap in rounds seven and eight, Whitaker's mathematical mountain again grew steeper in the ninth. With 1:09 remaining, Whitaker cracked Hurtado with a strong left to the jaw, but as Hurtado spun out of the corner he turned his back and retreated to ring center. Whitaker, in hot pursuit, threw two blows from behind. The first was blocked by Hurtado's glove but the second landed in back of the ear. Because they looked like rabbit punches Mercante deducted a point from an aghast Whitaker, who raised his gloves to his head with open-mouthed surprise. Hurtado, his spirits lifted, punctuated a four-punch flurry with a solid left to the jaw and ended the stanza by connecting with a short right. The point deduction couldn't have come at a better time for Hurtado or at a worse juncture for Whitaker, and each man was beginning to get a clearer picture of his ultimate fate. After a 10th round that saw Hurtado pelt a lunging Whitaker with two- and three-punch flurries, the challenger was ahead on all scorecards. John Stewart had the challenger leading 93-92 while Lazaro Carrasco saw the contest 94-92. Sergio Silvi viewed Hurtado as an unassailable winner at 96-91 and many in the crowd – including Oscar de la Hoya – were wrapping their minds around the possibility that the Whitaker-De La Hoya dream fight would remain only a dream.

"You need a knockout to win the fight," Shields told Whitaker matter-of-factly. Then he broke out the verbal whip: "You gotta get on top of this guy. You've got to let both hands go on this guy. You can't just throw one hand. You need a knockout to win the fight. Everything you've got now, you've got to go *'I need these last two rounds.'* You've got to put the pressure on this kid. You've got to show the kid who's boss. You've got to let your hands go."

But it was Hurtado who tried to show who was boss as the 11th began as he threw a combination and clinched. After Mercante commanded them to break, the desperate Whitaker popped Hurtado with a short right that drew a warning to "keep it clean." Whitaker caught Hurtado with two long lefts and the Cuban retaliated with a chopping right that forced a clinch. Whitaker banged a left to the body and an overhand left to the face, but none of the blows seemed to faze Hurtado much.

With less than five minutes remaining in the fight the clock had, for once, become an enemy for Whitaker. He was finally placed in the type of crisis situation that tested the mettle of all great champions and commanded them to produce the grace under pressure that transformed the greats of the game into bona fide legends. Sugar Ray Robinson saw his legacy flash before his badly cut eyes in his rematch with Randy Turpin and he responded by hammering his onetime conqueror into submission. Julio Cesar Chavez stared certain defeat in the face in his first match with Meldrick Taylor, and whether one agrees with Richard Steele's stoppage or not, Chavez still created the situation by producing a knockdown in the bout's final seconds. Jake LaMotta was outboxed by Laurent Dauthuille for 14-plus rounds, but saved his championship with a tidal wave of punches to score the knockout with just 13 seconds left on the clock.

Did Pernell Whitaker have it in him to save himself, save his title and complete his fistic resume?

The answer came with 1:23 remaining in the 11th in most resounding fashion.

Whitaker fell short with a right jab as Hurtado backed toward the corner pad, but that missed jab helped Whitaker tee up a monstrous left that snapped Hurtado's head and collapsed his legs. The stricken challenger fell into the corner pad and was completely at Whitaker's mercy – and "Sweet Pete" had none. Whitaker unleashed nine consecutive overhand lefts like a woodchopper whaling away at a mighty sequoia, his eyes ablaze with fury and a snarl creasing his lips. Hurtado's upper body fell between the second and third strands of rope and only Mercante's intervention – which could have come several seconds sooner – put a stop to Whitaker's animalistic assault. At 1:52 of round 11, Whitaker was declared the winner and he earned the right not only to face De La Hoya in April, but also the privilege of calling himself a champion of the highest order.

"It's not over until we say it's over," Whitaker told HBO's Larry Merchant. "I believe what my corner tells me. I didn't look past Hurtado, but I knew there was something bigger and better beyond him so I had to go through him. I couldn't go over or around the opponent, I had to go through him to get to Oscar. Oscar deserves the title shot, but I'm still the champion."

Indeed he was, and no matter what would happen against "The Golden Boy" in 78 days, he would always remain a true champion.

Epilogue: Whitaker lost the WBC welterweight title to De La Hoya in a verdict that is debated to this day, not only due to the result but because the judges saw De La Hoya a winner by four, six and six points. In fact, the Hurtado fight was the last official win of Whitaker's career.

Six months after dropping the belt to De La Hoya Whitaker was announced as a decision winner over Andrei Pastraev, but the result was changed to a no-decision after Whitaker tested positive for cocaine. Sixteen months later Whitaker challenged a peak Felix Trinidad for the IBF welterweight title, showing incredible grit by fighting more than half the fight with a broken jaw before dropping a wide unanimous decision. On April 27, 2001 at Caesars Lake Tahoe in Stateline, Nevada, the 37-year-old Whitaker lost by fourth round TKO to Carlos Bojorquez after suffering a broken clavicle. Whitaker's final record is 40-4-1 (17 KO) and was inducted – along with Roberto Duran and Ricardo Lopez – into the International Boxing Hall of Fame in 2007.

After losing to Whitaker, Hurtado won his next eight fights to earn a shot at Kostya Tszyu's WBC interim super lightweight title. Hurtado suffered a knockdown in the first round but decked Tszyu twice in that same round before losing by fifth round TKO. Hurtado earned a third title opportunity after going 6-0-1 in his next seven bouts, with the technical draw coming to future welterweight and junior middleweight champion Ricardo Mayorga. This time Hurtado made good as he whacked out WBA champion Randall Bailey in seven rounds. He lost the belt in his first defense to Vivian Harris (KO by 2) and would never again challenge for a belt. Following the loss to Bailey, Hurtado scored three knockout wins before taking a three-year hiatus. As of January 2010, the 36-year-old Hurtado is 4-0 on his comeback, with his most recent fight a unanimous 12 round decision over Manuel Garnica in June 2009 that raised his record to 42-3-1 (25 KO).

BACK FROM THE BRINK – GREAT COMEBACKS

Total Punches Landed/Thrown

Round	1	2	3	4	5	6	7	8	9	10	11	12	Total
Whitaker													168/448
													38%
Hurtado													131/429
													31%

Jabs Landed/Thrown

Round	1	2	3	4	5	6	7	8	9	10	11	12	Total
Whitaker													51/201
													25%
Hurtado													20/97
													21%

Power Punches Landed/Thrown

Round	1	2	3	4	5	6	7	8	9	10	11	12	Total
Whitaker													117/247
													47%
Hurtado													111/332
													33%

* Fight originally done by CompuBox, but the original HTML files with complete round-by-round statistics no longer exist.

Pernell Whitaker vs. Diosbelys Hurtado January 24, 1997, Atlantic City, New Jersey

Made in the USA
Charleston, SC
19 June 2010